D1590283

DESCARTES
A Biography

René Descartes is best remembered today for writing "I think, therefore I am," but his main contribution to the history of ideas was his effort to construct a philosophy that would be sympathetic to the new sciences that emerged in the seventeenth century. To a great extent he was the midwife to the Scientific Revolution and a significant contributor to its key concepts. In four major publications, he fashioned a philosophical system that accommodated the needs of these new sciences and thereby earned the unrelenting hostility of both Catholic and Calvinist theologians, who relied on the scholastic philosophy that Descartes hoped to replace. His contemporaries claimed that his proofs of God's existence, in the *Meditations*, were so unsuccessful that he must have been a cryptic atheist, and that his discussion of scepticism served mainly to fan the flames of libertinism. Descartes died in Stockholm in obscurity but soon became one of the most famous philosophers of the seventeenth century, a status that he continues to enjoy today. This is the first biography in English that addresses the full range of Descartes' interests in theology, philosophy, and the sciences and that traces his intellectual development through his entire career.

Desmond M. Clarke is Professor of Philosophy at the National University of Ireland, Cork. He received a D.Litt. from the National University of Ireland, was Jean Monnet Fellow at the European University Institute in Florence, and has been elected to the Royal Irish Academy. He is the author of a number of books on Descartes and the seventeenth century, most recently *Descartes's Theory of Mind*.

Descartes
A Biography

Desmond M. Clarke
National University of Ireland, Cork

CAMBRIDGE UNIVERSITY PRESS
Cambridge, New York, Melbourne, Madrid, Cape Town, Singapore, São Paulo

Cambridge University Press
40 West 20th Street, New York, NY 10011-4211, USA

www.cambridge.org
Information on this title: www.cambridge.org/9780521823012

First published 2006

Printed in the United States of America

A catalog record for this publication is available from the British Library.

Library of Congress Cataloging in Publication Data

Clarke, Desmond M.
Descartes : a biography / Desmond Clarke.
p. cm.
Includes bibliographical references (p.) and index.
ISBN 0-521-82301-3 (hardback)
1. Descartes, René, 1596–1650. 2. Philosophers – France – Biography. I. Title.
B1873.C57 2006
194 – dc22   2005008107

ISBN-13 978-0-521-82301-2 hardback
ISBN-10 0-521-82301-3 hardback

Contents

vi   Contents

Preface and Acknowledgments

Those who were best equipped in the past to write a biography of Descartes embarked on the project with great reluctance and explicit apologies. This pattern was set by the first major biographer, Adrien Baillet, in the late seventeenth century. As he began the task, he had on his desk more original documents by Descartes and his contemporaries than anyone has ever collected since then. Nonetheless, he suggested that Chanut, Clerselier, or Legrand would have been a more suitable biographer than himself.[1] Charles Adam was equally hesitant about writing his *Life of Descartes* (1910), even though he had just completed editing the eleven-volume edition of Descartes' works with Paul Tannery. 'In the current state of our knowledge', he wrote, 'it will not be possible for a long time to complete such a work properly.'[2] Adam thought that a good biography would require preparatory studies of philosophical and scientific topics in the early seventeenth century, and more research on those who influenced Descartes and on his personal relations with contemporaries.

When the late Terry Moore asked me if I were interested in writing a biography of Descartes, I answered too quickly in the affirmative. I did not appreciate adequately the unsatisfactory state of Descartes' correspondence, although I believed that many of the studies that Adam talked about had been done during the past century. My colleague in Utrecht, Theo Verbeek, was much better informed about these matters and told me with benevolent kindness that I was a fool! However, he also agreed to compensate as much as possible for my ignorance and temerity by sharing with me his wealth of knowledge about Descartes' life in the Netherlands, and about the Dutch authors in the seventeenth century who were significant for his biography.

I am particularly grateful to Theo Verbeek for making available his work in progress on Descartes' correspondence. I also thank Erik-Jan Bos and Theo for reading the first draft of the whole text and for making many valuable suggestions and necessary corrections. Dolores Dooley likewise read the full text and made detailed comments. Des MacHale and Oliver Ranner read various chapters and offered helpful suggestions. Jeroen van de Ven provided information about Helena Jans, and I borrowed extensively from the two-volume bibliography of Descartes' works prepared by Matthijs van Otegem. Letizia Panizza and John Sutton obliged with suggestions and material about the libertines and Digby. I consulted colleagues in the Departments of French and Ancient Classics at University College, Cork, for assistance with translations, including Matthew MacNamara, Patrick O'Donovan, and Keith Sithwell, and I am very grateful for their help.

Most of the research for this book was completed during the 2003–04 academic year, during which I had a Government of Ireland Senior Fellowship from the Irish Research Council for the Humanities and Social Sciences. I am grateful to the council for the financial assistance that made this work possible. I also acknowledge financial support from the Arts Faculty, University College, Cork, during the years 2002–04, which enabled me to consult material at the Bibliothèque Nationale, Paris, and at the British Library, London. During the past year, I also relied on the professional advice of Charles Shinkwin and David Pearson, each of whom contributed indirectly but significantly to the timely conclusion of this project.

Cork
November 2004

Note on Texts
and References

Most references to Descartes are to the eleven-volume edition of his *Oeuvres*, edited by Charles Adam and Paul Tannery, which was subsequently reissued with additions and corrections. Although this edition is usually identified in the literature as 'AT', I have simplified references by omitting this acronym and by providing only the volume and page numbers. Where I refer to alternative editions of Descartes' works, I use the same style of author/date that is used for other authors. I have used the usual prefix, 'CM', to refer to the standard edition of Mersenne's correspondence. Some relevant details of Descartes' correspondence remain uncertain, such as the date or addressee. I have followed the tentative suggestions of Adam and Tannery, indicating uncertainty by square brackets, unless the ambiguities have been resolved in Descartes (2003) or elsewhere.

The notes use the author/date system of reference. The corresponding entries in the bibliography refer to the editions that I managed to consult, rather than to first editions. Where there are standard English editions of primary texts readily available, I have also provided information on such editions.

Finally, I have translated into English the titles of all works that are mentioned in the body of the text.

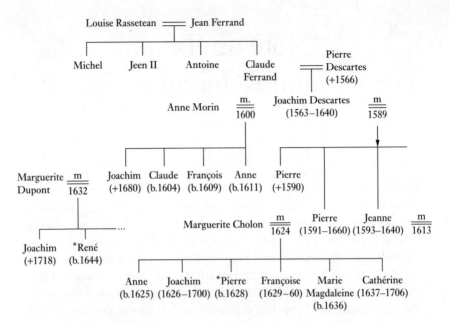

*René Descartes was godfather.

Descartes family tree.

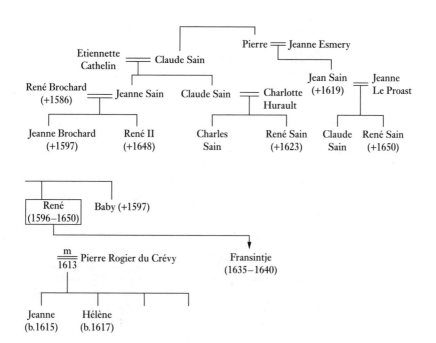

Introduction

D ESCARTES died in Sweden in 1650, a few weeks before his fifty-fourth birthday. He had spent most of his adult life in relative seclusion in what is now the Netherlands, while the Thirty Years' War waxed and waned around him. By 1667, when some French Cartesians arranged for the return of his remains to Paris, they had begun to publicize his works, to develop a characteristically Cartesian philosophy, and to be identified by critics as a 'sect'. These early supporters included many philosophers who, apart from Nicolas Malebranche, are probably remembered today only as marginal figures in the history of Western thought. The name of Descartes, however, remains readily recognizable. He has entered the canon of Western philosophy so securely that that there is no longer any dispute about his significance.

Why was he important? Hardly for the phrase by which he is popularly remembered today, both by students of philosophy and by other readers: '*I think, therefore I am*'. This was not an original insight on his part, and it had a relatively minor role in his work. During the past century, Descartes has often been read as a metaphysician or, perhaps as frequently, as a philosopher who took seriously the arguments of sceptics. Alternatively, he is classified as a philosopher of subjectivity, as someone who outlined an internal map of the human mind and defended the irreducibility of conscious experiences. Finally, there are those, especially feminist critics, who think of Descartes as having exaggerated the significance and capacity of reason at the expense of the emotional life. For them, Descartes was a mere 'rationalist'.

Descartes' life reveals a much more complex and interesting charac-ter than any of these labels suggests. As an intellectual in the early sev-enteenth century, he might have directed his energies toward political philosophy (as Hobbes did), to theological disputes (as Pascal did), or to the renewal of humanistic and classical learning for which Erasmus had earlier provided an outstanding model. Alternatively, he might have channeled his genius exclusively into mathematics (as his contemporaries Fermat and Roberval did); had he done so, he would surely have exceeded by far the novelty and ambition of their achievements. Although all these interests featured to some extent in his life, Descartes' primary focus was elsewhere. He is best characterized as a philosopher of the Scientific Revolution.

Two major events that helped define his intellectual odyssey occurred in the sixteenth century, one of them in Poland and the other in Trent, at the southern limits of the Holy Roman Empire. In Poland, Nicholas Copernicus published *The Revolutions of the Celestial Spheres* as he lay dying in 1543. Although it appeared with an unauthorized Preface by Andreas Osiander that seriously misled readers about the author's intentions, this book moved the Earth from its traditional place at the centre of the universe and relocated it as a relatively small planet circulating about the Sun. However, Osiander invited readers to minimize the significance of Copernicus' work by describing it merely as an 'hypothesis'. He compounded the mistake by reminding readers that 'hypotheses need not be true nor even probable. On the contrary, if they provide a calculus consistent with the observations, that alone is enough.'[1]

Osiander's cue reflected a tradition of instrumentalism that had been applied to astronomy since the time of Ptolemy. On this reading, astronomers do not try to describe or explain the real world. They merely construct mathematical devices for predicting regular changes in the apparent positions of the planets and for calculating, for example, when eclipses occur. This nonrealist reading of Copernicus was supported to some extent by the fact that he offered no physical explanation of why the Earth moves around the Sun. He assumed that the planets rotated on invisible but mechanically effective concentric spheres.

However, it was clear from other features of his book that Copernicus was doing much more than constructing a mathematical model. One sign of his realist intentions was his speculation about the dimensions of the universe, and about the infinitesimally small particles of matter from which visible bodies are composed. Although he stopped short of claiming that the universe extends to infinity, he acknowledged the change of scale required in the traditional picture of the 'world'.

This reasoning certainly makes it quite clear that the heavens are immense by comparison with the earth and present the aspect of an infinite magnitude, while on the testimony of the senses the earth is related to the heavens as a point to a body, and a finite to an infinite magnitude. . . . For that proof establishes no conclusion other than the heavens' unlimited size in relation to the earth. Yet how far this immensity extends is not at all clear. At the opposite extreme are the very tiny indivisible bodies called 'atoms'. Being imperceptible, they do not immediately constitute a visible body when they are taken two or a few at a time. But they can be multiplied to such an extent that in the end there are enough of them to combine in a perceptible magnitude.[2]

With these tentative steps, Copernicus introduced a genuine revolution in astronomy. Although he was a respected canon of his diocese at Cracow, he also raised a fundamental question about the role of biblical and other religious texts as sources of scientific knowledge.

Kepler was among the first to recognize the significance of the new theory. He concluded, in his *New Astronomy* (1609), that 'only Copernicus' opinion concerning the world (with a few small changes) is true, [and] that the other two views [those of Ptolemy and Brahe] are false.'[3] This unequivocal language, unmitigated by Osiander's qualification, made explicit the apparent conflict between the new astronomy and the Bible, which, on a literal reading, implied that the Sun moved around the Earth. Kepler addressed the problem directly. 'Now the Holy Scriptures, too, when treating of common things (concerning which it is not their purpose to instruct humanity) speak with humans in the human manner, in order to be understood by them. They make use of what is generally acknowledged, in order to weave in other things that are more lofty and divine.'[4] In other words, the Bible was never intended to teach astronomy. Instead, it spoke to people in a language that they understood. In the process, the Bible assumed the same views about the universe as its original readers. Kepler wrote this as a Lutheran, under the protection of the Holy Roman Emperor, Rudolph II, at Prague. The same issue arose in the Catholic world, and was addressed by Galileo in his *Letter to the Grand Duchess Cristina* (1615):

I question the truth of the statement that the Church commands us to hold as matters of faith all physical conclusions bearing the stamp of harmonious interpretation by all the Fathers. I think this may be an arbitrary simplification of various Council decrees by certain people to support their own opinion. . . . the Bible . . . was not written to teach us astronomy.[5]

This challenge from the new astronomy to a literal reading of the Bible coincided with a wider European discussion about the authority of the

Bible even as a source of religious faith. While the reformed churches, in general, encouraged Christians to read the Bible as the revealed word of God, Catholic bishops claimed to have exclusive, collective authority to interpret the Bible, and, in doing so, they relied on tradition and the teaching of the early fathers of the church. This appeal to tradition and authority was defended by the Council of Trent (1545–63) in uncompromising terms.

> Furthermore, to control petulant spirits, the Council decrees that, in matters of faith and morals pertaining to the establishment of Christian doctrine, no one, relying on their own judgment and distorting the Sacred Scriptures according to their own conceptions, shall dare to interpret them contrary to that sense which Holy Mother Church (to whom it belongs to judge of their true sense and meaning) has held and does hold, or contrary to the unanimous agreement of the Fathers, even if such interpretations are never to be published. Those who do otherwise shall be identified by the ordinaries [i.e., bishops or religious superiors] and punished in accordance with the penalties prescribed by the law.[6]

This set the stage for an inevitable confrontation between proponents of the new astronomy and the Vatican that resulted notoriously in Galileo's condemnation and subsequent house arrest in Florence. Those who defended Galileo publicly – and there were only two who did so – were also condemned by the church.[7] Paolo Antonio Forcarini wrote his famous *Letter* in 1615, and it was promptly condemned by the Congregation of the Index the following year. Tommaso Campanella was tortured by the Inquisition and spent almost thirty years in prison, some of it in solitary confinement, before escaping to France in 1634.

Descartes inherited from Copernicus and Galileo the intellectual conflicts involved in attempting to develop the new astronomy and, at the same time, to remain within the Catholic Church. He avoided church censure of his astronomy for almost two decades by dissimulation, self-censorship, and astuteness. However, his ambiguous support for Copernicus was merely a symptom of a much more radical problem that could not be camouflaged as easily. Descartes challenged the fundamental philosophy in terms of which both Catholic and Reformed theologians had expressed their teaching of Christian dogmas for centuries. That could not be marginalized, as a technical question in astronomy that only experts might be expected to understand. It went to the heart of the matter and eventually earned Descartes a delayed but almost inevitable listing in the *Index of Forbidden Books* in 1663.

Apart from the merits or otherwise of scholastic philosophy, Descartes was dispositionally querulous, a combative defender of his own ideas, and an unsympathetic critic of other people's theories. He fought consistently with mathematicians, philosophers, theologians, and anyone else who failed to acknowledge the significance or originality of his work. In fact, the dominant pattern of his life was combat, or, in his own words, an unrelenting intellectual 'war'.

This 'war' resulted in part from Descartes' sensitivity to criticism and the certainty that he claimed, prematurely, for his own views. However, the underlying reason for the extensive rows that distracted him for more than two decades was a conflict of cultures between a desiccated, obsolete scholasticism and the emerging philosophy of the Scientific Revolution. Descartes' major contribution to the history of ideas was made in articulating that conflict. He addressed many of the inherent weaknesses of traditional philosophy and championed a new way of thinking that implied the redundancy of earlier theories. In particular, he claimed that natural phenomena are explained ultimately by small particles of matter and their properties, rather than by the philosophical entities that his critics assumed.

The conceptual tension between the new ideal of scientific explanation proposed by Descartes and the moribund philosophy of the schools is much clearer in retrospect than it appeared during the early decades of the seventeenth century. This is especially obvious when Descartes falls back on many of the key concepts of traditional philosophy, such as the concept of a substance, even in the process of arguing for its replacement. He thus emerges from this revolutionary period as a reluctant participant in the Galileo controversy, as a very discreet critic of Catholic theology, and, especially, as a philosophical innovator who continued to exploit many of the scholastic concepts that his own work rendered problematic. He was a Frenchman who lived most of his adult life outside his native land. He was a recluse who kept in touch with intellectual developments all over Europe, mostly by correspondence with Mersenne. He lived alone, read few books, did his own scientific research, and fought with almost everyone he encountered while constantly announcing that all he wanted was 'the security and tranquility' required to complete his intellectual project. His less appealing personal characteristics did not prevent him from becoming the most original French thinker of the seventeenth century, and one of the most famous contributors to the history of Western philosophy.

A Lawyer's Education

I have been nourished by books since I was a child.

(Discourse on Method, vi. 4)

B READ and wine, and the seasonal changes that affect their production, were among the most familiar features of life in the Loire valley, in central France, in the sixteenth century. The appearance of the 'plague', although an infrequent event, was much more prominent in public consciousness. None of these realities was well understood. The range of grapes cultivated in this region was very extensive, and the wines produced were equally diverse. Growing grapes and producing wine relied on traditional techniques that had been passed on for generations. Those involved in viticulture could easily recognize a good season, with the right combination of spring rain and intense heat in midsummer, and they succeeded admirably without a scientific oenology. Likewise, the production of bread and other familiar foods did not presuppose biochemistry and any of its cognate sciences.

The plague, however, was a different story. In one province alone, in 1631, it killed 40,000 people.[1] No one understood what it was, how it arrived in a town, or why it eventually abated, although they noticed that it tended to vary in intensity with the seasons, being worst in summer. They also knew that it was likely to cause a very large number of painful deaths and that the best defence was to flee, preferably before the plague arrived in a town. Here was a natural phenomenon, then, that urgently required an explanation, with a view to providing a cure.

Bread and wine, of course, were not simply familiar foodstuffs that exemplified established French culinary traditions. They were also central to the Christian liturgical tradition that originated with the last supper of Christ. Their role in the Eucharistic service was one of the most contentious issues among different Christian churches and it was best left to the theologians of each church, who expounded at length the meaning of the words attributed to Christ in the gospel account of the last supper: 'This is my body', 'This is my blood'.

While it may have been possible for aspiring philosophers in the early 1600s to avoid any mention of bread and wine or their liturgical uses, it was almost impossible to avoid all controversy. Cautious philosophers repeated the well-worn formulas of their own local churches, especially if they coincided with the official views of the kingdom in which they lived. Those who challenged the received theological wisdom of the church or kingdom often paid a heavy price. Giulio Cesare Vanini, a wandering priest-scholar, was accused of atheism and other crimes in Toulouse in 1618. Having been imprisoned for six months, he was condemned to have his tongue cut out by the public executioner, and then to be strangled and burned at the stake. The immediate and very public implementation of the *parlement*'s judgment was meant to discourage others from similar obstinacy.

Vanini was not unique. There were many examples of the barbaric penalties that were applied to those who expressed dissident views in the early seventeenth century. Giordano Bruno's public burning was even more notorious, while Tommaso Campanella, who avoided execution, spent the best part of twenty-five years in jail for similar offences, during some of which he was tortured. However, Galileo is probably the most famous example of ecclesiastical punishment in the early 1600s; his case will be discussed in more detail.[2] The extraordinary penalties often imposed on those who expressed heterodox views might have been enough to persuade any sensible scholar to remain within the boundaries of what was locally tolerated. In the Loire valley, however, it was not as easy to do this.

Although most of the king's subjects were Roman Catholic, a significant minority was Huguenot. This made is difficult for philosophers to avoid theological controversy, either with one's own church or with those of another denomination, unless they observed a selective silence about contentious issues. However, any genuine attempt to understand a phenomenon such as the plague encouraged adventurous minds to question the traditional learning of the schools that had failed so signally to provide satisfactory explanations of natural phenomena.[3] At the same time, every inquiring mind of the period, whether described as a natural philosopher, theologian, or astronomer, was acutely conscious of the penumbra of theological controversy within which they had to work, and of the potentially lethal penalties that awaited those who strayed beyond the boundaries of orthodoxy that were locally enforced. This kind of censorship was not limited to any particular church or kingdom. Nonetheless, it was enforced more widely and more barbarously by the Catholic Church in all the kingdoms that fell within its ecclesiastical jurisdiction.

The penchant of the Catholic Church for condemning novel ideas was firmly and widely established when, on 20 November 1663, it forbade its members to read certain books by Descartes until they were corrected.[4] By this date, Descartes had been dead for thirteen years. The threat of such an unwelcome intervention from afar had been a constant source of concern for the French philosopher during the last seventeen years of his life, during which he tried as best he could to avoid this almost inevitable fate. However, when Rome eventually spoke, after his death, the effect was the opposite of what it hoped to achieve. As in the more famous case of Galileo, the church's condemnation provided a seal of recognition for the originality and pervasive influence of a style of philosophy that had by then acquired its own distinctive name as 'Cartesianism'. It was hardly worthwhile, even for an extremely censorious and interventionist church, to focus on the writings of someone whose ideas were likely to fade into a well-deserved oblivion. The problem with Cartesianism, even as early as 1663, was that it had become so widely known throughout Europe and so avidly adopted as a replacement for scholastic philosophy that it could no longer be ignored.

Here, then, was someone who presented himself as a loyal son of the Roman Catholic Church, and who succeeded throughout his life in at least avoiding public condemnation by his own church. In developing his ideas, he encountered more controversy that one might have expected, despite the extremely private and almost isolationist manner in which he lived his life. This life began in the comforting embrace of the Loire valley, and seemed destined by family expectations and education to lead to a secure, uncontentious career as a lawyer in the king's service. Instead, it culminated in the development of a new philosophy that eventually exceeded the most ambitious hopes of its author and, in the process, won the distinction of a censure from the Holy Office.

'Born in Touraine'

Catherine Descartes, the youngest daughter of Descartes' brother Pierre, constructed a rather poetic and fanciful summary of Descartes' origins some years after his death, which was intended to link her famous uncle with her own family in Brittany. She claimed that he had been 'conceived among the Bretons, and born in Touraine.'[5] In fact, Descartes' connection with Brittany was very much a retrospective recovery by his family, which had removed from Touraine to the former duchy of Brittany after his birth.

René Descartes was born on 31 March 1596, the third surviving child of Joachim Descartes and Jeanne Brochard.[6] He was born into a bourgeois legal family that had begun to consolidate its social position by service to the French crown. The circumstances of his birth and early childhood seem to have made a deep and lasting impression on René. Within fourteen months of his birth, the young Descartes was effectively an orphan, due to his mother's death and his father's lengthy absences from home.

The Descartes family was originally from the Poitou region of France, where many of its members had held royal appointments as tax collectors or members of provincial *parlements*, and where the philosopher's parents had established their impressive home on the Grand'rue in central Châtellerault. However, Joachim Descartes had been appointed to a post as counsellor in the *parlement* of Brittany in 1585 and had taken up his post in February 1586.[7] Given its somewhat marginal status, the Brittany *parlement* met each year for only one three-month session, which was extended in 1600 to six months. Thus Descartes' father spent part of the year at home in Châtellerault and the remainder at Rennes, 260 kilometres away. Jeanne Brochard's confinement coincided with her husband's annual absence in Brittany. Accordingly, she went to stay with her own mother, Jeanne Sain, at the small town of La Haye, about 20 kilometres from her home. Descartes' grandmother Sain had been widowed since 1586, and she provided a welcome haven for her grandson's delivery. Fourteen months after René's birth, on 16 May 1597, Descartes' mother died, three days after the birth of her fifth child (who also died at birth).[8] She left behind a family of three young children: Pierre (age six), Jeanne (age four), and René (age one).

Descartes was evidently confused or not accurately informed by his family about the details of his mother's death, because he wrote to Princess Elizabeth almost fifty years later that his mother had died a few days after his own birth. 'My mother died a few days after my birth from a disease of the lung caused by distress. I inherited from her a dry cough and a pale complexion which stayed with me until I was more than twenty, so that all the doctors who saw me up to that time condemned me to die young' (iv. 220–21). Immediately after his birth, baby René was entrusted to a nurse for breast-feeding, a practice that was customary at the time and was probably also required by his mother's relatively weak health. Thus, in his earliest years, the dominant people in his life were all women: his rather fragile mother, his maternal grandmother Sain, and his nurse. Descartes speculated much later in his career about the time at which first impressions are made on the mind of a young child, and he suggested that they begin when the child is still in the womb.[9] This claim may have been more a reflection on his earliest memories than the result of reliable medical research. His subsequent cool relationship with his father, Joachim, contributed to a retrospectively rosy picture of his infancy, marked for life by the influence of his mother and protected in the intimate family circle of his grandmother and nurse. Descartes never forgot his nurse and, even when dying, asked that she be included in his will.[10]

Descartes was baptized into the Catholic Church on 3 April 1596, at the nearby church of St. George in La Haye.[11] His father was still absent in Rennes, and his mother was presumably recovering from his delivery three days earlier; besides, it was not customary at the time for mothers to attend their children's baptism. The family was represented instead by three godparents, Jeanne Sain, Michel Ferrand, and René Brochard (who gave his Christian name to the young philosopher), as recorded in the baptismal entry:

The same day was baptized René, the son of the nobleman Joachim Descartes, counsellor to the King in his *parlement* of Brittany and of Damoiselle Jeanne Brochard; his godparents were the noble Michel Ferrand, the King's counsellor and lieutenant general of Châtellerault, the noble René Brochard, the King's counsellor and judge magistrate at Poitiers, and Jeanne Proust, wife of Mr Sain, the King's controller of taxes for Châtellerault.

These godparents reflected very accurately the family's status and the expectations for the newly baptized infant. Anyone interested in predicting his future would have said that he was destined to become a Catholic lawyer in the service of the crown.

French society in the late sixteenth century was clearly and rather inflexibly stratified into three classes or estates: the nobility, the clergy, and the rest of the population. Evidently the vast majority of the population belonged to the so-called third estate, and the opportunities for social promotion between estates were very limited. However, there was significantly

more flexibility for upward mobility within the third estate, in which there
was also an established hierarchy, in descending order, from (1) university graduates in law, medicine, theology, or the arts, to (2) lawyers, (3)
tax-collectors, (4) lower justice officials, (5) merchants, (6) shopkeepers,
and on through skilled craftsmen to the unemployed.[12] Even a hundred
years after Descartes' birth, most of the French population were illiterate;
as many as 86 percent of brides and 71 percent of grooms could not even
sign their names on their marriage certificates.[13] Thus, for most people,
the only hope of upward social mobility was by advancement within the
third estate, for example, from being a mere merchant or tradesman to
being a bourgeois gentleman. And the best way of realizing such ambitions was by acquiring an education and then purchasing or inheriting an
administrative or legal position within a mushrooming royal civil service.

Those in higher offices claimed the title '*Monsieur*' and recognition as
a squire or noble in a personal capacity. However, these were not genuine
nobles, and they were despised by those who inherited traditional family
titles.[14] This pattern of upward social mobility was so well established that
Montaigne comments in his *Essays*: 'What is more uncouth than a nation
where, by legal custom, the office of judge is openly venal and where
verdicts are simply bought for cash? . . . where this trade is held in such
high esteem that there is formed a fourth estate in the commonwealth,
composed of men who deal in lawsuits, thus joining the three ancient
estates, the Church, the Nobility and the People?'[15]

The original *parlement* of Paris was a relatively small group of special
political and legal advisers to the king. Apart from offering advice, they
were responsible for implementing royal decrees, overseeing the administration of justice, and for delivering final judgments on both civil and crim-
inal questions within their own jurisdictions. There were also *parlements*
in each of the provinces that had been fully integrated into the kingdom.
However, even among *parlements* there was a hierarchy, with Paris being
superior and closely associated with the crown. As France expanded and
became more centralized, similar *parlements* were established in regions
outside Paris. For example, the one in Brittany was established in 1554, and
its members were appointed so that half of them were natives of Brittany
and the remainder from outside the province, mostly from the centre of
power at Paris.[16] This was a well-recognized method of providing some
element of local autonomy while integrating such provinces more effectively into a kingdom whose continued unity remained insecure. Joachim

Descartes was among those who had been appointed from outside the region to help cement the relationship between Brittany and the crown.

However, the fundamental reason for multiplying these nominally royal appointments was the soaring demand for extra taxes to support the central administration in Paris. External wars, the suppression of internal challenges to the court's jurisdiction, and the constantly expanding demands of a highly centralizing system of government made ever-increasing demands on taxpayers. Royal appointments were effectively purchased, and they included an exemption from the extremely burdensome taxes that were levied on everyone else in the third estate.[17] Since the nobles and clergy were already exempt from taxes, there thus emerged a new bourgeois class of people who were exempt from taxes themselves while ensuring that all their social inferiors paid theirs. The range of royal officials who were involved in this complex administrative system included not only members of local *parlements*, but also various tax collectors and local police who were charged with enforcing their financial decisions.[18] In the period during which many of Descartes' immediate predecessors acquired their offices and titles, between approximately 1573 and 1604, the total number of royal offices in France increased significantly.[19] Although Descartes' paternal grandfather was a medical doctor, as was his paternal grandmother's father, Jean Ferrand I, most of his other ancestors were members of this newly emerging bourgeois class of tax collectors and lawyers that developed in sixteenth-century France. In particular, all three of his godparents were associated with this group of upwardly mobile legal office-holders.

Descartes' godmother at his baptism was Jeanne Proust, wife of Jean Sain, the comptroller of taxes at Châtellerault.[20] One of his godfathers was Michel Ferrand, his paternal great-uncle. He was brother of Claude Ferrand, the wife of Descartes' paternal grandfather, Pierre. Michel Ferrand was principal lawyer of the Châtellerault district at the time of Descartes' baptism. The third godparent was a son of Jeanne Sain and René Brochard I, and thus the maternal uncle of the philosopher. He also had a legal career, and became dean of the Présidial of Poitiers in 1621. With this symbolic representation at his baptism, the young Descartes might have been expected to follow the family tradition and become a lawyer. This is exactly what his older brother, Pierre, did. He became counsellor to the king in the *parlement* of Brittany in 1618, due to his father's influence; in the next generation, Pierre's son, Joachim, did likewise and followed his father and paternal grandfather into the Brittany *parlement* in 1648. This association with the legal profession was not uniquely confined to direct lines of descent. It was also customary at the time for men in the royal service to marry the daughters of others who had achieved the same social status.

The legal symbolism of the three family witnesses at René's baptism was not the only implication of the simple religious ceremony held at La Haye on 3 April 1596. One of the most disputed questions addressed by the Council of Trent was the role of baptism in the justification of those who were believed to have been damned by Adam's sin.[21] The council taught authoritatively that each individual is born in a state of original sin, that this sinful condition is removed only by the grace of Christ, and that the sacrament of baptism is a necessary condition of justification. The council also decreed that the sacrament be administered by pouring water over the child's head while a validly ordained minister said the words: 'I baptize you in the name of the Father, the Son, and the Holy Spirit.'[22] Since René was only three days old when this ceremony was performed, he could hardly have consented to assuming the duties that he automatically acquired. From the perspective of the church, however, his consent was unnecessary. His godparents consented on his behalf to his becoming a member of the Catholic Church. He was henceforth obliged to live according to the church's teaching, to obey its rules, and to believe its dogmas.[23] If he were ever to leave the church, he would be deemed to have done so despite the divine grace with which he had been assisted since baptism. He could never simply become a nonbeliever. Any deviation from the path that had been set for his life would make him either a heretic (if he denied the church's theological teaching) or a sinner destined for eternal damnation (if he refused to obey its moral teaching).

Whether Descartes remained true to his baptismal obligations, or to the way in which the Catholic Church understood those obligations, remains to be seen. Many years later, when writing the *Discourse on Method* (1637), he reflected on the strategy he had adopted in attempting to rebuild all his knowledge on firm foundations. 'I devised a provisional morality that included only three or four maxims. . . . The first was to obey the laws and customs of my own country, holding firmly to the religion in which, by the grace of God, I had been instructed since my infancy. . . .' (vi. 22–3). The intolerance of religious dissent in the seventeenth century makes it difficult to assess the genuineness of such apparently simple expressions of religious faith. At the time of his baptism, however, Descartes was destined by the rules of the Roman Catholic Church to be a compliant religious believer, and he seemed destined by his patrimony to become a lawyer.

René Descartes' father, Joachim, continued to divide his year between Rennes in Brittany and Châtellerault in Poitou for three years after his wife's death in 1597, and in 1600 he married Anne Morin de Chavagnes from Nantes. Anne Morin was the daughter of the First President of the provincial tax court.[24] Joachim and Anne had four children, including Joachim (who later acquired the same post as his father) and a daughter called Anne.[25] Descartes probably lived with his maternal grandmother for at least two years, or as long as his local nurse was feeding him, and he may have spent some time each year at his father's principal house in Châtellerault up to the age of four. But once his father moved permanently to Rennes in 1600, it is likely that Descartes remained with his brother and sister at his maternal grandmother's house, until her death in 1609 or 1610. He may have spent the holiday periods at the house of his godfather, Michel Ferrand, at Châtellerault, and he may have lived with his paternal grandmother, Claude Ferrand, who was the widow of Pierre Descartes, René's grandfather. While in the care of his two grandmothers, and in the company of his sister, Jeanne, Descartes acquired the elementary reading and writing skills that were normally learned at home, and thus began his preparation for formal schooling.

Even before attending school, however, he began to imbibe the social expectations of the class into which he had been born. Erasmus was the dominant exponent of Christian humanism in the sixteenth century and a master of expressing, in elegant, brief, Latin phrases, the social values of a pre-Reformation Europe. He had published a small booklet in 1530, which immediately became a best-seller and was translated into many European vernaculars. It appeared in English, in 1532, as *A Lytell Booke of Good Manners for Children*. Despite its relative brevity, Erasmus included detailed suggestions on how to eat and drink, how not to lick one's lips, what to wear, and how to conduct oneself in company, including a version of 'Little children should be seen and not heard.'[26] In the course of writing this primer in civility for young Christian children, Erasmus also captured in a pithy phrase the educational ambitions that motivated the hopes and expectations of the Descartes family: 'All those are to be considered noble who cultivate their minds by liberal studies.'[27] In fact, according to

Erasmus, those who become ennobled by education are more genuinely deserving of that status than those who merely inherit their titles from their ancestors.

One might think of the young Descartes, then, as enjoying a very peaceful life in a small village atmosphere, on the banks of the river Creuse, in the company of his sister, Jeanne (who was three years older), and his brother, Pierre (who was five years his senior). It may have been during these formative years that he became attached to the cross-eyed girl whom he writes about many years later. 'I loved a girl of my own age who had a slight squint. As a result, the impression made on my brain, when I looked at her cross eyes, became so linked with the impression also made there and which aroused the passion of love that, for a long time afterwards, when I saw someone with a squint, I was more inclined to love them than anyone else.'[28] With the passing of time he recognized that the girl's squint was a defect, and he moved beyond his childish infatuation. He was soon ready to leave his childhood behind, to leave his native village, and to take the first insecure steps in his education.

A Jesuit Education

The Jesuits had been expelled from France in 1595, following the assassination of Henry III in 1589, and they were expelled again more definitively, almost two centuries later, in 1763. In the intervening period, however, they enjoyed a public role – in education, in church and religious controversy, and in politics – that was unequalled by any other religious order.[29] Their readmission to France in the late sixteenth century and the founding of La Flèche College coincided with the official reconciliation of the king, Henry IV, to the Catholic Church and his reluctant acceptance by Catholic nobles as the legitimate successor to Henry III. The unusual circumstances of the Jesuits' readmission and the hostility of established educational and religious powers in France made them suspects in many of the controversies that took place during Descartes' life. Thus the Jesuits not only educated Descartes; their contentious role in French public life in the seventeenth century life made them one of the permanent points of reference for his professional career.

When a Dominican friar assassinated Henry III in 1589, the throne was claimed by Henry de Bourbon. At the time Henry was a Protestant, and his claim was not recognized by supporters of the Catholic League, by the

Pope (Sixtus V), or by the faculty of theology at Paris. Faced with such united political and ecclesiastical opposition by Catholics, Henry publicly abjured his Protestantism in 1593 and then wrote to the new Pope, Clement VIII, asking for absolution. This was eventually and somewhat grudgingly conceded two years later, in 1595. It remains a matter of dispute whether Henry IV was sincere in his change of religious allegiance, or whether he publicly changed sides in order to mollify his powerful political critics. It is at least clear that he remained sympathetic to the position of Huguenots in his kingdom, and he signed the Edict of Nantes in 1598 to provide them with minimal religious and political tolerance. Huguenots represented a minority in the kingdom at about 8–10 percent of the total population. However, they were particularly well represented in certain towns, where they had their own local representative bodies. La Rochelle was famously one of those, at least before the siege of 1627–28, and so was Châtellerault, where Descartes' family lived.

Following his conversion to Catholicism, the king acceded to a long-standing request from the Jesuits for permission to return to France, and in September 1603 he invited them to open a new college at La Flèche, where he himself had grown up as a young boy. Nonetheless, he also acknowledged the objections of the University of Paris against granting the Jesuits permission to reopen their former college, Clermont College, in Paris.[30] Thus La Flèche College was very much more than simply a college founded with formal royal approval. It was to be called 'The College of King Henry IV'; it represented a provisional substitute for the prestigious Jesuit college at Paris; and it was endowed with funds and prize money by the king so that students would not have to pay tuition fees. Finally, as a special mark of his interest, the king decreed that, after his death and that of the queen, their hearts should be preserved in the choir of the college chapel and that their portraits should be displayed there. In making this provision, he hardly anticipated the circumstances or the relative speed with which his decree would be implemented.

The college opened for new students in February 1604, and Descartes' older brother, Pierre, was among the first to enroll. Despite the official opening date, the school was still under construction for many years, and the church was not completed until 1621, long after Descartes had left. La Flèche accepted two kinds of pupils, those who were boarding and those classified as 'external' or day students. Within a few years, the total number of students increased to approximately 300 boarders and 1,200 day students, and these figures remained relatively stable during the time that Descartes attended.

The curriculum at La Flèche was set out in detail in the Jesuits' *Syllabus of Studies*, an educational curriculum that had been adopted by the order in 1599 and implemented in France in 1603.[31] The whole course of studies was divided into thirteen classes, which represented six years of preparatory studies, three for philosophy, and four years for theology. The inclusion of theology might seem unusual, but at the time there were no separate schools for those preparing for the priesthood. This policy was subsequently the basis for the sharp critique of Jesuit educational initiatives in France by Étienne Pasquier. 'Although they were not permitted either by the ancient custom of the Universities or by the novelty of their Bulls to open their schools to all kinds of students, or to have anyone other than seminarians in their Colleges, nevertheless they opened a College not only for members of their Order but also for all students.'[32] Thus Jesuit scholastics attended side by side with lay students, although only the former continued their studies for the final four years of theology. While many students left after the first six years, Descartes remained to complete the three-year philosophy course.

Another unusual feature of Jesuit schools in this period was that students were not classified by their age – a practice that is almost universal now – but by their progress in studies or their level of achievement. The elementary classes were numbered in reverse order, from sixth to first. In a typical school of the period, therefore, the pupils in fifth class (i.e., the second-lowest grade in the school) varied in age from eight to eighteen, with the largest number of them being age ten.[33] Thus students who were just beginning their studies may have joined the school at a higher class than the sixth, and some of those who made little progress in their studies may have remained in the same class for a number of years.

The first four years of study were mostly concerned with grammar, and with acquiring fluency in writing Latin and Greek. To support these academic objectives, the students and teachers were required to speak Latin during all their formal classes.[34] This must have been very difficult for some students, especially those who had no ambition to become clerics or to distinguish themselves in academic study. One of Descartes' contemporaries at La Flèche was so overwhelmed by the demands of Greek that he wrote to his father and asked permission to be taken out of school.[35]

Once the students had a firm grasp of the two classical languages, they concentrated in second class on the humanities and in first class on rhetoric. The devaluation of the vernacular changed only with the founding of the Académie Française in 1634, although many authors continued to publish in Latin well into the seventeenth century.

Apart from learning Latin and Greek grammar, students in the elementary classes were trained in rhetoric, and in reading and writing poetry in the classical languages. *The Art of Rhetoric* (1577), by the Jesuit Cyprian Soarez, was one of the standard texts used for rhetoric. It specified the function of rhetoric – to teach people how to speak effectively in order to persuade listeners – and it provided students with an introductory course in five parts: discovery, disposition, elocution, memorization, and pronunciation.[36] The contents were drawn primarily from Aristotle, Cicero, and Quintilian, a selection that was subsequently reflected in the 'Rules for Professors of Rhetoric' in the *Syllabus*: 'Only Cicero may be employed for orations, while Quintilian and Aristotle as well as Cicero may be employed for fundamental precepts.'[37] However, it is clear from the other authors recommended, and from independent evidence about their readings, that the students at La Flèche were exposed to a relatively wide range of classical authors, including Plato, Demosthenes, Thycidedes, Hesiod, Pindar, Livy, Ovid, Virgil, and some Christian authors such as Basil and Chrysostom. Those in the Higher Grammar classes were encouraged to read the more accessible books by Cicero, such as his *On Friendship* and *On Old Age*.

If Descartes studied Quintilian carefully, as he was expected to have done, he would have learned from one of its classical exponents those features of rhetoric that were especially important for lawyers. The objective of any rhetorical presentation was to convince one's hearers. Hence the need, according to Quintilian, for clarity and distinctness – two concepts that were to figure subsequently as key features of the Cartesian account of evidence.[38] When constructing arguments, a persuasive lawyer was expected to engage with the emotional content of his case and to try to stimulate an appropriate emotional response in the listeners. 'The prime essential for stirring the emotions of others is, in my opinion, first to feel those emotions oneself.'[39] Thirdly, effective arguments should be based on certainty. 'It has generally been laid down that, in order to be effective, an argument must be based on certainty; for it is obviously impossible to prove what is doubtful by what is no less doubtful.'[40] These themes, appropriately reworked in a different context, re-emerge in Descartes' theory of knowledge.

Elementary studies at La Flèche were followed by three years of philosophy. The first year was devoted to logic, the second to physics and mathematics, and the final year to metaphysics. Logic included two months on the basic logic of Toletus and Fonseca, the second book of Aristotle's *Physics*, and various suggestions about definition that are found in *On the Soul* and the *Topics*. The mature Descartes was consistently critical of the value of logic as taught in schools at the time. He reflected, in the *Discourse on Method*:

When I was younger, I had studied a little logic as part of philosophy and, in mathematics, I had studied geometrical analysis and algebra – three arts or sciences that seemed as if they ought to contribute something to my project. But when I studied them I noticed that, in the case of logic, its syllogisms and most of its other rules are more useful for explaining to someone else what one already knows than for learning them or even, in the Lullian art, for speaking uncritically about things that one does not know.   (vi. 17)

The study of physics and mathematics was even less satisfactory. The *Syllabus* gave the following rules for a mathematics teacher. 'Let him explain in class to the students of physics for about three-quarters of an hour the elements of Euclid. . . . after they have become somewhat familiar within two months, let him add something of geography or of the sphere or other matters which students are glad to listen to, and this along with Euclid either on the same day or on alternate days.'[41] Mathematics was a relatively late addition to the Jesuit curriculum, and in many of their schools there was no professor of mathematics at all. This seems to have resulted partly from opposition from the philosophers who were already established, and partly from a lack of experienced or adequately trained teachers.[42] One of the provisional remedies invoked was to exploit the talents of Jesuit theology students who were studying at the same college and who had already mastered the basics of mathematics. This was the solution adopted at La Flèche. Jean François was a theology student during the years 1612 to 1616, and he also functioned as a teacher of mathematics. At that time, the subject called 'mathematics' was not as narrowly defined or as clearly demarcated from its applications as it is today. It included, among other things, astronomy, optics, music, mechanics and hydraulics, surveying, and the art of fortification. The scope of the subject was not matched by an equally extensive student interest. As late as 1627, only sixty-four students were studying mathematics in the Jesuit colleges at La Flèche and Paris, which represented less than 0.5 percent of the total student enrollment and just over 7 percent of those in the philosophy cycle.[43]

In contrast with this training in skills that were relevant to the students, many of whom might have pursued careers in which applied mathematics was useful, their study of physics was based on certain books of Aristotle that were rapidly becoming obsolete. These included, in the second year, *On the Heavens*, Book I of *On Generation and Corruption*, and Books 6 and 7 of the *Physics*. The early seventeenth century was a period of intensive questioning of the fundamental efficacy and explanatory value of Aristotelian physics, and it would have been impossible for Descartes' teachers simply to read from Aristotle without any reference to recent challenges to his system. However, the basic concepts in terms of which Aristotle thought of the physical world, and the kinds of problems that were classified as physical, together with the perspective from which they were discussed, must have been taught to the young students. It was this general perspective, rather than any detailed solutions, that Descartes subsequently challenged with an intensity that could be explained only by personal experience.

Besides, the *Syllabus* required professors to respect Aristotle, even when they did not follow his teaching, and to refrain from presenting novel or dangerous views to their students. Rule 2 for professors of philosophy stated:

> In matters of any importance let him not depart from Aristotle unless something occurs which is foreign to the doctrine which academies everywhere approve of; much more if it is opposed to the orthodox faith, and if there are any arguments of this or any other philosopher against the faith, he will endeavour earnestly to refute them according to the Lateran Council.

The same conservatism was repeated in the rules for the prefect of studies, which specified the books that should be made available to students. 'He shall give to the students of theology and philosophy not all books but . . . besides the *Summa* of St. Thomas for the theologians, and Aristotle for the students of philosophy, some select commentary which they can consult in private studies.'[44] The rules for all professors of theology and philosophy required them to avoid 'new opinions' and not to introduce any opinion that 'does not have suitable authority' or is 'opposed to the axioms of learned men or the general belief of scholars.'[45] Descartes adverted to this conservative feature of Jesuit schooling many years after he had left school, when sending a copy of his first publication to one of his former Jesuit teachers. He wrote to Father Noël, in October 1637: 'Since I know that the principal reason why your colleges very carefully reject every kind of novelty in philosophical matters is your fear that they will also bring about some change in theology, I would like to emphasize at this point that there is nothing to fear on that count from my views' (i. 455–6). The fear of novel opinions, and the corresponding respect for Aristotle once his works were adapted to the needs of Christian theology, was not confined to the Jesuits or even to Catholics.[46] Philip Melanchthon, one of the founding theorists of the Lutheran Reformation, constantly exhorted his students in annual graduation speeches to cleave to their Greek classical heritage as a necessary condition for protecting their Christian faith.[47]

No brief summary could do justice to the complexity of Aristotelian physics or to the various compromises with which its official teachers worked in the period when Descartes was a student.[48] One of the central features of Aristotle's system was a distinction between what were called 'matter' and 'form'. If, for example, one carves a statue from a block of marble, the stuff of which the statue is made is evidently marble, but what makes it a distinctive statue is the shape or form that results from the artist's skill. Aristotelians thought that they could understand all material things by analogy with sculpting a statue, and that they could thereby explain how things acquired all their distinctive properties. They claimed that there was one propertyless stuff (corresponding to uncut marble) out of which all material things were made and which was called 'primary matter'. Various distinct forms are impressed on this primary matter, and the result is the great variety of things that we see around us in the universe, such as trees, fish, birds, and so on. Thus what makes something a bird or, even more specifically, a seagull is that it has the distinctive form of a seagull. All the properties of a seagull are said to result from its possession of this form. It follows that the best way to explain any naturally occurring thing or phenomenon is to understand the form that makes it into the kind of reality that it is. This theory of forms was complemented by a theory of four causes, and by a distinction between (a) natural or intrinsic change and (b) unnatural or externally caused changes.

The Aristotelian tradition repeated, for about two thousand years, that there were four types of cause: efficient, formal, material, and final. The form and matter just mentioned reappear here in a slightly different guise, as material and formal causes. Since the starting point for much of Aristotle's physics was his reflection on living things, he thought of them as emerging from matter, being guided in their development by their form, and tending toward some predetermined natural goal (which is the final cause of their development). Evidently, this way of thinking of the natural development of plants and animals, and of the changes they undergo in their maturation and eventual decline, fails to address the kind of change that occurs when, for example, one body bumps against another and causes some change in it. Here Aristotle's 'efficient' cause had to do the work required.

The original biological paradigm and the distinction between different kinds of cause gave rise to fundamental conceptual problems at the core of Aristotle's physics. Some changes were said to be 'natural', that is, caused by the internal form or inner nature of some reality. Others were 'unnatural', or caused by an external factor such as a foreign body that is already in motion. One of the implications of this division between radically different causes was that it was impossible to conceive of the motion of a projectile in a coherent way. If we throw a stone into the air or launch a rocket, its initial motion upward is an 'unnatural' motion caused by the stone thrower or the rocket launcher. Once the stone reaches its maximum height and begins to descend, however, its subsequent motion is a natural motion downward that is explained by its inner nature. In fact, even its initial motion upward is an unresolved issue for the Aristotelian tradition. Some thought that, for example, an arrow shot from a bow continues to move because it displaces the air in front of it, and that this displaced air constantly curls around behind the arrow to give it an additional push in the same direction. Others tried to convert this externally caused motion into an effect that is internally explained. Jean Buridan (d. 1358), for example, suggested that the initial projection from the bow imparted to the arrow what he called an 'impetus', and that this new property – a kind of inner tendency to motion – moved the arrow in a way that is similar to the natural downward motion of heavy bodies. Descartes later questioned, not so much the detailed solutions offered by this tradition, but the very assumptions on which it was based and its failure over many centuries to make significant progress in our understanding of natural phenomena.

The final year of the three-year philosophical cycle was devoted to metaphysics. This focused on other writings by Aristotle: Book II of *On Generation and Corruption, On the Soul*, and selections from Books 7 and 12 of the *Metaphysics*. This was a case, however, where the rule 'follow Aristotle' provided less than clear guidance. Aristotle's theory of the human soul had been a contentious issue for Christian philosophers since at least the thirteenth century. Some of his most insightful interpreters, such as the medieval Arabic philosopher Ibn Rushd (also known as Averroes), had challenged the ease with which Christian philosophers had adapted Aristotle to show that each individual human being has an immortal soul. Averroes understood Aristotle as proposing that there was a single world soul in which all thinking beings participate. However, such a shared active intellect did not fit easily with the Christian tradition, and it drew extensive critiques from Aquinas in *The Unity of the Intellect against the Averroists* (1269), and from Siger of Brabant in *The Intellective Soul* (1273).[49]

A similar attempt to return to Aristotle's original texts and their authentic meaning in sixteenth-century Italy persuaded a number of sympathetic commentators that, if the human soul is the 'form' that defines the nature of human beings, then the soul ceases to exist when an individual dies. Pietro Pomponazzi (1462–1525), the great Paduan philosopher, was notorious for defending this position.[50] While this avoided the one-soul-for-all approach of the medieval Arabic philosophers, it had equally unacceptable implications for those who wished to argue that each human being has his or her own distinct, immortal soul. Pomponazzi did not argue that the human soul cannot possibly be immortal. He defended the more modest position that, as far as human reason or philosophy can take us, there is no basis for believing that each person has an immortal soul, although it might be accepted on faith as part of the church's teaching.

The Lateran Council, a general synod of the Catholic Church, condemned these new interpretations of Aristotle in 1513.[51] Descartes' teachers were required to work within the principles and concepts proposed by Aristotle, and they were equally required to communicate to their young pupils the teaching of the Catholic Church as it was defined by Rome. They had to find a way, therefore, to present Aristotle's metaphysics in such a manner that it supported the two main contentions of Christian metaphysics, namely, the existence of God and the immortality of the human soul. Specifically, professors of philosophy were forbidden to teach Averroes, and if they found anything worth reporting in his philosophy they were encouraged to dissemble and pretend that they had found it elsewhere: a professor 'shall not treat of the digressions of Averroes . . . in any separate treatise, and if anything good is to be cited from him, let him bring it out without praise and, if possible, let him show that he has taken it from some other source.'[52] Twenty-five years later, Descartes adverts to this in his letter of dedication of his *Meditations* to the theology faculty at the Sorbonne.

School Days

The years during which Descartes attended La Flèche College are not certain, but it is most likely that he arrived there at Easter 1607, when he was eleven years old, and that he left school at the end of the philosophy cycle in 1615, when he was nineteen.[53] There had been an outbreak of some unspecified contagious disease at the school in 1605, and this, together with Descartes' own fragile health, may have delayed the beginning of his formal education.[54] When the day arrived to leave home and venture forth, Descartes travelled about 160 kilometres, by coach or on horseback, carrying the essential provisions for his first school year. Apart from prescribed books, each boarder brought their own cutlery and a goblet. They also needed enough money to pay for the services of a tailor, and for the hairdresser who visited the school twice a week to cut and powder their hair. The books alone were very expensive. They included Nicot's French–Latin dictionary, Cicero's *Letters*, the *Adages* of Erasmus, student editions of Cicero and Virgil, and various religious books used at the college, such as a life of St. Ignatius and Louis de Grenade's *Guide for Sinners.*[55] By far the largest number of students lived in rented accommodations in the town, although they followed the same daily schedule as the residents. Descartes, however, joined his brother Pierre as a boarder.

The Jesuits are widely credited with introducing many changes into schools that helped distinguish their curriculum from the monastic practices on which they had previously been modeled.[56] For example, they introduced a half-day holiday on Thursday, and annual summer holidays that varied in length from the junior to the senior classes. These were taken usually in September, so that students could return home and help with the harvest. Thus, apart from church holidays that had been traditional in schools, Descartes had annual summer holidays that varied from two weeks when he was in the junior grades to a maximum of two months when he was studying philosophy. The Jesuits also reduced the classes each day to about five and a half hours, leaving extra time for private study, recreation, and of course for prayer. However, even with all these progressive changes, the school week still appears extremely monastic from our perspective. There were minor variations from one school to another and for students of different classes, but the general structure of the school day was the following:

5:00/5:30 A.M.	Rise, pray, and repeat lessons to one's prefect
7:30/8:00 A.M.	Formal classes
10:00 A.M.	Attend Mass
10:45 A.M.	Lunch in the refectory
11:30 A.M.	Recreation
12:00 A.M.	Private study, and repetition of lessons with one's prefect
2:00–5:00 P.M.	Formal classes
6:00 P.M.	Dinner, and recreation until 7.00 or 7.15
7:00 P.M.	General repetition of lessons
9:00 P.M.	Visit to the church and prayer before retiring

This daily schedule applied seven days a week, although there were some variations on the weekend. Sunday included more formal religious services, and philosophy students had a weekly disputation for two hours on Saturday and, once a month, a disputation on a prearranged topic that extended over the morning and afternoon on Saturday.[57] Descartes seems to have been excused from the early rise by the college rector, Father Charlet, who was a distant relative of his. Many years later he wrote to him as someone 'who acted as a father to me during all my youth.'[58] Descartes' father had been dead for four years, at that stage, and he was able to tell Father Charlet, without exaggeration: 'I think of you as if you were my father, and I believe you will not be offended if I communicate with you as I would with him if he were still alive.' Unfortunately, there was not much difference, from Descartes' perspective, in the paternal care he received from his father while alive or dead.[59]

The college integrated students from various social classes, at least in the sense that it included some who were genuine nobles among the many

who were bourgeois.[60] For the most part, however, Jesuit schools reflected
the social stratification of French society in the early seventeenth century
and the lack of interest in formal education among merchants and peasants,
who did not see the benefits of having their children study Latin and Greek
for six years, much less philosophy. While some sent their sons to school
to support their aspirations toward upward social mobility, they usually
withdrew them after first class (that is, before beginning philosophy).
La Flèche also educated Jesuit scholastics and lay pupils together in the
same classes. It had originally been planned to establish a separate novitiate for young Jesuits in an adjacent Augustinian priory, St. Jacques,
but this plan was abandoned. The alternative was to integrate Jesuit students into the regular school, so that by the time that Descartes reached
the philosophy classes the school included fifty-five Jesuit scholastics and
approximately one hundred Jesuits in total.[61] One of the advantages of this
integration was that the senior Jesuit students could be used as tutors or
répétiteurs for lay students. This partially explains Descartes' comments,
in the *Discourse*, that his fellow students 'included some who were already
destined to replace our teachers' (vi. 5). The sheer size of the classes, some
of which included as many as two hundred students, made it necessary to
have some kind of tutorial system in place.

The predominant style of teaching was thus very much a study of
basic texts that were accessible even to the average student. The teacher
offered an initial reading of a text, explaining the meaning of words and
the implications of obscure passages, and the students then collectively
read the texts out loud and recited them in unison. Montaigne commented
sarcastically on his school experience that 'teachers are for ever bawling
into our ears as though pouring knowledge down through a funnel: our
task is merely to repeat what we have been told.'[62] Other periods during
the day provided an opportunity for private revision, and the students
were then required to meet their prefect and, individually, to recite or
explain their daily quota of lessons.

During at least part of his studies, Jacques Dinet was Descartes' principal prefect, and Etienne Noël was a theology student and part-time tutor
to whom he reported almost daily to show that he had completed his
lessons. The daily contact with these Jesuits explains the ease with which,
many years later, Descartes sent a copy of his first book to Father Noël,[63]
and asked Father Dinet, when he was provincial superior of the Jesuits,
to help deflect or restrain the criticisms of the *Dioptrics* that were written

by another Jesuit, Pierre Bourdin. Apart from Jean François (1582–1668), already mentioned as teaching mathematics, Descartes also knew François Du Ban as a contemporary in theology, and he was taught by Denis Petau (1583–1652), who was professor of rhetoric before moving to Paris to teach theology; Pierre Musson (1561–1637), whose dramatic compositions had been produced at the college during Descartes' school days, in 1608–12; and François Fournet (1581–1638), who taught philosophy from 1611 to 1614, as did Louis Lallemant (1588–1635) and Nicolas Caussin (1583–1651). Caussin subsequently became famous as the author of *The Holy Court* (1624) and other partisan writings.[64]

There are no reliable records of Descartes' studies at school. Many years later, Nicholas-Joseph Poisson – who by then had become an Oratorian priest and a loyal supporter of Cartesian philosophy – reports meeting a friend in Saumur, in 1663, who claimed to have attended La Flèche at the same time as Descartes. There is probably a certain amount of retrospective projection in the following description of the philosophical skills of the schoolboy René:

When there was a question of proposing an argument or disputation, initially he asked a number of times about the definition of terms. He then asked how various principles that were accepted in the schools should be understood. Then he asked if one agreed with various known truths, about which he wanted to have agreement, and from this he set up a simple argument from which it was very difficult to budge him subsequently.[65]

This may easily have been the standard format for a disputation, rather than an anticipation of the demand for clear and distinct ideas that later characterized the most famous alumnus of La Flèche.

The daily routine of studies was relieved slightly by dramatic productions that were composed by the professors, and evidently by various games that children commonly played in the early seventeenth century. The *Syllabus* included specific guidance for the 'tragedies and comedies' that were to be performed. They had to be done in Latin; they could not deviate from anything that was not 'sacred and pious'; and they could not include any 'feminine role or feminine attire.'[66] Before attending school, many children learned to ride a horse, to play music (for example, the lute or violin), to dance, and to play various board games or games that involved gambling.[67] They obviously did not renounce all these skills at the schoolhouse gate. Students at La Flèche enjoyed various ball games, including tennis and volley-ball, and they also engaged in various forms of board games or gambling, though gambling for money was officially discouraged.[68] The fact that the *Syllabus* explicitly forbade students from bringing to class 'arms, daggers, knives or other such things' might help put in context the society from which they came and the dangers to personal safety for which they had to be prepared on their journeys to and from school.

One other feature of the school day, perhaps the most important one in the eyes of the Jesuits, was the spiritual development or religious training of the students. The Council of Trent had underlined the importance of Catholic education as a means of consolidating the membership of the church against the influence of reformers. The Jesuits saw themselves as dedicated officers of the Counter-Reformation, and they took a special vow of obedience to the Pope. In the context of their schools, therefore, they were particularly conscientious in following the Tridentine model of religious instruction based on a catechism. The professor of rhetoric assumed this responsibility as a special feature of classes on Saturday. Teachers introduced each class with a prayer, and even external students were encouraged to 'confess their sins at least once a month, and to be present at the daily sacrifice of the Mass at the appointed hour and at the sermon on Holy Days.'[69] The students were also invited to become members of various confraternities, which met as religious clubs within the school. This was one of the ways in which they helped cultivate prayers to and special veneration of the Virgin Mary, including praying the rosary.[70] Finally, the students went on a week-long retreat once each year, under the guidance of the *Spiritual Exercises* of Saint Ignatius of Loyola.

Descartes named one of his most famous essays *Meditations,* in which he is often said to have given a special place to a form of pure thinking that contrasts with the deceptive illusions of the imagination. The *Exercises* of Saint Ignatius, however, relied very much on the imagination to represent scenes from the life of Christ, to reflect on the Christian's life as a journey toward God; and they systematically invoked the senses as a starting point for acquiring an appreciation or understanding of spiritual realities. The *Exercises* are divided into four principal sections, called 'weeks', and some of these in turn are divided into 'days'. Many exercises begin with an imaginative representation of a scene from the life of Christ. For example, the first exercise in the first week offers the following guidance to the retreatant:

Note. For a visual contemplation or meditation, the picture is an imaginative representation of the physical place where the event to be contemplated occurs. By physical place I mean, e.g., a temple or mountain where Jesus Christ our Lord is, as demanded by the subject-matter; where the subject-matter is not something visible, as in the present case of sins, the 'picture' will be the idea, produced by an effort of the imagination, that my soul is a prisoner in this corruptible body.[71]

This method of using the imagination to set the scene and to assist one's thought to focus on a specific issue is repeated throughout the *Exercises*. With unrelenting frequency and regularity, Ignatius asks retreatants to form an appropriate 'picture of the scene' in their imagination.[72] He also invites those who are making a retreat, at the very outset, to move through its various stages without knowing in advance what is to be done at later stages of the journey. 'It is a good thing for the retreatant in the first week not to know anything about what he will be doing in the second week: he should struggle in the first to get what he is looking for, as though he had no hope of getting anything in the second.'[73] There are obvious parallels with the first day of Descartes' *Meditations*, in which the meditator is left drowning in skeptical doubts as if there were no way out. However, in contrast with what Descartes later argued, Saint Ignatius expected readers to accept uncritically the teaching of the Catholic Church, even if it seemed to conflict with the most obvious deliverances of their own senses. 'To arrive at complete certainty, this is the attitude of mind we should maintain: I will believe that the white object I see is black if that should be the decision of the hierarchical Church. . . .'[74]

The Assassination of Henry IV

The repetitive daily life of students at La Flèche was interrupted by various unpredictable events that, despite a conscious implementation of the Jesuit curriculum, could not have been excluded from their otherwise cloistered and somewhat artificial environment. The country was subject to frequent outbreaks of disease, and one of these, described as involving both 'fevers and dysentery,' affected the college in 1613.[75] In the following year, France seemed as if it were on the brink of a civil war, and the young King Louis XIII visited the college. However, the event that was most prominent during the years that Descartes attended must have been the assassination of King Henry IV and the subsequent funeral ceremonies held at the college.

On Friday, 14 May 1610, King Henry IV was riding in an open carriage toward the royal palace in Paris (to visit his mistress, it was widely believed) when his carriage was accidentally blocked on a narrow street, rue de la Ferronnerie, by two parked carts. While waiting to have the street unblocked, his assassin, François Ravaillac, exploited the opportunity by jumping into his carriage and stabbing him with a knife several times in the chest. The king died almost immediately. Henry IV had been planning to leave Paris that day at the head of 30,000 troops to recover from the Austrian empire a disputed piece of territory on the German border near Cologne. This suggested initially a political motive for the regicide, but under questioning it emerged that Ravaillac was a disgruntled 'good Catholic' who claimed that the king was too sympathetic to Calvinists, and that he was waging war with the Pope by his opposition to the Austrian emperor. The most likely explanation of Ravaillac's motivation is that he was psychologically disturbed. He had joined the Benedictine order for a short time in his youth but had been encouraged to leave because he was having visions. He certainly had no connection with the Jesuits, and there was no evidence that they were in any way involved in the affair. Yet, despite that, there was a general suspicion that the Jesuits were in some way responsible for the king's assassination.[76]

The unfounded allegation against the Jesuits underlines the extent to which they were widely perceived to be supporters of the Pope against Gallican sympathies in the French church, or supporters of Spain in its war with France (since Ignatius and all the early Superior Generals of the order were Spanish). In summary, they were suspected of being secretly allied with foreign powers, political and ecclesiastical, in a way that compromised their allegiance to the French crown. When Henry IV had allowed them to re-enter France and had invited them to found a college at La Flèche, against the explicit advice of the *parlement* of Paris and the University of Paris, he had placed a senior Jesuit as a permanent member of his household as confessor to the king. At the time of his death, Father Pierre Coton was his confessor, a coincidence that gave rise to the quip that 'the king has cotton in his ears.' Given the widespread suspicion of the Jesuits, and the opposition of other interest groups to their apparently privileged role, their immediate response to Henry IV's death was an extremely public and obsequious expression of exaggerated grief and loyalty. This was an opportunity to implement the king's wishes about where his heart should be buried, and to win support with the

queen, Marie de Médicis, who would be regent during the minority of
Louis XIII.

On 1 June, following the principal religious ceremonies in Paris, the
king's heart was carried on a three-day funeral journey to the town of
La Flèche, accompanied by nobles, soldiers, and the Provincial of the
Jesuits in Paris, Father Armand.[77] Since the college chapel had not yet
been built, the ceremonies took place at the local parish church of St.
Thomas, at which Father Armand preached a lengthy sermon in praise
of the deceased monarch. Every year subsequently until the eighteenth
century, beginning on 4 June, the college held a three-day commemoration
of these events, in which the school pupils and the staff of the college
participated. This included a public procession carrying the king's heart
from the Church of St. Thomas to the college chapel, philosophical and
academic disputations, and, on the third day, a theatrical presentation that
honoured the memory of the late king.

The ceremonies for the first anniversary were published at La Flèche
under the title: *For the Anniversary of the Death of Henry the Great: the
Tears of the College of La Flèche, directed by the Society of Jesus.*[78] This
is no small pamphlet. It is a book of over four hundred pages, which
includes poems written by the staff and students in Latin, Greek, and
French, together with the text of the anniversary funeral oration.[79] The
commemorative oration begins with the words: 'Gentlemen: if this discourse, washed away by tears as soon as it emerges from the mind and
the pen, is interrupted by sighs, accept it as conceived and formed in a
heart that it broken by grief.'[80] The unrelenting rhetoric of sorrow and
copious tears makes it appear as if the preacher had just lost his most
intimate friend: 'How many times during this past year have tears welled
up in my eyes as I passed by the places and pathways of your tender
youth, of which these woods, these houses and gardens remind me every
day.'[81]

Among the relatively few verses written in French in *The Tears*, there
is a sonnet about the death of the king and the discovery, by Galileo, of
the moons of Jupiter. The fact that this is the very same year in which
Galileo's discoveries were published indicates that the sonnet's author
was well informed about recent developments in astronomy. The sonnet
contrasts the flood of tears that had been shed in France for the death of
the king, a deluge that was in danger of flooding the whole country and its
neighbouring provinces, with the benefits derived from the bright guiding

stars of Jupiter. There are connotations of the empty tomb associated
with the resurrection of Jesus, as reported in the Gospels, and the king's
empty tomb once God has raised him as a celestial flame in the heavens of
Jupiter.[82]

When Descartes completed his college education in September 1615,
he emerged from what he later described as 'one of the most renowned
schools in Europe' (vi. 5) with a classical education, but no university
qualification.[83] For, despite Henry IV's approval for establishing Jesuit
colleges, the universities retained the exclusive power of awarding professional qualifications in the various professions such as law and medicine. If
Descartes were to follow the family tradition, therefore, he needed a university degree, and for that reason he went to the University of Poitiers.
He seems to have been in Poitiers from 1615 to 1616, and to have lodged
with his maternal uncle, René Brochard. Poitiers was an obvious choice
for Descartes. Apart from his uncle's residence there and its nearness to
his home, his family had earlier connections with that university. Among
them, his great-grandfather, Jean Ferrand, had become rector of the university in 1568.

Following one year of study, possibly completed without attending lectures, Descartes registered at the University of Poitiers on 21 May 1616
and graduated on successive days, 9 and 10 November 1616, with a bach-
elor's degree and a licentiate in civil and canon law. It was customary to
defend publicly the theses on which the licentiate was awarded some weeks
after the official graduation. Thus Descartes' public defence was scheduled for 28 November 1616, and a poster to that effect, which listed the
forty theses to be defended, was displayed in Poitiers.[84] For some unknown
reason, the defence was delayed and was rescheduled for 21 December.
The theses were concerned with legal problems that arise in validating
wills and bequests, as befits someone who was studying to practice civil
law. Having completed his formal education, Descartes was twenty years
old; he was qualified for a career in law and could have followed his father
and older brother to Brittany to become a king's counsellor. Alternatively,
he could have envisaged a post as a teacher, since his qualification was
already the highest one given by a university, or he might have considered joining the ranks of the clergy or entering religious life (a choice that
emerged prominently among his nieces and one nephew). He chose none
of these. He summarized the uncertainty that caused his change of mind
in the *Discourse* as follows:

I have been nourished by books since I was a child, and because I was convinced that, by using them, one could acquire clear and certain knowledge of everything that is useful for life, I had a great desire to study them. But as soon as I had concluded the course of studies at the end of which one is usually admitted to the ranks of the learned, I changed my mind completely. For I found myself so overcome by so many doubts and errors that I seemed to have gained nothing from studying, apart from becoming gradually more conscious of my ignorance.   (vi. 4)

Thus, instead of pursuing a legal career, Descartes seems to have spent some time in Paris before departing on the first journey of what turned out to be almost ten years of travel and research. Since there are no contemporaneous indications from Descartes about this formative period of his life, one has to rely on his reflections twenty years later, when he was composing the *Discourse*. To some degree he may be describing the experiences of 1607–16 from the perspective of what occurred only much later. However, this text provides the only personal account, by this famous graduate of La Flèche College and of the University of Poitiers, of the significance he attached to his formal education.

Reflections on His Education

By the time Descartes came to reflect on his education and to assess its content and benefits, he had read Montaigne's *Essays* and had thus reviewed his early schooling through the eyes of a well-known critic of the schools. Montaigne contrasted the useless book-learning of the schools with relevant skills naturally acquired by practice: 'we often waste years training children for occupations in which they never achieve anything.'[85] He doubted the value of formal training in rhetoric, assuming that one could acquire the appropriate skills more naturally. 'All those fine "colours of rhetoric" are in fact easily eclipsed by the light of pure and naïve truth.'[86] Although Montaigne was a firm supporter of the merits of learning Latin, he thought that classical languages could be learned much more easily and inexpensively by the same practical methods by which we learn a vernacular language. 'There is no doubt that Greek and Latin are fine and great accomplishments; but they are both too dear.'[87] He especially recommended, instead of school attendance, that young people be exposed to the customs and traditions of different peoples. 'For this purpose [i.e., to learn how to speak and judge well] mixing with people is wonderfully appropriate. So are visits to foreign lands.'[88] Thus Montaigne was both supporting the kind of education that a gentleman required and sharply criticizing the means by which it was provided, especially the rote learning that was almost universally endorsed. Apart from the traditional professions that were available only to graduates, he argued, and the underlying motivation of making money that supported the whole system, young boys would be better advised to skip school completely, as girls did at the time. 'For without the unique goal which is actually set before us (that is, to get rich by means of jurisprudence, medicine, paedagogy, and Theology too, a goal which does keep such disciplines respected),' people in Montaigne's time would have been as uneducated as their equally successful ancestors.[89]

Descartes similarly acknowledged 'that law, medicine and the other sciences bring honour and riches to those who practise them' (vi. 6). However, 'neither the honour nor the profit that they promised were enough to persuade me to study them. For, thank God, my situation was not such that I had to earn a living from the sciences in order to supplement my income' (vi. 9). Descartes had a modest inheritance, and he therefore thought that he was financially secure enough to devote his life to addressing the fundamental questions about the sciences that had been motivated, at least in part, by his uncritical Jesuit education.

Descartes provides a characteristically ambivalent evaluation of his early education in which he is simultaneously both grateful and critical. He accepts that 'the languages learned in school are necessary in order to understand classical texts,' that 'the reading of all good books is like a conversation with the most eminent people of past centuries, who were their authors,' that 'oratory has incomparable powers and attractions,' and that 'mathematics contains very subtle discoveries that can help very much to satisfy those who are curious, to facilitate all the crafts, and to reduce human labour' (vi. 5–6). The only negative note to emerge when reviewing the benefits of all the subjects he mentions, including ethics and theology, occurs in his comments on philosophy, when he says: 'philosophy provides ways of speaking plausibly about everything, and of making oneself admired by those who are less educated' (vi. 6). Without rejecting the Jesuits' contribution to his development, he considered that, by the end of his schooling, he 'had already devoted enough time to languages and even to reading the classics, to their stories and fables, because conversation with people from other periods is like travelling. . . . if one spends too much time travelling, one eventually becomes a stranger to one's own country' (vi. 6). However, the fundamental issue in his reflections – at least when seen from the perspective of his subsequent research – was the insecurity of the foundations on which all the sciences were built.

Mathematics seemed to provide a paradigm of a reliable science, but, according to Descartes, even this discipline was compromised by the practical applications to which it was put. 'Above all else, I was interested in mathematics because of the certainty and self-evidence of the way it reasons; but I had not yet noticed its real use and, since I thought it was useful only for mathematical applications, I was surprised that nothing more noteworthy had been built on such solid and firm foundations' (vi. 7). The failure of mathematicians to develop its theory, and their distraction by the benefits of applied mathematics, both supported the promise of a foundational science and highlighted the extent to which philosophy, insofar as it offered such a foundation, failed to meet expectations.

I shall say nothing about philosophy, except that it has been practised by the best minds that have appeared over many centuries, and yet it still contains nothing that is not disputed and consequently doubtful; therefore I was not so presumptuous as to hope to succeed better in it than others. And when I considered how many different opinions there may be about the same thing which are defended by the learned, even though no more than one of them can ever be true, I regarded almost as false everything that was merely probable. Thus, as regards the other sciences, in so far as they borrow their principles from philosophy, I judged that it was impossible that anything solid could have been built on foundations that were so weak. . . .   (vi. 7–8)

It is impossible to avoid the impression that Descartes is retrospectively constructing a coherent development of his own career, seen from the perspective of twenty years of travel and (for much of that time) living outside France, and that he is offering as the fundamental motivation for a crucial choice in his life his estimation of the validity or certainty of the subjects that were taught as sciences in the universities. His logical next step, then, was to seek the truth elsewhere. Since he had manifestly failed to discover it in books and now understood why it was not likely to be found there, he decided to redirect his search for truth externally toward nature and, internally, within himself.

The immediate context in 1637 of these reflections on his school days was Descartes' attempt to avoid the debilitating impact of widespread scepticism in France and to launch his own intellectual project with a novel and reliable foundation. That explains the references to the uncertainty of what he learned at school and the inadequacy of his education. However, when he graduated from Poitiers University, he was still undecided about what to do with his life. He showed little warmth or affection for his father, who had more or less abandoned him as a child. Although he had other family connections in the legal profession and could have pursued that career without moving to Brittany, he seems not to have been attracted by that option either. It is likely that he was moderately content with his education but aware of its limitations, and that he considered travelling abroad a way of getting experience of alternative possibilities. He had some intimation of the scientific developments that were being reported from Italy, Denmark, the United Provinces, and from central Europe, and he decided to visit at least some of those places to learn at first-hand what he had heard about only indirectly at school.

In Search of a Career
(1616–1622)

What path shall I follow in life?

(Ausonius)[1]

DESCARTES made a decisive break with his past and a significant step toward his life's work – although this became clear only in retrospect – when he left France and travelled north to the United Provinces at the beginning of 1618. There is no evidence to suggest that he embarked on this journey with the intention of devoting his life to philosophy, or that he was considering emigrating permanently from France, as he did a decade later. His state of mind, in 1618, was that of a young man who was uncertain about a career. He had provisionally declined to follow his father and his brother into a legal career and had opted instead for the other standard path to social promotion in French life – as a gentleman army officer. He also seemed vaguely conscious of intellectual gaps in his education, and of the benefits of foreign travel to help remedy those deficiencies.

Descartes' formal education had been narrowly scholastic, and it had certainly not provided a basis for the fundamental reform of human knowledge that he eventually undertook. During this period of transition, the young Jesuit alumnus seems to have been willing to consider perspectives as disparate as the mystical and cabalistic writers of the Middle Ages and the astrologers and alchemists of the Renaissance. He mentioned authors as diverse as Ramon Lull, Johannes Kepler, and Thomas Campanella, and flirted briefly with the arcane philosophy of the Rosicrucians. On two occasions he considered purchasing a royal appointment, possibly as a reliable source of income rather than an alternative to amateur scholarly pursuits. In many ways he drifted, both intellectually and geographically, without any clear plan of where he was going or what precisely he was looking for. The uncertainty of his personal journey also meant that, in contrast with the years following 1628, he preserved very few traces, in correspondence or otherwise, of his intellectual itinerary. The one clear fact is that he travelled extensively, lived in a variety of different European centres, made new friends, and that his first steps on this uncharted journey were in the direction of the United Provinces.

The countries that are now called Belgium, Luxembourg, and the Netherlands, together with some regions of northern France and western Germany, were the scene of an intermittent war between Spain and the emerging Dutch Republic throughout the sixteenth century.[2] The Spanish Netherlands had been a loose confederation of seventeen provinces under Habsburg rule before the Reformation. However, during the early decades of the seventeenth century, the provinces north of the Rhine and Maas Rivers gradually acquired a distinctive political, linguistic, and social character that explains their positive response to Calvinism and, especially, their defensive reaction to the repressive Spanish Counter-Reformation of the 1570s that attempted to impose Catholicism as the official religion of the empire.

The Union of Utrecht in 1579 that brought together Holland, Utrecht, and Zeeland, was a public expression of this developing autonomy and an omen of the imminent emergence of the new Dutch Republic, with the province of Holland as its dominant member.[3] Following the addition over time of four new provinces, Overijssel, Gelderland, Groningen, and Friesland, the Twelve Year Truce (1609–21) signaled the effective establishment of the United Provinces as an independent political reality.

The emancipation of these provinces from Spanish rule left intact a significant portion of the former Spanish Netherlands in the south that included Flanders, Brabant, and Luxemburg. In contrast with the northern secessionists, the residual Spanish Netherlands remained loyal to the Spanish monarchy, spoke French rather than Dutch as the official language, and was officially Catholic. Given the religious and linguistic affinities with France, one might have expected a greater degree of political sympathy and perhaps even military support between the Spanish Netherlands and its southern neighbours. However, Philip II's intervention on behalf of the Holy Roman Empire in the civil war in France in 1590, together with the imperial ambitions of Spain for more than a century and its pressure on contested borders in eastern and northern France, ensured that the remnants of the Spanish Netherlands were seen as a common enemy by both France and the United Provinces. Accordingly, despite the appearance of paradox, Catholic France supported the emerging autonomy of the Calvinist United Provinces.

In 1618, therefore, when Descartes embarked on his first foreign journey, he had to travel through the Spanish Netherlands to reach his initial destination in Holland. He could have travelled by boat from a northern French port and sailed along the North Sea until he reached a safe port in Holland, such as Rotterdam. This was the route he recommended to Ferrier over a decade later.[4] However, he subsequently claimed that his first sea voyage was in 1619;[5] thus we must assume that Descartes completed his journey overland, by carriage or canal. His destination was still only a loose confederation of provinces, over which Maurits of Nassau had become *Stadtholder* (provincial governor) and, since the death of his half-brother in 1618, Prince of Orange. The religious identity of the emerging state had been defined initially by its rejection of an imposed Catholicism rather than by a popular adoption of Calvinism. However, that situation changed significantly during the first two decades of the seventeenth century, when Calvinist preachers and theologians identified the 'one true church' with the same degree of intolerance and commitment that their Catholic counterparts had exhibited since the Council of Trent. The result was a public policy of closing the churches and meeting houses of Catholics, Anabaptists, and all those classified as heretics, and a significant turn toward fundamentalism and religious intolerance.

The most public expression of this division and of its impact on the United Provinces was the long-running dispute between rival followers of Jacobus Arminius (1560–1609) and Franciscus Gomarus (1563–1641). Arminius had been appointed a professor of theology at Leiden in 1603, and he had begun almost immediately to express doubts about a strict understanding of the doctrine of predestination. The proponents of that dogma believed that God decides in advance that certain individuals will be saved or damned to eternal perdition. Accordingly, the church they join and the religious life they lead results from God's predestination, rather than from a free choice by the people involved. This theological dispute mirrored a similar and equally acrimonious division among Catholic theologians about the efficacy of God's grace, and about the compatibility of genuine free will with an 'irresistible' divine influence.[6] When Arminius questioned this doctrine, the implications of his challenge were not limited to speculative theology. To the extent that he defended human free will and the temporal dimension of God's interventions in human actions, he supported a more tolerant attitude toward other religious traditions whose members, according to his account of divine grace, retained the possibility of religious conversion and ultimate salvation.

This dispute, although initially concerned with one of the finer points of Reformed theology, divided Dutch society, its public representatives, and its city councils. It also threatened to destabilize the fragile unity of the United Provinces just at the time when their truce with the Spanish was about to expire (in 1621), because it drew unwelcome attention to the constitutional ambiguity of the new political entity. For, despite the depth and seriousness of the division of allegiance among Dutch Calvinists, it was unclear whether such a fundamental dispute should be resolved separately by each individual province, or whether it should be decided by the States General on their behalf. The Synod of Dordrecht (1618–19) decided after lengthy debates to support the anti-Remonstrant or Gomarist position. This led to the purging of Arminians from town councils, the imprisonment of the greatest Dutch jurist of the period, Hugo Grotius (1583–1645), his famous escape from Loevestein Castle in 1621, and his subsequent exile in France.

Descartes' first visit to the United Provinces, therefore, coincided with the deliberations of the Synod of Dordrecht, the consequent official repression of dissident religious sects, including Catholics and Lutherans, the uncertainty about the political unity of the secessionist provinces, and the early years of a Dutch recovery of its international commercial and shipping pre-eminence. It was also a time of significant immigration of refugee Calvinists from the southern provinces and from Germany, and of the consolidation of the religious ethos of the emerging republic. The relative instability and inhospitality of such a state did not deter the aspiring young Frenchman, when he arrived in Holland with vaguely military ambitions and a willingness to learn from what he called 'the great book of the world.'

Although one must have some reservations about the retrospective history of this period that Descartes provides in the autobiographical paragraphs of the *Discourse on Method*, his comments in 1637 have the feel of authenticity. For example, he recalls almost with disbelief that, on leaving college, he was naïve enough to think he knew the difference between valid sciences and their pseudo-competitors. 'As far as false doctrines are concerned, I thought that I already knew their value well enough not to be any longer subject to being deceived by the promises of an alchemist, the predictions of an astrologer, the deceptions of a magician, or the tricks and boasts of any of those who claim to know more than they really do' (vi. 9). The implication of this comment is that he was much less competent to make this distinction than he assumed confidently when he completed his formal studies. He needed to open his mind to alternative sciences, theories, and styles of life, which were likely to be at least as plausible as those he had learned uncritically at La Flèche.

That is why, as soon as I was old enough to leave the control of my teachers, I gave up completely the study of the humanities and, resolving not to search for any other science apart from what could be found in myself or in the great book of the world, I spent the remainder of my youth travelling, visiting courts and armies, meeting people of different temperaments and rank, acquiring different experiences, testing myself in meetings that came my way by chance, and everywhere reflecting on the things I observed so as to derive some benefit from them. . . . the greatest benefit I got from this was that, by seeing many things which were still widely accepted and approved by other great peoples, although they seemed very extravagant and ridiculous to us, I learned not to believe anything too firmly about which I had been convinced by example and custom alone. Thus I was gradually freed from many errors that can cloud our natural light and make us less capable of hearing reason. But once I had spent some years studying in this way in the great book of the world and trying to acquire some experience, I decided one day to study also within myself, and to use all the powers of my mind to choose the paths that I should follow. I was much more successful in this . . . than I would have been had I never left either my country or my books.   (vi. 9–11)

The extensive travel and experience of other cultures was the psychological fillip for what subsequently became his preferred method, namely, to look into his own mind for guidance about what he should or should not believe. This further transition occurred one year later, on the occasion of his famous dreams in 1619. Before then, however, he had to begin his journey in a more literal sense of the term.

Descartes in the United Provinces

Descartes arrived initially at Breda, one of the border garrisons in Brabant, which was on the truce lines between the warring parties in the north and south of the Netherlands. Here he met Isaac Beeckman (1588–1637), more or less by accident, in 1618.[7] Beeckman was seven years older than Descartes and, by the time of the latter's arrival in Breda, had already concluded his training as a Calvinist preacher, had graduated from Leiden University, and had received a doctorate in medicine from the University of Caen in Normandy. Beeckman had known Willebrord Snellius (1591–1626) – after whom the law of optical refraction is named – and had done some experiments with him. He was thus a most appropriate contact for someone like Descartes who was anxious to acquire as much scientific knowledge as possible during this somewhat unstructured period in his life. Beeckman was in Breda to visit with his girlfriend, Cateline de Cerf, while Descartes was officially enlisted in the army of Prince Maurits of Nassau.[8] Beeckman recorded in his journal that he met Descartes on 10 November, and that the Frenchman from Poitou discussed a mathematical problem with him.[9]

The terms in which Descartes expressed the problem suggest that he was still held captive by the language and style of argument of his scholastic training, and by the definitions of Euclid. He tried to prove that there is no such thing as an angle between two intersecting lines. He argued as follows. An angle is where two lines, AB and CB, meet at a point. However, if one were to divide further the angle ABC by the line DE, the point of intersection would also be subdivided into two parts. That is impossible, since, by definition, a point has no size and cannot be divided. Therefore, there is no point at which the original two lines intersect, and hence there is no genuine angle at their intersection.

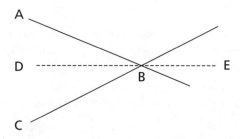

Despite such an inauspicious introduction, the two men struck up a friendship and began to exchange questions about mathematical problems and their solutions. Beeckman was the senior scholar, not only in age but in the extent to which he had thought about applying mathematics to the solution of physical problems. In the first months of their acquaintance, between November 1618 and April 1619, Beeckman shared a number of problems with Descartes and asked for his help with the mathematics involved. One of these was a familiar problem about the acceleration of falling bodies.[10] The other problem resulted from their joint discussion of an equally commonplace issue in theories of music. This resulted in one of Descartes' first essays, the *Compendium of Music*, which he completed in manuscript form and dated at Breda on 31 December 1618.

This apparent deviation from scientific investigations into music is easy to understand. Music had been taught as part of mathematics for generations, and was recognized as one of the four subjects in the medieval *quadrivium* (arithmetic, geometry, music, and astronomy). Philosophers since the time of Pythagoras had dreamed of discovering a natural harmony in the universe that would be expressed in mathematical terms. This suggested that, if one could crack that cosmological code and then express it in musical notation, one could use music to help bring the human soul into harmony with the universe. This Pythagorean and faintly mathematical-mystical inspiration was expressed, in rigorous form, in attempts to find an ideal mathematical division of a monochord to produce notes that would resonate, in some sense, with the harmony of the universe. One sees remnants of that tradition in some of Descartes' contemporaries, such as Kepler's *Harmony of the World* (1619) and Mersenne's *Universal Harmony* (1636). There was nothing novel, therefore, in the Cartesian attempt to match musical notes with lengths of a monochord; it had long been established that the pitch of a sound is related to the length of a vibrating string. Descartes' contribution, though minor, lay elsewhere.

The Pythagorean tradition assumed that the objective of musical studies was to express the natural harmony of the universe, even if only feebly, in musical harmonies. The tradition of tuning stringed instruments that resulted from this tradition limited the acceptable ratios of lengths of a monochord to 2:1 (the octave) and 3:2 (pure fifth), on the assumption that the simplest mathematical ratios could best capture the relations between different sounds. The problems associated with these limitations for keyboard instruments had been recognized as early as 1558 by Gioseffo Zarlino. One of Descartes' Dutch contemporaries, Simon Stevin (1548–1620), also made a modest contribution, in a posthumously published short treatise, to the production of a tempered intonation.[11] Thus the issues associated with devising an equal temperament were familiar to almost anyone working in this field in 1618. Descartes joined this debate as evidence of his mathematical skills, but primarily as an expression of his friendship for Beeckman. The subsequent row with Beeckman about the latter's alleged plagiarism of ideas from the *Compendium* throws more light on the character of its author than on the search for a tempered intonation in the early modern period.

However, despite the brevity and the relative lack of novelty of this essay, there are already some indications in the *Compendium of Music* of positions that Descartes adopted subsequently in his mature published work. The first line suggests that the objective of music is 'to please us and to stimulate various emotions in us' (x. 89). The second paragraph takes a decisive turn in the direction of distinguishing between the explanatory task of the physicist and a very different task, described in instrumentalist terms, of learning how to produce pleasant sounds without necessarily understanding adequately what causes them (x. 90). In complete contrast, therefore, with the Pythagorean project of discovery, the Cartesian analysis of music was designed merely to assist musicians to produce the sounds required to stimulate various emotions. In realizing that objective, there is no reason to limit oneself to simple mathematical ratios; the limits of one's musical skills are a function of the limits of one's mathematical abilities. Having rehearsed some of the standard ways of dividing a monochord, Descartes cuts short his discussion by pleading that an adequate treatment would 'exceed the scope of this small volume' (x. 140). Instead, he sends the draft essay to his friend Beeckman with these words:

I hope that this progeny of my mind, so imperfect and similar to a small bear which has just been born, will reach you as a testament of our friendship and a most certain token of my affection, but on one condition: that it remain forever hidden in the shadows of your study. . . . for it has been composed for you alone by someone who is free and idle in the midst of ignorant soldiers, but is concerned with entirely different thoughts and actions.   (x. 141)

Beeckman returned to Middelburg on 2 January 1619. When Descartes went to visit him in March, his return journey was delayed by a storm at sea that forced the boat on which he had set sail to return to port at Vlissingen. There is no evidence that they met again for another twelve years, until 1631.[12] Meantime, Descartes wrote to him (24 January 1619) that he was passing his time by painting, studying military architecture, and by learning Dutch. His efforts at language learning were successful enough that, in later years, he could write short letters in Dutch, though usually with apologies for his limited competence.[13]

Descartes seems to have spent the early months of 1619 in studying mathematics and, especially, in reflecting on ways to open up the discipline to new techniques. Descartes' mathematical training was probably elementary, and was based for the most part on the publications of Christopher Clavius (1537–1612), which included a well-known edition of Euclid's *Elements*.[14] Despite the recent applications of algebraic methods to geometrical problems, due mostly to François Viète (1540–1603), geometrical methods of construction were still limited to what could be realized with only straight lines and circles.[15] However, there were already some intimations of the Cartesian project in a startling claim at the conclusion of Viète's *Introduction to the Analytic Art* (1591). 'The analytic art . . . claims for itself the greatest problem of all, which is to leave no problem unsolved.'[16] Descartes wrote to Beeckman with similarly extravagant ambitions in March 1619.

Indeed, to tell you openly what I plan, I do not want to construct a Lullian *Brief Art* but a completely new science by which all questions that can be raised about any kind of quantity, either continuous or discrete, may be solved by a general method. However, each one must be solved in accordance with its own nature. In arithmetic, for example, some questions can be resolved using rational numbers, some only by surd numbers, whereas others can be imagined but cannot be solved. Likewise, I hope to prove, in the case of continuous quantity, some problems that can be solved by using only straight lines or circles; other problems can be solved only by using other curved lines which, however, result from a single motion and can therefore be traced by the new compasses, which I think are no less certain and geometrical than the common compass by which circles are traced. Finally, there are problems that can be solved only by curved lines traced by separate motions that are not subordinate to one another; such curves are certainly merely imaginary, such as the relatively well-known quadratrix. I think that it is impossible to imagine anything that cannot be solved by at least those lines. However, I hope to prove in due course which questions can be solved in one way or another, or not at all, so that there would be almost nothing left to be discovered in geometry. That is indeed an infinite task, and not for a single person. It is incredible rather than ambitious, but I have seen some light through the boundless obscurity of this science by which I think I can dispel the most dense clouds.   (x. 156–8)

Here Descartes tries to provide a complete classification of all mathematical problems, borrowing evidently from a tradition that bequeathed unresolved questions from one generation to another. In the case of arithmetic, he divided problems into equations whose solutions were (1) rational numbers, (2) surd numbers, and (3) complex numbers (i.e., those that involve the square root of a negative number, such as $\sqrt{-1}$). In the case of geometry, he assumes that all three kinds of problems are soluble, although only the first two – those that are constructible using a ruler and compass, or using one of the new compasses – belong properly to geometry. The neat division into three parallel types, for discrete and continuous magnitude respectively, might suggest that the problems in each group were mathematically equivalent, or that problems in geometry could be resolved by using equations of the corresponding level in algebra. However, Descartes seems not to have made enough progress in applying algebraic methods to geometry to realize that this was not the case.

What was new in this programmatic statement, apart from the scope and ambitiousness of the proposal, was the acceptance of 'new compasses' as valid instruments of construction, in addition to the traditional compass used in geometry for drawing a circle. These compasses made it possible to solve two kinds of problem that had been known in the literature for centuries: (a) constructing mean proportionals to given numbers, and (b) dividing a given angle into more than two equal parts. Apart from such technical issues that are specific to mathematics, however, the letter to Beeckman also shows that Descartes was thinking of mathematics as a model for resolving all kinds of theoretical problems, and that his primary interests in 1619 were mathematical or involved the application of mathematical techniques to problems in physics.

Beeckman appreciated the efforts of his younger collaborator enough to copy this letter into his journal. In the subsequent months Beeckman had other worries on his mind, both professional and personal. The Synod of Dordrecht concluded on 9 May 1619 and, in November of that year, Beeckman was appointed to teach at Utrecht. In April 1620, he married Cateline in Middelburg.

Beeckman as a 'Special Friend'

Following the relatively short boat journey in March 1619, when Descartes returned from Middelburg to Breda, he reported that he 'crossed the waves without getting sea-sick' and that, as a result, he felt 'more courageous about taking a longer journey.'[17] His new plan was to travel by sea to Denmark and onward by land to Germany. He was not deterred by stormy seas or troop movements associated with the early stages of the Thirty Years' War; however, he was forced to wait a little longer before embarking. He planned to sail northward and thereby bypass the battles that were rumoured to be occurring to the east in Germany. He wrote:

The troubles that have suddenly engulfed France [Germany?] have not changed my mind, but they will delay me here a little longer. I shall not leave for another three weeks. But I hope to reach Amsterdam and to go on to Danzig from there. Then by crossing Poland and part of Hungary, I shall reach Austria and Bohemia. This is a longer journey but I think it is safer. I shall bring my valet with me, and perhaps some friends that I have come to know.   (x. 158–9)

On April 29, he wrote to Beeckman again to say that 'I leave today to visit Denmark. I shall stay a while at Copenhagen, where I shall wait for a letter from you' (x. 151). The extent and duration of these travels remain uncertain. What is clear, at least, is that somehow Descartes arrived in Frankfurt during the ceremonies to celebrate the coronation of Ferdinand as emperor, which lasted from 28 July to 9 September, and that he had enlisted prior to that in the army of the (Catholic) duke of Bavaria.

Descartes' correspondence with Beeckman before his departure is unusually affectionate, even by the standards of the seventeenth century. For example, he inquires of Beeckman 'not only about your mind, although that may be the most important part of you, but about the whole man' (x. 151), and he mentions the Muses 'that attached me to you by an affectionate bond that could never break' (24 January 1619). Having inquired about Beeckman's health, he concludes: 'Meantime love me, and be certain that I would forget the Muses themselves rather than you, for they have bound me to you by a permanent bond of love' (24 January 1619).[18] The same affectionate sentiments are expressed in March and April, almost as if his impending departure heightened the anticipated feeling of separation. 'I write this letter so that your affection for me will have no occasion to be diminished. Love me, live in joy, and take care of yourself' (26 March). On 20 April, Descartes asks Beeckman for news about his personal life: 'how are you, what are you doing, are you still planning to get married . . . ? Good-bye, Love me.' On 23 April he writes again from Breda: 'I did not wish to leave here without once more renewing, by letter, the friendship that will endure between us' (x. 162). Finally, just before his departure (29 April), he writes: 'I do not want to lose any opportunity for writing to you, to show my affection for you, and to show that my memory of you cannot be erased by any of the distractions that occur during my travels' (x. 164).

There are fewer surviving letters in the opposite direction, most likely because Beeckman did not write as often to his junior colleague. However, he did write from Middelburg, in a letter addressed to Descartes at Copenhagen after his departure. In this letter Beeckman refers to Descartes as 'his special friend', and expresses the hope that they might join forces in future to collaborate on scientific projects. 'May God grant that we may live together for some considerable time to penetrate to the core of the kingdom of science. Meantime, take care of your health and be careful in all your travels, lest the only thing that you appear to lack is the practice of that science which you value so highly' (x. 167–8).

Given the evidence of the letters alone, it is difficult (almost four centuries later) to interpret Descartes' understanding of his relationship with Beeckman. At the time of this correspondence, he was twenty-three years old and seems not to have had any genuinely intimate friends, and none who were women. His relationship with Beeckman points to a pattern that is familiar to many young men, then and since, who are educated at a residential school for boys and who fail subsequently to establish genuine friendships with women as easily as their more socially experienced counterparts. Whatever the exact details of Descartes' friendship with Beeckman, he at least gives the impression in these letters of being emotionally immature, of having a strong affectionate attachment to an older and more experienced mathematician, and of writing to him with an intensity of feeling and immediacy that one would normally expect between lovers. As already mentioned, Beeckman married his fiancée the following year, and Descartes' correspondence with him lapsed until 1629.

The fact that Descartes was not married at this stage of his life is not itself significant. His brother, Pierre, who was five years older than him, married only in 1624 (at the age of thirty-one), and Beeckman married at the age of twenty-nine. Some of Descartes' other contemporaries, such as Pierre Fermat, married at about the same age, once they had established themselves in a career with a steady source of income.[19] Since Descartes had no career and had not even reached the age required to inherit the bequest from his mother, the mere fact that he remained unmarried at the age of twenty-three is insignificant.

The intensity of his initial friendship with Beeckman, however, is relevant in the context of his later career, and is confirmed by Descartes' emotional response when he heard, ten years later, of an exchange of letters between Mersenne and his special friend about musical harmonies. Descartes had apparently assumed that Beeckman was still living in Middelburg, but when he went there in 1628, hoping to renew his friendship, he found that Beeckman had been appointed to teach at Dordrecht in May of the previous year.[20] Mersenne visited Beeckman in 1629, in the course of a lengthy journey to the United Provinces that lasted until September 1630. During the visit his Dutch host discussed musical harmonies, one of Mersenne's favourite topics, with the Minim friar. Beeckman may have shown Mersenne some entries from his journal, and he subsequently wrote to him about the discussion of musical issues that he had had ten years earlier with Descartes.[21] On 1 October of the same year, Beeckman wrote again to Mersenne, and transcribed for him a section from Descartes' *Compendium of Music*. He did not claim to have written it himself, but clearly acknowledged that it had been sent to him by Descartes, 'our friend', who had written about the topic 'in his book'.[22] Mersenne lost no time in telling Descartes about Beeckman's correspondence, and the response from Descartes was a degree of outrage and apparent personal hurt that is almost inexplicable in its intensity. Descartes thanked Mersenne (8 October 1629) 'for alerting me to the ingratitude of my friend' (i. 24). By December, the incensed Frenchman had taken back the original text of the *Compendium of Music* from Beeckman,[23] and a full year later he wrote to Beeckman to explain his anger.

I retrieved my *Music* from you last year, not because I needed it, but because I was told that you talked about it as if I had learned it from you. I did not wish to write to you about it immediately, lest I appear to doubt too much the trust of a friend simply on the word of someone else. However, since many other things have confirmed that you prefer stupid boasting to friendship and truth, I shall warn you in a few words. If you claim to have taught something to someone, it is repulsive to do so even if you speak the truth; when it is false, however, it is much more repulsive; finally, if you yourself learned it from this person, it is most repulsive.   (i. 155–6)

This was as clear a signal as possible of the breach of trust and loss of friendship between the two men. Nonetheless, Descartes indicated at the conclusion of this letter that he could still regard Beeckman's indiscretion as a mistake rather than a fault, and that it might be possible for them to recover their previous amicable relationship.

However, all hope of a peaceful resolution was destroyed by an extremely querulous and cranky letter from Descartes on 17 October 1630, which seems to have been triggered in part by the fact that Beeckman implied that the former French 'pupil' would progress more quickly in his studies if he were to work with his former friend and adviser. The reply from Amsterdam is so full of self-justification that it throws considerable light on its author's state of mind at the time. It also reveals Descartes' suspicions about the way in which copies of letters could be used, by copying or showing them to others – a ruse to which he later succumbed himself.

You wrote to me recently, after a full year of silence between us, that if I wished to make progress in my studies I should return to you and that I would not be as well off anywhere else as with you, and other things along the same lines. You also wrote in familiar and friendly terms as if you were writing to one of your school pupils. What reason could I think you had for writing in this tone to me, except that you planned to show the letter to someone else before sending it, thereby giving them the impression that I usually come to you for instruction. . . . I could not have imagined that you are so stupid and ignorant about yourself that you really believe that I ever learned, or ever could learn, anything more from you than I usually do from all natural things – than I usually learn, I say, even from insects and flies – or that you could teach me anything.   (i. 157–8)

Descartes is either extremely sarcastic or intentionally hurtful, on this occasion, diagnosing Beeckman's mistake as the result of an illness rather than malice: 'I realize clearly from your recent letters that you have sinned, not from malice, but from some illness. Accordingly, I shall pity rather than blame you, and because of our former friendship I shall advise you about the remedies by which I think you can cure yourself' (i. 158). With that in mind, he introduces a distinction between things that can be taught to someone else and other things that cannot be learned by a pupil from a teacher. The former include languages, history, experiments, and certain and evident demonstrations that convince the mind, such as those found in geometry. In contrast, if one is led to believe something without convincing reasons or an authority on which one can rely, then 'one is not said to have learned it from someone, no matter how many times they may have heard it said' (i. 158). Using this distinction or the criteria used to make it, Descartes claims: 'you will easily see that I have never learned anything, apart from idle fancies, from your *Mathematical Physics*. . . . Has your authority ever moved me, or have your arguments convinced me? There were many things that you said, which I believed and endorsed once I understood them. You should understand that, just because I believed them immediately, it does not follow that I learned them from you. I approved them because I had already thought about the same things myself' (i. 159).

Adding further insults to those already hurled, the sarcastic correspondent asks if his former Dutch academic guide had 'ever discovered anything in your whole life that is genuinely worthy of praise' (i. 160). To help answer the question, he distinguishes three kinds of discovery: (a) those that are found by the sheer power of one's own mental ability; (b) those discovered by chance; and (c) those that resemble the bits of glass found by a blind man and mistakenly protected and concealed in a treasure chest as if they were precious stones.[24] Referring to Beeckman's journal, in which the Dutch mathematician carefully noted and dated various ideas as they occurred to him, Descartes wrote: 'I certainly do not wish to compare your manuscript with such a chest, for I can scarcely believe there could be anything better in it than bits of glass and debris' (i. 162). He then proceeds to reduce the two items for which Beeckman might have claimed originality, his work on music and on hyperbolas, to what was widely known to everyone who was familiar with the disciplines in question. Descartes concludes by claiming, rather implausibly: 'You should believe that I wrote this letter, not in a fit of anger or with any malevolent intentions towards you, but in a spirit of genuine friendship. For in the first place, why should I be angry with you? Because you think that you are better than me? As if I would care about that, I who am accustomed to place myself among the lowest. . . .' (i. 166). Having congratulated himself on his own 'characteristic modesty', Descartes concludes by hoping that his advice to an old friend will assist his recovery from whatever illness has affected his judgment and that, once restored to health, 'I shall not be ashamed to be your friend and you will not regret having received this letter from me' (i. 167).

This whole quarrel about the extent to which he was intellectually indebted to Beeckman was in stark contrast with what Descartes had written to his special friend, about the very same issue, before embarking on his travels in 1619. At that time he had acknowledged to his Dutch mentor that 'you roused me from my indolence' and that, if anything worthwhile were to result from his studies, Beeckman could rightfully 'claim it all as [his] own' (x. 163). The transition from being an immature, almost obsequiously grateful and amorous admirer of Beeckman to the tetchy and resentful independence of his mature years began with Descartes' travels to Germany.

The radical nature of the transition, however, is hardly explained by external factors. Descartes' relations with other friends and supporters suffered a similar fate in later years. Most notoriously, he cultivated Henricus Regius as one of the most supportive and insightful proponents of Cartesian ideas. Within a few years, however, he disowned him and decided to cut off all communications with him.[25] When one finds that Descartes disputed publicly with Fermat, Roberval, Voetius, Bourdin, and many others, the emotionally charged rift with Beeckman assumes the status of the first example of what subsequently emerged as a pattern in his personal and professional life. Descartes had a penchant for misunderstanding those who disagreed with him, attributing motives to their alleged mistakes that were less than complimentary, and then adopting the moralistic posture of someone who had been deeply wronged despite the virtues he claimed always to have exercised when attempting to resolve disagreements.

Travels in Germany

Descartes embarked on his travels on 29 April 1619. The young adventurer could not possibly have hoped to advance his studies by joining another army, or by idling in winter quarters with the billeted soldiers of various belligerent dukes and kings. Given the poor communications about military manoeuvres, he anticipated (23 April 1619) finding 'many men in arms but no combat. If that is so, I shall go to Denmark, then to Poland and Hungary, until I manage to reach Germany by secure routes that are not occupied by pillaging soldiers. Otherwise, I shall discover with certainty that they are really at war' (x. 162). One motivation for travelling to Bohemia was the renown of some central European scientists who were widely known to have contributed significantly to the new sciences. Some of these names were well known, even among those who had never read their works: thus Copernicus, Brahe, and Kepler were especially prominent on any list of famous scientists. While the first two were no longer alive, the centres where they had worked remained a promising source of inspiration for any aspiring young scientist in the early seventeenth century. Among those centres, Bohemia had been prominent for almost thirty years, and Descartes identifies that as his ultimate destination: 'I shall reach Austria and Bohemia' (x. 159).

The emperor, Rudolf II, an uncle to Philip II of Spain, had moved the imperial court from Vienna to Prague, where he was crowned in the Cathedral of St. Vitus, Prague, in 1575. During the following thirty-six years, he established Prague as a centre of culture and the arts, an international centre for the new sciences, and a welcome and supportive haven for those interested in mystical, hermetic, or astrological studies.[26] By the time of his death in 1612, he had turned the city into a research centre for those interested in scientific developments and a haven of religious toleration. For example, when the famous Danish astronomer Tycho Brahe (1546–1601) was forced to leave Denmark in 1597, he found a welcoming refuge at the royal court at Prague.[27] A Dutch physicist and friend of Beeckman, Willebrord Snellius, visited during the winter of 1599–1600, thereby establishing a model for Descartes' travels two decades later. Johannes Kepler (1571–1630) succeeded Brahe as royal astronomer at Prague in 1601, having spent almost one year previously as his assistant. During his research in Prague, Kepler published the *New Astronomy* (1609) and the *Harmony of the World* (1619), which made public for the first time his three laws of planetary motion.

Rudolph II has been variously characterized as melancholic or schizophrenic, but his refusal to take sides between Catholicism and various reformed churches provided a tolerant religious oasis in a very turbulent empire. Rudolph's fascination with clocks and similar machines meant that he employed some of the best clock makers in Europe, who designed technically advanced and artistically extravagant clocks (including the first to measure in seconds).[28] Perhaps the other side of his personality was expressed in his abiding interest in the occult. Paracelsus had died in 1541, leaving behind a heady mix of applied chemistry, medicine, and mystical philosophy derived from Neoplatonism and from various alchemical and astrological sources. Michael Maier (1568–1622), a friend of the English alchemist Robert Fludd and a follower of Paracelsus, was physician to the emperor and a consultant on a wide range of mystical, alchemical, and magical questions. During Rudolph's reign, the court welcomed the English alchemist John Dee (1527–1608) and his travelling companion and principal scryer, Edward Kelley. The royal visitors also included Franciso Pucci (1543–1597), who was executed as a heretic by the Roman Inquisition, and Giordano Bruno (1548–1600), who suffered the same fate at the Campo de' Fiori, Rome. Thus Prague was widely perceived not only as a religiously tolerant imperial centre, but also as equally receptive to a wide range of scientific and pseudo-scientific studies.

Apart from the exceptional religious toleration that characterized the imperial city, the intellectual climate that was explicitly cultivated in

Prague was an accurate reflection of the new sciences in the late sixteenth century. For some decades scholastic philosophy had seemed to many scholars to be 'dead, barren, outworn, and irrelevant.'[29] The response to this widespread intellectual effeteness emerged in two forms, religious and philosophical. The religious response was the familiar challenge of the Reformation to return to a form of Christianity that was closer to the Gospel, and to unshackle the church from the debilitating scholasticism that it had adopted as its official language.

The philosophical response was an equally radical search for new categories and new sciences that would put its practitioners in touch with a wide range of powers and natural forces and, through them, with the ultimate source of these occult powers, God. The philosophical revolution was supported by many of the same people who demanded religious renewal, but it was not by any means an exclusively Protestant movement. The exuberance of this intellectual movement, and its tolerance of many incredible or implausible variations, was evident in the interest shown in Neoplatonism, cabalistic literature, alchemy, astrology, and various kinds of magic and sorcery. With almost utopian zeal, countless writers and practitioners of magical arts found it difficult to camouflage their millenarian hopes and ambitious aspirations to discover the secrets of nature, thereby opening up a whole new era for mankind.

The first proponents of this new perspective on nature and its occult powers included Giovanni Pico della Mirandola (1463–1494) and Marsilio Ficino in Florence, Johannes Reuchlin (1455–1522) in Germany, and the Venetian friar Franceso Giorgi (1466–1540), who published his book, *The Harmony of the World*, in 1525. Although these authors varied in their identification with different forms of magic, they were united in their respect for mystical sources and Neoplatonist studies, which provided the social pressure required to challenge the established learning of the schools and to motivate the kind of mathematical work that was required by later scholars such as Brahe and Kepler. Descartes was vaguely aware of this undercurrent of ideas and wished to become more informed about it.

His first indirect acquaintance with the work and influence of Cornelius Agrippa (1486–1535) and John Battista della Porta (c. 1550–1615), and with the new art of memory allegedly discovered by Ramon Lull, occurred in 1619 immediately prior to his travels in central Europe. He wrote to Beeckman (26 March 1619) that he wished to construct 'not a Lullian *Brief*

Art, but a completely new science by which all questions that can be raised about any kind of quantity, either continuous or discrete, may be solved by a general method' (x. 156–7). He mentioned Lull again one month later, on 29 April 1619: 'The day before yesterday I met a learned man at an inn in Dordrecht with whom I discussed Lull's *Brief Art*' (x. 164). Since he had no access to the books required to check the theories of Lull and Agrippa, he asked Beeckman to investigate whether they provided a key to all knowledge, as they claimed (x. 165). Descartes' evaluation of the merits of Lull eighteen years later, in the *Discourse,* is entirely negative. 'I noticed that, in the case of logic, its syllogisms and most of its other rules are more useful for explaining to someone else what one already knows than for learning them or even, in the Lullian arts, for speaking uncritically about things that one does not know' (vi. 17).[30] However, in 1619 his knowledge of the new sciences was confined to what he had learned in the limited curriculum at La Flèche – which was almost nothing – and he may have been interested to learn about Lull's 'art' and its possible adaptation as a general method of discovering truths.

Ramon Lull (1232–1316) was a medieval mystic who dedicated his life to the conversion of Muslims and who conceived of his various 'arts' as rhetorical skills that could be used to discover 'the truth' and to persuade non-Christians of the validity of Christianity. He wrote and redrafted his basic insights in many different forms, in *The Art of Finding the Truth* (c. 1290), *The General and Ultimate Art* (1305–8), and in a greatly simplified and reduced version of the latter, the *Brief Art* (1308), which was written when he was shipwrecked at Pisa. Lull's enigmatic manipulation of words, symbols, and tables was very influential in Paris in the fifteenth and sixteenth centuries, and it gave rise to numerous commentaries and interpretations, including Jerome Sanchez's *Admirable and General Method for Learning all the Sciences more Easily and Quickly* (1613).[31] It is clear, in retrospect, that Descartes could not possibly have borrowed significantly from their contents to construct a new scientific method. However, he hardly knew the conclusion of his intellectual journey before its completion, and he seems to have had an open mind in 1619 about initiatives that he later rejected completely.

For example, Agrippa's work, especially the *Three Books of Occult Philosophy* (1531), provides a comprehensive summary of magic and a defence against its exploitation by those who are opposed to the true Christian religion. Agrippa argues, in his letter to the reader, that the term 'magician' does not mean 'a sorcerer, or one who is superstitious, or devilish; but a wise man, a priest, a prophet.' In fact, according to him, magicians were among the first who 'knew Christ the author of the world to be born, and came first of all to worship him.'[32] Agrippa divides reality into three ascending levels, 'elementary, celestial, and intellectual,' and claims that 'every inferior is governed by its superior.'[33] The three books of occult philosophy correspond to these three levels: (1) the world and its elements, (2) the celestial sphere, and (3) the upper level of intelligences, including angels. The study of magic, then, is the study of the powers that are man-ifested in these different levels of reality, and this study provides a route to 'the Maker of all things, and First Cause, whence all things are, and proceed.'[34] With frequent references to Plato, Agrippa conceives of the whole world as being informed by a 'soul of the world' through which the powers of natural phenomena are communicated from God. 'All virtues therefore are infused by God, through the Soul of the World, yet by a particular power of resemblances, and intelligences overruling them . . . in a certain peculiar harmonious consent.'[35]

The crowning achievement of magic, in this sense, is to teach people 'to know and understand the rules of religion.'[36] As Agrippa argues, in Book 3: 'to superadd the powers of religion to physical and mathematical virtues is so far from a fault, that not to join them is an heinous sin.'[37] Agrippa endorses the tradition, evident even in the early centuries of Christianity, of the 'discipline of the secret', according to which the most central mysteries of a religion should not be divulged to nonmembers.[38] Having defended an orthodox Trinitarian account of God, the author discusses the nature and powers of evil spirits, and the status of the human mind after death. On this question, as usual, he reports the opinions of the ancient philosophers, of 'the Cabalists of the Hebrews,' and of the New Testament.[39] Agrippa has no doubt that the common belief in the human soul surviving the death of the body is correct, and that it is consistent with the belief that souls may be imprisoned after death in the bodies 'of creeping things, and brutes, entering into them, what kind soever they be of, possessing them like demons.'[40] While acknowledging the continued existence of human souls after death, however, Agrippa also grants that such matters are obscure and that 'it is better to doubt concerning occult things, than to contend about uncertain things.'[41] This question, about the status of the human soul after death, emerges as one of the central questions of Descartes' metaphysics in the *Meditations* (1641).

Della Porta (1536–1605) claimed that, at the age of fifteen, he had written *Twenty Books of Natural Magic, in which the Riches and Delights of the Natural Sciences are Demonstrated*, and that he had enlarged it significantly for a second edition thirty-five years later.[42] A reprint of the latter was published in Hanover in the same year as Descartes' request to Beeckman (1619). Della Porta distinguished two kinds of magic, 'one infamous, and unhappy, because it hath to do with foul spirits, and consists of Inchantments and wicked curiosity. The other is Magick Natural . . . others have named it the practical part of Natural Philosophy, which produceth her effects by the mutual and fit application of one natural thing unto another.'[43] He argued that since magic is the practical part of natural philosophy, a magician (in this sense) should be 'an exact and very perfect philosopher.'[44] Della Porta's natural philosophy was still very much dependent on scholastic principles, such as the claim that all compound bodies are composed of matter and form.[45] Despite this, Book 17 provides a very competent and informed summary of discoveries in optics, including how external events may be represented on the wall of a dark room through a small aperture in the wall – which, he claims, helps to explain how vision occurs, and how the philosophical problem of 'intromission' is resolved – and how parabolic lenses can be used to transmit letters an infinite distance, even to the moon.[46] For della Porta, then, natural magic was equivalent to applied physics.

This tolerant and extremely heterogeneous intellectual climate, inspired by neoplatonic mysticism and magic, may seem to us in retrospect to be an unlikely birthplace for modern science. However, it unambiguously supported the study of the apparently hidden powers of natural phenomena even if it knew little of their precise nature, and it strongly encouraged the application of mathematical methods to astronomy. Descartes' limited exposure to this vast literature is reflected in some of his earliest writings, which are discussed in the next chapter. The vague hints of a general method proposed by Lull and reported in Sanchez's *Admirable and General Method* may also have inspired Descartes with the ideal of a single method by which all the sciences can be discovered and unified along the lines explored subsequently in the *Rules*.[47] However, within ten years of these fumbling inquiries, Descartes' initial hope of a privileged access to universal knowledge, discovered by an especially luminescent 'natural light', turned to suspicion about anyone who even mentioned secrets. He wrote to Mersenne, 20 November 1629: 'As soon as I even see the word *arcanum* [secret] in a proposition, I begin to think poorly of it' (i. 78).

Descartes eventually set sail for Copenhagen on 29 April 1619, and travelled overland through Germany during the initial skirmishes of the Thirty Years' War. Rudolph II had died in 1612, and his brother Mathias had succeeded him. Mathias's rule was short-lived, and the resulting contested succession was the immediate occasion of Descartes' travels. Ferdinand of Styria became king of Bohemia in 1617. His allegiance to the Counter-Reformation politics of Catholic supremacy prompted the electors to choose as emperor Frederick V, elector of the Palatinate in the Rhine. Frederick had married Princess Elizabeth, daughter of James I of England, in 1613 and had returned to Heidelberg the same year with his new wife. He accepted the invitation to become emperor on 28 September 1619, and was crowned in Prague Cathedral. However, the other contender, Ferdinand, had been elected emperor in Frankfurt in August, and the die was thus cast for a bloody resolution of the contest between Catholic and Protestant claimants to the imperial throne. During this winter, 1619–20, the so-called winter king of Bohemia exercised his disputed royal powers briefly while Descartes attended the coronation of his Catholic counterpart. The occasion is summarized as follows in the *Discourse*:

I was then in Germany, where I had been drafted because of the wars that are still being waged there and, as I was returning to the army from the emperor's coronation, the arrival of winter delayed me in quarters. Since I had no acquaintances to distract me there and, luckily, I had no cares or passions to trouble me, I used to spend the whole day alone in a room that was heated by a stove, where I had plenty of time to concentrate on my own thoughts.   (vi. 11)

Descartes was in the service of a Catholic army, and was temporarily lodged at Neuburg. He subsequently claimed that he had three dreams, on the night of November 10 (the same date assigned to his first meeting with Beeckman), which changed the course of his life.

Olympian Dreams

It is impossible to know whether Descartes actually had some significant dreams while billeted at Neuburg. The way in which he recorded them gives them the status of a major turning point in his life, a transition

par excellence from the uncertainty of searching for a career to having
a clear agenda for his life's work. The stage setting for the dreams is
unambiguous.[48] The dreamer is placed at a border town between the
contending forces of the Holy Roman Empire and the Protestant claimants
to the throne. The date is the eve of St. Martin's Day, 11 November,
when those involved in the harvest drank the new wine and celebrated
the transition to the winter season. St. Martin of Tours had a symbolic
meaning for all Frenchmen. For Descartes, however, he represented the
ideal of a Christian soldier, about whom many stories and myths were
told of his conversion to Christianity and his single-minded dedication
to his newly discovered vocation. Descartes anticipates an obvious and
plausible interpretation of his recollection: that he had drunk too much
wine that evening, as was the custom for Frenchmen, and that his dream
was nothing more than the effect of an inebriated sleep. Baillet writes, at
the conclusion of his account of the dreams: 'In fact, it was the eve of
St Martin, when it was customary to overindulge, as they do in France,
wherever one happens to be that evening. But he assures us that he passed
the evening and the whole day in great sobriety, and that it was about
three months since he had drunk any wine.'[49] In what he claimed was a
completely sober condition, then, Descartes fell asleep. He was 'full of
enthusiasm, carried away completely by the thought of having discovered
the foundations of a marvelous science', and while asleep at night, he had
a sequence of three dreams.[50]

He dreamt that he was walking along a road, confronted by shadows
that terrified him, and that he was forced to go left rather than right.
A great gust of wind, like a whirlwind, spun him about on his left foot
three or four times. He then saw a college gate open ahead of him, and
he retreated there to escape from the storm. He tried to reach the college chapel, so that he could pray for forgiveness for his sins. As he was
pushed violently by the wind, he noticed someone in the college yard who
recognized him and called him by his name in a friendly and helpful manner. This acquaintance gave him something for another unnamed person,
something that looked like a melon that had been imported from a foreign
country. While he was being constantly buffeted by the wind and finally
knocked down, those who spoke with him were all standing upright, unaffected by the storm. At this point Descartes awoke, and he thought the
whole experience might be the work of some evil genius who was trying to
deceive him.

Having lain awake for a while, Descartes fell asleep again and almost immediately had a second dream in which he heard a sharp, explosive noise that sounded like thunder. This caused him to reawaken, and he saw sparks from the stove fire flying about the room. He remembered having had this experience before, while awake, and he was therefore able to make sense of it and to return calmly to sleep. Within a short time, however, he had a third dream that was not frightening like the first two. He dreamt that he found a book open on his table, without knowing who had put it there. He opened it and, seeing that it was a dictionary, he was happy in anticipating that it could be useful for his studies. At the same time, he noticed another book under his hand that was just as unfamiliar, and he did not know where this one came from either.

On further inspection he found that it was a collection entitled *An Anthology of All the Ancient Latin Poets*, and he was curious to read something from it. He opened it at random and his eyes fell on a verse entitled '*Quod vitae sectabor iter?*' (What path shall I follow in life?).[51] At the same time someone whom he did not recognize presented him with a verse that he recommended highly, and which began with the words: '*Est & Non*' (It is, and it is not). Descartes told the stranger that he recognized that line as the opening of a poem by Ausonius, which was included in the anthology on the table. On leafing through the large book, he failed to find it. However, he told the stranger that he knew another poem by the same author with the opening line '*Quod vitae sectabor iter?*' This was a different edition from the one that he was familiar with, and at that point the stranger disappeared. The two lines that occurred in the third dream are indeed the opening lines of two different poems by the French poet Ausonius, and they are found on facing pages in a very large anthology of poets (an edition that had the dimensions of a dictionary) that was available to students at La Flèche.

If one assumes that Descartes actually had dreams to which he attributed great significance on 10 November 1619, they raise the question of who is best placed to interpret them. Freud famously declined to offer a confident interpretation, although he alluded to the symbolism of the first dream as suggesting deep anxiety, on the part of the dreamer, about possible deviations from his own strongly held rules of sexual morality, possibly with homosexual connotations.[52] With appropriate reservations about diagnosis at such a distance, he also conceded that the third dream could be understood as expressing unconscious concerns about how to live one's life in a more general sense. This Freudian analysis coincided with some elements of Descartes' own interpretation.

The Pythagorean dichotomy represented by the '*It is and is not*' has obvious connotations of the Y-shaped representation of life choices found in authors such as John Dee. In his *Monas Hieroglyphica*, Dee traces the development of individuals from infancy to adolescence, until they reach a fork in the road at which they have to choose between a life ruined by debauchery and a path that leads to wisdom.[53] Dee's own career illustrates Descartes' intellectual journey almost in reverse. Dee's earliest writings were unambiguously in natural philosophy.[54] In this context, he borrowed a metaphysics of light similar to that developed in the Middle Ages by Robert Grosseteste and Roger Bacon, and he used it to speculate about the influence of the heavenly bodies on human lives through some kind of mechanical force. In contrast, his later work shows a radical slippage into speculating about spirits that inhabit the world and communicating with spirits to help understand or foretell future events. The Monas symbol that he adopted was intended to signify a sharp dichotomy between the spiritual life of an adept and its opposite. By the time he joined forces with Kelley, he was fully committed to divination and to the reliability of the revelations that Kelley imagined while crystal gazing. In other words, he saw himself as having become an adept.

If Descartes were to borrow the Monas symbol from Dee, even in the course of a dream, he could have used it only to symbolize a development that went in exactly the opposite direction. Descartes had learned something about the astrologers and hermeticists of Bohemia, and he was about to face a choice between their inspired enthusiasm and an alternative path that would lead more reliably to scientific knowledge. It seems presumptuous to think that he understood clearly, in 1619, the alternatives that were available to him or that he realized the significance of the path on which he was about to embark.

What could Descartes have meant by the claim that he 'understood the fundamental principles of a wonderful discovery' (x. 216)? He is sometimes read as conceiving of a new method, inspired by mathematics, by which he could resolve all the problems of the age. This looks more like a retrospective interpretation made in the light of subsequent events, supported by some of Descartes' own remarks, than a reliable reading of events in 1619. The enthusiasm he experienced on his travels in Germany suggests the kind of holistic, metaphorical, and even cabalistic writing of della Porta or Lull, rather than the sobriety or self-composure of an applied mathematician.[55] The fragments that survive from his early writings often describe the effectiveness of poetic imagery in providing access to otherwise inconceivable realities and, in contrast, the relative sluggishness of philosophical thought in coping with what is not available to the senses.

It may seem surprising that there are significant judgments in the writings of poets rather than philosophers. The reason for this is that the poets write with the enthusiasm and strength of the imagination. We have within us the seeds of knowledge, as in a flint; philosophers extract them by using reason, but poets do so by using the imagination, so that they shine more brightly.   (x. 217)

Taking a cue from the success of poets, Descartes suggests that 'things that are perceivable by the senses help us to conceive of Olympian matters. The wind signifies spirit; temporal movement signifies life; light signifies knowledge; heat signifies love; and instantaneous activity signifies creation' (x. 218).

These early notebook jottings are also redolent of the kind of thinking that Descartes would have found in the mystical writers who were prevalent at the time and whose writings were widely reported in Bohemia. For example, he writes in a one-line paragraph: 'There is a single active power in things: love, charity, harmony' (x. 218). Together with brief, allusive reflections on God and creation, these suggest a young man who is concerned about his religious convictions, unsure about the future, and perhaps even overwhelmed by the uncertainty and ambiguity with which he is trying to cope.

Almost eighteen years later, Descartes reinterprets the events of 1619 as an invitation to look inward for the reliable foundations of knowledge that he had been thinking about for some years previously. He writes in the *Discourse on Method* that, as a result of his dreams, he began to compare buildings designed by a single architect to those that are cobbled together, over time, with contributions from many different hands. This contrast applies equally well to a whole town or a single building.

Thus I thought that the sciences found in books – at least those which are only probable and do not contain any demonstrations, since they were composed and developed gradually from the views of many different people – do not come as close to the truth as the simple reasoning that a person with common sense can perform naturally about things that they observe. I also thought that, since we were all infants before we became adults, and since we were necessarily governed for a long time by our appetites and our teachers, which were often at odds with each other and of which, perhaps, neither gave us the best advice, it is almost impossible for our judgments to be as clear and as well-founded as they might have been had we had the full use of our reason from the day we were born and had we never been guided by anything else.   (vi. 12–13)

The conclusion to which he was drawn was that it would not be reasonable for him 'to reform the body of the sciences or the curriculum established in the schools for teaching them' (vi. 13). That was a task for someone else. Descartes' project was to focus on instructing himself. 'My objective never extended beyond an attempt to reform my own thoughts and to build on a foundation that was entirely my own' (vi. 15). The appropriate method to be used in this reform of the self – as it is found in the *Discourse* – which was borrowed from the principles of reasoning that were fundamental to mathematics, is likely to have been articulated over the following years rather than in a single epiphany during a dream in 1619, and is best discussed in Chapter 3.

Whether he understood this method in detail or merely in outline, it was evident that its implementation would require a number of years' work, and that despite the emphasis on looking inward, the application of the method to natural phenomena would require observations and experiments.

I thought I should not try to complete it [i.e., to establish some principles of philosophy] until I had reached a more mature age than twenty-three, as I was then, and until I had spent a long time preparing myself for it, in advance, by rooting out from my mind all the incorrect views that I had previously accepted, gaining many experiences that would later serve as the subject matter of my reasoning, and practising constantly the method that I had prescribed for myself so as to improve more and more at it.

(vi. 22)

One of the factors that had led Descartes to travel abroad was the lack of agreement even among scholastic writers about most of the issues that they debated. Once he had travelled sufficiently and had read enough, it became clear that this diversity was compounded by the cultural differences that he noticed among 'the French or the Germans . . . the Chinese or cannibals' (vi. 16). However, the recognition of some degree of relativism did not turn him completely into a narcissistic or sceptical meditator. He anticipated, sensibly enough, that he would need some input from others.

Since I hoped to finish this task better in discussions with other people than by remaining shut up any longer in the stove-heated room in which I had all these thoughts, I set off again to travel before winter was completely over. During the following nine years [i.e., 1619–28] I did nothing other than wander around the world, trying to be

a spectator rather than an actor in the dramas that unfold there. I rooted out of my
mind all the errors that could have slipped into it. Not that I thereby imitated the
sceptics . . . on the contrary, my whole plan was designed only to convince myself, and
to reject the shifting ground and sand in order to find rock or clay. I think I succeeded
reasonably well in this because, by attempting to uncover the falsehood or uncertainty
of the propositions that I studied . . . by using clear and certain arguments, I found
none so doubtful that I did not always draw some reasonably certain conclusion from
it, even if only that it contained nothing that was certain.   (vi. 28–9)

Toward the end of 1619, when he was still at Neuburg, Descartes
received a copy of Pierre Charron's book *On Wisdom* from a Jesuit priest,
Johannes Molitor (1570–1626).[56] In February 1620, he recorded in his
notebooks that he was working on a treatise that he hoped to complete
before Easter of that year (April 19). He also wrote that he planned to
make a pilgrimage to Loreto before the end of November. Loreto had
been a traditional destination for Christian pilgrims who believed that the
house of the Virgin Mary had been transported there by angels from its
original site in the Holy Land. Descartes must have been familiar, from his
student days, with some of the extensive literature devoted to pilgrimages
and with the cult of the Virgin that was encouraged by the sodality in her
name at La Flèche. For example, the Jesuit father Louis Richeome had
written a detailed guide for pilgrims, *The Pilgrim to Loreto*.[57] Richeome
divided the pilgrimage into forty days, a symbolic number that coincided
with the duration of the church's pre-Easter penitential season of Lent.
Pilgrims were advised to set out on foot for their destination, to pace their
daily journies with prayers, doing penance and asking God's forgiveness
for their sins. At the conclusion of the pilgrimage, on the fortieth day,
the pilgrim was asked to reflect on the vanity of earthly kings and the
insignificance of working in their service, in contrast to being a soldier of
Christ: 'What do you expect in your vocation of an earthly army? What can
you earn thereby that is more precious than the friendship of an earthly
king, and the reward of some fickle, human saviour?'[58] The contrast with
worldly kings, their interminable wars, and the vanity of their ostentatious
celebrations would have struck a chord with Descartes. Accordingly, he
promised 'to reach Loreto on foot from Venice, if I can do so without
discomfort and if that is what is usually done. If I find it impossible to do
so, I shall at least bring to this pilgrimage all the devotion that is usually
involved' (x. 218). Despite the obvious enthusiasm of such good intentions, however, there is no evidence that Descartes fulfilled this promise.

He seems to have visited Italy three years later, but without any indication on that occasion of a pilgrimage to Loreto.

It is not clear whether Descartes continued his travels toward Prague, perhaps still in the service of the duke of Bavaria's army, or whether he witnessed the Battle of the White Mountain, in November 1620.[59] The defeat of Frederick meant that he had to evacuate the palace at Prague, but he could not return to Heidelberg – where he had left his wife and family – because it had meantime fallen to the Spanish. He moved initially to Berlin and then to The Hague, where his uncle, Prince Maurits, offered him accommodations. During this painful defeat and retreat, the daughter of Frederick and Elizabeth, also called Elizabeth, was barely two years old. Frederick subsequently died of the plague in 1632, and his wife and children remained in rather modest circumstances in The Hague for many years subsequently. The young exiled Princess Elizabeth of Bohemia was later to emerge in the 1640s as one of Descartes' most subtle critics and most favoured correspondents.

Descartes returned from Germany some time in 1621 or 1622, but there is no clear indication of where he went. He probably returned by a similar long detour, through Poland and across the North Sea to West Friesland, during the course of which he had an opportunity to display his fencing skills while crossing the river Elbe. He was travelling with his valet as his only companion, and naturally spoke French with him in the crowded confines of the sailing boat. The sailors on board mistook him for a foreign merchant and presumed that he must have been carrying a lot of money. So they conspired to rob him on the journey and to throw him overboard, but they made the mistake of assuming that the 'merchant' did not understand what they were saying to each other in his presence. As they were about to implement their nefarious plan, however, Descartes jumped up suddenly, drew his sword with unexpected ferocity, spoke to them in their own language, and threatened to kill them all. The story, as told by Baillet, concludes with the heroic safe return of the French cavalier and his valet to their chosen destination.[60]

Descartes was then about twenty-five years old. He returned from his long journey with a somewhat clearer picture of what he wished to do with his life. The period between coming to the United Provinces in 1618 and returning from Germany three or four years later helped to confirm him in his career choice. As he recalls in the *Discourse on Method*, 'I decided to review the various occupations that are open to people in this life, and to try to choose the best one' (vi. 27). None seemed more attractive than the one on which he had tentatively embarked. 'I thought I could do no better than to persevere in the very same occupation that I already had, that is, to use my whole life to develop my reason and to make as much progress as I could in discovering the truth in accordance with the method that I had prescribed for myself' (vi. 27). It may seem remarkable in retrospect that it took Descartes nine years, since the 'wonderful discovery' of November 1619, before he could formulate a sufficiently explicit and detailed strategy for realizing his vaguely understood objective. The length of time involved, and the relative lack of creative work that he completed during this period, suggest that he was still very much in search of a clear guide to his life's work during the years before he emigrated again to the United Provinces. The intermittent search for the right path eventually came to fruition. As Descartes records in the *Discourse*, 'I was much more successful in this, it seems to me, than I would have been had I never left either my country or my books' (vi. 10–11).

3

Magic, Mathematics, and Mechanics: Paris, 1622–1628

The entire method consists in the order and arrangement of the things to which the mind's eye must turn so that we can discover some truth.

(*Rules*: x. 379)

URING the years immediately prior to his second departure for the United Provinces, Descartes struggled unsuccessfully with a number of fundamental problems in mathematics and philosophy. The results of those efforts are recorded in the *Rules for Guiding the Mind in Searching for the Truth*, which was published posthumously, and in comments made in the biographical paragraphs of the *Discourse on Method*. The intellectual milieu in which Descartes lived was as fluid as the uncertainty of the initial steps on his intellectual journey suggests. His foreign travels confirmed at least the narrowness of the education he had received from the Jesuits. They also exposed him to a wide range of disparate views – religious, magical, and mystical – that were defended by apparently genuine believers. Descartes seems never to have been enamoured sufficiently of anyone's thought to consider seriously adopting it. This same general scepticism applied more vigorously in the case of authors such as Campanella and Bruno. His glancing encounter with their work, however, provided the conditions in which Descartes briefly considered and definitively rejected all forms of magic and mysticism in favour of an ideal of mechanical explanation.

He had planned to return to Paris in February 1622, but according to Baillet he was forced to change plans in order to avoid the plague that had afflicted the city for two years previously.[1] He went instead to visit his father in Rennes. Since Descartes was now twenty-six years old, his father was able to finalize the legal formalities of his inheritance from his mother's will. On 3 April of that year, he wrote to his brother, Pierre, about selling properties that he had inherited from his maternal grandmother, Jeanne Sain, from his mother, and from his aunt, Jeanne Brochard. Two-thirds of this bequest had earlier been divided between his brother and his sister, Pierre and Jeanne, and the remaining third was now due to the youngest child of the family, René. Descartes' share was the fief of Perron, which included a house at Poitiers, and three farms near Châtellerault (one called La Bobinière, a second called la Grand-Maison, and a third called le Mordais).[2] He sold the last two for 11,000 livres, and the fief of Perron and La Bobinière for 3,000 livres. The house at Poitiers was sold subsequently for 10–11,000 livres. The revenues from these sales were not enough to support him indefinitely, but they were sufficient in the medium term to fund his life as a gentleman; he continued to use the title "Sieur du Perron" that derived from a property that he no longer owned.

Having visited Poitou, he was now ready to return to Paris, without any specific plans for study but apparently with a vague ambition to contribute to the intellectual discussions of the day. He described this interlude in the *Discourse on Method* in general terms, although there is enough detail to offer some insight into how it seemed to him in retrospect, eight years later.

I continued to practise the method that I had prescribed for myself. For, besides taking care generally to guide all my thoughts in keeping with its rules, I set aside some hours from time to time that I used specifically to apply this method to mathematical prob-lems, or even to some others that I could almost convert into mathematical problems by detaching them from all the principles of the other sciences which I found were less secure.... Thus, apparently without living differently from those who are concerned only to lead an agreeable and innocent life[,] ... I continued to follow my plan and to progress in knowledge of the truth, perhaps more than if I had merely read books or spent my time in the company of the learned.   (vi. 29–30)

Two of the features that were to characterize Descartes' work during the following three decades are mentioned almost in passing here. Throughout his life he read few books, and he consistently avoided as much as possible the company of those who were regarded as learned. There was a sense in which his intellectual project was uniquely personal and solitary. However, it certainly was not an attempt to discover truths simply by looking into his own mind. He would set the questions he wished to answer, he would make observations and conduct experiments when required, and he would almost obsessively refuse to be convinced by arguments or evidence from others.

The years during which Descartes was travelling and studying 'in the great book of the world' (vi. 9) were a period when the familiar teachings of centuries – about religion, politics, and science – were publicly questioned and sharply disputed across a war-torn Europe. The Protestant Reformation of the sixteenth century and the on-going Catholic Counter-Reformation, together with the proliferation of religious sects and the foundation of new religious orders, highlighted the fragile intellectual foundations on which the apparent unity of Christianity had relied.

There were many symptoms of the widespread distrust of traditional learning, and of the openness to consider alternatives, in the early part of the seventeenth century. Francis Bacon, the lord chancellor, had published *The Advancement of Learning* in 1605, and there were intimations even there of a new age for mankind, of significant advances in understanding the natural world and its imminent exploitation for the benefit of humankind. One of the features that particularly characterized this period was a radical challenge to assumptions that the universe is finite and that human beings are located at its centre. Giordano Bruno had speculated about an infinite universe, and about a form of Christianity that could adapt to such a radically new world. He paid a heavy price for dabbling in dangerous speculations when he was condemned by the Inquisition and burned at the stake in the Campo de' Fiori, in Rome, in 1600. Many others contributed to this cacophony of modernist voices, all announcing the advent in some sense of a new era, the abandonment of traditional learning, and the emancipation of those who had been seduced into intellectual subservience by the cultivated obscurity of the schools.

Descartes was already aware of the fundamental challenge to the traditional picture of the universe that was implicit in the work of Copernicus. *On the Revolutions* (1543) was not just a new technical theory for astronomers. It was an emphatic displacement of man from the centre of creation and his relocation, on one tiny planet in space, as a much less significant creature than a literal reading of the book of Genesis had suggested to generations of Christians. Brahe and Kepler supported this redefinition of the human world and its consequent reduction in stature. Descartes was familiar with both of these authors, and he had heard reports of new observations in astronomy by a contemporary Italian mathematician and astronomer called Galileo. However, he almost certainly failed to acknowledge the significance of Galileo's contribution. While the great mathematician of Florence was 'revealing the existence of a wholly new

world, a new world not only unknown but not dreamed of before, even by
the ancients,'[3] Descartes focused his attention on disputes much closer
to home. In the immediate aftermath of inheriting and selling various
properties, Descartes set off once again to travel, this time to Italy.

In March 1623, Descartes heard of the death of René Sain, a cousin
of Descartes' mother, who had been commissary general of provisions for
the French army stationed near Turin. He travelled to Italy to wind up his
affairs and, perhaps, to look into purchasing the vacant post of intendant
of the army. Thus, despite his mathematical discussions with Beeckman
and his alleged dream about the foundations of an admirable new science,
Descartes was still considering the possibility of a royal administrative
appointment in which he could use his legal training to earn a secure
salary. However, he first took time to put his own affairs in order by selling
some inherited properties, and he then set out for the Alps and Italy [in
September?] 1623. He seems to have travelled first to Basel and Zurich in
Switzerland, where he was delayed by troop movements in Valtellina, a
strip of land that the Spanish had opened up in 1619 to provide a land link,
on the border of Italy and France, between Spain and the Habsburg empire.
Since 1625 had been declared a Holy Year for the Catholic Church, which
included special indulgences for those who visited Rome and prayed in
prescribed churches, Baillet assumes that Descartes reached Rome before
the beginning of Advent in 1624, and that he was present at the official
opening of the Holy Year on New Year's Eve, 1624.

When visiting Rome, Descartes may have heard about the condemnation of Marco Antonio de Dominis, although the frequency of such
convictions may have made them less newsworthy at the time than they
appear in retrospect. De Dominis, a former Jesuit and archbishop of
Spoleto, fell afoul of the Holy Office for views expressed in a book on
the rainbow. He was arrested and imprisoned, and he died while still in
prison in Rome in December 1624. Even his fortuitous demise in custody
did not satisfy the punitive ambitions of the Vatican. His body and writings were burned publicly, in the Campo de' Fiori, on the eve of the Feast
of St. Thomas.

There is no evidence that, on this occasion, Descartes fulfilled his earlier
promise to make a pilgrimage to Loreto. He reported thirteen years later,
in a letter to Mersenne,[4] that he had never met Galileo, and one can only
surmise that he travelled on this occasion primarily for personal reasons
and to acquire experiences in the more general sense discussed in the

Discourse. On his return journey through the Suse Pass in May 1625, he witnessed an avalanche, to which he later refers in the *Meteors*.[5]

On his return to France, Descartes went to Châtellerault, where he had another opportunity to acquire a royal appointment, on this occasion as lieutenant general of Châtellerault, at a price of 5,000 livres. He evidently considered this suggestion seriously and wrote to his father for advice. However, Joachim Descartes had already departed from Paris for Rennes, and his son seems to have given up the idea of pursuing this option.

During this period of foreign travel, the city of Paris was buffeted by a series of events that shaped the intellectual climate in which Descartes redirected his energies toward his life's work.

Paris, 1623–1625

The years 1624 and 1625 were not unique or atypical of the discussions that troubled the kingdom of France in the early part of the seventeenth century. The repressive measures adopted by the Council of Trent, in its combative Counter-Reformation, included a pervasive watchfulness over anything that was said or published which might challenge the traditional teachings of the church. Trent decreed that 'no one may print or have printed any books on sacred subjects without the name of the author, nor in future sell them or even keep them in their possession unless they have first been examined and approved by the local ordinary [that is, the bishop or religious superior], under pain of anathema and fine.'[6] The theology faculty at the Sorbonne provided the most authoritative test of theological orthodoxy in France, and its members figured prominently in helping to implement Trent's decrees.

One of the most public challenges to the validity of traditional learning was planned for 24–25 August 1624. A large crowd, estimated at about one thousand, turned up in Paris to hear three speakers criticize Aristotelian philosophy. Jean Bitault, Etienne de Claves, and Antoine Villon drew up fourteen theses against Aristotle and advertised a public disputation that was obviously critical of 'the Philosopher'. Before they even began, however, the meeting was banned and, at the instigation of the Sorbonne, the Paris *parlement* decreed that the theses in question be shredded, that the speakers be banished from the jurisdiction of Paris, and that no one be allowed to teach anything contrary to the ancient, approved authors 'on pain of their lives'.[7] This summary condemnation of all anti-Aristotelian ideas set a pattern that was repeated often during the subsequent decades. It was welcomed by two of the authors who were to figure prominently in Descartes' early writing, Marin Mersenne (1588–1648) and Jean-Baptiste Morin (1583–1656).

Mersenne had been teaching theology and philosophy at Nevers; in 1619, he was transferred to the Minim friary near the Place Royal in Paris, where he remained (apart from infrequent foreign travel) for the rest of his life. Mersenne had joined the religious order of Minims after completing his schooling at La Flèche. The Minims were one of the reformed branches of the Franciscans, in part inspired by the experience of their founder, Saint Francis of Paula, who had lived as a hermit in Calabria (c. 1435).[8] In addition to the traditional three vows of poverty, chastity, and obedience, they took a vow to live as vegetarians. Two centuries later, motivated by the Counter-Reformation ambitions of the Council of Trent, the Minims in France assumed the challenge to counter the arguments of libertines and atheists. The condemnation of the Italian priest Lucilio Vanini (1585–1619) was the occasion on which Mersenne moved to Paris and joined forces with the church's campaign against the libertines.

Vanini had been officially charged at Toulouse with atheism, blasphemy, and 'other crimes'.[9] Since he was a priest and the Inquisition was active in Toulouse, it would have been appropriate to bring him before such an ecclesiastical tribunal if he had been charged with heresy.[10] However, there were rumours that he had been expelled from Lyon for a crime that could not be mentioned, that 'he was rejected by the Friars and turn'd out of their monastery' and that he seemed 'to approve debauchery'.[11] One of the sources of these hints was Mersenne's commentary on Genesis. He was reported as writing that Vanini 'was turn'd out of the Convent for his disorderly behaviour; and among the rest, for a crime deserving of fire and faggot, which good manners forbid to name, and the Minime dares not to express himself but in Greek.'[12] Mersenne's reluctance about naming the alleged crime was such that most copies of his book omitted this passage completely.[13] Nonetheless, a number of authors communicated their message by innuendo; they referred to a couplet quoted by Vanini from a play by Tasso, in which one of the characters says: 'All the time that is not devoted to love is wasted.'[14] Since there had been questions raised about Tasso's sexuality, those who wished to insinuate that homosexuality was Vanini's real crime needed only to point to this quotation from Tasso and add a phrase such as: 'not being willing to dishonour himself by the love of women'.[15] The Toulouse *parlement* sentenced Vanini as follows, on 9 February 1619: that the public executioner should 'cut out his tongue, strangle him, and then burn him at the stake to which he is tied and scatter his ashes in the wind.'[16] The sentence was carried out immediately after the verdict was reached, when Vanini was thirty-four years old.

These events prompted Mersenne's move to Paris and his subsequent contributions to arguments in favour of God's existence.[17] When advised by a confrere, Claude Rangueil, that a published rehearsal of Vanini's views could do more harm than good, by drawing the attention of readers to problems they may not have noticed, Mersenne decided to cloak his discussion of atheism and magic in the guise of a commentary on Genesis.[18] His unrelenting dedication to the anti-libertine cause resulted in the publication of three extremely long books in quick succession, each one devoted to the same apologetic enterprise. *Important Questions about Genesis, with a correct Explanation of the Text; in this volume, Atheists and Deists are Combatted and Conquered* appeared in 1623; *The Impiety of Deists* appeared in 1624 as a two-volume book of almost 1,350 pages, and, in the following year, Mersenne published *The Truth of the Sciences, against Sceptics and Pyrrhonists.*

While Vanini's teaching provided the immediate motivation for Mersenne's commentary on Genesis, it must have been obvious that his subversive opinions did not disappear when he was burned at the stake. There were many other libertine authors in Paris who strayed into the protected space of theological discussion. Not only did they mock the pretensions of the learned, they also undermined the philosophical language in which theologians expressed their apparently profound and deeply obscure dogmas. For example, the legal proceedings against the poet Théophile de Viau (1590–1626) lasted for two years, until his death in September 1625. One of the most sensitive questions that provoked such an official response was the discussion of the mortality or otherwise of the human 'soul', a question that was later to ensnare Descartes too.

Church councils had defined their position on this question on numerous occasions. In response to various challenges, they had decreed that the rational soul is the form of the human body, that there is a distinct soul for each individual human being, and that each soul is immortal.[19] However, the church claimed that the immortality of the soul was not simply an object of religious faith. It also claimed that philosophical arguments were convincing enough to support the same conclusion. The connection between belief in the human soul and belief in God was too close to tolerate any ambivalence on the former, since the very concept of God depended on the concept of an immaterial soul. Any doubts about the latter were described as bordering on atheism, and supporters of the Counter-Reformation were invited to contribute as best they could to defeating atheism.

In addition to the prolix responses from Mersenne, there was an equally long, rambling discussion of these issues in a book written by one of Descartes' friends in Paris, Jean Silhon (1596–1667). Silhon published *The Two Truths* in 1626, and he returned to the same themes and arguments eight years later, in *The Immortality of the Soul* (1634). There is a significant overlap between the two books, since the full title of the first one was: *The Two Truths of Silhon: one concerning God, and his Providence, the other concerning the Immortality of the Soul*. In both books Silhon identifies Pyrrhonism – which he understood as the claim that 'that nothing is known, and that it is permitted to doubt everything' – as undermining belief in God and in the immortality of the soul.[20]

In a sense, these challenges to Aristotelian philosophy and to theological discussions of the human soul and God arose within a community of French intellectuals who were at least conversant with traditional scholastic philosophy. There was an even more worrying threat from the alleged arrival, in Paris, of a new sect of Protestant enthusiasts who claimed to draw their inspiration from the Bible and from esoteric sources that had little in common with scholastic philosophy.

The Rosicrucians

The astronomical theories that are now recognized, in retrospect, as genuinely scientific features of the intellectual revolution in the seventeenth century were developed in a convulsive flurry of changes that included studies of natural magic, witches, Paracelsus, and the enigmatic and obscurantist follies of those who claimed to represent divine or satanic interventions in human affairs. In this extremely fluid intellectual context, the myth of the Brothers of the Rose Cross spread in Germany during the second decade of the seventeenth century. Descartes was sufficiently interested in their claims to advert to the secret knowledge of nature that featured prominently in their manifestos.

This brotherhood was most likely merely a myth rather than an association of real individuals with implausible beliefs, but its mythical character did not prevent many people from believing its publicity and claiming to be secret members. The document that purported to reveal its origin and constitution had first appeared in 1614.[21] The title reveals unambiguously the millenarian ambitions of its protagonists: *A Universal and General Reformation of the whole World; together with the Report of the Fraternity of the Rose Cross, written to all the Learned and Rulers of Europe*.[22] The *Report* alludes to the recovery of an ancient form of wisdom that was originally made available to Adam after the Fall. It includes clear references to Paracelsus, and it has connotations of magic, the cabbalistic tradition, alchemy, and astrology. It was not just a new philosophy of nature; it also included a religious or mystical dimension that intimated the imminent discovery of a new world. This apparent hoax was compounded by the publication, in the following year, of *A Brief Consideration of the more Secret Philosophy written by Philip à Gabella, a student of philosophy, now published for the first time together with the Confession of the Rose Cross Fraternity* (1615).[23] The *Confession* repeated themes already included in the *Report*, such as the relative insignificance of transmuting base metals into gold, the importance of the Bible as a source of wisdom for its members, and the recognition of the Roman Empire as its political authority.[24] Its central message was that 'the book of nature stands open to all men',[25] and that most men fail to understand it because they are insensitive to its revelations and untutored in the arcane wisdom of the brotherhood.

It was particularly difficult during these years to distinguish between genuine advances in knowledge and the claims of soothsayers and mystics who exploited the general climate of uncertainty to further their dubious ambitions. The line of demarcation between the two that we might wish to project back into history was simply not there, and the ease with which authors oscillated from one to the other requires explanation only to those who look back from today's perspective. For example, Bacon's *New Atlantis* was utopian, as was Campanella's *The City of the Sun*. When Descartes returned to Paris in 1623, the city was posted with placards announcing the arrival of members of the Rose Cross who were both visible and invisible, and who claimed to be able to speak all the languages of the countries they visited without learning them from books or otherwise. 'The representatives of our principal college of the brothers of the Rose Cross, who are visiting this city, visible and invisible, in the name of the Most High, towards whom the heart of the just is turned. We teach all the sciences without books, writings or signs, and we speak the languages of the countries where we live in order to rescue men, our equals, from error and death.'[26]

These alleged mysterious and unwelcome visitors prompted trenchant critiques by a number of French authors, who ridiculed their claims but were also so worried by their potential for deception that they published tracts against them. For example, one anonymous tract, *A New Cabal*, argued that Satan was the source of the 'fraudulent impressions of some black and cabbalistic science, which consists only of certain characters, figures, rings, ablutions, sacrifices, invocations . . . and usurpations of divine names, so that its members think of themselves as little gods.'[27] Focusing on the new sect's use of magic in the service of religion, *A New Cabal* claimed that the whole aim of this diabolical stratagem was to deceive people and lead them away from the true faith, that is, the Roman Catholic Church. The same lethal combination of sorcery and deception was the target of another tract, *The Shocking Pacts*, which was published in the same year. Here the members of the brotherhood were described as signing an oath with their own blood and conspiring to undermine 'the immortality of the soul . . . and to go much further in claiming that there is no God.'[28] While acknowledging that the 'true church' had always been agitated by heretics and reminding readers of the fate of Vanini, who was burned as an atheist in Toulouse in 1619, the author asks: 'Should we fear today that a bunch of ignorant knaves, if ever there were such, could change themselves from being visible to invisible by some new doctrine, or by magic or necromancy; that they could bewitch holy souls, blind the eyes of faith, bury our faith and, by illusions and spells, make us renounce heaven in order to embrace hell?'[29] There were many similar replies to the perceived threat of the Rosicrucians. Among the best-known were those by Gabriel Naudé and François Garasse.[30]

Mazarin's librarian, Gabriel Naudé, published in 1623 an *Instruction to France about the Truth of the History of the Brothers of the Rose Cross*.[31] He castigated the 'useless drones and buzzards of the human race' who insinuate their 'useless venom and ridiculous opinion' into the imagination of sensitive minds in Paris and, as a result, compromise the reliability of their judgment.[32] Naudé thought that the authors of the *Manifesto* and the *Confession* were imposters. Either the tracts are hoaxes, he argues, or they provide a genuine account of a real confraternity. If they are hoaxes, then those who believe them are credulous simpletons; if they are genuine, those who accept them must resemble the Celts, who, 'when they see the ocean flooding their land, outrun each other to be first to be engulfed in the swollen tide of its waves.'[33] In the same year, Mersenne published his commentary on the book of Genesis. In the process of discussing Brahe, Campanella, musical harmony, and all the issues of the age that were among his encyclopedic interests, he warned readers against the cabalistic interpretations of the Bible proposed by the English natural philosopher Robert Fludd.[34] The Jesuit priest François Garasse added his voice to the universal condemnation in *The Curious Doctrine of the Acute Minds of this age, or those who pretend to be such* (1623), in which he analysed the dangers of the apparently new sect in Germany, 'the confraternity of the Cross of Roses.'[35]

Naudé's concerns, as Cardinal Marazin's librarian, were probably more political than religious, whereas Mersenne and Garasse were primarily interested in defending Catholicism against 'heretics'. They were worried that if people were gullible enough to believe the stories of the Rose Cross fraternity, they were also likely to question the credibility of mysteries that were taught equally dogmatically by the Christian churches and were accepted with similar credulity by their members. This sensitive issue – about the extent to which unintelligible mysteries should be accepted from any source on faith – would later reappear as a major question for Descartes.[36] What criteria should one apply as a safeguard against being foolishly credulous, and what evidence is appropriate in making judgments about issues that seem to transcend the limited abilities of the human mind?

Naudé's general suspicion about alchemists and magicians was initially cast so widely that it included nearly everyone in the past who had proposed any kind of novelty. The scope of his initial condemnation prompted him to return to the question two years later in an attempt to rescue, from the imputation of magic, many of the most eminent philosophers and mathematicians of the past. Thus in 1625 he published *An Apology for all the Great People who have been falsely suspected of Magic.*[37] Here Naudé distinguished four kinds of magic, each of which involves the human exercise of natural powers, and he identified only one variety as unacceptable magic, in which human capacities are allegedly supplemented by the assistance of a demon. He argued that the natural magic involved in using one's native powers to their limit is not objectionable, and by this strategy Naudé rehabilitated Aristotle, Pythagoras, Democritus, Cicero, and even Paracelsus.[38]

There is a paragraph in Descartes' early writings in which he seems to criticize the millenarian and somewhat mystical ambitions of the Rosicrucians, when he writes:

The mathematical thesaurus of Polybius, the cosmopolitan, in which are provided the true means of solving all difficult problems in that science and which demonstrates that human intelligence can discover nothing further about those questions. This work is directed towards certain people who promise to show us miraculous novelties, to challenge their sluggishness or to expose their temerity . . . This work is offered anew to learned men throughout the world, and especially to the distinguished brothers of the Rose Cross in Germany.   (x. 214)

Descartes had been suspected, on his return to Paris, of having met members of the Rose Cross fraternity and perhaps even of having joined their secret fellowship. He replied to such queries, according to Baillet, by showing himself visibly to everyone, especially to his friends.[39] To demonstrate that he was not a member of the 'invisibles,' he needed no proof except to appear very visibly in public. He used a variation of the same argument to demonstrate that he could not possibly have met or joined the fraternity while travelling in Germany, since, according to their own testimony, its members were invisible.[40]

Apart from the fact that it would have been impossible to do so, there is no evidence to suggest that Descartes was ever interested in joining the Rose Cross brotherhood. However, in 1643, when he was engaged in a bitter controversy with theologians at Utrecht, Martin Schoock exploited the vague suspicion about Descartes' passing interest in the Rosicrucians to focus attention on his penchant for hiding in the wilderness and changing address frequently.[41] Having first raised his possible membership of the Rosicrucians with readers, Schoock rejects the suggestion that Descartes had actually joined the fraternity, even if the reason offered for the negative verdict is less than complimentary: Descartes was so ambitious that he wished to have his name trumpeted to the four corners of the world, whereas the Rose Cross brothers preferred to remain modestly invisible. Schoock suggested, as an alternative explanation, that Descartes' seclusion and frequent changes of address were more likely due to immoral behaviour or to misanthropy.

However, if the Brothers of the Rose Cross were both alluring and invisible, the fate of Tommaso Campanella in prison in Naples was sufficiently real to catch the attention of anyone who supported novel and allegedly dangerous ideas in the 1620s. Campanella had been arraigned before the Inquisition in Padua in 1594, imprisoned, tortured, and released two years later. He was back in prison the following year, and was then returned to his native Calabria in chains. He spent the years 1599–1626 and 1627–29 imprisoned in Naples and Rome, and eventually fled to France in 1634, where he enjoyed briefly the luxury of life outside prison until his death in Paris five years later.[42] Campanella's unerring eye for controversy, his public defence of Galileo against the findings of the Inquisition in 1616, and, especially, his criticism of Spanish rule in the south of Italy prompted the church and the civil powers to co-operate in silencing him. The views he expressed about the infinity of the universe and the place of the Earth in the solar system were not in themselves so novel as to merit this extraordinary and sustained punishment. Cardinal Nicholas of Cusa (1401–1464) had expressed similar views and survived unscathed.[43] Whatever the real reasons why he attracted the attention of the Inquisition, they were overshadowed by the ferocious cruelty and duration of his mistreatment. He provided an unwelcome and very public reminder of the likely consequences of dissent or unorthodoxy.

Descartes probably did not know many of the relevant details of Campanella's case at this time. When he first read his works in 1623, the Italian friar was still in prison. He most likely knew simply that Campanella was publicly associated with Galileo, in support of whom he had written a *Defence*, and that, despite being a Dominican friar, he had suffered execrable punishment for views he had publicly expressed. Descartes later claimed that, although he had read Campanella fifteen years earlier, he could not recall anything from the book's content.[44] While he may have forgotten the details of Campanella's writings, he could not have forgotten the church's response to it later, when he abruptly decided not to publish the very first book that he had completed, *The World*.

Descartes subsequently came to be recognized as someone who was extremely unsympathetic to the arcane and mystical philosophies of those who dabbled in magic, hermeticism, and astrology. When writing to Beeckman in 1630 about the wide range of views that were defended by many disparate authors, he distinguished among the ancients between Plato, Aristotle, and Epicurus and 'Telesio, Campanella, Bruno, Basso, Vanini, and all the innovators' (i. 158) as a characteristic group of dissidents.[45] Perhaps this brief allusion to these Italian philosophers merely indicates Descartes' awareness of their fate and his own implicit concerns about expressing unorthodox religious views. However, when Huygens sent him one of Campanella's books in 1638, he did not mince his words. He declined to read it, and explained why.

> I confess that his language and that of the German who wrote the long preface [Adam Tobias] prevented me from daring to have a conversation with them before I had finished the letters that I had to write, for fear of being affected by their style. As regards the doctrine, it is fifteen years [i.e., in 1623] since I read the book entitled *The Nature of Things* [1620] by the same author, together with some other treatises, and perhaps this one was included among them. However, I found at the time so little solidity in those writings that I retained nothing at all from them in my memory. Now I can say nothing about them except that those who go astray while pretending to pass through extraordinary paths seem to me to be much less excusable than those who only go astray in the company of others by following the most well-worn paths.
>
> (ii. 660)[46]

The final sentence condemns the innovators as being even worse than traditional scholastics. Later in the same year, Mersenne offered to send Descartes another book by Campanella, and the response was the same. 'Given what I saw earlier by Campanella, I cannot hope for anything good from this book. Thank you for offering to send me a copy, but I have no desire to see it.'[47]

Descartes may not have had as clear an understanding as these texts suggest of what was creative or otherwise among the novel ideas that were widely reported in the early 1620s. The repudiation of all mysterious or arcane inquiries depended on an extremely restrictive concept of explanation that was not yet clear in his mind. Once it was adopted, however, Descartes became one of the most notorious critics of any writing that purported to explain matters mysteriously while in fact only adding to the reader's confusion.

France, 1625–1628

Descartes spent the years 1625 to 1628 in France, with a base in Paris. Despite the fact that Marin Mersenne had also attended La Flèche as a student, Descartes probably met him for the first time during this period.[48] Mersenne combined the religious life of a Minim with that of an intellectual who corresponded over a thirty-year period with almost every scholar in Europe. Given Descartes' own propensity for the life of a secular hermit, Mersenne provided him for approximately twenty years with reliable intellectual contacts and a clearinghouse for exchanges with many other correspondents, including even members of the Descartes family who lived in Brittany.

During this period Descartes began to work on a number of projects, all of which were left unfinished. He reflected on his apparent lack of resolution when he wrote to Mersenne in 1630: 'If you find it odd that I began a number of treatises when I was in Paris and did not finish them, I can explain why. As I was working on them, I gained a little more knowledge about them than I had when I began, and in trying to accommodate that I was forced to begin a new project. . . . ' (i. 137–8). The unfinished projects included: (a) an outline of a general method, usually called the *Rules for Guiding One's Intelligence in Searching for the Truth*; (b) an early draft of the mathematical papers that were eventually published as the *Geometry* in 1637; and (c) research on the theory and practice of grinding lenses. This last project was much assisted by Claude Mydorge, who introduced Descartes to a skilled lens grinder, Jean Ferrier. These draft essays and the discussion of solutions to various problems in mathematics and optics were shared with others, to such an extent that there are contemporary references inquiring about the progress being made by this otherwise unknown scholar.[49]

This apparently fallow period included a significant transition in Descartes' mathematical outlook. One of the standard challenges to mathematicians at the time was to devise a method for constructing mean proportionals. For example, if two line segments are given with lengths a and b, one is asked to find two other lengths x and y, such that $a : x = x : y = y : b$. Despite its apparent simplicity, this could not be constructed using only the traditionally accepted means of ruler and compass, and those who proposed solutions had to rely on sliding rules and comparative measurements that were generally regarded as too inexact to be acceptable in geometry. Descartes devised a solution to this problem using a circle and a parabola. He shared the results with Mydorge, who produced a proof of the result. When Descartes told Beeckman about the solution, in 1628, the Dutch physicist noted that 'Mr. Descartes thinks so much of this discovery that he claims to have never discovered anything more significant and that, in fact, nothing more significant has ever been discovered by anyone' (x. 346). Descartes' characteristic lack of modesty is evident here. In fact, this great 'discovery' represented a somewhat late recognition on his part of the significance of algebraic methods for solving geometrical problems, and a significant improvement on the strategies that he had preferred in 1619, when he had used new compasses to tackle such problems.

Descartes lodged initially with one of his father's friends, Nicolas le Vasseur, who had a royal appointment in the central tax office in Paris. However, the number of visitors at the house was such that the lodger could make little progress with his research, and he moved to a quieter and more private house elsewhere in Paris – an evasive pattern that he repeated throughout his life. On this occasion he moved to an address in the Faubourg St. Germain, at a lodging house called Les Trois Chapelets, in rue du Four. His plans for solitude were compromised when his valet accidentally met M. le Vasseur on the street, and felt obliged to show him where Descartes was living. According to Baillet's account, Descartes was accustomed to remain in bed during the morning while his valet went shopping for his daily needs. Le Vasseur went to Les Trois Chapelets, looked through the keyhole and saw Descartes, sitting up in bed with the window open and the shutters raised, thinking and writing at his leisure. Having watched him for about half an hour, the two uninvited observers left quietly, without disturbing the unsuspecting philosopher's privacy.

Among those who became his friends during his Paris stay were Jean Louis Guez de Balzac, who was author of a number of literary works and collections of letters addressed to eminent people in France, including Richelieu.[50] Father Goulu, the head of the Feuillant friary in Paris, criticized Balzac publicly – although he concealed his identity under the pseudonym 'Phyllarque' – and charged him with narcissism, religious insincerity, temerity, lack of judgment, stupidity, ineptitude, and much more besides.[51] Descartes came to Balzac's defence and wrote a short apology on his behalf that was sent to an unidentified common friend, possibly Jean Silhon (i. 7–11). Descartes praised Balzac's natural display of the ancient art of eloquence, and his truthfulness and fearlessness in commending or reproaching the mighty for their virtues or vices. Balzac's undying gratitude for this moral support is obvious from subsequent letters. For example, he wrote to Descartes in Amsterdam, 25 April 1631: 'I did not then live but in the hope I had to go see you at Amsterdam; and to embrace that dear Head, which is so full of reason and understanding. . . . It is now three years, that my imagination goes in quest after you; and that I even die with longing to be united to you, and never to part from you again.'[52]

During these years, Descartes also became acquainted with the mathematician Jean-Baptiste Morin, with whom he later discussed the Earth's motion, and with the Oratorian priest Guillaume Gibieuf (1583–1650). Gibieuf was thirteen years older than Descartes; he had enjoyed a similar Jesuit education at the college in his native town of Bourges, and he had subsequently joined the Oratory in 1612 following studies at the Sorbonne. He was thus ideally placed to offer Descartes the theological support that he needed when faced with challenges about his religious orthodoxy. This was especially true on the contentious issue of how human freedom is compatible with God's causal influence over human actions.[53] Descartes also first met the man who was usually identified as Abbé Picot, who acted subsequently as manager of his business affairs and who remained a friend to the end of Descartes' life.

There were two significant events in Descartes' life during this period: his meeting with Bérulle and the siege of La Rochelle, although the dating of the former remains unclear. In autumn 1627, Descartes attended a conference given by Chandoux in the presence of Cardinal Bérulle, the founder of the Oratory, and of the papal legate Cardinal Bagni. Descartes' intellectual skills in refuting point by point the various arguments proposed prompted Bérulle to ask him whether he had a method by which philosophical questions could be resolved. The young philosopher claimed that he was working on such a method – he had in his study an incomplete version of the *Rules*, about half the projected set of thirty-six rules of method – and he promised his host to make available the results of his reflections. He reported this event in a letter to Villebressieu in 1631:

You have seen the two results of my fine rule or natural method when I was obliged to apply it in the discussion I had with the Papal Nuncio, Cardinal Bérulle, Father Mersenne, and with the large and learned group that assembled at the home of the Nuncio to hear Mr. Chandoux's discourse about his new philosophy. That is where I made the whole group acknowledge the power that reasoning properly has over the minds of those who are only moderately learned, and the extent to which my principles are better established, more true and more natural than any others which are currently accepted among the learned.[54]

He apparently went to Brittany to spend the winter of 1627–28, hoping to complete that project. As we know now, that never happened. While he was with his family in Brittany, he became godfather to his brother Pierre's child at Elven, in Morbihan (22 January 1628), and he was still there at the end of March when Balzac wrote to him.[55] Twenty years later, he reflected

on his gradual adjustment to a life of solitude before leaving France for
the United Provinces. Despite the passing of time, these lines have the
appearance of authenticity. He was discussing the general question of how
one moves between two radically different positions and was suggesting
that such significant changes are realized best by degrees. In that context,
he used the example of his own conversion from a normal busy life to that
of a reclusive philosopher:

> That is why, it seems to me, it is best to move from one extreme to another only by
> degrees. Before I came to this country in search of solitude, I spent a winter in France
> in the country, where I did my apprenticeship. Although I had embarked on a definite
> direction in my life, in which my indisposition did not allow me to remain for any
> length of time, I did not wish to hide this indisposition. I preferred instead to make it
> appear greater than it actually was, so that I could honestly excuse myself from all the
> actions which could reduce it and thereby, by a series of easy steps, realize a complete
> freedom by degrees.[56]

The beneficial results of this apprenticeship in solitude became evident in
subsequent years.

There is no direct evidence that Descartes participated in the siege of
La Rochelle.[57] The St. Bartholomew's Day massacre, during the reign of
Charles IX, had been the worst example previously of the intermittent
ethnic cleansing of Huguenots in France. It began on 24 August 1572 and
continued for a number of days, during which thousands of Huguenots
were murdered in Paris and in various provincial cities, including the
famous professor of eloquence and philosophy Peter Ramus. This defining
moment in French history was followed by a period of relative toleration
under Henry IV, who was responsible for the Edict of Nantes. The complex
factors that led to the siege of La Rochelle are certainly not reducible
simply to intolerance of the Reformed Church by the majority Catholic
population. However, Richelieu recommended to the young Louis XIII
that he consolidate his power over the kingdom of France – to 'demolish
the Huguenot party, to humble the pride of the great, to subjugate all
subjects in their duties and to raise his name among foreign nations to the
status that it deserved.'[58]

La Rochelle, therefore, was not just a Huguenot city; it was also potentially a focus of dissent in a kingdom that was frequently threatened by
secession and disunity. At the beginning of the siege, 10 September 1627,
the city had approximately 28,000 inhabitants. The landing of the duke of
Buckingham at the nearby Ile de Ré in July 1627 gave the impression of an

alliance between Charles I and the unfortunate residents of La Rochelle, and precipitated the siege that lasted for more than a year. Buckingham sailed home in October 1627, and Charles I subsequently promised assistance to the besieged city on a number of occasions, in response to requests from La Rochelle. When the siege concluded, on 30 October 1628, approximately 15,000 of the city's citizens had died of hunger and associated sicknesses. The triumphant royal army entered the city, and Richelieu celebrated a High Mass in the cathedral, with a Te Deum in thanksgiving for their victory. It would help us to understand Descartes' political allegiance if he were found to have supported the siege, although those who place him at La Rochelle suggest that he merely visited – as many others did, almost like tourists – to study the architecture of the famous dyke erected around the city during the siege.[59]

The *Rules*

Descartes' writing during this period shows the indecisive search for a new method that was reflected in the wide range of authors he consulted, his interest in optics, and the first signs of an awareness that mathematics was only one science among many. The *Rules* were drafted and redrafted at various times during the decade 1618–28 and were then abandoned. However, Descartes kept the text and carried it with him throughout his travels and frequent changes of residence until his death, in Stockholm, more than two decades later. The inventory of his library includes a reference to 'nine notebooks, bound together, containing part of a *Treatise of Clear and Useful Rules for Guiding the Mind in Searching for the Truth*' (x. 9).[60] This manuscript was passed to Clerselier, who deferred doing anything with it until he had published other material from Descartes' manuscripts. Meantime, he showed it to Arnauld and Nicole, who included parts of Rule 14 in *The Art of Thinking* (1662), and he allowed Leibniz to have a copy made (in 1675 or 1676), before passing it on to Jean-Baptiste Legrand. After the latter's death in 1704, the original manuscript disappeared. Before its final disappearance, however, a Dutch translation appeared in 1684, and the Latin source of that translation was published for the first time in its original language in 1701.[61]

It has been recognized for many years that the surviving text of the *Rules* cannot disguise the extent to which it was edited and frequently recast before Descartes abandoned hope of completing it. It was originally

conceived as three sets of twelve rules.[62] Thus, toward the conclusion of
Rule 12, at a point where Descartes thought he had expounded general
principles that applied equally to the solution of all problems, he wrote:
'As regards questions, some may be understood perfectly, even if we do not
know their solutions, and we discuss those alone in the next twelve rules.
There are others, finally, that are not perfectly understood, and we defer
them to the final twelve rules' (x. 429). Unfortunately, the project lapsed
about halfway through the second set of rules, and Rules 19 to 21 are given
only in summary form without any detailed explanation. It is difficult to
avoid the conclusion that Descartes originally hoped to construct general
rules that would apply, with appropriate modifications, to all disciplines
and that he acknowledged eventually that such an ambitious project was
impossible to realize.

The almost utopian or, at least, naïve hope of finding a single method
by which all sciences could be guided was not a novel suggestion on
Descartes' part. Aristotle had begun this tradition, with his *Organon*, and
generations of Aristotelian commentators and critics had continued to
search for a single method for acquiring reliable knowledge of everything
possible. Even Galileo, during the early part of his career, drafted such
a general method in scholastic language, though for the most part he
later abandoned it.[63] Apart from inducements in Lull or Agrippa, which
may also have influenced Descartes, there was a more obvious contemporary exemplar in Francis Bacon. Bacon had notoriously composed a *New
Organon* in 1620. It was written in Latin rather than in English, to make
it accessible to schools across Europe, and was conceived as underpinning
the great restauration of the sciences toward which he worked. Descartes
was aware of Bacon's efforts; he acknowledged his death in 1626, and he
can be seen as attempting to construct in the *Rules* a method that could
compete in novelty and generality with Bacon's ambitions in the *New
Organon*.

The most startling implication of any of these methodological efforts,
including the *Rules*, was the hope of discovering a single method by which
the truth about any issue could be discovered. Descartes discussed the
widely assumed analogy between method and the arts in Rule 1. He conceded that the skills required for farming are not necessarily helpful for
playing music and, in general, that practical skills are not transferable from
one art to another. Some might think that the same lack of transferibility
applies in the case of the sciences but, according to the *Rules*, 'they are

completely wrong about this' (x. 360). Descartes' suggestion is that all the sciences are interrelated and dependent on one another, and that if anyone wishes 'seriously to investigate the truth about things . . . they should think instead only about increasing the natural light of reason ' (x. 360) by which the truth is discovered. The analogy to which he appeals is the Sun, shining brightly on all the objects that it illuminates. Similarly, the light of reason illuminates and reveals all the truths that await our discovery. It follows that we should not be distracted by specific disciplines, such as mathematics or astronomy, which are like different possible objects to be illuminated. The most fundamental thing required in a general method is subjective, namely, an ability to shine the light of reason appropriately on various objects, and that involves innate skills of some kind. If there are rules of method, therefore, they can be found by investigating what we would do spontaneously if left to our own naturally endowed intellectual dispositions.

This turns the project inward, to looking at the intellectual capacities of the human mind and to very elementary rules for using those capacities as best we can. However, that also raises a complementary objection that was discussed in Rule 4: perhaps no method at all is required. Descartes replies that studying without a method is how 'almost all chemists, most geometers, and quite a number of philosophers study' (x. 371). They are like people looking for a treasure who wander about the streets aimlessly and hope to stumble on the object of their search. They may be lucky, but the chances are that they will find very little. At this point one might expect Descartes to outline an alternative, systematic, and more reliable way of discovering solutions to problems. However, instead of offering an intellectual compass or guide for those who search for the truth, he immediately introduces a theme that remains with him for the rest of his life: that the natural light of reason is obscured or inhibited by traditional learning.

. . . it is much more satisfactory never to think about seeking the truth about anything, than to do so without a method, because it is very certain that the natural light is obscured and our intelligence is blinded by such disordered studies and obscure meditations. Anyone who gets used to walking in this way in the shadows weakens their eyesight to such an extent that they cannot subsequently tolerate daylight. This is confirmed by experience, for we see very often that those who have never studied judge much more reliably and clearly about simple things than those who have spent all their time in the schools. (x. 371)

This suggests something very different from what might have been expected. It is the first written indication of Descartes' disenchantment with traditional studies. Obviously, 'disordered studies and obscure meditations' include those that promised a privileged access to the truth through arcane symbols and mystical illumination. However, they also include most of the philosophy of the schools. In order to make progress in the sciences, therefore, one needs to escape from the complex restrictions of traditional disciplines and their subdivisions, and to begin anew with only the natural light of reason as one's guide.

The sudden change in strategy implies that, despite the explicit hints about a method and rules, one should not expect from Descartes anything that resembles a traditional method, that is, a set of detailed prescriptions for resolving problems in the various sciences. He offers instead some very general advice about simplifying problems into subproblems or analyzing complex realities into simple parts, and then understanding the parts clearly before moving on to more complex realities. According to Rule 5, 'the whole method consists in the order and arrangement of those things to which the mind's eye must turn so that we can discover some truth' (x. 379). It is not surprising, therefore, if the rules offered are so general in nature that one would be hard pressed to know, in a particular case, whether they had been observed or not.

In spite of the generality of the rules, however, there are some indications already of the scientific methods that Descartes would later recommend. The 'entire method' outlined in Rule 5 is illustrated with examples of practitioners who fail to observe it. The essence of the method is to begin with simple realities that we know, and then to move step by step to issues that are more complex. Descartes compares those who ignore this advice to people who try 'to go from the bottom of some building to its top in one step.' Unmethodical researchers also include philosophers 'who, neglecting experience, think that the truth will spring from their own brains as Minerva did from the head of Jove' (x. 380). Accordingly, the *Rules* do not recommend ignoring experience when doing research in physical science. On the contrary, the most obvious and simple things to be known in this context are known by experience. The same point is emphasized in Rule 8, which illustrates the proposed method by an example taken from optics. If someone wishes to find the anaclastic for a particular translucent medium, that is, the line at which parallel rays of light are refracted so that they intersect at a single point, they should follow a number of steps that will conclude with a question about the nature of light. Once this point is reached, they are forced to realize that light is a natural power, and, if they cannot make progress in understanding light by examining it directly, they may understand it indirectly 'by analogy' with other familiar natural powers (x. 395), all of which are known by experience.

This analogical approach matches the suggestions outlined in Rule 12 for understanding how we perceive things as being coloured, and it borrows on Descartes' earliest reflections in his notebooks on the way in which we conceive of immaterial things by analogy with familiar material realities. In Rule 12, he recommends that we avoid addressing directly the question about how colour perception occurs, for we do not know enough to provide an adequate explanation. Instead, we should model colours onto shapes, because we can understand shapes very well, and there are as many shapes available as there are colours in need of explanation (x. 413). This is the same point that was made, with a more general application, in *Olympics*:

> Just as the imagination uses shapes to conceive of bodies, in the same way the intelligence uses certain sensible bodies to shape spiritual things, such as the wind and light.... Man knows natural things only by analogy with those that fall under his senses. We even think that those who philosophize best, with greater truth, are those who most successfully assimilate the things that are sought with what is known to the senses.   (x. 217, 218–19)[64]

These concessions to the necessity of experience, both in conceptualizing the realities that we investigate and in gathering basic information about them, remained inadequately integrated into a theory of knowledge that still resonated, in 1628, with a model of scientific knowledge that had originally been borrowed from Euclid's geometry. Descartes, in the *Rules*, thus repeats what Aristotle had claimed in the *Posterior Analytics*, that 'every science is certain and evident knowledge' (x. 362), and that the only reliable way of acquiring such knowledge is by 'intuition and deduction' (x. 368). The rhetoric of certainty, of building knowledge on firm foundations through a series of deductive steps, leaves unchallenged a model of scientific knowledge that was about to be superseded by the overwhelming experience of empirical scientists.

One reason why Descartes may have abandoned the *Rules*, therefore, is that they were too general to provide any specific advice about, for example, how to develop theories in optics or physiology, and that they required a degree of certainty that was not feasible in natural science. These general rules of method, outlined in Rule 5, were later summarized and reissued in a very different context in the *Discourse on Method* in 1637. The other immediate reason for abandoning the project was Descartes' inability to construct a general problem-solving technique that would apply to all problems, including mathematical ones.

The discussion of method in the *Rules* changed suddenly at transitions between different ideas that were competing for attention in Descartes' still inchoate plans for a renewal of knowledge. One of those, already mentioned, is the relegation of scholastic methods to the past. Another version of this suggestion was that natural intelligence is a more reliable guide to the truth than the convoluted systems of thought invented by philosophers, and that the way to find the truth is to cultivate native intelligence rather than to learn a method from someone else. However, despite all these disclaimers, Descartes also had in mind a paradigm of what success in his enterprise would mean. This was summarized in the search for what he called a '*mathesis universalis*', or a universal rigorous method.

When these thoughts recalled me from the particular study of arithmetic and geometry to searching for a certain general mathesis, I first inquired what precisely everyone understood by that term, and why not only the disciplines already mentioned but also astronomy, music, optics, mechanics and many others are also said to be part of mathematics. . . . since the word 'mathesis' means the same as 'discipline', the other disciplines have as much right as geometry itself to be called mathematics. . . . Therefore, there must be some general science, which explains everything that can be learned about order and measure, which is not confined to any particular subject matter, and which is called universal mathesis.   (x. 377–8)

The *Rules* presents a very abstract version of the problems that seem to have been bothering Descartes at the time of its composition. It is reasonably clear that he is still thinking of a way of integrating arithmetic and geometry (or problems of discrete and continuous magnitude), and his new emphasis on the role of the imagination suggests that all soluble problems could be mapped onto problems in geometry or spatial extension. Part of the method envisaged is outlined in Part Two, which describes in general terms how to translate mathematical problems into equations. However, the underlying philosophical and mathematical problems remained unsolved – what methods of construction (apart from ruler and compass) should be accepted as genuinely geometrical; how to construct higher order algebraic equations; and ultimately, whether discrete and continuous quantity could be mapped perfectly onto each other.

This whole episode illustrates an important feature of Descartes' ambitious claims. The letter to Beeckman in March 1619 betrayed an exaggerated confidence in the extent to which the new compasses would resolve long-standing problems in mathematics. During the following nine years, Descartes began to appreciate the significance of applying algebraic methods to the solution of problems in geometry. However, before he had made the kind of progress that might have supported his claims on behalf of a general *mathesis*, he was once again promising to have discovered a method by which all problems in any discipline could be resolved. This involved two major moves, neither of which was justified by his work to date. The first was a reduction of problems in every discipline to the form or structure of a mathematical problem. Then, within mathematics, the ambition was to integrate arithmetic and geometry fully, so that the only remaining task was to find the appropriate equation for any given problem. This assumed that the solution of such equations was a relatively minor matter.

Having promised too much, Descartes had to acknowledge that he could not deliver on his overly ambitious plans. It simply was not the case that all problems are similar enough to mathematical problems that we could translate one into the other without significant loss. Even within mathematics proper, Descartes had made little progress over Viète's application of algebraic methods to geometry. It was time, therefore, to leave aside the misleading allure of a general solution to all problems and to look to the solution of particular problems, however that might be achieved.

A Mechanical World

This formative period in Descartes' life was dominated by uncertainty, both personal and professional. He was unsure of what career to follow, or where to live. He had rather vague ambitions about contributing to a radically new perspective on nature that many contemporary writers mentioned, but he was unsure about how best to get started on that project. He was briefly attracted by the promises of an arcane wisdom that was discovered, not by scientific work that any intelligent person could learn, but by initiation into a mystical tradition that reflected features of the early Christian Church as described by religious reformers. In the midst of this intellectual confusion, he had no conceptual resources with which to focus his speculative work apart from the scholastic philosophy that he had learned at La Flèche and the mathematical problems that he had attempted to solve as a self-taught practitioner.

However, these ambiguities were overshadowed by one clear suggestion from an unexpected source. In the spring of 1615, an engineer and architect in the service of the prince elector of Palatine, Salomon de Caus, published a book entitled: *The Explanation of Moving Forces, with various machines, both useful and decorative; to which are added various designs for Grottoes and Fountains.* This book was reissued and published in Paris in 1624, prior to its author's death there in 1626. Although Descartes does not mention De Caus in his subsequent correspondence, his later adoption of mechanical models makes it highly likely that he consulted his book during this period and that it sparked his interest in the possible adaptation of hydraulic models to his scientific ambitions.

De Caus defines a machine as 'a combination and firm connection of timber or other material, which has power and movement either from itself or from any other source,' and he distinguishes three kinds of machines: those for lifting weights, pneumatic machines that are powered by water or air, and machines such as windmills.[65] He argues, in Book I, that there is no vacuum in nature – a thesis later defended by Descartes – and he illustrates and supports this claim by various examples. The first argument is that water will not flow out from a container that is filled with water, which has a hole at the bottom, unless a tap is opened at the top to allow air to enter and fill the space left empty by the water. There is a similar argument in reverse, that one cannot pour water into a container that is already full of air unless the air is allowed to escape through some aperture.[66]

Book II, concerning grottoes and fountains, is dedicated to Princess Elizabeth, the mother of the princess with whom Descartes corresponded in the 1640s. This book is divided into 'problems', much like engineering exercises, which are arranged in sequence so that later problems are more complicated and presuppose the designs provided in previous solutions. For example, the first problem is to 'design a grotto which includes a satyr that will play the flageolet, and a nymph that responds to the satyr's musical cadences.'[67] Having discussed a wide range of machines, including pulleys for lifting weights, clocks controlled by a running stream, a water pump to quench a house fire, and a machine to simulate the singing of a bird, it is simply the next step of a natural progression to construct 'a machine by which a Neptune is represented, which turns in a circle around a rock, with other figures which squirt out water as they turn.'[68] Each solution is illustrated on a facing page with a detailed diagram of the proposed construction.

The implications of these models were evident in Descartes' approach to modeling animals as machines in the early 1630s. He wrote in the *Treatise on Man*:

The nerves of the machine that I am describing can be compared to the pipes in the mechanical parts of these fountains, its muscles and tendons to various other engines and springs which serve to operate these mechanical parts, its animal spirits to the water that drives them, the heart to the source of the water, and the brain's cavities to the apertures. Moreover, respiration and similar actions which are normal and natural to this machine, and which depend on the flow of spirits, are like the movements of a clock or mill, which the normal flow of water can make continuous. External objects, which by their mere presence act on the organs of sense and thereby cause them to move in many different ways ... are like strangers who on entering the grottoes of these fountains unwittingly cause the movements that take place before their eyes. For they cannot enter without stepping on certain tiles which are arranged in such a way that, for example, if they approach a Diana bathing they will cause her to hide in the reeds, and if they move forward to pursue her they will cause a Neptune to advance and threaten them with his trident. (x. 130–1)

De Caus's book on machines, including hydraulic machines that could simulate the movements and sounds of animals and human beings, provided a model of explanation that contrasted starkly with anything that Descartes might have borrowed from the Rose Cross fraternity. The contrast between mechanical and magical powers – and the corresponding contrast between explanations that use mechanical models and 'understanding' that presupposes mystical enlightenment – reflected the twin interests of the Holy Roman emperor, Rudolph II, and of the circle of dedicated researchers that gathered around the court at Prague. These two cultures were as incompatible as their subsequent history confirmed. Descartes had not reached a point, in 1628, at which he was sufficiently clear about the choice to be made, although the options available became very clear in the early 1630s. The transition was made after he returned to the United Provinces in 1628.

At the conclusion of this rather unstructured period of his life, Descartes was thirty-two years old. He had written little apart from an incomplete autobiographical sketch, and an incomplete draft of a general method that he was forced to abandon. He had lost much of his original enthusiasm for mathematics, and had begun to work in optics with the assistance of

skilled lens grinders. He had made new friends in Paris, some of whom
would continue to correspond with him for the next two decades. The
aspiring young philosopher had apparently given up hope of buying an
appropriate royal appointment in France and had decided to pursue his
intellectual interests abroad. He had a modest income from the proceeds
of the inherited properties he had sold, and he looked north again in the
direction of the United Provinces. Beeckman remarked, on one occasion,
that Descartes suffered from wanderlust [*peregrinandi cupidus*: i. 30]; that
was as plausible an explanation as any alternative for his return to the
United Provinces in 1628.

However, when he reflected on the period between November 1619
and 1628 in the *Discourse on Method*, he gave the impression that he had
purposefully travelled widely with a view to implementing his planned
restauration of human knowledge. He was convinced, he claimed, that
philosophy 'still contains nothing that is not disputed and consequently
doubtful' (vi. 8), and that there was 'nothing one could imagine which is
so strange and incredible that it was not said by some philosopher' (vi. 16).
He decided, therefore, to begin afresh or, in the metaphor he preferred,
to rebuild the house of his knowledge from the foundations up. Apart
from the provisional moral rules he adopted and 'the truths of faith that
have always been among my primary beliefs', he began the task of ridding
himself of all his other beliefs and of applying the rules or guides that
he had invented for himself. The period that he wished to describe, in
retrospect, as the time for practising his new method and acquiring the
experiences to which he could apply it lasted much longer than he might
have anticipated.

Those nine years passed by, however, before I had made up my mind about the questions
that are usually debated among educated people or had begun to look for foundations
for a philosophy that would be more certain than what is generally adopted. The
example of many excellent minds who had previously had this plan, but who seemed
to me not to have succeeded, made me imagine such great obstacles that I might not
have dared to embark on it so soon if I had not seen that some people were already
spreading the rumour that I had finished the task. . . . I thought I should try by every
possible means to become worthy of the reputation that I had acquired. It is exactly
eight years since this desire made me resolve to move away from all the places where I
had acquaintances and to retire here to a country where the long duration of the war
has resulted in a situation in which the armies involved serve only to make the fruits
of peace available with much greater security and where, among a great crowd of busy
people, who are more concerned with their own business than they are inquisitive

about that of others, I have been able to live as solitary and withdrawn a life as in the most remote deserts without lacking any of the conveniences that are available in the busiest town.   (vi. 30–1)

It may have seemed, from the perspective of 1637, that this transitional period in his life was part of a grand design. However, Descartes cannot have understood it that way in 1628, when it remained unclear whether anything of significance would result from further travel. He may have thought that a change of climate would remove some of the most obvious tensions in his life. One of those was a conflict between constructing a viable philosophy of nature and the dominant influence of a pious religious tradition according to which spirits were as real as stones or mountains.

Spirits in the World

Descartes' brief and passing interest in the writings of Lull, Della Porta, and Campanella provided an opportunity to reflect on the almost universal belief at that time in the existence of spirits and their alleged influence on the natural world. It was almost a truism for most of his contemporaries that God is a spiritual being, that angels exist, that human minds are spiritual, and that all these spirits have a significant impact on the observable realities of our experience. There was an equally widespread belief in witches and their nefarious powers.[69] The Rose Cross fraternity was completely unacceptable to its critics, not because of the powers that it claimed for its members, since nearly everyone believed at the time that such powers were commonly exercised, but because they were at the disposal of Protestant preachers and were being used to undermine the faith of uneducated Catholics or in some other way to cause evil.

Had anyone reported, in the 1620s, that various religious or mystical believers had visions or had exercised miraculous powers, hardly anyone in France would have said that such was impossible or incredible.[70] The Spanish mystical writers of the Carmelite tradition in the sixteenth century, Saint Teresa of Avila and Saint John of the Cross, were well known and widely admired. Seventeenth-century France was notable for the burgeoning religious devotion that was designed to counteract the effects of the Reformation. This emerged in many different forms that were adapted to the capacities of various types of believers. While most people did not know Latin and therefore could not understand what was being said in liturgical ceremonies, they were encouraged to revert to simple prayers in the vernacular that they had learned in childhood.[71] Francis de Sales wrote one of the standard manuals of religious devotion in 1608, *An Introduction to the Devout Life*. During the following decades, devotion to the Eucharist was fostered by the church, attendance at Mass was required, and the requirements of the Council of Trent for the use of the sacraments were widely implemented. The Jesuits were foremost in the design and dissemination of devotional practices. They were not alone, however. The Franciscans, Capuchins, Oratorians, Carmelites, and many others all joined in a concerted effort to turn France into a homogeneously Catholic kingdom. In this context, belief is spiritual realities was as uncontentious as belief in natural phenomena. It was accepted without question that there were both good and evil spiritual forces at work in the world, and that the real issue was not to establish their existence or otherwise but to join the battle between good and evil on the side of God and his angelic legions.

One option available to Descartes, therefore, was to establish a clear distinction between spiritual realities of any kind and the familiar phenomena of the natural world, and to focus his quest for understanding exclusively on the latter. This could best be done by adopting an official agnosticism with respect to spirits. Another way of doing the same thing was to consign the discussion of spiritual realities to theology and to avoid any entanglement with the seductive subtleties of its practitioners. It was not easy to do that in France. One of the reasons why Descartes may have looked north, then, was to find the intellectual freedom to pursue the inquiries about the natural world that most interested him. However, it was impossible even in the United Provinces to escape the intrusive attention of theologians who were constantly on hand to test the orthodoxy of all opinions. Descartes was therefore to find, during the subsequent two decades, that he was frequently under pressure from both Catholic and Calvinist theologians, and that his geographical isolation was a completely inadequate protection against their demands for conformity. It remains to be seen whether his religious faith was as central to his life as he claimed, or whether he retained his allegiance to the church of his nurse for other reasons.

4

A Fabulous World
(1629–1633)

Thus I shall be content to continue . . . as if my plan were only to tell you a fable.

(xi. 48)

I N late 1628, when he was thirty-two years old, Descartes set out for the United Provinces for the second time in his life.[1] The reasons he offered friends for his departure from France were that he wished to avoid the customary distractions of a gentleman's life (such as visiting friends and attending court), and that he wanted to escape the heat of the French climate. Descartes' subsequent frequent changes of address, and his almost obsessive efforts to conceal his precise location even from trusted friends, make the first reason more plausible than it might otherwise seem. During the period from 1629 to 1633, the new immigrant had at least five addresses, at Franeker, Amsterdam (twice), Leiden, and Deventer, and on two occasions he considered leaving the country either to return to France or to visit England.[2] Since he asked Mersenne not to reveal his address and seems even to have provided misleading return addresses on his letters, one must assume that he wished to enjoy the seclusion that he claimed was necessary for his studies.[3] His quasi-eremitical success is reflected in the pun used by some of those who were frustrated by his hiding, when they spelled his name as 'Monsieur d'Escartes' (Mr. Evasion). Apart from avoiding the unwelcome company of others, Descartes also seems to have preferred the temperate climate of northern countries, where he hoped to avoid 'the sicknesses caused by the heat of the air.'[4] He evidently believed that many of the plagues that affected cities were caused by warm weather.

Whatever the reasons for his obsessive reclusiveness, the intellectual results of this retreat were as significant as anything that he accomplished during the rest of his life. This was the time during which he first got a clear idea of constructing a general theory of the universe that would fundamentally challenge the traditional picture of the world that was almost universally taught at universities. For four years, he worked more or less exclusively on the manuscript of *The World*. He gave frequent reports to Mersenne of progress made, of unanticipated delays, and of the frustrations involved in collecting the experimental data required to complete various parts of the project. However, when the book was eventually ready to show Mersenne, Descartes heard about Galileo's trial by the Roman Inquisition and deferred its publication indefinitely. *The World* – the first fruits of many years of speculation – unfortunately remained unpublished until after the author's death.

Despite the self-censorship to which Descartes succumbed, this manuscript included the core of his entire philosophy and his most significant contribution to the scientific revolution. Nevertheless, it was not originally planned as such. Rather, it evolved gradually, over time, in response to reports of novel observations and requests for explanations of unusual phenomena, until the final scope of the enterprise was much wider than originally envisaged. It began, as might be expected, with Descartes' work on optics, which he had already initiated in Paris.

Franeker, 1629

Franeker had been a university city since 1585, and it provided a first, temporary lodging for Descartes in the United Provinces. He matriculated as a student in the arts faculty at Franeker on 26 April 1629, and lived in a small castle in the town that belonged to the Sjaerdema family. Descartes apparently lived there for about six months, within the walls of the city but separated from other houses by a moat. He thus enjoyed not only the privacy that he claimed to need for his studies, but also the secrecy required to attend Mass in a town that was officially hostile to Catholic religious services.[5]

Why Franeker, in the far north of Friesland? It may have been because Adriaan Metius (1571–1635) was professor of mathematics there, and Descartes was aware that his brother Jacobus, who lived in Alkmaar, had contributed to the discovery of the telescope.[6] It is clear from correspondence in June 1629 with Jean Ferrier, who lived in Paris, that Descartes' primary interest during this period was to develop a machine for grinding lenses. With this in mind, he tried to persuade Ferrier, an experienced lens grinder who was then in the service of the king's brother in Paris, to travel to Franeker and to work under his supervision. Descartes explained, sensibly enough, that many technical problems arise in the course of grinding lenses that cannot be anticipated in theory or adequately explained in correspondence. However, if Ferrier were to work side by side with him, they could resolve such problems more efficiently. The invitation naturally extolled the benefits of a remote place that the reluctant French lens grinder had presumably never even heard of:

> If you were gallant enough to make the journey and come to spend some time with me in the wilderness, you would have all the free time to train yourself, no one would distract you, and you would be removed from anything that could disturb your peace. . . . we would live as brothers, because I guarantee to pay your expenses for as long as you agree to stay with me, and to send you back to Paris as soon as you wish to return there.   (i. 14)

He would have to bring his own tools with him, Descartes tells Ferrier, but he need not incur any travel costs beyond Calais. From Calais it is possible to cross by sea to Dordrecht, and the trip from there to Franeker is as easy as going to church in Paris. Once arrived in Dordrecht, he should go to see Beeckman, who is rector of the local college, and he would supply him with money for his journey and anything else he needed. Descartes does not give Ferrier precise instructions about where to find him in Franeker, for fear that he might share the information with others in Paris. Beeckman is also designated as an intermediary for this purpose, to tell him how to complete his journey, but Ferrier must then keep secret the exact address of what is envisaged as a workshop for two French lens grinders. Almost as an afterthought, Descartes asks Ferrier to bring a camp-bed with a mattress, because the local beds are uncomfortable (i. 15).

This invitation failed to persuade the reluctant Ferrier, although it is clear that Descartes was very keen to exploit his talents. He commends his optical skills to another correspondent in September, claiming that he knows 'no one in the world who is as skilled as he is in his craft' (i. 21). In fact, Ferrier was said to be so gifted in the mathematics of manipulating light and air that 'he can cause all the illusions that magicians are said to cause with the assistance of demons' (i. 21).[7] Despite the warmth of the invitation and the exaggerated compliments about his skill, however, Ferrier preferred to work for the king, in Paris, rather than live with Descartes in an isolated town in the north of Friesland. He even asked Descartes to use his influence to help him to obtain a royal appointment. Descartes had told Ferrier previously that he should talk to Father Condren, a member of the Oratory who lived in Paris, and that he might be able to assist him at the court. But when Bérulle died while saying Mass on 2 October 1629, Father Condren was appointed Superior General of the order in his place and thus became unavailable as a potential intercessor. Accordingly, when Descartes wrote on 8 October, he suggested that two other priests of the Oratory might be able to assist his friend, either Father Guillaume Gibieuf or Father de Sancy.

Apart from counselling Ferrier about how best to exploit his time and talents, Descartes described in some detail a machine for grinding lenses that he had previously discussed with him before leaving Paris. With the onset of winter and little prospect of success with Ferrier, Descartes left for Amsterdam toward the end of October, although he wrote to Ferrier again on 13 November 1629 with detailed replies to queries about the proposed machine for grinding lenses. Descartes concludes his correspondence with the hope that, if the machine works, 'I would dare hope that we would see . . . if there are any animals on the moon' (i. 69).

Amsterdam (1629): Inventing a New World

Descartes was working on two other projects – one in metaphysics, the other in optics – during the first few months in Franeker, both of which eventually appear as significant parts of his published work. He began the treatise on metaphysics and, after jotting some notes over a period of about nine months, apparently left it aside until 1639. This excursion into metaphysics is first mentioned, in passing, in a letter to Father Gibieuf (18 July 1629):

I plan to bother you when I have completed a little treatise that I am beginning. I would not have told you anything about it until it was completed if I had not feared that the length of time involved would make you forget your promise to correct it and to put the finishing touches to it. For I do not expect to complete it for another two or three years, and I may then decide to burn it or, at least, it will not be allowed to escape from my hands and those of my friends without being carefully examined. For if I am not skilled enough to do something well, I shall at least try to be wise enough not to publicize my imperfections.   (i. 17)

Descartes told Mersenne the following year that, when he first arrived in the United Provinces, he worked almost single-mindedly at trying 'to demonstrate metaphysical truths'. 'The first nine months that I spent in this country, I worked on nothing else, and I . . . had planned to put some of it down on paper. However, I do not think it is appropriate to do so until I have first seen how my physics is received' (i. 144). This treatise was written in Latin, as were the *Meditations* into which it later developed, and it addressed the same two questions that eventually became the focus of the latter work, namely, 'the existence of God and that of our souls when separated from the body, from which their immortality results'.[8] Descartes' natural diffidence about metaphysical questions, especially those that impinged on theologically sensitive issues, may have persuaded him not to proceed with these metaphysical inquiries at that time.[9]

Another reason for this decision, suggested to Mersenne, was that many of the projects that had been initiated at Paris were overtaken by new discoveries by Descartes or by a change in perspective that was sufficiently radical that it required him to begin from scratch:

If you find it strange that I had started a few other treatises while I was in Paris, and that I did not continue with them, I will tell you the reason why. During the time that I was working on them, I acquired a little more knowledge than I had had when I began. When I wished to include that, I was forced to undertake a new project that was rather more extensive than the original one, like someone who begins a building that is intended as their home and then acquires unexpected riches which change their status, so that the building that had been started is now too small for them. No one would blame them if they were seen to begin another building that would more appropriately reflect their good fortune.   (i. 138)

One of the key items of 'new information' was acquired when Descartes was told about the appearance of parhelia near Rome. This provided the initial motivation for research directed to what he frequently referred to as a 'little treatise' and which eventually developed into *The World*.

The natural phenomenon of parhelia, or false suns, is a group of apparent spots on either side of the Sun, which are caused by light shining through ice crystals. It was observed by the Jesuit priest Father Scheiner, at Frascati on 20 March 1629, and reported by Cardinal Barberini to Gassendi's patron in the south of France, Nicholas Claudius Peiresc. He in turn passed on the information to Gassendi, who, during his travels in the United Provinces, told some of Descartes' acquaintances about it.

One of them, Henri Reneri (1593–1639),[10] asked Descartes for his explanation of the phenomenon, apparently in the hope of comparing it to what had already been promised by Gassendi. This sequence of events prompted Descartes to write to Mersenne, on 8 October 1629, asking for confirmation of the observation:

My mind is not strong enough to study a number of different things at the same time. . . . I have to concentrate exclusively on one subject when I wish to examine any part of it. This is what I found recently, in looking for the cause of the phenomenon that you wrote to me about. For it is more than two months since one of my friends showed me a reasonably adequate description of it and asked my opinion about it. I had to interrupt what I was working on to examine, in order, all the meteors, before I could satisfy myself about it. However, I think now that I can offer some explanation of it, and I have decided to turn it into a little treatise which will include an explanation of the colours of the rainbow – which cause me more trouble than everything else – and generally of all sublunar phenomena.   (i. 23)

This lengthy letter reflects the diversity of natural phenomena that Mersenne had asked him to explain, and it includes one of the earliest statements by Descartes of a principle of inertia.[11] During the next three years, Descartes wrote frequently to Mersenne about the extensive range of topics to be included in his treatise, the slow progress he was making, and the eventual reasons for suppressing its publication.

Within one month of writing to Mersenne about parhelia, Descartes extends the scope of his project to 'all the phenomena of nature' and expresses more enthusiasm about it than about any previous study:

Since I wrote to you a month ago, I have done nothing at all about it apart from outlining its structure, and instead of explaining only one phenomenon I have decided to explain all the phenomena of nature, that is, the whole of physics. I am more satisfied with my plan than with any other that I have ever had, because I think I have found a way of expressing my thoughts in such a way that they will satisfy some people while no one else will have an opportunity to contradict them.   (i. 70)

The extension in scope also meant that he would need more time for the 'little treatise' and that it would not be completed for 'more than a year' (i. 70).

One of the central principles on which the whole project relied was a principle of inertia for bodies in motion. Although Descartes wrote this letter to Mersenne in French, when he reached the point at which he introduced a principle of inertia he switched languages to Latin, so that the same idea is repeated in both languages. 'First of all I assume that the movement that is once impressed on some body remains in it perpetually, unless it is taken away by some other cause; that is, [in Latin] *whatever begins to move in a vacuum is moved for ever with the same speed*' (i. 71–2). It might seem trivial, in retrospect, that Descartes adopted this as a primary insight of his physics. However, that would seriously underestimate the significance of his discovery. Philosophers had tried to explain for centuries why bodies in motion continue to move as they do or, more usually, to slow down. They had speculated that bodies in motion acquired an impetus that continued to push them along from one moment to the next, or that they displaced the air in front of them in such a way that it rushed around behind them, nudging them forward incrementally. By adopting a principle of inertia, Descartes radically changed the focus of the question. Rather than ask: why does a body in motion continue to move? he asked: since bodies in motion remain naturally in motion, why do they slow down or otherwise change their condition? This change in perspective represented a revolutionary change in physics, the significance of which was minimally illustrated by the linguistic change in Descartes' letter. Instead of trying to explain why bodies in motion continue to move, it was assumed that a continuation of motion was 'natural', and that the reality that required explanation was any change in motion, in either its quantity or direction.

By December, Descartes was already expressing premature anxiety about publication of his treatise in the making. He first decided to withhold his name as the author from the title page, and to get advice from Mersenne and other reliable friends about its contents. The main source of worry was not his physical theories, but their possible implications for theology:

I wish to do this principally because of theology, which has been so ruled by Aristotle that it is almost impossible to explain any other philosophy without it seeming, initially, to be contrary to the faith. In this context, please tell me if there is anything decided in religion about the extension of created things, namely, whether it is finite or infinite, and whether there are created and real bodies in all those regions that are called imaginary spaces. Although I did not wish to discuss that question, I think nevertheless that I will be forced to investigate it.   (i. 85–6)

Apart from theological concerns, Descartes signalled other reasons for a potential delay in completing the 'little treatise.' One reason was that he had decided to widen its scope even more and 'to begin studying anatomy'

(i. 102). The other, more familiar reason was that his progress was slower than expected. He was ashamed to say that what he had written so far was hardly more than about half the length of his letter to Mersenne (i.e., about ten pages), and that the expected completion date was slipping further into the future.

One gets a good idea of the range of questions that were to be included in this treatise from Descartes' correspondence during the years of its composition. The law of falling bodies, the dissemination of sound, an explanation of condensation, the optics of mirrors, and generally all of the properties that are usually attributed to physical bodies, are all discussed at various stages of composition. The sources of the questions are equally varied. In the course of thanking Mersenne for providing a list from Aristotle of properties that required explanation, Descartes acknowledged that he had also drawn up a list himself, 'partly derived from Verulamius [Francis Bacon] and partly from my own head' (i. 109). Not only was he reading Bacon, but he had also dipped into Kepler's work on snow and had asked whether Gassendi might have any further comments to make on the same subject.[12] He had hoped to do further observations on meteorological phenomena, although an unusually warm winter had made it impossible to do any empirical research on ice or snow.

Descartes also began serious work in anatomy at this time. He described his investigations, nine years later, in a letter to Mersenne (13 November 1639):

It is not a crime to be interested in anatomy. I spent one winter in Amsterdam during which I used to go almost every day to the butcher's house to see him kill the animals, and I used to take home with me the parts that I wanted to dissect with more leisure. I have done the same thing on many occasions in all the places where I lived, and I do not think that any intelligent person could blame me for that. (ii. 621)

This work is reflected in the detailed references to an ox's eye in the *Dioptrics*, and in later correspondence with Mersenne.[13]

During this whole period of almost a year from his initial arrival in the United Provinces, Descartes continues to be excessively careful about concealing his address. He tells Mersenne that he is not concerned if people speculate about where he lives, provided that his exact location is not revealed.[14] In March 1630, he encourages Mersenne to ask anyone who remembers him whether they think he is still alive and where they think he is living.[15] The need for secrecy about his plans is repeated the following month.[16] He acknowledges that he had originally planned to spend about three years at Franeker, had he succeeded in persuading Ferrier to join him so that they could work together to construct a machine for grinding lenses. He had even hired a young boy who could cook in a French style to make life comfortable for his guest. But once that plan was abandoned, his interest in living in Franeker waned.

Meantime, the focus had changed to a much larger project, of writing a completely new and comprehensive physics, and by April 1630 the scale of this undertaking had become clearer. Descartes had begun to study chemistry and anatomy, and was now in a position to promise Mersenne that, 'unless I die, [I plan] to have it ready to send to you at the beginning of the year 1633' (i. 137). With a very significant change of projects, and a change of residence to Amsterdam, Descartes might have been expected to settle in one place and complete the major work that he had begun. However, his penchant for the peripatetic life interrupted plans once again. Although he was considering a journey to England, he told Mersenne in April 1630 that he would remain in Amsterdam for at least another month, presumably in anticipation of a visit from Mersenne. The wily Minim friar had been travelling since September 1629, using his friary in Paris for almost a year as a forwarding address, and he was close enough to pay Descartes a visit.

Leiden, 1630

If Descartes kept this promise, he stayed in Amsterdam until the middle of May 1630 but then left abruptly for Leiden. On 27 June, at the age of thirty-three, he matriculated as a student of mathematics at Leiden University.[17] He stayed in rented accommodations with Mr. Cornelis Heymensz van Dam, his wife and five children – one of whom was apparently lodged with neighbours to make room for paying guests. The reasons for moving temporarily to Leiden are as unclear as Descartes' original decision to live in Franeker.[18] He may have been attracted there by the fact that Golius had brought back from the Orient an Arabic translation of the *Conics* of Apollonius, or by his friendship with Henri Reneri.

Reneri had converted to Calvinism during his earlier studies at Leuven, and may have met Descartes later through their common acquaintance with Beeckman. Despite their different religious affiliations, Reneri remained throughout his life one of Descartes' most devoted friends.[19]

Thus, when he was later appointed to posts at Deventer and Utrecht, Descartes followed him to both towns. Reneri had been registered as a student of medicine at Leiden since October 1629 and was now in the process of looking for a suitable academic appointment there. While waiting for a decision on the vacancy at Leiden in 1629, Reneri accepted a post as tutor to a family with three children in Leiden in January 1630, and Descartes joined him there. Leiden University, at that time, included among its professors an impressive list of scholars: André Rivet in theology, Adolphus Vorstius in medicine, Frans van Schooten in mathematics, Jacobus Golius in oriental languages and mathematics, and Gerard Vossius in rhetoric and history. Descartes may also have thought that he could make progress on some of the numerous research projects on which he was working by discussing them with such outstanding scholars. Whatever the reason for the change, he moved to Leiden and seems to have met Mersenne there when he visited Holland during the summer.

After a relatively short interlude at Leiden, Descartes returned to Amsterdam and to the major project on which he had begun work. The themes that later appear in *The World* crop up frequently in correspondence. He proposes a general explanation of properties, in contrast with scholastic theories, which is later found in the first chapter of *The World*,[20] along with an explanation of gravity and another of how to derive light from the chaos.[21] One of the surprising features of his letters, during this period, is the extent to which he refuses to discuss mathematical problems because they take so much time to resolve and distract him from his main work.[22] With that one exception, however, there is hardly any issue in the whole of natural philosophy, from anatomy to music, that escapes his attention. The continued expansion in the scope of the project is reflected in further delays in its projected completion and in the single-minded dedication with which Descartes is beginning to focus all his intellectual efforts on this one interrelated network of problems.

I wish to add to it a discourse where I attempt to explain the nature of colours and of light, something that has held me up for the past six months and is not yet half finished; but it will also be longer than I expected and will contain almost a whole physics. Thus I hope to use it to fulfill the promise that I made to you, to have completed my *World* in three years, for this will be almost a summary of it. I do not think that, once this is finished, I will ever again decide to publish anything else, at least during my life. For I like the fable of my *World* too much not to finish it, if God allows me to live long enough to do so.   (i. 179)

Kepler died in 1630, acknowledged by Descartes as having been pre-eminent in his contribution to optics.[23] Meantime, Descartes' daily life continued in relative isolation in Amsterdam while he worked on what he called 'the most important occupation on which I could ever be employed' (i. 198). He slept very peacefully for ten hours every night, and then allowed his imagination to wander so that his daydreams merged with those of his sleep (i. 199). In the course of trying to persuade Balzac to choose Amsterdam as his retreat, he claimed that, since everyone apart from himself was engaged in commerce, he could live his whole life there without being seen by anyone. He took a walk daily through the busy commercial centre of the town, and saw ships laden with 'the produce of the Indies and the most rare items from Europe' (i. 204). Descartes was in fact living in one of the most active commercial and cultural centres in Europe – Rembrandt lived close by, but neither he nor any of his famous literary or artistic contemporaries is ever mentioned by Descartes. While in his 'retreat', Descartes was not in the habit of reading many books (i. 221); in fact, this reluctance to read books never changed, and it applied even to books written by his friends. For example, Father Gibieuf's book on God's freedom was published in 1630, but Descartes was still making excuses in October 1631 that he had not yet had an opportunity to read it, and he asked Mersenne to co-operate by keeping his procrastination secret. While in Deventer the following year, Descartes wrote that 'I have no books, and even if I had some, I would begrudge the time spent in reading them' (i. 251). Instead, he used the time available in thinking about the numerous scientific problems that he received from correspondents, and in doing experiments himself. The apparently single-minded commitment to writing *The World*, however, did not prevent him from further travel.

Descartes seems to have taken a trip to Denmark during the summer of 1631, accompanied by Étienne de Ville-Bressieux, a medical doctor from Grenoble who had come to spend some time with Descartes and had lived with him at 'our lodging of the Old Prince' (i. 215). In the course of that trip, he met Longomontanus and spent a whole day in philosophical discussion. Having failed to persuade him of his errors, he concluded that 'it is not worth while to go to him any more'.[24] Following this voyage, and in spite of the extremely acrimonious correspondence with Beeckman the previous year, Descartes went to visit his former collaborator at Dordrecht, who, according to Baillet, had been close to death because of old age and sickness.[25] However, Beeckman was only forty-three years old at that stage, and he was to live for another six years. Descartes also seems to have been ill himself during the summer of 1631. Although he returned to Amsterdam from Dordrecht in good health, Beeckman writes in October about his convalescing from a rather serious but unspecified illness.[26] This, together with the voyage to Denmark, may explain why Descartes writes to Mersenne, in October or November 1631, that he had done almost no work on his project 'for three or four months' (i. 228).

With a return to work on *The World*, Descartes takes up again some of the familiar scientific questions that had distracted him during the previous two years. He had discussed an explanation of the mercury barometer in June (i. 205), and he now plans to discuss gravity in what he invariably calls 'my treatise' (i. 222). He advises Ville-Bressieux that they are agreed about some basic principles; for example, that 'there is only one material substance which receives from some external agent the action or means of moving itself locally' (i. 216). The question about falling bodies, in a vacuum or in air, is still unresolved, although Descartes is quick to mention that he does not think there is any such thing as a vacuum (i. 228).

Descartes' friend Reneri, who had been appointed a tutor to children in Leiden, was appointed to a chair of philosophy at Deventer on 13 October 1631. Descartes commented that the new appointment was 'in an academy that was not very famous; however, the professors are better paid and live more comfortably than at Leiden or Franeker, where Mr Reneri could have been appointed earlier if he had not refused or neglected it' (i. 228–9). This was probably the reason why, in May 1632, Descartes moved once again, this time to Deventer.

Before departing, however, Descartes addressed one of the most intractable problems from ancient geometry, the so-called Pappus problem. Jacob van Gool (usually known as Golius), whom Descartes had met during his short stay at Leiden, had sent this problem simultaneously to a number of people.[27] Descartes' proposed solution to the problem was subsequently published in the *Geometry* (1637), but it was evidently formulated during the winter of 1631–32, since he told Mersenne in April 1632 that he had worked on it for 'five or six weeks' (i. 244). He was thus able to send his solution to Golius in January 1632, at the same time promising to send him the early part of the *Dioptrics* in which he had worked out the sine law of refraction.[28] Once that rather major mathematical puzzle was solved, he returned to his principal work, *The World*.

He tells Mersenne in April that, although he had promised to send him the long awaited 'treatise' before Easter, he would have to defer the delivery date a little longer to provide time for corrections and to complete some of the diagrams required. He repeats the request for a delay one month later, when he tells Mersenne that he has decided to spend the summer in the country, and that Mersenne should redirect his letters there (i. 248).

Deventer, 1632–1633

The next change of residence hardly interrupted the consistency with which Descartes pursued his primary goal. He had few books and relatively few personal items that required transport. He could thus move his residence with ease, and apparently without much advance planning. Once installed at Deventer, he wrote to Mersenne to acknowledge that his letters had arrived and that work on *The World* was still not finished:[29]

I am now in Deventer and I have decided not to leave here until the *Dioptrics* is completely finished. I have been wondering, for the past month, whether to include in my *World* a description of how animals are generated, and I have eventually decided not to do anything about it because it would take too much time. I have finished everything that I planned to include in it about inanimate bodies. It only remains for me to add something about the nature of man, and then I will make a clean copy to send you. But I dare not say when that will be, because I have failed so often in my promises that I am ashamed. (i. 254–5)

This tentative plan to include something about human nature was expanded within six months. The revised project, in November 1632, was to produce a comprehensive account of human nature and to outline a scientific explanation of various human faculties, such as the imagination and memory.

I shall speak about human nature in my *World* a little more than I had thought I would, for I plan to explain all the principal human functions. I have already written those sections that pertain to life, such as the digestion of food, the beating of the heart, the distribution of nourishment, etc., and the five senses. I am now dissecting the heads of various animals, to explain what the imagination, the memory, etc. consist in. I have seen the book *The Motion of the Heart*, about which you previously spoke to me, and I found that I differ a little from it, although I had not seen it until after I had written about this topic. (i. 263)

William Harvey's book, *An Anatomical Exercise concerning the Motion of the Heart and Blood in Animals*, had been published four years earlier and had been known in France since 1629, when Descartes had left for the United Provinces. Descartes was among the first to support Harvey's theory that the blood circulates continuously through the body and that the pumping action of the heart is its cause. While Descartes agreed about the main point – that the blood circulates through the body – he could not accept Harvey's apparently mysterious explanation of why the heart beats, which assumed in the heart a faculty for beating, and he subsequently suggested an alternative mechanical explanation.

The real significance of his letter to Mersenne, however, is not Descartes' agreement or otherwise with Harvey, but the extrapolation of the scientific project of *The World* to include human beings. What was envisaged was nothing short of a comprehensive explanation, or explanatory sketch, of all natural phenomena, including human beings. Even when the project had been concerned only with astronomy, in May of that year, Descartes had conceded that the project 'exceeds the scope of the human mind' (i. 252). The extended scope of *The World* now made its limitations much more obvious. He would discover, in time, that any attempt to explain human beings went far beyond not only the ability of the human mind, but also the limits of what ecclesiastical authorities were willing to tolerate.

There were already indications of possible problems with church authorities in summer 1632. Jean-Baptiste Morin (1583–1656), an established professor of mathematics at Paris, had published a book to support the theory that the Earth is stationary, under the title: *The Preferred Solution, to date, of the Famous and Ancient Problem of the Motion or Non-motion of the Earth* (1631). He argued that the hypothesis of the Earth's motion was not new, and that scripture, astronomy, and physics all supported the conclusion that the Earth is stationary.[30] 'The Sacred Scriptures show that it is far more certain and evident that the earth is stationary rather than in motion.'[31] Having outlined the scriptural reasons – summarized in the quotation from Ecclesiastes (1: 4) on the title page: 'The earth stands firm forever. The Sun rises, the Sun sets' – Morin borrows reasons from astrology to show that 'the earth is the receptacle or the passive subject of all the celestial influences' and is therefore stationary at the centre of the universe.[32] Descartes' comment on this was completely dismissive: 'I feel sorry, as you do, for the author who uses astrological reasons to prove the immobility of the earth. But I would feel even more sorry for a generation, if I thought that those who would make an article of faith of this view had no stronger reasons to support it' (i. 258).

The immediate context of this comment was the publication in February 1632 of Galileo's famous book *A Dialogue Concerning the Two Chief World Systems*.[33] Toward the end of that year, Descartes wrote to Mersenne, apparently in reply to queries about the extent to which he agreed with Galileo, that Galileo's account of falling bodies 'does not agree at all with my philosophy' (i. 261). However, he said he would be interested to find out what Galileo had said about tides, because that was one of the phenomena that he found most difficult to explain.[34] On 22 July 1633, Descartes was finally able to tell his patient correspondent in Paris that 'my treatise is nearly finished, but I still have to correct and recopy it' (i. 268). By the end of November 1633, however, Descartes had heard about the Roman Inquisition's condemnation of Galileo, and he changed his mind about even showing his manuscript to Mersenne.

The Trial of Galileo

The Galileo affair in 1633 was not directly concerned with astronomy or even with the interpretation of the Bible. It was sparked by an apparent challenge to the teaching authority of the church during a period, after the Council of Trent, when the church was acutely sensitive to any such threat. The council had decided, at the conclusion of its fourth session (8 April 1546), that the church reserved to itself the exclusive authority to interpret Scripture:

Besides, in order to control petulant minds, the Council decrees that, in matters of faith and morals that pertain to the edification of Christian doctrine, no one shall dare interpret the Holy Scripture by relying on their own judgment and by distorting sacred Scripture to their own meaning, contrary to the meaning which Holy Mother Church (to whom it belongs to judge the true meaning and interpretation of the sacred Scriptures) has held and still holds, or contrary to the unanimous opinion of the Fathers, even if such interpretations were never published. Those who contravene this decree shall be identified by their bishops and punished by the penalties established by law.[35]

The Holy Office had relied on this text, in 1616, to forbid Galileo from teaching that the Earth moved around the Sun, because it seemed to be inconsistent with the traditional interpretation of the biblical passage, in Joshua 10:12, in which the Sun is commanded to stand still.[36] The injunction to Galileo in 1616 mentioned the opinion 'that the sun is in the centre of the universe and is immobile, and that the earth moves,' and it forbade him to 'hold, teach, or defend it in any way, either verbally or in writing'.[37] When the *Dialogue* was published in 1632, therefore, the focus of attention was no longer on the alleged conflict between a scientific theory and the Bible, but on whether Galileo had disobeyed the original decree of sixteen years earlier. By June 1633, the almost inevitable decision was reached and Galileo was found guilty of having breached an explicit instruction of the Holy Office.[38]

News of the decision reached Descartes in his remote retreat in Deventer, and he wrote immediately to Mersenne to explain why he could not send him the long-promised results of his research.

I had planned to send you my *World* as a New Year's gift. . . . But I should tell you that, having inquired recently in Leiden and Amsterdam whether Galileo's *System of the World* [i.e., *Dialogue*] was available, since I thought I had heard that it was published in Italy last year, I was told that it had been published but that all the copies were immediately burned in Rome and that he had been fined. This surprised me so much that I more or less decided to burn all my papers, or at least not to allow them to be seen by anyone. For I could not imagine that, as an Italian and even, I have heard, someone who is in the good graces of the Pope, he could have been convicted for nothing more than attempting, as he surely did, to establish the earth's movement. . . . I acknowledge that, if that is false, then so are all the foundations of my physics, because it is easily demonstrated from them. It is so connected with all the parts of my treatise, that I could not detach it from them without undermining everything that remains. But since I would not wish for all the world to publish a discourse in which the least word was disapproved by the Church, I have for that reason preferred to suppress it rather than to have it appear mutilated.   (i. 270–1)

By February 1634, Descartes was more concerned about the fate of his own *World* than by minor disagreements with Galileo. Although he had decided to suppress *The World*, he revealed an insider's understanding of the workings of the Roman Inquisition by questioning whether its decisions were automatically a matter of faith, or whether they were merely an exercise of the church's teaching authority unless confirmed by the Pope or a general council of the church:

I hope that you will have greater respect for me when you see that I have decided to suppress completely the treatise that I wrote and to lose almost all my work over four years, in order to offer complete obedience to the Church insofar as it forbade the view that the earth moves. However, since I have not yet seen that the Pope or the Council

has ratified this prohibition, which was made by the congregation of cardinals that was
established for censuring books, I would very much like to know what people think
about it now in France, and whether their authority is sufficient to turn the prohibition
into an article of faith.   (i. 281)

Descartes suspected the Jesuits of having had a part in the condemnation,[39]
and he returned to the same concerns two months later. Convinced that
Galileo's scientific theory had been condemned as 'heretical', he could not
see any way in which to publish his own *World* because of the necessary
link between the motion of the Earth and the fundamental principles of
his physics.

I shall tell you that all the things that I explained in my treatise, among which is
this view about the motion of the earth, depend so much on one another that it is
enough to know that one of them is false to conclude that all the arguments that
I used are unsound. Although I thought that they were based on very certain and
evident demonstrations, I would not wish to defend them for anything in the world
against the authority of the church. . . . My desire to live in peace, and to continue the
life that I have begun by adopting the motto: *he lives well who lives in secret*, means
that I would prefer to rid myself of my fear of attracting more attention than I want
(as a result of my writing) than to have wasted the time and trouble that I used in
composing it.   (i. 285–6)

Descartes was astonished that any churchman should write in support
of Galileo, because the prohibition applied even to proposing the motion
of the Earth as 'an hypothesis in astronomy'.[40] However, given that the
condemnation was issued by a group of cardinals, rather than by the Pope
or a general council of the church, he still had reason to hope that his
World might some day 'see the light of day' (i. 288).

It is difficult to avoid the impression, from these letters, that Descartes
accepted the inerrancy of the Bible and even the authority of the Catholic
Church to interpret its meaning. This apparently deferential response
to the church's decree contrasts with that of Galileo. While the great
Florentine mathematician had accepted that the Scripture is infallible
about matters of faith and morals, he challenged Bellarmine's claim that
the motion of the Earth or the Sun had any essential connection with faith
and morals. He argued, instead, that when a scientific theory is supported
by the evidence and yet seems to contradict particular passages in the Bible,
we should not adopt a literal interpretation of those Biblical sentences
and, in that way, we can avoid the apparent contradiction.[41] By contrast,
Descartes seems to have accepted the authority of the church to decide

what the Bible means, even in passages about natural phenomena. However, he distinguished between the authoritative teaching of the church,
as expressed by the Pope or a general council, and the decisions about
what books should be published or censored, which was an administrative
decision by a small group of cardinals or theologians. That provided an
alternative resolution to the one proposed by Galileo, and it gave him
enough wiggle room to avoid Rome's decision without directly addressing
the fundamental issue about how to interpret Scripture.

Descartes soon began to show signs of paranoia or, at least, of extra
sensitivity (in May 1634), when he alerted Mersenne that some of their
letters had been intercepted, probably by people who recognized their
handwriting and who were hoping to intercept a copy of *The World*.[42] This
is more likely a symptom of Descartes' anxiety about the orthodoxy of his
physics, or of the unreliability of the messengers who delivered letters,
than evidence that some of his critics were planning to report him to the
Inquisition. Whatever the truth of the matter, Descartes had laboured for
over four years to write his first book, and, just as it was ready to be shown
to Mersenne, he felt constrained to hide it and to return to Amsterdam.
The World remained unpublished until thirty years later, when Descartes'
literary executor, Claude Clerselier, published a French edition of the first
part in 1664.

The World, or A Treatise on Light

It is not clear what was included in the treatise that Descartes promised
to send to Mersenne in 1633. The manuscript of *The World* was not found
intact during the inventory of Descartes' writings after his death.[43] Baillet
claims, but without providing supporting evidence, that the text of *The
World* that was published by Clerselier in 1664 was 'very imperfect' and
that it had been 'reduced to a very small summary'.[44] This may well be
correct. The frequent references in Descartes' correspondence during the
period 1629–33 suggest that he was working on a wide range of issues in
physics and physiology, and that he hoped to integrate many of these disparate studies into a comprehensive, unified theory. Some parts of this
large-scale project were later reworked and published as the *Dioptrics,
Meteors and Geometry* (1637), and some were recast to provide the main
ideas for Parts II–IV of the *Principles of Philosophy* (1644). The 1633

manuscript survived long enough to be partially published, in French, as *The Treatise on Light* in 1664. In the same year, *The Treatise on Man* was published (also in French).[45] Three years later, a more complete edition that included both treatises was published as *Le Monde* (*The World*). Descartes describes in retrospect, in the *Discourse*, how he had decided to limit the contents of *The World* to a few sample problems:

I was afraid that I could not include in my discourse everything that I had thought about. Thus I undertook to explain in it reasonably fully only what I understood about light and, at the same time, to add something about the sun and the fixed stars, because most light results from them; about the skies, because they transmit the light; about the planets, comets and the earth, because they reflect it; and in particular about all the bodies that are on earth, because they are either coloured, transparent or luminous; and finally, about human beings, because they are the perceivers of light.   (vi. 42)

The World raised one of the central issues in seventeenth-century theory of knowledge, in its very first chapter, concerning the possible difference between the way in which things are in reality and the way in which we perceive them. This question had already been raised by Galileo in 1623.[46] Its significance for the new sciences is difficult to exaggerate.

The spontaneous or naïve interpretation of our own perceptions is that the realities we perceive are exactly as they appear to us. This was the view that had been adopted since classical times, and which was expressed, for example, by Quintilian, an author who was prominently on the curriculum at La Flèche: 'We may regard as certainties, first those things which we perceive by the senses, things for instance that we hear or see.'[47] If this is questioned, we can no longer assume any direct access to reality, even in the simple perception of familiar things. Descartes addresses this question in the first sentence of *The World*. 'Since my plan here is to discuss light, the first thing that I want to bring to your attention is that there may be a difference between our sensation of light, i.e. the idea which is formed in our imagination by means of our eyes, and whatever it is in the objects that produces that sensation in us, i.e. what is called "light" in the flame or the sun' (xi. 3). Descartes illustrates his challenge by a number of persuasive examples, one of which had earlier been used by Galileo when he discussed the same question. If a child has a tickling sensation as a result, for example, of someone rubbing a feather against their lips, it would be an obvious mistake to assume that there is some quality in the moving feather that is similar to the child's sensation (xi. 6). The external cause of the sensation is nothing other than the motion of the feather when it touches the lips, but this is perceived by the child as a tickling sensation. There is therefore no reason to believe that there is a 'tickling quality' in the feather that resembles the child's sensation. Another argument is that words succeed in communicating their meanings to those who speak the language used, but there is no reason to think that the words actually resemble the realities to which they refer. Descartes argues: 'Now if words . . . are enough to make us think about things that do not resemble them in any way, why is it not possible that nature may also have established a particular sign that would make us have the sensation of light, even though such a sign contains nothing in itself that resembles that sensation?' (xi. 4)

With these and similar arguments, Descartes helped open the epistemic gap – between our subjective sensations and the external realities that cause them – that became one of the hallmarks of the Scientific Revolution. He later applied the same argument to so-called internal sensations, such as the sensation of hunger or pain. The significance of these apparently simple conclusions was that they opened up an 'appalling vista' for traditional science. Once this question was raised, it was impossible to adopt the naïve assumption of the scholastic tradition that our senses cannot err when they are applied to appropriate objects. It simply could no longer be assumed that the world that we experience, externally or internally, resembles our perceptions. Since we cannot legitimately project our sensory experiences onto reality, we have no alternative but to construct hypotheses about the kinds of realities that are likely to cause the sensations that we experience.

This ground-breaking initiative in theory of knowledge led to an equally original insight into the nature of explanation, although it was some years before Descartes made explicit its full implications. Where scholastic philosophers had assumed that a burning piece of wood must have properties such as the 'quality' of heat or light and the 'form' of burning, Descartes concluded that these were mere projections onto external realities of the subjective character of our sensations. He suggested, instead, that we imagine in burning wood a large number of very small, fast-moving particles, so that the conversion of the burning wood into ashes and the emission of light, smoke, and so on. are merely observable results of events that are too microscopic to observe with the naked eye. 'On condition simply that you grant me that there is some power which violently moves its finer parts and separates them from the larger ones, I find that this alone could cause it [the wood] to undergo all the same changes which are observed when it burns' (xi. 8). If we are forced to hypothesize what properties wood has, in virtue of which it gives off light when it burns, it is a short step to acknowledge that we could not possibly *explain* the phenomenon of burning and emitting light simply by attributing to the wood precisely those features that we set out to explain.

Later writers almost competed with each other to construct persuasive examples of this insight. Boyle argued, for example, that we cannot explain how a key opens a particular lock by ascribing to the key a 'lock opening' form. This argument was developed by later Cartesians, especially by Jacques Rohault (1616–1672), into a refrain about the emptiness of pretending to explain some event or phenomenon by attributing to it just those features for which the explanation was originally sought. One of the most famous examples, adapted by Molière and assigned to Doctor Bachelierus in *Le Malade imaginaire*, mocked the suggestion that one could explain how sleeping powder has its desired effect by saying that it has a 'dormitive power'.[48]

These complementary conclusions – about the invalidity of attributing qualities that resemble our sensations to the phenomena that cause them, and about the failure of scholastic forms and qualities to explain anything – implied that, when faced with explaining even such a familiar phenomenon as the experience of light, we have no choice but to guess at the nature of the reality in question. The kind of guesswork that Descartes was willing to tolerate was limited to those features of things that were both familiar and well understood, such as the size, shape, and movement of pieces of matter, and the whole project was inspired by a model that was borrowed from our understanding of machines.

Within a few short paragraphs, therefore, Descartes had proposed relegating the whole complex scholastic network of prime matter, forms, and qualities to a failed enterprise, and substituting hypothetical models that assume nothing more than the size, shape, arrangement, and motions of parts of matter. He was very conscious of not introducing more properties than are required in order to construct viable explanations of natural phenomena, and he suggested working with only three kinds of basic material particle that are distinguished by their size, shape, and motion. These were called 'elements'.

If you find it surprising that I do not use qualities that are called 'heat', 'cold', 'humidity'
and 'dryness' in order to explain these elements, as the philosophers do, I shall tell you
that these qualities seem to me to be in need of explanation themselves and, if I am
not mistaken, that not only these four qualities but all the others too, and even all the
forms of inanimate bodies, can be explained without having to assume for that purpose
anything else in their matter apart from the motion, size, shape and arrangement of
its parts.   (xi. 25–6)

The project of explaining natural phenomena is thus reduced to imagining
various combinations of parts of matter in motion that could conceivably
cause our perceptions of such phenomena.

Such explanations are evidently hypothetical. This feature of the enterprise is made explicit when Descartes invites readers to imagine a completely new world:

I wish to cloak part of my discourse in the invention of a fable through which, I hope,
the truth will appear sufficiently and will be no less pleasing to see than if I presented
it completely naked. Thus allow your thought to go outside this world, for a short
time, to come to see a completely new world that I shall bring to life before you in
imaginary spaces. The philosophers tell us that these spaces are infinite; we should
believe them in this case, because they themselves invented them. . . . let us suppose
that God creates anew all around us so much matter that, in whatever direction our
imagination may be able to stretch, it would no longer perceive any place in it [infinite
space] that is empty.   (xi. 31–2)

This imaginative ploy releases its author from the obligation to explain
immediately how the hypothetical world he constructs matches the world
of our daily experience. He can begin anew, tracing the steps of a hypothetical Creator, by placing matter in space, giving it an initial quantum of
motion, and imposing on matter in motion whatever laws are appropriate
to the creative designs of the Creator. The challenge then is to explain
how, from these modest beginnings, all the natural phenomena that we
experience could have evolved over time.

For God has established these laws so wondrously that, even if we were to imagine that
he created nothing more than what we have mentioned so far, and even if he imposed
on it no order or proportion, but made it like the most confused and disordered chaos
that poets could describe, the laws are enough to cause the parts of this chaos to
disentangle from each other and to become arranged in such a good order that they
would have the form of a very perfect world, in which one could see not only some
light but also all the other things, both general and particular, that appear in the real
world.   (xi. 34–5)

The extremely simple, and therefore readily intelligible, features of matter in motion were considered by its author to have a decisive advantage in comparison to the multiplicity and complexity of the forms to which scholastic philosophers appealed. By adding three laws of nature to this simple story, Descartes thought he had provided enough to construct a physical theory of the universe.

The first of Descartes' laws of nature is that 'each individual part of matter always continues to be in the same state, as long as it is not forced to change that state by collision with others' (xi. 38). He argued that almost everyone accepts that law when it is applied, for example, to the shape of a piece of matter or to the fact that it is stationary. Things do not change shape spontaneously or begin to move from a position of rest without some cause. All he did, therefore, was to extend the same rule to the motion of bodies. If something is in motion, then no new cause is required to explain why it remains in motion; but if its motion is changed – in speed or direction – then we must look for the factor that caused the change. The second law describes, in quantitative terms, how motion is transferred from one body to another on impact, and it is proposed as an hypothesis. 'When one body pushes another, it could not contribute any motion to the other except by simultaneously losing as much of its own motion, nor could it take away any of the other's motion unless its own motion increases by the same amount' (xi. 41). The third and final law of nature is the law of rectilinear motion: 'when a body moves[,] . . . each of its parts individually always tends to continue its motion in a straight line' (xi. 43–4).

These three laws of nature are qualified in two ways. They are not the only relevant laws, and they are inserted into a metaphysical or theological background that does little to confirm their truth but goes some distance toward separating nature from the Creator, who is normally regarded as the ultimate cause of all phenomena. On the adequacy or otherwise of the three laws, Descartes writes that 'I shall provide here two or three of the principal rules according to which one must think that God causes the nature of this new world to act and which will be enough, I believe, to let you know all the others' (xi. 38). Once the three rules have been proposed, *The World* acknowledges the need for 'many rules' to 'determine in detail when, and how, and by how much, the motion of each body may be diverted, and increased or decreased, by colliding with other bodies' (xi. 47). However, readers are left to work out these applications themselves.

At the same time, Descartes adopts a metaphysical background that attributes all these laws to nature, where the term 'nature' does not mean 'some goddess or any other kind of imaginary power, but . . . matter itself . . . on condition that God continues to conserve it in the same way as He created it' (xi. 37). Once God's activity is accepted as unchangeable, Descartes can avoid 'getting further involved in these metaphysical questions' (xi. 38). There is a clear distinction, then, between God as the ultimate cause of matter and motion, and the contingent events in the world that are the proximate causes of natural phenomena. 'One must say that God alone is the author of all the motions that occur in the world, in so far as they exist and in so far as they are rectilinear, but that it is the various dispositions of matter that make them irregular and curved' (xi. 46). The simplicity and immutability of the actions attributed 'by theologians' to God mean that God's agency can be omitted from a scientific account of natural phenomena, because the focus of attention is on those changeable conditions that explain differences between phenomena rather than on the general background that they all share in common.

With that distinction in place, Descartes speculates about the dispositions of matter in motion that would be required to explain such natural phenomena as the Sun and the stars, the motion of the planets and of comets, the weight of bodies, the tides, the nature and properties of light, and how the heavens would appear to inhabitants of the Earth. He cautions the reader that he will not provide 'exact demonstrations of everything that I say' (xi. 48) about such a wide range of phenomena, since that would diminish the pleasure of discovering them for oneself. He reverts, instead, to the notion of constructing a fable. Readers may then accept or reject his hypotheses by considering the progress made in explanation and the plausibility of alternatives. 'Thus I shall be content to continue the description that I have begun, as if my only plan were to tell you a fable' (xi. 48).

The fabulous character of the resulting discourse could not camouflage the fact that its author was clearly endorsing the same heliocentric system that had been proposed by Copernicus and Galileo. The whole structure of Cartesian cosmology depended on assuming an indefinitely extended space, in which there are indefinitely many suns or fixed stars, each of which is surrounded by whirling vortices. Each vortex includes masses of matter, or planets, that spin on their own axes and move in a circular motion around a central sun. Chapter 10 of *The World* thus unambiguously described the

Earth as simply one planet that is moving in a vortex around the Sun. It is easy to see why Descartes wrote to Mersenne, in the letter quoted earlier from November 1633, that the motion of the Earth around the Sun was an integral part of his cosmology and that it could not be adjusted without fundamentally recasting the whole theory. 'It is so connected with all the parts of my treatise, that I could not detach it from them without making everything that remains defective' (i. 271).

The official reason Descartes gave for withholding his *World* from publication was the church's condemnation of Galileo, and the fact that his own book assumed the same heliocentric theory that had provoked that judgment. However, the implications of the *Treatise on Man* for traditional theological beliefs were equally radical. Since no one read *The World* for many years, its implications for a theory of the human mind came to the surface only later in Descartes' life, in the course of answering critics of the *Meditations*. The scene for these later problems was clearly set in the early 1630s.

The *Treatise on Man* opens with the following sentence, in which the task of explanation is divided into two parts: 'These men [i.e. those described in this *Treatise*] will be composed, as we are, of a soul and a body. I must describe for you first the body on its own; and then the soul, again on its own; and finally I must show you how these two natures would have to be joined and united so as to constitute men resembling us' (xi. 119–20). The distinction of body and mind reflects Descartes' strategy of attempting to explain all natural phenomena by analogy with complex machines, and of leaving for further work those features of human experience that seem to be inexplicable in this way. 'We see clocks, artificial fountains, mills, and other similar machines which, even though they are only made by men, have the power to move of their own accord in various ways' (xi. 120). If the human body is created by God, then it follows that a divine artificer could construct a much more sophisticated machine than anything that results from human ingenuity. The apparently self-moving and self-controlling features of human bodies could therefore be explained by analogy with the machines in the royal gardens that had been designed to simulate the behaviour of animals and human beings.

As already mentioned at the conclusion of Chapter 3, these had been described by Salomon de Caus, and they provided a model for constructing mechanical explanations of apparently nonmechanical phenomena. The machines in the royal gardens, which were able to 'play certain instruments or pronounce certain words,' relied on a complex but hidden hydraulic system of pipes. Descartes invites his readers to imagine that the human body is similar, with animal spirits substituted for water as the dynamic fluid. Despite the connotations of the name, animal spirits were nothing more than 'a very lively and very pure flame' (xi. 129), that is, a type of subtle matter that was similar to the matter found in flames.

This subtle matter was generated in the heart from blood and was then distributed throughout the body by circulation through the veins. For Descartes, all those features of animals that included movement and that required an explanation – such as the transmission of sensations to the brain and the responses that they trigger, and the controls exercised automatically by any animal over its own body – are explained by variations in the movement of animal spirits throughout the body.

> I want to tell you first about the composition of the nerves and the muscles, and to show you how, from the sole fact that the spirits in the brain are ready to enter into certain nerves, they have the power to move particular bodily parts at the same instant. Then, after touching briefly on respiration and other similar, simple, and normal movements, I shall say how external objects act upon the sense organs. After that, I shall explain in detail all that happens in the cavities and pores of the brain, what route the animal spirits follow there, and which of our functions this machine can imitate by these means.   (xi. 132)[49]

With this plan in place, Descartes offers schematic explanations of how the muscles move and thereby control bodily movements, how animals breathe, how they swallow food and drink and convert them to nutrients, and how 'this machine is able to sneeze, yawn, cough, and to cause the motions needed to expel various excretions' (xi. 141).

The same model can explain how 'external objects that strike the sense organs can cause the machine to move its members' (xi. 141), and how the machine of the body can register these sensations in the brain. The mechanical explanations of hearing, feeling, smelling, and so on were sketched only in outline. In the case of sight, however, the work done in the years immediately prior to 1633 provided enough detail to hypothesize how an impression is formed on the back of an animal's eye by the optic lens, and how this pattern is communicated to a part of the brain in which inputs from various sensory organs are synthesized. This synthesizing feature of the brain was called the 'common sense', in deference to its function, although its exact location was a matter of speculation.

The hypothesis suggested by Descartes to account for sight was that the image formed on the retina causes a mechanically transmitted change in the centre of the brain. This pulling motion results in a release of animal spirits from the pineal gland in patterns that correspond, in some systematic way, to the images formed inside the eye. Descartes then suggested that the word 'idea' should be applied to the shape, form, or pattern assumed by this release of animal spirits. Descartes had argued, in the *Rules*, that there is an infinite supply of different geometrical shapes available by which one could model all sensations. He returns to this point in *The World* to suggest that the 'figures' or 'shapes' assumed by animal spirits, in response to various sensations, can vary systematically with the sensations themselves. These patterns, therefore, can provide an occasion for a human being 'to sense movement, size, distance, colour, sounds, smells, and other such qualities; and even things that can make it sense pleasure, pain, hunger, thirst, joy, sadness, and other such passions' (xi. 176).

It may come as a surprise that Descartes wanted to apply the term 'idea' to the flow patterns of animal spirits in the brain, but he is so explicit about this that it is impossible to avoid the implications of his claims. Objects that strike the senses cause many effects in the perceiver's body. However, 'it is not those imprinted on the organs of external sense, or on the inside surface of the brain, that should be taken as ideas, but only those traced in the spirits on the surface of the pineal gland, where the seat of the imagination and the common sense is' (xi. 176). Once ideas were understood as patterns in the flow of animal spirits to and from the brain, it was a short step to speculate about the imagination and memory as brain processes that resemble what happens in perception. Imagination is understood as an activity in the brain that results from those flows of animal spirits that arise spontaneously when an animal is not sensing any external stimuli; and memory is a disposition of the nerve ducts to conduct the spirits in patterns that resemble previous patterns.

Descartes said at the outset of this treatise that he proposed to explain the body first, and then the soul. Accordingly, he refers at various stages to the addition of a 'rational soul' to the body and to the ways in which the 'soul' functions in causing sensations.[50] However, the *Treatise on Man* concludes with an ambitious claim about the extent to which this rather speculative, hydraulic model has provided explanations of every animal function apart from those that are reserved for rational souls. Everything else about animal life is explicable in principle along these lines, and the outstanding features – for which a soul is required – remain to be specified and discussed further.

I desire that you consider that all the functions that I have attributed to this machine, such as the digestion of food, the beating of the heart and the arteries, the nourishment and growth of the bodily parts, respiration, waking and sleeping; the reception of light, sounds, odours, smells, heat, and other such qualities by the external sense organs; the impression of the ideas of them in the organ of common sense and the imagination; the retention or imprint of these ideas in the memory; the internal movements of the appetites and the passions; and finally the external movements of all the bodily parts that so aptly follow both the actions of objects presented to the senses, and the passions and impressions that are encountered in memory; and in this they imitate as perfectly as possible the movements of real men. I desire, I say, that you should consider that these functions follow in this machine simply from the disposition of the organs as wholly naturally as the movements of a clock or other automatons follow from the disposition of its counterweights and wheels. To explain these functions, then, it is not necessary to conceive of any vegetative or sensitive soul, or any other principle of movement or life, other than its blood and its spirits which are agitated by the heat of the fire that burns continuously in its heart, and which is of the same nature as those fires that occur in inanimate bodies.   (xi. 201–2)

When Descartes decided not to publish *The World*, and not even to show it to his most trusted friends, he had to face the reality that his life's work to date had come to a sudden halt. The fact that *The World* endorsed Galileo's astronomy was a minor problem compared to its radical suggestions about human knowledge, scientific explanation, and the extent to which human and animal behaviour could be explained without any of the 'souls' on which philosophers traditionally relied. Since he could not publish his ideas in the form in which they were written, he had to think of some way of salvaging his results, while at the same time protecting himself from church censure. Descartes the fabulist had to be transformed into Descartes the defender of the Catholic faith. This was the focus of his energies for the next four years.

At a personal level, the limited evidence suggests that Descartes lived a relatively isolated life, even in busy towns, and that he enjoyed the company of a small number of devoted male friends. Ville-Bressieux lived with him in Amsterdam in 1631, as he had done during his earlier residence at Amsterdam (1629–30). During his temporary domiciles at Leiden, Deventer, and Utrecht, he enjoyed the company of Henri Reneri. The other friend who is mentioned in similar terms, as a close disciple, was

Jean Gillot, a French Protestant refugee in the United Provinces. In later years, this pattern of having a few close personal friends and a wide circle of correspondents supported the French philosopher in his exile in the United Provinces. With the addition of powerful patrons, such as Huygens and various French ambassadors, he acquired the necessary protection against those among his Calvinist hosts who considered him as unorthodox as Galileo appeared to the Roman cardinals.

The Scientific *Essays* and the *Discourse on Method* (1633–1637)

I also noticed, about experiences, that the more we advance in knowledge the more necessary they become.

(Discourse on Method: vi. 63)

D URING the years immediately following the condemnation of Galileo, Descartes held fast to his initial view that the cardinals had made a mistake, though one that was potentially dangerous for himself. His fundamental idea was that the decision involved a misunderstanding of the role of the Bible as a source of scientific knowledge. He also argued that he was not bound to accept the Roman decision as a matter of faith, and he hoped that it would be reversed in due course so that he could publish his *World* without fear of censure. He had to concede, however, that as long as there was no change of mind about Galileo by the church, the *World* would remain 'out of season' (i. 324). Descartes' refusal to publish *The World* was therefore not as definitive as it seemed to people like Mersenne, to whom he wrote: 'If the reasons that prevent me from publishing it were to change, I could make a different decision without thereby being fickle' (i. 367). We know now, in retrospect, that there was no change in Rome's censure, and that there was none either in Descartes' decision. His first book remained unpublished throughout his lifetime.

In these circumstances, the next-best option was to consider ways in which parts of his work that were not theologically sensitive could be released to the public. Accordingly, during the years from 1633 to 1637, Descartes spent most of his time on this project. His efforts came to fruition with the publication of the *Discourse on the Method for Guiding one's Reason and Searching for Truth in the Sciences, together with the Dioptrics, the Meteors, and the Geometry, which are samples of this Method* (1637). Descartes was then forty-one years old. There may be signs of the author's reluctance about even this limited publication in his efforts to have his name omitted from the title page.[1]

Part VI of the *Discourse on Method* provides a rather lengthy, self-justifying explanation of Descartes' intention to publish some of his physics, at a time when he was still drafting the text in 1636.

> It is now three years since I reached the end of the treatise that contains all these things [i.e. questions that were discussed in *The World*, and mentioned briefly in the *Discourse*] and began to revise it for submission to a publisher, when I noticed that some people whom I respect, and whose authority over my actions can hardly be less than that of my own reason over my thoughts, had censured a physical theory which had been published a little earlier by someone else. I am not saying that I shared that view. However, I would not have noticed anything about it prior to their censure that I could have imagined as prejudicial either to religion or the state or, consequently, that would have prevented me from writing the same if I had been convinced of it by reason. This made me fear that I might have been mistaken about one of my own views, despite the great care I had always taken not to accept any new beliefs unless I had very certain demonstrations of them, and not to write anything about them that could turn out to be detrimental to anyone.   (vi. 60)

This is hardly an accurate account of what happened. Despite what he says in the paragraph just quoted, Descartes had supported the same heliocentric theory as Galileo, and he was convinced when he wrote *The World* that his supporting reasons were enough to defend it against misguided theologians.[2] Three years later, he begins to backtrack in the *Discourse* and writes with false modesty that 'I have never attributed great significance to what came from my own mind' (vi. 61). He then rehearses at length the reasons for and against publishing scientific theories when they are still in the process of being developed. He explains that 'two other reasons made me set down here some essays on particular issues and offer the public some account of my work and my plans' (vi. 74). These reasons were: (a) that many people who already knew about his work might conclude from a failure to publish that the theories had been shown to be false; and (b) that the completion of his research project needed much more observational and experimental work than he could do alone, and that he hoped to benefit from the contributions of others by sharing his provisional theories with the public.

The result of all this soul searching was the compromise represented by the 1637 book. It omitted what Descartes called the 'foundations of my physics' (vi. 74), that is, the controversial view of the universe that included heliocentrism. He offered instead some samples of the results that one could expect from his basic theory when applied to specific areas such as dioptrics. For good measure, he made sure that the book appeared anonymously. The lead-in period took more than three years.

Amsterdam, 1634–1635

During the years 1634 to 1637, Descartes lived in Amsterdam for about one year only, March/April 1634 to spring 1635, before continuing his peripatetic existence in Utrecht, Leiden, and Alkmaar. While at Amsterdam, he lodged with a bookseller and former French teacher, Jacob Thomasz Sergeant, in the house that is now Westermarkt 6, scarcely a hundred metres from another house that has since become much more famous as Anne Frank's refuge from German agents during the Second World War.[3] Toward the end of June, his former house companion, Henri Reneri, moved to Utrecht to take up his new post as professor of philosophy at the Higher School of Utrecht – which became a university two years later. This period was dominated by work on optics, an interest that paralleled Beeckman's research on lenses and caused the Dutch physicist to visit Amsterdam on a number of occasions to consult with an English lens grinder.[4] When Beeckman came as usual from Dordrecht, on Saturday, 13 August 1634, he brought with him a copy of Galileo's controversial book, which was not generally available in the United Provinces. He left again on Monday morning, so Descartes had the book for no more than 'thirty hours' and had an opportunity merely 'to glance through the entire text' (i. 304). When he reported his reading of Galileo to Mersenne, his reaction was generally positive, but dominated throughout by comparison to the unpublished *World*, the 'treatise that I decided to suppress' (i. 305). He then quoted for Mersenne part of the text of Galileo's condemnation that had been published by the papal legate at Liège on 20 September 1633:

The most eminent cardinals, inquisitors general, pronounced and declared that there seemed to be a serious suspicion that Galileo was heretical because he adopted a false doctrine, contrary to the sacred and divine scriptures. He claimed that the Sun is the centre of the world, that it does not move from dawn to dusk; that, on the contrary, the Earth moves and is not the centre of the world; and he believed that this theory could be defended as probable even though it had been declared contrary to sacred scripture.   (i. 306)

Since this put a temporary block on discussing the fundamental principles of physics or its underlying theory, Descartes turned his attention to specific phenomena, such as light, and developed some of the ideas on which he had been working for the better part of five years. He argued against Beeckman in August 1634 that light is transmitted 'in an instant' from its source to our eyes, and provided plausible arguments from eclipses that there is no perceptible delay between seeing light leaving the sun and seeing an eclipse of the moon. He rejected the alternative view, that light travels so slowly that we can notice a time lapse between waving a torch and seeing its reflection in a distant mirror, and concluded his statement with a dismissive greeting: 'If what I have written does not convince you, I must accept that nothing could do so. Goodbye' (i. 312).

Research on optics continued. Jean-Baptiste Morin had sent Descartes a presentation copy of his book on longitudes that had just been published in Paris.[5] As usual, Descartes wrote an effusive note of thanks, but without taking time to read the book. However, he sympathized with Morin's complaint that basic research was not rewarded financially. He offered a favourable comparison between his own commitment to research and that of Morin, and regretted that neither of them was likely to benefit financially from their efforts. 'A craftsman who makes a good pair of glasses would earn much more money from them than I would from all the reflections of my *Dioptrics* if I were to sell them' (i. 314). Twelve years later, Descartes was still concerned about the possible commercialization of his dioptrical work. In 1646 Huygens had sent him a copy of a book published in Paris, which proposed a method for making spectacles.[6] He wrote to both Mersenne and Huygens about this report, on the same day. To Mersenne he wrote:

I recently saw a book . . . of a certain Jacques Bourgeois, a mirror and lens maker to the king, who has his shop in Paris . . . from which I gather that this Mr. Bourgeois has made ordinary spectacles which are worn on the nose, concave on one side and convex on the other, in line with what I wrote at the beginning of the seventh and ninth discourses of my *Dioptrics*. I indicated there that the shape of the lenses need not be exact because we do not know exactly the shape of the eye, and besides it is not inflexible. I would be very interested to find out if these spectacles are more successful than what is normally available, if you have an opportunity to find out about them.[7]

With a shrewd insight into marketing strategies and, perhaps, his customary underestimation of others' work, he told Huygens that the book was merely the 'rigmarole of a charlatan', because 'if the spectacles worked as

well as he claims . . . he would not have to make such an intellectual effort
to sing their praises' (iv. 518–19).

The winter of 1634–35 was especially cold, thus offering opportunities
for Descartes to make detailed observations on the shapes of snowflakes –
and for adults and children to skate on frozen lakes and canals, as illustrated in the winter landscapes of a contemporary Dutch painter, Heindrik
Avercamp (1585–1634).[8]

During this period in Amsterdam, Descartes met one of the leading figures in the cultural and political life of the United Provinces,
Constantijn Huygens (1596–1686). Huygens was son of a refugee from
Brabant, one of the southern provinces that straddled the border between
the United Provinces and the residual Spanish Netherlands, and was the
same age as Descartes. He was married to Susanna van Baerle (1599–
1637), with whom he had five children – the second of whom, Christiaan,
became a famous physicist in the second part of the seventeenth century.
In stark contrast with the French philosopher, however, Huygens was a
committed Counter-Remonstrant, and an extremely successful administrator who functioned as private secretary to the *Stadtholder*, Frederik
Hendrik (from 1625). He was thus ideally placed to provide patronage and
support in a Calvinist society for the relatively impecunious, isolated, and
Catholic Frenchman. Huygens' interests extended well beyond politics
and religion. As an accomplished poet in his own right and translator of
the poems of John Donne, he acted as a cultural intermediary between
Prince Frederik Hendrik and many of the leading poets, artists, and archi-
tects of the time, including Rembrandt (whom he introduced to the prince
of Orange in 1629), Vossius, Hooft, and others. Despite his support for
the Counter-Remonstrant side in the division among Dutch Calvinists,
however, Huygens also acted as a catalyst in trying to reconcile divisions
between the provinces. For example, in a controversy fueled by Voetius'
attack on the use of organ music in the public church, Huygens wrote a
book in 1641 defending the appropriateness of the tradition and the use
of music in Calvinist religious services.[9]

Descartes first met Huygens in April 1632, after which he wrote to
David le Leu de Wilhem (1588–1658) – Huygens' future brother-in-
law – and asked him to pass on a letter to the intended recipient.[10] When
Huygens visited Amsterdam, 29 March–6 April 1635, Descartes read sections of the *Dioptrics* to him, as a sample of work in progress, and Huygens
offered to conduct some experiments to test the theory they discussed.[11]

This initial discussion gave rise to a lengthy, frequent, personal correspondence between Descartes and Huygens that was not interrupted even by the most pressing official demands on Huygens' time, including his frequent absences on manoeuvres with the army.

This began, however, after Descartes' next move in 1635, on this occasion to Utrecht. Before moving, Descartes must have turned at least some of his attention to the pregnant servant of his local host.

Descartes' Daughter, Francine

One of the servants in the Sergeant home, Helena Jansdr vander Strom, became pregnant by Descartes on 15 October 1634. A baby girl was born in Deventer on 19 July 1635 and was baptized into the Reformed Church on 28 July in the same town.[12] The birth certificate lists the father's name as Reyner Jochems – which is a Dutch version of 'René, son of Joachim' – and the child's name is given as Fransintge. The circumstances of Francine's birth, baptism, and subsequent short life are camouflaged by her father's dissimulations and by the accommodations to social expectations that her mother was forced to accept. Claude Saumaise claimed in 1640 that knowledge of the liaison originated with Descartes' valet, who 'complained about having to go to town too often on account of the infant and her mother.'[13]

Descartes' biographer, Baillet, addressed this issue rather delicately in the late seventeenth century. 'Mr. Descartes' marriage is, for us, one of the most secret mysteries of the hidden life that he led in exile from his native country, far from his relatives and friends.'[14] Baillet claimed that a life of celibacy was most appropriate for a philosopher, but that it would have been very difficult for anyone to remain strictly celibate while engaged in the most 'inquisitive investigations in anatomy'. On the other hand, he concedes that if Descartes did marry Helena, it was done so secretly that the most subtle and perceptive canon lawyers could not have distinguished it from concubinage.[15] These speculations inadvertently raise the obvious question about whether Descartes was even attracted to women. 'Mr. Descartes did not find anything in himself, *it seems*, which could have constituted an obstacle to his liberty to marry.'[16] When Baillet made that remark, he may not have been thinking of Descartes' sexual orientation, but he seems to concede the point made by some critics, such as Voetius, who later raised public questions about the French philosopher's alleged promiscuity.[17] 'One may fear that Mr. Descartes, in the depths of what he claimed was solitude, had provided the evidence to show to similar solitary people that not every hidden life is always innocent.'[18] Gustave Cohen, by contrast, explained Descartes' ambiguous relations with women by the loss of his mother in infancy. He compared him to another famous contemporary, Blaise Pascal, who was similarly reared 'without maternal tenderness.' Cohen thought that both philosophers exhibited a certain 'austerity and unease' in their relations with women, and that they were endowed with a 'soul that was not readily open to emotions which are not intellectual.'[19]

These biographers approach the question by trying to explain how a man of such outstanding virtue could have succumbed to the allure of a mere servant girl. However, it is probably a mistake to scrutinize the psychology of Descartes or the possibility of a clandestine marriage. It was more likely that he simply took advantage of a relatively young and inexperienced servant, a practice that was so common in the seventeenth century that Samuel Pepys used coded language in his famous diary to acknowledge frequent similar episodes.[20] The same practices appear in the diary of his contemporary Robert Hooke. Servants constituted a significant percentage of the total population in seventeenth-century Dutch society, in which between 10 and 20 percent of all households had at least one servant.[21] Their duties involved all the lowliest tasks in the house, including cleaning and cooking. Since maidservants were poorly paid, they had to depend completely on their employers even for basic food and accommodations, and their only alternative, if they were mistreated or dissatisfied, was to move to another household in the same servile role.

Many Dutch housemaids became pregnant in the households in which they worked. When that happened, there was strong social pressure on pregnant unmarried women to marry the father of the child, but only if the two people had the same social status. If the man refused to marry, it was even possible for unmarried women to sue the father for financial support. However, if the woman was socially inferior, her chances of legal redress or official marriage were minimal. It would therefore have been most unlikely, for both social and religious reasons, that Helena Jans could have persuaded Descartes to regularize her situation. That assumes, of course, that Descartes was as attracted to young women as Pepys and Hooke evidently were. If not, one is tempted to take Baillet's tantalizing suggestion about anatomical investigations one step further, and to relate the conception of Francine to the anatomical studies that Descartes continued when he lived in Amsterdam.

It is unclear how Descartes or Helena could have arranged for an official baptism for their child in the Reformed Church despite the fact that they were not married in that church, since the father at least was already well known in Deventer. One possibility, suggested by Charles Adam, is that Descartes first met Helena Jans in Deventer when he lived with Reneri, and that she followed him as a domestic servant to Amsterdam. Then, when her pregnancy could no longer be concealed, she returned to Deventer for the birth and baptism of the baby.[22] She may have enjoyed the complicity of a local Calvinist minister to camouflage Descartes' involvement in the whole affair. There is no indication of what arrangements were made for mother and child to be supported in the months after the baptism. It is worth mentioning that Francine was conceived in Amsterdam, born in Deventer, and that she died in Amersfoort. Descartes was never in any of these towns (apart from Amsterdam) at the same time as Helena. One possibility, then, is that Descartes' only child was cared for throughout her short life by her mother, who moved from town to town, in the annual cycle of hiring servants that then prevailed, as an unaccompanied servant and single mother. However, there is also evidence that he arranged for at least some of those years to share a house with Helena and her daughter.

Descartes seems to have lived in Utrecht beginning in the spring of 1635, and to have spent most of 1636 and the first months of 1637 at Leiden, overseeing the publication of his first book. Apart from his active correspondence with Constantijn Huygens, there are no surviving letters from the period March 1636 to March 1637. By the autumn of 1637, he had left Leiden for northern Holland, from which he wrote to an unknown correspondent about the possibility of arranging for Helena and her daughter to live with him. However, as usual, he disguised the reality of the situation by referring to Francine as his 'niece'.

Everything is going much better here than I had hoped. I spoke yesterday with my hostess to see if she wished to have my niece here and to find out how much I would have to pay her for that. She told me, without hesitation, that I should have her brought whenever I wished and that we would easily agree on a price, because it made no difference to her to take care of one child more or less. As regard the servant, she [my hostess] is waiting for you to provide one, and she is very anxious that it has not been arranged already. . . . In fact, it should be arranged for Helena to come here as soon as possible, for I am afraid that our hostess will get tired waiting too long without having a servant, and I would ask you to tell me what Helena thinks about it.   (i. 393–4)

Descartes adds in a postscript that he has included a letter for Helena, but that it is not urgent to deliver it. In fact, he suggests, it would be better if his correspondent were to retain the letter and deliver it personally to Helena rather than have it delivered by a messenger. That should happen, he thinks, about the end of the week, when Helena would come to give the intermediary some letters for forwarding to Descartes.

Descartes acknowledges the safe arrival of some books from the same correspondent, after a passage that included 'two nights on the water' (i. 394).[23] This may suggest that Helena and Francine had previously lived with him or near him in Leiden, and that he was now arranging to continue their camouflaged relationship in an even more remote corner of northern Holland.[24] It also implies that Helena was not an illiterate servant, since Descartes was writing to her and was expecting a number of letters in return, presumably written in Dutch. There is no indication of what happened after Helena and her daughter arrived in Alkmaar. Descartes may have remained in seclusion, probably at Egmond, until he became involved in the publication of his next book, the *Meditations* (when he returned once more to Leiden).

He left Leiden suddenly around 1 September 1640, and did not return for two weeks.[25] This coincided with the death of Francine, who died on 7 September 1640 at the age of five, on the third day after the onset of scarlet fever.[26] Baillet claims that Descartes was planning to send his daughter to one of his relatives in France, so that she could receive an appropriate education. Within eight days of Francine's death, Descartes was back in Leiden, focusing on the printing of the *Meditations*, and replying to scientific queries from Mersenne. It seems as if his intensely ambitious pursuit of another publication was only briefly interrupted by Francine's death.

Descartes cannot have been very surprised at the death of his daughter. Infant mortality was much higher in the seventeenth century than it is now, and everyone, young and old, was watchful for the infectious diseases that frequently devastated whole towns. For example, Descartes' earlier efforts to contact Elzevier as a possible publisher for his book, in October 1635, had been frustrated by the great plague that affected Leiden during the winter of 1635–36.[27] Apart from such plagues that affected people of

all ages, the diseases from which young children suffered made it especially challenging to survive childhood. Claude Clerselier, who was later
to become Descartes' literary executor, was not atypical in this respect. He
married at the relatively early age of sixteen and had fourteen children, all
but three of whom died in infancy.[28]

Once Francine had died, there are few indications later that Descartes
gave her life and early death much thought. He refers briefly, in a letter
to Chanut in 1644, to an occasion ten years earlier when he had lapsed
from the high Christian ideals by which he normally lived, and Baillet was
satisfied to set aside the whole episode as a unique episode in an otherwise
blameless life, a singular 'fall' from grace.

However, despite the uncertainty of their relationship during the intervening years, Helena Jansdr vander Strom reappears in Descartes' life
when he agrees to act as a witness to her wedding sometime after June 1644.
Helena married Jan Jansz van Wel, who was originally from Egmond, and
they settled in Egmond ann den Hoef. Prior to marrying, the two parties
filed a prenuptial agreement with a notary public in Leiden in May. They
made an inventory of the goods contributed to their common household
by each party, and then agreed that if either party were to die prior to their
having children, the other party would recover his or her original investment together with an extra thousand florins. As it happened, they had at
least one child, Justinus, who became the local chief of police in Egmond
between 1673 and 1683. In May 1644, Descartes had returned to live in
Egmond aan den Hoef, from which he travelled to Leiden on his way
to visit France. He had hoped to finalize the publication of the *Principles*
before his departure, but there were delays caused by the preparation and
printing of the diagrams.[29] However, he also had an ulterior motive, for it
seems that Descartes was in Leiden to facilitate the marriage of his former
servant. The prenuptial agreement mentioned that the groom's father had
provided a gift of 1,000 florins, which would be returned to that family if
Helena were to die without children. That amount of money – the equivalent of a university professor's annual salary – was unlikely to have been
donated by the groom's father, who owned a tavern in Egmond. Besides,
this clause was crossed out in the prenuptial agreement, suggesting that
some of the money may have been donated by Descartes, to help Helena
marry into a respectable and independent life. One likely interpretation
of this complex affair is that Helena Jans followed Descartes as a servant
to Egmond in 1637, and that she lodged with the parents of Jan Jansz

van Wel, whose mother, Reyntje Jansdr, had accepted Francine into her home at Descartes' request. Following her marriage, Helena Jans settled permanently in Egmond; she was widowed in the 1650s and married a second time, to Jacob van Lienen, who was the landlord of the Red Heart Inn that belonged to Jan Thomasz van Wel (her first father-in-law). She had three children by her second marriage, and she eventually inherited the Red Heart Inn.[30]

Utrecht, 1635

When Reneri took up his new post at the Illustrious School of Utrecht in 1634, one of his colleagues appointed at the same time was to have a central role in a subsequent dispute with Descartes. Gisbertus Voetius (1589–1676) was a Calvinist minister who had participated at the Synod of Dort and was the first professor of theology at Utrecht. When the Utrecht School was promoted to full university status, 26 March 1636, Voetius became professor of theology and Hebrew. Henricus Regius (1598–1679) was a medical doctor from Utrecht and was initially appointed Professor Extraordinary of Medicine and Botany in 1638 (and full professor in March 1639). Descartes followed Reneri to Utrecht one year after his appointment, and began a lengthy correspondence with Huygens (who was officially based in the Hague) in April 1635.[31] Descartes may have lived on the edge of the town, as was his custom, at a location that is now absorbed into the Maliebaan, an impressive avenue that was first designed and built after his departure in 1638. Within a few weeks of his arrival in Utrecht, however, Golius wrote to him in May 1635 from Leiden, where he was professor of mathematics and oriental languages, and offered to provide accommodations there. Descartes had been out of town for more than a week, probably on a trip to Friesland, and he had arrived in Utrecht probably only two months earlier.[32] Since he had only recently 'changed residence,' he had to decline the offer from Golius because, as he claimed, 'it would show fickleness on my part to leave so soon after I had arrived' (i. 320). The return trip to Amsterdam took him by boat across the Zuiderzee, during which he observed coronas around a lighted candle. He decided to explain this in his *Meteors*, which he had already begun to compose.[33]

In writing to Huygens as early as April 1635, Descartes apologizes for the draft material he sends, the poor quality of the diagrams, and the distraction from more pressing official duties that he is likely to cause

Huygens, who was then involved in military manoeuvres with the army of Prince Frederik Hendrik. France declared war on Spain in May 1635, and planned a joint offensive against the Spanish Netherlands, with the French marching from the south and the Dutch attacking from the north. Despite the urgent demands of the court and army, Huygens enters fully and personally into trying to persuade Descartes to publish some sections of his work. He writes from a military camp at Panderen, 28 October 1635, pleading with Descartes not to be impeded in his project 'by any of the imaginary considerations which have hitherto held you in scruples' (i. 588). He identifies an alternative publisher, Willem Blaeu in Amsterdam; he advises Descartes to use woodcuts rather than copper plates for printing diagrams; and he even suggests that the diagrams be printed throughout the text rather than collected all in one place at the end of the volume.[34]

Descartes reports to Mersenne, about the same time, that since the condemnation of Galileo he has completely revised a treatise that he had begun previously, presumably the *Dioptrics*, or at least those parts of *The World* that refer specifically to light.[35] In passing, he also criticizes the idea that weight is a 'real quality' in bodies (i. 323), a feature of his theory of explanation that recurs frequently in later years, and he expresses surprise that Mersenne would dare to criticize Morin's defence of the Earth's immobility.

By November 1635, Descartes' plans for his publication were beginning to come into focus. He decided to include the *Meteors* together with the *Dioptrics* and, for the first time, he mentioned his ambition to add a Preface to the book, which he thought was likely to delay completion by two or three months (i. 330). It is clear that the *Dioptrics* was already near enough to completion, by December 1635, to refer to its contents as if the structure of the book were fixed (i. 336). Descartes' correspondence seems to lapse in December 1635, and the date of the next surviving letter is three months later, in March 1636. By that time the plague that had affected Leiden during the previous winter had cleared, and he had finalized enough of his manuscript to show it to various printers with a view to publication.[36]

Leiden, 1636

Once arrived in Leiden, Descartes began to discuss publication of his book with Elzevier. The publisher raised many difficulties and assumed, since the prospective author had travelled so far to petition their services, that he had little choice but to accept his proposed terms. This bargaining strategy failed, and Descartes went to another printer in the same town, Jan Maire.[37] Although the book was still in the process of being written and edited, he described its contents to Mersenne with this ambitious, tentative title:

The Project of a Universal Science that could raise our nature to its highest degree of perfection. In addition, the Dioptrics, the Meteors, and the Geometry, in which the most surprising matters, which the author could choose to illustrate the universal science that he proposes, are explained in such a way that even those who have not studied will be able to understand them. (i. 339)

The first sentence here refers to the *Discourse on Method*, because he adds immediately as a commentary on the rather prolix title: 'In this *Project* I reveal a part of my method, I try to demonstrate the existence of God and of the soul separated from the body, and I add some other things which I think will not be unwelcome for the reader.' Descartes stayed constantly in touch with Huygens during the next twelve months. He visited him in The Hague on April 1, to discuss the new book after dinner, and he wrote frequently about Huygens' attempts to find a lens grinder who could produce a parabolic lens by constructing a machine similar to that described in the *Dioptrics*.[38] By 13 July 1636, the printer was promising to have all the illustrations ready within three weeks and to begin printing immediately. Frans van Schooten, the son of a professor of mathematics at Leiden of the same name, had agreed to make the woodcuts. The printer so treasured his expertise that he induced him to lodge in his house, partly to hasten completion of the project and partly 'for fear that he would escape' (i. 614). The printing of the *Dioptrics* was completed by 30 October, but since the engravings for the *Meteors* and the *Geometry* had not been done, the projected publication date was deferred to Easter 1637.[39] Meantime, Descartes spent his time 'with nothing to do except to read, now and then, a page proof full of mistakes' (i. 614).

Apart from the practical difficulties involved in having the book printed, Descartes encountered extra problems in getting the copyright protection (called a 'privilege') that his publisher required. The Dutch 'privilege' was granted without difficulty on 20 December 1636, but it proved much more difficult to get a similar privilege from Paris. Since the book was written in French, it was especially important to have the royal privilege from France, in order to protect the commercial interests of the Dutch publisher and to prevent French printers from copying the work without permission. Here again Huygens proved to be an invaluable patron and support. Descartes asked him (1 January 1637) to send to Paris a sample of fifteen or twenty folios of what had already been printed, using a diplomatic courier. Huygens readily agreed to have the material delivered into Mersenne's hands, as the person in Paris who was supposed to take care of the formal request for the privilege.[40]

Mersenne sorely tempted Descartes' patience during the negotiations to obtain the French privilege. Descartes had supplied copies of the three scientific essays, but not the *Discourse on Method*, which was the last part to be written and which had not yet been printed. He specifically asked that he not be identified in the privilege as the author of the book. Mersenne forwarded the application, in these terms, to the French chancellor, Pierre Séguier III (1588–1672). Séguier had been chancellor since 1635, and was generally sympathetic to the concerns of authors. He is credited with saying, 'If you wish to seduce me, all you need to do is offer me books.' However, the Cartesian request raised genuine difficulties, even for a sympathetic French chancellor, about authorizing an unexamined discourse that might contain sensitive theological or political opinions, written by an anonymous author, and destined for publication in French by a Dutch publisher. Even more challenging, Descartes was looking for a privilege for all the books that he planned to publish in the future and which had not even been written yet.

Séguier passed on the material at hand to his secretary, Jean de Beaugrand, who had published his own *Geostatics* the previous year and who was a severe critic of Descartes' geometry.[41] Beaugrand asked that the author provide a copy of the introductory 'discourse' for examination. Once he was informed about these problems, Mersenne summarized them in a letter to Descartes, and he suggested the solution of publishing simultaneously with a French publisher, such as Soly (who subsequently published the *Meditations*), who could then transfer legal protection to Jan Maire.[42] Descartes turned to Huygens once again, and accepted reluctantly that he might have to compromise his anonymity, since the French chancellor 'did not wish to put the King's name on a book where the author does not put his own' (i. 623). He also sent him a copy of the *Discourse*, requesting that it be sent by diplomatic courier to Mersenne, and inviting both Huygens and his wife to read the proofs and make corrections.

Since he was reading samples of the text in proofs, Mersenne objected to the plan of publishing the scientific essays without the fundamental theory on which they depended (namely, *The World*), and he questioned whether Descartes had revealed enough about his method in the Preface. In response to the second problem, Descartes wrote a lengthy clarification of what he was trying to do.

> I could not understand your objection to the title. For I do not say: *Treatise on Method*, but *Discourse on Method*, which is the same as *Preface or Advice about Method*, to show that I have no intention of teaching it but merely of speaking about it. It is apparent from what I say about it that it consists more in practice than in theory, and I call the subsequent treatises *Illustrations of this Method*, because I claim that the things they contain could not have been found without it, just as I also include something about metaphysics, physics and medicine in the first discourse, to show that it [the method] applies to matters of all sorts.   (i. 349)[43]

However, in reply to continuing pressure to publish *The World*, Descartes laughed at the suggestion, apparently made by Mersenne, that he owed it to the public to kill himself so that his writings could be released for publication. He assured the importunate Minim friar that the manuscript of *The World* was hidden so securely that, even if he were killed, it would not be found 'for more than a hundred years after my death' (i. 349).[44]

Given the lengthy negotiations involved in getting the French privilege, Mersenne was not the only one who had a sneak preview of parts of Descartes' book. Beaugrand showed the *Dioptrics* to Pierre Fermat (1601–1655), who in turn sent some critical comments to Mersenne, and Descartes sent extra copies of the *Dioptrics* and *Meteors* to Huygens for his wife and his sister.[45] When Huygens tried to read the *Geometry*, in March 1637, he found it almost impenetrable.[46] Mersenne's apparent involvement in releasing parts of the book, his request to the chancellor's office that an embarrassingly effusive privilege be written, and his evident compromising of the author's anonymity, tested Descartes' patience almost to the breaking point.[47] The reclusive philosopher in Leiden began to refer to him as 'the good monk', and, although he acknowledged that he was one of his best friends, he told Huygens that he had never read more of any book by Mersenne than was possible to complete in half an hour – a significant comment on such a prolix author.[48] Eventually, he reached the limits of his patience, and he wrote as follows:

You urge me to publish other treatises [*The World*], but at the same time you impede the publication of this one [the *Discourse* and essays]. I dare not write everything I think about this. I beseech you, however, in the name of God, to arrange either that it can be published as soon as possible with the privilege, in whatever form that may be given, or at least that you write and tell us that the privilege was refused. . . . (i. 364)

Descartes asked Mersenne to send the privilege directly to his publisher in Leiden, if he was successful in his request, perhaps because he had already decided to leave Leiden in frustration, since the whole book had already been printed apart from the final page. He moved north to some location near Alkmaar, probably to Egmond.[49] Meantime, Mersenne's efforts were further delayed because the chancellor was absent from Paris, attempting to suppress a mutiny in Rouen.

Apart from his most trusted friends, so many others anticipated the imminent publication of Descartes' first book that it casts some suspicion on the author's apparent determination to remain anonymous. Evidently, Mersenne was partly responsible for disseminating the news to many of his other correspondents. For example, he wrote to André Rivet (15 September 1636) that Descartes was still living in Leiden and that he was about to publish 'something from his excellent speculations.'[50] Likewise, Saumaise wrote from Leiden to Jacques du Puy, in April 1637, that 'the printing of Mr. Descartes' book has been completed but it has not yet appeared because of the privilege that they await from Paris' (i. 365). He expanded on this by giving his impression of Descartes as extremely reclusive, as among the most zealous of Roman Catholics, but as someone whom the local intellectuals characterized as 'without equal'.

Descartes had scarcely left Leiden for his new residence near Alkmaar when Huygens' wife died. Susanna Huygens had given birth to her fifth child, a daughter who was named after her mother, on 13 March 1637, at the age of thirty-eight. She fell sick soon afterward and died on 10 May. Descartes might have assisted at the funeral had he still been in Leiden (and thus within a short journey to The Hague), but it was impossible for him to arrive in time for the funeral from his new northern hideaway. Instead, he wrote a long and genuinely sympathetic letter of condolence, though, inappropriately, he included a few lines toward the end about his own minor frustrations. 'I do not understand Father Mersenne's way of proceeding, because he still has not sent me the privilege and seems to wish that I should be indebted to him while he does the exact opposite of what I request' (i. 373, 634). Descartes' former friend, Isaac Beeckman, died ten

days later at Dordrecht, on 20 May 1637. On hearing that news, Descartes
wrote a rather brief and unemotional letter to Colvius, a Calvinist minister
at Dordrecht.

In passing through this town [Leiden] on my return from a journey that took more
than six weeks, I found the letter that you took the trouble to write to me, in which I
learn the sad news of Mr. Beeckman's death. I regret it, and I am certain that, as one
of his best friends, you will be distressed. However, Sir, you know much better than
I do that the time we live in this world is so short in comparison with eternity, that
we should not worry ourselves too much if we are taken a few years earlier or later.
Since Mr. Beeckman was extremely philosophical, I have no doubt that he had been
resigned for a long time to what has happened to him. I hope that God enlightened
him so that he died in his grace.   (i. 380)

Beeckman's passing is acknowledged with a rather detached, philosophical reference to the brevity and unpredictability of human life. At about
the same time, Descartes mentions Beeckman's name when writing to
Mersenne about those who 'try to acquire a reputation by false advertis-
ing' (i. 375). It is clear that, whatever the deep source of their dispute, it
had merely been camouflaged during the intervening years by a respectful and intermittent correspondence about matters of common scientific
interest.

The long-awaited privilege for Descartes' first book was given in Paris
on 4 May 1637, and Jan Maire was able to print the last folio on 8 June,
using an abbreviated version of the privilege that omitted the author's
name.[51] Descartes returned to Leiden and sent the good news immediately to Huygens. He asked him to present a copy to 'his Highness' the
prince of Orange, though not in the name of the author, who had succeeded in remaining anonymous.[52] Huygens co-operated with the request
before Frederik Hendrik embarked on a new siege of Breda in July, which
concluded successfully on 10 October. Descartes had contracted with his
publisher to provide him with two hundred copies of the book, which he
would be free to distribute to his friends and correspondents, and which
would allow the publisher to sell as many copies as he wished during the
term of their contract.

The proud author began immediately to distribute copies of his first
book to supportive friends and potential patrons. One copy was sent to
the French ambassador to the United Provinces, Baron de Charnacé, who
was also commander of a French regiment that was assisting at the successful siege and recapture of Breda. Huygens told Descartes that the

ambassador was about to send him serious objections, and he was assured by return that they would be very welcome. Unfortunately, Charnacé was killed on 1 September in the course of the siege without having sent his comments. Descartes sent a copy to Balzac in the middle of June, from an unidentified address in 'Holland', with a letter of regret for his silence and lack of correspondence 'for a number of years'. He also imitated the ornate literary style that was typical of Balzac in excusing the defects of his work:

I eventually took the risk of printing the writings that you receive with this letter. Although I do not think that they are at all worthy of being read by you, and although I am very much more ashamed of the unsophisticated style and simplicity of my thoughts before you than before others who would not be as well able to recognize them, nevertheless the affection which you deigned to show me for so long suggests that this book will receive more protection and support from you than from anyone else, and that you will even oblige me by informing me of the errors you notice in my writings and the ways in which they could be remedied. For, since I did not let the book carry my name, I think I can still disown it if necessary.   (i. 381)

He wrote an equally effusive letter to one of his former Jesuit teachers at La Flèche, Father Étienne Noël.

I am sure that you will not have retained the names of all the students you had twenty-three or twenty-four years ago, when you were teaching philosophy at La Flèche, and that mine is among those which were erased from your memory. However, I did not think that, for that reason, I should erase from mine the obligations that I have to you. I have not lost the desire to acknowledge them, although I have no other opportunity to do so except that, having had the book that accompanies this letter published recently, I am very happy to offer it to you as a fruit that belongs to you and of which you had spread the first seeds in my mind, just as I owe to members of your order all the little knowledge of good literature that I possess. If you take the trouble to read this book or to have it read by those of your order who have more leisure for the task, if you notice any errors (which will undoubtedly be found in large numbers), and if you do me the favour of alerting me to them and thus continue to teach me, I would be very much obliged and would do my utmost to correct them in accordance with your good suggestions.   (i. 385)

Apart from those to whom Descartes sent copies of the book after publication, others had seen earlier versions of the text that had been sent to Mersenne as part of the request for a French privilege. Some readers presumably bought their own copies from booksellers, and within a relatively short time Descartes was faced with objections and criticisms from far and near.

The Scientific *Essays* (1637)

The standard practice among scholars in the seventeenth century was
to write in Latin, since that was the normal language for instruction at
universities, and thus to make their publications accessible to academic
readers all over Europe. Descartes, however, decided to publish his first
book in French, and he explained the choice as follows:

> If I have written in French, which is my native language, rather than in Latin, which
> is the language of my teachers, it is because I hope that those who use only their pure
> natural reason will be better judges of my views than those who trust only ancient
> books. Those who combine common sense and study . . . will not be so partial to Latin,
> I am sure, that they refuse to listen to my arguments because I explain them in the
> vernacular.   (vi. 77–8)

Evidently, some of his local readers at universities in the United Provinces
did not read French as easily as Latin. This problem was remedied seven
years later, when Descartes arranged for a Latin translation of the book
(without the *Geometry*) to be published by Elzevier.[53] In the short term, he
preferred to write in French not only because he found it easier to do so, but
also because he wished to dissociate his work from the scholastic tradition
that it criticizes, and because he trusted readers (including women) who
had not been contaminated by school learning more than academic readers.
The relative openness of women to new ideas later became one of the
central features of Cartesian arguments in favour of women's education.

   Despite the author's plans, Descartes' three essays – on dioptrics, meteorology, and geometry – are rarely read today.[54] By contrast, the *Discourse
on Method* has been adopted as part of the canon in Western philosophy,
as an independent text from which modern readers are expected to distill
its author's seminal contribution to modern thought. This reversal began
even with Descartes' most sympathetic reader, Constantijn Huygens. He
wrote in March 1637, prior to publication: 'In passing, I devoured your
Discourse on Method, which is truly the most digested piece, the most ripe,
and as the Italians seem to express themselves vividly, the *piu saporita* [the
most flavourful] that I have ever seen. If you need to know my opinion, I
assure you that it satisfied me extremely well' (i. 626). The relative acces-
sibility of the *Discourse*, and the fact that the essays have lapsed with the
passing of time into obsolete texts in the history of science, has even had
the remarkable effect of transforming retrospectively the original core
of the book into what are often referred to as its 'appendices'. Yet it is

obvious that the scientific essays are the main text, and their relative size alone confirms that fact.[55] More fundamentally, it is clear from the history of its publication that the *Discourse* was planned merely as a Preface to the scientific essays, and that it was written when the book was being printed partly as a concession to Mersenne's importunate requests for publication of the underlying physical theory on which the essays were based.

None of these reasons, of course, will persuade most readers today to change their reading habits and to read the *Essays* together with the famous Preface on method. On the other hand, if one reads the *Discourse* out of its original context it is almost impossible to understand what the book was about or why its author wrote it in the form in which it finally emerged from the printer at Leiden in 1637. For those who wish to understand the *Discourse*, it is necessary to consider the essays for which it provided a Preface.

The traditional distinction between catoptrics and dioptrics represented a division between studies of light reflection and light refraction or, in simpler terms, between studies of mirrors and lenses. Descartes' *Dioptrics* is designed as a discussion of the extent to which the invention of telescopes or other lenses can assist human vision. In fact, however, it is just as much a philosophical discussion of sensation and a reworking of some of the themes about perception that had been presented in the initial chapters of *The World*. Since he still had no definite plans for that book in 1637, Descartes offers readers a glimpse of his fundamental rejection of scholastic theories of perception by including in the *Dioptrics*, in the fourth discourse, a discussion of 'The Senses in General'.

The *Dioptrics* repeated an evasive ploy that had been first adopted almost ten year earlier in the *Rules*, when Descartes claimed that he did not need to explain the true nature of light. Here again he says that he is concerned only to explain how its rays 'enter the eye and how they can be bent by the different bodies that they encounter' (vi. 83). This suggests that we think of the action of light by analogy with how a blind man perceives objects by using a stick, or how wine tends to flow through holes in the bottom of a barrel. The first analogy helps the reader not to think of light as a something that moves from a visible object to our eye, just as nothing needs to pass along a blind man's stick in order for him to 'perceive' things. The implication of the analogy is that there is no reason to assume that 'there is anything in these objects which is similar to the ideas or sensations that we have of them' (vi. 85). In this way, readers' minds will 'be delivered from

all those little images flying through the air, called "intentional species ",
which worry the imagination of philosophers so much' (vi. 85). Instead,
Descartes asks his readers to think of light simply as a feature of subtle
matter best described as a tendency to move, and to assume that this
tendency is transmitted in straight lines.

This almost instrumentalist attitude allows Descartes to focus on the
geometry of how light rays are bent. He presents a mathematical analysis of
how light is reflected from smooth surfaces, such as mirrors, and how it is
refracted when it travels from one medium to another (e.g., when it passes
from the air into glass). In the case of reflection, Descartes argues that the
angle of incidence is equal to the angle of reflection. In the case of refraction, he develops a mathematical analysis that concludes with the sine law
of refraction, the same conclusion that resulted from independent work by
the Dutch physicist Snellius. Having established these laws of reflection
and refraction, Descartes needs to describe the anatomy of the eye.

It is hard to avoid the conclusion that the description of a cross-section
of the eye, presented in the third discourse of the *Dioptrics*, is based at
least in part on anatomical dissections that Descartes had done during
the previous years. Without using technical terms such as 'iris', 'pupil',
or even 'optical lens', he describes the various parts of the eye, including
what he calls the 'optical nerve', with only enough detail to make it possible
for readers to follow the discussion in subsequent chapters. However, as
promised to Huygens, he does provide many diagrams to illustrate the
points being made in the text. This is in stark contrast, for example, to
a book on the same subject written by one of his contemporary critics,
Vopiscus Fortunatus Plemp (1601–1671). Plemp had studied medicine,
first at Leiden and later at Bologna, one of the best medical schools in
Europe. Having practised medicine at Amsterdam for six years, he was
appointed professor of medicine in Louvain. In 1632, Plemp published
his *Ophthalmographia, or the structure, action and use of the eye according
to the common opinion of physicians and philosophers.*[56] This relatively short
treatise explains the functioning and diseases of the eye without using even
one diagram to illustrate the text.

The fourth, fifth, and sixth discourses of the *Dioptrics* provide a summary of the Cartesian theory of vision and, by extension, of sensation in
general. Descartes concedes at the outset that 'it is the mind which senses
and not the body' (vi. 109), or, more exactly, it is the mind insofar as it is
'in the brain, where it exercises the faculty called common sense' (vi. 109).

This claim requires an account of how the nerves work and how they can transmit information from the external senses to the brain. Descartes adopts the common opinion of anatomists, that a cross-section of nerves shows three distinct parts: an outer membrane, an inner filament, and a very subtle matter (called animal spirits) that lubricates the gap between the outer and inner layers and thereby allows the inner tube to move smoothly within the outer membrane. If one assumes that information is transmitted from the external senses to the brain by the motion of the inner filament, one can exploit the analogy of the blind man to show that the mind can acquire reliable information without having an image of perceived objects. At this point Descartes repeats an argument from *The World*, and, since that book remained unpublished, he could present it to the public as if for the first time. 'There are many other things apart from images which can stimulate our thought such as, for example, signs and words, which do not in any way resemble the things they signify' (vi. 112). The argument is that, if words can stimulate the mind to think of specific things without resembling them – the word 'horse' does not in any way look like a horse! – then why would it not be equally possible for the mind to think of a horse as a result of patterns of information from the optical nerves, without this information resembling a horse?

The optical part of this discussion is presented in the fifth discourse, in which Descartes accepts that an optical image resembling an object of perception is formed on the back of the eye. However, the novelty of his contribution is in the sixth discourse, in which he constructs a theory about how the information presented in this optical form can be transmitted to the centre of the brain. He repeats the general principle that 'our soul is of such a nature that the force of the movements' of the optical nerves 'makes it have the sensation of light', although 'there is no need, in this whole process, for any resemblance between the ideas that the soul conceives and the movements that cause those ideas' (vi. 130, 131). The Cartesian theory is that the brain receives information from many sources apart from the optical image on the retina – for example, from the muscles that move the eyes, from muscles that adjust the focal length of the ocular lenses, from the degree of brightness of images received, and from changes in the size of the pupil.

The most explicit example of ways in which information is made available to the brain is developed by analogy with a blind man who estimates the distance of some object by using two sticks. The blind man knows that

his hands are about two feet apart, and he turns his two sticks inward so
that they both reach the same object in his vicinity. If he estimates the
angle by which he bends his sticks from a parallel position, it is an easy
mathematical problem, at least for Descartes, to calculate the distance of
the invisible object.[57] This suggests that there is a form of spontaneous
triangulation involved in our estimation of the distance of objects that we
can see, because we turn our eyes from their normal parallel position to
focus on objects of perception that are more or less close to us.

The remainder of the text discusses the ways in which lenses of different shapes are suitable for various optical instruments, and especially
the merits of hyperbolical and elliptical lenses, which Descartes claims are
'preferable to any others that can be imagined' (vi. 195). It is easy to appreciate from the *Dioptrics*, in retrospect, the urgency of Descartes' invitation
to Ferrier to follow him to the United Provinces when he first arrived in
1628, and the frequency with which he had written to Huygens, in the
1630s, requesting assistance in finding a lens grinder who could produce a
uniformly ground hyperbolic lens. His theory of vision and his research on
dioptrics could be tested only by using well-ground lenses. Accordingly,
the final discourse of the *Dioptrics* reproduces a design for a good lathe for
lens grinding, similar to that described in lengthy correspondence with
Ferrier in October and November 1629.[58] Descartes still had not yet found
a sufficiently skilled lens grinder. But, in the meantime, he was publishing
a theory that could be confirmed or otherwise by experiment.

The *Meteors* is, like the *Dioptrics*, a somewhat eclectic collection of
explanations of meteorological phenomena, most of which had been discussed by Descartes in correspondence during the previous nine years. In
addition to discussing the disparate phenomena mentioned, it also had as a
centerpiece a prominent new discovery, namely, the Cartesian explanation
of the rainbow. It is clear from the outset – a point reiterated in the concluding sentence of the book – that Descartes' objective was to demystify
the apparently strange phenomena that occur in the space between the
Earth and the heavens and that had been interpreted by others as omens
or prophetic messages. 'That makes me hope that, if I explain the nature
of clouds here[,] . . . it would be easy to believe that it is possible, in the
same way, to find the causes of everything that is most admirable above
the earth' (vi. 231).[59] The explanations that are suggested are contrasted
with the 'superstition and ignorance' (vi. 324) that compromises even the
very description of many meteorological events.

There are two other general qualifications of the nature of this project, both of which were to give rise to serious discussions and critiques in the following years. One was that Descartes had to present his results in a hypothetical manner because the general principles of physics, on which the explanations relied, could not be divulged yet.

It is true that, since knowledge of these things depends on general principles of nature that have not yet been well explained, as far as I know, I have to use some assumptions at the beginning, as I did in the *Dioptrics*. However, I shall try to make them so simple and easy that, perhaps, you will have no difficulty in believing them, even though I have not yet demonstrated them.   (vi. 233)

This refers to the three laws of nature and the general assumptions that had been presented in *The World*, on which most of the explanations in the *Meteors* relied. The effects of this self-imposed limitation become evident, for example, in the explanation of winds in the fourth discourse. Had he been able to refer to the daily revolution of the Earth, he might have explained more readily the movement of air around the Earth 'from east to west'. As long as he had to remain silent about that sensitive topic, he could only invite readers to accept that assumption, because its explanation 'cannot easily be deduced without explaining the whole fabric of the universe, something that I have no intention of doing here' (vi. 269).[60]

The other caveat had similar connotations of the earlier unpublished work. Descartes was very conscious of the extent to which he was replacing traditional scholastic explanations of natural phenomena, which relied on what were called 'qualities' and 'forms'. In place of the multiplicity of such exotic entities, he asked his readers to accept that there was only one matter in the universe, that it was divisible into indefinitely small parts, and that all the natural phenomena mentioned in this treatise could be explained by reference to the size, shape, disposition, and movement of parts of matter. He could obviously anticipate the reaction of his learned contemporaries in the universities, and he lamely tried to avoid controversy by suggesting that he was not arguing against their theories but merely proposing an alternative, simpler theory.

Finally, you should know that, to avoid breaking the peace with philosophers, I do not at all wish to deny anything they imagine in bodies over and above what I have talked about, such as their 'substantial forms', their 'real qualities', and similar things, but it seems to me that my explanations should be approved to the extent that I make them depend on fewer things.   (vi. 239)

This was a key text to which he returned, years later, in a very public controversy between Regius and his university rector.[61] Descartes did not really believe that his approach to explanation was compatible with that of scholastic philosophers, a point that became clear in subsequent discussions and was obvious even to his earliest readers. Here he is merely trying to avoid controversy, but the seeds of future acrimonious disputes are barely hidden in this somewhat wishful peace token.

Much of what is explained in the *Meteors* derives from specific experiences that are dated by Descartes himself. Thus he refers to the shapes of snowflakes that he observed in Amsterdam, during the winter of 1635 (vi. 298); to the avalanches he observed when crossing the Alps in May 1625 (vi. 316); to the coronas around a lighted candle that he had recently seen while crossing the Zuiderzee (vi. 351–2); and to parhelias observed in Rome in March 1629 (vi. 361). It was not merely a coincidence that Descartes tried to explain various phenomena that he had witnessed himself. He often argued that observations made by others are unreliable; accordingly, he conceded in the *Meteors* that he could speak only conjecturally about 'things that happen on the oceans, which I have never seen and about which I have only very imperfect descriptions' (vi. 315). Apart from explaining very unusual phenomena, therefore, he also constructed explanations of familiar things such as clouds, winds, rainfall, thunder, and so on.

The focal point of the *Meteors*, however, was the explanation of the rainbow that presupposed the sine law of refraction presented in the *Dioptrics*. Descartes acknowledged some of the familiar features of rainbows that require explanation, for example, that they are bow-shaped, that they occur at a definite angle in the sky relative to the observer, that there is often a secondary bow that is less bright than the primary bow, that the colours appear in reverse order in the two bows, and so on. The explanation he offered relied on an assumption that light is a tendency to move imparted by the Sun to the subtle matter that fills up all the apparently empty spaces between larger parts of matter, and that our perception of colours results from the different ways in which those subtle particles modify their spins when they tend to pass from one medium to another. Even though this 'assumption' was very wide of the mark, Descartes could still successfully calculate the ways in which light is refracted as it passes through raindrops, because that depended only on the refractive index of the rain rather than on any more general theory of what light is. In an ingenious suggestion, Descartes explains how the two bows appear. If light strikes a raindrop, it can be refracted twice (on entering and exiting the drop), and reflected once at the back of the raindrop that faces the observer (see diagram 1). Likewise, it may be refracted twice and reflected twice, and this explains how the secondary bow appears at a different height, why it is less vivid (since only some of the light rays are reflected in this way), and why the colours appear in the opposite order in which they are seen in the primary bow (diagram 2).

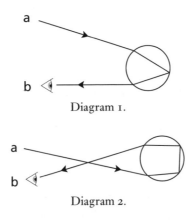

Diagram 1.

Diagram 2.

One of the reasons Descartes offered for publishing this first book in French was to make it accessible to as wide a readership as possible.[62] However, despite its being in French, the mathematical language in which the *Geometry* was written was bound to inhibit many readers. Descartes acknowledged this, by inserting a special 'notice' at the beginning of the text:

Up to this point I have tried to make myself intelligible to everyone. However, for this treatise, I fear that only those who already know what is in geometry books will be able to read it. The reason is that they contain many truths that are very well demonstrated, and I therefore thought it would be superfluous to repeat them and, for that reason, I have taken the liberty of using them.   (vi. 368)

The caution was appropriate. Only those who were trained in mathematics could understand what the problems were. Besides, it is clear that Descartes had been working on some of these problems for at least ten years, that he had shared his interim conclusions with various correspondents, and that he had written the *Geometry* in its published form 'only when the *Meteors* was being printed' and had 'even invented part of it at that time'.[63]

One of the most obvious features of the *Geometry* is that it is not a series of proofs of theorems, similar to the familiar methods used by Euclid.[64]

It was inspired by a well-established tradition in geometry that accepted only lines and circles as legitimate elements for constructing all geometrical figures.[65] Another way of expressing the same restriction is that one must be able to construct any geometrical figure by using only a compass and ruler. There were well-known problems that could not be solved given these limitations, such as constructing a square with the same area as a given circle or finding two lines that were mean proportionals to two given lines. The extent to which geometry, as a discipline, could express problems that it could not solve was made even more acute by the publication, in 1588, of a Latin translation of Pappus' problem.[66] Descartes' ambition was to release geometry from such limitations or to introduce new methods that could address previously insoluble problems. The focus of his contribution was to develop algebraic methods for describing geometrical figures, especially curves, and to propose novel approaches for solving problems of construction.

The ambition of his previous engagements with these problems, dating back to 1619 and the mid-1620s, reappears in the first sentence of the *Geometry*. 'All the problems of geometry can be reduced easily to such terms that we then need to know only the length of certain straight lines in order to construct them' (vi. 369). What catches the eye immediately is the 'all' and the 'easily'. It is true that, in the *Geometry*, Descartes displays the power of his new curves to solve the Pappus problem for five lines, and that he endorses the use of algebraic equations as the criterion of exactness for the construction of curves. However, there is an element of wishful thinking in the claim that he has provided a method of solving all problems in geometry, and he was much too good a mathematician not to have seen some of the fundamental problems that remained in the discipline. Rather than take more time to tackle them, however, he returned to the fundamental philosophical issues that featured in the unpublished *World*; and while he defended his significant contribution to mathematics and scorned the claims of many of his contemporaries, he effectively stopped doing new work in mathematics once the *Geometry* was published.

The *Discourse on Method* (1637)

The *Discourse* was a rather hastily written Preface designed to introduce the three scientific essays of 1637. Its rambling, repetitive, and uneven character is easily understood from the context of its composition. As in the case of the three scientific essays, Descartes borrowed some of its content from material that he had written over a number of years and that still remained unpublished. These sources included a draft autobiography that he had discussed with Balzac in 1628; the *Rules*; an early draft of a treatise on metaphysics; and, most of all, *The World* and the *Treatise on Man*, in which his general approach to natural philosophy had been developed.[67] He may have written the final section (Part VI) first, because it is the only section that refers to the accompanying essays. Having done that, he then added autobiographical material, four rules that summarize his method, eight pages of a detailed description of blood circulation that seems oddly out of context, and a somewhat protracted account of his frequent changes of plan about publishing or not publishing *The World*.

Descartes' correspondence with Mersenne and Huygens, while the scientific essays were in production, shows that he changed the content of the *Discourse*, and that he modified his original ambition from a 'project of a universal science' to a 'preface or advice about method'. This scaling down of plans is reflected in the text of the *Discourse* itself, when he writes in Part I: 'my plan here is not to teach the method that everyone must follow in order to guide their reason, but merely to explain how I have tried to guide my own' (vi. 4). Since no one can argue that a fable is not true, he lapses into that metaphor again to characterize his comments on method. 'Since I am proposing this work as a history or, if you prefer, a fable . . . I hope it will be useful for some readers without being harmful to others, and that everyone will be grateful for my frankness' (vi. 4). The same diffidence or defensiveness reappears in Part II, where he claims that his aim was never more ambitious than 'an attempt to reform my own thoughts and to build on a foundation that was entirely my own'. He does not advise 'anyone else to imitate it' (vi. 15). With all these disclaimers in place, he then summarizes four rules that are borrowed from the *Rules*, but that in fact give very little indication of how to realize the significant results of the three essays.

Descartes thought that he could also illustrate the range of disciplines to which his new method applied by giving examples of the progress that he had made in metaphysics, physiology, and generally in natural philosophy. The brief digression into metaphysics, by which he meant arguments about the existence of God and the immortality of the soul, outlined the approach to which he returned later in the *Meditations*. Likewise, the claim that he had discovered explanations of many natural phenomena was supported by reference to the unpublished *World*. Such explanations were radically different from what was widely taught in schools, for, according to Descartes' concept of matter, it contained 'none of those forms or qualities about which they dispute in the schools' (vi. 43).

In the final section of the *Discourse* (Part VI), Descartes eventually addresses one of the fundamental questions raised by his scientific essays, namely, the extent to which the theories presented there could be confirmed by evidence, and the kind of evidence that would be relevant to the task. The solution he offered was a compromise that was excused by the provisional status of the publication. In other words, Descartes claimed to have a fundamental theory of nature in *The World* that could 'demonstrate' all the theories outlined in the 1637 book. At the same time, he could not publish that work yet. He therefore had no option, he claimed, but to begin the *Dioptrics* and the *Meteors* with various 'assumptions' that, had *The World* been published, could have been established more certainly. He explained the compromise as follows:

If some of the issues that I have spoken about at the beginning of the *Dioptrics* and the *Meteors* shock people initially, because I call them assumptions and seem not to want to prove them, they should have the patience to read the whole text attentively. . . . For it seems to me that the arguments are interconnected in such a way that, just as the last ones are demonstrated by the first, which are their causes, the first arguments are demonstrated reciprocally by the last, which are their effects.   (vi. 76)

Descartes knew that this looked like what philosophers had traditionally called a vicious circle, or using **A** to prove **B** and then using **B** to prove **A**. However, he claims not to fall into that trap because the relationships between cause and effect are not equivalent. We know the effects or the natural phenomena that we are trying to explain, and that knowledge is used to *confirm* the truth of our theories. Working in the opposite direction, the theories are not meant to confirm the truth of our descriptions of phenomena (which we already know), but are designed to *explain* the phenomena in question. Besides, he adds, 'I only called them assumptions to let it be known that I think I can deduce them from those first truths that I have explained above' (vi. 76), but that have not yet been revealed to the public.

This attempt at revelation and concealment, with some self-justifying comments on method, failed miserably. One of the reasons was that the *Discourse* contained enough hints about the general theory proposed in

The World to make potential critics very uneasy. It was clear, even in these prefatory remarks about method, that Descartes was explicitly rejecting the scholastic tradition of philosophy that was firmly established in French and Dutch universities, thereby attracting the ire of professors in both countries. He had developed an account of animal behaviour that made animal souls redundant, even if he stopped short of its apparent implications for human beings by including arguments in defence of the rationality and distinctiveness of the human soul. He said enough about proving God's existence to attract the interest of theologians who thought that his proof was not sufficiently robust or, more likely, who thought that questions about God should be reserved for religious faith rather than philosophical argument. In fact, the only concession to vested interests was to dissemble about his agreement with Galileo, thereby avoiding direct conflict with the Roman Inquisition.

The cloak of official anonymity did little, either, to protect Descartes from critics. Every reasonably well-informed reader in France and the United Provinces knew the identity of the author. The stage was set for enthusiastic applause from a few devoted fans, and for unrelenting criticism from the learned establishment. Descartes even invited such, by inserting the following comment toward the conclusion of the *Discourse*: 'I ask all those who may have objections to them [i.e., my writings] to take the trouble to send them to my publisher. Once the publisher tells me about them, I shall try to append my response at the same time and, in this way, readers will see both of them together, and will find it so much easier to make a judgment about the truth' (vi. 75). He promised to admit his mistakes frankly and, if replies were appropriate, to write them as briefly as possible. The next two years provided a more stringent test of his sincerity in that regard than he might have assumed was possible when he first penned the invitation to critics.

6

Retreat and Defence
(1637–1639)

There is still hardly anyone who has understood fully what I wrote.

(i. 502)[1]

DESCARTES spent the years immediately following publication of the
1637 *Essays* in seclusion in the north of Holland. As usual, he concealed the various addresses he used from anyone who might disturb him.[2]
He moved north from Leiden some time during spring 1637, perhaps as
early as April. By May, he reported that he was living in an unidentified
location in the Alkmaar region, possibly at Egmond, 'but without being
there because I do not think that I shall remain there' (i. 634).[3] None of the
letters during the following eighteen months, even those sent frequently
to his patron, Huygens, gives any indication of his precise address. Thus
when Huygens was writing to him from the siege of Breda (which lasted
from 23 July to 6 October), he borrowed one of Descartes' phrases from the
Discourse to tease his elusive correspondent about the 'imaginary spaces'
he inhabited.[4] On 29 January 1639, however, Descartes acknowledged that
he was in Santpoort, a small village north of Haarlem, though it remains
unclear whether he had moved there recently or had been living there for
some time previously.[5]

The reasons for the extra secrecy during these years may have been
that Helena Jans and her daughter, Francine, were still living with him,
although there is no independent evidence to support that suggestion.
Descartes' own explanation of his seclusion during this period was the
same one he had offered on previous occasions. For example, he wrote to
Mersenne (27 May 1638):

Finally, between ourselves, there was nothing more incompatible with my plans than
the Paris air, because of the infinite number of distractions that are unavoidable there.

As long as I can live as I wish, I shall always remain in the country – as I currently do in a corner of north Holland – in some region where I cannot be pestered by my neighbours' visits. That is the only reason that made me prefer this country to my own, and I am so used to it now that I have no desire to change.   (ii. 151–2)

The peaceful life in pastoral surroundings described here fails to mention the extent to which Descartes was distracted, not by intrusive neighbours, but by epistolary interventions from afar. His geographical seclusion was interrupted by sustained criticisms of his work and by his equally vigorous defence of the views expressed in the *Essays*.

Each week the messenger delivered a steady stream of letters in response to the public invitation to readers, in the *Discourse*, to submit objections so that the author could either reply to them or correct his writings. He even considered publishing the objections and replies together, 'as soon as there are enough of them to make a book' (i. 449).[6] While this plan was eventually abandoned, it helps explain why Descartes wrote so many detailed and lengthy letters during these transitional years. There were objections to almost everything he wrote in the *Essays*. Some of the most interesting queries concerned the kind of evidence Descartes claimed in support of his theories, while the most acrimonious by far related to his mathematics.

An Invitation to Critics

When Descartes published the *Essays* he did not follow the customary practice of dedicating his book officially to a powerful patron. However, he tried to realize the same goal unofficially by arranging to have copies sent to influential readers and potential patrons in the United Provinces, in France, and even in Rome.[7] He also sent copies to a number of Jesuits, hoping perhaps that his ideas might filter into their school curriculum in France and, possibly, elsewhere in Europe.[8] There was a third privileged group who got complimentary copies: those who were prominent in the artistic and academic life of the United Provinces, including the few readers whom Descartes thought were capable of reading the *Geometry* and for whom he reserved specially bound copies of the work.[9]

To all and sundry he sent the same official message: please send me your frank comments on the enclosed, to help me correct errors. The style of the invitation to Father Noël may have been more deferential than usual,

but the underlying content was similar to what he wrote to others. To the
Jesuit he wrote: 'My only objective is to instruct myself, and those who
reproach me for some error [*faute*] will always please me more than those
who praise me' (i. 455). The French term used in all these requests was
faute, which could be translated as 'mistake' (with connotations of a simple
slip that could easily be corrected), or as 'defect' or 'error' (words that have
implications of something being seriously wrong). Descartes had written
in a similar vein to Mersenne, in spring 1637:

> I am very grateful for the objection that you sent me and I beseech you to continue
> to tell me about any others that you hear, in a manner that is as much as possi-
> ble unfavourable to me. That will please me as much as you possibly can, for I am
> not accustomed to complaining while my wounds are being treated, and those
> who are kind enough to instruct me and to teach me something will always find
> me docile.   (i. 349)[10]

There is nothing unusual in the style of this open invitation to Mersenne.
The Minim friar was his most loyal correspondent, on whom he relied
for continued representation in Paris and for the indirect communication
with many other scholars that he provided. However, Descartes wrote to
other selected correspondents in a similar way. He invited Balzac to tell
him about 'the errors [*fautes*]' that he noticed in the essays (i. 381). He
encouraged Plemp to send 'objections' to his account of blood circulation
and to request, on his behalf, the strongest possible objections from an
unnamed Jesuit reader (i. 477). Finally, he asked Father Antoine Vatier
to encourage others to forward 'all the difficulties that are encountered in
what I have tried to explain', since that would provide the shortest route to
'discovering all the errors [*erreurs*] or truths in my writings' (i. 561, 562).

   This all sounds open-minded and genuinely impartial about the possible
merits of the theories proposed in the 1637 book. Together with these
requests for objections and corrections, Descartes provides a self-serving
description of his attitude to criticism. Not only is he 'docile', as he claimed
above, but he is reluctant to speak in his own defence. 'I am not comfortable
if I am obliged to speak favourably about myself' (i. 478). While offering
a spirited reply to Froidmont's objections, he tells Plemp that he had to
overcome his natural reluctance to engage in controversy in order to reply
adequately to the problems raised. 'To some extent I forced my own nature,
which in other circumstances is averse to all controversy' (i. 475).[11] He
even claims not to care whether others have anticipated his discoveries,
thereby implying that he would not get involved in priority disputes. Thus,

when Father Vatier wrote that he was happy that others had not published similar ideas before Descartes, he replied: 'that is something that I have never feared. Apart from the fact that it is unimportant whether I am the first or the last to have written the things that I have written, on condition that they are true. . . . ' (i. 562) In sum, he constantly requested comments on his work, claimed to welcome them in proportion to their strength and efficacy, and described himself as a docile author who was receptive to criticism.

The reality was rather different. Descartes conceded nothing to any objection made by any of his correspondents. There is no example, in response to comments on the *Essays*, where he agreed to correct his views or to amend his theories. In fact, he wrote dismissively that the strongest objections raised against him were no better than the weakest of those he had thought of himself, and that the objections of others served merely to confirm his original opinions.[12] Rather than welcoming criticisms, he deeply resented them and did not readily forget or forgive their authors. For example, six years after receiving objections from the Louvain professor Plemp, Descartes was still complaining that 'in bad faith, he [Plemp] published my replies in a mutilated and distorted form.'[13]

However, that does not mean that the detailed replies he wrote were mere stone-walling. In the course of answering critics, Descartes was forced to address one of the central issues in any account of knowledge, namely, how to provide evidence to support one's views and what degree of certainty may be claimed on their behalf. There is nothing to suggest that Descartes had worked out this strategy in advance. He seems to have been genuinely groping for an answer to an extremely difficult question, and his response is understandably unsatisfactory from the perspective of readers today. One constant feature of his reply was to situate explanations of specific phenomena in the wider context of a full development of his natural philosophy, and thus to defer replying adequately to criticism until he had an opportunity to publish *The World*. He could therefore acknowledge the weakness of the published version of his theories and, at the same time, claim that he had a much stronger but as yet unpublished defence available.

A Network of Beliefs

Huygens was among those who continued to ask Descartes to release *The World* from the embargo under which it lay concealed. Descartes replied (5 October 1637) that 'I have hidden my *World* a long distance from here'

(i. 645) in order to avoid the temptation to complete and publish it. Huygens' disappointment was obvious. He wrote again in November, requesting that Descartes publish his other writings because they were destined to 'cleanse the world of a universal flood of errors and ignorance' (i. 462). However, this request was no more successful than Mersenne's of the previous year. The author's determination to keep *The World* secret was confirmed when Descartes told Pollot, in 1638, that the original reasons for suppressing publication 'seemed to get stronger from one day to the next' (i. 518). If he had to choose, he would prefer that people blame him for his silence rather than for the alleged unorthodoxy of what he had written. Nonetheless, while he continued to resist requests to publish *The World*, Descartes frequently appealed to the unpublished text to support replies to objections to his *Essays*. This cannot have been a satisfactory response for his critics, who were told in effect that he had stronger arguments to support his assumptions than they had seen but that they could not read them.

This studied appeal to general principles that had been outlined in *The World* took the form of claiming, as Descartes had already intimated in the *Discourse*, that all the apparently disparate elements of his natural philosophy fitted together into a coherent whole. Consequently, his conclusions could not be examined piecemeal, independently of the fundamental, unpublished insights on which they depended. For example, he wrote to Mersenne (January 1638): 'I would be very pleased if those who wished to raise objections took their time and if they tried to understand everything that I wrote before judging one part of it, because the whole fits together and the conclusion serves to prove the beginning' (i. 484–5). He provided a longer version of the same argument for Father Vatier:

As regards light, if you consult page three of the *Dioptrics*, you will see that I said there explicitly that I would speak about it only hypothetically. In fact, the treatise that contains the whole body of my physics carries the name *On Light*, in which I explain light more fully and in greater depth than anything else. Therefore I did not wish to repeat the same things elsewhere. . . . my thoughts are so interconnected that I dare to hope that my principles – once people have studied them enough to become familiar with them and to consider them all together – will be found to be as well proved by the consequences that are drawn from them as the waxing and waning of the moon proves that its light is borrowed.   (i. 563, 564)

There is an obvious sleight of hand involved here. It is true that Descartes had used *On Light* as an alternative title for the first part of *The World*, and that he had outlined his theory of light in more detail there than in the *Dioptrics*. However, it is equally clear that *The World* itself had also been drafted as a hypothetical enterprise, and that the style of argument used to support its theory of light was exactly the same as that being questioned by critics of the *Essays*. The appeal to something in *The World* that his readers could not check – not even his most trusted friends, such as Huygens – merely camouflaged the fact that Descartes could not provide the kind of confirmation of his theories that he describes in the letter to Vatier as '*a priori*' (i. 563).

This raises a question about what Descartes thought he had achieved by linking all his thoughts together into a coherent network of beliefs. There was no suggestion that any of his scientific opinions about specific items – such as the circulation of the blood, the explanation of why the heart beats regularly, the nature of light, and the explanation of colour perception – could be deduced in some rigorous way from axioms. Nor did he claim that beliefs about the material world are intrinsically uncertain and require a metaphysical foundation. Descartes did mention, when writing to Vatier about proving God's existence, 'the uncertainty of all the knowledge we have of material things' (i. 560). However, this was not an endorsement of a general scepticism about empirical beliefs. Descartes supported claims about all the scientific items that he discussed during this period by reference to experiments and observations. For example, in one of his letters to Plemp (15 February 1638), he not only describes an earlier vivisection on a rabbit's heart but also says that he repeated the experiment as he was writing the letter (i. 526).[14] The problem that emerged here was one that had been recognized for centuries, and Descartes was trying to evade it by appeals to the coherence of his belief system. It arose from the indirectness with which theories are confirmed by the evidence that is used to support them.

A Theory of Confirmation

There is a form of argument that is so obviously invalid that it had its own proper name for centuries before Descartes.[15] The mistake can best be seen from an example. An amateur sleuth might argue as follows, on finding the body of an apparent murder victim called Murphy. 'If Murphy had been killed by Estragon, then Murphy would be dead. Murphy is certainly dead, since I just found his dead body. Therefore, Estragon killed him.'

Evidently, the conclusion does not follow. Murphy would be equally dead had someone else killed him, had he died of natural causes, had he died by accident, and so on. Descartes was unavoidably entangled in the structure of this type of argument, and he was consciously trying to avoid the sleuth's misguided logic. In the case of each natural phenomenon that he claimed to explain, he began with a description of the observed effects (comparable to observing that Murphy is dead), and then tried to imagine an appropriate cause that may have given rise to the effect. However, he knew, as every student of philosophy knew in the seventeenth century, that he could not argue from an observed effect to the truth of a hypothetical cause without being exposed to a notorious fallacy.

One of the first readers to submit objections to Descartes was Libert Froidmont (1587–1653), also known as Fromondus. Froidmont was a professor at Louvain who had written a commentary on Saint Paul's epistles and a book on meteorology published in 1627.[16] Froidmont had also published an anti-Copernican book called *Anti-Aristarchus* in 1631, with a 'privilege' from Philip IV of Spain. Thus from the perspective of those in the United Provinces, including Descartes, this was a publication from enemy territory by a vociferous defender of the church's stand against Galileo.[17] It did not augur well for a meeting of minds between Froidmont and Descartes. However, when Plemp received three copies of Descartes' book, he passed on copies to Father Fournet and to Froidmont (who had earlier been his professor of natural philosophy at Louvain), and kept the third copy for himself.[18] Plemp acted as an intermediary in the ensuing correspondence between Descartes and Froidmont, almost apologizing for Froidmont's replies because of the fundamental philosophical differences that emerged. When he was forwarding his colleague's objections, he acknowledged that the professors in Louvain philosophized in a different (traditional) style, and that this did not necessarily imply that Descartes was mistaken. 'We think differently, because when we were new pots we were filled with a different smell, which we have retained' (i. 400).

The Louvain professor was fundamentally shocked by the Cartesian attempt to explain the operations of what he called 'the sensitive soul' (i. 403). In the case of animals, Descartes had suggested that their hearing, seeing, and their ability to move about could all be explained by a single factor, the heat of their blood. Froidmont could not see how such 'noble actions' could result from such an 'ignoble and brute cause', and he wished to retain the 'intentional species' that scholastics imagined as mediating between observers and objects of perception.[19] More seriously, he raised the concern that Descartes' philosophy might be a first step toward the position endorsed by 'atheists', who substitute a purely material soul even for the operations that should be attributed to a rational soul. Having listed many worrying features of Descartes' philosophy, which had connotations of what he described as the 'heretical' views of Calvinists, Froidmont concluded his letter as follows: 'what I like most about him is that he is a Catholic and that he may hope, after this short life, to enjoy an eternal life with us [Catholics] . . . which is something we cannot say about Reneri' (i. 408).

Descartes tried to answer these objections without explicitly disagreeing with scholastic philosophy.[20] He offered a combative defence of his distinction between the rational souls of human beings and the kind of explanation that would be more appropriate for animal sensations. He even quoted various texts from the Old Testament that, he claimed, corroborated his identification of the blood of an animal with its 'soul'. He concluded, with an obvious reference to Froidmont's use of Scripture against Galileo: 'These passages [i.e., those quoted from Scripture by Descartes] seem much clearer to me than those that are cited against certain other opinions, which some people condemn simply because they contradict Holy Scripture, or seem to contradict it' (i. 415).[21]

Apart from the concern about making souls redundant, in animals or in human beings, Froidmont took exception to a number of Descartes' detailed explanations of natural phenomena, especially to the hypothetical character of such explanations. In reply, Descartes expressed surprise at any criticism of the one feature of his work of which he was most proud: 'I use a style of philosophizing in which all reasoning is mathematical and evident, and in which the conclusions are confirmed by true experiences' (i. 421). He then spelled that out in more detail. Froidmont should reflect, he thought, on what Descartes said in Part VI of the *Discourse*, concerning the assumptions used at the beginning of his scientific essays and the ways in which they are confirmed by all the observed phenomena that they are used to explain. If he wished, Froidmont could even transform the Cartesian presentation into a series of syllogisms that would correspond to the style of argument that he preferred. They would then read as follows:

If water is more fluid and freezes less easily than oil, *that is a sign* that the latter is composed of parts that adhere to each other more easily, similar to the branches of trees, while the former is composed of parts that are more lubricated, similar to those that have the shape of eels. However, experience shows that water is more fluid and that it freezes less easily than oil. Therefore, . . .   (i. 422–3)

Descartes leaves the final sentence dangling with an incomplete 'therefore', and then gives three similar incomplete syllogisms. He concludes that, although each syllogism when considered separately provides only a probable conviction, 'all of them taken together provide a demonstration' (i. 423). The logical difficulties in dispute between the two philosophers are camouflaged by the phrase 'that is a sign', because it allows Descartes to reverse the two parts of the first sentence (which he hopes his scholastic critic will accept as a major premise), and to recast his argument in a valid form. However, once the sentence is rewritten without ambiguity, it is clear that he is arguing as follows: '*If* water were composed of fluid particles like eels, etc., *then* water would freeze more easily than oil. Water does freeze more easily than oil. Therefore, . . . ' As Descartes knew very well, nothing follows from *that* syllogism about the truth of the first assumption. It suffers from the same logical defect that emerged earlier with the amateur sleuth.

This problem was made explicit by Jean-Baptiste Morin, a professor of mathematics at the Collège de France. Morin wrote a very friendly but detailed critique of the Cartesian theory of light, in February 1638. He quoted extensively from various parts of Descartes' text which had suggested that light is a movement, a mere tendency to move, or an 'action' that tends to cause motion, and that this tendency affects a subtle matter that is said to fill up all the apparently empty places between larger particles of matter, including the spaces between particles of translucent bodies.[22] Morin also aligned himself with Descartes as an anti-establishment scientist, by reminding him of his own [Morin's] earlier failure to persuade a royal commission that he had solved the problem of how to calculate longitudes at sea by relying on lunar observations. Having praised the excellence of Descartes' work in mathematics, he contrasted it with his work in physics, where he should not be surprised to have critics because he had withheld knowledge of 'the principles and universal notions of your new physics, the publication of which is passionately desired by all the learned' (i. 537).[23] With these preliminary expressions of admiration and caution in place, Morin identified the central issue about the logic of confirmation:

You know very well that the appearance of celestial movements results equally certainly from the assumption that the earth is at rest as from the assumption that it is in motion. Therefore, the experience of this appearance is not sufficient to prove which of these two causes just mentioned is the true cause. . . . There is nothing easier than to adjust some cause to a given effect, and you know that this is familiar to astronomers, who by means of different hypotheses, of circles and ellipses, come to the same conclusion. The same thing is very well known in your *Geometry*. However, in order to prove that the cause of an effect is the true and unique cause, it is necessary to prove at least that such an effect could not be produced by any other cause.   (i. 538, 539)

Morin also raised queries about many details of the Cartesian theory of light, and even about the fundamental model of light that underpinned the *Dioptrics*. In the passage just quoted, however, he was focusing primarily on the logic of confirmation. Even if Descartes' hypotheses were readily intelligible, and even if one could construct a plausible account of how they cause the various optical phenomena that they are supposed to explain, it remained an open question whether this theory was correct or whether some alternative hypothesis might work equally well.

Descartes took almost five months to prepare a lengthy reply to this challenge. He may have delayed sending his response because he had planned to avail of Morin's permission to publish his objections, together with the replies, without showing them to their author.[24] Once that plan was abandoned, he sent detailed, sequentially numbered replies to each of Morin's objections. Descartes had to accept the general point, that the observed phenomena about light could have been explained as easily by an alternative theory. 'If light can be imagined in some other way by which one can explain all of its properties that are known by experience, one will see that everything that I have demonstrated about refractions, vision, etc. can be deduced from it as well as from the way that I proposed' (ii. 197). Likewise, he could hardly have disagreed that it is always easy to imagine a specific cause that is tailor-made to explain a given effect. 'There are truly many effects to which it is easy to adjust different causes' (ii. 199). Having conceded this much, however, he went on to defend both the logic of his scientific method and all the particular explanations that Morin had challenged.

There was no way to avoid the appearance of circularity – and there is still none, more than three centuries later – that is involved in making an observation (for example, observing the colours of the rainbow), imagining some cause that could explain this phenomenon, and then using the observed evidence to confirm the hypothetical explanation. Descartes explains why this is merely an appearance of circularity by distinguishing between *proving* and *explaining*.

> You also say that 'to prove effects by a cause, and then to prove this cause by the same effects, is a logical circle'. I hold the same. However, I do not accept, for that reason, that it is a logical circle to explain effects by a cause and then to prove the cause by the effects, because there is a big difference between 'to prove' and 'to explain'. I add that it is possible to use the word 'demonstrate' to mean one or the other, at least if one understands it according to common usage and not with the special meaning that philosophers give it.   (ii. 197–8)

In a word, there is no vicious circle involved because the relations between hypothetical causes and observed effects are more complicated than they initially appear. The effects are known by observation or experience, and the fact that we know these is used *to confirm* the hypothetical cause that we invent or construct. Once the cause is in place, there is no suggestion that it is used to confirm the truth of the effects. That would certainly be circular. The hypothetical cause *explains* the effect.

Avoiding circularity was the easier of the two problems identified by Morin. The real challenge was to avoid committing a fallacy by claiming that the success of a given explanation confirms the truth of its assumptions. Here Descartes appealed to the fact that he explained so many effects with so few causes that the very simplicity of his theory helped to confirm it. 'It is not always as easy to adjust one single cause to many different effects unless it is the true cause from which they result' (ii. 199).

The other line of defence was to compare the mechanical models on which Descartes relied to the vast profusion of special entities invented by traditional philosophy.

> If one compares the assumptions of other philosophers with mine – that is, all their 'real qualities', their 'substantial forms', their 'elements' and similar things, the number of which is almost infinite – with this one assumption, that all bodies are composed of various parts (something that can be observed with the naked eye in some cases and can be proved by an infinity of arguments in the others) . . . and if one compares what I have deduced from my assumptions concerning vision, salt, the winds, the clouds, snow, thunder, the rainbow, and similar things, with what others have derived from theirs about the same phenomena, I hope that this will be enough to persuade those who are not too prejudiced that the effects that I explain have no other causes apart from those from which I deduced them.   (ii. 200)

This is an honest attempt to salvage the logic of confirmation from the potentially lethal objection that it is fundamentally fallacious. The appeal to a range of factors – the intelligibility of what he assumed, the small number of hypotheses used, and the fact that the same assumptions explain a wide range of apparently disparate phenomena (rather than having a new hypothesis for each thing that needs to be explained) – was the only recourse available in the seventeenth century in defence of scientific method.[25]

Mersenne raised the same kind of general problem about confirmation, and he was rewarded with a summary of all the strategies already offered to Morin. Descartes' reply is worth quoting at length:

> You ask if I claim that what I wrote about refraction is a demonstration. I think it is, at least insofar as it is possible to provide a demonstration in this subject without having first demonstrated the principles of physics by metaphysics (something that I hope to do some day . . .), and insofar as any other question in mechanics, or optics, or astronomy, or another subject which is not purely geometrical or arithmetical, has ever been demonstrated. However, to ask me to provide geometrical demonstrations in a subject that depends on physics, is to ask me to do the impossible. . . . It is sufficient, in subjects such as these, if the authors presuppose certain things that are not manifestly contrary to experience, and if they reason coherently and without making logical mistakes, even if their assumptions were not strictly true. Now what I claim to have demonstrated concerning refraction does not depend on the truth about the nature of light . . . but only on the assumption that it is an action or a power that obeys the same laws as local motion. . . . As for those who are content to say that they do not believe what I wrote, because I do not deduce it from certain assumptions that I did not prove, they do not know what they are asking for, nor what they ought to ask for.   (ii. 140–4)

Descartes clearly distinguishes here between the kind of demonstration or proof that is appropriate to mathematics and the kind that it is possible to realize in physics.[26] Once that point is conceded, however, there is little effort made to explain the degree of certainty that can be expected in optics or meteorology. Evidently, Descartes wanted to claim as much certainty as possible for the results of his work, and to challenge critics to explain what alternative methods they might use.

Morin and Mersenne both raised two types of objection, one of which was the general question just mentioned about the logic of confirmation. The other type of objection involved detailed reservations about specific explanations. Morin accepted that it would have been impossible for Descartes to give an adequate explanation of any optical phenomenon as long as he refused to disclose the fundamental theory of light on which it depended.[27] However, he also wished to persuade Descartes that he should consider using scholastic distinctions to resolve some difficulties, such as distinguishing between 'act' and 'potency' and thus recognizing that light is a 'faculty' by which the Sun illuminates (ii. 296). This type of resolution was fundamentally inconsistent with the Cartesian project. Descartes replied that the substantial form of the Sun, insofar as it is distinct from the qualities that are found in its matter, is 'a philosophical entity that is unknown to me.'[28] Thus there were radical differences in the type of entity that they were willing to include as contributing to an explanation. Accordingly, Descartes resisted all the objections raised by Morin, although their conversation was always polite and cordial, and he eventually acknowledged to Mersenne that Morin's views were 'further from mine than they were at the beginning, so that we will never agree.'[29]

This might lead one to hope that, when discussing objections to Cartesian mathematics rather than physics, it would have been easier both to identify the reasons why his critics objected and to resolve the resulting disagreements. The evidence of his long-running disputes with Fermat, Roberval, and Pascal shows the extent to which logic and mathematical skill were relatively marginal considerations in those disputes also.

Pierre Fermat and the French Mathematicians

Like Descartes, Pierre Fermat (1601–1665) was effectively a self-taught amateur in mathematics. He had become familiar with the analytical methods developed by François Viète (1540–1603) during a period spent in Bordeaux, and had then embarked officially on a legal career, in 1632, in the Toulouse parliament. With such apparently unpromising educational resources, Fermat thought of linking indeterminate algebraic equations in two unknowns with two-dimensional geometric curves, an idea that Descartes seems to have stumbled on some years earlier. Despite their subsequent fame, neither Fermat nor Descartes had ever heard of each other during the years prior to publication of the *Essays*. Fermat was working in a remote corner of the kingdom of France, while Descartes was hiding in an even more remote corner of Holland. The contact point between the two mathematicians was their common friends in Paris. Fermat sent the manuscript of his *Introduction to Plane and Solid Loci* to his mathematician friends in Paris, including Roberval and

Étienne Pascal, while Descartes sent the manuscript of the *Essays* to Mersenne.

Before the unlikely coincidence of two mathematicians independently developing analytical methods inspired by Viète, Descartes had already criticized both Beaugrand and Roberval. When Beaugrand claimed that Descartes had plagiarized some of his results from Viète, the author of the *Géometrie* commented very negatively on Beaugrand's *Geostatics*. Gilles Personne de Roberval (1602–1675) was an outstanding mathematician, six years younger than Descartes, who had been appointed to the Ramus Chair of Mathematics at the Collège Royal in 1634. The chair was filled by open competition, and the successful appointee had to re-enter the competition every three years in order to maintain his post. Roberval managed to do this for thirty-four years, until he died in 1675; however, he could maintain his advantage over the other competitors only by not publishing his results and reserving them for the triennial competition. During the first competition for appointment in 1634, when candidates were set various questions to resolve, Descartes commented acidly that he should have been asked 'a more difficult question, to see if he could resolve it – such as, for example, the Pappus problem that I was given three years ago by Mr. Golius' (i. 288). It is obvious that Descartes thought of Roberval as an inferior mathematician, and he seems to have been jealous of the high respect in which their common correspondent, Mersenne, held him.[30]

The first contact between Descartes and Fermat occurred when Beaugrand received the text of Descartes' *Essays* in his capacity as secretary to the French chancellor. He passed on a copy of the *Dioptrics* to his friend Fermat, and invited him to comment. Fermat penned his comments in April or May 1637.[31] It is clear from the style of this first letter to Descartes that Fermat did not know the author of the *Dioptrics*, that he was unaware of earlier animosities between Descartes and Roberval or Beaugrand, and that he was stumbling into a potentially explosive situation based on a very brief perusal of a book that was destined to become famous.[32] The initial correspondence between the two mathematicians was also compromised because the *Dioptrics* had been released without authorization by Beaugrand, before its official publication, and because Fermat implied that Descartes was 'groping about...in the shadows' in search of the truth, a procedure that he had explicitly disavowed in the unpublished *Rules*.[33]

Mersenne seems to have been embarrassed by the lapse of confidentiality involved in this misunderstanding, and he delayed until the following September before forwarding the uncomplimentary comments to Descartes. Fermat disputed Descartes' assumption that a 'tendency to move' obeys the same laws as a body that actually moves, 'because there is as much difference between them as between potency and act' (i. 357). More seriously, he questioned the geometrical analysis proposed in the *Dioptrics* to support the laws of reflection and refraction, and he argued that Descartes' analysis (into two components at right angles) of what he called the 'determination' of a ray of light presupposed the conclusion that he was attempting to demonstrate. He summarized his objections with the comment: 'as far as I am concerned, I could not accept his reasoning as a legitimate proof and demonstration' (i. 358).

This unsolicited and obviously unwelcome intervention sparked a controversy that continued to resonate long after Descartes' death. Descartes seems to have been as uninformed about Fermat as the Toulouse counsellor was about him. Thus, without knowing the identity of his critic, Descartes replied reasonably calmly in his first letter (5 October 1637) and asked Mersenne to forward his response to the critic identified simply as 'one of your friends' (i. 450). Already, however, he antagonized Fermat by accusing him of culpably misunderstanding what he read. Where Descartes had written: 'it would be easy to believe that the tendency to move should follow the same laws as movement,' the 'Toulouse counsellor' had taken that to mean that it was probable – a reasonable interpretation, one might have thought. The pedantic response from 'north Holland' must have sounded like a cranky teacher rebuking a careless student. 'I classify as almost false everything that is merely probable. And when I say that something is easy to believe, I do not mean to say that it is merely probable, but that it is so clear and distinct that there is no need for me to take time to demonstrate it' (i. 451). How was Fermat supposed to know that?

The tone of the dispute became more acrimonious with each new letter. This progression seems to have been facilitated by Mersenne, when he shared confidential letters that he had been asked to reserve while failing, at the same time, to forward letters in a timely manner. It thus seemed to each somewhat sensitive mathematician that he was being snubbed by the silence or delayed response of the other correspondent.[34] When Mersenne sent Descartes a short mathematical text in Latin written by Fermat, which discussed tangents to curves, Descartes did not realize that it had been written about eight years previously and that it was therefore not representative of Fermat's most recent work.[35] Descartes replied: 'I would be happy to say nothing about the text that you sent me, because I could not say anything about it that would be favourable to whoever wrote it' (i. 486).[36] The controversy was exacerbated when two of Fermat's supporters in Paris, Étienne Pascal and Roberval, joined the fray in support of the Toulouse parliamentarian. Étienne Pascal (1588–1651), the father of the more famous Blaise (with whom Descartes would also cross swords later), had sold his tax-collecting office at Rouen in 1634 and moved to Paris, where he was associated temporarily with the Mersenne circle. Descartes assumed – mistakenly, it seems – that these two 'defenders' of Fermat had joined the discussion as uncritical friends of his opponent and that their opinions were thus compromised.[37] He puffed, at a great distance from local events in Paris and without knowing the situation: 'I despise those who get involved in slandering my *Geometry* without understanding it' (ii. 13).

While Descartes described the dispute in terms of a combat and demoted Roberval and Pascal to Fermat's 'seconds' in the protracted duel, he simultaneously excused himself from being responsible for the animosity between them.[38] 'If there is any special animosity between him [Fermat] and me, as they [Roberval and Pascal] claim, it is entirely on his side. For, from my point of view, I have no basis to complain against those who wish to challenge me in a combat in which one can often be vanquished without infamy' (ii. 12). Descartes even suspected his opponents of making minor but important changes in the disputed texts, and advised his own supporters to protect against this by holding onto the original manuscripts and giving only copies to critics.[39] This distrust is matched by the uniformly sharp and uncomplimentary comments he made about all those who disagreed with him throughout the dispute. He thought that Beaugrand's *Geostatics* was 'so impertinent, ridiculous and despicable that I am surprised that any honest person has ever taken the trouble to read it'.[40] He described the Calvinist ministers in the United Provinces as 'mute like fish' in response to his book, and he claimed that Martinus Hortensius (1605–1639) was 'not only very ignorant, but was a very black and malicious soul' who feigned friendship with Descartes while simultaneously slandering him in secret.[41] Roberval did little to calm the controversy by writing that Descartes had evidently failed to understand Fermat's method. According

to Professor Roberval, Descartes 'made absurd objections against it in his
first writing, to which we replied in keeping with our understanding of the
same method, [and] he replied in such a way that he got entangled in other
objections which are as absurd or more so than the first ones' (ii. 104).
When Roberval sent a discussion of the cycloid to Mersenne, Descartes
in turn scoffed at the significance of the discovery. 'I do not see that he
has any reason to boast so much about finding something that is so simple
that anyone who knows the least amount of geometry could not fail to find
it simply by looking for it' (ii.135).

There was no sign of a resolution of these mathematical disputes in 1638.
In fact, Descartes seems to have been preparing himself for a lengthy duel
by itemizing, in a letter to Mydorge (1 March 1638), all the letters and writings
exchanged by both sides.[42] There were promising signs of a thaw and
of a suppressed magnanimity on Descartes' part, when he discovered that
Fermat had not received his earlier replies (because, as usual, Mersenne
had failed to forward them), and that the Toulouse mathematician had
been offended by the vigour of Descartes' reply.

As regard the fact that he [Fermat] says he found sharper words in my first reply than
he would have expected, I ask him very humbly to forgive me and to believe that I did
not know him. His *De maximis* arrived as a challenge from someone who had already
tried to refute my *Dioptrics* even before it was published – as if to choke it before its
birth – by getting a copy of it that I had not sent to France for that purpose. . . . Those
who disguise themselves at the carnival are not offended if people laugh at the mask
they wear and if they do not salute them when they pass them on the street, as
they would if they were dressed in their normal clothes. Likewise, it seems to me,
one should not object if I replied to his writing completely differently than I would
have replied to him in person, as someone whom I esteem and honour as his merit
requires.   (ii. 175)

This apparent change of mind merely illustrates the frequent oscillations
in Descartes' attitude to Fermat. In the same letter as that just quoted, he
suggested that Fermat's actions confirmed completely what he [Descartes]
had suspected from the beginning, 'that Fermat and those in Paris had
conspired together to try to discredit my writings as much as possible'
(ii. 193).

The following month Descartes wrote to Fermat in phrases that seemed
once again to augur a cessation of hostilities.

I was no less happy to receive the letter in which you do me the favour of promising me
your friendship than if it had come from a mistress whose favours I had passionately

desired. Your other writings which preceded it reminded me of the Bradamente of our poets, who was unwilling to accept anyone as a servant unless they had previously been tested against them in a duel. . . . I assure you that I have great respect for your merit, and when I look at the most recent way in which you find tangents to curved lines, I have nothing else to reply except that it is very good. If you had explained it in this way at the beginning, I would not have contradicted it at all.   (ii. 281)

This apparent reconciliation was unfortunately short-lived. One month later (23 August 1638), Descartes writes to Mersenne about Fermat's continued objections. He says he is slow to displease him, given the compliments that had been exchanged. However, 'the enthusiasm with which he continues to claim victory for his method and to persuade people that I did not understand it . . . forces me to express some truths here that seem to me will not be to his advantage' (ii. 320). But by 11 October, he writes sympathetically to Fermat to inform him 'frankly that I have never met anyone who showed me that he knew as much as you do in Geometry' (ii. 406), and that the residual items of dispute were comparable to 'small imperfections in diamonds, in contrast with great blemishes in ordinary stones' (ii. 408).[43]

During this dispute with critics in France who were often vaguely identified, Descartes seems to have reserved his harshest comments for Pierre Petit (1598–1677). Petit had circulated objections to the *Discourse* and the *Dioptrics* beginning in March 1638. Descartes thought he was a charlatan, that there were as many 'impertinences and mistakes as there are lines in his writing,' and that if he lived in a country where the Inquisition was active, he would have reason 'to fear the flames' (ii. 266). By April 1639, he was punning on his name (Mr. Little) by describing him as a little barking dog. 'I think you pay too much attention to Mr. Petit by contradicting him. One should allow little dogs to bark without bothering to resist them' (ii. 533).[44] His estimation of the mathematical talents of Roberval and Fermat was almost as negative. He thought Roberval was as vain 'as a woman who puts a ribbon in her hair in order to appear more beautiful' (ii. 274). He asked Mersenne not to bother him any further with Fermat's letters. 'I am completely disgusted with his discussion, and I find nothing reasonable in anything he says' (ii. 274–5). By August of 1638, Descartes writes in confidence to Huygens – there was no risk here, as with Mersenne, that his comments would be reported back to their targets – to tell him that he had done no significant work during the whole summer. There were 'certain people who dabbled in geometry' and who, without understanding

Cartesian mathematics, were doing their best to discredit it. Given their limited ability, their objections did not make him work hard. However, they did enough to distract him 'in the same way that two or three flies, flying around the face of a man who tries to relax by lying in the shade of a wood, are often able to prevent him from doing so' (ii. 671).

In retrospect, the row between Fermat and Descartes was sustained by misunderstandings on both sides, by the extreme sensitivity of Descartes to any criticism of his *Geometry*, and by a difference in temperament that made it difficult for either of them to sympathize with the other. Fermat was primarily a mathematician rather than a physicist, and his initial reaction to Descartes' *Dioptrics* shows that he suspected its author of constructing an a priori proof of the sine law of refraction. He was unaware of the background principles on which Descartes based his work, because they were available only in the unpublished *World*, and his own natural tendency was toward an empiricist approach to optics.[45] Since Fermat was unwilling to have his mathematical results published, he is probably best understood as a relatively innocent and reluctant critic of an extremely defensive opponent who thought of his reputation as depending on the originality of the analytic methods that he had independently developed in the *Geometry*.

The lack of resolution in the dispute with the French mathematicians contrasts with the pragmatism and diplomacy involved in resolving another mathematical row between supporters and critics of Descartes in the United Provinces. Johan Stampioen (the younger) was highly respected as a mathematician by his contemporaries. He taught mathematics at a 'higher school' in Rotterdam, and he issued a number of public challenges, on placards, in 1638 to Dutch engineers to calculate the most effective angles for shooting canon shells at a fortress wall. He then published a book, dedicated to Prince Frederik Hendrik, in which he claimed to provide the only solution to such problems.[46]

These claims were challenged by Jacob van Waessenaer, who not only offered an alternative solution for extracting cube roots, using Descartes' mathematics, but also claimed that there were 'gross errors' in Stampioen's book. In defence of his honour and reputation, Stampioen challenged his critic to support his claims by a wager. This challenge was accepted, and both disputants lodged six hundred guilders with an impartial referee and agreed on a three-person jury of mathematical experts to decide the question.[47] Stampioen argued in favour of a one-person jury, claiming that the nature of mathematics was such that everyone should agree with the judgment of any competent referee. However, this view was undermined by his efforts to nominate a mathematician who would support his side in the dispute. Descartes argued, on behalf of Waessenaer, that since Stampioen and Waessenaer disagreed, it was just as likely that others would fail to agree also. He asked: 'why should he fear accepting the judgment of a plurality of votes, if he hopes to find that they will all agree with him?' (ii. 698). The money was lodged with the rector of the University, and judgment was given in May 1640 – in favour of the Cartesian side.[48]

Supporters in Utrecht

During what seemed like an interminable and insoluble row with the French mathematicians, Descartes lost one of his best friends, and acquired a new convert to Cartesian philosophy at Utrecht. The convert was Henricus Regius (1598–1679). He was born in Utrecht, and first came to know about Descartes through lectures by Reneri. He began to provide lessons privately to other students and thus came to be appointed to the Extraordinary Chair of Theoretical Medicine at Utrecht on 21 July 1638.[49] Regius wrote immediately to Descartes, to explain that his academic success was due to the influence of Cartesian ideas on his education. Since Reneri frequently visited Descartes in his seclusion in the province of Holland – he must have been one of the few people who knew where he lived at that time – it was agreed that Regius would visit Descartes, accompanied by Reneri, and that he would be introduced personally to the philosopher who was allegedly responsible for his academic success. Reneri did visit Descartes on 19 August 1638, and was able to tell him the height of the Dom tower at Utrecht.[50] This visit coincided with the worst period of controversy with the French mathematicians, during which Descartes borrowed the words of Saint Paul to express his feelings of rejection. 'At the end of the day, if the French are too unjust to me, *I shall turn to the Gentiles*' (ii. 334). In this context, he consoled himself by reflecting on the fact that his philosophical efforts were appreciated at least in Utrecht.

I am determined to have my Latin translation of this material published soon, and I tell you that I received this very week some letters from a Doctor whom I had never known or seen, and who nevertheless thanked me very warmly for having made him become a professor in a university in which I have neither friends nor influence. But

I hear that, having privately taught some of what I had published to some students there, they liked it so much that they all asked the magistrate to appoint him their professor.   (ii. 334)

Descartes was obviously contrasting the spontaneous welcome his theories had received in Utrecht with the stubborn resistance of critical mathematicians in France. However, the rhetoric of the contrast camouflages an obvious dissimulation. He knew that Regius had learned what he knew about Descartes from one of his most ardent and loyal supporters, Reneri, and Utrecht was not therefore 'a university in which I have neither friends nor influence'.[51]

Despite the plans for frequent visits to Descartes and an introduction of the new recruit to Cartesianism, Reneri seems to have been sick throughout most of the following winter and was unable to take up Descartes' invitation. Regius thus wrote to him in February 1639, thanking him for his invitation the previous year and accepting a new offer to visit on his own because of Reneri's continued indisposition.[52] Unfortunately, this revised plan was frustrated by Reneri's death the following month. Regius wrote again, on 29 March 1639, informing Descartes that his friend had died and that the funeral oration, pronounced by Antonius Aemilius, professor of rhetoric and history, had been in praise of Descartes as much as of the recently deceased Reneri.[53] Regius' own plans for visiting Descartes in September of the same year were cancelled because his wife was more than eight months pregnant and expected her husband to remain at home in Utrecht.[54]

Descartes confirmed the extent of his support at Utrecht when he was asked by Debeaune for advice (in the autumn of 1638) about where he should send his son to study. Having first mentioned La Flèche as the best place in France, Descartes evaluated the merits of various Dutch universities. His earlier experience at Leiden led him to believe that the food and accommodation were good but that the teaching was poor. In contrast, he thought that Utrecht University would be much better. It had been built 'only four or five years ago';[55] therefore 'it had not yet had time to get corrupted, and there is a professor there, Mr Reneri, who is my intimate friend and, in my judgment, is better than all those at Leiden' (ii. 379).[56]

Apart from dedicated supporters in Utrecht, however, some other early readers of the *Essays* wrote supportive letters. It is difficult to gauge how representative of a wider readership these comments may have been. The publisher sold relatively few copies during the first two years, which made it unlikely that it would be reissued soon afterward.[57]

A Reclusive Life

Descartes' life during the period 1637–39 was dominated by research and letter writing. Between May 1637 and December 1639, he wrote approximately two hundred pages of detailed letters in reply to the French mathematicians. Apart from this work, he wrote almost weekly letters in reply to an extraordinary array of disparate queries from Mersenne. Each letter from Mersenne typically asked for explanations of a long list of itemized phenomena that ranged from the limited efficiency of water pumps to optical phenomena and musical theory. Descartes then took these letters, sometimes more than one at a time, and answered the queries in order, using the same numbering system for his replies as Mersenne had used for his questions. Evidently, he could not give as much time to each query as it may have deserved, although he tried valiantly to reply to all queries by writing even on Christmas Day of 1639, when he offered this general excuse for his replies. 'Having sometimes to reply to you concerning twenty or thirty different things in one evening, it is impossible for me to give a lot of thought to each one' (ii. 634). In addition to such extensive correspondence, he continued to conduct anatomical experiments, including vivisections. 'This is an exercise that I have often performed during the past eleven years and I think there is hardly any physician who has made such detailed observations as I have.'[58]

One might expect that Descartes spent much of his time reading while in seclusion in Holland. However, he claims to have had only about 'half a dozen books' in his house, and he was too busy to take the time required to read most of those that were sent by various correspondents.[59] Among the authors that he declined to read or, despite their merits, could not find time to read were Campanella, Beaugrand, Galileo, Roberval, Stevin, Hortensius, Herbert, and Bouillau.[60] When the controversy with the French mathematicians showed no signs of abating, he tried to cut it short by denying that he had any further interest in geometry. In fact, he claimed to have given up studying geometry as early as 1623. 'You know that it is already fifteen years since I professed to give up geometry' (ii. 95).[61] This means that his original work in that discipline, especially his contribution to the Pappus problem, had been completed many years earlier. Despite these protestations, however, he continued to write what amounted to hundreds of pages of mathematics in defence of his *Geometry*.

Descartes was forty-two years old in 1638, and for the first time he began to refer to his age, his health, and his limited life expectancy. Forty-two was hardly old age in the seventeenth century. Some of Descartes' contemporaries lived much longer, although many others succumbed to the plague or other illnesses at an even earlier age. When Susanna Huygens died during the summer of 1637 (at the age of thirty-eight), Descartes addressed some of his first reflections on his mortality to her widower. 'The white hairs that I am rapidly acquiring warn me that I should study nothing other than ways of delaying them. That is what I am doing now. . . . This task takes up so much time that I am resolved to concentrate on that alone.'[62] He returned to this theme two months later, when writing to Huygens again, by suggesting that he might live for a hundred years and that it would not require extraordinary interventions to realize that ambition.

I have never taken greater care of my health than I am doing at present. Whereas I used to think that death could deprive me of thirty or forty years at most, it could not surprise me now unless it took more than a century from me. I think I see clearly that if only we protect ourselves against certain mistakes that we are accustomed to make in the way we live, we could reach without further inventions a much longer and happier old age than we currently achieve. However, since I need more time and more experiences to investigate everything that is relevant to this subject, I am now working on a compendium of medicine. . . . I hope to be able to use it to obtain some delay from nature.   (i. 649)

He told Mersenne in September 1638 that he was surrounded by fevers on all sides, that everyone in his neighbourhood was affected, and that 'I am the only one in this house who has escaped' (ii. 361). The following January he gave a more complete summary of his condition and expectations, in reply to concerns about his health expressed by Mersenne and other correspondents when they had not heard from him for some time.

It is thirty years, thank God, since I had any illness that could be called an illness. And since age has taken away the heat in the liver that formerly attracted me to the army, I no longer profess anything but cowardice. Since I have learned a little about medicine, I feel well, and take as much care of myself as a rich man with gout, it seems to me that I am further from death now than I was in my youth.   (ii. 480)

These rather ambitious hopes about living long were challenged by the death of local friends and acquaintances. Reneri ('my dear friend') had died at the age of forty-six the previous year, and Martinus Hortensius (not a friend of Descartes) had died the same year at the relatively early age of thirty-four. In thinking about their deaths, Descartes was prompted to acknowledge that 'one can find death without going to war' (ii. 570). The only indication of ill health that Descartes mentions, during these years, is that he is 'almost deaf' (ii. 699).

Despite these sober reflections on mortality, Descartes seems to have been relatively content during this period of his life. He had a domestic male servant whom he usually referred to simply as 'my Limousin'. This native of Limousin was presumably the same one named as Clément Chamboir in Descartes' letter to his cousin, Marguerite Ferrand, of 24 February 1634.[63] Chamboir had returned to Paris on one of his frequent errands in spring 1638, and he seemed slower than usual in returning to Holland. Descartes asked Mersenne to intercede and to try to persuade the reluctant valet to resume his duties. However, he was not willing to wait indefinitely for a decision, and so he told Mersenne: 'I know someone else here whom I have promised to hire if the Limousin does not come by the end of April or if I do not hear that he is on the way' (ii. 96). This extra pressure had the desired effect, because the servant 'eventually arrived eight or ten days' (ii. 190) before the end of June. Descartes also had some very reliable friends who visited frequently. Gillot visited for three days (27–30 June 1638), and Reneri was a frequent visitor before August 1638. After that, he was too sick to travel the distance from Utrecht to the vicinity of Alkmaar.

During this period Descartes also seems to have lost interest in maintaining contact with his own family in Brittany. His brother, Pierre, had apparently sent him two letters, using Mersenne as an intermediary, and Descartes acknowledges that only one of them arrived, courtesy of his local publisher.[64] Descartes uses the same indirect route to reply, asking Mersenne to make sure to forward the letter before July, when his brother usually left Brittany at the close of parliamentary business.[65] He also acknowledged that he had lived so long outside France that he was ignorant about many features of French life, including ordinary usage in writing the French language.[66]

The picture that emerges from his correspondence is that of a philosopher very much out of touch with his native country and with his family, relying on a Limousin for domestic support, and visited infrequently by a few close friends and supporters with whom he shared the secret of his address. He had become a reclusive, cantankerous, and oversensitive loner, who worried incessantly about his place in history and the priority he claimed for various discoveries.[67] His famously black hair was turning grey, and he began to wear a wig. He continued this habit until his death, always sourcing his wigs in Paris, even when he was living in Sweden.[68]

One feature of his hidden life that attracted unfavourable comment was his religious practice. Claude Saumaise (1588–1653), who held a chair at Leiden beginning in 1631, had written that he was 'one of the most zealous Roman Catholics.'[69] During this period when he lived in north Holland, Descartes had two friends who were Roman Catholic priests, Jan Albert Bannius and Augustine Bloemaert, on whose behalf Descartes wrote to Huygens in October 1639. Descartes first met them because of their shared interest in music and his reputation for having written a short treatise on that topic many years earlier.[70] In writing to Huygens, Descartes acknowledges that some of his critics in France reproached him for living in 'this country, because the exercise of my religion is not tolerated there' (ii. 585), and that he did not even have the excuse that he was living abroad as a member of the French army that supported the United Provinces. However, he explains that one can be a true Catholic without 'supporting the side of the king who is called Catholic' (ii. 584), and that he could enjoy the company and friendship of some clerics in Holland, so that his conscience was free.

The tone of this letter was appropriate to that of a request addressed to the secretary to the Dutch prince. When writing to Mersenne, however, Descartes conceded that he was equally distrusted by both Catholics and Calvinists. 'The Huguenots hate me as a papist, and those of Rome do not like me because they think I am entangled in the heresy of the earth's movement' (ii. 593). His problems with Roman Catholics were not limited to his endorsement of Copernicus. Many also accused him of being a cryptic Calvinist and of attending their religious ceremonies. In November 1639, he wrote to Mersenne at great length to counter this accusation with a written version of his examination of conscience. He listed all the occasions on which he had attended a 'sermon' by anyone other than a Catholic priest. On one occasion, in the company of two friends, he had visited the site outside Leiden where, on the first Sunday of each month, many 'enthusiasts' gathered to speak in tongues and to preach the Gospel.

'Each one preaches as they wish, both men and women, according as they feel inspired, so that within one hour we heard sermons from five or six peasants or working people' (ii. 620). He also acknowledged hearing a sermon by an Anabaptist minister and, much more recently, he had attended a service of thanksgiving at The Hague at which a Calvinist minister preached.[71]

None of these comments explains whether Descartes practised his religion in the manner required, at the time, by the Council of Trent. When Descartes wrote to Huygens in support of his local priests, his letter assumed that it was not necessary to make explicit what was being requested, since the primary petitioners had already made known their request. However, the final sentence of his letter says: 'If you wish to leave a few priests here for us, I ask that it would be these rather than any others' (ii. 699). This is consistent with what is known independently of the unofficial toleration of Roman Catholics in the United Provinces at that time. Although all public religious meetings apart from those of the Calvinist Church were officially banned, other religions were tolerated as long as they were discreet. In some towns in the province of Holland, for example, the majority of the residents were Roman Catholics. They were able to attend religious ceremonies, such as the Mass, as long as they did so without public display and with the co-operation of local officials, who often needed to be bribed.

Descartes was still planning during the autumn of 1638 to publish a selection of objections and replies to his *Essays*, although he anticipated that it would take another three months' work to get all his papers in order.[72] It was initially unclear whether they would appear in French or in Latin, or in parallel editions in both languages. However, since most of the objections or, at least, most of those that he thought worth publishing had been written in Latin, he asked in July 1638 that any other outstanding objections be written in Latin too.[73] At the same time, he was encouraging Mersenne to prepare corrections of the French edition of the *Essays*, although it was evident by January 1639 that, given the poor sales of the first edition, the publisher was unlikely to reissue the book in French.[74] Despite these unfavourable omens, Descartes seems to have still been committed to his original plan, as he explained to Mersenne in the same letter in January. 'I have planned a study for the rest of this winter, which will not tolerate any distraction. For that reason I humbly ask you to allow me not to write to you again before Easter' (ii. 491–2).[75] Although he did not mention explicitly what he proposed studying on that occasion, he wrote unambiguously to Huygens at the end of the month that he had sent him more than 235 pages of objections and replies, and asked him to cast his eye over the whole lot and to suggest corrections.[76] By May, he had to send a reminder, asking for a return of the 'bundle' of objections (ii. 677), because he planned to have them published that summer. Huygens, however, was busy with preparations for the departure of the prince's army from The Hague.

By this time it seems clear that Descartes was discussing with Huygens the publication of a Latin version of the *Essays*, together with selected objections and replies. It remains unclear when work on the Latin translation began. Descartes referred to discussions of a Latin edition as early as 1637, and there is evidence that a Latin version of the *Meteors* was being circulated in early 1639.[77] For example, Descartes had sent a copy of this Latin text to a Dutch theologian, Caspar van Baerle (1584–1648), in the autumn of 1639, in the hope of provoking him into writing objections. Unfortunately, that ploy failed, and one year later he had to request that the manuscript be returned.[78] The text that eventually appeared in Latin, in 1644 from Elzevier in Amsterdam, was most likely done not by Descartes himself, but by Étienne de Courcelles, a French Huguenot who earned his living as a translator. Between 1639 and 1643, therefore, there is good reason to think that some parts of a Latin translation of the *Discourse*, the *Dioptrics*, and especially the *Meteors* were circulating among those Dutch readers who did not read French, and that Descartes was concerned that he would lose control of its publication.[79]

Huygens advised Descartes, on 15 May 1639, to publish *The World* rather than 'these objections and solutions' (ii. 679). Descartes seems to have accepted more or less immediately the second part of this advice, not to publish objections and replies to the *Essays*. Huygens left The Hague with the army on 23 May, and wrote from an army camp five days later with a new argument in favour of publishing *The World*.[80] 'You will die. After your death, this *World* will see the world' (ii. 680), and there will be no opportunity at that stage to rebut the objections and misinterpretations that will result from the 'ignorance and envy' of readers. Descartes, however, was not impressed by this new argument. He had not decided never to publish *The World* while he was alive, no more than he planned to arrange for a posthumous publication. Besides, although death might surprise him at any moment, 'I feel that my teeth are so good and so strong, thank God, that I do not think I need to fear death for more than thirty years, unless it were to surprise me' (ii. 682).

With these optimistic anticipations about his health, Descartes concluded that it would be best not to publish the objections and replies, and to defer once again any final decision about publishing *The World*. His recent studies in anatomy and medicine prompted the reflection that, had he been composing *The World* in 1639 rather than in 1630–33, he would not have avoided trying to explain the formation and birth of animals by assuming a body already fully formed.[81] Thus, almost nine years after he had begun to work systematically on a general renewal of natural philosophy, *The World* remained in the background as the key to understanding his philosophy, often requested by sympathetic readers, but destined to remain unpublished unless Rome changed its mind about Galileo.[82] Meantime, the period 1637–39 had been consumed by objections from critics to the *Essays* and by detailed and lengthy replies that would appear, posthumously, only in Descartes' correspondence. If Descartes were to realize his ambitions, he needed a new strategy that would not compromise his standing vis-à-vis Rome and would support his claim to be recognized as a distinctive voice in the already crowded competition for novel ideas in the 1640s.

Metaphysics in a Hornet's Nest (1639–1642)

There are few people who can understand metaphysics.[1]

A T the beginning of the year 1640, Descartes was still living in Sant-poort. He had given up the idea of publishing a selection of objections and replies to the *Essays*, and had been working instead for some weeks on what he described as 'An Essay on Metaphysics'. Although this was not his first incursion into metaphysics, it represented a significant departure from what he had been doing during the previous decade and a return to a project that had been deferred since 1629. In that year he had writ-ten to Father Gibieuf, a theologian and member of the Oratory in Paris, that he would hold him to his promise to correct 'a little treatise' that he hoped to complete within two or three years.[2] Descartes had evidently intended to contribute to the anti-libertine literature, in which the names of Mersenne and Garasse were so prominent, and to write about atheism and the human soul. The following year, 1630, he told Mersenne that he had worked on almost nothing apart from metaphysics for nine months after arriving in the United Provinces – adding, on that occasion, that it would not be appropriate to publish anything about metaphysics until he first saw how his projected book on physics was received.[3]

Since his 'physics' [i.e., *The World*] was never published, he had no indication from its success or otherwise of how his metaphysical specula-tions might be received when he returned to the project in 1639. During the intervening years, he had tried to avoid theological disputes as much as possible, especially after 1633. That implied avoiding metaphysics too, because he understood the term 'metaphysics' as denoting questions about the nature of the human soul and the existence of God. Although Descartes argued that one could discuss these questions without appeal to revela-tion or religious belief, it was difficult in practice to say anything about

either one without attracting unwelcome notice from theologians. There
was one exception to this self-imposed restriction – the brief summary in
Part IV of the *Discourse on Method* of his earlier work from 1630. Apart
from that, Descartes devoted all his intellectual energies in the early 1630s
to completing *The World*.

When *The World* was withdrawn and the *Essays* published as a provisional substitute, many sympathetic critics, such as Plemp and Morin,
and especially his unwavering admirers such as Huygens and Mersenne,
pleaded with him to release the hidden treasures of his physics so that
they could appreciate better the foundations of the scientific explanations
developed in the *Essays*. France was not subject to the Inquisition, and
the United Provinces were even less so. It is not clear, therefore, why
Descartes resisted these encouraging requests.[4] Claude Saumaise speculated that, had he not been such a devout Catholic, he would have published his metaphysics long before then. Saumaise may have exaggerated
Descartes' allegiance to the Catholic Church, by confusing fear of censure
with religious faith. However, whatever the reason, Descartes held firm to
his original decision, prompting Mersenne to write: 'There is no way to
get hold of his physics and metaphysics, where his foundations are.'[5]

Nonetheless, ten years after his original draft essay, Descartes returned
to metaphysics while still refusing to reveal the basic principles of physics
that remained hidden in *The World*. It was unclear how metaphysics could
provide a 'foundation' for physics or whether such foundational studies might require a number of layers, the deepest of which would be
metaphysics.[6] The occasion for the change of mind may have been his
reading of the French edition of Edward Herbert's *On Truth*.[7] When
Mersenne first sent him a copy of this book in August 1639, he was too
busy to read it, but he found time to reopen it two months later and to give
his first impressions to the donor.[8] Since Descartes notoriously read only
what interested him and politely refused to read most of the books that he
received as gifts, the mere arrival of *On Truth* cannot have been the real
reason for his renewed interest in metaphysics. His first reaction to the
book was that Herbert was discussing a subject on which he (Descartes)
claimed to have worked 'all my life' (ii. 596) – a lifelong interest that is
certainly not reflected in the frequency or detail with which metaphysics
is mentioned in his correspondence. However, he must have given some
thought to metaphysical questions before 1639, because, within a month
of its first mention, he began to refer to a draft essay that was almost

completed. The initial plan was to print twenty or thirty copies of the
draft and to circulate it privately for comments.

> The part of the mind that is most useful for mathematics, namely the imagination, is
> more of a hindrance than a help in metaphysical speculations. I now have in my hands
> a *Discourse* in which I tried to clarify what I had previously written about this subject.
> It will consist of no more than five or six sheets of print, but I hope that it will contain
> a significant part of metaphysics. In order to realize that goal better, my plan is to have
> printed only twenty or thirty copies and to send them to twenty or thirty of the most
> wise theologians that I can find, to get their opinion of it and to find out from them
> what I should change, correct, or modify in it before making it public.[9]

The extreme caution involved in this circuitous method of publishing
shows that the lessons learned in 1633 were still very much on his mind.
With advance theological support, he could protect his work from sub-
sequent criticism. Mersenne sent him comments on 4 December, and
Descartes thanked him on Christmas Day for his advice concerning the
'Essay on Metaphysics' (ii. 629).[10]

Between December 1639 and August 1641 (when the first edition of the
Meditations was printed), Descartes worked consistently on two related
features of the new project. One was to collect objections from theologians and to reply to them in writing, so that the objections and replies
could appear together in the first edition. The other was to approach the
theology faculty of the Sorbonne for an official endorsement that would
provide a guarantee of its orthodoxy. Both strategies were motivated by
the same concerns about theological disputes, especially those originating
with Jesuits, that had made him avoid this subject for so long. These legitimate concerns further reinforce the question why he decided to engage
with metaphysical questions at all.

One possible explanation is that Descartes had been thinking about a
Latin edition of the *Essays* since 1637. This was eventually published –
without the *Geometry* – in 1644 as *Specimens of Philosophy, or a Dissertation
on the Method for Guiding Reason properly and for Investigating Truth in
the Sciences*. However, there were frequent changes of plan before the final
decision to publish the *Specimens of Philosophy*. He had considered, at
one stage, including selected objections and replies in the Latin edition
but later abandoned that idea. At about the same time as that decision
was made, draft versions of the Latin text began to circulate. These drafts
included the *Meteors*, which would have been an ideal textbook in Latin for
Jesuit schools, and they probably included a Latin version of the *Discourse*

on Method. Such a Latin text – which made the *Discourse* available to Dutch theologians, many of whom did not read French – revivied the kind of objections that Part IV had provoked when it was first published. Descartes had acknowledged the inadequacy of his discussion of metaphysics in the *Discourse*, and the need for a more extended discussion.

As regards your second objection – that I have not explained sufficiently how I know that the soul is a substance that is distinct from the body and that its nature is only to think, which is the only thing that obscures the proof of God's existence – I admit that what you say is very true and also that it makes my proof of God's existence difficult to understand. However, I had no better way of dealing with this question than by explaining at length the falsehood or uncertainty that is found in all judgments that depend on the senses or the imagination, in order to show subsequently which judgments depend only on pure understanding and the extent to which they are evident and certain. I omitted this intentionally, after due consideration, mainly because I wrote in the vernacular and was afraid that, if weak minds avidly embraced the doubts and scruples that I would have had to propose, they might not be able to understand as fully the arguments by which I tried to remove them.[11]

This implies that an adequate discussion of metaphysics would have to include a comparison between the kind of certainty available in empirical studies and the apparently greater certainty available in metaphysical arguments that rely on 'pure understanding'. For Descartes, the viability of metaphysics as a distinct enterprise presupposes a discussion of related questions in theory of knowledge.

Descartes repeated another version of this argument in a letter (May 1637) to an unnamed correspondent who is assumed to have been Jean Silhon.

I agree . . . that I have not adequately presented the arguments by which I think I prove that there is nothing that, in itself, is more evident and certain than the existence of God and of the human soul. However, I did not dare to attempt this, because I would have had to explain at length the strongest arguments of the sceptics to show that there is no material thing of whose existence one is certain. At the same time, I would have accustomed the reader to detach their thoughts from things that are perceived by the senses, and then I would have shown that if anyone doubts everything material, they still cannot have any doubt about their own existence. It follows from this that the person – that is, the soul – is a being or substance that is not at all corporeal . . . and also that it is the first thing that one can know with certainty. Indeed, if one spends enough time on this meditation, one acquires gradually a very clear and, dare I say, intuitive notion of intellectual nature in general. This idea is the one that, if considered without limitation, represents God. . . . I was afraid that this introduction, which could have appeared as if it were designed to introduce the views of sceptics, would disturb

weak minds, principally because I was writing in the vernacular. . . . Most intelligent
people, if they take the trouble not only to read but also to meditate in an orderly way
on the same topics on which I claim to have meditated myself . . . will draw the same
conclusions as I did. I shall be glad, the first time I have an opportunity, to try to
explain this matter further.   (i. 353–4)

These letters introduce some of the key features of the *Meditations*. They
acknowledge the special difficulties involved even in acquiring an idea of
God, and the extra challenges that arise in proving God's existence.

Many of Descartes' contemporaries assumed that we acquire our ideas
by observing things in the world around us and that we refashion some of
those ideas by adding or subtracting various features in our imagination.
For example, we might see a tree and then imagine one that is not resistant
to other bodies – something like the shadow of a tree that we could walk
through. If we were to think of God along those lines, we might refer to
paintings of Christ and assume that God is some kind of ghostly man,
with a shadowy halo about his head, and so on. Descartes was suggesting a
radically different approach. He thought that we could get an idea of God
only by reflecting on our own experience of thinking. If we could form
some idea of what thinking is, we might then manipulate that idea to form
what is still an obviously inadequate idea of God.

The other suggestion in these letters is that we might exploit the arguments of sceptics to show how uncertain is all knowledge of the natural
world. Descartes does not have to endorse those sceptical doubts. He
can simply acknowledge that they are used effectively by many thinkers
to undermine unfounded claims about the certainty of empirical knowledge, and he can contrast that with the certainty we experience when we
reflect on our own thoughts. Therefore, if people think that, despite sceptical arguments, our knowledge of the natural world is certain, they must
accept that we are even more certain of our own inner experiences. Unfortunately, this approach requires some discussion of scepticism. Given the
fact that he had written the *Discourse* in French, Descartes was concerned
that people who were not trained in philosophy might be so persuaded by
sceptical arguments that they would fail to understand their subsequent
refutation. There was an unresolved tension, then, between discussing
scepticism at the risk of seeming to endorse it (because it is a necessary
step on the road to proving God's existence), and failing to answer the
arguments of sceptics and leaving one's readers worse off than when they
started. Finally, Descartes mentions at least twice in the letter to Silhon

that this kind of argument requires a 'meditation'. The only way to embark on this project is to stop looking at the familiar objects of our experience and to look instead within ourselves, at our own thoughts. This requires a form of mental training, for which the *Spiritual Exercises* of Saint Ignatius might provide a model. Given the risks involved, this was something that he thought should be deferred in 1637. He might come back to it again some other time.

This opportunity arose in 1638. In fact, even before the *Discourse* was published in French, the question of preparing a Latin translation has been raised, and in that context Descartes mentioned that he had written a draft of a treatise on metaphysics eight years previously. 'If there is a Latin version of this book, for which preparations are being made, I could have it [a discussion of metaphysical questions] included there' (i. 350). By late 1639, Descartes had given up hope of reprinting the *Essays* in French or of publishing an expanded Latin translation that would contain objections and replies. However, it was too late by then to halt the project of preparing a Latin version of the text, one that would certainly be accessible to a much wider academic readership than the original French text. Hence the need to return to those metaphysical questions that were partly revealed in Part IV of the *Discourse* and that required a more extended discussion and defence.[12] As already acknowledged by Descartes, such a metaphysical essay would also mean that he had to discuss scepticism.

Pyrrhonism

There is no indication in Descartes' work prior to 1640 that he was remotely persuaded by sceptical doubts about the possibility of knowledge. His studies in optics, physiology, and meteorology, and his earlier work in mathematics, give no indication that he ever worried about the possibility that all human knowledge might collapse because it was built on faulty foundations. More accurately, he seems to have had no reservations about the veracity of his own theories or the reliability of the 'proofs' he offered to support them. Impartial readers at the time were likely to believe that he was too confident about his philosophical views rather than the opposite, and that he was unwilling to listen to genuine objections.

He had indeed raised questions about foundations in the *Discourse*, but they were doubts about other people's theories and, in general, about the traditional learning of the schools that continued to be taught uncritically to generations of students. This attitude of complete confidence in his own work and a consistent failure to acknowledge the contributions of others, including such luminaries as Galileo, was slightly modified in the course of replying to objections to the *Essays*. Then, for the first time, he acknowledged the indirectness of the evidence that supports scientific theories, and the lack of parity between mathematical proofs and scientific 'demonstrations'. During 1640, in particular, a new phrase – often written in Latin, for emphasis – appeared in his correspondence, in reply to queries about scientific questions: '*Est quaestio facti*' (that is a factual question).[13] Nonetheless, this explicit recognition of the need for empirical evidence, in addition to speculative explanations, did nothing to reduce Descartes' confidence in the validity of his work. Nor did he experience a crisis of confidence, an emotional collapse, or anything faintly similar to a mental breakdown, as had been reported in the lives of other philosophers. The explanation of this late interest in scepticism is much simpler. Once a Latin version of the *Discourse* was in circulation, he could no longer avoid discussing contemporary scepticism and its relevance to metaphysical questions.

Descartes was already familiar with Jean Silhon's book *Two Truths*, which had been published in 1626 when he was still living in Paris. In 1634, Silhon reworked many of his earlier ideas in a new book entitled *The Immortality of the Soul*, in which he discussed Pyrrhonism as undermining belief in God and the soul. However, his interest in those questions was not purely metaphysical; he argued that the social order depends on belief in the immortality of the soul. 'Without it, the political order and civil society, which flourish . . . by the just relation and faithful correspondence between the right of Sovereigns and the duty of subjects, will soon dissolve.'[14] There was nothing novel about these remarks in the 1630s. What was surprising, however, was the argument developed by Silhon to establish at least one truth that he considered to be beyond doubt.

Here is a piece of knowledge that is certain, no matter what direction one turns it or from what perspective one considers it, and is such that it is impossible for any person capable of reflection and discussion to doubt and to fail to be convinced about it. Every person, I say, who has the use of judgment and reason can know *that they are*, that is to say, that they have a being and that this knowledge is so infallible that, if all the operations of the external senses were deceptive in themselves, or if one could not distinguish between them and the operations of a disturbed imagination; or if one could not be fully convinced that one is awake or asleep and that what is seen is true or is an illusion and pretence, it is impossible to be mistaken in this judgment and *that they not be*, for any person who has the capacity to enter into themselves, as some people have, and to make the judgment *that they are*. It is a truth – as perceptible by reason as the Sun is to healthy eyes – that action presupposes being, that it is necessary for a cause to exist in order to act, and that it is impossible for something that does not exist to do anything.[15]

Silhon anticipated the Cartesian project at least in this sense. He saw clearly the impact of sceptical doubts on proofs of the soul's immortality or of God's existence, and he believed that he had to address those doubts adequately before he could make any progress with those two questions. It would be merely a change of emphasis if Descartes were to argue that scepticism about knowledge of nature, whether it is adequately countered or not, provides a foil against which the relative certainty of self-awareness is obvious.

The most likely source of these sceptical problems was the publication in Paris in 1562 of a Latin translation of Sextus Empiricus.[16] Theologians and philosophers exploited its riches to undermine the claims of adversaries, irrespective of what was being debated or who the adversaries happened to be. Catholic theologians, for example, could use such sceptical weapons against what they considered undue reliance on reason by Calvinists, and could then encourage the faithful to put their trust in the traditional teachings of the church. Calvinists, for their part, could appeal to sceptical arguments to challenge the alleged credulity of Catholics, some of whose beliefs seemed to verge on magic. Marie de Gournay could deploy similar sceptical arguments to challenge received views about the inferiority of women.[17]

A more immediate source of sceptical arguments, however, were the very influential *Essays* of Michel de Montaigne, published in various editions between 1580 and 1588. Montaigne rehearsed, in his *Apology for Raymond Sebond*, all three of the famous sceptical arguments that appear in the first of Descartes' *Meditations*. He argued that our senses often deceive us, that we cannot be sure if we are awake or asleep, and that we cannot use our cognitive faculties to establish their own trustworthiness without arguing in a circle.[18] Thus one factor in Descartes' decision to structure the *Meditations* as he wrote them, with the First Meditation rehearsing the strongest possible sceptical arguments available, was the popularity of Montaigne's *Essays* and the fashionable scepticism that they endorsed.

Apart from these popular discussions of scepticism and metaphysics, Descartes may also have seen a need for a pre-emptive strike in defence of his philosophy of human nature, much of it still unpublished. His criticism of scholastic philosophy and his novel studies on human and animal behaviour raised doubts about the traditional account of the human soul. Descartes acknowledged this danger by including a lengthy discussion of the essential distinction between animals (and other automata) and human beings in the *Discourse*. Unfortunately, this merely drew attention to the possibly unorthodox implications of his anthropology for those who, otherwise, might never have noticed them. Accordingly, in the years between 1637 and 1640, he often had occasion to explain the distinction between 'animals without reason . . . automata' and human beings,[19] and he tried to do this without reverting to the scholastic language of forms.

In contrast with these efforts, the Jesuit priest Louis Richeome published a typical treatise on the soul in 1621, which he dedicated to Richelieu: *The Immortality of the Soul, certified by natural reasons, by human and divine testimonies, for the Catholic Faith against Atheists and Libertines*.[20] Richeome referred to the Lateran Council (1513), as Descartes also does, which condemned those followers of Aristotle who claimed that the 'intellectual soul is mortal, or is one in all human beings'.[21] The Jesuit apologist argued that God created human souls naturally immortal. Therefore, although it would have been possible for God to annihilate them, it would imply an unreasonable change of mind on God's part if He were to do so.[22] As one might expect, Richeome's description of the human soul does not deviate significantly from what had been taught at La Flèche when Descartes was a student. The soul was said to be 'the primary act and form of the human body, substantial and spiritual.'[23]

Richeome explains the scholastic term 'form' as follows: 'the form of gold is the essence and perfection of gold which gives, with its essence, its accidents, the colour yellow, the low sound, and the softness for melting.'[24] In a similar way, the human soul determines both the essence of what counts as human and explains why we have our characteristic properties. Richeome assumed some version of the body/soul distinction to conclude that 'no soul is bodily, even though the soul of animals and plants is material'.[25] There were innumerable ways in which the language of the scholastic tradition – of forms, essences, and suchlike – could have been used to express the conclusion that Pope Leo X had invited Catholic philosophers to defend. Richeome's book was merely one example of how it could be done. The question for Descartes was whether, having abandoned scholastic philosophy, he could find any acceptable way of describing the soul and defending its immortality within the scope of his natural philosophy.

This question was highlighted by another book that appeared in Paris in 1637. François La Mothe le Vayer's *A Small Christian Discourse on the Immortality of the Soul* reviewed the arguments for the soul's immortality developed by philosophers and mentioned once again the decree of the Lateran Council. Having surveyed many philosophical arguments, La Mothe le Vayer concluded that it would be preferable to rely on faith rather than philosophy to support the doctrine of immortality. 'Rather than attempt to compel the more incredulous to acknowledge such an important truth by the power of reason alone, I believe it would be better to acknowledge frankly its weakness and to capture their acceptance gently by obedience to the Faith.'[26] Despite its explicit deviation from the expectations of the Lateran Council, this libertine book won the official approval of the theology faculty at the Sorbonne, which was subsequently denied to Descartes.[27]

Descartes joined this debate about the human soul that had intermittently dominated theological concerns in Paris since the 1620s. In doing so, he adverted explicitly to the Lateran Council, in the "Letter of Dedication" that introduced the *Meditations*:

As regards the soul, many people thought that its nature cannot easily be investigated, and some have even dared to say that human reason shows us that the soul dies with the body and that the contrary view is held by faith alone. However, the Lateran Council, held under Leo X (Session 8), condemns them and explicitly commands Christian philosophers to defeat their arguments and prove the truth to the best of their abilities, and therefore I too have not hesitated to take on this challenge.   (vii. 2–3)

Thus the author of the *Meditations* presents himself as a Catholic philosopher who assumes the invitation of the Lateran Council to construct arguments in support of the soul's immortality.[28] This unwise intrusion into theologically sensitive questions, contrary to a rule of thumb by which Descartes had avoided controversy in the past, was encouraged by a suspicion that the Jesuits, collectively, had targeted him for special criticism.

War with the Jesuits

Descartes wrote to Mersenne (30 July 1640) that he had not yet published his 'five or six sheets of metaphysics, even though they have been ready for a long time. What stopped me from doing so is that I do not want them to fall into the hands of pseudo-theologians or, in future, into those of the Jesuits (with whom I foresee that I am going to go to war)' (iii. 126).[29] Descartes was reflecting on his experience of publishing the *Essays*, when parts of the book were distributed to readers in France and the United Provinces even before they were officially published. On this occasion he was being extra careful, given the sensitivity of the subject matter, that no one would see his metaphysics until he had had an opportunity to have it 'read and approved by various doctors [i.e., theologians] and, if possible, by the Sorbonne as a whole' (iii. 126–7). The reason for identifying the Jesuits as a likely source of opposition in Paris was that one member of the society had already engaged in a public criticism of the *Dioptrics*. The reverberations of this controversy appeared in the second edition of the *Meditations* in 1642.

Clermont College (renamed Louis-le-Grand in 1682), which was the Jesuit college in Paris, organized a two-day disputation on Descartes' *Dioptrics* on June 30 and 1 July 1640, under the direction of Father Pierre Bourdin (1595–1653). Bourdin had entered the Jesuit novitiate in 1612, and he had probably attended La Flèche as a student while Descartes was there, before becoming a teacher in the same college in 1618. Meantime he had been promoted, in 1635, to lecture in physics and mathematics at Clermont College. Mersenne notified Descartes, who was still in Leiden, about this disputation almost immediately after it was held, since it was obviously critical of some of the main features of his optics. Descartes thanked Mersenne for passing on the news and asked him to pretend that he had not told him the name of the Jesuit involved.[30] This ruse would allow Descartes to write to the rector of the college and refer anonymously to the author. He could not restrain himself, however, from commenting that he had heard that Bourdin was a relative of Petit, and that the Jesuit had possibly become involved in the controversy out of affection for a relative whom Descartes had earlier compared to a small barking dog.

Descartes then wrote to Father Hayneuve, the Jesuit rector of Clermont College, on the same day as his letter of thanks to Mersenne – but in a different language (Latin). He explained to Hayneuve, with profuse apologies, that he was evidently the author of the theses that had been attacked at the Jesuit college, although he did not know the name of his critic. He lied: 'I assure you that no one has written me the name of whoever proposed those theses, nor even the name of the discipline that he teaches, although I can guess easily from the reasoning used that it is physics or mathematics' (iii. 98–9). He then revealed the real reason for his worries. Descartes imagined, not without some basis in reality, that the Jesuits acted collectively and cohesively on all matters. There was therefore a danger that the critique of a relatively obscure professor at Clermont College was likely to represent the considered judgment of the whole Society of Jesus on his physics.

Since I know that all the members of your Society are so tightly united together that nothing is ever done by one member that is not approved by all, and therefore that whatever is written by one of you has much more authority than what is written by individuals, I think it is not unreasonable for me to ask and expect from your reverence – or, rather, from your whole society – what has been promised publicly by one of your members.   (iii. 99)

Having explained that he was willing to be taught once again by the Jesuits, as he had been instructed earlier at La Flèche, the apparently docile alumnus requested a written version of the objections that had been disputed in his absence in Paris.

A letter from Huygens on 24 July provided another opportunity for Descartes to reflect on his ambivalent relations with the Jesuits. Huygens was on military manoeuvres again. On this occasion he was camped at Reek, where he was taking refuge in his tent from 'a great storm of wind and rain', and he was embarrassed to have heard a rumour that Descartes had published something 'about the soul and the divinity' without even telling him about it (iii. 750). Descartes dismissed the rumour as false. He confirmed that he had not yet written anything that could be given to a publisher, and that he was trying 'to clarify what I wrote in the fourth part of the *Discourse on Method*' (iii. 751). He also repeated the phrase he had used the same day, when writing to Mersenne, that he was about 'to go to war with the Jesuits' because of what one of their mathematicians had said about his *Dioptrics*. 'I have known the proverb for a long time: *do not stir up the hornets*. Nonetheless, since they get stirred up all on their own and I cannot avoid it, I believe that it is better if I confront them all together, once and for all, than wait for them one at a time, which would never finish' (iii. 752).[31]

In retrospect, it is obvious that this was a relatively insignificant criticism, by one Jesuit priest, of features of Cartesian optics that many other contemporary commentators had also questioned. Descartes characteristically turned a minor skirmish into a 'war' and misread the situation as if the whole Jesuit order collectively had authorized Father Bourdin to speak on its behalf. There are many similarities in the pattern of this controversy to the earlier row with French mathematicians and to later disputes with Dutch theologians. Descartes now contrasted unfavourably the support that he experienced at Utrecht with the carping reaction of readers in Paris, just as he would subsequently contrast the ignorant critics at Utrecht with the those who turned out to be receptive supporters in France.[32] Once again, as in the other disputes, he used Mersenne as an intermediary for correspondence in both directions. Thus, he wrote a lengthy rebuttal of Bourdin's objections from Leiden (29 July 1640), and asked Mersenne to forward the letter to the Jesuit college.[33] He also found, as on previous occasions, that Mersenne compromised his communications by failing to forward letters in a timely manner. By 30 August, Mersenne had still not forwarded the letter of 22 July that he had intended for Father Hayneuve, and Descartes felt obliged to send him another letter in Latin for transmission to the Jesuit rector.[34]

This was a ruse that Descartes often used. He wrote two letters together, one for a trusted correspondent to whom he revealed what he really thought about something, and the other accompanying letter to be passed on to someone else as his pretended or official position. So he sent two letters to Mersenne, one for himself and one to be forwarded to Father Hayneueve. The letter to Mersenne reveals the extent of Descartes' fear of a conspiracy to undermine him, and his dishonesty in providing inconsistent interpretations of the same event on the same day.

Having finally realized, both by Father Bourdin's action and those of many others, that a significant number of them [Jesuits] speak about me unfavourably and that, since they have no way of harming me by the strength of their arguments, they have undertaken to do so by the number of their voices, I have no desire to address them individually – which would be an infinite and impossible task for me. My plan is to coerce them either to reveal, once and for all, all the arguments they have against what I wrote . . . or else to refuse to do so, which they cannot do without admitting that they have nothing worth saying. (iii. 161)

In the accompanying letter for Hayneuve, Descartes acknowledged that Bourdin had written his critique without consulting other Jesuits, that it was never his (Descartes') intention to suggest otherwise, and that he was merely hoping to provoke the Jesuits collectively into an examination of his work. Stretching credibility to its limits, he added: 'I am clearly not someone who is offended if my views are refuted. On the contrary, those who oppose them with serious and solid arguments make me very grateful' (iii. 171–2). Although these letters were both written on 30 August, they were not given to a messenger until Descartes returned from Francine's funeral on 15 September.

Descartes' duplicity is evident again in October, when he uses Mersenne to entrap the reluctant Jesuit critic. He asks that Mersenne make sure that the Jesuits have copies of all the relevant correspondence, and that they know that Descartes knows that they have them. If they reply only orally, thereby depriving Descartes of a record of their response, he asks Mersenne to make a Latin summary, to give it to the Jesuits, and to mention 'in passing' when writing to Descartes that he has shown the summary to the Jesuits. Descartes is almost artificially fomenting a contest with extremely reluctant adversaries, in the course of which he vows 'to interpret in future everything that comes from one of them as if it came from their whole society' (iii. 206).[35]

The first edition of the *Meditations* was published in August 1641 without any contribution from the Jesuits, despite Descartes' importunate efforts to extract from them either an official endorsement or written objections. This did not deter him, however, from continuing his efforts to provoke them. He wrote to Mersenne in December, with another letter to be shown to the superior of the Jesuit province in Paris, suggesting that any comments from these learned religious should be written down, so that they could not retract them later.[36] This unrelenting badgering eventually worked. In January 1642, Descartes received a letter from Father Bourdin, but it did not quite satisfy his anxious requests. He was evidently expecting a set of objections to the *Meditations*, written by Bourdin – with the assistance, perhaps, of other Jesuits – and he was relying on Huygens to guarantee their safe delivery by messenger. He increased the pressure on the Jesuits by threatening to use one of their textbooks as a target for a sustained critique of scholastic philosophy, although he had already decided by this time not to implement that plan.[37] He also wrote to Huygens, as another useful intermediary, that the printing of the second edition of the

book was nearly completed and, if he received Bourdin's objections, that
he should send them immediately to Van Hogelande's house in Leiden.[38]

The long-awaited objections arrived about 26 January 1642. Descartes
expressed his reaction in the following colourful military metaphor: 'I
received the writing of the Jesuits four or five days ago. It is a prisoner
who is under my control and whom I wish to treat as courteously as I can.
However, I find it so guilty that I cannot see any way to save it. Every day
I assemble my council of war on this topic, and I hope that you will see
the trial within a short time' (iii. 523). The 'trial' in question was made
public when Bourdin's objections, together with Descartes' replies, were
printed in the second edition of the *Meditations* as the Seventh Objections
and Replies (vii. 451–561).

In general, Bourdin's objections were as quibbling or nitpicking as
Descartes had complained. They relied excessively on the kind of rhetorical tricks that might have been effective in oral disputation, by focusing
on individual words, quoting texts inaccurately, and using sarcasm or
funny stories to sway listeners. That style did not work as well for readers.
Descartes' reaction was correspondingly acerbic. He regretted that this
'reverend Father' was so anxious to quibble that he imitated 'the vilest
comedian on the contemporary stage by raising a laugh by his own ineptitude' (vii. 492). However, Bourdin made some telling points against the
Meditations, especially by showing that the argument that the mind is not
material assumes, unjustifiably, that we already know all the properties of
matter. Unfortunately, he expressed even this valid point by telling a story
about a peasant who knew only four kinds of animal, and then argued,
on seeing a novel animal, that it must not be an animal because it did not
correspond to anything in his previous experience.[39]

Descartes' dismissive attitude to Father Bourdin is complemented by
a lengthy and obsequious letter to his superior, Father Dinet, which was
written as an Appendix to the second edition of the *Meditations*.[40] Here
Descartes acknowledges that Bourdin could not have been acting on behalf
of the Jesuits, since his objections fail to display the charity, understanding, and scholarship that characterize that religious order. 'It is very evident from the dissertation of the reverend father that he did not enjoy
that good health that is found in the rest of your body [i.e., the Jesuits]'
(vii. 565). Once again, Descartes explains that he is in the process of writing a new book (i.e., the *Principles of Philosophy*) that would benefit from
the advice of the Jesuits. Their suggestions would be so highly esteemed

that, if they were to make a negative recommendation, he would even consider not publishing the book at all (viii. 603).

The famous letter to Father Dinet concluded one episode in Descartes' unrelenting efforts, during the publication of the *Meditations*, to protect his project from potential theological objections. Unfortunately, it also opened hostilities on another front – with Calvinist theologians in Utrecht – which are discussed in Chapter 8.

Publishing the *Meditations*

Descartes returned to writing metaphysics, after an interval of ten years, in part because his discussion of God and the human mind in the *Discourse* had raised objections that were inadequately discussed there. From the outset, he was keenly aware of danger from theological critics, and this fear was magnified by what he understood as an imminent threat of criticism from the Jesuits in France. These exaggerated worries are reflected in the way in which he carefully managed the publication of his metaphysics and sought an official approval from the theology faculty at the Sorbonne. After all, the Sorbonne had been very critical of the Jesuits in France and had made sure that they were not allowed to confer degrees in their colleges.[41] Its theology faculty was also more closely aligned than the 'foreign' Jesuits with the bishops in France, so that if they approved his *Meditations*, he could confidently ignore whatever the Jesuits might say.

By March 1640, although Descartes was still in Santpoort, he was planning to move to Leiden 'in about five or six weeks time' to oversee the printing of the *Meditations*.[42] This cannot have been a very firm plan, since on 1 April he speaks openly about the possibility of visiting England.[43] He did move to Leiden sometime before 7 May,[44] and he sent his draft metaphysics to Utrecht, to Regius and Aemilius, who were reported as being 'charmed to ecstasy' by the essay.[45] Descartes mentions during May that he might visit Utrecht to hear Regius' lectures. Since the local critics of Regius thought that Descartes was the main source of the erroneous views taught at Utrecht, if the French visitor were to attend the lectures, he acknowledged that he would have to hide behind the curtain used by Anna Maria van Schurman when she listened to lectures given by Voetius.[46] By the end of the month, he was considering leaving Leiden to live in Amersfoort, which is about 20 kilometres northeast of Utrecht, and offering to visit Regius en route when passing through the university city.[47] Given that he was also thinking about visiting France at the end of July, Descartes was obviously unsettled. He had lived in Sant-poort, moved to Leiden, had thought seriously about visiting England and France, and had considered changing residence again to Amersfoort, all within the space of three months. In fact, he remained in Leiden until March 1641, when he moved to the castle of Endegeest. However, as long as he lived in Leiden and still planned to visit France during the summer of 1640, Descartes decided to defer printing his draft metaphysics until immediately before departing. In that way, he would reduce the chances of allowing any copies to fall into the wrong hands.[48]

This plan was apparently abandoned sometime between July and September 1640, when Descartes was involved in controversy with the French Jesuits. He had left Leiden suddenly, for two weeks, at the end of August, probably because of the death of his daughter, Francine. On his return on September 15, he still had on his desk two letters about the Jesuit controversy that he had written on 30 August and had not dispatched by messenger. At that stage, his plan was still to travel to France, perhaps within about six weeks (i.e., toward the end of October).[49] By the end of the month, however, Descartes had rethought his strategy for publishing the *Meditations*. Even if initially he printed only twenty or thirty copies at Leiden, he could not guarantee to limit their distribution only to those to whom he sent them. In fact, even the printer might make extra copies and distribute them without permission as he wished. Rather than publish in Leiden, therefore, it was decided to send the manuscript to Mersenne in Paris and to ask him to consult with Father Gibieuf and a number of theologians of his choice.[50] Descartes hoped that they would examine and approve his treatise, and he decided that he would then dedicate it (if Mersenne thought it was a good idea) to the Sorbonne theologians. 'I will tell you that Bourdin's caviling has made me resolve to arm myself in advance as much as possible with the authority of others, because the truth on its own is not appreciated very much' (iii. 184). Given his exaggerated estimate of how important the dedication would be for the success of the book, Descartes even asked Mersenne how he should address a letter of dedication to the Sorbonne (iii. 185).

Descartes seems to have recognized how close he was sailing to theolog-ical disputes, even though the official plan was merely to discuss various metaphysical claims that could be known by reason, independent of reve-lation. He alluded to the Galileo affair, and to the fact that his contribution to that discussion remained hidden in *The World* (iii. 180). Since he was awaiting a detailed reply from the Jesuits, which he did not expect for another 'four or five months', he had to accept that the projected trip to France would not occur before the end of 1640. In preparation, he planned to read a little of 'their philosophy, something I have not done for twenty years', and he asked Mersenne for suggestions about scholastic authors who were then popular. Apart from the Coimbra commentators, and Toletus and Rubius – whom he vaguely remembered from his school days – he thought there was some 'Carthusian or Benedictine' who had recently written a summary of scholastic philosophy, although he could not remember his name.[51] The author in question, Eustace of St. Paul, had written a popular four-part summary of philosophy that had been published in numerous editions in Paris, most recently in 1626. This was the first mention by Descartes of Eustace of St. Paul, and the first time that he gave serious thought to what eventually became his *Principles of Philosophy* – all in response to anticipated objections from the Jesuits.

Descartes eventually sent his draft *Metaphysics* to Huygens and asked him to forward it to Mersenne on 10 November 1640.[52] Apart from the somewhat grandiose plan for the future, the immediate literary aim was to publish the *Metaphysics*. Since Descartes had sent the manuscript to Mersenne without any title, he now suggested as a title *The Meditations of René Descartes on First Philosophy*. This seemed appropriate, he thought, because he did not discuss God and the soul in detail, but 'in a general manner, all the first things that can be known when one philosophizes' (iii. 235).[53]

Although more than eleven years had passed since Descartes had written to Father Gibieuf about a 'little treatise', he contacted him again (11 November 1640) to say that he had drafted a 'writing on metaphysics' and that Mersenne would supply him with a copy.[54] He asked Gibieuf to advise Mersenne about how best to get the protection of the Sorbonne, because the project on which he had embarked was to defend 'God's cause' (iii. 238). Descartes' detailed plan was outlined to Mersenne, to whom he wrote twice on the same day. He asked him to have the text of the *Meditations* printed, to copy by hand his letter of dedication to the Sorbonne, and to present the theology faculty with both together (providing as many copies of the printed draft as they needed so that it could be examined simultaneously by all their theologians). The theology faculty might wish to establish an expert group to examine his writing, and, if they had any objections, they could send them to Descartes in Holland and he would reply. Such corrections and the author's replies could be printed at the back of the book.[55]

Descartes allowed Mersenne plenty of latitude in arranging for the publication of the *Meditations*. He gave him permission to 'correct or change everything that you think is appropriate' (iii. 265), and he left it to Mersenne to choose those who would be invited to submit objections. When sending the text in November 1640, Descartes included a model of what appropriate objections might look like. He had already requested some from 'a priest at Alkmaar' who wished to remain anonymous, although he also divulged his name as Caterus.[56] Given the anticipated problems of making copies available to relevant theologians, Descartes suggested that it might be more practical to have twenty or thirty copies printed in advance – a plan he had abandoned earlier when he could not trust the local printer, because he did not wish the text to be seen by 'the ministers of this country before our own theologians see it' (iii. 267). This decision, of limiting circulation to Catholic theologians, was evidently compromised when Mersenne invited Thomas Hobbes to compose objections. Descartes, however, clung to his original decision. When Huygens suggested, much later, that he might invite objections or comments from Caspar Barlaeus (1584–1648), a Remonstrant theologian and professor of philosophy at Amsterdam, Descartes politely declined.[57]

Between December 1640 and August 1641, when the first edition appeared in Paris, Descartes corresponded frequently with Mersenne about the sets of objections that he had collected, the problems involved in correcting printer's errors at such a distance from Paris, and the need to win the approval of the Sorbonne as a protection against future possible objections. It is clear that, given the distance involved and the unreliability of the messengers, Descartes lost control of the project in more senses than one. For example, he informed Mersenne that he should not be surprised if he did not find in the book 'one word about the immortality of the soul', because he demonstrated only that the mind was completely distinct from the body. Thus the human soul was not naturally subject to death as the body was, although he could not demonstrate that God could not annihilate it.[58] Despite this clarification, the subtitle of the first edition was printed as follows: 'in which God's existence and the immortality of the soul is demonstrated'. One might assume that this was supplied by Mersenne, because Descartes quite intentionally changed the subtitle, in the second edition, to read more accurately: 'in which God's existence and the distinction of the human soul from the body are demonstrated'. There are also signs that, in the course of publication, Descartes had second thoughts about the extensive scope for editing that he had granted to Mersenne. Although he had originally made Mersenne 'the godfather' of the book and had given him 'the power to baptize' it,[59] Descartes now reverted to discussing detailed amendments and even typographical corrections.[60]

Descartes thought that it might take 'two or three years' to gather the objections envisaged for the first edition. He eventually received five more sets of objections, in addition to those of Caterus, which he asked to have published in the order in which they were received. The Second Objections were written by Mersenne, although Descartes seems not to have been aware of that when he received them by messenger. Their arrival in Leiden was delayed by icy weather conditions, and Descartes thanked anonymously 'those who took the trouble to write them'.[61] Mersenne apparently sent copies of the *Meditations* to a number of people simultaneously. The invitation to Thomas Hobbes (1588–1679) precipitated a lengthy and rather bitter controversy about the *Dioptrics*, during which Hobbes raised objections that resembled those already made by Fermat.[62] Hobbes had fled to Paris in 1640 to escape from the political turmoil that was about to erupt in the English civil war, and he remained there until 1652 as a member of the informal Mersenne circle. During his Paris years, Hobbes wrote some of his most famous political works, including *De Cive* (1642) and the *Leviathan* (1651). He hardly fitted Descartes' profile of a Catholic theologian, since he was neither a Catholic nor a theologian, and the mismatch that resulted is evident in the hostility of Descartes' response.

Descartes' initial reply to Hobbes (21 January 1641) implied that he thought the objections had been sent from England, and he initially referred to their author, without appreciating who he was, as 'the Englishman'.[63] During the following three months, Hobbes continued to dispute the Cartesian theory of light; he also independently provided objections specifically against the *Meditations*, which arrived in Leiden on 22 January 1641.[64] As often happened, the controversy between Hobbes and Descartes included a priority dispute. In this case, they disagreed about which of them would be acknowledged by subsequent generations as the one who had first thought about the subtle matter that allegedly transmitted light.[65] Descartes seems never to have acknowledged any merit in Hobbes's point of view. He regretted that his first reply was not sufficient to terminate the correspondence and, having reviewed the material again, he concluded: 'As a final word, I have not found the slightest argument in this whole paper which differs from mine and which appears to be true and valid' (iii. 313–14, 318). By 4 March, Descartes was asking Mersenne to discontinue the discussion with 'the Englishman': 'I think that it would be best if I had nothing to do with him and, with that in mind, that I refrain from replying to him' (iii. 320).

Descartes received a fourth set of objections in March 1641, written as usual at Mersenne's request, from Antoine Arnauld (1612–1694). Arnauld was subsequently to figure prominently in support of the Jansenist cause against the Jesuits, but at this point in his life he was a relatively young theologian who was about to receive a doctorate in theology from the Sorbonne.[66] Despite his youth, Arnauld impressed Descartes with the detailed suggestions he made; 'I think these objections are the best of all . . . because he has penetrated more than anyone else into the meaning of what I wrote' (iii. 331). As a result of his objections, Descartes agreed to make a number of changes to the original text, and he sent those to Mersenne.[67] In particular, he adopted Arnauld's advice about the sensitivity of the Catholic doctrine of transubstantiation, and he agreed to check the official teaching of the church in its general councils. However, he still maintained that the church's teaching about the Eucharist could be explained best by using Cartesian principles, and that it was poorly served by those who 'mixed together Aristotle and the Bible and wished to abuse the authority of the Church to exercise their passions' (iii. 349). Despite this conviction, Descartes omitted a few paragraphs from the conclusion of his Replies to Arnauld, on Mersenne's advice, athough he restored them again in the second edition after he failed to obtain the Sorbonne's approval.[68]

Pierre Gassendi (1592–1655) was a Catholic priest from Aix-en-Provence, and he visited Paris in January 1641 to arrange for publication of his Life of Peiresc. He seems to have been given a copy of the Meditations in March, and he eventually found time to write his extremely lengthy comments before sending them to Descartes about 19 May 1641.[69] Not only did Gassendi write the longest objections, he went further than anyone else in antagonizing the author of the Meditations by mockingly addressing him as 'O Mind'. Not surprisingly, this triggered an equally sarcastic response from Descartes, who addressed his critic as 'O Flesh' (vii. 336, 385).[70] The sharpness of this exchange is reflected in Descartes' instructions to Mersenne. He told him not to show the replies to Gassendi before publication lest he change his mind, and to print the author's name so that he could not take refuge in the kind of anonymity offered to others.[71] The final set of objections was collected from various theologians by Mersenne, as the second set had been earlier, and they were sent to Descartes during the summer of 1641.

The Sorbonne Approval

Throughout this whole process of inviting objections and drafting replies, Descartes referred frequently to his hopes of getting some kind of official approval from the Sorbonne.[72] He told Mersenne (4 March 1641) that he had sent him the text 'to get the judgment of the Sorbonne people about it, [and] not to delay me in disputes with all the little minds who would like to get involved in sending me objections' (iii. 328). He reminded Mersenne of the same objective at the end of March, and thanked him in July for the suggestion that he omit some paragraphs about transubstantiation 'if that can help to get an approval' (iii. 416). Since they were already printing the book at that stage, he had to acknowledge that he might not get the Sorbonne's endorsement in time, and he claimed that it would not bother him much if it failed to arrive. On 1 August 1641, the Sorbonne appointed four of its members to read and report on the *Meditations*.[73] There is no evidence of what the subcommittee recommended. Meantime, the printers had completed their task on August 28, and the *Meditations* appeared without any official response from the Sorbonne. Evidently, both the author and the printer had anticipated a different decision, because they included on the title page the phrase: 'With a Privilege, and the approbation of Doctors'. The second edition, published in Amsterdam, omitted this phrase. A Dutch edition did not need a French privilege, and it was clear by that time that the Sorbonne had remained silent in response to Descartes' request.

Descartes' reaction to this failure was characteristic of his duplicity in other matters. He claimed both that he did not need the approval of others, and that he had never even requested it. He had anticipated a negative decision on 22 July 1641, when he thanked Mersenne for all his assistance in arranging for the book's publication, and accepted the modifications of the text suggested by Arnauld, to facilitate the approval of the Sorbonne. 'Even if we do not receive it, I am certain that it will not bother me very much' (iii. 416). Two months later, after the *Meditations* had been published, he again thanked Mersenne for his assistance, and then added the following characteristic comment. 'For my part, I have known for a long time that there are fools in the world, and I have such little respect for their judgments that I would be very sorry to lose one moment of my leisure or my rest in thinking about them' (iii. 436). It seems strange that, only one month after the book was published and before he had even seen a copy, he claims to have put it completely out of his mind.[74]

However, despite such face-saving denials, the failure to obtain the Sorbonne's approval continued to weigh on his mind. Four months later (19 January 1642), he wrote to Father Gibieuf, whom he had hoped might sway the Sorbonne in his favour, about the small number of theologians who had supported his cause, including Arnauld. 'My hope was not to get their collective approval. I knew very well and I predicted, a long time ago, that my thoughts would not be to the liking of the multitude and that, wherever a majority rules, my ideas would be promptly condemned' (iii. 473). Neither claim is true. Had Descartes received an ecclesiastical endorsement, there is no doubt that he would have exploited it fully when the second edition was published.

The first edition of the *Meditations* was published by Michael Soly in Paris. The complexity of the publishing project is reflected in the final product. While Descartes was in Leiden and Mersenne was soliciting sets of objections from his friends in Paris, the author lost control of the book. This applies especially to the many detailed corrections that would normally have been done, in the seventeenth century, by showing page proofs to the author in the course of printing. The most obvious feature of the Soly edition is the number of printer's errors. Descartes claimed that he was not very concerned about them, but he cannot have been happy with the final product.[75] The publisher seems to have experienced financial problems in the course of completing the work, which may explain the extraordinary delay in providing Descartes with copies of his book. Soly had promised to supply one hundred copies, but five months after publication Descartes had still not received even one copy.[76] They were to arrive eventually only in May 1642. Long before then, however, Descartes had decided to have a second edition printed 'in this country' (iii. 448), and he agreed to have it done by Elzevier in Amsterdam and Leiden.

The reason given was that the French privilege would not prevent pirate editions from appearing in the United Provinces; if there were to be other editions, he might as well take advantage of the circumstances to make corrections.

Since the first edition had been published only in late August, 1641, and Descartes mentions that a second edition is already being printed as early as 17 November, one must assume that he was extremely disappointed with the Paris edition. He had made a number of compromises in that edition in the interest of getting the Sorbonne's approval. When that strategy failed and the threat of a Jesuit critique continued, Descartes decided to amend the second edition in two ways. He omitted from the cover page any mention of an approval and restored the missing paragraphs about Eucharistic theology in the Replies to Arnauld. The amended text was printed for Elzeviers in Leiden, by working from corrected page proofs of the Paris edition, and it was completed as expected by January 1642.[77] Meantime, Bourdin's objections finally arrived in January, and this precipitated further amendments. Descartes added the objections from Bourdin, together with his own interpolated replies, and, as a final Appendix, he included the open letter to Father Dinet. Since these appendices were printed as a second volume in Amsterdam, Elzevier had to send a messenger with page proofs to Endegeest, where he would await Descartes' corrections.[78]

The second edition appeared with a modified subtitle as: '*Meditations of René Descartes concerning First Philosophy, in which the existence of God and the distinction of the human soul from the body are demonstrated. In addition, various objections of learned men to the demonstrations about God and the soul, together with the author's replies. Second Edition, augmented by the seventh objections not previously published.*' Descartes commented to Huygens: 'This edition is more correct than the Paris edition, and even a bit larger, primarily towards the end of my reply to the fourth objections, where I unfettered myself to write that the common view among our theologians about the Eucharist is not as orthodox as mine, something that Father Mersenne had withdrawn in order not to displease our theologians' (iii. 785). Descartes went out of his way to underline the extent to which the *Meditations* represented the foundations of his whole philosophical enterprise. He claimed, in reply to Father Bourdin, that this building project was not the work of an ordinary mason, but that it required the skills of a church architect and the kind of secure foundations that are necessary for tall buildings in marshy Holland.[79]

The marshy soil of the United Provinces was a metaphor for the rampant scepticism that Descartes had to acknowledge in his ambitious building plans (vii. 548–9). Readers were advised that they should not conclude that he was supporting scepticism. This would be as misguided, he argued, as assuming that medical authors offer prescriptions for falling ill simply because they describe the symptoms of the diseases they discuss.[80]

Meditations on First Philosophy

The most obvious features of this book are that it is written in Latin rather than in French, and that the first part is presented in the form of meditations. Descartes should have found it almost as easy to write in either language, given his classical education at La Flèche. However, he read and wrote French with greater facility than Latin.[81] The linguistic change and the extra effort were evidently warranted because he wished to reach an international audience, including readers in England and the United Provinces, many of whom did not read French. The switch to Latin may also have been influenced by remnants of his reservations about the discussion of these questions in the *Discourse on Method*, that metaphysical questions should not be made accessible to uneducated readers. Thus by appearing in Latin from an international publisher, the *Meditations* were available to every student of philosophy in Europe and, at the same time, they avoided the risk of misleading uneducated readers who might stumble unwittingly into metaphysical problems from which they could not easily escape.

While writing in Latin was the norm at the time, writing in the form of meditations was far from standard practice. The *Spiritual Exercises* that Descartes practiced at La Flèche were designed by Saint Ignatius as a way of breaking habitual patterns of thinking, and of redirecting a Christian's attention to episodes in the life of Christ and to the moral and religious implications that may be drawn from them. Descartes seems to have understood the principal obstacle to doing metaphysics in similar terms. According to him, the human mind is immersed in the immediately pressing demands of the body, almost constantly from birth, and it finds great difficulty in reaching the level of abstraction required to notice its own thinking. Descartes' strategy was, in one sense, extremely simple. To get an idea of the human mind and, by analogy, an idea of God, it is necessary first to become aware of our own thinking activity. The *Meditations* are meant to coach the reader into reflecting on his or her own thinking, and to guide the reader into that kind of reflection. Descartes outlined the method involved, in reply to a correspondent's query about the metaphysical overtures of the *Discourse*: 'Thus I would have you spend enough time on this meditation to acquire by degrees a very clear and, I would say, an intuitive notion of intellectual nature in general. This is the idea which, if considered without limitations, represents God, and if limited, is the idea of an angel or a human soul' (i. 353).

The simplicity of this strategy was obscured by the language of innate ideas, when Descartes claimed that the idea of God is innate in human minds. He was forced to clarify this by saying that he did not hold that infants are born thinking about God, but that they are born with an innate capacity to generate an idea of God by reflecting on their own intellectual activities.[82] According to the argument developed in the *Meditations*, we acquire some idea of what thought is by reflecting on our own thinking. Since this is an intellectual activity, we thereby form an admittedly indirect and somewhat impoverished concept of what is meant by a 'thinking thing' (because the activity of thinking cannot exist without belonging to some subject or other).[83]

All this effort is required simply to acquire an idea of a thinking subject. This cannot be done by listening to a lecture, by looking at a painting or representation of a thinker, or by reading a book. It can be done only by reflecting on the activity of thinking that we take for granted when we normally focus our thoughts on external things. Cartesian meditations are therefore intended to guide untrained metaphysicians to 'look' in the appropriate place for the fundamental idea on which the whole enterprise depends, or to put them in an appropriate frame of mind to notice what is already going on inside themselves. If the method works, the result is an inner experience rather than a concept, to which Descartes attaches the name 'idea of thinking', because the idea is not distinct from the activity itself of thinking.

Descartes seems to take more seriously than usual the fact that sceptical arguments could be launched against metaphysical thinking of this kind. None of his readers – or, at least, none who also read French – could have failed to notice the similarities between his argument against universal doubt and that of Jean Silhon. The more familiar version of that argument occurs in the *Discourse*. 'When I noticed that this truth, "I think, therefore I am", was so firm and certain that all the most extravagant assumptions of the sceptics were unable to shake it, I judged that I could accept it without scruple as the first principle of the philosophy for which I was searching' (vi. 32). Of course, Silhon was neither the first nor the most famous exponent of this argument. It is found as early as Aristotle, and more famously in Saint Augustine.[84] When Andreas Colvius (1594–1671), a friend of Beeckman at Dordrecht, pointed out the similarity to Augustine's argument in *The City of God* (xi. 26), Descartes consulted the book in the university library at Leiden and replied:

> I am obliged to you for alerting me to the passage in Saint Augustine with which my 'I think, therefore I exist' is somewhat similar. . . . I find that he used it to prove our existence, and then to show that there is an image of the Trinity within us insofar as we exist, we know that we exist, and we love this being and this knowledge within us. However, I use it to show that this *I* which thinks is an *immaterial substance* and that there is nothing corporeal about it. These are two very different things.   (iii. 247)[85]

Descartes' correspondence about the similarities to St. Augustine imply that he was not familiar with Augustine's work and that he did not borrow the argument directly from this source.[86] Of course, he may have been dissembling again and exaggerating the novelty of his argument.

According to their subtitle, the *Meditations* were written to demonstrate that the human mind is distinct from the body and that God exists.[87] Descartes aimed for the first conclusion by showing that the activity of thinking cannot be explained in terms of the properties of matter.[88] He could not produce an argument to show that mental activity cannot result from some complex activity of the brain and the senses. His task was more modest and feasible: to examine the evidence that supports what we would today call a scientific explanation of mental activity. He concluded that we might eventually discover that, in human beings, 'there is one nature that is both intellectual and corporeal', but it was impossible in 1641 to explain mental activity in terms of bodily events.[89] As long as this gap obtained in our theory between mental events and what we know about physical events – as it still does – Descartes thought that the only intellectually honest conclusion to draw was that mental properties are distinct from physical properties. There was thus a residual dualism in the incomplete Cartesian theory of human beings. However, Descartes was not proposing dualism as a successful theory. He was not arguing that we could *explain* thought by attributing a 'thinking faculty' to human beings. That would have been as uninformative as explaining how sleeping pills work by saying that they have a 'sleep-inducing faculty'. They undoubtedly have such a faculty, but it explains nothing if one simply redescribes what needs to be explained in apparently technical, scholastic language.

The conclusion that the soul and body are distinct was therefore, for Descartes, a temporary or conditional position. He may have borrowed from ancient sceptics by asserting this conclusion while leaving open the possibility that the opposite was true. The evidence available implied that the activity of thinking could not be explained by reference to pieces of matter in motion. As an activity, it had to be predicated of something or other, and since it could not belong to a material substance, it had to belong to an 'immaterial' substance. However, that left open the possibility that, at some future date, new evidence would become available. If that were to happen, it would require a change of opinion. The interim conclusion, then, was that, based on evidence available in 1641, the activity of thinking must depend on some kind of immaterial substance.

Descartes' treatment of the other question, about God's existence, was less successful. He included two proofs of God's existence in the *Meditations*, a novel argument in the Third Meditation, and a reworking of a famous argument from Saint Anselm in the Fifth Meditation.[90] In the course of writing the *Meditations*, he received a copy of Jean-Baptiste Morin's book *That God Exists*.[91] However, as usual, he found nothing helpful there, especially since Morin supported his proof of God's existence by claiming to refute the Earth's movement.[92] Descartes' first argument is generally seen as a failure, since it relies on a crucial premise that is both difficult to understand and even more difficult to accept.[93] The second argument, usually called the ontological argument, claims that God's existence is included in the very concept of God, since the idea of a nonexisting God would be a contradiction in terms. However, even if that premise were accepted, it would show only that we could not have a coherent idea of a nonexisting God. It would remain to be proved that, because we conceive of necessary existence as an essential feature of God, there exists a necessarily existing God who corresponds to our idea.

It is difficult to avoid the conclusion that the *Meditations* fell far short of their author's expectations. All six sets of objections rejected Descartes' claim that thinking could not possibly result from some complex physical process of which we are not aware. Even his more sympathetic readers, such as Arnauld and Mersenne, persisted in saying that he had failed to prove that conclusion. In the case of Mersenne, he put the point somewhat

sharply as follows, in the Sixth Objections: 'No one has been able to com-
prehend your demonstration, by which you think you have demonstrated
that no bodily motion can be what you call thought. Can you show us –
for we are attentive and, we think, sufficiently intelligent – that is it impossible for thoughts to emerge from those motions?' (vii. 413) The other
principal objective of the *Meditations*, to prove the existence of God, was
so unsuccessful that some of his critics claimed that he was trying deviously
to support the opposite conclusion by illustrating the obvious weakness
of the strongest arguments he could find. Finally, Descartes' discussion
of scepticism suffered precisely the outcome that he hoped to avoid. The
sceptical arguments that he borrowed from familiar contemporary sources,
and which he outlined so successfully in the First Meditation, caught the
imagination of readers then and since to such an extent that most remained
unconvinced that he had adequately addressed them. To the first generation of readers, the book seemed to be a failure, both commercially and
philosophically.

Leiden and Endegeest

Descartes lived in Leiden for about eleven months, from April 1640 to
March 1641.[94] The original reason for moving there was to arrange an
advance printing of the draft *Metaphysics*. Once that plan was abandoned,
he decided to visit France and arrange for publication there instead. However, the ongoing row with the Jesuits convinced him that he should remain
where he was – so that, if they were to send written material, Mersenne
would be able to forward it immediately. This holding pattern continued
throughout 1640, until Descartes' financial situation improved and the
expected 'war' with the Jesuits failed to erupt.

Descartes had a number of very good friends in Leiden, including
Gillot, to whom Mersenne was asked to forward letters before Descartes'
arrival in 1640, and Cornelis van Hogelande.[95] Van Hogelande was a
Catholic medical doctor, who apparently offered free drugs and medical
services to the indigent and, it seems, free accommodations to Descartes.[96]
On one occasion, Descartes even assisted Van Hogelande in his medical
practice. One of De Wilhem's daughters, most likely Johanna, who was
still a baby of less than a year old, suffered from rickets, which causes
a softening of the bones and distortion of the spine and legs. She had a
consultation with Van Hogelande and Descartes on 6 June 1640. They

wished to have a surgeon present and therefore asked that De Wilhem and his child remain until the following day at Gillot's house, where they promised to apply their medicinal skills as best they could.[97] Two weeks later, Descartes writes on behalf of Van Hogelande that he could send medication for the infant to The Hague, but that he could better judge the strength of the dose required if he could examine the young patient again.[98]

During this period at Leiden, three of Descartes' relatives died. His daughter, Francine, died on 7 September 1640, and his father died just over a month later.[99] At about the same time, Descartes' sister, Jeanne, died. She was three years older than he and one of his closest companions during his early years. Descartes evidently knew nothing of his father's death, since he wrote ten days after his death to explain the delay in visiting France and the reasons why he preferred to live in Holland (to avoid the attention of scholastic philosophers who targeted him as a critic of their philosophy). It took some time for news of his father's death to reach Leiden, in a letter from his brother, Pierre. Pierre also informed Descartes about their father's will. This prompted the exiled philosopher to appoint one of his friends to act on his behalf in this matter, and to complain eight years later of Pierre's conflict of interest in claiming to act impartially on behalf of his absent brother.[100] In writing a letter of condolence to Pollot, on the death of his brother, in January 1641, Descartes was reminded of his own recent bereavements: 'I recently experienced the loss of two people who were very close to me' (iii. 278). While this may refer to Francine's death, it more likely alludes to the deaths, at about the same time, of Descartes' father and of his sister, Jeanne.

One assumes that Descartes' daily life during this period was relatively unaffected by the major political events and minor social distractions in his immediate environment. He acknowledges in the autumn of 1640 that Huygens has had a 'very bad campaign with the army', and mentions the severe weather, when winter seems to return in March 1641 and local people are forced to get about on sleighs.[101] He has infrequent visitors, one of whom was certainly Claude Picot (1601–1668), who visited in March 1641 and remained in the United Provinces until the following summer.[102]

Picot is an enigmatic character who is usually referred to as the Abbé Picot. The title 'abbé' simply indicates that he was a Catholic priest, although the date of Picot's alleged ordination is unknown. If he was in fact the libertine who lived in the bohemian company of others, such as Jacques

Vallée des Barreaux, Damien Milton, and Jacques Bordier – who notoriously enjoyed all the delicacies of France – it would be understandable in
retrospect that his biographical details are obscure.[103] His visit to Descartes
was sufficiently memorable that, five years later, Descartes recalled his
earlier lengthy visit to Holland when they returned to live together at
Egmond-Binnen during the winter of 1647–48.[104] In 1641, Descartes had
already begun to sketch what eventually became the *Principles of Philosophy*, and he acknowledged in March that Picot 'liked my *Metaphysics*'
(iii. 340). It is most likely, therefore, that they discussed together his work
in progress. Picot was later responsible for the French translation of the
Principles.

Without independent evidence, one must think of Descartes during
this winter as a relatively isolated and lonely figure, spending hours each
day at his escritoire while he waged an epistolary war with Jesuits and
foreign critics, in many cases not fully appreciating the identity of his
correspondents. Even Pierre Fermat re-emerges as a potential critic, when
Descartes gives firm instructions to Mersenne not to show him a copy of
the *Meditations*. 'I consider Mr. Fermat one of the least capable of offering
good objections to it. I believe he knows mathematics, but in philosophy I
have always noticed that he reasons poorly' (iii. 328). As often happened,
it was too late because Mersenne had already given him a copy.

Descartes' attorney in Brittany wrote to him in January 1641, and his
brother, Pierre, wrote at the end of February 1641, possibly reporting
on the settling of their father's will.[105] Very soon afterward, Descartes
arranged to rent a small castle at Endegeest, which was owned by Pieter
van Foreest van Schouwen (who was still a minor and living in Rome
at the time).[106] The Van Schouwen family was Catholic, and the nearby
village of Oegstgeest had a small Catholic church where Descartes could
worship without hindrance. Many years later, when Descartes' correspondence was being published, Samuel Sorbière recalled this period
in Descartes' life when he seemed more at peace than usual. He was
ideally located, because he could travel to The Hague and return the
same day, and he could travel by canal to Utrecht, Delft, Rotterdam,
Dordrecht, Haarlem, or Amsterdam. 'He had a sufficient number of
domestic servants . . . a rather attractive garden, with an orchard at the far
end, which was surrounded on all sides by open fields from which one could
see emerge a number of more or less elevated church towers' (iii. 351).
Baillet reported that Descartes was also more receptive to having visitors

than before, possibly because he had been 'humanized by age or disputes or because . . . he had to accord some recognition to his beautiful residence.'[107]

The work involved in publishing the *Meditations* seems to have concluded an important phase in Descartes' life. He had failed to get official church approval for his metaphysics, thereby leaving him exposed to unpredictable criticisms from theologians in the future. If the Sorbonne would not co-operate, he could change allegiance once more and try to reconcile with the Jesuits instead. He began to take them into his confidence by writing about a new project that he had already begun, which emerged in due course as the *Principles of Philosophy*.

The Principles of Philosophy

In the course of explaining his grievances about Father Bourdin to the rector of Clermont College, in August 1640, Descartes acknowledged that the Jesuits could avoid controversy with him by distinguishing between mathematics and philosophy, and by claiming special expertise only in the latter. He went on to say, surprisingly, that he had written about many things that are usually classified only as philosophy, 'among other things, about all the meteors' (iii. 173). It is obvious that the boundaries between mathematics, physics, metaphysics, and theology were rather fluid at the time and that Descartes was exploiting that fluidity to promote his own ideas. During the year 1640, he continued to discuss all the issues in physics that had originally motivated him to write *The World*. He wrote to Mersenne about the explanation of gravity; about sensitive plants, which he was hoping to cultivate in Leiden if the Minim would send him seeds from Paris; about the tides, although this should be kept secret to protect the novelty of *The World* if it were ever published; about constructing machines that fly like birds, which seemed to Descartes to be possible in principle but physically impossible; and about the force that makes the Earth revolve around its own axis each day and around the Sun each year – something that could also be explained only in *The World*.[108]

He decried the baneful influence of astrology, because it seemed to have contributed to the death of one young man and caused another to languish in depression after their horoscopes had been cast in Italy.[109] He cast doubt on the suggestion that a sister of one of the Minims suffered convulsions because of some kind of supernatural intervention. The cause

was most likely medical, he suggested, and Mersenne was too credulous if
he believed otherwise. Indeed, Descartes was confident that he could even
diagnose the illness himself if the patient were to consult him.[110] During
all this time, Descartes seems to have continued his interest in anatomy,
especially in response to queries about the pineal gland.[111] This suggests
a continuation of the pattern of investigations adopted from his early days
in the United Provinces, which is reflected in the surprising plans for a
new book that emerge during the months when the *Metaphysics* was being
published.

On 11 November 1640, Descartes began to sketch the idea of writing
a general summary of his philosophy, which might even include a parallel
summary of scholastic philosophy. This was outlined in the context of
explaining to his Minim correspondent that many phenomena could not
be explained without revealing 'the principles of my philosophy':

I will tell you that I have decided to write them [i.e., the *Principles*] before I leave this
country and to publish them possibly within a year. My plan is to write, in order, a
whole textbook of my Philosophy in the form of theses where, without any redundant
discussion, I will include only all my conclusions, with the real reasons from which I
deduce them, something that I think I can do in relatively few words. I also plan, in
the same book, to print a textbook of the common Philosophy such as, possibly, that of
Brother Eustace, with my notes at the end of each question where I will add the various
opinions of others . . . and, in conclusion, I might add a comparison between these two
philosophies. But I beseech you not to say a word about this to anyone, especially not
before my *Metaphysics* is published. . . . it might inhibit the approval of the Sorbonne,
which I desire, and which I think could be extremely helpful for my plans.   (iii. 233)

The vague reference to 'my plans' revealed his hopes of having this book
accepted as a treatise on metaphysics that could serve as an alternative to
those usually used in colleges. The same ambition was repeated in similar
words the following month. On this occasion Descartes asked whether
Brother Eustace was still alive, so that he could ask permission to reprint
his philosophy course.[112] As usual, Mersenne did not keep the news to
himself. On 9 December 1640, Villiers wrote to him to say how happy he
was to hear that Descartes' metaphysics was about to appear and that 'it
might perhaps be the fore-runner to his Physics.'[113]

By the end of 1640, Descartes had apparently made enough progress
on the draft *Principles* to write to Mersenne as follows:

Apart from issues that are relevant to my *Metaphysics* . . . I would be very happy to have
as few distractions as possible, at least for this year [i.e., 1641], which I have decided

to use for writing my Philosophy in such an order that it can be taught easily. The first part, which I am doing at the moment, contains almost the same things as the *Meditations* that you have, except that it is in a completely different style, for what is spelled out at length in one is more abridged in the other and vice versa.   (iii. 276)

He wrote about the same time to a Jesuit, telling him dishonestly that one of his friends was preparing a book in which Descartes' philosophy was compared to what was taught in the schools, and asking advice about what to include or exclude.[114] However, while he was still trying to provoke the Jesuits into writing a response to the *Meditations*, and reserving the option (if all else failed) of targeting one of their texts in his systematic critique of scholastic philosophy, he gave up entirely the idea of including Eustace of St. Paul's textbook, with Cartesian notes, in a future publication.[115]

In January 1642, Constantijn Huygens was still asking 'for some news of *The World*' (iii. 780). Descartes seemed willing to consider publishing *The World*, partly in response to what he called 'these scholastic wars' (iii. 782). However, if he were to publish it he would first 'teach it to speak Latin, and . . . would have it called a *Summa of Philosophy*, so that it could be introduced more easily in the discussions of the people in the schools' (iii. 782). He had to admit, however, that the same scholastics were currently trying to smother it before it was born, and that this applied equally to Jesuit priests and Calvinist ministers. Of course, he had already embarked on rewriting both the *Meditations* and *The World* in a format that would be suitable for use in schools, and he wrote confidently about this plan to Father Dinet in May 1642 (vii. 577).

In the meantime, Descartes was to become involved in controversy again, on this occasion with the rector of Utrecht University, Gisbertus Voetius. This was a very public controversy in which he pitted his energies against one of the best-known Calvinist theologians at the time in the United Provinces, and in which he provided unstinting support for his philosophical protégé, Henricus Regius. Within a few later years, Descartes was to turn his wrath on Regius too. The pattern of his life was degenerating into a sequence of lengthy unresolved controversies, in the course of which he accused both friends and foes of failing to understand him.

8

The French Liar's Monkey
and the Utrecht Controversy

Descartes has no reason to object when he is compared with Vanini, because he does exactly the same as him in everything.[1]

ACCORDING to his own account, Descartes had gone 'to war' with the French Jesuits in 1640. While that controversy was still active, he opened hostilities on a second front two years later with the rector of Utrecht University, Gisbertus Voetius (1589–1676) and, eventually, with the Utrecht city council. At the height of this controversy, Regius was described in a student's Latin rhyme as the 'French liar's monkey'. The 'French liar' himself, Descartes, was characterized by a somewhat reluctant critic as follows: 'The man lacks all modesty, is proud, supercilious, scandalous and quarrelsome.'[2] The unusually sharp language used by both sides, even when judged by the standards that prevailed at that time, shows the depth of the rift involved.

As usual, Descartes offered a benign and self-serving interpretation of his motivation. 'All I ask for is peace . . . but I see that, to obtain it, I have to wage war a little.'[3] It is hardly credible however that, while living in comparative solitude in a rented castle at Endegeest (in the province of Holland), he had to engage in public controversy with influential Dutch theologians in another province (Utrecht) in order to protect his tranquillity. It is much more likely that he blundered into this theological and political minefield by making careless comments about Voetius in an appendix to the second edition of the *Meditations*, which was published in Amsterdam. Admittedly, the appendix, entitled *A Letter to Father Dinet*, avoided any explicit mention of the name of the university or of the rector involved.[4] However, this pretence at official anonymity hardly prevented the participants from recognizing themselves in Descartes' very public and nasty criticism. For example, this is how he describes the rector of the 'anonymous' Dutch university to his Jesuit correspondent in France:

He passes for a theologian, a preacher, and a dialectician. He has become very famous and influential among the uneducated because he displays his indomitable and protective religious zeal by inveighing against the Roman religion or other religions that differ from his own, or against the powerful, all the while caressing the ears of the masses with his scurrilous comments. He also publishes, daily, many tracts that no one reads, citing many authors (most of whom oppose him rather than support him, and are possibly known only from the indexes of books), and he writes about all kinds of sciences as if he were an expert in them. By speaking very confidently, but ignorantly, he appears very learned to the uneducated. However, those who are more educated know how importunate he has always been in provoking others; how often, in disputes, he has offered insults rather than arguments and then retreated in disgrace and defeat. If they differ from him in religion they openly mock and despise him, and some have treated him in that way so publicly that it seems as if nothing new could be written against him. If however they share his religious beliefs, although they excuse and tolerate him as much as possible, they do not agree with him in their hearts.   (vii. 584–5)

Here was Descartes, a French Catholic immigrant in the United Provinces, offering a portrait of the professor of theology at Utrecht, rector of the university (until 26 March 1642), a prominent member of the Synod of Dort on the anti-Remonstrant side and, therefore, an extremely orthodox, influential, and public proponent of Calvinism. The lack of diplomacy involved was compounded by the fact that a French philosopher was trying to win support from Jesuits in France by regaling their provincial superior with stories about the ignorance, ineptitude, and moral weakness of a Dutch Calvinist theologian. Descartes went on to describe Voetius as bullying other faculty members into agreeing with his condemnation of the professor of medicine, and as acting as both judge and prosecutor in the academic senate's condemnation of Cartesianism.[5]

This critique of Voetius in the letter to Father Dinet was the immediate cause of the Utrecht controversy. It began, however, with Descartes' friendship with Regius and the latter's support for the introduction of Cartesian natural philosophy into Utrecht University.

Regius and Descartes

Regius first became acquainted with some of Descartes' ideas from one of his university colleagues in Utrecht, Henricus Reneri, and by reading the *Discourse* and *Essays* of 1637. As mentioned earlier, he planned to meet Descartes in person in 1639, in the company of Reneri, but this visit had to be abandoned because Reneri fell ill. After Reneri's death in March 1639, Regius began to communicate regularly with Descartes, without relying on an intermediary, and to discuss with him various questions from natural philosophy on which he was working independently. By July 1639, there were early signs of conflict at Utrecht University between supporters and critics of traditional philosophy, at a thesis defence by Florentius Schuyl (1619–1669).[6] Following his graduation in arts at Utrecht, Schuyl was later to study at Leiden and, in 1662, to edit the first edition (in Latin) of Descartes' *Treatise on Man*. However, as a young student at Utrecht, he defended a thesis about magnetic powers that provoked the standard Cartesian criticism, namely, that it relied on occult powers that merely redescribed what needed to be explained.[7] These were the first signs that Cartesian philosophy had infiltrated Utrecht, and they pointed to an imminent confrontation between traditional philosophy and its Cartesian critics.

Despite his promotion to full professor in March 1639, Regius was still being paid only about half the salary of comparable professors at Utrecht. He therefore asked permission to give extra lectures on physics, and, with the support of Voetius and without any objections from the professor of philosophy, he assumed these extra duties in May 1640. This allowed Regius to lecture on topics on which, for some time, he had been composing a textbook of physics that eventually appeared, in 1646, as *Physical Foundations*. These lectures were complemented by a series of disputations that Regius arranged for his students. Even the first of these, on blood circulation (20 June 1640), was so controversial that he was advised in advance to focus on some more traditional topic in medicine.[8] Regius was not renownded for subtlety or an ability to avoid controversy. He proceeded more or less as he had planned, and received suggestions from Descartes before the disputation was held.[9] The relations between Regius and Descartes at this stage were mutually supportive and sympathetic. For example, even when Regius raised critical objections to the text of the *Meditations*, Descartes rejected them with uncharacteristic expressions of gratitude and a solicitous understanding of why they disagreed.[10]

The disputation in support of the Cartesian theory of blood circulation provoked hostile comments, both in Utrecht and elsewhere in Europe.

James Primrose (1598–1659) wrote a detailed refutation in England, to which Regius replied in a published pamphlet. The very title of this reply reveals the kind of nasty personal attacks that were typical of the polemical language used in academic disputes at the time: *A Sponge with which to clean the filth of the Objections that James Primrose, Doctor of Medicine, recently published against the Theses in support of Blood Circulation that were recently disputed at Utrecht University*.[11] Having expanded the scope of his lectures from medicine to natural philosophy, Regius asked Voetius and Descartes, in Spring 1641, whether it would be better to publish a book on physiology or to present his ideas in the form of disputations. Voetius, who had become rector of the university on 26 March 1641 (for a one-year term), advised that a book would be less likely to antagonize his colleagues, whereas Descartes encouraged Regius to proceed with further disputations, so as to clarify his views before publishing them as a monograph.[12] Regius adopted Descartes' suggestion and continued to send him advance copies of proposed disputations.

In response to one such draft disputation, Descartes suggested, probably in early May 1641, that Regius should not confuse what some people called a 'soul' in animals with what is called a 'mind' in human beings. 'I do not accept that the power of growing and sensing in animals deserves to be called a soul, as the mind does in the case of human beings. Those who are not well educated wished to do so because they did not know that animals lack a mind and that the word "soul" is therefore equivocal when applied to animals and humans' (iii. 370). Since Descartes' name was included on the title page of these disputations, he felt obliged to read the texts very carefully lest they attribute views to him publicly that he did not hold. Apart from many other detailed suggestions, he reminded Regius that, for Catholics, it would be heretical to suggest that human beings had a 'triple soul'.[13]

Regius apparently did not appreciate the sensitivity of these questions about the human soul and its relation to the body. The widely accepted Christian view at the time was that the soul is immortal, while the human body evidently is not so. However, Christians also believed in what was called 'the resurrection of the body', which was to occur after a final judgment by God in which the sins and virtues of all mankind are reviewed. This theological position required some way of thinking of the soul as an entity that could exist on its own, after the individual's death and, at the same time, as something that does not exist separately during one's life because it is intimately related to the activities of the body. Theologians had turned to philosophy for an appropriate way of describing this unusual kind of entity. Scholastic philosophers had divided all realities into two classes, substances and accidents. They used the word 'accident' for qualities of things, such as the colour of a cat or the shape of a tree. It would not make sense to think of a colour as existing on its own, without being the colour of something or other. By contrast, they applied the word 'substance' to things that are not necessarily predicated of other things and that could be thought of as existing on their own. That raised the problem: is a human mind a substance? It would seem that it is, if it can survive the death of the body. However, it would also seem that it is not a completely independent reality in its own right, because it depends on the human body for many of its characteristic functions.

This conundrum was avoided temporarily by appeal to another distinction that was used in the schools. Philosophers had distinguished between (a) the principal or defining feature of any substance in virtue of which it is the kind of thing it is, and (b) the matter of which it is made and which it shares with other things. The term 'substantial form' was used to describe the former. This provided theologians with a provisional compromise. The human mind was said to be the 'substantial form' of human beings, because it was the ultimate, quasi-substantial reality that distinguished humans from nonhuman animals. However, as a form, it was necessarily united with some appropriate matter. Thus this Aristotelian distinction of form/matter was mapped onto the corresponding Christian belief in an immortal soul/mortal body. This solution implied that, if there was any tampering with the borrowed philosophical language, it would raise serious theological objections.

In a disputation over which Regius presided on 18 December 1641, Henricus van Loon (c. 1617–1659) proposed that a human being is some kind of accidental union of two distinct substances, a soul and a body. 'Together with the body, the human mind does not constitute a being that is one in itself [*unum per se*] but a being that is accidentally one [*unum per accidens*], because they [body and soul] are individually complete or perfect substances.'[14] Descartes was alarmed by this, and he advised Regius with some urgency: 'There is hardly anything more unacceptable, or anything that would provide a greater opportunity for offence and accusation, than to put the following in your theses: "man is an accidental being" ' (iii. 460). Descartes also suggested a way of correcting the apparent implications of this provocative suggestion; in particular, he listed various philosophical views that could not be denied on pain of 'offending the theologians' (iii. 461). On this occasion, Descartes correctly anticipated the main source of opposition. For, despite local attempts to avoid a public confrontation, Voetius presented a sustained defence of substantial forms on behalf of Reformed theologians, and against all those supporters of the new philosophy (including Regius) who wished to eliminate such forms from their natural philosophy.[15] Regius wrote once again (24 January 1642) for advice and support from Descartes.[16]

Descartes' lengthy and detailed suggestions about how to reply to Voetius provide a revealing insight into the apparently duplicitous strategy that he had used himself in previous controversies – of praising his critics in public, while rejecting their comments and reviling them behind their backs. He encourages Regius to thank Voetius profusely for the opportunity to serve the cause of truth, and to acknowledge the 'great piety, incomparable learning and all the other excellent qualities' (iii. 495) of his opponent. In general, he advises him to use every opportunity to praise Voetius. For example, he should say that his theses were 'very learned, very excellent and very subtle', and that Voetius himself was 'a great man' to whom he was grateful for his 'patronage and his favourable friendship' and for the 'civility and courtesy' displayed in his critical comments (iii. 494, 497). This almost obsequious attitude should be reflected even in the way he addresses him. He should not call him Mr. Voetius but 'Magnificent Rector', and he should use 'the most respectful and favourable titles possible' (iii. 498). Moreover, Regius should imply that the real source of Voetius' concerns was not the views held by the professor of medicine and botany, but rather those held by others whom he described as follows: 'young people who, minimally acquainted with the basic elements of philosophy . . . spit out the whole philosophy of the schools before they have understood its vocabulary and, without that understanding, read authors from superior faculties [i.e., theology] without benefit' (iii. 498). Rather than become associated with such ignorant critics, Regius should adopt a conciliatory attitude and thank Voetius for the opportunity to resolve apparent misunderstandings without public controversy. This was good advice, even if given disingenuously.

On the specific issue that was central to the dispute – whether or not to accept substantial forms as a way of talking about the human mind – Descartes advised that, rather than rejecting substantial forms explicitly,

Regius should provide arguments from which informed readers could conclude that they are redundant.

I would wish above all that you never propose any new opinions but, while retaining all the old ones in name, that you offer only new arguments. No one could object to that, and anyone who understands your new arguments properly will conclude immediately from them what you mean. Thus, why did you need to reject explicitly the substantial forms and real qualities? Do you not remember that, in my *Meteors* (vi. 239), I expressly said that I did not reject or deny them at all, but only that I did not need them in order to explain my arguments?   (iii. 491–2)

One might commend Descartes for encouraging Regius to avoid public controversy as much as possible, especially when his opponents included a renowned theologian who happened to be the rector of the university in which he worked.

When Descartes offers specific suggestions about Voetius' theses, he goes beyond the general guidance just offered – that he not deny substantial forms and that he merely offer alternative explanations of natural phenomena that would make them redundant. He argues that there is no mention of substantial forms in Scripture (iii. 502), and that those who accept them are more likely than Cartesians to compromise the uniqueness and immateriality of the human soul. Descartes also advised Regius to consult two local sympathizers in Utrecht, Gijsbert van der Hoolck (a town councillor) and Antonius Aemilius. When he did this, Van der Hoolck gave a rather alarmist interpretation of events. He thought that Regius was in danger of being dismissed from his professorial chair and that the apparently conciliatory suggestions of Descartes might even be interpreted by critics as sarcasm. Aemilius read the situation in a similar way. It would be better, he thought, not to reply to Voetius, and to calm the situation by silence. Regius consulted Descartes once again (2 February 1642). His reply revealed what he really thought of Voetius. 'I did not know that he ruled over Utrecht . . . and I feel sorry for the city that it is willing to be subject to such a vile pedagogue and such miserable tyranny' (iii. 510). However, he advised Regius (as had Van der Hoolck and Aemilius) not to publish any reply that might compromise his tenure at the university.

At the same time, Descartes also offered apparently contradictory advice with further detailed comments about Voetius that had occurred to him since he had written the previous month. The argument here was that if the so-called forms of purely material things are shown to be nothing more than various dispositions of matter in motion, there is a danger that the same conclusion might apply to the human mind (iii. 503). For example, 'all the arguments used to prove substantial forms can be applied to the form of a clock, although no one claims that it is substantial' (iii. 503). He returns to this type of argument when he tries to formulate an argument against substantial forms.

It is clearly unacceptable that any substantial form would begin to exist unless it were created afresh by God. However, we see every day that many of the forms that are said to be substantial begin to exist, although the people who think they are substances do not think that they are created by God. They are therefore mistaken. This is confirmed in the case of the soul, which is the true substantial form of human beings, because it is thought to be created immediately by God for no other reason except that it is a substance.   (iii. 505)

The other reason used by Descartes, which has echoes of his discussion ten years earlier in *The World*, was that, even if substantial forms were accepted, they would fail completely to provide the kind of explanations for which they were invented by their supporters.

Philosophers had no reason to introduce substantial forms except that, by using them, they were able to explain the characteristic actions of natural things, of which they would be the principle or source. . . . But clearly one cannot explain any natural action by such substantial forms, since even their proponents admit that they are occult and that they do not understand them. For if someone claims that a natural action results from a substantial form, that is the same as saying that it results from something that they do not understand, which explains nothing.   (iii. 506)

There is an obvious sense in which the problem raised by Voetius was insoluble within the terms used by scholastic philosophy. If the soul is classified as a substance, it compromises the unity of human nature. If, however, one focuses on the unity of human experience, it is difficult to understand how this could result from some inexplicable union of two distinct substances. It was this latter problem that tempted Regius into describing the relation between mind and body as 'accidental'. In an attempt to avoid criticism, Descartes encouraged him to acknowledge the limits of our understanding, and to admit that he may have misunderstood technical terms in scholastic philosophy. Above all, he should continue to press the point that human bodies and souls are joined together by a 'real substantial union', that the resulting union constitutes a 'single entity in itself', and that the union of body and soul is 'not accidental but essential' to both parts (iii. 508).

Regius had resisted attempts in the past by his colleagues to cancel disputations or to change their content significantly. On this occasion his characteristic stubbornness reappeared. Despite the possible threat of losing his chair and the unanimous advice of friends that he not reply publicly to Voetius, he published a pamphlet on 26 February 1642, under the title: *A Reply or Notes on the Appendix to the Theologico-Philosophical Corollaries*. The reaction of Voetius was hardly surprising. Within days, he called on the university senate to initiate proceedings against a book that had been published without permission, by a Remonstrant printer and that, he claimed, had libelled him personally and disrespected the office of the rector.[17] The senate agreed to send a delegation to the city magistrates to request seizure of Regius' pamphlet and the suppression of the new philosophy that it endorsed. This was agreed; the remaining copies of the book were confiscated; and the city council issued a condemnation of the 'new philosophy' on 4 April 1642.

It was in these delicate and most inopportune circumstances that Descartes published, as an appendix to the second edition of the *Meditations*, the letter to Father Dinet that included the provocative comments about the University of Utrecht and its rector.

Letter to Father Dinet

The primary purpose of this appendix to the *Meditations*, in the style of an open letter, was to bring about a reconciliation between Descartes and the Jesuits in France. The Jesuits were not allowed to function in the Dutch Republic, and there was therefore no possibility that they would raise objections locally to what Descartes had written. In fact, they showed little enthusiasm for criticizing him even in France, and this silence on their part may have been as much the issue as anything else. The reality was that the Jesuits had not responded, critically or otherwise, to the two books that Descartes had already published, namely, the *Discourse and Essays* (1637) and the *Meditations* (1641).

However, Father Pierre Bourdin – a relatively insignificant professor at the Paris Jesuit college – had arranged a disputation in which some features of Descartes' optical theory were criticized. Descartes' exaggerated response at the time, which coincided with his failure to win approval from the theologians at the Sorbonne, was to contrast the hostility to his ideas in France with the emerging sympathy and support for Cartesian philosophy in the United Provinces. During the final months of 1641 and the first months of the following year, however, he was distracted by a reversal of fortune in the gathering storm of opposition from theologians and philosophers at Utrecht. Accordingly, when he was drafting replies to Bourdin's objections, in preparation for the second edition of the *Meditations*, he was acting as chief philosophical advisor to Regius. It is understandable, then, that when focusing on winning Father Dinet's support, he lapsed into the same kind of contrast that he had used earlier, only this time between the support and advice he hoped to get from France and the petty, ignorant, and uninformed comments of Calvinist theologians at an unnamed Dutch university. This was not the first time that Descartes had expressed regret publicly at the failure of others to acknowledge his philosophical contributions. The lapse of judgment involved here was not out of character. On this occasion, however, it carried a heavy price, both personally and professionally. Utrecht had been the first university to hire a professor who supported Cartesian philosophy. It was now to become the first of many to condemn Cartesianism and to prohibit its teaching.

Any impartial reader today cannot fail to be struck by the bitterness and intensity of the language used by Descartes. Voetius is described as directing his 'machinations' against a rather defenceless Regius, attempting to dismiss him from his chair, of being 'stupid' and 'malicious', of proposing arguments that were 'ridiculous, vicious and false', and of being a 'quarrelsome and incompetent Rector' (vii. 584, 586, 596, 603). He is also described as abusing his position as university rector to defeat Regius by immoral strategies rather than by open argument. For example, Descartes claims that Voetius complained to the theology faculty about the content of Regius' pamphlet and also arranged, at the same time, to have it confiscated so that no one could check the validity of his complaints.[18] When Descartes analyzed the arguments used by Voetius and the theology faculty, he claimed that 'the Rector maliciously tried to conquer his opponent by authority, having been vanquished by his arguments' (vii. 594). In a word, Voetius was presented as an immoral, quarrelsome, stupid, malicious, vindictive, and unfair theologian who abused his temporary authority as rector in order to suppress philosophical ideas simply because they were novel.

Descartes opened up a much bigger 'hornet's nest' on this occasion than anything that might have resulted from Jesuit criticism in France. The reason why he told Father Dinet about this whole episode in such detail, however, is obvious. He wanted to describe what happens when those in authority abuse their power in order to suppress the free discussion of ideas that is required for philosophical inquiry. Since he was trying to persuade Father Dinet to act against Father Bourdin, he stopped short of describing the latter in the same terms as Voetius. However, the implied analogy between the two critics was obvious. Descartes was inviting all those who disagreed with his philosophy to publish their criticisms, and he was particularly requesting that his views not be criticized in private (for example, in disputations in Jesuit colleges), in circumstances in which he could not reply. The suppression of Cartesian ideas at Utrecht was just another recent, relevant, and particularly galling example of the behaviour about which he complained. He evidently hoped that the French Jesuits would not follow the same pattern as his Calvinist critics in a neighbouring Dutch province.

In the course of defending the freedom of philosophers to propose novel ideas, Descartes also quoted from the university's decision, which was sufficiently well known to undermine the appearance of confidentiality or anonymity that he adopted:

The Professors of the Academy of *** . . . reject this new philosophy. Firstly, because it is opposed to the traditional philosophy which universities in the whole world have hitherto taught on the best advice, and it undermines its foundations. Secondly, it turns young people away from the ancient, sound philosophy and prevents them from reaching the pinnacle of erudition because, by relying on this pretence of philosophy, they can no longer understand the technical terms used in the books of renowned authors and the lectures and disputes of their professors. Finally, various false or absurd views either follow from the new philosophy or can be deduced rashly from it by naïve young people, which are inconsistent with other disciplines and faculties and especially with orthodox theology.   (vii. 592–3)

Descartes had stretched the limits of Dutch hospitality by publishing an open letter to Dinet in Amsterdam. Local readers might not have noticed his critical remarks initially, since they were written in Latin. However, Jean Batelier (1593–1672), a Remonstrant opponent of Voetius, translated into Dutch the part of the Dinet letter that concerned Voetius and published it in 1642. It was impossible subsequently for the theology faculty at Utrecht to ignore Descartes' criticism or to fail to reply. While they were considering a measured response, Voetius also decided to initiate his own response, and he asked one of his former colleagues, Martinus Schoock (1614–1669), to write a reply to Descartes.

The University Response

The text of Descartes' letter to Dinet was communicated to the academic senate of the University of Utrecht on 29 June 1642. The professors at Utrecht followed the typical pattern in such matters; they set up a committee to look into the issues raised and to report back to the senate. The committee was comprised of four professors, including the new rector, Antonius Matthaeus.[19] Almost one year later, 16 March 1643, the report of this committee was presented to the senate as an 'historical narrative' of the relevant events.

While the university's official response was still pending during the summer of 1642, Descartes seems to have enjoyed a temporary respite from the controversies involving Regius and Voetius. He wrote to Mersenne (March 1642) to put all the blame for the controversy on Voetius' jealousy, because of the popularity of the new philosophy.

His great animosity towards me results from the fact that there is a professor at Utrecht [Regius] who teaches my philosophy. His disciples, having experienced my way of reasoning, despise the common philosophy so much that they mock it publicly. That has provoked all the other professors, with Voetius as their leader, to be extremely jealous of him. Every day they request the magistrate to prohibit this way of teaching.   (iii. 545–6)

The word in Leiden, which was the nearest large town to where Descartes lived, was that Regius had already been dismissed from his chair, although Descartes was reluctant to believe that.[20] When the academic senate of the university decided, on 25 March 1642, that Regius should restrict his teaching to medicine and to traditional authors, Descartes advised him to observe scrupulously the university's decision. He even counselled that he should adopt the same ploy for avoiding dangerous questions that Descartes himself had used to good effect. If students asked him to discuss questions that were outside the scope of medicine, he should explain that such issues are so interrelated that it is impossible to explain one of them adequately without getting involved in many others.[21] It is evident that, during this summer of 1642, Descartes was on the margin of events in

Utrecht and that, at least for a short time, he enjoyed the tranquillity
required to devote himself to writing the *Principles*.

This picture of a respite in hostilities emerges from a number of independent witnesses. Samuel Sorbière (1615–1670) wrote from The Hague,
25 August 1642, about his visit with Descartes 'five months earlier'. He
described him as a reclusive figure in the castle of Endegeest, pursuing his
studies with the equanimity of a detached scholar.

> Descartes lives near Leiden in a comfortable retreat, like another Democritus. He is
> taken up with his speculations and he communicates his thoughts and experiences to
> no mortal, except to Picot and to a chemist from Leiden, Hogelande. He will publish
> his Physics in two years time. Meantime, he maintains a rigorous silence about it, lest
> those mysteries be profaned. Hence, during the two hours I spent in his company, I
> learned nothing at all about them. I came away, however, admiring him, for he is a rare
> individual about whom later generations will speak.[22]

Descartes provides a similar description of himself when writing to
Huygens, 1 September 1642. He acknowledges that there is a 'truce' in
the attacks from his enemies, at least insofar as no one is attacking him
publicly. 'For that reason, I am philosophizing here very peacefully and in
my usual way, that is, without rushing myself' (iii. 792).

The leisurely drafting of the *Principles* was interrupted dramatically in
December 1642, when Descartes saw the first pages of a book that was
in the process of being printed under the working title *Cartesian Philosophy*, and which he assumed was being written by Voetius.[23] He wrote
to Mersenne that he would not deign to reply to it if he considered only
his own interest. Altruism, however, required him to respond. According
to Descartes, Voetius was exceeding his authority by governing the city
of Utrecht, which included a number of citizens who were friends of the
French philosopher and who would be happy to see a challenge to Voetius'
authority. For their sake, he would 'reply on their behalf' (iii. 599), and
would publish his reply as soon as the whole book was printed.[24]

In the meantime, since Voetius had asked Mersenne naïvely to support his critique of Descartes as theologically heterodox, Descartes took
advantage of that strategic slip to request Mersenne's assistance. He got
copies of the Voetius letters from Mersenne and kept them safely until he
died, in case he needed to quote them against their author.[25] Secondly, he
asked Mersenne to write to Voetius in defence of Descartes and to share
the contents of that reply with him.

If you are so inclined, I have a very effective way of confounding him. For example, if you were to write him a very short letter, in which you tell him that you have been informed that there is a book against me in production, on page 44 of which are the words, etc. [Descartes had quoted a sentence from the book, in which he is described as seeking the protection of the Jesuits, against the criticism of Mersenne and other French theologians and philosophers.] You were very surprised at this, because when you saw that he had said something similar in his theses [on substantial forms, 23 and 24 December 1641], you had written to correct him, etc. You might also mention in this letter that he had already written to you two or three years ago, to request that you write against me. You replied, however, that you would do so very willingly if you had any reason to do so, and if he were to send you details of what he or his associates found objectionable in my writings, and that he had not replied to you. You had therefore concluded that it was purely out of malice that he wished to provoke you against me, and you were now writing him this letter, and sending it to me, open, for forwarding to him, to let me know that you were dissociating yourself from what he wrote about me. If you were to write such a letter, and if I were to have it published, that would undermine his credibility.   (iii. 600–1)

This is typical of the clever manipulation of supportive friends that Descartes used against his critics. Mersenne wrote the letter as requested on 13 December, in Latin (so that Voetius could read it without difficulty).[26] However, rather than forward it to Voetius as originally agreed, Descartes claimed that he was embarrassed by the generosity of Mersenne's compliments, and he decided instead to ask Huygens to act as an intermediary with Voetius.

Descartes now approached Huygens (5 January 1643) to tell him that when he had alerted Mersenne to some of the claims made by Voetius, Mersenne had volunteered to write a letter in his defence. This concealed from Huygens the fact that the suggestion about writing the letter had come originally from Descartes, who had asked Mersenne to send it unsealed to Descartes so that he could forward it to Voetius. His clever ploy now placed him in a quandary. 'However, since that could involve him [Mersenne] in controversy if the other person [Voetius] found out that the letter passed through my hands, I am taking the liberty of putting it in your hands. I ask you to agree to assume that it was Father Mersenne who sent it to you directly from Paris and who commended it to your care' (iii. 800). This was also designed, as Descartes wrote, to undermine the credibility of Voetius as publicly as possible. However, despite the objective of silencing his Dutch critic, Descartes had an even stronger desire to engage in a public row with Voetius. He therefore suggested that Huygens burn the compromising letter from Mersenne if he thought it might discourage Voetius from completing and publishing the critique of Descartes. Huygens agreed to this ruse, and he sent the letter from Mersenne to Voetius with a cover letter in his own hand.[27]

While awaiting publication of what he understood to be a book by Voetius about Cartesian philosophy, Descartes became aware of a different theological dispute among Calvinists in 's-Hertogenbosch, when he saw the first pages of another book in the course of printing, in January 1643.[28] The town of 's-Hertogenbosch had been the scene of a famous siege in 1629. It was a highly fortified town in Brabant, on the northern border of the Spanish Netherlands, and it had fallen to Dutch troops under Prince Frederik Hendrik in September 1629 after a five-month siege that subsequently acquired an almost mythic status. After this highly symbolic rout of the Spanish, there was a general Calvinization of the town, with the establishment of a local Reformed Church (about which Voetius had been consulted) and the official suppression of the public exercise of the Roman Catholic religion.[29] In general, the town and surrounding territory were integrated into a regime similar to what obtained in the rest of the United Provinces. However, the legal rights of established corporations were guaranteed, and this applied equally to a confraternity that had been established in 1318, evidently under Roman Catholic auspices, to promote devotion to Mary, the mother of Jesus. Over time, the confraternity had evolved into something more than merely a religious association. It was also in some sense a club or venue for social gatherings. When the new Calvinist governor of the town, Johan-Wolfert van Brederode, requested admission to the confraternity after the siege, together with thirteen other administrators, none of whom were Catholics, it raised delicate questions about religious sensitivity on both sides.

The local spokesmen on behalf of Calvinist orthodoxy objected to church members joining a club that, in their eyes, condoned idolatry and superstition, and this condemnation triggered publication of a number of books. Samuel Desmarets (1599–1673), a prominent member of the Walloon Calvinist Church and a theologian in the local Illustrious School, wrote a *Defence of the piety and sincerity of the Den Bosch patricians in the affair of the Confraternity named after the Holy Virgin* in 1642. Voetius articulated the objections of the other side in an extremely prolix book that was eventually published in March 1643, thereby contributing to a public dispute within Dutch Calvinism. Even an abbreviated version of the title of Voetius' book extends beyond reasonable limits. *Example of the claims, partly ambiguous and ridiculous, partly dangerous, extracted from a Treatise recently written in Defence of the Establishment and Institution among the Reformed of Confraternities of St. Mary, . . . offered by G. Voetius to the Dutch churches, their faithful pastors and elders.* Voetius argued, predictably, that there were never circumstances that could excuse Calvinists if they joined such a popish sodality and compromised their faith by superstition and idolatry. This intervention by Voetius into the affairs of a town that was outside the jurisdiction of Utrecht provided Descartes with more evidence to support his characterization of the one-time rector as someone who thrived on controversy.

The Principles of Philosophy

By focusing on the Utrecht controversy one gets the mistaken impression that Descartes devoted almost all his energies, during this period, to quarrels with his Dutch Calvinist hosts. In fact, he had been working consistently on a major book that was to be published in 1644 as *The Principles of Philosophy*. Descartes reported to Huygens on 5 January 1643 that he had reached the sections of the *Principles* in which he discussed magnetism.[30] Huygens thought he might assist by sending him a copy of a book by Athanasius Kircher (1601–1680), entitled *The Magnetic Art*, which had been published in Rome in 1641. In characteristic style, Descartes took 'enough patience to leaf through it' by reading only 'the chapter titles and the marginal notes', and he then suggested that the Jesuit author was more 'a charlatan than an expert' (iii. 803).[31]

This reluctance to be distracted by reading the work of others – or, perhaps, Descartes' disdain for their work – is illustrated by the number of books that he refused to read during this period. It is understandable that, when he was extremely busy completing the text of the *Meditations*, he had not read one of the most famous theological books of the time, the *Augustinus* of Jansen, which had been published in Louvain in 1640.[32] However, he also declined to read Fermat's geometry, and a new publication by Gassendi on motion, entitled *Two Letters on Motion impressed by a Body in Motion*. 'I have more or less read only the index that he put at the beginning, from which I learned that he did not discuss any subject matter that I need to read' (iii. 633).[33] He refused to read Hobbes' essay on the tides, with the dismissive comment: 'I am not interested in seeing the writing of the Englishman' (iii. 633).

Despite his unwillingness to read publications by others, Descartes remained open to answering many detailed queries about experiments that were sent almost weekly by Mersenne. In this context, he adverted to the recent death of Richelieu (4 December 1642), commenting that he would have needed to bequeath two or three of his millions to support the range of experiments required 'to discover the specific nature of every body' (iii. 610). The stark contrast within French public policy – between raising taxes to wage war and failing to support scientific research from royal funds – provoked the comment that such an investment 'could lead to great discoveries, which would be of much greater benefit to humanity than all the victories that one could win by waging war' (iii. 610).

By the following month, Descartes was sufficiently confident of progress that he planned to put the *Principles* into production during the summer, although he reminded his correspondent that it had taken a year to complete printing of the *Dioptrics* and that he could expect a similar delay in this case.[34] He continued to perform experiments, including those that Mersenne claimed to have done already, because he refused to rely on experimental results that he had not replicated himself.[35] He was reworking the sections on astronomy that appeared in Part III of the *Principles*, in April 1643, and inquired about Galileo's telescope, then in the possession of Gassendi, and whether it could be used to examine the moons of Jupiter.[36] However, just when he had nearly completed the text, he was forced to return 'from the heavens to earth' by the publication of Martin Schoock's critique of Cartesianism.[37]

The Admirable Method

Martinus Schoock's long-winded, personal attack on Descartes, under the title *The Admirable Method of the New Philosophy of René Descartes*, appeared in late March or April 1643.[38] Schoock had supported Voetius previously in controversies within Dutch Calvininism, especially against Remonstrants, and had subsequently moved from Utrecht to a chair of rhetoric at Deventer and eventually to a chair of philosophy at Groningen.[39] He had begun work on his anti-Cartesian critique during the summer holidays in 1642, at Utrecht, where he could collaborate more conveniently with Voetius on the content and style of the pamphlet. By the end of the year, when he returned to Groningen for the new academic year, he had completed only part of the response, and he sent that to the printer, pending delivery of the remainder. This allowed Descartes to get an advance copy of part of the text, and to have his own reply ready almost immediately upon the publication of *The Admirable Method* in spring 1643.

The Admirable Method is a prolix, sustained, personal attack on Descartes. Schoock calls Descartes 'a lying biped', the 'prince of Cretans', 'king of the Cretans', and someone who 'has a habit of lying'.[40] This direct critique of his alleged immorality was complemented by an equally damaging, indirect inquiry about why the French philosopher changed his address so frequently. Schook offered a few possible reasons: that he belonged to the fraternity of the Rose Cross, that he was a misanthrope, and that he changed residence to escape the consequences of an immoral life. Since he also questioned whether Descartes practised his religion and compared him to Vanini, who, he reminded readers, had been 'burned at Toulouse', the implications of the comparison were very clear to informed readers.[41] With both explicit and implicit charges, he was characterizing Descartes as a lying, irreligious, homosexual atheist.[42]

When he addresses Descartes' philosophy, Schoock claims that it leads him to scepticism, atheism, and enthusiasm.[43] Rhetoric, rather than evidence, was likely to be most effective in this kind of personal attack. Schook, probably at the instigation of Voetius, got his point across to readers by suggesting that Descartes was a member of the Rose Cross fraternity and that he was acting like a follower of Lull. Even the Cartesian contribution to mathematics provided an opportunity to imply that those who trust numbers so much are like those who attribute magical powers to inanimate objects.[44] With a colourful reference to the role of the serpent in the Garden of Eden, he writes of Descartes: 'This man competes with Vanini in this sense; while giving the impression of combating atheists with his invincible arguments, he injects the venom of atheism delicately and secretly into those who, because of their feeble minds, never notice the serpent that hides in the grass.'[45] Many of these suggestions amount to not much more than name calling or guilt by association with those who were already generally recognized as anathema to the Christian tradition. However, Schoock also manages to raise one or two questions that have genuine merit.

For example, he questions how Descartes can apply his extremely demanding standards of intelligibility and certainty to any of the central mysteries of Christianity. If Descartes requires everything that we believe to be intelligible, then he would reject all the central dogmas of the Christian tradition, such as the Trinity, the divinity of Christ, and the resurrection of the body, and that would make him equivalent to a Socinian.[46] If however Descartes were a genuine Christian, he should acknowledge that revelation is much more certain than anything one learns in medicine and that it would be a fundamental mistake to confuse the type of certainty that is available, in principle, in one context with that available in the other. In pressing this argument, Schoock makes a point that is similar to Descartes' response to Morin in 1638: 'Just as it would be a mistake to demand of medicine a degree of certainty that is comparable to the dogmas of theology, so likewise one could not excuse those who would demand, for all the dogmas of physics, that their demonstrations achieve the exactitude that is found only in mathematics.'[47]

This challenge reflects a debate within Calvinism between those who put their trust in reason and then adjusted the teachings of the church so that they were 'reasonable', and those who trusted religious faith so much that, if necessary, it could be used to override conclusions based on rational argument. Moise Amyraut (1596–1664) was a prominent proponent, within the French Huguenot community, of the first option. He published a book in the same year that Descartes' *Meditations* appeared, under the title: *The Elevation of Faith and the Lowering of Reason when Believing the Mysteries of Religion* (1641). Amyraut argued that faith and reason were compatible and complementary, and that it was never necessary to reject reason – as in the Roman Catholic doctrine of transubstantiation – in order to retain genuine religious faith. Descartes was being accused by Schoock of joining the Amyraut side of the debate and using reason as a touchstone of what may be accepted on faith.

Schoock also claims that, despite his explicit statements to the contrary, Descartes is unduly influenced by the scepticism of Sextus Empiricus, that he wishes to undermine proofs of God's existence by offering manifestly ineffective arguments, and that his invitation to readers of the *Meditations* to clear their minds of all previously held beliefs is a mere disguise for deluding them into accepting Cartesianism.[48] The image of Descartes portrayed here is not that of a philosopher who is grappling with genuine metaphysical questions, but rather that of a shrewd manipulator of credulous followers whose primary interest is to found a new 'sect' and to control its members by the authority of his word.

Descartes' *Letter to Voetius*

Descartes had been aware for some time of the imminent publication of *The Admirable Method*, since he had seen the first few pages of the text, presumably through some contact with the printer, in December 1642. By 23 March 1643, he had the full text of the book, and he began writing his reply in April. He concluded his *Letter to the distinguished gentleman, Mr. Gisbertus Voetius, in which two books recently published at the same time for Voetius of Utrecht are examined: one concerning the Marian Confraternity, the other concerning Cartesian Philosophy*, toward the end of May 1643.[49] He arranged to have it published both in Latin and in a Dutch translation.[50]

Descartes opens his reply to *The Admirable Method*, which he claims was written with the active collaboration of Voetius by one of his supporters, with a spirited defence of freedom of thought. This type of argument is familiar in the version later presented by John Stuart Mill in the nineteenth century. Mill constructed a lengthy argument, in *On Liberty* (1859), to support the fullest possible freedom of expression. Part of the argument was that, if certain views happen to be false and are expressed publicly, their publication will cause no harm (except in special cases). However, if they happen to be true and are still suppressed, the whole of humanity suffers the harm of being denied access to the truth.[51] Descartes offers a similar defence of freedom to publish philosophical views:

Philosophizing has always been so free and so many have erred before us without causing harm to anyone that, if I am mistaken like them, one should not fear that the human race will be harmed as a result. However, if I happen to discover the truth, one could expect great benefits. That is how it happens that those who love the truth, in the tenuous and doubtful hope of finding truth in my writings, invite me to publish them.   (viii-2. 3)

Descartes also proposes, as he had done in previous disputes, a completely favourable description of his own role in the controversy. He describes himself as living in relative obscurity in the country, as avoiding as much as possible the company of others, and as having tried his best to avoid cultivating disciples.[52] Besides, as he repeats a number of times – in an obvious reference to the *Principles*, which were almost complete – he has not yet published his philosophy; he has merely made available some samples that might help readers to determine if they were interested in seeing his whole system.[53] Not only does he live in the country and withhold publication of his philosophy, but he is also naturally a peace-loving person!

'It is known that I am a lover of peace and quiet more than anyone else, that I have never instituted legal proceedings against anyone or engaged in controversy with anyone. I have often even condoned the injuries I suffered rather than try to avenge them' (viii-2. 109–10). He offers the same explanation that he had given on previous occasions of why he is living in the United Provinces, rather than in France, where he could have enjoyed the protection of his own nation:

As many people know, I lived in relative comfort in my native country. My only reason for choosing to live elsewhere was that I had so many friends and relatives whom I could not fail to entertain, and that I would have had little time and leisure available to pursue the studies which I enjoy and which, according to many people, will contribute to the common good of the human race.   (viii-2. 110–11)

In contrast with this retiring, peace-loving, and tolerant scholar who minds his own business, Voetius is presented as someone who is very much involved in the public life of the new Dutch republic. He is a preacher and professor, and was for a time rector of the university.[54] He is known as being 'most querulous, bitter, and troublesome' (viii-2. 110), and he has looked for 'rows and controversies to destroy other people's reputations, and to appear so implacable, obstinate and terrifying, that no one would subsequently dare to challenge him' (viii-2. 130).[55] Descartes illustrates Voetius' penchant for meddling in the affairs of others by reference to the Confraternity of the Blessed Virgin.

This intervention by Voetius into the internal affairs of another town, in a different province (Brabant), helped support Descartes' claim that he was a meddling, dogmatic, and quarrelsome theologian who found reasons to dispute in public even with members of the Calvinist Church. Descartes usually avoided becoming involved in theological controversies, even within his own church, and it was a new – possibly unwise – step on his part to engage in what seemed like an internal dispute within Dutch Calvinism about the extent to which they should tolerate social interaction with Roman Catholics. Wise or otherwise, Descartes took full advantage of the opportunity to brand Voetius as a troublemaker. 'Nothing can tend to civil unrest more readily than if someone relies on the authority of one town to condemn what has been done in another town – and not just anything done there, but something that was done for the good of the republic – in a public writing which, rather than reproach with reasons, afflicts them with insults' (viii-2. 133).[56] Descartes uses this obscure theological dispute within Dutch Calvinism to draw attention to one of the implications of Voetius' conduct, namely, that he assumed a theocratic authority by telling the magistrates of another civil power how to behave in their social lives. The rhetorical effect of this claim was greatly enhanced by an independent and on-going tension, between different provinces, about decisions concerning war and peace. After August 1643, the states of Holland signaled their independence with respect to foreign policy by withholding from their delegates to the States General the authority to negotiate with other provinces without specific instructions from Holland.[57]

Voetius emerges from Descartes' *Letter to Voetius* as someone who changes roles from one scene to another, but always with the same fundamental objective. 'Your skills as a mime artist are well known; you adopt the role at one time of the Faculty of Theology, at another of the University, at another of the city Senate, then of the whole Republic, then of the Dutch Church, then as a Prophet or as the Holy Spirit, or finally as one or other of your disciples' (viii-2. 159). In conclusion, having painted an extremely unfavourable picture of a dogmatic, interfering minister who disputes even with senior civil members of the Dutch Calvinist Church in another jurisdiction, Descartes appeals to the religious freedom that he is guaranteed under the law. 'I need not invoke the religious freedom that is granted to us [i.e., French residents] in this republic' (viii-2. 193). The book published by Voetius, or published in his name by Martin Schoock, is so filled with 'culpable lies, scurrilous insults, and odious calumnies' (viii-2. 193) that no one could express them, even against an enemy or an infidel, without revealing his own depravity.

The *Letter to Voetius* repays him in the same currency of personal attack that had marred the whole discussion from the beginning. Contemporaries were almost embarrassed by the intensity of the public row. Huygens, as usual, was sympathetic, complimenting Descartes on the justice he displayed toward Voetius and his 'aide-de-camp', Schoock.[58] He even applied to this theological dispute a comment that he had heard previously: 'theologians are like pigs; when you pull the tail of one of them, they all squeal together.'[59] Andreas Colvius was more impartial, regretting the fact that two renowned scholars were publicly accusing each other of atheism, while each of them displayed the lack of charity of which he accused the other.[60] He suggested that Descartes would have been better advised to concentrate on delivering to the world the work on natural philosophy that he had long promised. However, in replying to Voetius, Descartes did more than match the insults and charges that were so liberally scattered throughout *The Admirable Method*; he also answered some of the genuine criticisms it contained.

One of the most dangerous objections against Cartesian philosophy was that it was conducive to atheism. Schoock had argued that Descartes was a secret atheist who appeared to provide arguments for God's existence but whose real intention, since the arguments offered were demonstrably so poor, must have been to undermine belief in God and his Providence. Descartes' reply is both apposite and effective. He refers to theological disputes published by Voetius in 1639, on the theme of atheism, and to the efforts of many theologians to construct the best arguments possible in support of God's existence. The nub of his argument, then, is this. 'If someone tries to refute atheism and offers arguments that are inadequate to the task, he should be accused of incompetence only, but not of atheism' (viii-2. 175). However, even this judgment is too harsh. As Voetius himself had acknowledged in his discussions of atheism, the refutation of atheists is extremely difficult, and therefore those who argue ineffectively against atheism are not necessarily guilty even of incompetence (viii-2. 176). In a word, if Descartes' arguments in support of God's existence fail, he is no more unsuccessful than many famous theologians who preceded him, and he should definitely not be accused of atheism.

Descartes' letters during the controversy confirm that the most worrying feature of Schoock's long book was the suggestion that he was some kind of cryptic atheist, and that he deserved the same fate as Vanini. This had also been the initial response of Mersenne, when he read the *Admirable Method* in May 1643.[61] Mersenne must have been particularly sensitive to the implications of the comparison to Vanini, since he had dedicated so much effort to refuting Vanini in is own books and was one of the main sources of the rumours about his homosexuality.[62] For his part, Descartes wrote to the French ambassador in The Hague (22 January 1644) and mentioned twice the concern about atheism and Vanini. 'Simply because I demonstrated the existence of God [in the *Meditations*], he tried to convince people that I secretly teach atheism, in the same style as Vanini who was burned at Toulouse.'[63] He wrote the following month to the University of Groningen, where Schoock was a professor, complaining about the same accusation. 'There can truly be no greater crime than the atheism of which he accuses me. . . . He proves that I am an atheist by no other argument except that I wrote against atheists and, according to many people, my efforts were not poor' (iv. 178).

The report of the committee established by the Utrecht university senate was completed and submitted in March 1643. It might have remained confidential to the senate had Descartes not further antagonized the Utrecht faculty members by his public letter to Voetius at the end of May.[64] The interim decision of the Utrecht magistrates was a demand that all sides observe a truce and that no books for or against Descartes be published in Utrecht. 'The Vroedschap of the city of Utrecht prohibits and forbids very rigorously printers and booksellers in this city and within its jurisdiction to print or to have printed, to sell or to have sold, any small booklets or writings for or against Descartes, under penalties to be decided. Enacted: 12 June 1643.' The university senate might have accepted a similar compromise. However, Descartes' second public attack on Voetius provoked its members into publishing their version of events and their commentary on the merits of both sides in October 1643.[65]

The committee's report would seem to impartial readers today to be a matter-of-fact and balanced account of the various disputes that had been reported to the university. It is clear that the report objected especially to the personal attack on Voetius and to the accusation that he abused his authority as rector in order to muster support from the academic senate for himself. While recounting the background to the controversy, it mentions an earlier controversy that involved Regius when he was teaching at the Latin school of Naarden. His controversial views on that occasion about the immateriality and immortality of the soul had raised theological objections that, at the time, he was able to avoid by retracting some opinions and accepting orthodox Calvinist teaching. There were also suggestions that Regius had contributed to the public disorder that occurred during some of the more contentious disputations. However, the central feature of the narrative was a listing of the reasons why members of the theology faculty at Utrecht were concerned about Regius' current teaching. While the 'historical narrative' did not attempt to support its concerns with arguments, it mentioned and endorsed the same fundamental concern that had earlier provoked Voetius. The orthodox teaching of the Calvinist Church was expressed in scholastic language. Therefore, if this set of concepts were abandoned, it could undermine basic Christian beliefs in the nature of God, the immateriality of the human soul, the resurrection

of the body, and even, in the case of Galileo's astronomy, in the truth of
the Scriptures.

Egmond aan den Hoef

During the time when Descartes was putting the final touches to *The
Principles of Philosophy* and writing a reply to Martin Schoock's critical
book, he mentioned without any explanation that he was 'about to move
from here and to go to live near Alkmaar op de hoef where I have rented
a house' (iii. 647).[66] Sometime during the month of May 1643, he left
Endegeest and moved north again, to Egmond aan den Hoef, which was
considerably more isolated than his former residence.[67] He repeated, in
February of the same year, the reasons he had often given since 1628 for
deciding to live in the United Provinces. Picot had written to say that
he was going to the Touraine region of France with a view to buying a
property there. Descartes claimed that he would prefer, for his part, to
purchase land in a poorer country where, for the same price, one could
get a larger piece of property, and 'thus I would not be as easily disturbed
by my relatives' (iii. 616). He presumably did not have the resources to
purchase property anywhere. One might read into his comments that he
could more easily afford to rent property in Egmond than close to Leiden,
and that the dominant motivation for his move was, as usual, to avoid
being disturbed by friends or relatives. His relocation may also have been
encouraged by the turn of events in Utrecht, where there was suddenly a
danger of being brought before a civil court and charged with libel.

Descartes had been summoned by the municipal council of Utrecht in
June 1643 to answer the charge of libel against Voetius. The principal participants in this complex dispute lived in different provinces – Descartes
in Holland, Schoock in Groningen, Desmarets in Brabant, and Voetius in
Utrecht – and it was unlikely that any one province could have successfully enforced a summons against those who lived elsewhere. Descartes
refers to this in a formal letter of reply to the *Vroedschap* of Utrecht.[68] He
complained about the public nature of the summons, as he was well known
in the United Provinces, especially in Utrecht. Consequently, they knew
where he lived if they wished to contact him directly. He also hinted that
they lacked jurisdiction over him, since he lived in north Holland (iv. 12).
However, Descartes was also concerned enough about his personal safety
to look for legal advice, to ask Pollot for advice about getting local support,

and to write to a number of potential defenders, including Huygens, to help resist the new pressure from Utrecht.

Pollot advised that he contact Dirck Graswinckel, whose role was similar to that of an attorney general for the province of Holland. He suggested wisely that Descartes not make matters worse by writing provocative letters to Utrecht or Groningen.[69] Pollot also advised Descartes to seek the protection of the French ambassador to The Hague, the Marquis Gaspard Coignet de la Thuillerie, and, through him, to request that the *Stadtholder* intervene in the case.[70] The *Stadtholder* was sufficiently sympathetic that the Utrecht magistrates agreed, informally, to close the case. The ambassador's secretary wrote to Descartes, regretting that the Dutch republic had not forced him to leave the country, because France would thereby have gained a benefit equivalent to their loss.[71] The ambassador also wrote on his behalf to the states of Groningen, probably in March 1644, arguing that the public interest required that Descartes be allowed to enjoy the freedom and noninterference required to complete his intellectual project.[72]

Descartes was equally anxious to achieve a satisfactory resolution with Groningen. He explained to Pollot that he did not wish to harm Schoock, whom he always understood as a relatively naïve pawn in the controversy. His main objective was to put a stop to menaces from Utrecht.[73] Accordingly, he wrote a letter to explain his situation, without any addressee, and he sent it to Pollot to ask advice about who to send it to: the French ambassador, the academic senate at Groningen, or the states of the corresponding province.[74] Descartes' original claim about the authorship of *The Admirable Method*, perhaps initially based on a mistaken hypothesis about its author before the title page was added, was to some extent vindicated when Schoock accepted, two years later (20 April 1645), that the initiative to write the book came from Voetius. This late development included a number of acknowledgments that were very damaging for Voetius.

(1) Schoock undertook to write *The Admirable Method* only because he was asked to do so by Voetius, who in turn suggested a number of criticisms of Descartes, including the charge of atheism.

(2) While most of the text had been written by Schoock in Utrecht, another unidentified hand had added some of the most virulent accusations to the text.

(3) The tone of the work was unbecoming a scholarly debate; in particular, Schoock had never meant to compare Descartes to Vanini.

(4) He had been pressured into saying that he was the author of the controversial book, whereas in fact he was responsible only for the order of the
sections and chapters.[75]

Descartes was reluctant to conclude this controversy without getting some
apology or formal acknowledgment of innocence of the various charges
levelled against him. He was willing to accept a reconciliation with Schoock
because, he claimed, 'there is nothing in life that is sweeter than peace'. In
fact, he would not even 'reject the friendship of Voetius if I believed that he
offered it in good faith'.[76] In this frame of mind, he sent the Utrecht magistrates a number of documents in 1645, including the letters from Voetius
to Mersenne that invited the Minim to testify against Descartes' orthodoxy, and the results of the Groningen inquiry.[77] However, the *Vroedschap*
was reluctant to become involved in further controversy and deferred
making any decision by requesting its secretary to prepare a translation of
the Latin request.

Descartes' final effort to get satisfaction from Utrecht, the *Apologetic
Letter to the Magistrates of Utrecht*, was drafted probably in the spring of
1647 and sent to the magistrates in February 1648.[78] The word 'apologetic'
was evidently used in the sense of 'vindicatory' or 'self-defensive'. The
immediate cause of drafting a fresh appeal to Utrecht was a lawsuit taken
by Voetius against his former collaborator, Schoock, whose testimony at
Groningen had publicly exposed the extent to which Voetius had inspired
The Admirable Method. It was also motivated by the final rift with Regius
(to be discussed in Chapter 11) and the new controversy with theologians
at Leiden (discussed in Chapter 12). As a last straw, Voetius published an
amended version of his disputations in the first volume of his *Theological
Disputations* in 1647, and reopened old wounds by addressing accusatory
questions to Descartes about his alleged atheism.[79]

Descartes' letter identifies some of the charges that evidently continued to rankle despite the passing of time. He had been accused of being
a disciple of the Jesuits, of attacking the great defender of the Reformed
religion, G. Voetius, in order to win their favour, and of being sent by
the Jesuits to the United Provinces to stir up trouble there (viii-2. 221
[French], 292 [Latin]). He repeats his charge that Voetius must have
been the real author of *The Admirable Method*, since Schoock disavows
its content while Voetius continues to defend it (viii-2. 264–5 [French
only]).

By this time, despite the involvement of Voetius' son, Paul, the temporary arrest of Schoock after church services while visiting Utrecht, and
the lawsuits that were threatened on all sides, the city council of Utrecht
decided, very wisely, simply to repeat their earlier decision. Descartes
arranged that the letters from Voetius to Mersenne would be preserved,
if he were to die on his travels to Sweden, and that his associates would
have the evidence to defend his good name even after his death.

Mind and Body

The Utrecht controversy was sparked by Regius' attempts to describe
human nature without respecting the traditional philosophical account
that was widely taught in the schools and was presupposed equally
by Roman Catholic and Calvinist theologians. It was also triggered by
Descartes' undiplomatic efforts to win the support of Jesuit readers in
France. Jesuit opposition eventually waned, or at least the French philosopher in exile accepted that it was not significant enough to warrant his continued concern. He wrote to Father Bourdin, 7 September 1642, to encourage him to publish both his own objections and, if he wished, Descartes'
replies.[80] He concluded this letter with the warm, though possibly insin-
cere, acknowledgment: 'As regards those who love the truth, among whom
I include all the fathers of the Society: I have no doubt that they are all my
friends' (iii. 577). Descartes then arranged to send a copy of the same letter
to Mersenne, with the following instructions. 'If he publishes something
against me . . . or if he misrepresents the history of our dispute, you will
know that it is not because I failed to warm him not to do so' (iii. 584).
Two months later, he wrote to another Jesuit in Paris, Father Vatier, with
whom he had corresponded after publication of the *Essays* (1637). 'You are
the one among all the members of your Society whom I have the honour
of knowing from whom I could have hoped for a favourable judgment' (iii.
595). He may have overdone the charm offensive on this occasion.

I have always had a great affection and respect for your Society. . . . I am extremely
obliged to Revered Father Dinet for the frankness and prudence that he showed on
that occasion [the row with Bourdin] . . . for I know that it is only those who are most
eminent in prudence and virtue who are usually chosen for his office [as superior of
the province]. . . . The only favour I ask is that people refrain from blaming what they
do not understand and, if there is anything to say against me or my writings, that
they would be kind enough to say it to me directly rather than to slander me in my
absence.   (iii. 597)

This healing of the strained relations with the French Jesuits continued during the subsequent years. When Descartes visited Paris in the summer of 1644, he had an opportunity to visit with Father Bourdin and to report later to Father Dinet that Bourdin gave him reason to hope that they could be friends.[81] When the *Principles* was published in 1644, Descartes sent a dozen copies to Bourdin and asked him to distribute them among the Jesuits in France. Given these developments, it was not surprising that Descartes' final contribution to the Utrecht controversy, his *Apologetic Letter* of 1647/8, referred to the Seventh Objections and his own replies in these words: 'That whole book was written against a certain Jesuit whom, however, I am now happy to have as my friend' (viii-2. 222 [French], 293 [Latin]).

The philosophical problems about the nature of the soul were not resolved as easily as the apparent hostility of the Jesuits. Descartes remained an implacable critic of real qualities and substantial forms, because he thought they were useless for explaining any natural phenomenon. For example, he wrote to Mersenne in April 1643:

I do not assume that there are any 'real qualities' in nature which are added to a substance like little souls to their bodies and which could be separated from them by divine power. . . . My principal reason for rejecting these real qualities is that I do not see that the human mind has within itself any notion or specific idea by which it conceives them. Thus when we name them and claim that there are such things, we assert something that we do not conceive and we do not understand what we are saying ourselves. The second reason is that philosophers assumed these real qualities only because they believed that, otherwise, they could not explain all the phenomena of nature. On the contrary, I find that one can explain such phenomena much better without them.   (iii. 648–9)

The philosophers who proposed philosophical entities such as 'real qualities' and 'substantial forms' thought of them as two different types of reality. Descartes, however, tended to discuss them together, as postulated entities that had been invented to explain natural phenomena but that failed miserably in their intended function. Despite this consistent criticism, Descartes continued to speak of the human mind as an exception to his general rejection of substantial forms, and this is reflected in the letter just quoted in which he compares real qualities in other natural phenomena to 'little souls'.

Thus, in parallel with the critique of substantial forms in other contexts, Descartes continued to defend a real distinction between the soul and the body, especially when he suspected that Regius was willing to fudge that distinction. For example, he wrote to him in June 1642:

> You acknowledge that thought is an attribute of a substance that includes no extension and, conversely, that extension is an attribute of a substance that includes no thought. You must accept, therefore, that a thinking substance is distinct from an extended substance. For we have no criterion by which we know that one substance differs from another except that we understand one without the other. God can patently bring about anything that we understand clearly. . . . However, we can understand clearly a thinking substance that is not extended and an extended substance that is not thinking, as you acknowledge. Even if God joins and unites them as much as he can, he cannot thereby deprive himself of his omnipotence, nor therefore can he take away his ability to separate them, and therefore they remain distinct.   (iii. 567)

This real distinction between mind and body was destined to reappear in subsequent discussions and correspondence. It proved to be a source of contention between Descartes and Regius in later years. However, long before Regius went public with his disagreement with Descartes, Princess Elizabeth was to take up the same question in 1643, and to raise it as something that she genuinely did not understand.

9

Descartes and Princess Elizabeth

The very friendly letter, which showed that you were thinking of me, is the most precious thing that I could receive in this country.

(Descartes to Elizabeth)[1]

THE people who were most influential in Descartes' early life were all women. His mother died when he was one year old. That might have provided a context in which he could have formed close family ties with his two siblings, Pierre and Jeanne, or with his father, Joachim. Apart from Jeanne, however, he seems to have been estranged from his immediate family and to have directed his affections from infancy toward others. The first person with whom he bonded closely was his nurse, with whom he maintained a residual emotional link for the rest of his life. According to his niece, Catherine, Descartes specifically asked as he was dying that those who managed his estate 'take care of the living expenses of his nurse, whom he had always cared for when he was alive'.[2] This final token of gratitude should not be exaggerated. It probably indicates a redirected love for his mother rather than a deep, authentic love for someone whom he had not seen for more than fifty years.[3] The other people most closely involved in Descartes' early life were his grandmothers. Since his father, Joachim, worked in Rennes for part of each year from 1596 to 1600 – when he remarried and moved permanently in Brittany – Descartes was effectively cared for until he went to college by his two grandmothers, Jeanne Sain and Claude Ferrand. The evidence of later years suggests that he was also close to his sister, Jeanne, from his infancy. One has to think of Descartes, therefore, in the first five or six years of his life as playing with his older sister, in the care of his grandmothers, and devoted to his nurse, who occupied the role of a mother for the first few years of his life. Neither his father nor his brother seems to have established in his childhood any basis for an enduring, emotionally strong relationship.

In complete contrast, once Descartes reached maturity, he lived a rather nomadic life in which he had no genuine women friends.[4] It is true, of course, that he had conceived a daughter, Francine, with the maidservant of his landlord in Amsterdam in 1634. He might have developed an appropriately paternal affection toward his daughter had she lived long enough to reach adulthood. But that was not to be. His concern for Helena Jans was evident, as late as 1644, in his financial support for her marriage – to someone else.[5] He had briefly become acquainted with Anna Maria van Schurman, one of the most learned women at the time in the United Provinces, but he was very disparaging about her intellectual interests and, especially after 1642, her alliance with Voetius. Finally, in 1643, Princess Elizabeth of Bohemia, who enjoyed political asylum from her native Bohemia in The Hague, read the *Meditations* and initiated an intellectual correspondence with Descartes that resulted in some of the most revealing replies on his part to her searching questions.

This lack of genuine women friends would not require any special explanation if the French philosopher were simply a misanthrope, as Schoock had suggested. However, Descartes' reluctance about friendships and social contacts was not so general or undiscriminating that it would merit that description. He was certainly reclusive, and he was consistently secretive about where he lived. He frequently changed residence, often moving from one town to another rather than renting new accommodations in the same town or city. Nonetheless, throughout most of his adult life, he cultivated relatively intense and exclusive friendships with a small number of male friends, beginning with Beeckman. Balzac was among the first to show a genuine affection for Descartes, while Baillet described Villebressieu as a 'special friend'.[6] Reneri was later to merit the same status, when he lived 'in great intimacy' with the philosopher in Deventer, and Regius was temporarily classified as a friend at a distance before his public falling out with Descartes.[7] In fact, the impression one gets from his correspondence is that Descartes cultivated special friendships with a small number of loyal supporters who shared his philosophical views. He also acquired a wider circle of correspondents who were instrumental in various ways in making his life's work successful.

The most obvious person among the latter was Marin Mersenne. Despite a few occasions when his patience with Mersenne was exhausted and he expressed his frustration in letters to others, Descartes treated Mersenne throughout his life as an indispensable source of scientific information and as a mediator with the wider world of European learning. Mersenne kept him informed about scientific developments in Italy and France; he helped arrange for publication of the *Meditations* in Paris (with a rather unsatisfactory outcome); and he frequently provided copies of new books that he thought were relevant to Descartes' work. This explains the frequency of letters exchanged between the two men. Of course, Descartes was not the only one who corresponded in this way with Mersenne, whose extraordinary correspondence extended to many others who shared his encyclopedic interests in theology, music, and all the physical sciences. The Minim's penchant for letter writing was such that it prompted Huygens (no mean correspondent himself) to comment that he 'filled the air of the universe with his letters'.[8] Besides writing to Mersenne frequently, Descartes also displayed the respectful deference that was customary toward clerics in the seventeenth century, as he did even toward the Jesuits whom he was criticizing. Despite the frequency of their correspondence, however, and their mutual dependence, one would hardly have described Mersenne as a friend of Descartes. He was more like a Catholic apologist who was anxious to enlist Descartes' assistance in his religious propaganda, while Descartes, for his part, was happy to exploit Mersenne's co-operation while trying to become recognized as a successful philosopher.

Within the United Provinces, Constantijn Huygens was more a patron of the exiled Frenchman than a friend. Descartes took advantage of Huygens' office as secretary to the *Stadtholder* to send letters and draft manuscripts to and from France with the added security and lack of expense of diplomatic messengers. Huygens viewed himself as a general patron of the arts and sciences in the United Provinces, and his solicitude in relation to Descartes reflected the widely acknowledged expectations of the French philosopher's potential contribution to the sciences. Just as Mersenne had many other correspondents apart from Descartes, Huygens had many other artists and men of letters – mostly Dutch – whom he patronized. Descartes, for his part, was appropriately deferential toward such a central figure in the administration of the emerging Dutch republic.

In the case of the few women who figured in any way in Descartes' life, therefore, one has to ask whether they were friends (as were Van Hogelande and Reneri), whether they were useful contacts or patrons (such as Mersenne and Huygens), or whether they were rejected as inferior scholars who exaggerated their intellectual accomplishments, such as almost all those who responded to the Cartesian invitation to submit corrections to his work (including Beaugrand, Fermat, Hobbes, and many more). Maria van Schurman fell into this latter category, while Elizabeth of Bohemia is most accurately described as an intellectual patron.

Anna Maria van Schurman

Van Schurman's parents had moved from Antwerp to Cologne during the Spanish occupation of the city, and she was born there into a strict Calvinist family in 1607. She moved later to Utrecht (1615) and subsequently to Franeker (1622–23), where her brothers were attending university. However, with her father's death in 1623, the young woman returned to Utrecht, where she lived with her mother and aunts for many years.[9] During this period she became well known for her work as a miniaturist artist and even more famous for her learning and knowledge of languages. She attended theology lectures given by Voetius at the university, while hiding behind a curtain, since women were not allowed to register officially for university studies. It is clear from the theological writings of Voetius that Van Schurman must have listened to a strictly orthodox account of Calvinism. He inveighed against the kind of probabilism that he associated with Jesuit moral theology, demanding that moral queries be answered with 'categorical and absolute' rules.[10] Not surprisingly, when he illustrated his morality with examples, his discussion lapsed into an extended complaint about the social customs of the time. He reproached those who 'lend money for usury, or drink as much as others at parties . . . or wear their hair long and curled, or dress up like whores . . . by adorning, or deforming, not only the top of their head but also their face and arms'.[11]

It is a tribute to Van Schurman's independence of mind that, despite the oppressive influence of Voetius, she wrote an articulate tract in support of women's education, which was published in the same year as Descartes' *Meditations*.[12] Van Schurman's *Dissertation on the Aptitude of Women's Intelligence for Learning and Advanced Studies* is a systematic attempt to answer the question raised at the very beginning of the book: 'are studies in the humanities necessary or appropriate for a Christian woman?'[13] She argues that such studies are both necessary and appropriate, and she is very inclusive about the range of studies involved.

One should include especially those sciences or arts which are most closely connected
with sacred theology and moral virtues. . . . we think that the following are included
in this class: grammar, logic, rhetoric . . . physics, metaphysics, history, etc. and also
languages, especially a knowledge of Hebrew and Greek, all of which can lead us to
a fuller and better understanding of Sacred Scripture. Others, such as mathematics
(which also includes music), poetry, and painting, and other liberal arts . . . [14]

Van Schurman can be read as adopting, for rhetorical purposes, the
extremely negative view of women that she learned from Voetius, and
then showing that women have a correspondingly greater need to be educated than men. 'Whoever is most in danger of vanity, because of imbecility
and fickleness of natural temperament' is most in need of education. Likewise, whoever has a weaker intelligence has a greater need for education.
But, according to common opinion, women are vain, foolish, fickle, and
so on.[15] There is no reason to think that Van Schurman endorsed these
negative assumptions about women. However, she wished to show that,
according to the logic of misogynists, women needed education much more
than men. Her own view was that the natural abilities of men and women
differ from one person to another, and that nothing else is required for
study apart from what Descartes had called 'common sense'. This reads
very much like a sympathetic expression of the Cartesian view that native
intelligence, rather than familiarity with Aristotle, is the only prerequi-
site for study. In spite of their shared opinion, however, Descartes was
unequivocally and consistently critical of Van Schurman's contributions
to contemporary debates.

Descartes must have known about Van Schurman when he lived on the
outskirts of Utrecht in 1635–36, because she lived in a prominent location
in the shadow of the Dom Cathedral, in Cathedral Place. He evidently
knew about Van Schurman's attendance at the theology lectures given by
Voetius, because he refers to her concealed attendance in a letter to Regius
in 1640.[16] Since Descartes had already begun to target Voetius as a critic of
Regius, it is most likely that his intense dislike of Voetius was transferred,
to some extent, to one of his most devoted followers.[17] By November
1640, Voetius had contacted Mersenne directly in the hope of gathering
evidence to show that Descartes' theological views were unorthodox, even
by the standards of Roman Catholics in France. As one might expect
of Mersenne, who was always willing to facilitate controversies, he told
Descartes immediately about the request. Descartes replied by referring to
Voetius as the 'most arrant pedant on earth' and then added the following

comment about Van Schurman: 'This Voetius has also ruined Miss Van Schurman. Whereas she had an excellent mind for poetry, painting, and other similar niceties, he has totally dominated her for the past five or six years so much that she is interested only in theological disputes, which has caused her to be excluded from the conversation of respectable people.'[18]

At about the same time, Descartes seems to have learned enough Hebrew to read the first chapter of *Genesis* in the original language. However, this brief venture into biblical studies failed to provide him with clear and distinct ideas of what Moses intended to teach, and he gave up the enterprise as a waste of time. This was surely the principal source of his disagreement with Van Schurman, as described by a contemporary.

Mr. Descartes went to visit her at home in Utrecht. . . . he found her occupied with her favourite study, which was Holy Scripture, in the original Hebrew language. Descartes was surprised that such an outstanding woman devoted so much time 'to something that was so unimportant.' These were the very words he used. When this lady tried to show him the great importance of this study for knowledge of the word of God, Descartes replied that he himself had had the same thought and, with that in mind, that he had learned the language that is called sacred. . . . when he read the first chapter of *Genesis* . . . he was forced to acknowledge that he found nothing clear and distinct in it. . . . This response surprised Miss Van Schurman very much, and she acquired such an antipathy to this philosopher that she avoided ever having any contact with him since then.[19]

There is independent evidence that Van Schurman devoted much effort to studying the Bible in its original languages. For example, when Marie de Gournay questioned the benefits of learning languages in 1647, Van Schurman replied that she only spent her 'spare time' studying languages. 'However, I make an exception, if you permit, for the sacred languages of the Bible.'[20]

It is true that Van Schurman subsequently became enamoured of the dubious mysticism of a French cleric, Jean de Labadie (1610–1674), and that she joined his community of enthusiasts, having cast off the restrictions of strict Calvinist orthodoxy. Perhaps Descartes recognized early symptoms of this disposition toward religious enthusiasm when he tried to discuss theology with her. She certainly thought of him as a profane man, as someone who was more confident about clear and distinct ideas than about the word of God as found in the Bible. It also seems as if there was a genuine basis for each one's assessment of the other. Just as Van Schurman was much more trusting of religious teaching then Descartes, the French philosopher was less willing to accept religious beliefs if they were not supported by rational arguments. For example, when he wrote to Huygens to express his sympathy on the death of his older brother, Maurits, he consoled him with the thought that we would meet our relatives again in the afterlife and that we would remember each other from this life. However, he added the revealing comment: 'Although religion teaches us many things about this subject, I must acknowledge a weakness in myself which seems to me to be common to most people, namely, that although we wish to believe and even think we believe very strongly everything that religion teaches us, we are usually moved by religion when we have very evident natural reasons that convince us.'[21]

In his response to Van Schurman, the conflict in personalities, in religious affiliations, and more fundamentally in their assessments of the role of reason in religious belief meant that Descartes found it impossible to befriend one of the most genuinely talented, intelligent, and independent women that he ever had the opportunity to meet during his life.

Princess Elizabeth of Bohemia

Elizabeth had been living in exile since 1621 in The Hague, where she was privately educated. She remained there by agreement with the House of Orange until 1646. There had been rumours about an arranged betrothal with the king of Poland since she was fifteen years old. However, Elizabeth was a committed Calvinist, while Ladislaus IV was a Roman Catholic, and she seems to have been as reluctant about the plan as he was unenthusiastic about its implementation. Elizabeth's first languages were French and English, although she also read Latin and Dutch. Thus when Descartes' *Meditations* were published in Amsterdam in 1642, it was almost inevitable that Elizabeth got a copy and began to read it.

Descartes was still in the castle at Endegeest, in October 1642, when Pollot advised him that Elizabeth was reading his *Meditations* and that she was interested in discussing the book with him. He replied enthusiastically that he would value her opinion much more than that of university professors, who adopt as their criterion of truth the opinions of Aristotle rather than the evidence of reason.[22] He added, to Pollot: 'I shall not fail to go to The Hague, as soon as I know that you are there, so that, with your introduction, I may have the honour of offering her my respects and hearing her commands' (iii. 578). This indirect introduction initiated one of the most productive intellectual conversations in Descartes' mature years, which eventually amounted to fifty-nine letters. Even when Elizabeth left the United Provinces in 1646, her departure did not interrupt her correspondence with her philosophical tutor. Many years later (in 1667) she was appointed abbess of Herford, to which she welcomed Anna Maria van Schurman together with her suspiciously close spiritual advisor, Jean de Labadie, in 1670.

Elizabeth's first letter to Descartes (6 May 1643) mentioned that she had asked Regius a philosophical question when he had visited The Hague earlier, and that Regius had referred her to Descartes for an expert opinion.[23] The question was central to the Utrecht dispute, so that Elizabeth's reading of the *Meditations* merely helped to underline the intractability of that controversy. Descartes had argued in his physics that any communication of motion from one body to another occurs because of a collision between the two bodies. Yet it seems that, when we decide to perform some action – where the decision is understood as a mental act – the mental act affects the flow of a subtle fluid in our nerves (called animal spirits) and that this, in turn, moves our muscles. This was a case, therefore, of a mental act causing the motion of a physical body. Elizabeth had identified a fundamental anomaly in the interaction between mind and body, and she asked her question as follows:

How can the human soul, which is only a thinking substance, determine the movements of the animal spirits in order to perform a voluntary action? It seems as if every determination of movement results from the following three factors: the pushing of the thing that is moved, the manner in which it is pushed by the body that moves it, and the quality and shape of the latter's surface. The first two presuppose that the bodies touch, while the third presupposes extension. You exclude extension completely from your concept of the soul and, it seems to me, it is incompatible with being an immaterial thing. That is why I am asking for a definition of the soul that is more specific than what is provided in your *Metaphysics*. . . .   (iii. 661)

Descartes' immediate reply (21 May 1643) was wrapped in diplomatic formalities, acknowledging the honour of receiving commands from his royal correspondent and offering to travel to The Hague, at her convenience, to explain himself orally. Apart from the obsequious compliments, Descartes also provided the first genuine effort on his part to philosophize about how the human mind and body interact.

Descartes suggested that, when we think about any reality, such as the human mind or material bodies, there are a few fundamental concepts in

terms of which we structure our thinking. Thus there is one basic concept
available for thinking about the mind, namely, the concept of thought; and
there is one basic concept that must apply equally to all bodies, namely, the
concept of extension. It would therefore be a mistake to confound these
concepts, since they are equally basic, and it would also be misleading to
think about any reality whatever by applying the wrong concept. The same
kind of conceptual embargo applies when thinking about the interaction
of mind and body. 'We have confused the notion of the soul's power to act
on the body with the power by which one body acts on another' (iii. 667).
Descartes advised, rather, that Elizabeth not think of the mind acting on
the body by analogy with one body colliding with another. She should
conceive of the way in which the mind affects the body in a completely
different way.

Elizabeth found this reply unsatisfactory. She made excuses for her
failure to understand Cartesian philosophy by referring to the unwelcome
distractions and unavoidable duties of her social life. It is clear, however, not
that she had failed to understand, but that Descartes had failed adequately
to address the problem she raised. Descartes had hoped to explain how
the mind moves the body by analogy with the way in which gravity moves
bodies towards the centre of the Earth, because no one is tempted to
think of gravity as another body that pushes heavy bodies by impact. In a
similar way, he suggested, one might think of the mind causing the human
body to move without being itself another body that moves by impact. On
Descartes' own acknowledgement, however, the proposed analogy was
unhelpful because it tried to resolve a problem by analogy with something
else that we do not understand. Elizabeth presses home her objection: 'I
confess that it would be easier for me to attribute matter and extension to
the soul than to attribute the ability to move a body, and to be moved by a
body, to an immaterial being' (iii. 685).

Descartes' reply to this letter (28 June 1643) includes a surprising demo-
tion of the role of metaphysics in resolving problems encountered in philosophy. He acknowledges that he had never spent more than a few hours
a day in thinking about things by using his imagination, nor had he given
more than 'a few hours a year' to thoughts that occupy the understanding on its own, although the latter is evidently what is involved in doing
metaphysics.[24] He returns to the same suggestion at the conclusion of his
letter, in a passage that is so at odds with the standard image of Descartes, as
an apologist on behalf of 'pure reason', that he might almost be suspected

of adapting the rigour of his method to the limited ability of an uneducated woman:

Although I think that it is very necessary to have understood well, once in a lifetime, the principles of metaphysics, because they provide us with knowledge of God and of our soul, I also think that it would be very harmful to occupy one's understanding by frequently thinking about them, because the understanding could not as easily be available to the imagination and the senses. It is best to be satisfied with retaining in one's memory and one's belief the conclusions that have once been drawn from the principles of metaphysics, and to devote one's remaining study time to those thoughts in which the understanding acts together with the imagination and the senses.   (iii. 695)

However, apart from underlining the contribution of the imagination and the senses to most of the knowledge we acquire, and the extent to which a little metaphysics goes a long way, this does little to answer Elizabeth's original question.

Descartes is slightly more helpful when he writes about the interaction of mind and body, and about how we might conceive of their union. He emphasizes that we conceive of the union of mind and body by using our experience, rather than by relying on the thoughts that result from metaphysical speculation. Those 'who never philosophize and who use only their senses have no doubt that the soul moves the body and that the body acts on the soul. But they think that the body and soul are both the same thing; in other words, they conceive of their union, for to conceive of the union of two things is to conceive of them as one thing' (iii. 692). In other words, we know that the soul and body interact, since we have direct experience of their interaction in almost everything we do. If this is taken together with the advice offered in his first letter, Descartes seems to be suggesting that we use different concepts, which are acquired in different ways, for thinking about the mind or body separately and for thinking about their intimate union. He confirms this, although the sense of what he is saying is not much clearer, in the same letter of 28 June.

The human mind is incapable of conceiving very distinctly, and simultaneously, both the distinction and union of body and soul. The reason is that, in order to do so, it would be necessary to conceive of them as one single thing and, at the same time, as two things – which is inconsistent... since your Highness suggested that it is easier to attribute matter and extension to the soul, than to attribute to the soul the ability to move and to be moved by a body without having any matter itself, I beseech you to take the liberty to attribute this matter and extension to the soul, for that is nothing more than conceiving of its union with the body.   (iii. 693, 694)

Despite the obscurity of these suggestions, this is as close as Descartes had ever come to addressing the apparent inconceivability of an immaterial mind acting on a material body, and vice versa, when the two interacting entities are defined in such a way that they have no common properties.[25]

As one might expect, Descartes' acute correspondent returned to the same question within a matter of days. She wrote (1 July 1643) about a problem that had already been raised in a number of the objections to the *Meditations* and to which Descartes had formulated a reply that satisfied none of his critics. Elizabeth pointed out that, according to Descartes' own analysis in the *Meditations*, the main reason why we make mistakes and hold false beliefs is that our judgments overstep the evidence that supports them or, in her words, that we make judgments 'about things that we do not perceive adequately' (iv. 2). When Descartes constructs a theory of mind, therefore, he may feel confident that there is no overlap between the concepts of extension and thought. However, it is still possible that, despite his best efforts to think about these realities clearly, there is a covert relation between thought and extension that he has simply failed to notice. 'Although extension is not necessary for thought . . . it may contribute to some other function of the soul which is no less essential to it' (iv. 2).

The obvious person to have raised this objection was Thomas Hobbes. In his objections to the *Meditations*, the English philosopher had pressed the suggestion that thought is nothing more than some complex physical activity, and that Descartes was mistaken in claiming that thinking is really distinct from all bodily processes. Descartes' unsympathetic reply to Hobbes was that we do not know whether thinking is or is not explained by complex brain processes. Rather than jump to conclusions, therefore, he suggested that the question be deferred until we can provide some plausible account of how processes in the senses and the central nervous system result in the experience of thinking. Meantime, we should talk about the subject that supports the activity of thinking and the subject that supports properties that are known to be physical, and we should decide later whether these are two distinct subjects or the same reality under different descriptions. 'It is very reasonable and in keeping with common usage that we apply different names to those substances that we recognize as the subjects of completely different acts . . . and that we examine later whether those different names signify different things or one and the same thing' (vii. 176).[26]

This seems like a reasonable argument, and it might have been accepted as such had Descartes not attempted to develop it into an argument in favour of the immateriality of the human mind when he was pressed further by other objections. Not only the objections of Hobbes – whose view might have been predictable – but all the other five sets of objections to the *Meditations* included versions of the same question. Caterus, Gassendi, Arnauld, and Mersenne all requested more convincing reasons to support the Cartesian conclusion. Mersenne put the point as follows, in the Sixth Objections: 'Someone might maintain . . . that you are nothing else but bodily motion. Can you show us . . . that it is impossible for thoughts to emerge from these motions?' (vii. 413). Descartes acknowledges the impact of these objections to the *Meditations*, in the 'Preface to the Reader'.

The first objection was: from the fact that the human mind reflecting on itself does not perceive itself as anything other than a thinking thing, it does not follow that its nature or essence consists merely in the fact that it is a thinking thing, where the word 'merely' excludes everything else that might also be said to belong to the nature of the soul. I reply to this objection that, in that context, I did not wish to exclude other things with respect to the truth of the question . . . but merely with respect to my own perception. . . . I will show below how, from the fact that I do not know anything else that belongs to my essence, it follows that nothing else does in fact belong to it.   (vii. 7–8)

This attempted defence captures neatly the transition that worried critics. Descartes claimed that, from the point of view of our subjective experience, thinking lacks many of the features that normally characterize a physical process. For example, it makes no sense to think of a thought as having a particular size or shape, as being coloured or plain, as being at rest or pushed about by impact with other bodies. His reply to Hobbes supported only the cautious conclusion: one should not assume in advance that thinking is, or is not, a physical process. However, he evidently thought that he had supplied an argument in the *Meditations* for the much stronger conclusion that the human mind is in fact as immaterial as it appears to be. That is the focus of Elizabeth's question.

Unfortunately, either Descartes failed to reply to this question from Elizabeth or his reply has been lost. He was distracted in the following weeks by the summons from the *Vroedschap* of Utrecht to appear before them to answer charges of defaming Voetius. His energies were therefore

channeled into finding political support to resist the new pressure from
Utrecht, while he was simultaneously putting the final touches to the
Principles of Philosophy. The apparent pause in the correspondence with
Elizabeth is interrupted five months later, in November 1643, when
Descartes writes about resolving a mathematical problem.[27] There are
no surviving letters for almost another year, when Elizabeth writes to
Descartes in August 1644. Between those two dates, Descartes published
the *Principles of Philosophy* and dedicated the book to Princess Elizabeth.[28]

Descartes had published his first book in 1637 and had intentionally
withheld the author's name from the title page. His second book, the
Meditations, had appeared in 1641 with the author's name and an introductory letter of dedication to the theology faculty at the Sorbonne, from
whom he had unsuccessfully sought some kind of guarantee of theological
orthodoxy and thus an indemnity against Jesuit criticism. There is no significant change, during the intervening years, in the caution with which
Descartes attempted to protect his publications from criticism or official
censure. His recent experiences in Utrecht, which were still unresolved
as he prepared the *Principles* for the printer, and the political intervention
that protected him from legal action in Utrecht suggested the need for a
prominent Calvinist patron in the United Provinces. The obvious person
for this role was Princess Elizabeth, even if she was not Dutch and not
directly in the ancestral line of the House of Orange. Descartes accordingly dedicated the book to 'her most Serene Highness, Princess Elizabeth,
eldest daughter of King Frederick of Bohemia, Count Palatine and Elector of the Holy Roman Empire'. At the time, Elizabeth was twenty-six
years old. Descartes acknowledges her previous correspondence about the
Meditations, the scope of her interests in natural philosophy and mathematics, and the extent to which she had engaged him in genuine scholarly
debate despite her lack of a formal university education.

Most Serene Highness: The most rewarding result of my previously published writings was that you deigned to read them and, by making your acquaintance in this way, I
discovered that your natural gifts were such that I was convinced that it would benefit
the human race if I publicized them as an example for future generations. . . . Those
in whom a very firm will to act rightly is combined with a very acute intelligence and
the greatest devotion to discovering the truth are much more eminent [than those
who are ignorant but loyal to their religious faith]. It is obvious that Your Highness
possesses such great devotion, because neither the distractions of the court nor the
customary education that normally condemns young women to ignorance was able to

prevent you from studying all the worthwhile arts and sciences. Besides, the supreme and incomparable acuteness of your intelligence is apparent from the fact that you have examined in depth the mysteries of all those sciences and learned them accurately in such a short time. I have even greater evidence, which I alone possess, in support of that claim because I have found that you alone have understood perfectly all the work that I have published to date. My publications seem to be very obscure to many other people, including those who are very learned and gifted. In the case of most people it is true that, if they are well versed in metaphysics, they hate geometry, whereas if they are trained in geometry they do not understand what I wrote about first philosophy. I recognize that your intelligence is the only one to which all these disciplines are equally clear, and for that reason I describe it as incomparable. When I also consider that such a varied and perfect knowledge of everything is found, not in some professor who is already old and has spent many years in contemplation, but in a young princess who in beauty and age is more like one of the Graces than an ageing Minerva or one of the Muses, I cannot avoid being lost in the greatest admiration.   (viii-1. 1, 3–4)

This dedication, together with the book for which it was written, gave rise to a new, more frequent correspondence between Descartes and Elizabeth and helped to change the focus of their letters from metaphysics to natural philosophy.

Mental Health

Elizabeth signed off her letters to Descartes, from the beginning of their correspondence, with a phrase such as 'your affectionate friend' or 'your very affectionate friend'.[29] Descartes, for his part, reflected the difference in their social status with concluding sentences about his willingness to serve her and to obey her commands.[30] Elizabeth compensated for her superior social status by mentioning frequently that she was 'ignorant and indocile', by acknowledging her 'stupidity' and the inconveniences that resulted for Descartes because he had agreed 'to instruct a stupid person like me'.[31] This artificially constructed balance, between a princess in need of instruction and a philosopher in need of a patron, fostered a mutual understanding that eventually allowed Elizabeth to share with Descartes some of the more personal features of her family life and, especially, the various indispositions that required 'expert' medical advice. However, even the most pressing personal problems never distracted Elizabeth so much that she lost sight of the philosophical problems that both developed her interests and helped to distract her from the tedium of her life in exile.

Descartes wrote to Elizabeth, 18 May 1645, expressing regret that she had been sick for quite some time and that he had not known about it sooner because of his 'solitude'. However, he had heard from Pollot that the princess was suffering from a fever and a dry cough, and since she had asked him the previous year for advice about 'the conservation of her health', he felt emboldened enough to inquire about the details of her sickness.[32] While acknowledging that he is not a physician, Descartes offers a psychosomatic diagnosis even before he hears directly from the patient. 'The most usual cause of a low fever is sadness. The stubbornness with which fortune persecutes your house provides you continuously with reasons to be angry. These misfortunes are so public and striking that it requires little guesswork . . . to judge that they are the primary cause of your indisposition' (iv. 201). Descartes then appeals to his assumptions about mind-body interaction to suggest a remedy, in the course of which he makes one of the first references to the passions, a topic that later emerges as central to his philosophy. He suggests that common or 'lowly' souls allow themselves to be dominated by their passions, and that they are happy or sad simply because they have pleasant or unpleasant experiences. In contrast, those with 'superior' souls, who may be subject to even more violent passions than normal, make sure that reason remains master of the passions and that natural afflictions contribute toward 'the perfect felicity they enjoy even in this life' (iv. 202). In a word, Descartes recommends that Elizabeth use her mind to overcome the baneful effects of negative emotions and that she rally her mental strength to combat an illness that results from an underlying mental state.

Elizabeth replies gratefully with the following description of her indisposition:

You should be aware that I have a body that is very much imbued with the weaknesses of my sex. It feels very easily the disturbances of the soul and is not strong enough to recover as the soul does because its temperament is subject to obstructions, and I live in a climate that affects its condition greatly. I also live with people who cannot take much exercise, so that the heart does not require a long oppression by sadness before the spleen is obstructed and the rest of the body is affected by its vapours. I imagine that the low fever and dry cough from which I am still suffering results from that, although the season's heat [in May] and the walks I take are renewing my strength a little. That is why I have accepted the advice of physicians, to drink the Spa waters within a month (which they will deliver here . . .), because I have found by experience that they clear obstructions. However, I shall not drink it before

I get your opinion, because you are good enough to agree to cure me both mentally
and physically.   (iv. 208)

This request opened up a new line of discussion that soon returned
to the original question that had caught Elizabeth's attention, namely,
the ways in which body and mind are so related that each affects the
other.

Descartes' extended discussion of the blood and the spleen, in May
or June 1645, presupposes the kind of close interaction between mind
and body that their earlier discussion had failed to explain. He uses an
example that was familiar from his school days to explain the effects
on an audience of watching a tragedy on stage. When people go to the
theatre, they know intellectually that the scenes performed on the stage
are 'imaginary fables'. Nonetheless, once their imagination is caught up
in the experience, various bodily consequences follow automatically. He
speculates that thicker particles in the blood may cause an obstruction
in the spleen, while the more subtle and active particles travel to the
lungs and trigger a cough.[33] He then develops a theme that became a
constant feature of his account of the imagination. We cannot directly
affect our imagination simply by deciding to change it, any more than we
can affect our passions by a simple decision. However, our imagination
may be indirectly controlled if we imagine other things that can displace
harmful images or at least counteract their influence. As confirmation
of this theory, Descartes gives the example of the 'dry cough and pale
complexion' that he inherited from his mother, as a result of which most
doctors told him that he would die young. He claims to have overcome the
effects of his unlucky inheritance by always considering things from the
most favourable perspective – which sounds implausible, based on the evidence of many of his letters – so that his inherited indisposition gradually
disappeared.[34]

This kind of psychotherapy, however, did not preclude other traditional
medical therapies. Accordingly, Descartes recommends that Elizabeth also
take the spa waters, and follow the usual advice of physicians when doing
so. He seems to have been interested in pursuing such physical therapies
in parallel because, according to one of his contemporaries in Utrecht, he
'investigated night and day without intermission the nature of things by
trying to explain the properties of plants and animals'.[35] Since Elisabeth
evidently knew about these investigations into the therapeutic properties

of plants, she wanted to visit Egmond and hear about the truths that
Descartes was discovering in his 'new garden', but she was prevented
from doing so by 'the malediction of my sex'. [36]

Seneca: *The Happy Life*

Descartes decided suddenly, in July 1645, to offer Elizabeth a guided
reading of a book entitled *The Happy Life* by the Roman philosopher
Seneca (d. 65 A.D.).[37] The objective was to get her to meditate on 'the
means by which philosophy teaches us to realize the supreme happiness
that common souls vainly expect from fortune and which can be acquired
only from within ourselves' (iv. 252). It might seem strange that such a
consistent critic of the ancients would revert to these philosophers as a
source of wisdom, even with the qualification that he would 'try to advance
beyond them by adding something to their rules' (iv. 252). He was careful
to point out that Seneca was 'not enlightened by religious faith and had
only natural reason as a guide' (iv. 263).

Once this plan was agreed upon, both correspondents seem to have
read Seneca and exchanged comments about his philosophy of the good
life. Descartes emphasized that happiness is ultimately 'a perfect contentment of the mind and an inner satisfaction' (iv. 264). This might imply
that misfortune is irrelevant to happiness, or that those who are mentally
strong could ignore misfortune and achieve this inner happiness despite
what happens to them. Such a view exaggerated the insignificance of fortune. Accordingly, Descartes qualified the apparently naïve view he had
proposed by acknowledging that there are two kinds of thing that make
us happy: those that depend on ourselves, such as virtue and wisdom,
and those that depend on good fortune, such as health, riches, and so on.
However, if two people are equally virtuous and wise, then the one who
enjoys good health and wealth could enjoy a more perfect contentment
than the other. Despite this concession, Descartes wished to argue for the
relativity of contentment to the needs of individuals, so that 'the poorest
people and those who are least blessed by fortune or nature' (iv. 264–5) are
capable of being completely content and satisfied.

Descartes then offers three rules to guide people toward inner contentment, independent of the effects of external factors such as wealth, health,
and social status, which are reminiscent of the three rules of morality proposed in the *Discourse on Method*.[38]

The first is to try always to use one's mind, as much as possible, to discover what should be done or not done in all life's situations.

The second is to have a firm and constant resolution to implement whatever reason recommends without being diverted by passions or desires. . . .

The third is to keep in mind that, while acting in this way according to reason, as much as possible, all the goods that are not possessed are completely and equally outside one's power, and in this way one gets used to not desiring them.   (iv. 265–6)

Descartes concludes that 'the greatest human happiness consists in the right use of reason' (iv. 267), and that Seneca should have taught the principal truths required to practise virtue and to control desires and passions.

Elizabeth might have been consoled by the length of Descartes' letters and the detailed instructions that he provided. However, she was not convinced by the basic ideas on which his morality depended. She objected that some bodily indispositions are such that they compromise the very application of reason on which the Cartesian rules depend.

I still cannot rid myself of doubt about whether one can realize the happiness about which you speak without the assistance of what does not depend completely on the will. There are illnesses that take away completely the ability to reason and, consequently, the ability to enjoy a rational satisfaction. There are others that reduce our strength and prevent us from following the maxims which sound judgment has formulated, and which leave the most moderate person subject to being carried away by their passions and less capable of extricating themselves from the accidents of fortune, which requires a firm resolution.   (iv. 269)

Elizabeth gives as an example the fact that she had spent the previous eight days in the company of her sick brother, trying to persuade him to follow the doctor's advice and hoping to comfort him by her presence. During that time, she could not concentrate enough even to write a response to Descartes. Bodily indispositions, she concluded, do indeed inhibit the functioning of reason.

Before this reply from Elizabeth arrived in Egmond, Descartes continued writing his intermmitent commentary on Seneca. He repeated the advice he offered as the second maxim of morality in Part III of the *Discourse on Method*, that, in practical matters, one should follow the best advice available without waiting for certainty. 'One satisfies one's conscience and is assured that one's views about morality are the best available . . . as long as one takes care to get advice from the most capable people and to use all one's mental powers to examine what one should do'

(iv. 273). While Descartes 'strongly agrees' with Seneca about that, he also claims that Seneca's proposal about living in conformity with nature is rather obscure. It might mean following all one's natural desires, even though Seneca has already explained how such a policy could make one miserable. The ancient philosopher must therefore have been using the term 'nature' to mean something like the order established by God, and 'living according to nature' could then be translated, into Christian terminology, as submitting oneself to the will of God (iv. 273).

This provides an opportunity for Descartes to comment on the connection between the supreme good and the motivation required to seek it. Descartes distinguishes among three different things in this context: (a) the supreme good, (b) happiness, and (c) the final goal of all human actions. Happiness is not itself the supreme good, but presupposes it, because happiness is the inner contentment that results from possession of the supreme good. However, one could think of either (a) or (b) as the goal of all human actions. In one sense, the supreme good is the goal of human actions, but the resulting happiness is the attraction that motivates us to seek it, and it may therefore rightly be called the goal of human actions.

At this point in their correspondence, Descartes' letters and Elizabeth's replies followed so closely that the messengers who delivered them often passed each other in opposite directions. Descartes accepted that some illnesses take away the power of reasoning and consequently the ability to enjoy the contentment of a rational mind.[39] This led to a further admission, that an indisposition of the body can result in a loss of free will. Descartes draws the initially surprising conclusion that 'it is worse to lose the use of one's reason than to lose one's life'. The reason is as follows: 'Even without the teachings of the faith, natural philosophy alone gives the soul reason to hope for a happier state, after death, than the one it currently enjoys. It makes it fear nothing more distressing than being attached to a body which takes away completely its liberty' (iv. 283). This anticipation of the pleasures of an afterlife helps to reinforce the distinction made by Descartes between bodily pleasures and mental pleasures. The latter can be as immortal as the soul itself on condition that they are based on reliable knowledge.[40]

This almost inevitable drift into dualism about happiness is qualified by the impact of the passions on the life of embodied minds. Descartes distinguishes between pleasures that are exclusively mental and those that reflect human embodiment, that is, those 'that belong to the mind insofar as it is united to the body' (iv. 284). The mind-and-body pleasures are presented to the imagination, confusedly; they tend to appear much greater than they are in fact, and thus they are potentially misleading. 'This is the source of all the evils and all the mistakes of life' (iv. 284). This leads naturally to a discussion of the way in which passions represent goods that are misleading. 'Passions often make us believe that certain things are much better and more desirable than they really are. When we have taken a lot of trouble to acquire such things . . . their enjoyment reveals to us their deficiencies, from which result dissatisfaction, regrets, and remorse' (iv. 284).[41] The principal role of reason, in this context, is to assist individuals to examine their goals critically and, if necessary, to override the impulses that result from misleading passions.

By this stage, Descartes not only found that he was replying to letters sent before his own most recent replies; he was also unsure about the address of his royal correspondent, because he suspected that she might have changed residence.[42] Elizabeth reassured him, on September 15, that she was living temporarily at Ryswijk, at the house of the prince of Orange, while her usual accommodations were being refurbished.[43] Descartes provides a summary of his Senecan morality by listing four truths on which Elizabeth should focus. These are: (a) that God controls all things; (b) that the human soul 'subsists without the body and is nobler than it' (iv. 292); (c) that human beings are relatively insignificant entities in a vast universe; and (d) that, despite the fact that each of us is a distinct person, we should 'always prefer the interest of the whole, of which we are part, to the interests of a particular person' (iv. 293). This advice was obviously designed to provide a wider context within which Elizabeth might review some of the relatively minor problems that made her anxious. It suggested that God was ultimately the cause of everything, that we should accept what happens to us as an expression of His omniscient will, and that the promise of immortality should prevent us from fearing even death.

This must have seemed to Elizabeth almost like a string of clichés. Theologians had discussed the compatibility of human choice with God's Providence since the time of Augustine's *On the Free Choice of the Will*, in the fourth century, and the problem had acquired an added urgency in the recent acrimonious debates between Arminians and Contra-Remonstrants within Dutch Calvinism. It was predictable that Elizabeth would ask her philosophical tutor to explain the role of human choice in a world in which, according to Descartes, everything that occurs is ultimately an expression of God's will.

God's Providence and Human Choice

Elizabeth identified genuine philosophical problems in almost every suggestion made by Descartes in his latest letter (15 September 1645). The most obvious one was his bland suggestion that we accept whatever misfortunes we experience as, in some sense, caused or approved by God. She reminded him of a familiar distinction between natural evils and moral evils, and of the Calvinist belief in God's predetermination of the fate of each individual.

> Knowledge of God's existence and of his attributes can provide consolation for the misfortunes that befall us from the ordinary course of nature and the order that he established in it, such as losing one's goods in a storm, losing one's health because of infection from the air, or losing one's friends through death. But it cannot console us for the misfortunes that are inflicted by other people, whose choice seems completely free. Only faith can convince us that God takes care to rule human wills, and that he has determined the fate of each person before the creation of the world. (iv. 302)

Elizabeth did not need to spell out the problem, since it was already familiar within Christian theology, both Calvinist and Roman Catholic. Apart from the general Providence that God exercises over the whole of creation, there remained a contentious question about whether He exercised a 'special Providence' over individuals.

Elizabeth also pointed to a problem that subsequently became a standard issue in utilitarianism in the nineteenth century. When Descartes recommended that she should prefer the interests of the community to those of the individual, he failed to provide any agreed measure of the relative weights of each set of interests. Elizabeth claimed, reasonably, that individuals are likely to give a much greater weight to their own immediate needs, of which they have a clear knowledge, than to the less well-known interests of others in the community to which they belong.[44] She wanted to know, therefore, why any individual should be impartial between his or her own interests and the interests of others.

Descartes' reply to the query about human choice and God's comprehensive causality was unsatisfactory, as it was bound to be. One reason for this deficiency was that the concepts that we use when talking about God were invented originally to describe the mundane realities of everyday experience, and they apply only by analogy (and with significant disclaimers) to God, who transcends human experience. For example, we know what it means for one thing or event to cause another, because we have experience of apparent causal connections in our day-to-day exposure to natural phenomena. Even here, however, we have no guarantee of perfect knowledge. Therefore, if we are bold enough to stretch the meaning of the term 'cause' so that it applies to God's actions, we cannot conclude that the original causal connections in nature are redundant or inefficacious, because that would undermine even the limited use of the very concepts on which their analogical application to God depends.

Descartes had argued the previous year, in the *Principles of Philosophy*, that we have a direct experience within ourselves of causal activity when we decide to perform some action, such as walking, and then find that we are walking as we had decided. He had no coherent account of how God is the ultimate cause of everything and, at the same time, of how human beings are the causes of their voluntary actions. In fact, there were independent reasons to argue that God so transcends the limits of human intelligence that we could never understand His free causality. The solution recommended in the *Principles* was to hold onto both claims – that we make free choices, and that God causes everything – while conceding that we cannot understand how they are compatible. 'It would be absurd just because we do not understand one thing which, of its very nature, we know should be incomprehensible to us, to doubt something else of which we have an intimate understanding and which we experience in ourselves' (viii-1. 20).

Something along those lines might have satisfied Elizabeth in reply to her query. Instead, Descartes simply states that the same reasons that show that God exists and is the immutable cause of all natural events also prove that He is 'the cause of all the effects that depend on human free will'.[45] Thus God is the cause of every event, free or otherwise, and 'nothing can occur without his will' (iv. 314). This merely restated the problem, without providing any resolution. Elizabeth was quick to point this out in her next letter (28 October). She agreed that it was possible for God not to have given human beings free will. But, having done so, 'it seems to me to be inconsistent with common sense to believe that free will depends on God, in its actions, in the same way that it depends on God for its existence' (iv. 323).

Descartes makes two further attempts to reply to this question.[46] The first effort repeats the resolution adopted in the *Principles*, more or less acknowledging that this is a problem that exceeds the limited powers of human intelligence. 'Just as knowledge of God's existence should not prevent us from being certain of free will, because we experience and feel it in ourselves, likewise knowledge of our free will should not make us doubt God's existence' (iv. 332–3). Without resolving the problem in any way, this encouraged Elizabeth to hold onto both parts of an apparently contradictory conjunction. However, one of the features that was central to the debate within Calvinism was the compatibility of (a) God's knowing in advance that human beings will perform evil actions, and (b) without any remedial divine intervention, God's deciding in advance on the reward or punishment of such actions. Descartes tried to address this issue, unsuccessfully, in his letter of January 1646.

His effort involved telling the following story. Suppose a king prohibits dueling in his kingdom, and assume that he also knows that two of his subjects (who live in different towns) are very likely to duel if they meet. If he gives orders to these two individuals that cause them to meet and, despite the king's orders, to duel, one could see how the duel results both from the free will of the two individuals and from the king's order. Descartes tries to apply this story of the king to God, in order to distinguish within God two different acts of the will. 'In the same way, theologians distinguish in God a will that is absolute and independent, by which he wills that all things occur as they do, and another will which is relative, which applies to the merit or demerit of men, and by which he wills that his laws be obeyed' (iv. 354). This attempt was bound to fail, for reasons that Descartes himself had acknowledged elsewhere. One reason was that, according to the Cartesian account, there are no real distinctions within God between different acts of the will, and therefore the analogy with the king limps too much to be of any assistance. The more fundamental reason was the one already mentioned, namely, that we genuinely do not understand God, and we cannot hope to provide a coherent account of His thoughts and actions by borrowing the completely inept concepts that apply to human beings.

The question about God and free human actions had obvious implications for an account of how Christians understood the efficacy of prayer.

A naïve account of prayer suggests that God hears the prayers in which we make various requests and then answers some of them by granting what is requested. This seems to make God's will depend on human actions, whereas Descartes is evidently claiming the opposite. He returns to this question in reply to Elizabeth's concern about God's special Providence. 'I do not think that you mean [by special Providence] some change that occurs in God on the occasion of actions that depend on our free will' (iv. 316). Descartes argues, in a manner that would be acceptable also to Calvinists, that we do not pray to God to inform Him of our needs (since He already knows them), nor to attempt to change anything in God (which would be impossible). God's eternally unchanging will and omniscience are not affected by anything that we do. Thus, unless we classify this issue among the mysteries that we do not understand, we have to say something about God's anticipating our needs and our prayers and granting the reliefs sought independently of the fact that we request them.

Apart from such theologically sensitive truths, Descartes was willing to concede that moral decisions are not usually based on certain knowledge. On various occasions he returned to the same theme, that we have to make moral decisions about matters that remain uncertain. 'Although we cannot have certain demonstrations of everything, we should still make a decision and endorse the opinions that seem most probable to us about practical issues, so that, when we have to act, we will never be irresolute' (iv. 295). We have to be satisfied with what he called a 'mediocre knowledge' of the more necessary goods from among which we must choose.[47] 'Leaving aside what we are taught by the faith, I confess that by natural reason alone we can make many conjectures which are to our advantage and we can have great hopes, but no certainty.'[48]

The Passions of the Soul

Elizabeth was twenty-two years younger than Descartes. Despite the sharpness of her intellect and her intuitive knack for finding the weakest points in his arguments, her letters give the impression of someone who needed good practical advice in addition to philosophical tutoring. She continued to experience various medical complaints, and she was scandalized in 1645 when her brother, Edward, converted to Catholicism when he married a French Catholic.[49] On this occasion, Descartes could not hide the fact that, as a Catholic, he approved of the change of religious allegiance as would the majority of people in Europe who were also Catholic.[50] However, his usual attitude was to encourage his royal correspondent 'to adopt a more carefree attitude' to things, and to engage in a kind of mental training to alleviate the scruples from which she suffered. This was consistent with the advice about making decisions about matters that remain uncertain. Descartes tried to persuade her that probable knowledge was sufficient to make practical judgments and that, once such decisions had been made, she should accept that these were the best ones she could have made in the circumstances. For this reason Elizabeth needed to acquire practice in making decisions, together with the kind of resolution required not to second-guess those decisions subsequently.[51]

Apart from such typical counselling, Descartes was drawn by Elizabeth's letters into discussing an issue that was subsequently to emerge as an important part of his philosophy, namely, an explanation of human emotions. He embarked on this project explicitly in October 1645 by telling his royal correspondent that she was the ideal person with whom to have that discussion.[52] The reason was that she had already had a preview of a draft treatise on animals that he had written, and she was therefore familiar with his earlier speculations about how both external and internal stimuli trigger impressions in the brain when, for example, animals see an object or feel hungry. Descartes claimed that exactly similar physiological changes occur in human beings, with similar results. If the term 'passion' is used to refer to states that we experience passively and over which we have no control, then all these experiences should be classified as passions. For example, when we perceive external objects, when we feel thirsty or tired, when we dream while asleep or daydream while awake: in all these cases, the person who has such experiences is passively subject to events that do not result from any choice on his or her part. Likewise, in all such cases, the mental state that is experienced – the feeling of thirst, or the awareness of our dreams – results from some corresponding state of the body.

However, Descartes was starting out with a wide sweep in this context before focusing on passions in a much narrower sense that corresponds to what are now called emotions. He wanted to classify and to explain experiences such as feeling sad or joyful, and he needed to distinguish, for example, between feeling a pain and feeling sad while one is in pain, or between feeling thirsty and having a desire to drink. In both examples, only the second feeling is an emotion properly so called (although both are passions in the wider sense).[53] This effort soon resulted in a draft treatise on the passions, which Descartes wrote during the winter of 1645–46.[54] He apparently gave Elizabeth a copy of this draft treatise in March 1646, when he visited The Hague, and she began to read and comment on it in April 1646.[55]

Elizabeth, as usual, both apologized for her 'stupidity' and raised some telling objections to the Cartesian speculations. Descartes had suggested that there is a small number of basic passions, such as wonder, love, hatred, desire, joy, and sadness, and that each of these results from a specific flow of animal spirits from the heart to the brain.[56] Elizabeth asked, reasonably, how he could determine which flows of animal spirits cause different emotions.

I do not see how it is possible to know the different movements of the blood which cause the five primitive passions, because the passions never occur alone. For example, love is always accompanied by desire and joy, or by desire and sadness, and as love gets stronger the other emotions increase too. . . . How is it possible, then, to distinguish the difference in the beating of the pulse . . . and in other changes in the body, which are used to discover the nature of these motions? The motion that you mention, for each of the passions, is not the same for every temperament. In my own case, sadness always takes away my appetite even though it is not accompanied by any aversion, which I experience only on the death of some friend.   (iv. 404–5)

The mind-body connection continued to crop up in subsequent correspondence between Elizabeth and Descartes. When she told him about a stomach illness in June 1647, he agreed that an appropriate diet and exercise were a good idea. However, the remedies 'of the soul' are even better.

The structure of our body is such that certain bodily movements follow naturally from certain thoughts, as one sees that blushing follows from embarrassment, tears from sorrow, and laughter from joy. I do not know of any thought that is more appropriate for conserving one's health than the strong conviction and firm belief that the structure of one's body is so good that, on condition that one has been healthy once, one cannot easily fall ill unless one accedes to some significant excess or unless the air or other external causes harm us. If someone then falls ill, they can easily recover their health by the sheer force of nature, especially when they are still young.   (v. 65)[57]

Descartes was exploring how the natural unity of mind and body was central not only to metaphysics but to human health. He was encouraged in that enterprise by Elizabeth's questions about health, happiness, and philosophy. The culmination of his gradual enlightenment is found in *The Passions of the Soul* (1649).

It is also obvious from these letters that Elizabeth adopted the role of the untutored junior partner, as someone who experienced many of the weaknesses that were typically attributed to women, and that she welcomed the advice of Descartes as both an expert in philosophy and a wise life coach. It seems equally clear, however, that Descartes learned much more from Elizabeth's letters than she did from him. Her questions were invariably precisely on target with respect to the gaps in his arguments and weaknesses in his theories. Both correspondents continued to play their assumed official roles, while acknowledging the reciprocal benefits that they both enjoyed.

This correspondence continued even after Elizabeth's abrupt departure from The Hague and Descartes' extremely reluctant departure from Egmond in the service of another young royal female, Queen Christina of Sweden. Descartes' letters expressed extravagant claims about his feelings of duty and service toward the young princess. For example, he wrote from Egmond in May 1647, when she was living in Berlin: 'The letter that I have had the honour of receiving from Your Highness makes me hope that you will return to The Hague towards the end of summer. I can say, however, that it is the principal reason which makes me prefer living in this country rather than in any other' (v. 15). In fact, Elizabeth never returned to Holland, and Descartes never met her again. They continued to correspond, intermittently, until his death.

Descartes' language throughout these letters might give the impression of someone who may have been in love with the princess or, at least, of having such respect for her that he was willing to follow her wherever she lived and to provide counselling and philosophical guidance despite the inconvenience involved for himself. However, the letters he wrote to Queen Christina in 1649 – at that stage, to someone he had never even met, and about whom he knew relatively little – put a different complexion on his extravagant prose style. In the case of Queen Christina, Descartes will write parallel letters to Chanut and the queen in which he cancels in the former what he pledges with apparent sincerity in the latter. This duplicity or, at least, this exaggerated use of diplomatic obfuscation suggests the need to reread his letters to Princess Elizabeth in the same way. She was a potential patron, and she was certainly an able intellectual critic. She was also perhaps the unwitting object of an immature affection on the part of someone who was almost a total recluse and who had failed to develop relationships with mature women who were his social equals. This would explain why Elizabeth insisted, after Descartes' death, on retrieving the letters she had written to him for seven years and that he had brought with him to Stockholm. She may have recognized more clearly than Descartes the ambiguity of their relationship and how it might appear to a third party who had an opportunity to read both sides of the correspondence.

Before reaching that conclusion, however, she acted as an intellectual midwife for publication of Descartes' book on human emotions, *The Passions of the Soul.*

The Principles of Philosophy (1644)

Since all natural phenomena can be explained in this way ... I do not think that any other principles of physics should be accepted or even desired.

(Principles: viii-1. 79)

D ESCARTES' correspondence during the two years prior to publishing the *Principles* is almost silent about the wider political and military turmoil within which he conducted his own intellectual war. Charles I had been king of England since 1625. He was formally challenged by Parliament in June 1642, in a document called the 'Nineteen Propositions', because of the arrogance and arbitrariness with which he allegedly exercised his royal powers. His formal reply, 18 June 1642, did little to satisfy his critics.[1] The civil war that resulted brought Cromwell to power and, in January 1649, led to the public execution of the king by order of Parliament. During these tumultuous years, a number of royalist intellectuals emigrated to France and subsequently became correspondents with Descartes and, in some cases, supporters of his philosophy. They included Kenelm Digby and the two Cavendish brothers, William (marquis of Newcastle) and Charles.

The situation in the United Provinces was politically more stable than in England but, militarily, was just as unpredictable. The *Stadtholder* was constantly under pressure, both at home and on the battlefield, because he failed to synchronize military successes with political support, especially in the largest and most economically powerful province, Holland, as he carried on an increasingly stalled campaign against the Spanish Netherlands in the south. Descartes made minimal reference to this wider world as he lived in relative seclusion in the north of Holland.

He had moved from the castle of Endegeest (near Leiden) to a small village on the North Sea coast called Egmond aan den Hoef, in the early part of May 1643. Apart from a few short local trips, he remained there for the next year, until he embarked on his first visit to France after sixteen years of living in exile.[2] This latest place of seclusion was so isolated that it took eight days for letters to reach him from Leiden.[3] Most of his time and energies during the remaining months of 1643 were consumed by the Utrecht controversy (discussed in Chapter 8). During this period, he also began the lengthy correspondence with Princess Elizabeth in which he tried to clarify many unresolved and fundamental questions in his metaphysics. Descartes was then forty-seven years old. He had published two books, the scientific *Essays* in 1637 and the *Meditations* in 1641, both of which had stimulated more public criticism than he welcomed. Following publication of the *Essays*, he had fought a long-running and unresolved battle with French mathematicians about the novelty of the method used in the *Geometry*, and he had tried unsuccessfully to lure the French Jesuits into open controversy about the *Dioptrics*. The *Meditations* introduced its author to a new set of critics, especially Hobbes and Gassendi, each of whom was at least as well-known among contemporaries as Descartes. Now, in 1643, he was involved in an extremely public and nasty controversy with the rector of Utrecht University and its city council, while coping simultaneously with a new dispute about the objections to the *Meditations* that had been written by Pierre Gassendi.

Gassendi was unhappy that his objections, together with Descartes' replies, had been published in the first and second editions of the book (1641, 1642). Gassendi explained that he had addressed Descartes as 'Spirit' only in an ironic way, and that he had no objection if the author of the *Meditations* were to return the compliment in kind, by addressing him 'not only as Flesh . . . but even as Stone, Lead, etc. or anything you think is more obtuse'.[4] Like many other disputes that involved Descartes, this one acquired an independent dynamic that became impossible to control. It also shared its immediate origins with the Utrecht controversy. Descartes had triggered the bitter row with Voetius by his ill-considered comments in the letter to Father Dinet. The same text seems to have annoyed Gassendi so much that he took up his pen in defence of his philosophical reputation.

Gassendi was so annoyed by the way he appeared in the *Meditations* that he wrote an extended version of his original objections (i.e., the Fifth Objections), together with new objections to Descartes' replies. This manuscript seems to have circulated among sympathetic friends during the winter of 1641–42. This kind of surreptitious criticism particularly grated on Descartes' sense of fair play, as was evident in the earlier exchange with Father Bourdin. His initial complaint against Bourdin was that he criticized the *Dioptrics* in private, and that he refused to divulge his criticisms even when challenged. In the course of recounting this niggling concern to Father Dinet, Descartes compared Bourdin's behaviour with that of other unnamed critics who wrote 'whole books, not for publication but – what I think is much worse – to be read in private by the credulous' (vii. 600). This reference to Gassendi was as transparent as the 'anonymous' reference to Voetius in the same letter. He went on to explain that he had originally thought that the best way to have an informative debate was to follow the pattern adopted in the *Meditations*. In that case he had invited critics to send him their comments in advance; he would reply, and would publish both the objections and the replies together in the same text. Gassendi, however, complained about this arrangement because it deprived him of the opportunity to respond to Descartes' replies. In other words, Descartes always had the last word. Descartes rehearses the core of this dispute in his letter to Dinet, and then suggests a new procedure for future discussions of his work.

I now ask and encourage all those critics to publish what they have written. For experience has taught me that this would be better than if they were to send them to me, as I had requested. . . . Some might think that I have injured them, if I publish their comments and add my own replies because, as someone recently told me about his own case, that would deprive them of the advantage they would enjoy if they arranged for publication themselves. In other words, they would be read for a number of months and have the full attention of many minds, before I would be able to reply to them.   (vii. 600)

Descartes added the barbed comment that many critics did not deserve any reply, because their quibbles and abuse were irrelevant to the questions being discussed.

Following Descartes' minimally camouflaged public complaint to Father Dinet, Gassendi authorized Sorbière, in June 1643, to publish the rather large book of replies to Descartes that had been circulating privately. By August, Rivet was able to report to his correspondent in Paris that 'Blaeu has begun to print . . . Mr. Gassendi's writing against the philosophy of Descartes'.[5] One of Huygens' friends, Johan van der Burgh (1599–1660), even offered to provide a copy of the book as it was being printed, page by page, and Huygens in turn offered to act as intermediary by sending the text to Descartes.[6] In February 1644 the printing was completed, and Gassendi's extended critique of the *Meditations* appeared from his Amsterdam publisher as: *A Metaphysical Disquisition: Or Doubts and Counter Objections to the Metaphysics of René Descartes, and his Replies.*[7]

Descartes reacted to this book as he did to most large tomes and, indeed, to many rather small books: he did not read it. He had started to read it on or about 21 February 1644 and, having glanced over the Preface and 'five or six pages', he had decided initially that it deserved a reply.[8] He was especially annoyed that Gassendi was complaining about publication of his objections to the *Meditations*, for, according to Descartes, Gassendi had asked to have his name included – when all the other authors of objections were anonymous – and he had availed of the opportunity even to correct the proofs before publication. However, once Descartes had read about a hundred pages of the *Disquisition*, he changed his mind. He found that there was nothing in the book that was worth reading and he lacked the patience required to persevere to the end. He decided instead to retaliate against Gassendi by deleting the Fifth Objections from the next edition of the text, and to insert instead a brief explanation of why he had dropped them, together with a reply to Gassendi's new book.

Meantime, Descartes had begun to write a summary of his philosophy in late 1640, and he had planned to devote most of 1641 to completing the task. Although he originally thought of including in his new book an exposition of scholastic textbook philosophy, he changed his mind about that during 1641. The revised and reduced plan was to summarize his metaphysics and physics in a format that would make it suitable for college teachers. The time spent preparing a second edition of the *Meditations* and, even more distractingly, the time consumed by his row with Voetius frequently displaced the *Principles* to the margins of his agenda. Nonetheless, he seems to have continued working on it in his spare moments, as is evident from his correspondence. This research included his own observations of natural phenomena and, with his usual reluctance, a cursory review of what his contemporaries were publishing about topics in natural philosophy that he planned to explain.

Descartes and Digby

Kenelm Digby (1603–1665) and Thomas White (1593–1676) were two English Catholics who had settled in Paris, where they were introduced to Mersenne and Hobbes. When Digby was only three years old, his father,

Everard, was executed for his involvement in the famous Gunpowder Plot, when a group of Catholics planned to blow up the walls of the Parliament buildings in London in November 1605. Despite this inauspicious start to life, Kenelm Digby survived to win royal approval and to be entrusted with an official diplomatic mission to Spain. He emigrated from his native country in 1635, following the death of his wife, Venetia, and remained in Paris more or less continuously until after the Restoration. However, he returned to London briefly in 1638 and 1640, and during the latter visit invited Descartes to England.

Digby had read Descartes' *Essays* when he first arrived in Paris, and he subsequently wrote to Hobbes about them, with glowing praise that was unlikely to be shared by his English correspondent:

> I come now with this to make good what I promised you in my last: which is to putt Monsieur des Cartes ... his book into your hands. I doubt not but you will say this is a production of a most vigorous and strong braine; and that if he were as accurate in his metaphysicall part as he is in his experience, he had carried the palme from all men living; which yet neverthelesse he peradventure hath done. I shall be very glad to heare your opinion of him.[9]

Digby's enthusiasm for Descartes' philosophy was such that he claimed to have crossed the Channel from London to visit Descartes in Egmond sometime in 1641. He recounted the story of his visit to Charles de Saint-Denis, also known as Saint Evremond. According to his account, he travelled to Egmond and arrived unannounced and evidently uninvited at Descartes' door. The details of the visit are so obviously favourable to Digby that one must reserve judgment about their accuracy. For example, Digby claimed that, after he arrived at Descartes' house, he talked for quite some time without identifying himself. At that point, Descartes, 'who had seen some of his works, said to him that he had no doubt but he was the famous Mr. Digby'.[10] However, in 1641, Digby had published nothing that Descartes could have recognized or admired. Then, slightly more credibly, Digby is supposed to have told Descartes:

> Our speculative sciences are indeed wonderful and agreeable, but after all they are too uncertain and too impractical to constitute a man's total occupation. Life is so short that we barely have enough time to get to know what is necessary, and it is much more worthy of someone, who understands well the structure of the human body, to research the means of prolonging life than to spend time in the simple speculations of philosophers.[11]

Descartes is said to have endorsed this sentiment, and to have assured his uninvited guest 'that he had already thought about this question, that he did not dare to promise to make human beings immortal, but that it was well within his power to extend the span of his life to equal that of the patriarchs'.[12]

Digby returned to London from Paris in 1642, to support Charles I in the hope of winning tolerance for Catholics, and was arrested twice and imprisoned – once for only a week, and the second time for almost a year (November 1642 to July 1643). Evidently, Mersenne was well informed about these developments, since Descartes expressed his regret about Digby's imprisonment and, subsequently, his delight on hearing of his release.[13] During his second period in captivity, Digby drafted the book that eventually appeared, in 1644, as: *Two Treatises in the one of which, The Nature of Bodies; in the other, the Nature of Mans Soule: is looked into: in way of discovery, of the Immortality of Reasonable Soules.*[14] Digby was evidently supportive of the objectives of the *Meditations*, namely, to establish the immortality of the soul and the existence of God. Not surprisingly, then, there were obvious points of agreement between Digby's *Two Treatises* and Descartes' metaphysics. Unfortunately, Descartes was unable to read English, and although Princess Elizabeth suggested having some chapters translated for him by her chaplain, Descartes never had an opportunity to read Digby's book. It appeared in a Latin translation only the year after Descartes' death.[15]

However, one of Digby's companions in Paris, an English priest named Thomas White, published a book that Descartes was able to read in Latin, under the title *Three Dialogues about the World* (1642).[16] Mersenne sent two copies of this book to Huygens, one of which was forwarded to Descartes.[17] In contrast with his usual disdain for other authors, Descartes took a whole day to read White's *Three Dialogues*. He reported to Huygens that, although there were some sections in White's book where he acknowledged the pre-eminence of Descartes, there was little he could learn from it.[18] White addressed a number of philosophical questions that coincided with issues that appeared later in Descartes' *Principles*, such as the compatibility of human liberty with divine Providence.[19] In contrast with Descartes, however, his attitude toward astronomical theories was sceptical. He argued that the relative rarity of the evidence available makes it difficult to draw reliable conclusions in astronomy, that those who exceed the scope of the evidence are constructing dogmas, and that we have no reason to believe in an indefinitely large universe or in a plurality of worlds (both of which were Cartesian hypotheses).[20]

There are intermittent references to progress on the *Principles* between 1642 and 1644. Descartes acknowledges a request from Charles Cavendish about grinding lenses as an implicit compliment on his own work and an encouragement to publish what he calls 'my Physics'.[21] He summarizes his explanation of magnetism, which postulated imperceptible particles that pass through the Earth from the North and South Poles, in both directions, and re-enter the Earth at the complementary pole. Again, this is something he promised to explain more fully in what he called 'my Physics'.[22] Descartes briefly consulted a new book on magnetism by the Jesuit Athanasius Kircher (1601–1680), but found nothing significant in it either.[23] By September 1643, he was able to tell Huygens that Van Schooten's son, who had drawn the diagrams for his *Dioptrics*, was about to prepare the diagrams for 'my Philosophy', and that the printer had promised to have all the work completed by Easter 1644.[24]

During the final months of preparation, Descartes further reduced the scope of the *Principles* by omitting two parts that were intended to discuss animals and human beings. Pollot and Huygens evidently heard about the change of plans, and this prompted Huygens to write, in October 1643, that he had heard that Descartes was withholding part of his 'Physics'.[25] By the following month, he was pleading with the author not to ruin the book by omitting the section on human beings. 'Mr Pollot and I would strongly advise that, in publishing your Physics, you should not mutilate it of the part on human nature, and that you anticipate the likelihood that what you conceal will always provide material for slander, as has happened to you up to now.'[26] Descartes did not follow this advice for reasons that, on this occasion, seemed plausible. The author was very distracted by the ongoing controversy at Utrecht, and he had not made enough progress in his study of animals and human nature to include those sections in the text. He explains the revised project in those terms in Part IV, Chapter 188, of the *Principles*.

I would not add anything else to this fourth part of the *Principles of Philosophy* if, as I had previously intended, I were to write two other parts, the fifth part about living things, animals and plants, and the sixth part about human nature. But since I have not completely examined all the things that I want to write about there, nor do I know that I will ever have enough time to do so, I shall add a few things here about the objects of the senses rather than delay further the earlier parts or omit from them what I would have deferred to the later parts.   (viii-1. 315)[27]

Descartes had written to Huygens in January 1643 that he was drafting the sections of the *Principles* that discuss magnetism. Given the major distractions emanating from Utrecht during 1643, it is not surprising that it was almost a full year before he could report to Pollot, in January 1644, that he was finishing the paragraphs on magnetism.[28]

The imminent publication of the text caused Mersenne to defer a trip to Italy that he had planned to make in early 1644, and to announce the anticipated appearance of the *Principles* in the dedication of a book he published that year.[29] He wrote on that occasion:

When I hear that you are about to edit very soon the Physics that is awaited so impatiently by the learned, and which is more perfectly compatible than peripatetic physics with the mysteries of our faith and theological dogmas, I address to you, in the name of all Catholics, the greatest gratitude possible, to you who happily take under your protection not only philosophical truths but also those of theology.[30]

From Mersenne's perspective, Descartes was about to provide a more reliable basis for Catholic apologetics than scholastic philosophy. Huygens was equally enthusiastic about the imminent appearance of what he hoped would be a comprehensive and authoritative summary of Descartes' philosophy, one that might redeem the damage caused by suppressing *The World* eleven years earlier. He sent Descartes a poem entitled 'In praise of The Principles of Philosophy of René Descartes', which subsequently appeared in a collection of his poems called *Desultory Moments*.[31]

Descartes had hoped to have copies of the *Principles* ready before he embarked on his visit to France. In preparation for the visit, he wrote to various friends and potential supporters to arrange meetings. Unfortunately, he knew in advance that he would be unable to meet one of his most sympathetic readers. In August 1643, Antoine Arnauld had published his famous book *On Frequent Communion*, in which he publicly supported Jansenism in the increasingly bitter dispute between Port Royal and the Jesuits.[32] Arnauld's theological critics arranged for him to go to Rome, to give an account of his allegedly heterodox views. They also hoped to confirm his exile by making a return to France impossible. However, Gallican supporters of the autonomy of the French church provided a refuge for him in France, presumably as a solitaire in Port Royal des Champs or some similarly safe Jansenist haven. Descartes expressed his sympathy for Arnauld's predicament, acknowledging that Arnauld's 'enemies' (i.e., the Jesuits) were, for the most part, also his own.[33] He consoled himself with the thought that he did not quite understand the subtleties of the theological controversy in which Arnauld was trapped, and that his own writing did 'not impinge on theology, neither from a distance nor at close range', and that he 'did not think they could find any pretext in them for blaming me' (iv. 104).

Although he had no hope of meeting Arnauld in hiding, Descartes hoped to see Picot and to enjoy the kind of intellectual conversation that he lacked in Egmond. Despite his letter of support for Arnauld against Jesuit hostility, he also planned to visit a number of Jesuits and, possibly, to persuade them of the merits of his new physics. He wrote to Father Mesland (2 May 1644): 'I hope to go to France soon where, if possible, I will have the honour of meeting you' (iv. 120). In the case of Mesland, Descartes' lengthy letter included discussion of a number of philosophical issues, especially human freedom, in response to detailed queries that had been sent by this genuinely interested Jesuit correspondent. As usual, he had to acknowledge that he had not read a book on which he was asked to comment – on this occasion, a book on free will by another Jesuit, Father Denis Petau.[34] However, he could refer Mesland to his own book, 'my treatise of philosophy, the printing of which is almost complete' (iv. 113). He wrote to a third Jesuit, Father Grandamy, in similar terms.

The printing of the *Principles* of my philosophy should have been completed two months ago, if the publisher had kept his promise. However, it was delayed by the diagrams, which he was unable to have engraved as quickly as he hoped. Still, I hope to send you a copy soon, unless the wind carries me from here before the printing is completed.   (iv. 122–3)

By this stage (2 May), Descartes had already left Egmond and had arrived in Leiden on his way south to arrange a passage by sea to France.[35]

The *Principles* was being printed by Elzevier in Amsterdam, and Descartes apparently visited his publisher before leaving for France without, alas, getting a final copy of his book. The same printer was interested in publishing a Latin edition of the *Discourse on Method*, together with the *Dioptrics* and the *Meteors* – in other words, the 1637 book without the *Geometry*. It made sense commercially and editorially to omit the *Geometry*. The *Geometry* probably required a more specialized translator (and Van Schooten had already embarked on that task), and it was likely to have a more limited readership. The other two (more accessible) essays were translated by a French Huguenot refugee, Etienne de Courcelles (1586–1659). Meanwhile, the *Principles* was eventually completed on 4 July 1644, with two separate 'privileges' to cover France and the United Provinces.

On his journey south, Descartes also visited Johan van Beverwijck (1594–1647) in Dordrecht, from where he embarked by boat for France. Beverwijck had graduated in medicine from Padua and, having returned to Dordrecht, had been administrator of the city orphanage for ten years before being appointed professor of anatomy and medicine at the local Illustrious School. He had asked Descartes (10 June 1643) to contribute to a collection of essays, *Epistolary Questions*, in which prominent intellectuals would write about topical issues.[36] Descartes wrote about the circulation of the blood. While acknowledging the originality of Harvey as the first to discover and publish the fact that blood circulates, he dissented from the English physician concerning the explanation of circulation. For, according to Descartes, all the factors that explain blood circulation are 'genuinely mechanical'.[37]

Despite the relative isolation in which Descartes lived, there was rarely a time when he felt free to undertake a journey that required more than a few days. He invariably felt that he had to remain 'at home' to complete some project, to avoid the swiftly changing contingencies, on land and sea, of the war with Spain, or to finalize a long-running dispute in which he almost obsessively hoped to claim victory. The summer of 1644 was no different than usual. He was anxiously awaiting the final printing of the *Principles*, and he was watching equally anxiously the way in which Groningen University was handling his complaint about Schoock. He could do nothing about the former – the books could be forwarded to him in Paris. He asked Tobias Andreae to keep a watchful eye on Groningen in his absence, and to pass on word of any developments through Van Hogelande (in Leiden).[38]

Just before departure, Regius wrote to Descartes to wish him a safe journey and to express his concerns about a possible long-term separation between them, which he compared to the separation of the soul and body. This seems slightly exaggerated in the context of their growing estrangement, which was to be confirmed in 1646 with the publication of Regius' book on physics. For the moment, at least according to Baillet, Regius worried that Descartes might remain in France and that they would never see each other again.

The whole of philosophy could not inspire him [Regius] with the constancy required to accept this separation [from Descartes], the pain of which he expressed in words that are all the more touching insofar as he did not trust Descartes' promise to return to Holland. Having given greetings from his wife, his daughter, Mr. Goodefroot van Haestrecht, Mr. Peter van Leeuwen, Mr. Anthony Charles Parmentier and Mr. Peter van Dam, the celebrated physician of Utrecht, in his letter of goodbye, protested that had he not been bound by obligations to his wife, his children and his profession, he would have followed him everywhere and that he would have attached himself to Descartes in a manner that he hoped to achieve, in his heart, for the rest of his life. (iv. 124)

This is probably a more reliable indication of Descartes' uncertain plans for the future than of Regius' state of mind in June 1644. He cannot have failed to notice, at that time, that his former protector and counsellor was putting some distance between himself and a less-than-docile disciple.

Visit to France

Descartes arrived in Paris some time toward the end of June 1644. His long absence from France, especially the relative isolation in which he lived, must have made his re-entry almost like a first visit to a foreign country. During the years since 1628, he had acknowledged losing confidence about French social customs, and even the fluency and unreflective skills expected of a native speaker of French. He most probably travelled by sea from Dordrecht to Calais, and then overland to Paris.[39] He seems to have gone to Paris initially and, according to Baillet, he then travelled south to the Loire valley, where he met Florimond de Beaune in Blois and his younger-brother in Tours. He wrote from Paris (9 July) that he was about to leave the city to visit Brittany and that his journey would last two months.[40] Given the long distances involved and the relatively slow pace of overland travel by coach – the trip from Paris to Tours, Nantes, and Rennes was over 500 kilometres – he most likely did not return to Paris until he was about to leave for Holland again.

One of the reasons for this long-deferred return home was personal.[41] He simply did not get on well with his older brother, Pierre, and there was little affection between them. Since Descartes' father and his sister, Jeanne, had both died four years previously, his closest family members were his half-sister, Anne, his brother-in-law (Jeanne's widower), Mr. Rogier, and his half-brother, Joachim. Since Anne lived in Nantes, she was not able to join the family reunion near Rennes. While visiting his family,

Descartes got news that copies of the *Principles* had arrived in Paris from Amsterdam.[42] He remained in Brittany until the feast of Saint Louis (25 August), after which he returned to Paris. While en route, in September 1644, he consulted a lawyer who finalized the transfer of property and rental income from his brother, Pierre.

Once he returned to Paris, Descartes initiated a marketing strategy for his new book and at the same time accepted Picot's offer to prepare a French translation based initially on a defective copy (without diagrams) that he had brought with him from Amsterdam in June. The marketing strategy coincided neatly with efforts to repair the somewhat fraught relations with the Jesuits that, only four years earlier, he had described as a 'war'. Descartes wrote to three Jesuits, Fathers Charlet, Dinet, and Bourdin, with similar expressions of good will and rather surprising interpretations of what he thought he was doing in the *Principles*. In the case of Bourdin, he had an opportunity to meet him in person for the first time and to bring some closure to their earlier dispute.[43]

One of the Jesuits to whom he wrote, Father Charlet, had been rector of La Flèche from 1606 to 1616, when Descartes was a student there. Having acknowledged his educational debts,[44] he went on to explain – implausibly and very surprisingly – how his philosophy assumed no principle that is not found in Aristotle.

I know that people believed that my views were novel. However, they will see here that I do not use any principle that was not accepted by Aristotle and by everyone who ever philosophized. People also imagined that my plan was to refute the views that are taught in the Schools, and to try to make them ridiculous. But they will see that I do not mention those views any more than if I had never learned them.   (iv. 141)

This was surely an extraordinary commentary on the novelty of his ideas and the motivation of his whole intellectual project. He gave a similar commentary to Father Dinet, whom he credited with resolving the dispute with Father Bourdin. He suggested that some unidentified people had tried 'to smother [his philosophy] before its birth' (iv. 142), but that they would now find that it was 'more innocent than they anticipated'. However, readers might still find reason to criticize it, because it omitted any explanation of animals and plants and dealt only with inanimate bodies. This suggests another reason for the omission of these topics. It was not simply that Descartes had not yet completed the research required to discuss them adequately; it was also evident that they raised more sensitive questions than an explanation of inanimate bodies. Thus Descartes was implicitly acknowledging to Dinet, in the same paragraph, that readers would find his book 'innocent' because it did not contain any discussion of controversial topics about living creatures.

The letter to Father Bourdin was accompanied by a rather generous gift of twelve copies of the *Principles*, one for himself and the others for distribution to various Jesuits who knew Descartes. He mentions Father Charlet and Dinet – evidently, he was expecting Father Bourdin to forward a copy of his book and the accompanying letters to both of them (iv. 143). Other copies were intended for Father Jean François, who had taught philosophy and mathematics at La Flèche when Descartes was a student, and Fathers Vatier, Mesland, Fournier, and Grandamy. Once these gifts were dispatched, Descartes would return to the challenge, in early 1645, of encouraging the Jesuits to adopt the *Principles* as a basis for the philosophy courses they taught in colleges throughout France.

Descartes seems to have spent less than two weeks in Paris in October 1644, since he was anxious to return to the reclusive life he enjoyed near Alkmaar. Before leaving, he met Kenelm Digby, who was then resident in Paris as chancellor to the English queen in exile, Henrietta Maria. Digby was about to publish his *Two Treatises* of 1644, in which he had adopted a line of argument about the human soul that was similar to Descartes'. Digby's project was more explicitly an attempt to enhance the status of the human soul by emphasizing the limitations of material bodies – so much so that he thought he should justify the apparent paradox in the first of two Prefaces to his book. Digby's worry was the following. If one explains mere bodies and their properties by reference to 'powers', simply because they are not understood well enough for us to provide genuine explanations, and if one subsequently discovers that such powers are nothing more than relatively complex material properties, critics are likely to draw the same conclusion about the human soul. In a word, the widespread tolerance of forms and qualities as explanatory entities in natural philosophy is likely to undermine arguments for the immateriality of the soul.

For what hope could I have, out of the actions of the soule to convince the nature of it to be incorporeale; if I could give no other account of bodies operations, then that they were performed by qualities occult, specificall, or incomprehensible? Would not my adversary presently answere, that any operation, out of which I should presse the soules being spirituall, was performed by a corporeall occult quality: and that as he must acknowledge it to be incomprehensible, so must I likewise acknowledge other qualities of bodies, to be as incomprehensible: and therefore could not with reason presse him, to show how a body was able to doe such an operation, as I should inferre must of necessity proceede from a spirit, since that neyther could I give account how the loadestone drew iron, or looked to the north, how a stone, and other heavy thinges were carried downewardes: how sight or fantasie was made; how digestion or purging were effected; and many other such questions, which are so slightly resolved in the schooles.[45]

The obvious danger in this approach to explanation is spelled out in the Preface to the second treatise (on the soul). Scholastic philosophers, according to Digby, had turned 'all bodies into spirits, making (for example) heate, or cold, to be of it selfe indivisible, a thing by it selfe, whose nature is not conceivable'.[46] Having thus collapsed the fundamental distinction between matter and spirit by using 'spiritual' explanations of merely material phenomena, they risked supporting those who argue from the same mistake to the opposite conclusion. If purely material things are mistakenly given a spiritual explanation, then those features of human experience, such as thought, that require a similar spiritual explanation are likely to be no more than complex material processes that are not currently understood.

Digby, in opposition to scholastic philosophy, was anxious to show that 'our Soule is a substance, and Immortall'.[47] Although in natural philosophy we should rely on the evidence of our senses and avoid postulating unnecessary forms or substances, the opposite applies here. 'We are now out of the boundes that experience hath any iurisdiction over: . . . we must in all our searches and conclusions rely only upon the single evidence of Reason.'[48] One of the arguments he used was borrowed from 'Monsieur des Cartes in his Methode'.[49] This was the argument that the mind by definition does not have the properties that are characteristic of material things. By appealing to an experience that was relatively familiar to soldiers at the time, Digby reminds readers that even if one is missing a leg or an arm, one is still a 'thinking thing'.[50] Descartes and Digby both knew that a similar argument does not work in the case of the brain; without a brain, one ceases to think. Their argument showed only that arms or legs are not necessary for thinking, while a brain is obviously necessary. However, they supported their position by arguing that it makes no sense to think of half a mind, whereas it always makes sense to think of half a body. The fragility of the argument was beginning to be exposed.

There is no record of what Descartes and Digby discussed in Paris. The Englishman may have shown his visitor an advance copy of his new book. Had he done so, Descartes could not have read it. More significantly, he could not have known (in October 1644) that Digby's book would be published later that year with the Sorbonne's approval, something that Descartes had requested for the *Meditations* so importunately and unsuccessfully three years earlier. Digby got a '*nihil obstat*' for his book only on 10 November.[51]

Digby continued to live in Paris, to undertake diplomatic missions, including a lengthy unsuccessful visit to Rome, 1647–48, to request the Pope's assistance on behalf of Queen Henrietta Maria. He eventually published an extremely popular book that confirmed, for many critics, the implausibility of his natural philosophy and the conclusions about the soul's immortality that depended on it: *A Late Discourse Touching the Cure of Wounds by the Powder of Sympathy*.[52] Here Digby argued that bodies of the 'same nature' can affect each other at a distance. The crucial observation on which he relied was that the 'powder of sympathy', when applied to a bandage from a soldier's wound, can cure the wound itself because of the 'faculty and force' with which it affects the blood in the wound, even without coming into contact with it.[53]

According to Baillet, Descartes also visited Roberval, with whom he had disputed after publication of his *Geometry*, and they found enough common ground to reconcile.[54] He then travelled overland to Calais, a distance of approximately 260 kilometres, where he was delayed for twelve days by bad weather while he awaited a boat for Dordrecht. He used the enforced interruption to read over Picot's draft French translation of Parts I and II of the *Principles*. He told Picot, in a letter since lost, that he found the translation to be excellent and that he could not have hoped for anything better.[55] This translation, when completed, was to appear three years later. Meantime Mersenne, who had deferred a journey to Italy so that he could be in Paris when Descartes arrived, set off at about the same time on a journey that was to last for 'eight or nine months'.[56] That implied that his almost weekly correspondence with Descartes was broken off for more than a year. The next letter available between the two Frenchmen dates from 2 March 1646. Mersenne seems to have returned from Italy in July 1645, and to have set out again for the same destination during the winter, coming back to Paris only in September 1646.[57]

The Principles of Philosophy

The printing of the first edition of the *Principles* was completed by Elzevier in Amsterdam, 10 July 1644. The book was designed as a compact and comprehensive survey of Cartesian philosophy, with the exception of his thoughts about plants, animals, and human beings. The most obvious way in which the first edition differs from many subsequent translations is that it is divided only into four parts; the text of each part is not further subdivided, as is usually done today, by the titles of paragraphs or articles. Instead, the content of each paragraph is summarized in numbered marginal notes that correspond to the Index at the beginning of the book. Besides, Descartes also adopted the advice given by Huygens for the *Essays*, to include diagrams at appropriate places in the text rather than collect them all at the end of the book.

The first part of the *Principles* is entitled 'The Principles of Human Knowedge'. This represents a second attempt to provide a metaphysical foundation for Descartes' system of philosophy or, as he described it five years later, a 'summary of what I wrote in my *Meditations*'.[58] The reluctance of Catholic supporters in France and the extreme hostility of Calvinist critics in the United Provinces to the proofs of God's existence, in the *Meditations*, may have persuaded him to change his presentation of this issue in the *Principles*. Whereas the *Meditations* offered an a posteriori proof in the Third Meditation and a version of the ontological argument in the Fifth Meditation, the *Principles* reversed the order in which they were presented and condensed each argument to a mere outline. There is no suggestion in the *Principles* that God may be a deceiver – a possibility that was briefly mentioned and almost immediately retracted in the *Meditations*, and which attracted vehement objections from Dutch theologians – and the apparent dominance of sceptical concerns in the 1641 book is avoided. Instead, the necessity of God's existence is included in the very concept of God (I, 14), whereas the argument based on the intentional reality of the idea of God is presented, succinctly, by integrating some of his earlier replies to Caterus in the *Meditations* (I, 17, 18*)*.[59]

Part I of the *Principles* is also more explicit and extensive in its discussion of human freedom, and this may have provided counter-Remonstrant critics with an independent basis for their objections to Cartesianism. Descartes claimed that the scope of the human will was in some sense infinite 'because we never notice anything that can be the object of someone else's will, or even of the immense will of God, which is outside the scope of our will' (I, 35). While repeating the analysis of error already offered in the *Meditations* – that we err only when we make judgements about things that we do not adequately understand – Descartes was anxious not to hold God responsible for human error. There is nothing in human nature that necessarily causes error. Although Descartes does not mention the sin of Adam, it is obvious that Calvinists and even some Catholic followers of Augustine would have distinguished between the capacity of the human mind in its pristine, prelapsarian condition and the error-prone faculties with which sinful human beings were subsequently endowed. However, there is no suggestion of such theological qualification in the *Principles*, when it argues: 'That there is freedom of our will and that we are able to assent or not assent . . . is so evident that it should be counted among the first and most common notions that are innate in us' (I, 39). At the same time, God is all-powerful, and everything is preordained by Him. 'The power of God by which He not only knew eternally everything that exists or could exist, but also willed and preordained them, is infinite' (I, 41). Descartes has to admit that he cannot reconcile God's preordination and human free will, as he had explained in correspondence with Princess Elizabeth.

Part I concludes with a summary of the degrees of certainty that we can claim for our beliefs. There is a descending hierarchy of reliability from (a) revealed truths, to (b) what is critically examined, to (c) what we spontaneously and uncritically believe based on our experiences.

Although the light of reason, however clear and evident it is, may seem to suggest something different to us, we should put our faith exclusively in divine authority rather than in our own judgment. However, in the case of things about which divine faith does not teach us anything, it is very inappropriate for a philosopher to accept anything as true that they have never perceived as true; and it is even more inappropriate to trust in the senses, that is, in the uncritical judgments of childhood, than in mature reason.   (I, 76)

Part II of the *Principles*, entitled 'The Principles of Material Things', provides a summary of the Cartesian concept of matter and of the most fundamental laws of nature by which changes in material things occur. Descartes outlines, in this context, his argument against the possibility of what he calls an 'absolute vacuum'. The argument is that if God were to remove all the matter from a vessel, its sides could not remain apart because the distance between them would then be a property of nothing, and 'nothing' does not have any measurable size (II, 18). This would later provide a basis for common cause between the Jesuit Father Noël and Descartes against Blaise Pascal.

Descartes uses the opportunity provided by publication of the *Principles* to reveal, for the first time, three 'laws of nature' that he had already formulated (in a slightly different way) in *The World*.[60] The three laws are proposed as the fundamental principles that explain all natural phenomena in terms of the motions and interactions of various parts of matter that swirl around in an atmosphere that is filled with matter. The motion of any particular body (i.e., a part of matter that, at least temporarily, moves without joining with other parts or shedding any parts from itself) is therefore similar to that of a fish swimming in water. The motion of the fish does not presuppose any empty place into which it moves, or any empty space left in its wake after its departure. Rather, by the force of its own motion, it displaces water that, in turn, displaces other matter that fills the space left unoccupied by the moving fish. Descartes further developed the three laws into seven rules that help determine what happens when, in idealized conditions, one body collides with another. Some of the rules appear to be counterfactual, although Descartes tries to explain away this impression by arguing that, in the real world, all bodies constantly interact with an indeterminate number of others in their immediate environment and, therefore, no actual collisions occur in the idealized conditions envisaged by the rules.

Having outlined the extremely parsimonious list of items that would be acceptable in a Cartesian theory of the natural world – parts of matter of varying sizes and shapes, moving with more or less speed in different directions – and, by implication, the kinds of reality that would not be acceptable, such as scholastic forms, qualities, and anything that was equivalently 'occult' or poorly understood, Descartes aspired to explain all natural phenomena by reference to these few items and the three laws of nature. The concluding paragraph of Part II gives the following programmatic statement of his intentions:

I freely acknowledge that I know of no matter in bodily things apart from that which can be divided, shaped, and moved in every way. . . . I consider nothing in that matter apart from those divisions, shapes and motions. . . . And since all natural phenomena can be explained in this way, as will appear in what follows, I do not think that any other principles of physics should be accepted or even desired.   (II, 64)

The most contentious issue that Descartes had to face, at the beginning of Part III, was whether to offer any opinion about Galileo's heliocentric theory and, if so, how to phrase his views without risking the wrath of the Catholic Church. He had very carefully avoided public discussion of this topic since 1633, and he continued to repeat his original explanation of his silence – that he was waiting for signs of a change of mind in Rome. He provides a context for the Cartesian solution by warning readers against reducing God's power, and the universe He created, to the limits of human intelligence. He also rejects as 'clearly ridiculous and inappropriate' any kind of anthropocentrism that would imply that God created the whole universe only for human beings.

Descartes was convinced that, among the various models of the planetary system, Galileo's was most consistent with observational evidence and with the laws of nature that he had outlined in Part II. He also thought that it was not enough for an astronomical theory to *describe* the motions of the planets, that is, to say which planets move, what paths they describe, and so on. It also had to provide some explanation of *how* the planets move or what makes them move as they apparently do. Most of all, he wished to avoid conflict with Rome over its prohibition on teaching that 'the Sun is in the centre of the universe and is immobile, and that the Earth moves'. He took care of this restriction easily. According to the relativist definition of motion proposed in Part II, paragraph 25, a body is said to be in motion when it is transferred from being close to the bodies in its immediate vicinity to being in the vicinity of other bodies.[61]

According to Descartes, all the matter of the planetary system is whirling about in a vortex around the Sun, and it is carried along by the vortex of which it is a floating part. This allows him to 'save the phenomena' by having the Sun at the centre and the planets in orbit around the Sun, as Galileo claimed. It also explains how such large bodies move, without invoking gravity or action at a distance. Finally, Descartes could maintain that, despite its motion around the Sun, there is a genuine sense in which each planet is at rest relative to the immediately contiguous matter that moves in the same vortex as itself.[62]

The conclusion of this convoluted redefinition of terms and of his dynamical theory of planetary motion, he claimed, was that he had 'resolved every scruple about the Earth's motion' and that 'all the matter of the heavens in which the planets are located turns constantly like a vortex, in the centre of which is the Sun' (III, 30). This released him to speculate about the nature of light, the stars, magnetism, and all the natural phenomena that had occupied his attention for almost fifteen years. The final paragraphs of Part IV address the niggling worry, raised even by sympathetic readers of the *Essays*, that his hypotheses might turn out to be false. Descartes bets both ways on his physical theory, and still leaves open the possibility that it may be false if it contradicts the teachings of the church.

He argues in paragraph 205 that his hypotheses are 'at least morally certain', that is, that 'they have the kind of certainty required for daily living' (IV, 205). The concept of 'moral certainty' was already familiar in the seventeenth century. If wine is bought from a reputable producer, it is not necessary to get a chemical analysis before drinking a glass of it. Most of what we do in our daily lives relies on a degree of certainty that is far short of proof, but is sufficient to make it possible to carry on without undue anxiety. Descartes gives another example to support his understanding of the degree of certainty that could be claimed for his hypotheses. If one imagines a letter written in code, and if one discovered a translation manual that turns unintelligible strings of signs into meaningful words, one could feel confident that the translation was correct, even if it were discovered merely by conjecture. Likewise, 'those who notice how many things about the magnet, fire, and the whole fabric of the universe are deduced here from so few principles . . . will acknowledge that it could hardly have happened that so many phenomena were consistent with those principles if they were false' (IV, 205).

Stepping up the pressure, Descartes argues in the next paragraph that some of his principles are 'absolutely, and more than just morally, certain'. He is not very specific about which claims 'even about natural phenomena' enjoy this kind of metaphysical certainty, and he concludes that 'at least the more general things that I wrote about the world and the Earth can hardly be explained otherwise than as I have done' (IV, 206). The final paragraph of the book, perhaps the most telling symptom of his continuing concerns about censorship from Rome, is as follows:

Nonetheless, mindful of my weakness, I affirm nothing. However, I submit all these things both to the authority of the Catholic Church and to the judgment of more prudent men. I do not wish anything to be believed by anyone, unless they are convinced by evident and invincible reason.   (IV, 207)

Wooing the Jesuits

Descartes had visited a number of prominent Jesuits based in Paris during his visit in October 1644. He distributed twelve copies of the *Principles* specifically to the Jesuits, and left behind with Picot some extra copies for other French supporters. On his return to the United Provinces, he went back to northern Holland and settled in one of the three villages that included 'Egmond' in their names, possibly in Egmond-Binnen. In early 1645, he took up again the charm offensive toward the Jesuits, to try to have his *Principles* adopted as a college text. He pursued this plan so aggressively that, on a single day, he wrote four lengthy letters to different Jesuits in Paris, all with the same objective.

Despite the lapse of almost thirty years since he had been a Jesuit student, Descartes seems to have received a reply from Father Charlet, his former college rector, to his letter of October 1644. He wrote in February 1645 to acknowledge that he had received a number of similar letters from various Jesuits and that he felt very much obliged to them.[63] The fact that Father Charlet was now assistant to the Father General of the Jesuits in France made it all the more important that Descartes exploit this connection to his advantage – an effort that, on this occasion, he was uncharacteristically honest in acknowledging. He tried to persuade Charlet that Cartesianism would eventually emerge as the preferred philosophy of the schools, and that the Jesuits had the power to facilitate that recognition or, alternatively, that they could delay it by their lack of interest.

For, although this philosophy [i.e., Descartes'] relies so much on demonstrations that I cannot doubt that, in time, it will be generally approved and adopted, nevertheless, if a lack of interest prevented them [the Jesuits] from wishing to read it, I could not hope to live long enough to see that day because they are the largest group who are competent to evaluate it. However, if their goodwill persuades them to examine it, I dare to hope that they will find in it so many things that will appear true to them, and which can easily be substituted for what is commonly taught and can be helpful in explaining the truths of the Faith, that – without contradicting Aristotle's text – they will even accept them and thus, within a few years, this Philosophy will acquire the kind of credibility that it would otherwise not acquire for a century. I acknowledge that this is something in which I have an interest; I am a man like other men, and I am not so insensitive that I am not affected by success.[64]

The letter to Father Dinet acknowledges his assistance in converting what initially seemed like a concerted Jesuit attack, led by Bourdin, into a promise of goodwill from the Society. The pitch to win Jesuit support for the *Principles*, which is identified as his 'Philosophy', is similar to the overtures to Father Charlet.

Having taken the trouble to write a Philosophy, I know that your Society [i.e., the Jesuits] alone can do more than the rest of the world to make it valued or despised. That is why I do not fear that people who are competent judges, and who think that I am not completely lacking in judgment myself, will doubt that I shall do everything I can to deserve their evaluation. I was very glad to hear that you took the trouble to read it. . . . I fully acknowledge that views that are very different to those that are commonly accepted surprise readers initially, and I did not hope that mine would be accepted immediately by those who read them. But I hoped that, bit by bit, readers would get used to them and, the more they examined them, the more they would find them credible and reasonable.[65]

This conveys a completely implausible estimate of how the *Principles* compare to the philosophy that was widely taught in Jesuit colleges. While acknowledging that Cartesian philosophy was sufficiently unfamiliar to surprise or shock readers initially, Descartes suggests that patience and the familiarity gained by persistent reading would be enough to win their approval.

Descartes' letter to Bourdin, apart from the extravagant compliments and the conventional blandishments of French epistolary style, explains why he cannot return to Paris again, in the near future, to benefit from the stimulation afforded by intellectual conversation with his recently acquired correspondent. The reason given is the usual one: he needs to spend as much time as possible on research and writing.

The Theology of the Eucharist

The letters to the fourth Jesuit, Father Mesland, were completely different from the other three just mentioned. Descartes acknowledged that they had not known each other before the publication of the *Meditations*, and that it was Mesland's careful reading of that book and subsequent questions about it that had first put them in contact with each other. Mesland had evidently asked Descartes about the Tridentine theology of the Eucharist, in particular about the way in which Christ was supposed to be present in the Eucharist after the liturgical consecration. In general terms, the reformed churches made a distinction between the manner in which God exists (in Heaven?) and the way in which Christ is present in the Eucharist (in some other sense, which might be called symbolic or sacramental). In stark contrast, the teaching of the Council of Trent implied a presence of Christ in the Eucharist that was 'substantial' or 'real'. Most reformed theologians thought that the Catholic view was not only mysterious but incomprehensible, because it implied that the same reality could be present, simultaneously, in thousands of different places.[66]

Descartes recognized the sensitivity of the questions raised. He prefaced his comments by disclaiming: 'it is not up to me to explain how one can conceive that the body of Jesus Christ is present in the Holy Sacrament' (iv. 165). However, he also quoted, in Latin, from the Council of Trent the passage that conceded that 'we can hardly express in words' the kind of existence that is involved here.[67] Since the Council did not teach that we could not express the reality in words, but merely that we could hardly do so, Descartes ventured, foolishly, to make such an attempt. However, mindful of what might happen if others heard about their discussion, he asked Mesland not to communicate his views to anyone unless his correspondent thought they were orthodox and, if he were to share them with anyone else, that he not attribute those views to Descartes.

Descartes' confidential commentary on the theology of the Eucharist was motivated by a desire to show that belief in transubstantiation was not irrational.[68] 'I shall risk telling you in confidence a way of . . . avoiding the slander of heretics [Calvinists] who object to us [Catholics] that we believe, in this matter, something that is completely incomprehensible and implies a contradiction' (iv. 165). The proposed solution was to focus attention on the identity of familiar bodies, despite the changes they undergo over time. The matter that composes the human body may change completely, over a number of years, as each particle is replaced by other particles by nutrition. However, a person is still said to have 'the same body' because, despite its piecemeal substitution, it continues to be united to the same soul. There is thus a sense in which the matter we ingest when we eat and drink is 'transubstantiated' into the body of a human being. Descartes thinks that a similarly elegant and easily comprehensible account is available for the teaching of Trent about the Eucharist. The bread and wine used in the liturgy is joined, by divine power, with the spiritual reality of God. Despite maintaining all the usual properties of bread and wine, such as the familiar size, shape, and texture of the bread or the colour and taste of the wine, they are transformed into the body and blood of Christ by the spiritual presence of Christ in what is apparently bread and wine.[69] Descartes summarizes his conclusion as follows:

> The whole miracle of transubstantiation...consists in this...that the soul [of Christ] informs the particles of bread and wine...by the power of the words of consecration.... This explication will no doubt shock those initially who are used to believing that, in order for the body of Jesus Christ to be present in the Eucharist, it is necessary for all parts of his body to be there with their same quantity and shape.... nothing like that has been decided by the Church.... the soul of Jesus Christ informs the matter of the host.   (iv. 168–9)

Descartes thinks that this avoids the obvious difficulty of claiming that the body of Christ, which Christians believe was assumed into Heaven three days after his crucifixion, is present at each Mass in the same way that Christ's body was present on Earth during the first century A.D.

Descartes returned to this topic on a number of occasions in later correspondence. He wrote to Mesland again, after he had been sent to the Jesuit missions in Canada, expressing the hope that he would return to Europe at some stage and that his talents might not be wasted on the relatively unsophisticated residents of that foreign land. He repeated the suggestion that the identity of a human body does not depend on the matter of which it is composed but on the fact that, despite changes in the body, it remains joined with the same soul.[70] His further thoughts on how a host could have been consecrated successfully during the period when Christ's body was in the tomb helps illustrate the intractability of the position adopted by Trent rather than the limitations of Descartes' ingenuity.

However, Descartes also replied, in response to a query about transubstantiation from Clerselier in 1646, as if he accepted the traditional account of transubstantiation. On this occasion he suggested that God could substitute one piece of matter for another – for example, a piece of gold for a piece of bread or one piece of bread for another piece of bread – and that such changes would involve merely transferring the 'accidents' (i.e., the nonessential properties, such as its size, shape, etc.) from the original piece of matter to its substitute. In theory, that would mean that a piece of gold would look like a piece of bread, or that one piece of bread would assume the characteristics of a different piece for which it was substituted. 'However, there is something else in the Holy Sacrament; for, besides the matter of the body of Jesus Christ, which is placed under the original dimensions of the bread, the soul of Jesus Christ – which informs this matter – is also there.'[71] The suggestion about the qualitative features of bread or gold being attached, even by divine power, to different underlying substances was inconsistent with the account of substances that Descartes had developed over a number of years.[72]

There is a slightly more honest acknowledgement of the problems involved in this issue, in another letter of 1646. Here Descartes identified two problems for the traditional account of changing a substance while leaving the observable qualities unchanged.

> There are two principal questions pertaining to this mystery [of the Eucharist]. One is how it can happen that all the accidents of the bread remain in some place where the bread is no longer present and there is a different body in its place. The other question is how the body of Jesus Christ can be present under the same dimensions as the bread.   (iv. 374–5)

Descartes concedes that, in reply to the first question, he should provide an answer different from the one taught in the schools, because he had a different account of how qualities are related to the subject of which they are qualities. However, he declines to repeat what that answer should be. As to the second question, he claims that he has no obligation to look for a new explanation and that, even if he could find one, he would not wish to tell anyone about it, 'because in such matters the more common views are the best ones'.[73] However, even here he could hardly resist intimating the way in which both he and the traditional theologians ought to answer the question.

> When one bodily substance is changed into another and when all the accidents of the first substance remain, what has been changed? They [theologians] should reply, as I do, that nothing at all of what is observable has been changed nor, consequently, nothing of whatever is the basis for giving different names to those substances. For it is certain that the differences in names that have been given to substances result only from the fact that different observable properties have been noticed in them.   (iv. 375)

If this is translated into plain language, it means that we give different names to various physical things because of the observable qualities that we notice in them. For example, we call one liquid 'wine' not only because of its liquidity, but because of its colour, taste, viscosity, and so on, while we call another liquid 'water' because it has some different properties. Thus, if none of the observable properties of a glass of wine have changed, then it is still what we call 'wine'. Descartes leaves open the possibility that the body in question has changed into a different reality despite the fact that none of its properties has changed. However, we have still no reason to call it anything other than wine, based on the only criteria available for applying different names to different things, which are their observable qualities.

Baillet had commented in another context that, in constrast with Sorbière, 'Mr. Descartes did not have the gift of dissimulation'.[74] It is difficult to avoid the conclusion here that Descartes is avoiding saying explicitly what he believes and that he is implying the opposite of what was taught by Catholic theologians at the time. They standardly claimed that the observable properties of bread and wine remain unchanged while the unobservable, underlying substances are changed. Someone as well informed as Mersenne had even based one of his arguments in natural philosophy on this reading of the Council of Trent. In *The Impiety of Deists*, he had argued that each body must be a substance in its own right and have its own characteristic form. Otherwise, two distinct bodies would be only one substance, and the church's teaching about transubstantiation would be undermined unless each body is a distinct substance.[75] This unwise intervention by Descartes into an insoluble theological problem was one of the reasons why the Vatican condemned his work in 1663.

Reactions to the *Principles*

The favourable response to the *Principles* that Descartes expected from French Jesuits did not materialize, and the reactions of other readers were equally mute or critical. For example, Gassendi was unlikely to be among the fans of the new book. When asked by Rivet what he thought of it, he declined to comment on Descartes' physics as he had done, with contentious results, on his metaphysics. 'However, I shall add the following, so that you can think of me as dealing with you in confidence, that this work will be seen to be extremely empty when it is seen to die before its author. I certainly do not know anyone who has the courage to read it from cover to cover who does not find it extremely tedious, and who is not amazed that it contains such time-consuming trifles.'[76]

The Cavendish brothers were more positive in their assessment, though probably less well informed. William Cavendish had been head of a regiment in the battle of Marston Moor, in July 1644, and was frustrated by his lack of military success. He left almost immediately afterward, with his two sons and his brother Charles, and landed at Hamburg on 8 July. He remained there until February 1645, when he travelled to Paris and may have met Descartes on route. Charles Cavendish had wished to visit Holland immediately, where he hoped to see Descartes, but he was informed that the French philosopher had already left for France.[77] Instead he wrote to John Pell and asked him to send a copy of the *Principles*.[78] He reported to Pell in September that he was 'extreamlie taken with Des Cartes his newe booke', although he thought that 'Kercher the Jesuit of the loadestone hath prevented Descartes, for they differ little as I remember.'[79] He was also able to report, in October 1644, about Hobbes' assessment of the *Principles* and of his own response.

I received yesterdaie a letter from Mr. Hobbes, who had not seen De Cartes his newe booke printed, but had reade some sheets of it in manuscript, and seems to receive little satisfaction from it, and saies a friend of his hath reade it through, and is of the same minde; but by their leaves I esteeme it an excellent booke, though I think Monsieur Des Cartes is not infallible.[80]

While the first readers were giving their opinions of the new book, Descartes returned to the relative isolation of Egmond. From there he had to acknowledge that he was not quite sure what various readers thought about the *Principles*. To protect it from inappropriate objections, he makes the same proposal to Father Mesland as he had made eleven years earlier about *The World*, that readers think of it as a 'fable'.

I would have wished that you had had enough time to examine my *Principles* in greater detail. I dare hope that you would find in it at least that the parts are linked together coherently so that one would have to reject everything that is contained in the two final parts and to accept it only as an hypothesis or even as a fable, or else accept the whole thing. Even if one accepted it only as an hypothesis, as I suggested, it seems to me, nonetheless, that it should not be rejected until one has found a better hypothesis to explain all the phenomena of nature.

However, I have no reason yet to complain about my readers. For since this last treatise was published I have not heard of anyone who has undertaken to criticize it. . . . Nonetheless, I do not know what is said in my absence, and I am here in a corner of the world where I would not fail to live very much at peace and contented even if the judgment of all the learned were against me.[81]

He also suggested, as he had on a similar previous occasion, that most of his potential readers were so ignorant that their views were irrelevant to him. 'Although when one publishes a book one is always very anxious to know what readers say about it, I can assure you however that it concerns me very little. Indeed, I think I know the ability of most of those who pass for learned so well that I would think little of my views if they approved them.'[82] Having dismissed the significance of his critics, Descartes offered a defence of the empirical character of his work and, as in earlier letters to the Jesuits, of the extent to which his new physics complemented that of the ancients.

What I find most surprising is the conclusion of the evaluation that you sent me, namely, that what will prevent my principles from being accepted in the schools is that they are not sufficiently confirmed by experiences and that I have not refuted the explanations of others. For I am amazed that, despite the fact that I have demonstrated in detail almost as many experiences as there are lines in my writings and, having offered a general explanation, in my *Principles*, of all the phenomena of nature, I explained in the same way all the experiences that could be performed on inanimate bodies, whereas in contrast no one has ever explained any of them by using the principles of school philosophy, those who follow the latter accuse me of a lack of empirical support.

I also find it very surprising that they want me to refute the reasoning of the scholastics. . . . Because those who have most at stake here are the Jesuit fathers, the esteem of Father Charlet – who is a relative of mine and is currently the superior of their company . . . – and that of Father Dinet and of some of the other prominent members of their order, whom I believe are genuinely my friends, was the reason why I refrained from doing so to date. I even composed my *Principles* in such a way that one could say that they do not in any way contradict scholastic philosophy, but that they merely enriched it with many things that it lacked. Since they accept indefinitely many views that are mutually inconsistent, why could they not also accept mine?   (iv. 224–5)

Descartes' hopes for a rapprochement with the Jesuits and for the adoption of his *Principles* as a philosophical textbook was not about to be satisfied in the short term. His impatience for recognition, despite his explicit comments to the contrary, caused him to recede even further into seclusion in Egmond-Binnen.

The Hermitage

In the immediate aftermath of publishing the *Principles* and the initially promising reception he received in Paris, Descartes returned to the refuge in Egmond-Binnen that he called his 'hermitage', to continue the research required to complete his account of all natural phenomena.[83] He concentrated on two projects: cultivating plants for research purposes in his garden, and performing anatomical dissections in order to make progress with the explanation of animal life that he had begun many years earlier.[84] He wrote to Tobias Andreae in July 1645 that he was dedicating all his resources and energies to anatomical experiments for a full year. Apart from a short visit to Leiden and the Hague, 'he did not leave his house at Egmond, to which he had brought from Alkmaar and other places all kinds of animals that were suitable for dissection.'[85] One gets the same impression from his communications with the marquis of Newcastle. William Cavendish seems to have been interested almost exclusively in whatever Descartes could contribute to an understanding of animals. Years later, as he waited in Antwerp for the Restoration, he published a book on dressage.[86] This abiding interest was reflected in his conversations and correspondence with Descartes.[87] In October 1645, Descartes mentions to Newcastle 'a treatise on animals on which I began to work more than fifteen years ago'.[88] He concedes that he has not had an opportunity to do all the experiments required to complete that work, that he still has not done so, and that it is unlikely that he can finish the treatise in the near future.[89] Sorbière provides a snapshot of this period in a letter to Petit, written more than a decade later.[90]

One of his friends went to visit Descartes at Egmond. This gentleman asked him, about physics books: which ones did he most value, and which of them did he most frequently consult. 'I shall show you', he replied, 'if you wish to follow me.' He led him into a lower courtyard at the back of his house, and showed him a calf that he had planned to dissect the next day. I truly believe that he hardly read anything any more.

Borel gives a slightly different account of this event, in his biography of Descartes, in which he has Descartes point to the dissected calf and proclaim: 'this is my library!'[91] Sorbière acknowledges that the dissecting of animal or human bodies was not unusual, and he mentions various other practitioners whom he met.[92] However, whereas others applied themselves 'to dissecting animals without a theory, Descartes applied himself to theory without having all the observations that it required'.[93]

Borel's version of the story, that Descartes thought of his laboratory as his library, was even more explicit than Sorbière's in mentioning that, in this phase of his life, he 'did not wish to have many books because he knew that, apart from mathematical books, they were not truthful'.[94] This declining lack of interest in reading books is confirmed by Baillet's account of the inventory taken after his death in Sweden. 'One must acknowledge, however, that he did not read very much, that he had very few books, and that most of those that were found by his inventory after his death were presents from his friends.'[95]

This unwavering focus on anatomy and physiology was confirmed by Descartes' reply to a request from one of his most loyal and supportive friends, Constantijn Huygens, who asked him in July 1645 to do some work on chemistry. Descartes replied, with regret:

> It was difficult for me to decide to send you this letter without including a discourse on chemistry, as you had requested. For there is nothing that I would not do very willingly to obey you, on condition that I was capable of doing so. However, having already written what little I know about this subject in Part Four of my *Principles* . . . I cannot write anything more about it without running the risk of making mistakes, because I have not done the experiments that would be required to acquire detailed knowledge of each thing. Since I have no opportunity to perform those experiments, I renounce this study for the future . . . and all other studies for which I require the assistance of others. For I still have enough other studies, which I can do myself, and which will occupy me happily for the rest of my life.　　　　　(iv. 260–1)

Since Descartes was given to making dramatic claims that had the appearance of finality, one has to read this letter to Huygens with some caution. However, there are obvious intimations in his correspondence that he was becoming increasingly aware of the limited time that might remain to him and of the need to channel his energies to complete the more urgent of his projects. In contrast with earlier predictions of a long healthy life, Descartes also began to acknowledge explicitly his advancing years and their impact on his well-being. From about the age of forty-three he had taken to wearing a wig, to protect his head from the cold.[96] He began to feel that, 'since my trip to France [in 1644], I have got twenty years older than I was last year, so that to go from here to the Hague is now a greater journey than it was previously to travel to Rome.'[97] This reticence about travel did not prevent him from making two further journeys to France, in 1647 and 1648, nor from accepting the invitation from Queen Christina of Sweden that eventually led to his death. His state of mind, in the final years in Egmond, was one of uncertainty about the future and of a growing reluctance to publish anything at all. Even his desire for victory in the long-running dispute with Voetius was waning. Having heard no response from Groningen to his complaint about Martin Schoock, he wrote to Pollot in May 1645: 'I am completely indifferent to what happens there, and I have resolved to let them do what they wish without even bothering to take the slightest further action or to write or say anything to anyone about that issue.'[98]

The Quarrel and Final Rift
with Regius

The book by Mr. Regius does not contain a word about Metaphysics that is not exactly the opposite of my views.[1]

T HE two years immediately following his visit to France – 1645 and 1646 – were a transitional period in Descartes' life in many senses of that term. In Paris he had met a number of potentially supportive scholars, and he had begun almost immediately to cultivate their friendship. However, once returned to the north of Holland, he seemed to lapse into a general malaise. He heard on 25 November 1644 that his friend Bannius had died during his absence.[2] During the following months he wrote relatively little; he tried with limited success to complete the missing parts of the *Principles*; and he completely sundered his friendship with one of his most loyal and committed followers, Regius. There was some compensation for this intellectual stagnation in the preparation of French translations of his two Latin books, the *Meditations* and the *Principles*, although the work involved in translating them was done by others. Midway through this period he also began to work on a completely new project – which he called the passions of the soul – partly at the request of Princess Elizabeth and partly in response to queries from Chanut. Even here, however, his tentative explorations were qualified by a lack of interest in publishing the results. It was consistent with this mood that, for the first time in almost two decades, he began to consider seriously returning to France or finding alternative ways to enjoy the stimulation of intellectual discussions with his fellow countrymen.[3]

It is clear from Descartes' earliest days in the United Provinces that he had a weakness for losing friends and, in the case of those who criticized him, for making permanent enemies. One notable exception to this general pattern was Cornelis van Hogelande (1590–1676). Van Hogelande was, according to Sorbière, 'a great Catholic gentleman' who provided free medical care and drugs to the poor of Leiden.[4] Descartes had lived with him briefly in 1640 and, since then, had used his services as a reliable intermediary for many correspondents who were unable to contact him directly. They sent their letters or books to Van Hogelande, who in turn could be relied on always to pass them on to the reclusive philosopher.[5] Descartes was later to leave a trunk containing letters and other documents in the care of Van Hogelande when he travelled to Sweden. He was therefore one of the few close friends of Descartes who remained such throughout his life.

During his visit to Paris in 1644, Descartes met two other sympathetic readers who were subsequently to become instrumental in publicizing his work and defending it against critics. Claude Clerselier (1614–1684) was a lawyer in the *parlement* of Paris. Although he had fourteen children, only three of them survived. One of his daughters, Geneviève, subsequently married Jacques Rohault, who was a prominent proponent of Cartesian natural philosophy for decades after Descartes' death. Once introduced to Descartes, Clerselier also acted as an intermediary for some of Descartes' relatives who lived in France and who wished to communicate with him by letter in Holland.[6] Descartes also met Pierre Chanut (1601–1662), Clerselier's brother-in-law, who later became one of his cherished correspondents and, as the senior resident French diplomat in Sweden, the intermediary between Queen Christina and Descartes who encouraged him to accept the queen's invitation to travel to Stockholm.

When Chanut was first appointed a diplomat in Sweden, he travelled overland from Paris to Denmark and passed through the United Provinces with his family in early October 1645. This provided Descartes with the opportunity to renew their acquaintance on 4 October. The two Frenchmen spent four days together and consolidated their friendship for life.[7] Descartes recalled their visit five months later, when he wrote to Chanut in Stockholm. Apart from complaining about the 1645–46 winter, which was the coldest since 1608, and the detrimental impact of the weather on his plans to grow plants for research, Descartes expressed his warm feelings toward Chanut.

If I had availed of the honour of writing to you every time I wished to do so, since you passed through this country, you would have been pestered very often by my letters. For there has not been a single day that I did not consider writing to you a number of times. . . . If you have deigned to examine what I wrote [i.e., the *Principles*], you would oblige me enormously if you were to alert me to the mistakes that you will have noticed. For I have not been able to meet anyone, so far, who has told me about them and I see that most men judge so poorly that I should not bother with their views. However, I would treat yours as oracles.[8]

Three months later he writes along the same lines to Chanut, asking him to review the *Principles* and to point out the many mistakes and obscurities he would almost certainly find there, since 'I cannot hope to be advised as well about them by anyone else.'[9] He had to acknowledge, however, that the French resident in Sweden was more interested in moral philosophy than in physics, and that he might lose interest very quickly in reading the *Principles*, which had little to say about morality.

By 1 November 1646, Descartes mentions that Chanut is waiting to get a copy of the French edition of the *Meditations*, to present it to Queen Christina. This provoked Descartes into a lengthy reflection on the disadvantages of publication, a theme to which he returned often during these years.

If I had only been as wise as savages are supposed to believe that monkeys are, I would never have become known to anyone as someone who writes books. For savages are said to imagine that monkeys could talk if they wanted to do so, but that they abstain from talking so that they are not required to work. I have not been as prudent by abstaining from writing, and therefore I no longer have as much leisure or as much rest as I would have if I had been smart enough to keep quiet.[10]

Since it was then too late to turn back the clock, and since there were countless scholastics waiting to object to what he wrote, he thought he would benefit by having a patron to protect him by their 'power and virtue' (iv. 535). Despite this overture toward royal protection from afar, Descartes did not consider travelling to Sweden at that stage. 'I do not believe that I shall ever go to the places where you live [Sweden], nor that you will retire to where I am [Holland]' (iv. 537). The most likely way in which they could meet and discuss philosophical issues of common interest, he thought, would be if Chanut were to return to Paris and travel through Holland en route. Descartes evidently changed his mind about this in 1649, and travelled to Stockholm on his final journey.

During these transitional years, 1645–46, there was also a change in Descartes' correspondence with Mersenne and Princess Elizabeth. Mersenne had deferred a planned journey to Italy in 1644, so that he could be in Paris when Descartes visited. Soon after Descartes' departure, however, Mersenne embarked on his travels. He was absent from Paris on two extended journeys, and there was no communication from Descartes again until the autumn of 1646.[11] In the case of Princess Elizabeth, she was forced to leave The Hague in August 1646, following an altercation in which her brother Philippe was accused of involvement in the death of a French citizen in The Hague. Descartes seems to have visited her for the last time, perhaps in August of that year, when she asked him to read and comment on Machiavelli's *Prince*.[12] Descartes continued, nonetheless, to correspond with Elizabeth in Germany, although he now had to address his letters to her younger sister, Sophie, for forwarding to Elizabeth.[13]

French Translations

In 1644 Descartes seems to have agreed to suggestions, rather than to have initiated the projects himself, to have French translations of his two major works published in Paris. The *Meditations* had been republished in 1642, in a corrected Latin text, with the addition of the Seventh Objections (from Father Bourdin) and Descartes' replies, together with the source of so much subsequent controversy, the infamous letter to Father Dinet. Likewise, the *Principles* had been published in Latin with a view to its potential use in colleges as a textbook of philosophy that might compete, for readers, with scholastic texts. Louis Charles d'Albert, duke of Luynes (1620–1690), had prepared a French translation of the six Meditations. Since this represented only about fifteen percent of the book that appeared in 1642, Claude Clerselier was responsible for most of the work involved, because it fell to him to translate all of the Objections and Replies.[14] Descartes reviewed the translation and took advantage of the opportunity to add clarifications to the text and to reduce the predominance of scholastic jargon that had been used in Latin.[15]

There still remained a question about what to do with Gassendi's original objections, or with the much more extensive response to Descartes' replies that Gassendi had published (in Latin) under the title *Metaphysical Disquisition*. Descartes had initially considered omitting Gassendi's Objections completely from the French version, especially since their author had complained about their inclusion in the Latin text. Thus he wrote to Huygens, long before the French translation had been completed, that 'when they print my *Meditations* in future, I shall unburden them of the fifth objections [Gassendi's], which are useless and which comprise almost a third of the book.'[16] In their place, he planned to substitute a short explanation of why Gassendi had been omitted. In January 1646 he sent Clerselier this explanatory note, which amounted to a brief reply to the *Metaphysical Disquisition*.[17] It was not based on his reading of Gassendi's large book – since, as usual, he had not read it – but on a selection of passages that his friends had brought to his attention as deserving a reply.[18] Descartes also added a 'Note from the Author', which alerted readers who might have seen the original Latin text and might have wondered about the missing objections and replies from Gassendi. Despite these explicit plans and consequent adjustments, when the French edition of the *Meditations* appeared in Paris it also included, as an appendix, a translation of the original objections and replies, possibly because Clerselier had devoted so much time to translating them that he did not wish to waste the results of his work. Besides, the practical arrangements for the publication in Paris were being taken care of locally by Clerselier, and the author probably had very little input into any final decisions about its contents. Descartes' only specific request was that copies be sent to his three nieces who were in religious life, two in Brittany and the third in Poitiers.[19] By November, it seems as if publication of the French edition of the *Meditations* was imminent, since Chanut was waiting to present a copy to Queen Christina.[20] This deadline was missed, however, because Clerselier was indisposed during November and December 1646, with an illness that began as gout and developed into epileptic fits.[21] This probably delayed publication, and the book finally appeared in Paris in February 1647.[22]

The translation of the *Principles* had been initiated by Picot in 1644, and by February of the following year Descartes was writing to thank him for sending his version of the third part of the text (there were four parts in total). Although he had not yet read the whole manuscript, he was able to assure his trusted translator that his version was 'as good as he could have hoped' and that he had 'understood the material perfectly'.[23] More than a year later, however, in April 1646, Descartes asked Mersenne to convey his apologies to Picot for causing a delay in the translation. Picot had apparently requested clarification of the laws of motion in Part II, and Descartes pleaded, somewhat implausibly, that he was unable to find 'a quarter of an hour, during the whole year since he [Picot] looked at that article, to clarify my laws of motion'.[24] However, the real cause of the delay seems to have been the malaise that he mentions in the next sentence – a malaise to which he referred on different occasions in 1646. 'I am so fed up

with the profession of writing books that it hurts me even to think about it'
(iv. 396). One must assume, however, that despite his own loss of interest,
work on the two French translations continued. He planned to reuse the
French privilege that had been granted for the *Essays* of 1637, because it
applied to 'all the books that he had written and that he would write'.[25]

Before these projects could be completed, however, Descartes had to
address the painful reality that his most devoted and most public philosophical supporter, who had risked his career at Utrecht University to
publicize Cartesian ideas, was about to publish a book in which he disagreed publicly with Descartes' metaphysics. In the language of Baillet –
which might have been more appropriate for a religious dispute, than for
a philosophical disagreement – Regius was about to become 'not so much
the first plagiarist of Mr. Descartes, as the first rebel among his disciples
or the first schismatic among his followers'.[26]

Regius: *Physical Foundations*

Regius had drafted a book under the title *Physical Foundations*, and he
sent Descartes an advance copy during the summer of 1645 to ask for his
advice. Descartes' first reaction, in July of that year, was simply to sound
a note of caution about the danger of confusing readers by combining
what Regius had borrowed from Descartes with what he was proposing
in his own name. The Utrecht professor initially accepted the legitimacy
of these concerns and offered to publish a Foreword to his book in which
he would acknowledge publicly that, on some questions, he differed with
Descartes.[27] Descartes repeated his concerns in a second letter the same
month, in which he made those original worries very explicit. During
the intervening days he had read more than the first few pages of the
manuscript, and he was particularly worried by the style – more suitable,
he thought, for disputations than for a book – in which the author's ideas
were presented in a paradoxical fashion and without the supporting arguments that might help to convince readers. However, when he reached the
section of the book devoted to human nature, his worst fears were realized.
He felt obliged to repeat the reservations that he had expressed in 1642,
at the beginning of the Utrecht crisis.

But when I reached the Chapter 'On Man', and when I saw what you have about
the human mind and about God in that section . . . I was completely astounded and

saddened. . . . Please forgive me if I say what I think as freely as if I were talking to a friend. . . . I must say publicly that, in metaphysical questions, I disagree with you as much as possible, and that I shall even testify to this publicly when one of my books is edited, if your book is ever published. I am indeed grateful to you for showing it to me before publication. However, I am not grateful that you have been teaching in private what is contained in this book without my knowledge. I now fully endorse the opinion of those who wanted you to confine yourself to medicine. Why do you have to confound metaphysical and theological matters in your writings, since you cannot mention them without falling into some error or other?   (iv. 249–50)

The real source of Descartes' worry was that, when writing about the human soul, Regius strayed a long way from what was acceptable to the Catholic Church. He had previously described the human soul as an 'accidental reality' in 1642. He was now making matters much worse in 1645 by talking about the human soul as merely a 'mode of the body', that is, as a quality or feature of a physical body rather than as a distinct spiritual reality in its own right, as it was understood by Christian theology. Regius was obviously free to publish that opinion in his own name, if he wished, but he should not include Descartes' name under any circumstances, as if the French philosopher were the source of such ideas or as if he agreed with them.

One of the underlying differences between Regius and Descartes that emerged at this juncture was about whether the Christian belief in the soul's immortality was based exclusively on the Scriptures, or whether human reason could provide arguments to support the same opinion. Descartes had accepted the challenge of the Lateran Council, in the dedicatory letter to the Sorbonne that prefaced the *Meditations*, to support the church's teaching about the soul with philosophical arguments. Regius now claimed that this was a mistake. He argued that religious faith teaches that the soul is immortal, but, as far as we know when we use reason alone, the human mind may be merely a 'mode of a body'.[28] This consideration suggested another line of argument, which was even more troubling for the defensive Descartes.

According to Regius, Descartes had presented the arguments in the *Meditations* as if they contained nothing that was not 'clear, certain, and evident' (iv. 255). The fact that many competent readers thought otherwise was enough to show that these arguments were 'obscure and uncertain', and the disputes triggered by the *Meditations* had served only to 'multiply the doubts and clouds of uncertainty'. Adopting the rhetorical strategy used in Martin Schoock's book, Regius suggested that there was no 'religious enthusiast, no impious person or buffoon, who could not make the same claim for their folly and madness'. All this suggested that Cartesian metaphysics was, in some sense, inconsistent with the general philosophical framework within which it was developed and that its author actually believed in private the opposite of what he published, as Schoock had suggested.

> You will not be surprised at my conduct when you realize that many honourable and intelligent people have often told me that they had too high an opinion of the quality of your mind to believe that you did not hold, in the depths of your soul, opinions that are the opposite of those that appear in public under your name. Without any dissimulation, many here [in Utrecht] are convinced that you have greatly discredited your philosophy by publishing your metaphysics.   (iv. 255)

Despite these extremely provocative comments, Regius agreed to make the changes in the text that Descartes requested, out of respect and 'love' for his former tutor. However, he also suggested that if Descartes were to implement his threat – of dissociating himself publicly from what Regius had written – it might cause more harm to Descartes' reputation than to that of Regius.

Descartes responded predictably to this allegation. While accepting that it was sometimes prudent not to reveal exactly what one thought about a controversial subject, he thought it was 'despicable and immoral' to publish the opposite of what one genuinely believed.[29] Although infuriated by the charge of intellectual dishonesty, he simply reminded Regius of the possible outcome of publishing the book, since he had sent it to him in advance to ask his opinion. 'I cannot fail to tell you openly that I do not think it is in any way in your interest to publish anything about philosophy, not even about the part that deals with physics. First of all, because you were forbidden by your Magistrate from teaching the new philosophy in private or in public . . .' (iv. 257). If Regius were to transgress the decision of the magistrates, he would provide a good reason for his enemies to apply various penalties and, possibly, to deprive him of his post as professor of medicine at Utrecht.

At this point (July 1645) the correspondence between Regius and Descartes comes to an abrupt end, or at least there is no trace of any further letters between the two former friends. Despite Descartes' advice and his threat to disown the book in public, Regius proceeded as planned and published his *Physical Foundations*. He included a dedication to Prince Frederik Hendrik dated 10 August 1646, on the second page of which he defended his right to depart from the philosophical path set out by his master.[30]

Unfortunately, *Physical Foundations* was as far from Cartesian metaphysics as Descartes had feared. However, it was also an accessible and compact introduction to a range of philosophical problems, and it was presented in a style that provided competition for Descartes' *Principles*. The final and longest chapter, Chapter 12, was devoted to human nature.[31] Here Regius suggested that it would be redundant to ask how the mind thinks; its nature is to think, just as the nature of matter is to be extended.[32] He argued that we know from Scripture that the human mind is a distinct substance that can exist apart from the human body, although this is not something that we can discover by using our reason.[33] By contrast, we definitely know from experience that our mind is very closely joined to the body 'in a single substance' and that its nature is such that it is affected by the body and, in the opposite direction, that the mind affects the body.[34] He also introduced a descriptive phrase here that would be the subject of further dispute with Descartes in 1648: that 'the human mind, although a substance that is really distinct from the body, is nevertheless *organic* as long as it exists in the body,' and that this so-called organic connection is confirmed by epilepsy, apoplexy, and other similar conditions in which the mind cannot avoid being affected by an injury to the brain.[35] Many of Regius' specific suggestions about mental functions were similar to those found in Descartes – for example, that the activity of remembering depends on vestiges of prior thoughts that remain in the brain, or that the will is a form of thought by which the mind accepts or rejects something that it has understood.[36]

Regius also addressed the fundamental question that had been raised by Princess Elizabeth in 1643 as a criticism of Descartes' *Meditations*: how can a mind (which is apparently purely spiritual) move the human body simply by deciding to move it, if 'deciding' is understood as a form of thinking? Regius adopted a solution that was very similar to what was implicit in Descartes' earlier work and that became explicit only later, in the *Passions of the Soul*.[37] The 'solution' involved two steps, the first of which was that there is a 'natural' coincidence between the occurrence of certain thoughts in the mind and corresponding motions in the body. According to Regius, 'we are equipped in this way by nature.'[38] The second step was to exploit the 'natural' coincidence of some thoughts and brain states in order to direct animal spirits in the patterns required for appropriate bodily motions.

The mind, although it does not have the power of moving a body from one place to another, has nevertheless in itself the power to direct spirits that are in motion into one place or another in the same way as it has in itself the power of understanding or willing. Nor is it necessary to attribute to the mind a power of moving bodies, when the motion of animal spirits is sufficient to cause motion in different parts of the body.[39]

Regius completed his physicalist account of the human mind by openly denying one of the most characteristic theses of Cartesian philosophy, that the mind has innate ideas.

It seems as if the mind does not need any innate ideas, images, notions or axioms in order to think. Instead, the innate faculty of thinking alone is enough for it to perform all acts of thinking. This is evident in the case of sorrow, colour, taste, and the perceptions of all similar ideas, which are genuinely perceived by the human mind even though none of these ideas is innate in the mind. Nor is there any reason why some ideas, rather than others, should be innate by nature.[40]

As is implicit in this quotation, Regius suggested that what other people call 'innate ideas . . . arise from the observation of things'.

It may have been painful for Descartes to lose the support of someone like Regius, on whose behalf he had become embroiled in the Utrecht crisis. However, the source of this new dispute was not simply a stubbornness on the part of Regius or an inability to follow subtle metaphysical arguments. This personal parting between former friends was primarily a symptom of a real tension within Descartes' own philosophy, which was merely made explicit when Regius borrowed some of the implications of the *Treatise on Man*. Descartes complained to various correspondents in October and November 1646 that Regius had borrowed material about the action of muscles from an unpublished Cartesian work, and that he had understood it poorly. His letter to Mersenne (23 November 1646) was typical in this respect.

It is twelve or thirteen years [i.e., 1633/4] since I described all the functions of the human body, or of an animal, but the paper on which I wrote is so confused that I would have difficulty myself in reading it. However, that did not stop me, four or five years ago, from lending it to one of my closest friends, who made a copy which, in turn, was transcribed with my permission by two others but without me checking or correcting them. I asked them not to show the copies to anyone, and I never wished that

Regius would see it because I knew what he was like. Besides, since I was considering publishing my views about that matter, I did not want anyone else to deprive them of their novelty.   (iv. 566–7)

This was Descartes' perspective when it was already too late to retrieve the situation, when he was accusing Regius of borrowing his ideas and misunderstanding them. However, there was another equally plausible interpretation available.

Regius may have put his finger on a genuine problem in Descartes' work when he pointed to the apparent anomaly of his metaphysics. It was not that Cartesian metaphysics was inconsistent with the natural philosophy that it was designed to support. It was almost as if the two parts of his work represented the writings of two different people. Everything that Descartes had written, both published and unpublished, about the role of the brain in perception, memory, and imagination suggested that a theory of the human mind would be an explanation that relied on detailed work in physiology and neurology. On the other hand, the discussion of mental events in the *Meditations* constituted a first-person description of how thinking appears to the individual subject, and it failed completely to persuade any of those who wrote objections that it is impossible for this mental activity to be a complex activity of the central nervous system. There was therefore a genuine sense in which Regius was not disagreeing with Descartes but articulating a view that resulted from Descartes' own work, one that he found impossible to integrate into the metaphysical foundation offered in the *Meditations* and the *Principles* (Part I).

Intimations of Mortality

In contrast with the confident expectations of a long, healthy life and with the combative confrontations with almost all his correspondents that characterized the early 1640s, Descartes acknowledged a growing awareness of advancing years and a willingness to resile from controversy in 1645–46. Even his lifelong penchant for travelling seems to have abated, as he settled into the comparative isolation of Egmond-Binnen and complained about the effects of the long, cold winters. To modern eyes, he seems to have suffered from depression.

There were intimations of mortality as early as February 1645, when he thanked Huygens for the poem in honour of the *Principles*. He refrained from answering in verse, he explained, because 'Socrates never wrote verse until he was close to his death' and 'it might be a bad omen' if he were to follow his example.[41] The following winter was particularly cold, which caused him to defer until spring trips he wished to make earlier.[42] By June 1646, he admitted to Chanut that his *Principles* did not address directly the questions about morality that his diplomatic correspondent wished to raise. However, he assured him that the *Principles* provided foundations for a morality that were so secure that he could talk about the problems raised there with more confidence than he could about medicine, on which he had laboured much longer. 'Thus, instead of finding ways to conserve life, I have found another, much simpler and more certain, way which is not to fear death' (iv. 441–2). This new focus on how to live and how to prepare for death featured in another letter to an obviously receptive Chanut in November 1646, when Descartes quoted Seneca with approval: 'A painful death awaits him / Who, known too well to all, / Dies unknown to himself.'[43] This growing awareness of advancing age was matched by a confirmation of Descartes' unwillingness to read books by other authors, to respond to criticism, or, in general, to engage with the wider world in the way he had notoriously done throughout his writing career.

Baillet provides an insightful description of Descartes in northern Holland, although, as usual, he anticipates the obvious interpretation of the facts and makes sure to reject it. The agreed facts are as follows. Descartes slept late each day. 'He spent a lot of time in bed and he used to sleep a lot in every season and everywhere he lived. . . . He often used to remain ten or sometimes twelve hours in bed.'[44] His lengthy sleeps were complemented by a 'taciturn' wakefulness, which Baillet attributes to his dedication to meditation.[45] In his correspondence with others, Descartes was reported as 'always slow to write. . . . his customary neglect caused him always to defer writing until the messenger was about to depart.'[46] Consistent with his own reports, Descartes read very few books, and thus, after his death, 'the few books found during the inventory' confirmed the nonreading habits of his later years.[47] These would seem to an impartial observer today to be signs of clinical depression. However, lest anyone draw this conclusion, Baillet tried to assure readers that 'one could not even say that melancholy had any influence on his extraordinary resolution' to hide in the solitary conditions of Egmond-Binnen.[48] When read carefully, of course, Baillet was denying only that Descartes was depressed before he arrived in Egmond, and that his state of mind prior to going there explained his decision to live in isolation. However, even when read in that way, Baillet's defence is weak. Besides, Descartes' own letters during this period suggest that his state of mind did change soon after his arrival.

There was no significant change in Descartes' reluctance to read other people's books, since he had always been that way. He told Mersenne in April 1646 that he had read only 'the first four pages' of Roberval's book and that it would have been extremely tedious for him to write more about it and for Mersenne to have to read what he wrote.[49] Evidently, Roberval was a special case, because he was described so often by Descartes as having nothing worth reading. But during this period Descartes also repeated, frequently, that he had lost interest for a long time in doing mathematics. In general, he wished neither to read what others sent him, nor to write anything in reply. Nor did he plan to write anything else himself, apart from the letters that he drafted just in time for departing messengers. He must have mentioned this decision to write no more to Chanut, during their discussions in Amsterdam in October 1645, because Chanut complimented him on his apparent change of mind, in August of the following year, when he heard that Descartes had written something about the passions. 'I was delighted to see in your letter a change in the chagrin that you told me about in Amsterdam.'[50] Unfortunately, this reversal to his former active lifestyle was short lived, for he wrote to Mersenne, in October 1646:

Finally I declare that, from now on, I do not wish to read any writings apart from letters from my friends, in which they give me news about themselves. . . . likewise, I shall never write anything again apart from letters to my friends, the subject of which will be 'If you are well, that is good.' I shall not get involved in any science, except to instruct myself. I ask you to persuade all those who boast about having something to object to my writings that, rather than send them to me, they should publish them. Let them publish books against me as much as they wish; unless I find that the more intelligent specimens are very good, I shall not even read them.[51]

By November of 1646, in the same context in which he had quoted Seneca to Chanut, he told him that 'the best thing that I can do from now on is to abstain from writing books' (iv. 537). He still wished to pursue his studies but only for his own instruction, and he offered to communicate his thoughts privately to his trusted friends as he had earlier promised to Mersenne.

Finally, Descartes gives the appearance of calling a truce in the long-running row with Voetius. 'With regard to Voetius, he is someone that I never think about any more.'[52] The members of his own church could call Voetius the 'ornament and glory of the Dutch Church' (iv. 437) if they wished, but nothing would entice Descartes into any further comments about him. However, this almost reluctant concession to peace did not prevent Descartes from entering the fray, once again, when he heard about criticisms of his philosophy at Leiden in 1647. Descartes was evidently in a psychological state in which he wanted to cease hostilities, but he could not resist the temptation to engage his 'enemies' on a new front. What he wanted to do shows his state of mind; what he actually did follows the patterns of a life engaged almost continuously in controversy.

Egmond-Binnen

Despite the apparent depression that hindered his normal output of work, Descartes continued to grow plants in his garden, and to perform the anatomical investigations that were required to complete work on what he referred to as a treatise on man and/or a treatise on animals.[53] Although he wished for nothing other than 'security and tranquility', he became involved in local affairs when Meeus Jacobs stabbed to death his stepfather, Jacob Clopper, in the course of a row at an inn in Egmond-Binnen in August 1645. The results of the trial were appealed by the prosecutor, and the convicted Jacobs fled the jurisdiction rather than risk appearing and being given a harsher sentence. In his absence, he was sentenced to being banished forever from Holland, Utrecht, and Zeeland, and to having all his goods seized. Descartes seems to have been persuaded that Jacobs was being harshly treated and, in particular, that the effect of the sentence would be to harm his wife and children. In those circumstances, he wrote a lengthy plea to Huygens, requesting that he intervene with the *Stadtholder* on behalf of his unfortunate neighbour.

I appreciate that you have so many more important things to do than to interrupt your work to read the greetings of a man who associates here only with peasants, that I would not dare interfere by writing to you unless I had a reason to trouble you. The reason I write is to give you an opportunity to exercise your charity towards a poor peasant, who is a neighbour of mine, and who had the misfortune to kill someone else. His relatives would wish to have recourse to the clemency of His Highness [Prince Frederik Hendrik], to try to obtain his favour, and they also wish me to write to you about it to ask you to put in a good word on their behalf if you have an opportunity of doing so.[54]

Descartes pleaded that the dead man had been battering his wife, that she had separated from him, and that Jacobs had intervened in a brawl between his stepfather and his brother-in-law. Jacobs was described as having led a blameless life before this incident, and that provoked Descartes to inquire into the causes of his uncharacteristic behaviour, since (he wrote to Huygens), 'as you know, I usually philosophize about everything that I notice, (v. 263). This provided an opportunity to speculate about the affects of the passions on otherwise blameless people, especially the commendable passion to protect one's own family, and to indicate the benefits of moderating justice with clemency. He concludes: 'If you do anything to allow this poor man to return to his children, I can say that you will perform a good action and that will be another reason for my being in debt to you' (v. 265).

Descartes did not realize that the *Stadtholder* was very sick and that he could hardly have been interested in the sentence passed on a peasant from Egmond-Binnen.[55] Huygens acknowledged Descartes' intervention in February 1646, and that provided an added incentive for the French philosopher to write a second time on behalf of the Jacobs family.[56] The details of the subsequent process are unclear, but the court of appeal issued a more lenient judgment in January 1647.

In the meantime, Descartes was contending with the harsh weather conditions and the slow pace of his work. There were many obstacles to completing the two sections that had been omitted from the *Principles*. Although the word '*expérience*' in French was used for both experiments and observations, there was a big difference between observations that could be done without any preparatory work and experimental tests that required both equipment and skilled assistants. Descartes explained the distinction to Chanut, by comparing his unplanned observation (in February 1635) of hexagonal snowflakes that simply fell from the sky, and the sophisticated experimental observations that were now required to complete his physics. 'If all the experiences that I need for the rest of my physics could fall from the clouds in that way, and if I needed only my eyes to know them, I would hope to finish it [my physics] shortly. But since one also needs hands to do them and since I do not have any hands that are appropriate to the task, I am losing completely the desire to do any further work on it.'[57]

These frustratingly incomplete projects were interrupted by a request from Charles Cavendish about pendulums with asymmetrical bobs. Mersenne had also sent him a similar query, and the two invitations provoked Descartes to return to the dispute he had had with Roberval nine years earlier, following publication of the *Geometry*.[58] One of the crucial features of that correspondence, apart from his obvious disdain for Roberval, was Descartes' recognition that his mathematical calculations had to coincide with experimental observations and that any solution to the queries that he received relied essentially on observations. 'My reasoning does not agree with the observations that you were kind enough to send me, and I acknowledge honestly that I cannot yet see why not.'[59]

The renewed controversy with Roberval was mediated, as before, by Mersenne, who forwarded Roberval's criticisms and Descartes' replies. Descartes had the impression that, when they met in Paris in 1644, Roberval had offered to explain why he thought Descartes had not fully solved the Pappus problem. This was evidently something to which he did not wish to return two years later. Out of politeness, however, he offered to review Roberval's *Aristarchus* and to explain his principal reservations about it if Roberval, for his part, would promise to write his residual doubts about the *Geometry*.[60] The subsequent discussion of Roberval's mathematics was confused by the fact that they were discussing two distinct problems – the oscillations of asymmetrical pendulums, and the relative merits of Descartes' *Geometry* and Roberval's *Aristarchus* – and by a background disagreement about the significance of experiments intended to resolve the former issue.

Descartes consistently claimed that the anomalies observed in the oscillations of different pendulums was due entirely to variations in the obstruction caused by the air, and that this factor was so complicated that it could be known only from experiments.

That is why I shall say nothing more here about it except that the great difference between (a) the oscillations of very obtuse triangles or those that are suspended by their bases and (b) the calculation that I did for all triangles in general, results only from the cause that I have called the obstruction of the air which . . . is much greater in the case of obtuse triangles than in others. Now I believe that one can quantify this obstruction only by experience. . . . All I claim to do is to try to make sense of what someone else has experienced; but I think the most appropriate way to examine experiences is to choose those that depend on fewer distinct causes and of which one can more easily discover the true cause.[61]

This caveat appears almost as a refrain in later letters on the same topic. 'I have said that the quantity of this obstruction can be determined only by experience.'[62] 'I distinguish between what moves a body and what impedes it, and between what can be determined by reasoning and what can be determined only by experience.'[63]

The enforced revisiting of Roberval's *Aristarchus* provided Descartes with another opportunity to articulate more clearly than on many other similar occasions his understanding of what counts as an explanation of a physical phenomenon and, by implication, what does not count as such. He wrote to Mersenne, in April 1646:

Whenever we assume something in order to explain something else, the assumed reality must always be more probable, more evident, and simpler, or it should be better known in some way. Otherwise, it could not enlighten us about the thing to be explained. However, if one were to assume, for each of the things that one wishes to explain, not only the same number of equally unknown things but many more less credible things, and if moreover what one wished to explain by such assumptions did not follow from them, one should surely not claim to have achieved anything worth while.   (iv. 398)

Descartes illustrates this kind of mistake by describing as 'very absurd' the assumption that 'there is some property in every part of the earth's matter in virtue of which they are drawn to each other and attract each other', and that there is another property in every part of the same matter with respect to other particles that does not impede the first property. This provoked the usual Cartesian objection: that it was equivalent to thinking of each part of matter as having a soul, and even a number of souls, by which each part could know what was happening in distant places and exercise its powers there.

Roberval's interventions, either about the Pappus problem or about the calculation of pendulum oscillations, were dismissed by Descartes as worthless. It seems clear, despite their friendly meeting in Paris two years before, that Descartes' opinion of the professor of mathematics at the Collège de France had not changed since 1638. To Mersenne he wrote: 'I shall tell you, between ourselves, that I have so many proofs of the mediocrity of the knowledge and intelligence of its author [Roberval], that I am amazed at the reputation he has acquired in Paris.'[64] As one might expect, Roberval dismissed Descartes' explicit appeal to observational evidence and claimed that 'reason and experience support my side. If Mr. Descartes does not wish to accede to either one, I leave it to others to decide what to expect from him.'[65] This dispute was predictably doomed to irresolution. Descartes suggested to Cavendish that he ask Roberval for the correct analysis of the problem; he himself could not contribute further, and eventually Cavendish could take his pick between Descartes' analysis and that of Roberval.[66] In fact, Descartes was so reluctant to think

about mathematical problems, which were about the furthest thing from
his mind, that he hoped to turn Roberval's critique to his own advantage.
If Roberval prevailed, his success might at least have the beneficial effect
of persuading everyone that Descartes had completely forgotten how to
do mathematics.[67]

Although Descartes made no progress with Roberval, he completed a
first draft of what was eventually published as the *Treatise on the Passions
of the Soul*. He had visited The Hague on 7 March 1646 and had left
for Princess Elizabeth a first draft of this book.[68] He exaggerated the
modesty of his efforts with the excuse that he had never studied the subject
previously.[69] However, the underlying theory on which his account of
human emotions depended was the still-incomplete *Treatise on Man*. This
had been drafted as part of the more comprehensive project called *The
World*, which Descartes had withdrawn in 1633. He probably made some
amendments to this draft as he did further work in anatomy during the
intervening years. Sometime in 1642, he allowed copies of the *Treatise on
Man* to be made, probably by Van Surck and by Pollot.[70] He had shown
a copy of this draft to Princess Elizabeth, sometime before October 1645,
which provided an outline theory of how thoughts are associated with
brain states.[71] He was thus able to borrow from that work to express one
of the fundamental insights of his account of mind-body interaction, the
novelty of which he was attempting to protect from any prior unauthorized
publication by Regius.

There is such a close liaison between our soul and our body that the thoughts that
have accompanied certain movements of our body from the beginning of our lives still
accompany them today. Therefore, if the same movements are triggered afresh in the
body by some external cause, they also stimulate the same thoughts in the soul and,
reciprocally, if we have the same thoughts, they produce the same bodily movements.
Finally, the machine of our body is constructed in such a way that a single thought
of joy, or love, or some other similar thought, is sufficient to send the animal spirits
through the nerves into all the muscles that are needed to cause the movements of
blood which, I claimed, accompany the passions. . . . One can move the hand or the
foot almost at the instant that one thinks of moving them because the idea of this
movement, which is formed in the brain [*cerveau*], sends the spirits to the muscles that
are appropriate for this movement.[72]

This is a long way from the speculations about 'pure thought' that distracted and misguided readers of the *Meditations*. Descartes relies on a

very primitive understanding of nerves as long thin tubes through which a subtle material, called spirits, moves very quickly. The way in which it moves is determined by brain states, and the results of its movement are the great variety of bodily motions that are controlled by the muscles. The key to the complex puzzle is a primitive link between certain fundamental thoughts and the corresponding motions of animal spirits, a link that was established by nature soon after our birth. This allows Descartes to write as he does here without compromising his theory of mind, that such thoughts are formed in the brain rather than in the mind. Once in place, he has the elements of a solution to the problem of mind-body interaction that had been raised by Princess Elizabeth in 1643.

The Rift with Regius

Since Descartes had told Regius what he thought about the draft version of his *Physical Foundations* and Regius had published it despite those strong reservations, it was merely a matter of time before Descartes publicly dissociated himself from the book and its author. While waiting for this opportunity, when the French edition of the *Principles* appeared, Descartes told as many correspondents as possible about his assessment of Regius and about the way in which, he claimed, their friendship had been exploited. The frequency with which he mentions this issue gives some indication of how deeply it affected his trust and, perhaps, his confidence in finding anyone in the United Provinces on whom he could he rely to support his philosophical ideas without compromising their integrity.

He gave Mersenne a rather disingenuous account of earlier discussions with Regius when he wrote to him in September 1646. Mersenne had heard indirectly, from an unreliable source, that someone called Jonsson (who had been a chaplain to Princess Elizabeth's mother) was about to publish a book based on Cartesian principles. Descartes was quick to correct him.

It is Regius, the professor at Utrecht, on whose behalf I had such quarrels with Voetius, who now has such a book in press, as far as I know. It should be published soon, although I do not know what it will include and I tried my best to persuade him not to publish it. I did this, not for my own sake, but for his, because I understand that his metaphysics is unorthodox and there are many enemies in that city who would be very happy to find a pretext for harming him.[73]

Evidently it remained possible, until he saw the published book, that
Regius might have introduced amendments as a result of his earlier discussions with Descartes. However, even prior to seeing the book in print,
Descartes' report to Mersenne was less than honest. He should have told
him that Regius had visited him, that he had given him an advance copy
of the book, and that one of his main reasons for objecting to its contents
was that it was likely to misrepresent Descartes' own views.

Descartes returns to the same theme a month later in another letter to
Mersenne, when he explains at greater length his objections to the book
by Regius. On this occasion, his own interest is much more prominent.

I recently saw a book that will make me more cautious in future about communicating
my thoughts than I have been up to now. It is a book by a professor at Utrecht, Regius,
entitled *Physical Foundations*. While repeating most of the things that I put in my
Principles, my *Dioptrics*, and my *Meteors*, he piles into it everything that he was ever
able to get from me in private and even everything that he was able to learn through
indirect means that I did not want him to know about. Besides, he recounts the whole
lot in such a confused manner and provides so few reasons that his book can serve
only to make these views appear ridiculous and to leave me open to criticism in two
ways. Those who know that he has hitherto professed such friendship with me, and
that he has followed blindly all my views, will wish to hold me responsible for all his
mistakes. Secondly, in respect of the things that I have not yet published, if I ever
wish to publish them people will notice that they resemble what he has written and
will say that I borrowed them from him. But the worst of all is that, although he has
followed what he believed were my views in physics . . . he has done the exact opposite
in metaphysics, and in four or five places where he writes about metaphysics he takes
completely contrary positions to what I wrote in the *Meditations*.[74]

The real source of Descartes' concerns is clear in this more honest letter.
He was worried that he would suffer collateral damage if readers attributed
the same views to him as they did to Regius. He was also anxious to protect
the novelty of his own theories and not to allow Regius to publish them
prematurely; and he was especially concerned by the unorthodoxy of the
metaphysical views about the human soul that Regius had published in
his new book. He wanted to make it clear that Regius was no longer his
friend, and he suggested to Mersenne that, if he had not already bought
a copy, he could save himself the cost of the book, which would otherwise
be wasted.[75]

The damage limitation exercise continued for a number of months.
Descartes wrote to the Jesuit, Father Charlet, in December that he would
have preferred it if 'one of his friends' had expressed his criticism of school

philosophy more diplomatically. Because he had failed to do so, Descartes
now felt that he should distance himself from his friend in the Preface to a
book that was about to appear. Implausibly, he told Charlet that, if he had
followed his own inclinations, he would never have published anything.[76]
He likewise warned Princess Elizabeth about 'the book by Regius that has
eventually been published', and he used it to illustrate a general point, that
if ideas are used by people who do not understand them properly they are
converted from truths to errors.[77]

The letter to Father Charlet provides another insight into the reasons
why Descartes was so unhappy with Regius' book. His efforts to win
the favour of the Jesuits in 1644, immediately after publication of the
Principles, seem to have had no success. Descartes heard from Mersenne
that two Jesuits had published philosophy books, Father Etienne Noël
(rector of the Jesuit college in Paris) and Father Honoré Fabri, and he was
anxious to see both books and, if necessary, to reply to them.[78] Noël's book
mentioned Descartes by name, although he had not yet received the copy
that Mersenne had sent, whereas Fabri had published a compendium of
philosophy that was apparently more widely received among the Jesuits
than the *Principles*. Descartes was very anxious, therefore, 'to discover
the terms in which members of the Society speak about my writings'
(iv. 498). There were also signs here of his earlier paranoia, that all the
Jesuits collectively supported the views of one of their members. Given the
time he had wasted in disputes with Roberval, he reflected that 'I would
prefer to spend my time examining Father Fabri's book and defending
myself against the whole Society [of Jesus] than against Roberval on his
own' (iv. 499).

In fact, Father Noël wrote to Descartes on 28 September 1646, and
sent him copies of his two new books.[79] Descartes had already received
a copy of one of them, *The Sun as a Flame*, three weeks earlier when he
had visited Huygens in The Hague, and he was gratified to find that Noël
was at least willing to discuss novel views that differed from traditional
scholastic theories.[80] The copies sent by Noël must not have arrived with
his letter, and he therefore had not yet had an opportunity to read the
other book, *Physical Aphorisms*, which was evidently a compendium of
scholastic physics. Descartes had read enough of Noël's book to see that
his own work had been cited on page five, and that 'the Fathers of your
Society are not so attached to ancient views that they do not also dare to
propose novel opinions' (iv. 584). Having mentioned Father Charlet and

Mesland, and having recognized that the former was then the provincial superior of the Jesuits in France, Descartes expressed his confidence that none of the Jesuits, 'especially those in France', would abuse their position by misrepresenting him to others.[81] Once again, Descartes was happy with the apparent implications of these obsequious letters in which he implored the Jesuits for their support and favour. He reported in December to Princess Elizabeth – hardly someone who shared his esteem for the Jesuits – that he had 'even received compliments from the Jesuit Fathers, whom I have always believed would be most interested in the publication of a new philosophy and who would pardon me least if they thought they had reason to find something wrong with it'.[82] Descartes was evidently still hoping that his *Principles* would be adopted as a more satisfactory philosophy of nature by the Jesuits, and that they would find a way to reconcile it with their scholastic tradition. For this reason, if for no other, it was most important that the new French edition dissociate itself from the unorthodoxy of Regius. This is exactly what Descartes did in a letter addressed to the translator of the French version, Claude Picot, which could function as a Preface to the *Principles*.

In this Preface, Descartes was conscious of the diplomacy required to win the support of his intended readership. Thus, while he claimed that the schools had blindly followed Aristotle and, as a result, had failed to discover true principles, he was equally keen to point out his respect for the ancients. 'Although I respect all those thinkers and do not wish to make enemies by finding fault with them, I can provide a proof of what I say which I think none of them would reject.... nonetheless, I do not wish to diminish the reputation that each of them can claim' (ix-2. 7–8). With these concessions to tradition in place, Descartes set out his famous metaphor about philosophy being like a tree. 'Thus the whole of philosophy is like a tree, the roots of which are metaphysics, its trunk is physics, and the branches that emerge from this trunk are all the other sciences, namely, medicine, mechanics, and morality' (ix-2. 14). Descartes had to admit that, if he were to provide a complete philosophy, he would have to include sections on 'plants, animals and especially man' (ix-2. 17). However, reflecting the same reservations that he had expressed to a number of correspondents, he thought he was not so old or so frail that it would be impossible to complete the project. However, to do so would have required 'all the experiences that I would need to support and justify my theories' (ix-2. 17). These in turn would involve great expense, and he had little hope of receiving the financial support necessary to complete the project. With such an apology, he could hope only to offer humanity the incomplete results of his labours on their behalf.

The public repudiation of Regius came in the penultimate paragraph of the new Preface. Descartes acknowledged that he had written previously that his high esteem for the intelligence of Regius was such that he could accept any of Regius' views as his own.[83] That situation had now changed completely.

Last year he published a book entitled *Physical Foundations* in which, although he seemed not to include anything concerning physics and medicine that he had not got from my writings – those that I published, and another one concerning the nature of animals that was still incomplete and which fell into his hands – nevertheless, because he transcribed the material inaccurately and changed its order, and denied certain metaphysical truths by which the whole of physics should be supported, I am forced to disavow the book completely. I must ask readers never to attribute any view to me unless they find it explicitly in my writings; nor should they accept any of them as true – either in my writings or in those of others – unless they see very clearly that they are derived from true principles. (ix-2. 19–20)

The French edition of the *Principles* was to be published by Pierre Des-Hayes in Paris, in spring 1647. Descartes wrote the prefatory letter to Picot while visiting him in Paris, with the title: 'Letter by the Author to the translator of the book'.[84] By May 1647, it had been published as: *The Principles of Philosophy, Written in Latin by René Descartes, and Translated into French by one of his Friends*, and a copy had been sent to Princess Elizabeth.[85] The die was now cast for the final public disagreement between Descartes and his former protégé, when Regius published a list of theses in the form of a short booklet or manifesto.

An Explanation of the Human Mind

Regius planned to respond to Descartes' criticisms by adding corollaries to a medical disputation scheduled for 2 October 1647.[86] When the university senate suppressed these extra theses, on the advice of the rector, Regius and his respondent, Petrus Wassenaer, decided to publish their controversial comments on Cartesian metaphysics as a manifesto, under the title *An Explanation of the Human Mind*. This provided a list of contentious claims about human nature that differed significantly from the Cartesian account, some of which had already appeared in the *Physical Foundations*.

At about the same time, Voetius published the first of four volumes of the-ological disputations, in which many of the disputed questions involved in the earlier row with Descartes and Regius were reopened.[87] Descartes replied to the Regius/Wassenaer pamphlet with his *Comments on a Certain Manifesto*, which seems to have been written toward the end of December 1647 and was published in January 1648.[88] One of the principal objec-tives of the *Comments* was to state publicly that Regius did not speak for Descartes, and to dissociate their author from any collateral dam-age that might result from the apparent unorthodoxy of Regius' views. 'The other pamphlet . . . contained views which I think are pernicious and false . . . [and] includes the name of someone, as author, who is believed by many people to teach views which are the same as mine. Therefore, I am forced to expose its errors so that they will not be attributed to me' (viii-2. 342). They also included some references to an independent dis-pute with theologians in Leiden (which is discussed in the next chapter) and a clarification of the relationship between faith and reason.

The *Comments* add little to what had already been rejected by Descartes on previous occasions. They included a slightly clearer-than-usual expla-nation of why he defended innate ideas and what he meant by the term, so that he could claim with some justification that he disagreed with his critic only verbally.

When he says that 'the mind does not need innate ideas or notions or axioms' while conceding to it a faculty of thinking (apparently, natural or innate), he clearly affirms the same reality as I do although he denies it verbally. I never wrote or claimed that the mind needs innate ideas that are anything other than its faculty of thinking. How-ever, when I noticed that I had certain thoughts, which did not come from external objects or from the determination of my own will, but which resulted exclusively from my faculty of thinking, I called them 'innate' in order to distinguish the ideas or notions, which are the forms of those thoughts, from others that were acquired or constructed.   (viii-2. 357–8)

Descartes repeats the regret expressed in the Preface to the *Principles* (in French), about having praised Regius in the past and having appeared to endorse what he wrote as if it were a genuine reflection of his own position (viii-2. 364). He is now forced by his regrettable experience to admit that Regius is motivated, not by a love of truth, but by a love of novelty.

Once it emerged into the public domain, this dispute followed the usual pattern of replies to replies until one side or the other lost interest or died. Regius responded to the Cartesian *Comments* with another booklet that set out his metaphysical views about human nature, under the title: *A Brief Explanation of the Human Mind or the Rational Soul, in which is explained what it is and what it may be*. The subtitle indicated that it had been 'formerly proposed for public examination and was now significantly clarified by the work of Henricus Regius of Utrecht and claimed by the notes of the very noble Descartes'. The book carried a dedication to the 'Very Noble René Descartes', which must have aggravated the situation still further.

This pamphlet included the same theses about the human mind that had already alienated Descartes in 1642 and 1646. They were numbered for easy reference, on this occasion, and the starkness with which they were expressed, with a minimal commentary, confirmed the danger of misinterpretation that had concerned Descartes in their earlier manifestations. For example, the second thesis reads: 'As far as the nature of things is concerned, it seems possible for the soul to be either a substance or the mode of a corporeal substance.'[89] Regius concludes, with an obvious though implicit reference to Descartes: 'therefore those who claim that we can clearly and distinctly conceive of the human mind as necessarily and really distinct from the body are mistaken.'[90] Besides, 'the fact that we can doubt the body even though we cannot truly doubt the mind does not prevent the mind from being a mode of the body.'[91] As in his earlier, more complete version of this argument, Regius adds for good measure that 'in order to think, the mind does not need any innate ideas, notions, or axioms that are distinct from the faculty of thinking,' and that 'the idea of God, which exists in our mind, is not a sufficiently valid argument to prove the existence of God.'[92] It was a calculated irony on his part to dedicate this tract to Descartes and to acknowledge with an ambiguous term, on the title page, that it was either claimed by Descartes as his own or repudiated by him as the exact opposite of some of his main theses in metaphysics.

Descartes made one final contribution to this intractable dispute, when he summarized the history of the row with Voetius in *The Apologetic Letter to the Magistrates of Utrecht* in February 1648 (discussed in Chapter 12).

Thought in Animals

Descartes' anatomical investigations continued during 1646, despite his frustrating failure to complete the outstanding research required for the missing sections of the *Principles*. He describes experiments that involved immobilizing chickens, and observations of the development of chickens in eggs.[93] He even arranged for the slaughter of a pregnant cow so that he could examine the foetus at an early stage of its development. When he noticed that Dutch butchers often slaughtered pregnant cows, he took advantage of their carelessness to further his investigations: 'I arranged for them to bring me more than a dozen wombs in which there were small calves, some as big as mice, others as big as rats, and others again like small dogs, in which I could observe many more things than was possible in the case of chickens because their organs are larger and more visible' (iv. 555).

This on-going work in anatomy coincided with the Marquis of Newcastle's interest in the apparent capacity of animals to think. Unfortunately, when Cavendish wrote to Descartes to ask his opinion about the matter, his letter took ten months to arrive in Egmond-Binnen.[94] Despite the delay, Descartes took the question seriously and, in the process, wrote one of his clearest comments yet on whether animals are capable of thinking.

This question developed naturally from the theories that Descartes had been exploring in the *Treatise on Man* in the 1630s. He had argued then that many features of human perception, imagination, memory, and intentional action are explained by reference to the flow of animal spirits in the nerves. He assumed, of course, that many nonhuman animals have similar brains and that the complex ways in which they react to their environments must be explained in the same way. Thus when he offered readers a summary of the contents of that (unpublished) *Treatise* in the *Discourse on Method*, he took advantage of the opportunity to make as clear a distinction as possible between human beings and other animals. The significance of the question at issue could hardly be exaggerated. The theology of the Christian churches depended on the assumption of a life after death, in which sin is punished and a virtuous life is rewarded. For many Christians, those beliefs presuppose that each person has an immortal soul. By contrast, the behaviour of animals – no matter how sophisticated it may be – can be explained without attributing an immortal soul to them. Newcastle's question thus reopened the metaphysical questions that had been addressed in the *Meditations*, where Descartes had tried to establish 'the distinction between the human soul and the body'.[95]

Descartes' account of human nature, in the *Discourse*, was not much different from what he wrote seven years later in the *Principles*. He had to concede in the *Discourse* that, when he discussed human nature, he 'did

not have enough knowledge . . . to speak in the same way as about the rest'
(vi. 45). However, the lack of specific knowledge did not prevent Descartes
from speculating, in great detail, about how the human brain works both
in receiving information from outside and in causing the body to react
appropriately in response to its perceptions.

> Then I had shown . . . what the structure of the nerves and muscles of the human
> body would have to be in order for the animal spirits in the body to have the power
> to move its members . . . what changes must be made in the brain to cause waking,
> sleep, and dreams; how light, sounds, odours, tastes, warmth and all the other qualities
> of external objects can impress different ideas [idées] on it through the senses; how
> hunger, thirst, and the other internal passions can also send their ideas there; what
> part of the brain should be taken as the 'common sense' where these ideas are received;
> what should be taken as the memory, which stores the ideas, and as the imagination,
> which can vary them in different ways and compose new ones and, by the same means,
> distribute the animal spirits to the muscles and cause the limbs of the body to move in
> as many different ways as our own bodies can move without the will directing them,
> depending on the objects that are present to the senses and the internal passions of
> the body.   (vi. 55)

This would not surprise those who know anything about automata, he
thought. Without any explicit reference to the work of De Caus he
surmised: if human engineers can construct automata that move like animals or sing like birds, then surely a body made by God would be 'incomparably better structured' (vi. 56), and one could anticipate explaining all
the phenomena about human beings that were mentioned in the passage
just quoted by a sufficiently advanced anatomy and physiology.

    This is precisely the line of development that caught the attention of
Regius and, when pushed to its apparent conclusion, would suggest that
souls are redundant even in the case of human beings. The *Discourse* tried
to block that conclusion, however, by offering two arguments to show
that human beings are so different from other animals that they must
have a soul or mind. One argument relied on the distinctive character
of human language. One could easily imagine a machine that uttered
words or phrases in response to specific stimuli. However, according to
Descartes, a machine 'could not arrange words in different ways to reply
to the meaning of everything that is said in its presence, as even the most
unintelligent human beings can do' (vi. 56–7). The other reason was that,
although machines may perform specific tasks better than we do – such as
clocks telling the time – they always do so in a way that is determined in

advance by their design. By contrast, 'reason is a universal instrument' that allows us to respond appropriately to an almost unlimited range of situations. Descartes appeals at this juncture to the fact that machines need to be designed or programmed for each specific task that we want them to perform. His argument hinges on the assumption that it would be close to impossible for any machine to store in its memory all the responses that it would need in order to simulate human behaviour. 'It is morally impossible for a machine to have enough different dispositions to make it act in every human situation in the same way as our reason makes us act' (vi. 57).

This argument was not an attempt to decide whether animals are conscious, or to describe what the subjective experiences of animals may be like from the perspective of the animals. The argument focused exclusively on an *explanation* of the overt behaviour of animals, and on what must be postulated about their brains and sensory systems in order to explain their behaviour. Descartes could not deny that animals listen and respond to sounds, that they call out to each other, and, in many ways, that they seem to behave as human beings do. However, he distinguished between natural signs – such as the cry of pain of a wounded animal – and the conventional signs used by human beings. As long as this distinction holds, between the creativity of human language and the inflexible, 'natural' signs used by animals, Descartes concluded that animals 'have no intelligence at all and that it is nature that acts in them in accordance with the disposition of their organs' (vi. 59).

When asked by Newcastle to address this question again nine years after publishing the *Discourse*, Descartes identifies two of the most prominent protagonists of animal thought as Michel de Montaigne and Pierre Charron (1541–1603). He had been given a copy of Charron's *Three Books of Wisdom* in 1619, and, perhaps contrary to his usual practice, he had read some of it on his travels during the winter of 1619–20. In the case of Montaigne, it was impossible for any educated Frenchman not to have perused some pages of his voluminous *Essays*. Both authors had extolled the ingenuity and even the superiority of animals over man and had claimed that animals have their own languages that we fail to understand in the same way that they fail to understand us. It was not surprising that they were viewed in Paris as more or less discreet advocates of the libertine cause. Descartes' defensive response, therefore, was consistent with his apologetic objectives in the *Meditations* on behalf of the immateriality of the human mind.

Montaigne relied on this claim about animal languages to support an argument in favour of animal souls in the *Apology for Raymond Sebond*. 'From similar effects we should conclude that there are similar faculties. Consequently, we should admit that animals employ the same method and the same reasoning as ourselves when we do anything.'[96] In other words, if it is necessary to attribute a soul to human beings in order to explain their linguistic behaviour, we must attribute the same kind of mind or soul to animals who use language in a comparable manner.

Charron appealed to the same kind of argument. He conceded that we do not understand animal language. However, we do not understand most human languages either, but we could hardly deny that other nations use genuine languages simply because we fail to understand them. In the case of other human languages, the reality of mutual incomprehension is undeniable. The same thing is true of animals and human beings.

Just as we speak by gestures and by moving our eyes, our head, our hands, and our shoulders (by which those who are mute become wise), animals do the same, as we observe in those which have no voice but nonetheless engage in mutual exchanges; and just as animals understand us to some extent, we likewise understand them. . . . We speak to them, and they speak to us, and if we do not understand each other perfectly, who is responsible for that? They could easily judge, by the same reasoning by which we judge them, that we are animals. However, they also reproach us that humans do not understand each other. We do not understand the Basques, the Bretons . . . [97]

Descartes tells Newcastle, however, that he 'cannot share the opinion of Montaigne and others who attribute understanding or thought to animals'.[98] He returns to the argument he used in the *Discourse*, which relies on the distinctive character of human language.

He concedes that animals may excel us in many respects. Therefore, 'none of our external actions, apart from spoken words or other signs . . . could convince those who examine them that our body is anything more than a machine that moves itself, and that there is also within it a soul that has thoughts' (iv. 574). Descartes specifies the kind of 'spoken words or other signs' that characterize human language. They may be the kind of signs used by mute people, but they have to be relevant to the context in which they are used and cannot be like the talk of parrots when they utter the same limited sounds no matter what is said to them. Descartes assumes that the use of signs by animals is limited to occasions on which they express their 'passions', such as a need to eat or to avoid pain, and that any extension of this limited usage is achieved only by training them

to associate other situations with those in which they naturally express
their passions. 'There has never been any animal so perfect that it used
some sign to make known to other animals something that was not related
to their passions' (iv. 575). Descartes' conclusion is the same one he had
drawn in the *Discourse*, appropriately qualified to acknowledge that it is
no more certain than any hypothesis that one might construct to explain
other natural phenomena. 'This seems to me to be a very strong argument
to prove that the reason animals do not speak is that they have no thought,
rather than that they lack the appropriate organs' (iv. 575).

The success or otherwise of Descartes' argument about animals depends
on making a sharp distinction between thinking and not thinking, so that
human beings who think have an immortal soul, while animals fail on
both counts. Here, however, in response to Newcastle, he opens up the
possibility for the first time that there may be different degrees of thought
and that animals may enjoy some less perfect form of thinking. 'One can say
only the following: although animals perform no actions which convince
us that they think, nonetheless, since their bodily organs are not very
different from ours, one could hypothesize that there is some thought
associated with these organs, as we experience in our own case, even if
their thought is much less perfect' (iv. 576). Descartes seemed willing to
concede this possibility, with the qualification that 'if they thought like us
they would have an immortal soul just like us' (iv. 576).

This discussion – of what kind of thought must be attributed to animals
in order to explain their behaviour – was obviously inconclusive. It seemed
to some critics that Descartes was not only denying that animals think like
human beings, but was also contending that they lack sensory experiences,
such as pain or hunger. On the other hand, he seemed to concede that
animals enjoy a low degree of thinking that breaches the sharp dichotomy
between thinking and not thinking at all. That suggested that human
beings were in many ways similar to nonhuman animals. He returned to
that question on a later occasion. In the meantime, he had to cope with
another extremely cold winter in 1646–47 that forced him to remain at
home, in Egmond-Binnen, more than he would have wished.

12

Once More into Battle: The Leiden Theologians (1647)

I shall ask only for justice. If I cannot obtain it, it seems best that I prepare myself very calmly to retreat.[1]

T HE winter of 1646–47 was too cold for Descartes even to travel to The Hague. His last visit there had been toward the end of November 1646, and he deferred his next trip for another four months, until the end of March 1647.[2] As in the previous winter, this reluctance of a formerly inveterate traveller was not due exclusively to the weather. He was also beginning to feel old and infirm, and his thoughts turned once more to considerations of mortality. Thus when Huygens mentioned the musical compositions of their late friend Bannius, Descartes told him that he did not value them highly, and then added: 'If I die only of old age, I would still like some day to write about musical theory.'[3] At about the same time, he told Picot about changes in his daily routine. He had reduced his evening meal, he said, because his usual eating habits made him feel heavy and disturbed his night's sleep. That might have seemed trivial in other circumstances. Now, however, Descartes thought it was a warning sign of imminent ageing and a more reliable indicator of advancing years than his grey hair.[4] Baillet noticed a number of related symptoms of Descartes' awareness of ageing. He lost interest in writing; he changed his long-established pattern of working late into the night; and he limited overland journeys to those he could complete with less physical effort.

During the last two or three years of his life, he seemed a little more opposed to the work involved in writing. . . . he gave time willingly, after dinner, to conversation with his friends, to cultivating plants in his garden, or to walking. He previously liked physical exercise well enough and he often took exercise during his recreation time. He used to ride a horse willingly, even when it was possible to travel by barge on the canals. However, his sedentary lifestyle made him so unaccustomed to this kind of effort that,

337

since about 1645 [at the age of forty-nine], he was unwilling to tolerate any kind of transport apart from a carriage or a boat.[5]

These initial signs of ageing, and Descartes' awareness of the reduced options that he would enjoy in the future, helped turn his mind once more toward the possibility of visiting France in 1647.

Although this plan was initially somewhat vague, and was possibly inspired by loneliness and by memories of the positive reception he had received in both Paris and Brittany in 1644; it soon evolved into thinking about returning to France permanently. For example, he wrote to Elizabeth in March 1647 that he did not plan to travel south for another two months, and that he would return before winter.[6] By May, however, he was considering leaving the United Provinces for good. The decisive factor in this change of mind, after living for almost two decades in the United Provinces, was the public attack on his metaphysics by theologians at Leiden, and the implicit threat that they might use their political power to bring him before what seemed to Descartes like a Dutch Calvinist version of the Spanish Inquisition. This was enough to override completely the reasons he had consistently given, since 1628, for his self-imposed exile. 'As regards the peace that I came here to seek, I anticipate that I shall not be able in future to enjoy it as much as I would have wished because, not only have I not yet received all the redress that I should have had for the injuries I suffered from Utrecht, but I see that they have attracted further trouble. There is a group of scholastic theologians there, who seem to have conspired to oppress me with slanders' (v. 15–16). Descartes had had the experience of a long drawn-out struggle with Voetius in Utrecht. In his view, this had not yet been resolved satisfactorily, and he was anxious to avoid a recurrence in Leiden. If he failed to get satisfaction, therefore, he would be 'forced to retire completely from these Provinces. However, since everything happens rather slowly here, I am certain that more than a year will elapse before that occurs' (v. 17).

Before getting involved in that controversy, however, Descartes wrote a lengthy letter on the nature of love for Chanut that attracted the interest and respect of Queen Christina of Sweden and, indirectly, led to his death in Stockholm three years later.

An Essay on Love

Chanut had told Descartes almost as soon as they first met in 1644 that he was not very interested in natural philosophy and that it would be preferable if Descartes were to devote more of his intellectual effort to moral philosophy. Consistent with these limited interests, he now asked Descartes to write something about love that would help respond to queries from Queen Christina.[7] Descartes analysed Chanut's query into three parts, in a lengthy letter of 1 February 1647: (1) What is love? (2) Does the natural light of reason alone move us to love God? (3) Is love or hatred more damaging if it gets out of control?

He distinguished initially between (i) a purely intellectual love and (ii) a passion or emotion that is also called love. Descartes understood the first of these as the spontaneous response of the will toward anything that the mind perceives as good. 'When our soul perceives some good, whether absent or present, which it considers appropriate to itself, it joins with it voluntarily, that is, it thinks of itself and of this good as a single whole of which itself and the good in question are the two parts.'[8] This purely intellectual form of love would be possible even for minds that are not embodied, such as those of angels. 'However, when our soul is joined to our body, this rational love is usually accompanied by another kind of love which could be called sensual or sensuous' (iv. 602). Sensual love, like all other human emotions, is a reality with both mental and physical features. The physical events associated with an emotion are a rush of animal spirits through the body and, in the case of love, a warm feeling around the heart. These bodily changes are always accompanied by a specific feeling that, according to Descartes, is necessarily a mental phenomenon.

Descartes tries to explain the complexity of this feeling by comparison to another example in which the characteristic features are easier to separate. If we feel dryness in the throat, we are likely to desire a drink. There are three distinct realities here: (a) the physical condition of the throat; (b) the feeling of dryness, which is a mental state; and (c) the desire to drink, which is a different mental state. It seems clear, in this case, that one could experience the feeling of dryness without having a desire to drink. Equally, someone could have a desire to drink – for example, because he or she planned to do demanding exercise and anticipated the subsequent dehydration that is familiar from previous occasions – without having any experience yet of a dry throat. Similar distinctions apply in the case of love. There is a characteristic bodily feeling that inclines the subject to experience what Descartes had already described as intellectual love.[9]

Descartes used this opportunity to repeat a thesis that he had outlined in his draft treatise on the passions and that was to emerge later as a central feature of his account of the unity of mind and body in human nature. The

fundamental intuition was that certain mental events and corresponding
bodily events become linked when the mind is first joined with the human
body, and that they remain correlated in pairs in such a way that, in later
life, the occurrence of either member triggers the occurrence of the other.

There is nothing surprising in the fact that certain movements of the heart are naturally
linked in this way with certain thoughts, which they do not resemble in any way. For,
since the nature of our soul is such that it was capable of being joined to a body, it also has
the property that each of its thoughts can become associated with various motions or
other dispositions of the body in such a way that, whenever the same dispositions occur
in the body again, they induce the same thoughts in the soul. Conversely, when the same
thought returns, it prepares the body to have the same disposition again. Similarly,
when one learns a language one links the letters or the sounds of certain words,
which are material things, with certain meanings, which are thoughts. As a result,
when one later hears the same words, one conceives of the same things, and when one
thinks about the same things one is reminded of the same words.   (iv. 603–4)

This allows Descartes to speculate that the human soul must experience
joy and love as its first thoughts when it is joined with an appropriately
disposed body – because its earliest sensations result from the pleasurable
feeling of being fed – and that it feels hatred and sadness only later. There
is no attempt here to explain how this natural coincidence of bodily states
and mental states occurs. It is simply a fact of nature.

The second question that was prompted by Chanut's letter involved
deep theological divisions that had troubled christianity since the time of
Saint Augustine. While it seemed like an innocent question to ask 'whether
the natural light, alone, teaches us to love God and whether it is possible
to love Him by the power of this light' (iv. 607), it was obvious that any
answer he gave could become entangled in disputes about the necessity
or otherwise of divine grace. Descartes tried to defend his own intuitions
and, at the same time, to avoid theological controversy by replying: 'I have
no doubt that we can truly love God by the power of our nature alone. I do
not guarantee that this love is meritorious without grace, and I leave the
theologians to disentangle that' (iv. 607–8). Given his trust in the powers
of reason, unaided by divine grace, Descartes explained the way in which
we can conceive of God by analogy with our own mind. However, he was
also careful to point out that God is infinite and that we are constantly
in danger of reducing God's infinity to dimensions that we can imagine.
Those who reduce the greatness of God's creation and who 'would like
to think that the world is finite' (iv. 609) make that mistake. Descartes

recommends, instead, that they acknowledge God's infinite greatness and universal Providence. From that perspective, one can see that nothing occurs without God's decree and that one need not 'fear death, pain or disgrace' (iv. 609).

The Cartesian account of love included a brief reflection on love of country, which motivates individuals to recognize their role as a very small part of a much greater reality and willingly to risk their lives for their prince. The sacrifice of one of its parts to save the body politic as a whole is illustrated by the way in which people accept 'a little blood-letting from the arm in order to ensure that the rest of the body is improved' (iv. 612). This was stretching the point a little, since Descartes was never a fan of blood-letting and resisted attempts to apply that therapy as he lay dying.[10] In fact, his lack of trust in the generally accepted medical therapies of the period extended even to the use of drugs. 'As for drugs, either from apothecaries or empirics, I have such a low opinion of them that I would never advise anyone to use them.'[11]

Chanut was unqualified in his gratitude to Descartes for replying to his queries and in his praise of the extensive letter of 1 February.[12] He shared these grateful sentiments with the queen's physician, another Frenchman named du Ryer, on whom Queen Christina depended so closely that she allowed him home visits to France only on condition that he left his wife in Stockholm as a guarantee of his prompt return to Sweden. The physician in turn told the queen about Descartes' letter, so that she also wanted to read it and discuss it with Chanut. Having indicated that she had never experienced the passion of love and therefore could not comment on the merits of the Cartesian analysis, she raised two questions about whether Descartes' account of the indefinite extent of the universe was compatible with Christianity. Christina claimed that, if one denied that the universe is finite, it would be difficult to reconcile its indefinite duration with the biblical account of God's creation and with the Christian understanding of a final judgment. In other words, the Earth as described in the Bible seemed to have a beginning in time and a definite end. She was also concerned that the Christian account of the Incarnation would seem less credible if the traditional view of the human race as being the centre of creation were surrendered. Why should God be united with human nature if there were many similar species on other planets and if mankind, therefore, were no longer the primary or exclusive focus of God's benevolence?

Chanut's letter reached Egmond three hours after Descartes had departed for Paris, in May 1647, with The Hague as the first stop on his journey south. Once he arrived there, he heard that the Chanut letter had already passed through The Hague and been dispatched north. Since it included royal queries, he decided to wait for the letter to be returned from Egmond. Descartes remained in The Hague to answer it as best he could, although his accommodation 'in the room of an inn' was not ideally suited to the intellectual challenge involved.[13] In his reply, Descartes provides an extensive answer to all the objections raised by Queen Christina. He also invokes the authority of Nicholas of Cusa, who – although he was a cardinal – had also argued that we have no reason to believe that the universe is finite (iv. 51).

Descartes repeats the style of argument he used in the *Principles* to show that the universe has no spatial boundaries. If we imagine the universe with a finite boundary and then try to describe what lies beyond it, we are forced to think of an empty space that has the same property of extension as matter. Descartes concludes that we cannot imagine the universe as being spatially bounded and, for that reason, that we should describe it as indefinitely extended (rather than infinite, which is a feature that applies properly only to God). He does not claim that indefinite extension in space implies that there was an indefinitely extended time, in the past, during which God might have created the universe had He wished to do so. However, the Christian doctrine of the resurrection of the body suggests that time must extend indefinitely into the future. 'For the faith teaches us that, even though the Earth and the heavens will perish – that is, will change their appearance – nonetheless, the world (that is, the matter of which they are composed) will never perish. This is apparent because the faith promises eternal life after the resurrection for our bodies and, consequently, for the world in which they will exist' (v. 53).

Descartes disposes more easily of the other objections that Queen Christina drew from Christian faith. Genesis, according to Descartes, tells the story of creation from the perspective of human beings and gives us the impression that we are the centre of the universe. However, even if there were indefinitely many worlds like ours, the mere fact that we are not unique would not imply that the significance of human life is devalued. God could have created an indefinitely extended universe, with creatures similar to us on many other planets. Yet the core of the Christian account could remain intact. As usual, Descartes follows his philosophical intuitions to their logical conclusion, and then looks for a way to make them compatible with Christianity. If necessary, he was willing to adjust the ways in which theologians had understood the Christian faith when they combined it with elements of scholastic philosophy. Even if his arguments were generally unwelcome to theologians, his contention was well founded that scholastic philosophy was not an essential part of the Christian faith and that it should not have been protected as unchallengeable by various churches.

The kind of difficulty mooted from afar by Queen Christina, about the possible implications of Cartesian philosophy for school theology, was raised more forcefully, and much more dangerously, closer to home at Leiden University.

Theological Objections at Leiden

The objections of two Calvinist theologians at Leiden University to what they presented as Cartesian metaphysics gradually developed, during 1647, into a very public controversy. It was not as bitter or as lengthy as the earlier row in Utrecht, but it seemed to be potentially more dangerous from the perspective of Descartes. While the French philosopher was as defensive as ever before, there was a new dimension in this controversy because the contestants could not agree about the reason for their disagreement. The theologians certainly gave everyone the impression that they were objecting to Cartesian philosophy, whereas the target of their hostility claimed consistently that the theses to which they objected could not in fact be found among his writings. As had happened on other occasions, the controversy was marked by personal antagonisms between members of the teaching faculty at Leiden, by claims of misquotation or misrepresentation, by appeals to public officials and politicians to resolve what was essentially an intellectual dispute that they probably understood poorly, and by an underlying threat of civil penalties for those convicted of serious theological unorthodoxy.

Adriaan Heereboord (1614–1661) was appointed Professor Extraordinary of Logic at Leiden in 1640 and subsequently became assistant regent to the *Statencollege* that had been founded in the same city by the states of Holland.[14] Heereboord began to show signs of sympathy for Cartesian ideas as early as 1644, when Descartes commented favourably on his support in contrast with the ebbing loyalty of Regius.[15] The regent of the

college was Jacobus Revius (1586–1658), a theologian of such modest
ability that he is remembered now, if at all, as a poet rather than as a theologian, or as one of the two unremarkable culprits identified by Descartes
as instigators of opposition to his metaphysics at Leiden.

At the time of his appointment, Heereboord seems to have been a
relatively competent Aristotelian philosopher, but one who also showed
early signs of intellectual independence. Among the disputations that he
arranged for his students, as Descartes acknowledged, was one in which
the validity of substantial forms was defended against the Cartesian criticisms that were emanating at the time from Regius in Utrecht.[16] However, while defending central features of the Aristotelian tradition, as it
was taught in Dutch universities at the time, Heereboord also strayed
into theses that sounded vaguely Cartesian, and some of them opened up
well-known problems about the relationship between religious faith and
reason. This was an issue that had troubled Calvinist theologians for some
time. Moise Amyraut, for example, had defended a radical view in 1641
that acknowledged the privileged role of reason.[17]

One way of understanding religious mysteries, such as the Trinity,
is to consider them intelligible claims for which, apart from revelation,
human beings lack supporting evidence. When understood in that way,
they are not inconsistent with reason. However, it is a much stronger
claim to suggest that religious mysteries cannot be understood at all, even
if they are revealed by God, and that religious faith requires Christians
not only to accept them without independent evidence but also to believe
something that they cannot even understand. Heereboord showed both
his independence and his Cartesian sympathies by supporting the first of
these two alternatives, in corollaries to a disputation on the role of reason
in philosophy.

10. The principle from which one begins in philosophy is reason, mind, the natural
light of the human intellect, by means of principles that are naturally innate in the
human mind and through conclusions that are deduced from them or, in other words,
through innate and adventitious ideas.
11. Those who ban the use of reason and mental reasoning from theology are mistaken because, in this case too, reason deduces conclusions from principles which are
revealed.
12. Those who claim that the mysteries revealed by Holy Scripture must be held by
faith alone and not also by reason do not speak with sufficient accuracy.
13. Nothing is held by faith unless it is also held by reason, because 'reason' means
that by which we know, not the source of our knowledge. . . .

16. The mysteries of faith are above reason insofar as they cannot be known without the light of revelation and insofar as, once revealed, they are not comprehended fully, although they are understood.[18]

The intellectual independence that Heereboord displays in these corollaries was challenged by the arrival of Adam Stuart (1591–1654), as professor of philosophy at Leiden in 1645. Stuart was not only an orthodox Scot, he was also appointed with responsibility for metaphysics and physics, and with seniority over Heereboord (even though the latter was promoted in June 1644 to a full professorship). The personal rivalries and simmering antipathies between Heereboord and Stuart came to the surface in September 1646, when another theologian, Jacob Trigland (1583–1654), objected to the introduction of Cartesian-style doubt as an appropriate starting point for a nonsceptical philosophy. As had happened in similar circumstances in Utrecht, the university senate tried to avoid controversy by deciding that only Aristotelian philosophy should be taught or discussed in official disputations in Leiden.

Despite that decision, Revius arranged for a number of disputations in February and March 1647, which addressed what he suspected were heterodox theological implications of Descartes' philosophy. These theses focused particularly on Descartes' concept of God and his apparent ambivalence about proofs of God's existence. Revius objected especially to the suggestion that a Christian could doubt God's existence, since this was something that was taught by the Scriptures. He was equally concerned by the apparent implications of a short passage that Descartes had written about the scope of the human will. Revius argued: 'It is false that we have an idea of free will and that it is formally and specifically greater than the image or likeness of God, as he [Descartes] claims in the same context. This exceeds all forms of pelagianism.'[19] The worry about Pelagianism reflected Calvinist beliefs in the limits of human free will and the predetermination by God of each individual's salvation or perdition. The Cartesian trust in human freedom seemed to imply the redundancy of divine grace and an arrogant confidence in the natural powers of human nature. According to Revius, that was equivalent to eliminating God and enthroning free will in His place.[20]

These concerns within Calvinist theology were confirmed by another disputation arranged by Trigland in March 1647. Trigland focused on the brief consideration by Descartes, in the *Meditations*, that God may be a deceiver (an idea that had been dismissed almost as soon as it was mentioned). By appealing to the Calvinist doctrine of the inner certainty about salvation that is provided to the faithful, he challenged Descartes with these words: 'It is not permissible to doubt temporarily or under any pretext whatever, the internal testimony of the Holy Spirit concerning the certainty of salvation, much less to think or imagine that the Holy Spirit (or God himself as is wickedly done by Descartes) is an impostor or a deceiver, which is clearly blasphemous.'[21]

When Descartes was told about the disputations taking place at Leiden, he became concerned immediately about their possible implications for himself. He accordingly wrote to Heereboord, 19 April 1647, asking him if he had heard local reports that he (Descartes) had 'written that the idea of our freedom is greater than the idea of God' [22] Descartes followed this with a long letter to the curators of the University of Leiden and the consuls of the city, on 4 May 1647. In his official complaint he acknowledged the freedom of university professors to question his philosophy and to arrange disputations in which his opinions were discussed. However, he did not accept that the professor of theology could accuse him falsely of 'the most odious and most seriously punishable crime of blasphemy' (v. 2). In an effort to win the sympathy of his correspondents, Descartes told them that he was using the most discreet option available to him to get satisfaction, but that he would resort to other means if his request was not granted.

The core of Descartes' complaint was that he had been accused of blasphemy and Pelagianism. The basis for the latter objection was a passage that was not actually in the *Meditations* and that allegedly said: 'The will or freedom of choice is the only thing I experience in myself as so great that I cannot conceive of any greater idea' (v. 4).[23] On the charge of blasphemy, he quotes from the disputation scheduled for 27 March, and concedes that one would be guilty of this crime if one described God as a deceiver. However, he had not done so. He also accepted that, if his critics had refrained from naming him, they could have legitimately exercised their freedom of thought by discussing this question as a speculative hypothesis. His objection, therefore, was not to theological speculation or philosophical criticism, but to the fact that he had been described publicly as guilty of a crime that was 'horrible, impious and blasphemous' (v. 7).

When challenged to produce evidence for such a serious charge, the only text that his accusers were able to quote was a passage from the

First Meditation that reads: 'Therefore I shall suppose not that God, who is the source of truth, but some evil mind who is all powerful and cunning, has devoted all their energies to deceiving me' (v. 8 and vii. 22). Descartes refers, in passing, to a similar calumny to which he had been subjected from another hostile source, namely Voetius (v. 9), who accused him of atheism merely because he had argued against atheists. He demands the freedom of conscience that he should enjoy in the United Provinces. He has been accused of serious crimes by two prominent members of the Calvinist Church, the professor of theology at Leiden and the dean of the *Statencollege*. The curators need not get involved in any subtle theological disputes, for the issue he wishes to put before them is not a question of doctrine but a question of fact: do the words about which the theologians complained appear in any of his writings?

The real source of Descartes' concern was his fear of a Calvinist inquisition, of being denounced to a synod of Calvinist theologians who would almost certainly support the charges brought against him, and of being handed over subsequently to the magistrates or a civil court. He expressed these fears to Princess Elizabeth a week after writing to Leiden University. 'I am told that the theologians wish to be judges, that is, to subject me to a more severe inquisition than was ever seen in Spain, and to turn me into an enemy of their religion' (v. 18). He had been advised by friends in Leiden to appeal to the French ambassador and to the authority of the *Stadtholder*, as he had done previously to protect himself against the onslaught from Utrecht. However, he told Elizabeth, on this occasion, that he would simply appeal to the good judgment of the Leiden University curators. In fact, he had no sooner sent this letter to Elizabeth than he changed his mind again. Prince Frederik Hendrik had died on 14 March 1647, and had been succeeded by his son, Prince William. Unfortunately, the French ambassador, La Thuillerie, was absent at this time, and Descartes wrote instead to Abel Servien, who temporarily represented the French crown in the United Provinces from January to July 1647. Servien, however, was posted there with a very specific mission: to persuade the United Provinces not to make a separate peace agreement with Spain without consulting their French allies. He was therefore much too busy to bother with relatively minor theological disputes that involved one of his countrymen who lived in the far north of Holland, and to protect the freedom of conscience of a French Catholic who had formerly served in the Dutch army.

Despite the poor timing, Descartes still pleads his case with Servien. He asks him to request that Prince William, who was responsible for appointing the Rector of the University, to prevent Calvinist theologians from making a judgment on the orthodoxy of a French Catholic. He also spells out the political implications of the case.

> I am certain that the curators will not accept that, after the French have spilled so much of their blood in helping them to dislodge the Spanish Inquisition from here, a French-man, who also formerly carried arms in the same cause, would be subjected today to an Inquisition of [Calvinist] Ministers from Holland. . . . I claim that the theologians have no right to examine what I wrote in their ecclesiastical assemblies, that is, in their theology faculties, consistories, classes and synods. My reason is that there is nothing to be found in all my writings that is relevant to the religious controversies between them and us. As regards issues that involve the Christian religion in general – such as the existence of God, which I dealt with – the freedom which they owe me in this country, because the [French] King gives them a similar freedom in France, requires them to leave any decision about those matters to the superiors of our own Church.   (v. 25–6)[24]

As supporting evidence of his willingness to be judged by Catholic theologians, Descartes claims disingenuously that he had left the *Meditations* – which was the main target of Calvinist attacks – in the hands of the Sorbonne theologians for more than a year before its publication, and that they had found nothing objectionable to faith or morals in it. It was true that he had submitted it to their judgment, but they had not reported anything at all about its contents, favourable or otherwise.

This request to Servien fell on deaf ears, for obvious reasons. However, the curators replied on 20 May, and informed Descartes that they had explicitly forbidden their professors to speak of him in future in their lectures or disputations. They also requested the complainant, for his part, to refrain from proposing the views that, allegedly, had been attacked by the Leiden theologians. This hardly satisfied Descartes. He tried once more to clarify his position.[25] He could not refrain from repeating the views that had been attacked by the Leiden theologians, since he had never expressed them in the first place. The reason for his concern was, as he had explained earlier, that these theologians exercised a public authority in Holland, and therefore he could not simply ignore their public statements as 'ridiculous calumnies' (v. 37). In fact, Descartes worried that there was a wider conspiracy against him, involving the other professors of theology at Leiden, namely, Spanheim and Empereur.[26] He continued to insist that the theologians be required to compensate him for the harm caused to his reputation. As in his other letters, he explained that anyone with even a smattering of Latin would be able to decide the factual question, whether the words complained of by the theologians were or were not in his writings (v. 39). Having replied to the university officials, Descartes also wrote to Jan van Wevelinchoven, the secretary of both the Leiden burgomasters and the Curators, to request assistance in explaining his position to the curators.[27]

Descartes must have felt under threat from a number of simultaneous attacks on his philosophy at the time. The very public falling out with Regius (discussed in Chapter 11) was on-going, and it was concluded on Descartes' side when he wrote the *Comments on a Certain Manifesto* in December 1647. In October of the same year, Voetius had rejoined the fray by publishing the first volume of his *Selected Theological Disputations*.[28] Although many of these disputations had been held years earlier, Voetius took advantage of publication to update them and to include easily recognizable references to Descartes and his philosophy, especially in the disputations on atheism. In defence of his own very public row with Descartes, he justified his reaction to 'some Papist, living in a reformed Republic, [who] proceeds to abuse with his libellous writings theologians and ministers because of sermons and books in which, if the occasion requires, they censure Papism for its heretical, idolatrous, magical, atheistic, and libertine consequences'.[29] Voetius' criticisms were as sharp as ever, but they were familiar. Those of Regius were also familiar, and were very disappointing. The most recent attack by the Leiden theologians, in the same province in which Descartes hoped to find a peaceful retreat, was more worrying than any of the others and included threats of unspecified imminent punishment.

While Descartes was invited by the Leiden curators to do the impossible – to refrain from repeating claims that he denied ever making – the professors of theology who were forbidden to mention his name found it almost as difficult to comply with their university's decisions. Adam Stuart presided over a disputation on 23 December 1647, in which one of the theses for discussion was obviously aimed at Descartes. 'There are certain philosophers addicted to novelties who withdraw all reliable trust in the senses. They contend that philosophers can deny God and that it is possible to doubt his existence, while at the same time they acknowledge that there are actual ideas, species, or notions of God that are inserted by nature in the human mind.'[30] The principal respondent that day was Johannes de Raey (1622–1702), who, in the course of defending his views, provoked Revius into breaching the university ban by naming Descartes as one of the suspect philosophers. The report of the disputation by Heereboord depicted Stuart shouting like a madman and ordering de Raey to 'shut up', while audience members stamped their feet and supported noisily both sides of the argument as if they were attending a public spectacle.

The general prohibition on arguing for or against Descartes was also breached, at least in spirit, by the publication in 1648 of a new book by Revius, *A Theological Consideration of the Cartesian Method*.[31] This included comments on many of the points in the *Discourse* and the *Meditations* that Revius considered to have objectionable implications for theology. The style was characteristically acerbic and aggressive, as illustrated by this comment on Descartes' rejection of scholastic logic. 'We are offered a very petulant invective against the art of logic, such that it would not be mistaken to describe it as both puerile and damaging, indeed as extremely damaging, while he withdraws logic from all those who have any semblance of judgment or of a sound mind.'[32] He examined in turn each of the claims that he identified as Cartesian theses, and found them all wanting.

The curators met again on 8 February 1648 and, once again, confirmed their original decision of 20 May 1647 that only Aristotelian philosophy may be taught in Leiden. By this time, however, Stuart had tried to persuade them that, improbably, he had not been informed of the earlier embargo and therefore had not realized the misconduct involved when he continued to dispute about Descartes. Revius and Heereboord were also reprimanded, so that none of the principal protagonists at the university emerged unscathed. The most important feature of the curators' decision was that they focused their attention almost exclusively on restoring peace among their own faculty members and that they took no initiative against Descartes. On 21 February 1648, Descartes submitted his lengthy review of the whole Utrecht controversy and the statement of his own defence, the *Apologetic Letter to the Magistrates of Utrecht*. It arrived at its destination in the middle of March, and no action was taken. This controversy simmered just below the surface of public debate throughout 1648. It almost erupted again when Trigland gave the funeral address for Constantijn L'Emperur in July. Pollot informed Brasset that they 'had made the dead speak against [Descartes], without a miracle' by telling the

congregation that a student of the deceased had become an atheist by reading Descartes' work.[33] Brasset was able to reassure Descartes, however, that
he had informed the *Stadtholder* and that silence had been restored.

This was the second occasion on which Descartes had felt threatened by
a very public controversy with Dutch Calvinist theologians who were based
in a local university. At the time he feared for his safety, especially given
the threatening connotations of comparison to Vanini. Before concluding
these rows, he had occasion to pay two more visits to France, the first of
which was in summer 1647.

Visit to France (Summer 1647)

Descartes began to anticipate, in April 1647, the inconveniences associated
with a journey to France that he hoped to make during the summer. On
his previous trip in 1644 he has used the services of Dutch valets, or of
French assistants who had lived for some time in the United Provinces. He
was unhappy with both, since they were unable to adapt quickly enough
to the customs and expectations of French polite society. Accordingly, he
now wrote to his host in Paris, Picot: 'The Dutch are troublesome on a
journey, and the French people who have been in this country are of no use
in France. That is why I would very much like if one of your acquaintances
were willing to look for a young boy for me who would be able to assist me
during the journey' (iv. 641).

Descartes' threat to leave permanently the country that had provided a
welcome retreat for almost two decades, together with talk about another
journey to France, prompted a worried response from Princess Elizabeth
in May, before his departure.[34] Elizabeth compared Descartes' growing
reluctance to return to Holland to a similar change of plans she herself was
contemplating. She had hoped to go back to The Hague toward the end
of 1647, but she thought now that it would be better to await the outcome
of the Treaty of Münster and see if she might be able to return instead
to her 'homeland' (i.e., the Palatinate). The war had abated, at least in
some parts of Germany, although there was much residual fire damage
to property, and they were plagued by such large swarms of midges that
some people went blind and deaf.[35] By 6 June, Descartes had arrived
at The Hague en route to Rotterdam, from which he wrote to Chanut
and to Princess Elizabeth. He was still considering a permanent change of
residence, especially if the Leiden theologians became 'unbearable' (v. 60).

However, he was somewhat consoled by the fact that the French version of the *Principles* was almost ready for distribution. The dedicatory letter to Elizabeth had been printed last, and he was about to send her a copy in case she wished to suggest amendments. He left for Rotterdam on 7 June, travelled overland to Middelburg, and left by boat from Vlissingen on 9 June. The journey to Paris was expected to take about two weeks.[36]

The original plan had been to lodge with Picot for a short time and then to travel to Brittany toward the beginning of July, when he would take care of various financial matters that required his personal attention. However, he now had to hand the almost complete French *Principles*, and it urgently required the final touch of another short Preface, that is, the 'Letter of the Author to the Translator of this Book, which can serve here as a Preface' (ix-2. 1–20). While he took time to complete this, he visited with very few people. They included Mersenne, as usual; Mydorge (who was to die before Descartes' return to Paris in September); and Claude Clerselier, who had recovered from the serious illness of the previous winter and had seen the French version of the *Meditations* through the press in Paris about four months earlier.[37]

While still in Paris in July, Descartes received a letter that had been forwarded from Elizabeth, in which she told him about further health problems. He confirmed his plans to travel to Poitou and Brittany 'within four or five days' (v. 66). However, he seems to have had another change of mind about either remaining in France or returning to Holland. The apparent vacillation might be nothing more than a symptom of the customary obsequious language with which he expressed his gratitude to Elizabeth for writing to him and honouring him with her inquiries. 'As soon as I put my affairs [in Brittany] in some order, I would like nothing more than to return to the places where I was so happy to have the honour of speaking sometimes with your Highness. For, although there are many people here [in Paris] whom I honour and esteem, I have nevertheless not seen any yet who could keep me here' (v. 66). This desire to return to the United Provinces was consistent with the conditional nature of his earlier plans. If the Leiden theologians could be forced to retract their accusations, Descartes would be willing to remain in Holland. And since it would take some time to get a decision on that issue – given that the controversy at Utrecht was still not resolved to his satisfaction four years after it had erupted – he could count on a sufficiently long delay and, meantime, he could return provisionally to Egmond.

Descartes spent the next six months in the company of Picot, who accompanied him to Rennes, to Poitou, and then back to Egmond. His financial affairs were concluded at Rennes on 26 July, after which the two companions journeyed to Poitou and then returned to Paris through Touraine. Baillet recounts the story of Descartes accepting the hospitality of a Mr. de Crenan, who was so happy to have such a famous visitor that he wanted to share his company with his friends and neighbours. Descartes, however, remained aloof, was never seen before midday, and even when he should have respected his host's expectations for the evening, went walking alone and left Picot to entertain the invited guests.[38]

Picot and Descartes returned to Paris toward the beginning of September. There they found that Mersenne had fallen ill in late August, and his condition was exacerbated by an incompetent surgeon who cut an artery in his arm while attempting to bleed him. Mersenne was concerned that his arm would become gangrenous, a danger that subsided only the following month.[39] However, his recovery was relatively short-lived, because he died the following year in Paris. Mydorge, unfortunately, had died while Descartes was in Brittany, about two weeks before his return to Paris.[40]

The most memorable person to meet Descartes on the occasion of this visit, however, was Blaise Pascal, the relatively young son of Étienne Pascal, who had supported Fermat's critique of Descartes' *Geometry* ten years earlier.

Descartes and Pascal

Blaise Pascal (1623–1662) was only twenty-four years old, and already in poor health, when Descartes visited him at his home in Paris on 23 and 24 September 1647. Pascal is usually remembered today as the author of famous, randomly collected jottings in draft form that he prepared in defence of his religious faith and that were published posthumously under the title *Pensées*, or as the scourge of the Jesuits in a series of *Provincial Letters* that were published anonymously in 1656–57 in defence of Jansenism. However, when Descartes came to visit Paris in 1647, the young Pascal had acquired a modest reputation primarily as a mathematician, as the inventor of a mechanical calculating machine, and as someone who had recently become interested in pneumatics.

Pascal's younger sister, Jacqueline – who later became a nun at Port Royal – wrote to her older sister, Gilberte, with a detailed description of

Descartes' visit. Gilberte had been married since 1641 to Florin Périer, and they lived in the Auvergne. The sisters were frequently worried about their brother's delicate health; they were great protagonists of his genius and, in later years, they disseminated stories about his religious life that gave the impression of sainthood. It was understandable, then, that Jacqueline would report in detail to Madame Périer about a visit by one of the leading French philosophers of the time who usually lived in seclusion in northern Holland. One of Descartes' friends had called at Pascal's family home, while he was at church on Sunday, and suggested that he return the following morning at nine o'clock accompanied by Descartes. Somewhat implausibly, Gilberte reports that Descartes had great esteem for both her father and her brother. Given the delicacy of Pascal's condition, his houseminders suggested that ten-thirty would be a more suitable time, since Blaise found it difficult to talk and to entertain people early in the morning. Meantime, Roberval – a friend of Pascal and one of his father's mathematical friends who had criticized Descartes' *Geometry* and much else – was tipped off to attend, along with a number of others. Pascal's admiring sister reports the visit as follows:

After the initial greetings, they spoke about the instrument [the calculating machine], which was much admired as Mr. de Roberval demonstrated it. They then discussed the vacuum, and Mr. Descartes was very serious as they described an experiment to him. When they asked what he thought had entered into the syringe, he said it was subtle matter. My brother replied as much as he could at that point, and Mr. de Roberval, believing that my brother would have difficulty speaking, challenged Descartes enthusiastically but civilly. He replied somewhat sharply that he would speak to my brother as much as he wished because he spoke reasonably, whereas he would not speak with him [Roberval] because he spoke prejudicially.[41]

When the discussion seemed to have deviated from Pascal to Roberbal, Descartes looked at his watch, noticed that it was already midday, and told the assembled group that he had a dinner appointment at Faubourg Saint-Germain. Since Roberval had to leave at the same time, Descartes offered him transport in his carriage, and the two philosophers abused each other verbally en route much more than they had in Pascal's company (or so, at least, Roberval reported when he returned to Pascal's home after dinner).

Descartes asked if he could return the next morning at eight o'clock to continue the discussion with Pascal, who was reluctant to agree because of his ill health. Descartes did come, in fact, although we have no record of what was discussed during a three-hour conversation. Pascal's sister, Jacqueline, was unable to be present, and she failed to get a summary from her brother later, because she and her assistants spent most of the afternoon trying to bathe him. She subsequently asked Mersenne why Descartes objected to Pascal's account of air pressure. The unfortunate Minim, who was still suffering the effects in his right arm of his surgeon's inept blood-letting, replied in hardly legible writing. Jacqueline's account is helpful about the domestic circumstances of the meeting between her brother and Descartes. However, she understood very little about why they disagreed, which was acknowledged when she discovered, later, that it was Roberval rather than Descartes who opposed the theory of air pressure.

It had been known for some time that when a tube (closed at one end) is filled with mercury, and when the tube is inverted with the open end submerged below the surface of a dish of mercury, the mercury does not flow out of the tube completely. Instead, it drops to a height of about thirty inches, leaving an apparently empty space above the mercury. Scholastic philosophers explained this phenomenon by saying that 'nature abhors a vacuum'; in order to avoid having a vacuum, the mercury rises in the tube to the observed height. Descartes had been criticizing such explanations for almost two decades. Any reference to nature's 'abhorrence' either mistakenly attributed intentional states to nature when they belonged properly only to people, or it camouflaged a failure to explain the phenomenon by appeal to a metaphorical abhorrence. In addition to these objections to pseudo-explanations, there was a significant amount of experimental work being done at the time on this phenomenon. It was obviously important for understanding the theoretical limits of even the most efficient pumping devices, such as those used in the United Provinces for draining marshes. The Florentine physicist Evangelista Torricelli (1607–1647) had experimented with mercury tubes in 1644. Once news of his work began to spread around Europe, there were attempts to duplicate it by a number of independent experimentalists, including Pierre Petit (who had earlier criticized Descartes' *Dioptrics*) and an obscure Capuchin friar, Valeriano Magno, who published his results in Warsaw.[42] Thus when Pascal began to do experiments with Torricelli tubes, he joined an ongoing experimental and philosophical dialogue that had been initiated in Florence.

Pascal published a short booklet entitled *New Experiments Concerning the Vacuum* in October 1647, after Descartes had returned from Paris to Egmond.[43] He also wrote one month later to his brother-in-law, Florin

Périer, asking him to conduct what became one of the most famous experiments of the seventeenth century. Poor weather conditions and Périer's
professional duties delayed the planned experiment for almost ten months.
However, in September 1648, Périer set off to test the theory that a column
of mercury is supported in a Torricelli tube by the weight of the column
of air that presses on the surface of the mercury. The experiment worked
perfectly. Périer set out in the morning, with five reliable witnesses, to
measure the height of mercury in an inverted glass tube at the bottom
of the mountain called the Puy-de-Dôme and at various intervals as they
climbed to the top. They brought two similar tubes, filled with mercury
and inverted in the usual way. The height of mercury was equal in both
tubes, and it was measured and recorded. Périer left one tube in position at the bottom of the mountain, in the care of a Minim friar who was
charged with watching it during the day and recording any variations in
the height of the column of mercury. Meanwhile, Périer and his assistants
climbed the mountain and took measurements at various places until they
reached the top. At that point, the mercury had dropped 'three inches and
one and a half lines'. This was the anticipated result, which so excited the
participants that they repeated the measurement a number of times in various weather conditions throughout the day. The team of observers then
descended the mountain until they reached the friary garden, where Father
Chastin reported that his column of mercury 'had remained unchanged
all day, despite the fact that the weather was very changeable, sometimes
calm, sometimes rainy, sometimes very foggy and sometimes windy'.[44] To
the delight of all concerned, the other column of mercury, which had been
carried up and down the Puy-de-Dôme, returned to its original reading.
The results were reported in a pamphlet entitled *Description of the Great
Experiment on the Equilibrium of Liquids* in 1648.[45]

The conclusion for which Pascal argued was that the mercury is supported to a height of about thirty inches by the column of air above it
that presses down on the surface of the mercury. Since the weight of that
column of air should be reduced as one climbs a high mountain, the height
of the mercury in the tube should decrease proportionately. By contrast,
if nature's abhorrence of a vacuum were the correct explanation, there
would be no reason to think that nature would abhor a vacuum less on
top of a mountain than lower down, and there should therefore be no corresponding change in the column of mercury. Descartes agreed that the
phenomenon should not be explained by reference to nature's apparent

moods. He even claimed subsequently to have suggested the Puy-de-Dôme experiment to Pascal during their meeting in September 1647. However, Pascal and Descartes differed about how to describe the apparently empty, enclosed space at the top of a mercury column in a Torricelli tube. Pascal thought it contained a vacuum, whereas Descartes had argued for at least two decades that there is no such thing as a genuine vacuum in nature.

Descartes' argument about the vacuum was metaphysical rather than something he had concluded from observation or experiment. He argued consistently throughout his career that an apparently empty space has dimensions, and that dimensions cannot be predicated of a complete nonentity. He had recently developed this argument in reply to Queen Christina, arguing that the apparently empty spaces beyond the solar system cannot be absolutely empty and that they must contain some matter. In a similar way, the apparently empty space above a column of mercury must contain some kind of matter, which is invisible to the naked eye but has very specific dimensions. He was joined in this debate by an unlikely ally, his former Jesuit teacher Father Étienne Noël.

Noël corresponded with Pascal in the autumn of 1647, following publication of the *New Experiments* but before the Puy-de-Dôme experiment had been done. The fact that he was a Jesuit cannot have helped his cause in criticizing the rather irascible Pascal. He accepted the validity of Pascal's experiments – although others doubted that he could have performed them as described – and he agreed with him that columns of liquid are not supported by nature's fear of a vacuum.[46] However, he could not see how an absolute vacuum could have the physical properties that were observed in the apparently empty space above the mercury.

I read your experiments about the vacuum, which I find very good and ingenious, but I do not understand this apparent vacuum which appears in the tube after either the water or mercury has dropped. I say that it is a body, because it acts like a body, it transmits light with refractions and reflections, it retards the movement of another body, which can be observed in the descent of the mercury when the tube that is filled at the top with this vacuum is inverted.[47]

Thus Noël's arguments closely mimicked those of Descartes and were most likely influenced by his reading of Descartes' work. His style of argument, however, remained more scholastic than that of his former pupil. For example, he could not understand what kind of reality a vacuum was supposed to be, because it did not fall within either of the two most general types of reality that were accepted by scholastics, namely, a substance or a property. Worse still, if Pascal were so keen to accept only what was observable, a vacuum should be rejected because it is invisible, inaudible, and so on.[48] Despite these metaphysical objections, however, Noël acknowledged the significance of Pascal's experimental results. He conceded that he had learned much from them and had even modified his own scholastic views accordingly[49]

Descartes, for his part, had returned to Holland before the publication of Pascal's *New Experiments*. However, the author sent him a copy, and Huygens as usual acted as a postal intermediary. When forwarding the book to Egmond, in November 1647, Huygens advised that Descartes say nothing in public about the disagreement with Pascal until 'the young author has published his views about the whole matter'.[50] Descartes accepted that Pascal's 'booklet' was, on his own account, merely an abridged version of what he promised to publish later. However, this did not prevent Descartes from expressing a provisional evaluation, even while hoping to see the fuller presentation in the near future. 'It seems to me that the young man who wrote this booklet has the vacuum a bit too much in his head and that he is in a great hurry. I wish that he had already published the volume that he promised, so that his arguments could be examined. Unless I am mistaken, they will be as unconvincing as what he has tried to prove.'[51]

The following week he told Mersenne that Pascal had sent him a copy of his publication, in which 'he seems as if he wishes to attack my subtle matter.'[52] As usual, Descartes reserved the right, at some unspecified 'time and place, to explain everything that I consider relevant to defend myself' (v. 98). He asked Mersenne if he knew whether Pascal had done the experiment that they had talked about in late September (i.e., the Puy-de-Dôme experiment). While waiting for news about that, he suggested that the Minim friar could assist by doing a joint experiment, for which he sent instructions. Descartes had noticed that the height of the mercury column varied with weather conditions, and he made two long strips of paper, about two and a half feet long, on which he had marked exactly similar intervals. He sent one of them to Mersenne in Paris, so that while Pascal was checking changes in the height of the mercury column at different heights above sea level, Mersenne and Descartes could do a parallel experiment to see if the mercury level varied with changes in weather conditions at the same place.

In order for us to know also if variations in the weather and place do not affect the [height of the] mercury, I am sending you a strip of paper two and a half feet long, on which the third and fourth inches above the two-foot mark are divided into lines. I shall keep an exactly similar one here, to see if our observations agree. I am asking you, then, to observe the point to which the mercury rises on this scale when the weather is warm and when it is cold, and when the wind blows from the north and from the south. In order to let you know that there will be variations, and to persuade you to report your observations to me very honestly, I will tell you that, on Monday last, the height of the mercury was exactly two feet three inches on this scale. Yesterday, which was Thursday, it was a little above two feet four inches. Today, however, it has dropped again by three or four lines. I have a tube that remains attached to the same place day and night, in order to make these observations. However, I think it would be best not to tell anyone about them yet, and to wait until Mr. Pascal's book is published.   (v. 99–100)

Since Descartes was equally confident that the apparent vacuum in these glass tubes was some kind of body, he asked Mersenne to conduct another experiment by setting fire to a piece of sulphur – which could be set alight by using a mirror or lens – suspended by a string in the 'vacuum'. He needed Mersenne's help because the Sun was not strong enough, at least not in December, to do that kind of experiment in Egmond.

Descartes' observations contrast markedly with those reported eventually by Florin and Pascal, that there was no change in the height of the mercury despite fluctuating weather conditions on the Puy-de-Dôme. Descartes did not publish his results, and almost two years later (after Mersenne had died) he was still inquiring about the results of the Puy-de-Dôme experiment.[53] When he was told about those results, in July 1649, he was delighted to hear the news. He claimed that the results were entirely consistent with his principles, and even that he had suggested the experiment to Pascal, who otherwise would never have attempted it, since he had expected the opposite result. Since Pascal had promised to refute the Cartesian subtle matter in his first publication, *New Experiments concerning the Vacuum*, Descartes asked Carcavi to tell Pascal, if he met him in Paris, that he was still waiting for the promised refutation.[54] This request remained unanswered. By the time Carcavi looked for Pascal to pass on the request, Pascal and his whole family had left Paris to live with his sister and brother-in-law in Clermont, and Descartes had left Egmond to visit Stockholm. Pascal did not return to Paris until after Descartes' death.[55]

This unresolved debate about the metaphysical status of the apparently empty space at the top of a Torricelli tube, between Descartes and Noël on one side and Pascal on the other, corresponded closely to a later dispute between Robert Boyle – a defender of the vacuum theory – and his equally adamant critics, Hobbes, More, and another Jesuit called Father Linus.[56] In both disputes, there were misunderstandings, charges of irrationality, appeals to observational evidence that was inadequate to resolve the questions involved, and an underlying failure to recognize the extent to which the disputes were incapable of resolution in the terms in which they were framed.

Before leaving Paris, Descartes was awarded an annual pension of 3,000 livres, in recognition of his contribution to philosophy and as financial support for the experiments required to complete his research. There were no conditions attached – for example, he was not required to live in France. Toward the end of September, then, with a promise of added financial security from a royal pension, he set off again in the company of Picot.

A Temporary Return to Egmond

Despite earlier misgivings, Descartes returned to Egmond with Picot about the middle of October 1647.[57] They lived together in what Baillet described as 'amiable solitude . . . and a laziness that was completely philosophical'.[58] Huygens heard about the royal pension from some independent source, and he wrote almost immediately to ask Descartes if he was now tempted to live in France.[59] Huygens also added a second query. He had been asking Descartes for many years to study chemistry – a request that fell on deaf ears – and he now asked if it was also true that, while in France, he had met some renowned chemist and had brought him back to Holland with him. If so, what did they plan to study together? Descartes' reply to the first question was sufficiently ambivalent to leave everyone in the dark about his future plans. He used it as another opportunity to complain about the recent threats by the Leiden theologians, and to remind Huygens of the protracted row with Voetius. His answer to the second question was a simple denial.

As regards the famous chemist that you said I brought back with me from France, I can assure you that I know nothing about him, unless one wished to honour with such a title one of my intimate friends who does not at all claim to deserve it. It is Mr. Picot who previously lived for more than a year at Endegeest when I was there, and who has come once again to spend the winter here. He did this only on condition, and after having made me promise, that I would also go with him to spend next winter in France. It is only that promise and a few other special considerations that will make me return to Paris within a few months, without being obliged by anything that I promised the king and without having decided to spend the rest of my days there. . . . It is true that the person who informed me about the royal pension added that I might expect other favours if I agreed to live in France. Although that is not a decisive factor with me, I think it would be unreasonable if I did not prefer to be in the country where I was born, and in which they provide testimony of their respect for me, than to remain in another country where I have been unable for nineteen years to obtain the status of a freeman [*bourgeois*] and in which, in order to avoid oppression, I am forced to appeal on every occasion to our ambassador. That does not prevent me from thinking that I have some special friends here whom I honour and cherish very much. However, my relations with them are almost exclusively by letter, something that I could continue if I were in Paris more easily than I can at Egmond, and to which I would still hope to return.   (v. 653–4)

Descartes is obviously exploiting Huygens' unwavering friendship over many years to pressurize him here, once again, into providing a defence against the Leiden theologians. When the Jesuits in Paris seemed to criticize Descartes in 1640, he contrasted their negative response with the favourable support of Regius at Utrecht. When Regius became critical some years later, Descartes contrasted his disloyalty with the esteem and friendship he then found in Paris. Now that he had been promised a French royal pension, he is back to his old tricks of threatening to leave Holland, possibly permanently, to live among those in his native country who appreciate his contributions to philosophy and who confirm their appreciation with financial support.

Descartes' strong desire for public recognition of his work was encouraged by a further request from Queen Christina, who asked Chanut to get his comments about the supreme good.[60] His reply reworked themes that he had mentioned on previous occasions, when he distinguished between (a) goods of the body and of the soul, and (b) those that depend on luck or nature and those that are under the control of each individual. Since we can dispose absolutely only of the will, he argued, it follows that the supreme good for each individual 'consists only in a firm will to do what is good and in the contentment which that produces' (v. 82). The argument that the most satisfactory contentment results from virtuous action had echoes of the thesis that had attracted charges of Pelagianism from Leiden. 'Free will is in itself the most noble thing that we can have insofar as it makes us, in some way, equal to God and seems to exempt us from being His subjects. Therefore the good use of the will is the greatest of our goods; it is the good which is most properly our own and which is most valuable to us. It follows that our greatest contentment can result only from the will' (v. 85). Descartes added that he was sending Chanut some papers that the queen might wish to consult. They included an early, incomplete version of the treatise on the passions, which he had to transcribe from a rather rough draft, and copies of six letters to Princess Elizabeth in which he had provided a running commentary on Seneca's *The Good Life*.[61] Apart from the obvious efficiency involved in not having to compose this material from scratch, he anticipated any objections that Elizabeth might have to sharing this material with Queen Christina by explaining that it might persuade the queen to think more highly of her in future.

The French diplomat Henri Brasset, who was based in The Hague as permanent representative from Paris, wrote to Descartes in December with apologies for disturbing his 'solitude'.[62] Among other items of diplomatic news, he told him about Louis XIV's illness and about recent developments in England that were moving quickly toward their inevitable conclusion and the execution of Charles I. The king of France was only nine years old at this stage, and he had been suffering from smallpox since 10 November. When he experienced fainting fits later in the same month, his doctors began to fear for his survival, and they bled him four times without any noticeable improvement in his condition. By the end of November, however, he had begun to show signs of recovery, and diplomatic delegations throughout Europe were authorized to announce the imminent recovery of the king.

Descartes passed through The Hague on 15 January 1648, without meeting anyone there. He was on his way to Rotterdam, simply to accompany Picot on the overland part of his return journey to France.[63] Since he had said he wanted to avoid such uncomfortable journeys, especially in midwinter, one might wonder at the desire for companionship that motivated a round trip journey of 200 kilometres. Whatever the reason for this extended journey, Descartes returned immediately to the solitude of his northern outpost. During the previous month he had been faced with the final irritant in his disagreement with Regius, and with the new book by Revius that systematically criticized his metaphysics. He ignored Revius – according to Rivet, he was not worth getting angry with – and drafted a short reply to Regius in the *Notes on a Certain Manifesto*, which was published officially in January 1648. There are signs in his response to both events that he was losing interest in battling with his critics. For example, he described the *Notes* as 'a booklet of little significance' and seemed unconcerned when others added a Preface and verses that he had neither approved nor welcomed.[64] However, he was not entirely idle, even if he was losing his characteristic combativeness.

Descartes continued to regret that he had been unable to complete those parts of the *Principles* that were intended to discuss living creatures. Research on plants was proceeding slowly, using the garden attached to his house. The outstanding and most contentious issues involved an explanation of animal life, beginning from conception. This was not a central focus of his work as he oscillated between a number of projects that were incomplete or, in the case of one of them, not even begun. The latter was a 'Treatise on Learning' that he had apparently mentioned to Princess Elizabeth in terms that provoked an enthusiastic response from her about 'how much the world needs the *Treatise on Learning* that you formerly planned to write'.[65] Descartes' reply indicated that he had dropped the idea completely, for a number of reasons. None of them was very convincing, and Descartes' customarily effusive and subservient reply was that he would get back to work immediately on the treatise if Her Highness wished.[66] This was most unlikely. In excusing his relative indolence, however, Descartes refers in passing to taking up again a project that he had worked on in the mid-1630s.

I am now working on another essay, which I hope will be more agreeable to your Highness. It is a description of the functions of animals and human beings. What I drafted on that topic twelve or thirteen years ago (and which your Highness has seen), got into the hands of a number of people who transcribed it inaccurately and therefore I thought I should make a better copy (that is, that I should rewrite it). I have even ventured (but only in the last eight to ten days) to try to explain in it the way in which an animal is formed from the beginning of its conception. I write 'animal' in general because, in the specific case of human beings, I would not dare to tackle that problem since I do not have enough experience to conclude the project.   (v. 112)

Descartes had worked intermittently on a general theory of animal functioning since the early 1630s, when he had expanded the scope of *The World* to include a section on human beings. The suppression of *The World* and the subsequent publication of reworked excepts meant that, during the years 1632 to 1648, the original manuscript was mined for many of its best insights while its publication as an integral work was neglected or indefinitely deferred. On the most recent occasion on which Descartes had referred to it, in a letter to Mersenne in November 1646, he had acknowledged that it was in such poor condition that he even had trouble in reading it himself.[67] He had also dated the original work, in 1646, as about 'twelve or thirteen years ago'. In 1648, therefore, he should have added another two years to his estimate, and that would date the original work to approximately 1633, the year in which *The World* was completed in draft.

It seems as if Descartes finally returned to work on the poorly preserved copy of his *Treatise on Man* in the winter of 1647–48, and that the fruits of his new initiative were the essay entitled *A Description of the Human Body*, which was published (posthumously) with the first French edition of the text in 1664. Rather than simply make a clean copy of his original work, however, he embarked on a more ambitious project of writing a comprehensive treatise on animal life. This is reflected in a letter he wrote about one year later, to an unknown correspondent:

As regards the description of animals, I gave up the idea a long time ago of editing it, not because of negligence or for want of a good intention, but because I now have a better plan. I had intended simply editing what I thought I knew most certainly about animal functions, because I had more or less given up hope of finding the causes of animal formation. However, in thinking about it, I have discovered so many new things that I have almost no doubt about being able to complete my whole physics as originally planned, on condition that I have enough free time and the opportunity to do some experiments.[68]

The revised plan was to do further experiments to explain how animals are conceived and how they develop from the very beginning of their lives.[69] He anticipated that the rest of the winter (1647–48) would be 'the most peaceful time that I shall possibly enjoy in my life' (v. 112–13). Picot had left, and the intellectual rows of the past five years seemed to be abating. If it had been implemented as outlined, Descartes might have considered adding the results to a revised, expanded edition of the *Principles*. For reasons that remain unknown, perhaps because the plan was too ambitious and his experimental and observational techniques were limited, this project remained in draft form and was never published during his life.

Meantime, his thoughts continued to turn toward his native country and toward the lack of research time that he was likely to experience with the arrival of spring. 'I am obliged to return to France in summer, and to spend the coming winter there too' (v. 113). The reason he gave was that his 'domestic affairs and other reasons' required it. By his own admission, the royal pension did not impose any condition on where he lived. The only basis for the apparent obligation, therefore, was that he had promised Picot to spend the winter of 1648–49 with him in Paris. If there were any reasons not to publicize that promise, Descartes observed the proprieties of confidentiality by camouflaging his plans under the cover of generalities.

Thoughts of Retirement

Although there is nothing to keep me here [in Holland] – except that I know of no other place I would prefer to be – I realize that I am in great danger of spending the rest of my days here' (26 February 1649).[1]

I N contrast with the previous year, the winter of 1647–48 was one of the mildest that Descartes had experienced since his arrival in the United Provinces.[2] In other circumstances, this would have been a welcome change for the resident Frenchman. However, in January 1648 Descartes was recording variations in barometric pressure and comparing his results to those obtained by Mersenne in Paris. For scientific reasons, therefore, he would have welcomed a cold spell.[3] His correspondence with Mersenne in the early months of 1648 showed a continued interest in the issues that had been raised by Pascal during the previous summer, and in the debate about barometric measurements and the so-called vacuum at the top of a Torricelli tube. He even claimed to have been looking forward to seeing a new book on the subject by Father Noël, entitled *Gravity Compared*, despite his legendary reluctance to read other people's publications.[4]

What was even more evident, at the beginning of 1648, was Descartes' indecision about where he planned to live during the following years. He had promised Picot to spend the winter of 1648–49 with him in Paris. This plan was now in the process of being changed. He now hoped to visit Paris much earlier in the year and, possibly, to remain there indefinitely. Thus when Mersenne experienced practical difficulties in an experiment that involved lighting a flame inside the top of a Torricelli tube, Descartes suggested that they could do the experiment together 'during the summer, when I shall be in Paris, if you have not done it before then' (v. 116). His immediate plan was to continue his scientific investigations at Egmond, since he feared that he might never again have the leisure required to complete them.[5] However, there were simultaneous intimations of a final departure from Holland, especially in his parting shot to those in Utrecht who had accused him of heresy and who implied that he was persona non grata in a Calvinist country.[6] Accordingly, Descartes wrote to Chanut (21 February 1648) that he planned 'to go to Paris at the beginning of next month [March]' (v. 131).

In fact, he remained in Egmond until early May. During this relatively calm period of his life, he was visited by a young theology student who recorded Descartes' detailed replies to questions about Cartesian philosophy.

Conversation with Burman

Frans Burman (1628–1679) had matriculated as a theology student at Leiden in 1643, and he was still studying there during the controversies of 1647–48, when the Leiden theologians targeted Descartes and his philosophical sympathizers. As a pupil of the *Statencollege* in which Revius was dean, Burman had an opportunity to participate in disputations in which Heereboord and his critics, Revius and Spanheim, presided.[7] He must have been aware, therefore, of the extent to which Descartes' views were the source of constant wrangling at Leiden University and the subject of official inquiries by the university curators. In contrast with other students, however, Burman took the initiative to travel north to Egmond and asked Descartes to clarify many of the central claims of his philosophy. He also came well prepared. He seems to have brought with him copies of four of Descartes' publications, with eighty-two passages marked for ease of reference. Most of Burman's queries were taken from the second edition of the *Meditations* (including the objections and replies). However, he also marked some passages from the *Principles of Philosophy*, the *Discourse on Method*, and, with obvious relevance to the recent controversy at Leiden, Descartes' reply to Regius, the *Comments on a Certain Manifesto*. With these books in hand, all published in Latin in the United Provinces, Burman met Descartes on 16 April 1648, and joined him for dinner.

Burman probably pointed out the passages that he had marked in advance and asked their author to clarify each one in turn. In some cases, when Burman was dissatisfied with the reply, he followed his initial query with a supplementary question. The young student took notes in the course of the conversation and brought them to Amsterdam where, on 20 April, he met with Johannes Clauberg (1622–1665), who was subsequently to become a well-known exponent of Cartesian philosophy. Clauberg produced a clean copy of the interview, possibly with some additional editorial contributions, and this in turn was copied by an unknown hand at Dordrecht in July 1648.

Burman was son of a Calvinist minister and was himself a student of theology. It was not surprising, therefore, if many of the queries he raised with Descartes reflected the controversies that had emerged from disputations at Leiden University. For his part, Descartes seems to have used the occasion to redirect the young student away from misleading interpretations of his work that Burman was likely to have learned from his theology professors. For example, when the problem of scepticism was raised, Descartes explained that he was introducing 'not only the objections that are usually raised by sceptics but also every objection that they can possibly raise so that, by doing so, he would completely remove all doubts' (v. 147). In a word, he was trying to defeat scepticism rather than to promote it.

Some of the other questions that featured as major sources of contention at Leiden were also raised. Thus, Descartes denied that God could be a deceiver, despite the impression that careless readers of the *Meditations* might have got, because he now argued that 'supreme power and malice are not compossible' (v. 151). He also explained, once again, the limited sense in which 'the will is greater than the intellect and more similar to God' (v. 159). The point here was simply that judgments of the intellect always suffer from some degree of ignorance, whereas the will is absolutely free. Two of the most obvious implications of the Leiden controversies appear in Descartes' reflections on the relative insignificance of metaphysics, and on the necessity for theologians not to contaminate the simplicity of God's revelation with complex, contested scholastic views.

The comment about metaphysics seems to have been made by Descartes at the conclusion of a long list of queries that were all taken from the *Meditations*. Having answered each one in turn patiently, Descartes offered the following spontaneous advice without any prompt from Burman.

It should be noted that one should not devote so much effort to the meditations or to metaphysical things, nor should one expand them in commentaries and the like. Much less should one study them more than the author has done – which is what some people try to do – for he has discussed them in sufficient depth. It is enough to have known them once in a general way and simply to remember the conclusion. . . . The author has pursued metaphysical things sufficiently in the *Meditations* against the sceptics, and so on, and has established their certainty, so that it is not necessary for everyone to try to do the same work or to tire themselves in meditating on those matters at length. It is enough to know the first book of the *Principles* [*of Philosophy*], in which one finds whatever is necessary from metaphysics for knowledge of physics etc. (v. 165)

This might have seemed like an overreaction to recent disputes, or even the kind of advice that one would give an anxious student. However, it matches exactly the reply that Descartes had given Princess Elizabeth five years earlier, when she attempted to get a more detailed explanation of how the mind and body interact than he was able to provide at the time.[8] It is also consistent with Descartes' reflection in his conversation with Burman on the relative significance of the work he had done, many years earlier, in *The World*. In retrospect, this now seemed to include the most memorable and innovative ideas he had ever had. 'The author concedes, however, that he remembers with the greatest pleasure those few thoughts he had about the world, that he values them most highly, and that he would not exchange them for any other thoughts that he has had on any other subject.'[9]

Descartes' attempt to distinguish philosophy from theology was even more indicative of his recent travails. However, even on this question, there was no radical departure from views he had expressed frequently since the early 1630s. Descartes told Burman that 'theology should not be subjected to our reasoning' and that the simpler we keep it the better (v. 176).

If the author [i.e., Descartes] knew that anyone would apply certain arguments borrowed from his philosophy to theology and abuse his philosophy by doing so, it would make him regret the work he had done. However, we can and ought to show that theological truths are consistent with philosophical truths, but we should not scrutinize the former in any way. This is how monks have provided an opportunity to all sects and heresies, namely, by means of their scholastic theology, which should have been obliterated before anything else. Why should we put so much effort into theology, when we see that peasants and simple people can get to heaven just as easily as we can? This should surely warn us that it would be much better to have a theology that is as simple as they are, than one which is plagued with many controversies and corrupted in such a way that it opens the way to disputes, quarrels, wars, and so on. (v. 176)[10]

This reply to Burman had obvious connotations of the recent disputes with theologians at Utrecht and Leiden. Descartes added that theologians were so expert in denigrating their opponents that it had almost become their specialty.

In keeping with his earlier views, Descartes was arguing for a clear distinction between (a) philosophical theories (including natural philosophy), which must be understood and supported by evidence, and (b) the truths of revelation. The latter should be accepted at face value, without drawing any conclusions from them for philosophy. One of the implications of this way of doing theology was to read the Scriptures as if they were written in a style that was adjusted 'simply to our way of understanding' (v. 169). In that way, the six days of Genesis should be understood metaphorically. By quoting parts of the text in Hebrew, Descartes showed signs of his efforts some years earlier to study Hebrew and to read the Bible in the original language. However, he also argued that one should be free to use philosophy at least to show that what is believed on faith is not unreasonable, as Descartes had tried to do in the case of transubstantiation. Whatever approach was adopted, one could find no advantage for religion or for the faith of Christian believers in leading theology down the cul-de-sac of scholastic controversies.

A Visit to Paris during the Fronde

Descartes' friends in Paris arranged for a certificate of his royal pension, written on parchment and ornately sealed, to be delivered to him in Holland as an inducement to return to his native country. As Baillet pointed out, it was very improbable that the court under Mazarin's control had issued the same pension twice.[11] However, Descartes confirms the story in a letter he wrote to Chanut the following year, in which he expresses his great disappointment with almost every feature of what he had expected to be a triumphant return to his fatherland. The theme of his letter was fortune, which had disappointed him on each of the three visits he had made to Paris 'since I retired to this country, but particularly on the most recent one, which I was commanded to undertake as if on behalf of the king'.

To convince me to make the journey, I was sent letters written on parchment and ornately sealed, which contained eulogies that were much more generous than I deserved and the gift of a rather significant pension. Besides, in letters from those who sent me the king's letter, I was promised a lot more as soon as I arrived in Paris. However, as soon as I was there, the unexpected troubles resulted in the fact that, instead of seeing those promises implemented, I found that one of my friends had had to pay the costs of sending me the letters and that I had to repay him. Thus I seem to have gone to Paris simply to buy a parchment, the most expensive and most useless one that I have ever received. . . . Still, the thing that most disgusted me was that none of those [who invited me] showed any interest in seeing more than my face. So I have reason to think that they wanted me in France only like an elephant or a panther, because they are rare animals, rather than because they are useful for anything.[12]

The circumstances of Descartes' hesitant return to Paris in May 1648 reveal not only his continued uncertainty about living in Holland, but a lack of awareness about political events in France that underlines once again the extent of his isolation in Egmond.

The intermittent military successes of France in its long-running war with Spain, beginning in 1635, were compromised by a series of revolts at home that occasionally escalated almost into civil war. The exorbitant taxes required for the war effort, and for the expansion of royal power in the provinces, were one of the main causes of these revolts. The revolts of the *croquants* in the Southwest in 1636–37, and of workers (*nu-pieds*) in the salt flats in Normandy in 1639, were among the most notorious popular revolts against high taxes. They were also symptoms of a more fundamental political instability that was contained precariously only by the forceful exercise of royal power.[13] Thus, when Richelieu died in 1642 and Louis XIII died the following year, the balance of power changed sufficiently that the regent, Anne of Austria, and Richelieu's successor, Mazarin, faced unpredictable internal obstacles to ruling a kingdom in the name of the boy king, Louis XVI (born in 1638).

Disputes over the burden of taxes continued throughout the 1640s. When they surfaced in Paris in 1648, in the form of a confrontation between the regent and the Paris *parlement*, the issues involved were no longer merely about taxes. There were now constitutional questions about the role of the *parlement* and the absolute discretion claimed for the king's powers. The fact that the king was only ten years old, and that the kingdom was being ruled in his name by a Spanish princess, Anne of Austria, and an Italian, Cardinal Mazarin, helped underline the extent to which loyalty to an adult French king had provided the main source of political stability during the previous years. The conflicts, which continued from 1648 to 1653 (usually called the Fronde), were almost predictable and were manifestly insoluble in the short term. The citizens of Paris erected barricades in support of the *parlement* during the night of 26–27 August 1648, and the confrontation between the members of *parlement* and the regent continued until 24 October. Even this temporary settlement did not resolve the underlying issues. With the outbreak of open war between the two sides, the young king and his mother had to flee Paris during the night of January 5–6, and the hostilities in Paris ceased only with the Peace of Ruel in March 1649.

Descartes seems to have been unaware of the political situation in his native country, and he was taken by surprise by the unfolding events in Paris during his visit in the summer of 1648. The French resident in The Hague, Brasset, had written to him a few times in spring 1648, usually to pass on letters that arrived from Chanut in Stockholm.[14] In the course of discussing questions that were relevant to Descartes' philosophy and Queen Christina's interest in it, Brasset mentioned the preliminary discussions that led to the peace of Münster, the success of French troops against the Spanish at Naples, and the willingness of France to continue the war unless the terms of the proposed settlement were satisfactory. Thus he was not completely out of touch with news of military operations. Perhaps Descartes and his contemporaries had become so accustomed to a war that had been waged off and on for thirty years that they failed to recognize the significance of changed circumstances in France. Besides, there were no indications in letters received during spring 1648 that the political situation was particularly unstable in Paris. Hence Descartes' surprise, and his extreme disappointment, when he reached the French capital.

The returning Frenchman had given clear indications, before arriving in Paris, of where he wished to lodge and how he hoped to spend his time there. He told Picot in April that he preferred not to accept his kind invitation to lodge with him, and that he would prefer more central accommodations, perhaps on rue Saint Honoré or the Faubourg St-Germain. He also requested facilities that would allow him 'to be served on his own and to dine alone as usual'. If that was impossible, he would accept accommodation in a residence owned by very respectable people and in which he was the only guest. He would need at least three rooms, one in which to study, one properly furnished in which he could receive guests, and a third room for his valet. Finally, he would not require horses, a stable, or even a carriage entrance, but he would require use of a carriage for journeys within the city.[15] Picot found a suitable place for him, which also provided ready access to a Catholic church where he could attend mass.[16] Descartes was about to leave The Hague for Rotterdam and, from there, to travel by sea to France on 8 May when he received a letter from Chanut.[17] His reply (quoted earlier), after he had arrived in Paris, shows the extent of his disappointment.

Descartes' first impression of Paris was that there was something in the air that disposed him 'to conceive of chimeras rather than of philosophical thoughts'.[18] However, he also noticed so many other people who were misguided in their views and plans that their lack of direction seemed to him 'a universal sickness' (v. 183). In an obvious reference to the political events that he had unexpectedly encountered, Descartes began to talk about returning to Egmond almost as soon as he arrived in Paris. 'I very much prefer the innocence of the desert that I came from, and I do not think that I can prevent myself from returning there within a short time' (v. 183). He relented on his earlier demands for private accommodations and accepted hospitality from Picot for the remainder of his visit.

Descartes remained in Paris for about three months. There are few indications of how he spent his time there. Arnauld sent him a number of philosophical queries, and, as in the case of his objections to the *Meditations*, Descartes welcomed them as informed comments from a sympathetic critic. Although he offered to meet Arnauld personally, this proved to be as impossible as it had been on his visit in 1644, because the Sorbonne theologian was still in hiding because of his Jansenist sympathies.[19] Arnauld was concerned about a number of issues, including the manner in which Christ is present in the Eucharist and the nature of what Descartes had called 'intellectual memory'.

The query about Christ's presence in the Eucharist revived discussion of a problem that had caused considerable difficulty in the objections and replies to the *Meditations*. This was a very contentious theological issue that Descartes would have preferred to avoid, and he had already established boundaries to prevent himself from straying unwittingly into theological disputes.[20] Arnauld phrased his question as follows:

You claim that an extended thing cannot be distinguished in any way from its local extension. I would like to know, therefore, if you have thought of any explanation by which you can reconcile that doctrine with the Catholic faith, which requires us to believe that Christ's body is present on the altar [at Mass] without its local extension, since you have shown successfully how the lack of a distinction between accidents and their substance is consistent with the same mystery. Otherwise, you can easily see the danger to which you expose the most sacred reality.   (v. 190)

Descartes replied, cautiously, that even the Council of Trent did not attempt to explain how Christ is present in the Eucharist and that he could not be expected to do better than a general council of the church.

However, he would be willing to discuss the issue orally with Arnauld, so that no record of his views would become public.

Since the Council of Trent itself did not wish to explain how Christ's body is present in the Eucharist, and since it wrote that 'it was present with a type of existence that we can scarcely express in words', I would be afraid of being accused of temerity if I dared to decide anything about that question. Besides, I would prefer to explain my conjectures orally rather than in writing.[21]

Arnauld replied that he could not meet Descartes personally for such a tête-à-tête, since he was 'out of the city' (v. 212), but that he would take advantage of the opportunity to raise his questions in letters. He had to accept Descartes' reluctance to write to him about Christ's presence in the Eucharist. However, he tried once more to persuade his cautious correspondent to say something about the topic in a letter.[22]

Apart from the request to clarify what he meant by an intellectual memory – an obscure argument that seemed to hinge on the fact that we succeed in remembering things of which we do not have images and therefore, presumably, cannot have memory traces as physical events in the brain – Descartes replied to a number of other queries from Arnauld. One concerned the way in which mind and body interact, and this pro- voked one of the clearest statements by Descartes of the reality of this interaction, even if he acknowledged that he did not understand it.

However, the most certain and evident experiences – rather than any reasoning or comparison with other things – shows us daily that the mind, which is incorporeal, can move the body. This is one of those self-evident things that we make obscure when we try to explain it by reference to other things.[23] Nonetheless, I shall use an analogy here. Most philosophers who think that the heaviness of a stone is a real quality, which is distinct from the stone, believe that they understand well enough how that quality can move the stone towards the centre of the earth, because they think they have a clear experience of it. However, I am convinced that there is no such quality in nature and, consequently, that there is no true idea of it in the human mind. Consequently, I think that they use the idea they find in themselves of an incorporeal substance to represent this heaviness to themselves. Therefore, it is no more difficult for us to understand how the mind moves the body than for them to understand how such a heaviness moves a stone downwards.   (v. 222–3)

Descartes exploits the comparison further by arguing that the mind may be described as corporeal if we understand the term to mean 'whatever belongs to a body', because the mind is adapted for being united with the body. However, if we describe as 'corporeal' only what has the nature of a body, then even the heaviness that scholastic philosophers talked about is not genuinely corporeal. It is not clear how this reply could have helped Arnauld. He was not a traditional scholastic philosopher, and he did not believe in the existence of a distinct quality called heaviness any more than Descartes did.[24] He might have accepted that Cartesian talk about mind-body interaction was just as intelligible as scholastic talk about heaviness moving bodies toward the centre of the Earth. This, however, was a very low threshold for success, similar to the strategies used in a scholastic disputation when one defends one's position merely by showing that an opponent's view is even less credible.

In his replies to Arnauld, Descartes also qualified the apparent rationalism of his discussion of God. It invariably seemed to theologians who talked at length about the mysterious features of God that Cartesian philosophy relied on the limitations of human intelligence to decide what God could or could not do. Descartes explicitly rejects that suggestion, by turning the argument around, just as he was to do a year later for Henry More. On this occasion he rejects the idea that God might be able to create a space beyond the boundaries of the universe where, according to scholastics, there is no matter.

For my part, I do not think that we should ever say about something that God cannot do it. . . . I would not dare say that God cannot arrange that there would be a mountain without a valley or that one plus two would not be three. I merely claim that he has endowed me with a mind such that I cannot conceive of a mountain without a valley or that the sum of one plus two would not equal three, etc., and that such things imply a contradiction in my thought. I think that the same should be said of a space that is completely empty or of a nothing that is extended, and of a universe of things which is limited.   (v. 224)

Descartes could not conceive of a limit or boundary to the universe without thinking of matter beyond it. Nor could he conceive of a completely empty barrel that has the property of being extended, although the extension is predicated of nothing. 'For wherever there is extension, there is also necessarily a body' (v. 224). In the case of God, likewise, there is no suggestion that God's powers are limited by our conceptions. It is simply that there are logical limits to what we can or cannot conceive. If there are realities that exceed our powers of conception, we simply cannot say anything intelligible about them.[25]

Descartes also had an opportunity during his stay in Paris to visit Mersenne, who was still living at that time in the Minim friary near the

Palais Royal. He wrote to him in June or July, in his usual style of answering detailed questions about physics, although on this occasion the queries had been borrowed by Mersenne from some unidentified book that was critical of Descartes' optics.[26] However, Mersenne fell ill on 27 July and never recovered. He suffered from an abscess that was initially diagnosed as a false pleurisy, and his condition deteriorated during the following month. He died on 1 September 1648, at the age of sixty, surrounded by his confreres at the friary of Saint Francis of Paula, in central Paris, where he had lived for most of his religious life. Although Mersenne was still alive when Descartes left Paris, his health was evidently so precarious that, when Descartes arrived in Amsterdam on his return journey, he wrote to Picot to inquire about him.[27] By then, unfortunately, the Minim friar had died.

Descartes had little opportunity to reflect on Mersenne's contribution to his work and on the often-strained relationship between them. However, within a few months he realized that he no longer had someone in Paris to whom he could direct his queries and from whom he could get reliable information. Thus, when he wondered in June 1649 whether Pascal had ever done the experiment on the Puy-de-Dôme, he tried to find in Pierre Carcavi a plausible substitute for his erstwhile informer. In doing so, he had occasion to reflect on the services over many years provided by Mersenne.

I had the benefit, when the good Father Mersenne was alive, that although I never asked him about anything, I never failed to be informed in detail about everything that was exchanged among the learned. Thus, although he sometimes had questions for me, he repaid me very liberally with his replies by informing me about all the experiments which he or others had performed, about all the unusual inventions which had been found or sought, about all the new books that people thought were worthwhile, and finally about all the controversies which occurred among the learned.[28]

There was a real sense in which Mersenne was irreplaceable to Descartes. No one else enjoyed the same stability (having lived in a friary in the centre of Paris for thirty years), had contact with so many learned people both in France and in other European countries, or had the time and energy to write letters daily almost like a one-person clearing house for the dissemination of ideas. There were occasions when he caused controversies that might have been avoided, and, in the opinion of some correspondents, the depth of his intelligence did not always match the scope of his interests.[29] Once he had died, however, his personal failings seemed relatively insignificant in comparison to the service he had provided as a communicator between scholars, some of whom had no other means of sharing information.

There was closure in a different sense to the long-running mutual antipathy between Descartes and Pierre Gassendi during the Paris visit. These were two very different personalities whose philosophical perspectives made a meeting of minds difficult. However, they had at least two things in common – an abiding interest in new discoveries in natural philosophy and, at least officially, a common allegiance to the Catholic Church. A young priest named César d'Estrées arranged for the two protagonists to meet during Descartes' stay in Paris. The initial visit by Gassendi was reciprocated by a return visit from Descartes in the course of which, according to Baillet, the two philosophers 'renewed their protestations of eternal friendship with the greatest sincerity'.[30] There is no evidence of any further communication between Descartes and Gassendi, who was to outlive his compatriot by five years.

Descartes' correspondence with Princess Elizabeth during this period was, as usual, more revealing about his personal plans and his concerns about the political instability he was witnessing and, on her part, about the possibility of returning to The Hague if the war were concluded. Elizabeth told him in June about further health problems – on this occasion, a swelling in her arm that resulted from a surgeon cutting a nerve in the course of blood-letting.[31] Elizabeth was watching carefully the way in which the parliamentary forces were conducting their campaign against Charles I in England, and the unfolding of military events in Germany. Hope for the former and despair about the latter were equally relevant to the prospects for her return to Holland. Descartes' reply shows that he felt likewise at the mercy of uncontrollable events in France. In his case, however, the immediate reaction was flight, and a return to Egmond.

The *parlement* [of Paris] together with the other sovereign courts assemble every day at present to deliberate about certain decisions that they claim should be made about the management of finances. This is happening with the Queen's permission, so that it seems as if the whole affair will drag out for a long time, though it is difficult to imagine how it will conclude. . . . However, while waiting for a resolution, I would be better off taking myself to a country which is already at peace and, if these storms fail to clear soon, I plan to return to Egmond in six weeks or two months, and to remain there until the situation in France calms down. In the mean time, holding to my plans, with one foot in one country and the other in another, I find that my condition is very happy insofar as it is free.[32]

Later in the summer, Elizabeth thought that the situation in England and Germany seemed to be moving toward a 'crisis', and she was unable to make any immediate decisions about the future.[33] After his return to Holland, Descartes wrote to Elizabeth to confirm that he had followed through on his intuitions and had returned to the tranquility of northern Holland.

> For my part, thank God, I accomplished what I had to do in France. Although I do not regret having gone there, I am much happier now that I have left it again. I met no one there whose situation was such that I would envy them, and those who seemed to be most influential appeared to me most pitiable. I could not have gone there at a time that would better have helped me realize the happiness of a tranquil and retired life, and the richness of the most mediocre fortunes.[34]

Descartes had not clarified in advance of his visit why he felt obliged to travel to Paris in May 1648. The confusion about his royal pension and the allusion in a subsequent letter to Chanut to a visit that he was 'commanded to undertake' hardly explain the urgency or necessity of the travel. On previous occasions he had used such trips to visit his relatives in Brittany and to finalize legal arrangements about property. His maternal uncle, René Brochard, died at the beginning of August, leaving his estate to his wife and children. Descartes also had an interest in this will, and he authorized Picot to act on his behalf, even to the extent of intercepting letters from Brittany and Poitou that concerned his financial affairs and making decisions without forwarding them to Egmond unless it was absolutely necessary.[35] Disputes about the distribution of the estate continued for some time, because Descartes' brother, Pierre, claimed a bigger share than his legal entitlement. Pierre also offered to represent Descartes in the negotiations about the will in which he had a competing interest. This prompted the younger sibling to complain to Picot that Pierre had played the same trick when distributing their father's estate years earlier. On this occasion, even an otherworldly but somewhat impoverished philosopher could not 'accept a loss rather than plead his case' (v. 235). It prompted him to quip to Picot that Pierre's objection was 'like that of a wolf which complains that a sheep commits some injury to the wolf by fleeing, when it fears it is about to be eaten'.[36] Descartes seems to have planned his customary trip to Brittany to visit his relatives, and perhaps even to resolve problems about his inheritance. However, he cancelled those plans abruptly following the night of the barricades, and he left Paris suddenly on 27 August.[37] The wisdom of his decision was confirmed, on his return to Egmond, by news of continued political disturbances associated with the Fronde in September.[38]

This episode sparked a number of reflections about the reasons for the sudden change of mind and, just as much, a certain amount of brooding about where Descartes was likely to spend his remaining days. Having spent most of the winter in relative isolation in Egmond and having failed to keep his original promise to spend the winter of 1648–49 with Picot in Paris, he wrote to three different correspondents in February 1649 about the pressing issue of where he would live. He explained to Picot that he was living in 'the solitude of Egmond as peacefully and with as much contentment as he had ever enjoyed' (v. 280), and that his main reason for leaving France was the political instability that continued to disturb his native country. When such considerations were combined with what he described as 'a dread of ever undertaking another journey', Descartes acknowledged that he seemed destined 'to spend the rest of his life in Holland, that is, in a country which no longer possessed the attractions that it previously had to retain him' (v. 280).[39]

The public beheading of Charles I in London, 9 February 1649, was reported within a week to The Hague. Although the events that led up to this regicide were in many ways peculiar to England and Scotland, and were particularly influenced by the dominant personality of Oliver Cromwell, the climax of the confrontation between the English king and Parliament confirmed the general political uncertainty that was equally evident in France. Descartes wrote to Elizabeth on 22 February to offer his condolences on the execution of her uncle, which he describes obliquely as 'the fatal conclusion of the tragedies of England' (v. 281). In the course of claiming that such a public death is much more glorious than dying in one's bed, he refers once again to his own decision to remain in Egmond.

As far as I am concerned, since I am not attached to living in any particular place, I would have no difficulty in exchanging these provinces or even France itself for that country [i.e., the Palatinate] if I could find there an equally secure peace, even if I were drawn there by nothing more than the beauty of the countryside. However, there is no place in the world, no matter how primitive or inconvenient, where I would not think of myself as happy to pass the rest of my days if your Highness were there and I were able to serve you in some way. (v. 285)

Apart from the more factual comments on life in Egmond, this is another case in which literary style and deference to nobility induced Descartes to say much more than he really meant. He had no more intention of embarking on a new life in the German lands than he had of returning to his native France.

Descartes' letters to Chanut during the same month give a more accurate impression of how he felt about where he lived and the likelihood of change in the coming years. Five months after his return from France, he felt free to express his great disappointment about the visit, whereas immediately after his return, he had restrained himself from writing about the reasons for coming back suddenly to Egmond.

I was very glad not to write anything on my return, so that I would not appear to reproach those who invited me to France. I thought of them as friends who had invited me to dine at their table and, when I arrived at their house, I found their kitchen in disarray and their cooking pot turned upside down. That is why I came back here without saying a word about it, so as not to make them more vexed. However, this experience has taught me never to undertake another journey which relies on promises, even if they are written on parchment. And, although there is nothing to keep me here, except that I know of no other place I would prefer to be, I see that I am in great danger of spending the rest of my days here. For I fear that our commotions in France may die down soon and I am daily becoming more lazy, so that it would be difficult for me to decide to suffer the inconvenience of another journey.[40]

He hoped that Chanut might return to France in due course and pass through the United Provinces, and that they could arrange to meet then without Descartes having to travel a great distance.

Descartes' consistent hints about the political uncertainty of France, his desire for solitude, and his unwillingness to travel all suggested that he would remain in Egmond for the rest of his life. He had spent more time there than in any other place during his adult years, and, on balance, it had fewer disadvantages than other places he might live in. Somewhat unpredictably, however, the same correspondence with Chanut in which he made these feelings explicit was to result soon afterward in an invitation from Queen Christina to visit Stockholm.

Invitation to Sweden

When Gustavus Adolphus died at the Battle of Lützen in 1632, his throne was inherited by his only child, a six-year-old daughter named Christina. Christina had challenged the competence of her nurses to identify her sex at birth, since they had first identified her as a son and only later as a daughter. Although the precise reason for the misidentification remains unknown, Christina's subsequent life seemed to confirm the unusual circumstances of her birth with what was at least an ambiguous sexual orientation. Following the king's death, Sweden was ruled for twelve years by a five-person regency until, in December 1644, Christina reached her maturity and assumed her royal duties as queen. She began almost immediately to foster diplomatic initiatives with Mazarin against the Habsburgs, an otherwise improbable alliance between a Lutheran kingdom and a staunchly Catholic one. Pierre Chanut was thus favourably placed, in Stockholm, to have access to the queen and to respond to her newly acquired interest in all things French.

Chanut had given the queen an advance copy of the *Passions of the Soul*, which was not yet published, and he had evidently shared with Christina the lengthy letter about the sovereign good that Descartes had written in response to an earlier royal request. The queen seems to have been more interested in humanist culture, especially what she could learn of Greek and Roman civilization, rather than in the religious beliefs and observances of her Lutheran kingdom. Descartes unwittingly satisfied both these interests, and she wrote to him accordingly on 12 December 1648, when she was just twenty-two years old. She thanked him for his opinions about the sovereign good 'in the letter that you were kind enough to write to me, and also for the *Treatise on the Passions* that you enclosed with it' (v. 251). Chanut reported on the same date that he had accompanied the queen on a journey to visit copper and silver mines, during which she relieved her boredom by reading. The French resident had brought his own reading material on the journey – a copy of Descartes' *Principles* – and he entertained or distracted the queen by reading the Preface to her. This caught her attention, and she requested assistance in making sense of it. Chanut suggested that her librarian, Johann Freinsheim, might provide this service, but the queen insisted that Chanut should also help. The French resident thus found that one of his official duties in Stockholm was to read Descartes' *Principles* and tutor the queen so that she could understand it too. When reporting all this to Descartes, whom he mistakenly believed was still in Paris in December 1648, Chanut added ominously: 'Her Majesty is very interested in your fortune and in whether they are taking care of you in France. I do not know if, once she has acquired a taste for your philosophy, she may tempt you to come to Sweden' (v. 254). This was the first hint of a possible invitation. It was followed soon after by an official royal request.

Descartes' reply to Chanut, which he enclosed with a second letter that could be shown to the queen, helps to put in context his obsequious writing to Princess Elizabeth during the previous six years. The accompanying note to Chanut says: 'the enclosed letter is nothing more than a sterile compliment. Since I was not asked about any specific issue, I did not dare discuss any, out of respect . . . but I thought nevertheless that I had to write something [for the Queen].'[41] The letter to be shown to Christina, however, is so excessively adulatory that one is tempted to think that Descartes rarely meant anything he wrote to royal correspondents. He began his letter as follows: 'If I happened to be sent a letter from heaven and saw it descend from the clouds, I would not be more surprised and I could not receive it with more respect and veneration than I received the letter that it pleased your Majesty to write to me' (v. 294). This opening line was followed by waves of exaggerated compliments and references to the virtues of 'her majesty', who was so burdened by affairs of state and 'the common good of the whole earth' that it would be a great honour for Descartes to provide her with any service she requested. Having thus committed himself in general terms, Descartes concluded: 'I dare to protest here to your Majesty that she could not command me to do anything that is so difficult that I would not always be ready to do everything in my power to obey her command' (v. 294). It is the very same style that he had practised for years in corresponding with Elizabeth. On this occasion, however, although he thought of it only as a 'sterile compliment', he left himself open to a royal invitation to visit Sweden, to tutor this alleged paragon of virtue and wisdom.

Without realizing that their letters had crossed in the post, Chanut wrote again to Descartes (27 February 1649), inviting him on behalf of the queen to visit Sweden.[42] Given the uncertainty about where the French philosopher was living, it took some time for this letter to reach him in Egmond. Meantime, the queen got impatient and demanded that Chanut send another invitation on 6 March. There was a Swedish ship under the captaincy of Admiral Herman Fleming en route to Holland, and she asked Descartes to take advantage of the opportunity to return with Fleming to Stockholm. This plan suffered the same fate as the previous one. By the time Fleming arrived in person at Egmond, Descartes had not even received the royal letter of invitation, and he certainly was not yet ready to travel to Sweden.[43]

There followed another letter from Chanut (27 March) to indicate that the queen would like to have Descartes travel north in April, and that she guaranteed to have him back in Egmond before the winter if the Swedish climate proved to be too harsh for him. By this stage, the importunate queen began to show signs of accommodating the requirements of the philosopher, who was surely not obliged to respond to any of her demands. Descartes meantime replied to the earlier invitation with two letters to Chanut, one that he would be free to show to the queen and one in which Descartes expressed his true feelings. He was reluctant to make a short visit to Sweden, he said, for fear that it would not satisfy the queen, and he was especially reluctant to spend the winter in Stockholm. This alternative plan would suit him best for various reasons.

I would realize the following benefit – which I acknowledge is significant for a man who is no longer young and whom a twenty-year seclusion has rendered completely unaccustomed to fatigue – namely, that it would not be necessary for me to embark on my travels at the beginning of Spring or at the end of Autumn. I could also use the most secure and most convenient season which, I believe, will be towards the middle of Summer. Besides, I hope in the mean time to have the leisure to finalize a number of projects that are important to me.[44]

In this letter, which could be shown to the queen, Descartes makes it very clear that he plans to remain in Egmond until he receives further instructions by letter from Chanut. While Descartes was awaiting such confirmation, Admiral Herman Fleming turned up and his invitation had to be graciously declined.

In another letter of the same day, which was confidential to Chanut, Descartes was more honest about his reservations. 'I shall give you, if I may, the trouble of reading two of my letters on this occasion. For, assuming that you may possibly wish to show the other one to the Queen of Sweden, I have reserved for this one what I thought she does not need to see, namely, that I have much more difficulty in deciding to take this journey than I would have imagined myself' (v. 326). One reason was that few people understood his philosophy, even those with 'an excellent mind and a great desire for knowledge'. Christina, as a relatively young woman with little formal education, might fall into that category. The second reason was that, if the queen understood his opinions, they might not seem as attractive or innovative as she might have expected. He was hinting diplomatically that

Christina was more likely to be interested in novel fancies, as her study of ancient languages might suggest. In this context he acknowledged that 'those who boast of having secrets, for example in chemistry or judicial astrology, no matter how impudent and ignorant they may be, never fail to attract curious people who buy their very expensive impostures' (v. 327). What he could offer was so far removed from the kind of occult knowledge that stimulates wonder and desire in people that the queen might be disappointed.

The final reason for Descartes' reluctance was his great disappointment on his most recent visit to Paris, which was quoted earlier. He was worried that a visit to Sweden might simply be another cause for regret.

I do not imagine that anything similar will happen where you are. But the limited success of all the journeys that I have taken during the past twenty years makes me fear that, on this one, I shall only meet robbers who will strip me of everything, or that I shall be caught in a shipwreck which will rob me of my life. Nonetheless, that will not deter me if you judge that this incomparable queen persists in wishing to study my views. . . . But if that is not the case, and if she was simply experiencing a temporary curiosity, I beseech and urge you to arrange, without displeasing her, for me to be excused from this journey. (v. 329)

These parallel letters, like the earlier pair of similar letters on 26 February, show Descartes at his dissembling best. He writes publicly that he is anxious to serve the queen in any capacity that she may choose, and that he is ready 'to obey very exactly everything that is commanded on behalf of her Majesty' (v. 325). In private, he suspects that she may not understand his philosophy, may not find it exciting enough, and that her passing fancy is hardly a sufficient reason for someone in his state of health and semiretirement to undertake a long journey into the northern cold.

The alternative and much more attractive option for Descartes was to remain in Egmond and to complete a number of unfinished projects. One of those was the *Passions of the Soul*. This was closely connected with the unfinished sections of the *Principles*, in Parts V and VI of which he had hoped to include a discussion of living things and animals. His renewed interest in physiology during the previous year gave him reason to hope that he could complete both projects, and possibly publish his treatise on animals as a fully worked-out version of an earlier draft treatise on human nature.

Meantime, he also had inquiries from a new correspondent, the Cambridge Platonist Henry More.

Henry More

More wrote two letters to Descartes, 11 December 1648 and 5 March 1649, at a time when Brasset was reporting open hostilities between the royal court and the *parlement* in Paris.[45] More was interested primarily in Descartes' conception of immaterial realities, such as God and the human mind, and in his definition of matter as extension. The two questions were interrelated. The courteous replies sent from Egmond testify to Descartes' respect for the Cambridge Platonist and his acknowledgment of a kindred spirit in Christ's College.

Descartes was anxious to clarify that he conceived of God and angels as powers rather than as bodies of some kind. 'Thus it follows clearly that no incorporeal substances are, in a strict sense, extended. I conceive of them, rather, as certain powers or forces which, although they affect extended things, are not themselves extended because of that' (v. 270). This conception of God and angels was reinforced by a programmatic statement about how to conceive of God, and about the limitations of human thinking in attempting to formulate an adequate concept of God.

However, since I know that my intellect is finite and that God's power is infinite, I never determine anything about the latter. I consider only what I can perceive and what I cannot perceive, and I am very careful that my judgment never differs from my perception. Consequently, I boldly assert that God can do everything that I perceive as possible; however, I do not boldly deny, on the contrary, that he is capable of doing what is inconsistent with my conception. I say simply that that implies a contradiction.   (v. 272)

This was fundamentally the same reply that Descartes had given Arnauld the previous year.[46] It was a commentary not directly on our knowledge of God, but on the limitations of human understanding. It was also consistent with the answer that he had given Burman in April 1648, when he asked Descartes about the concept of matter. Descartes had told Burman that we cannot claim to have adequate knowledge of anything, even of bodies, and that we are constrained to work within the limitations of our concepts even if we recognize their limits.[47] This may have been a late discovery or acknowledgement on Descartes' part, but such intellectual humility was better late than never.

The other topic that attracted a lengthy reply to More was the status of animals. Here Descartes distinguished clearly, in explaining human actions, between (a) what he called the 'purely mechanical and bodily principle which depends exclusively on the force of animal spirits and the structure of the body' (v. 276), and which could be called a 'bodily soul', and (b) 'the incorporeal principle or mind, or that soul that I defined as a thinking substance' (v. 276). Evidently, Descartes had extended the scope of the first of these principles so that it functioned as an explanation of nearly all the activities of human beings, apart from thinking. The question about animals, then, was whether one needed to postulate a thinking substance in order to explain their activities. Descartes thought not. However, he also conceded that we cannot prove that there is no thought in the strict sense of the term in animals. Rather, when he examined 'what is most probable in this context' he found no reason in support of thought in animals. He could appreciate the reasons for thinking that they have sensations that are similar to ours, but there was one outstanding reason for resisting the idea that they have genuine thoughts. 'It has never been observed to date that any brute animal has achieved such a degree of perfection that it used genuine speech, that is, that it indicated anything by voice or signs which could be referred exclusively to thought rather than a natural impulse' (v. 278).

More's further queries about the nature of the body and its definition in terms of extension raised very few new questions. Descartes retained his conception of God and angels as powers rather than as bodies of an unusual kind. It was an important clarification of the direction in which this argument was developed: we conceive of our own minds more easily and more readily than we conceive of God, and we can conceive of the latter only by analogy with the former. Even the way in which God moves bodies can be conceived only by analogy with the way in which a human mind, inexplicably, moves a body. 'I concede that I find no idea in my mind, which represents the way in which God or an angel can move matter, which differs from that which shows me the way in which I am conscious of being able to move my body by my thought.'[48]

Descartes wrote these lines, in haste, in the middle of April 1649, excusing himself to More by saying that he would prefer to write quickly and inadequately rather than fail in courtesy by not replying at all. In the course of his reply he referred to his on-going research on animals, which was required for completion of what he called his 'philosophy' (i.e., the *Principles*). He was not certain that the results of his work would ever 'see the light of day' (v. 344). However, he hoped to publish during the summer of 1649 'a short treatise on the passions, from which it will be apparent how I think that, even in our own case, all the motions of our limbs which accompany our emotions are caused, not by the soul, but exclusively by the machinery of the body' (v. 344). He was indeed stretching to its limits the scope of a mechanical account of human activity.

A Treatise on the Passions

Descartes' book on human emotions was published in Amsterdam and Paris, toward the end of November 1649.[49] He had drafted a large part of it during the winter of 1645–46 and had sent it to Elizabeth. Elizabeth's reply included suggestions for improvement that, almost out of character, were accepted by the author. Even with additions and corrections, however, this still amounted to only about two-thirds of the final text. Descartes made a clean copy of the revised text and sent it to Chanut, with permission to show it to Queen Christina. At about the same time, he had a request from an unidentified correspondent who had met him on his trip to Paris, had heard about the essay on the passions, and had apparently offered to assist the author in getting the final version into print.[50] Descartes explained that his reluctance to release the manuscript had nothing to do with an unwillingness to serve his reading public. He wanted to keep the essay confidential as long as possible, partly because it had been composed originally 'only to be read by a princess whose mind is so above the norm that she easily understands what seems most difficult to our doctors' (xi. 324). However, Descartes relented and promised 'to revise this writing on the passions, to add what I think is necessary to make it more intelligible. After that, I shall send it to you and you may do what you wish with it' (xi. 324).

In the spring of 1649, Descartes also sent a copy of the revised manuscript to Clerselier in Paris. Clerselier advised him that it was too difficult for ordinary readers. This prompted a further revision and plans for the addition of most of the material that was published as Part III of the book.[51] When he wrote to Clerselier, in April 1649, he probably still had done little more than think about the additions that remained to be written.

As regards the *Treatise on the Passions*, I do not expect it to be printed until I have arrived in Sweden. For I neglected to revise it and to add the things that you thought were missing, which would have increased its size by a third. It will contain three parts, of which the first will be about the passions in general and, as required, the nature of the soul, etc.; the second part will be about the six primitive passions, and the third part about all the others.[52]

Descartes seems to have been procrastinating at this stage, and to have been concerned primarily with a decision about going to Sweden – whether he would go at all and, if so, when would be the best time to travel.

His importunate correspondent of the previous year wrote again, in July 1649, bemoaning the fact that 'it has been such a long time that you have made me wait for your *Treatise on the Passions* that I am beginning to lose hope of getting it' (xi. 324).[53] This correspondent had hoped to facilitate Descartes' ambition to complete the unfinished parts of the *Principles*, and he suggested that, if he were to publish this essay, it might prompt those who had access to public funds or private donors to provide the money required to complete the necessary experiments.[54] One reason for Descartes' reluctance to part with the text of the *Passions*, which his correspondent could not have known about, was that he was worried about publishing a book that he had previously shown to Queen Christina without dedicating it to her and without her permission to make public something that he had shared with her as if with a privileged reader. This scruple was resolved by writing to the queen's librarian and asking him to inquire discreetly about whether she might take offence.[55] Once that was cleared, Descartes replied to his anxious editor that he was not so lazy that he feared the challenge that would result if he had adequate funds for his scientific work. However, he was now able to report that he had worked on the revisions he had promised and was ready to release the work for publication. He thus wrote on 14 August 1649, two weeks before his departure for Sweden:

I confess that it took more time to revise the little treatise that I am sending you than it previously required to write it. Nonetheless, I added very little to it, and I changed nothing in the argument, which is so simple and brief that it will show that my plan was not to explain the passions as an orator or even as a moral philosopher but only as a natural philosopher. I foresee, therefore, that this treatise will not do any better than my other writings. Although its title may possibly attract more people to read it, only those who take the trouble to study it carefully can find it satisfactory. Such as it is, I place it in your care.   (xi. 326)

It seems as if there was another short delay before the manuscript was finally dispatched.[56] It found its way to Louis Elzevier in Amsterdam sometime between August and November 1649. Elzevier printed copies for the Dutch market and also sent copies to Paris with an amended title page, to be published officially by Henry La Gras. It was translated into Latin by 'H.D.M.' (Henri Desmarets) and was published posthumously by the same Dutch printer the following year.

The comments in the anonymous letters apparently addressed to Descartes in the Preface to the volume were accurate. They linked the *Treatise on the Passions* with the unfinished *Principles*, in particular with the writing on animals and human nature that Descartes wished to complete. The *Treatise on the Passions* was thus a foretaste of what might have been realized if Descartes had had the financial resources to pursue his research project and if he had made the progress that he thought, less plausibly, was being inhibited only by a lack of observations and experiments. It is difficult to estimate how successful that project might have been had Descartes lived longer, in a more suitable research environment. Apart from such guesswork, the context in which the *Passions* should be read was captured perfectly by Descartes' prefatory letter. There was nothing unusual about a philosopher writing a book on the passions. However, it was distinctive to approach the topic as a '*physicien*', that is, as a natural philosopher or, in today's language, as a scientist. In doing so, Descartes came as close as he had ever come to addressing directly the question of how mind and body interact.

Emotions or, in the traditional language he chose to use, passions were classified by Descartes as a special kind of feeling. The nearest equivalent were the sensations we have when we are affected by external stimuli (such as hearing a sound) or the internal sensations we have when stimulated by our own bodily conditions (such as feeling hunger or pain). The most characteristic feature of such sensations, for Descartes, was that the subject is not in control of what is experienced. Apart from very unusual situations, one cannot simply decide not to feel pain or not to hear loud noises. In that sense, the subject is passive, and the sensations in question are therefore 'passions'. Descartes wanted to maintain the close connection between such sensations and emotions by also classifying emotions as passions. The only difference, then, between emotions and other kinds of feeling or sensation was that emotions are stimulated by what Descartes called 'animal spirits'.[57] Since one of the primary functions of animal spirits was to transmit signals throughout the body – a function performed by the nervous system in more recent medical theory – the emotions were

understood as feelings that a subject passively experiences because of
information that is transmitted to the brain from relevant stimuli.

This suggests a distinction between primitive or primary emotions and
others that are either more complex or that result from combinations of
simple emotions. This approach also relied on a distinction between some
emotions that are innate in human beings from birth, and others that are
learned or acquired in some way. For good measure, Descartes included
at this stage of his discussion a comment on the function of the passions.
He thought of them as dispositions, built into our nature, which help us
to seek things that are naturally good for us and to avoid things that are
naturally harmful. 'The function of all the passions consists in this alone:
they dispose the soul to choose things which nature determines are ben
eficial to us and to persist in this choice. Besides, the same movement of
spirits which usually causes such emotions disposes the body to the movements which implement those choices' (xi. 372).[58] Despite Descartes'
famous objection about not reading God's wishes from nature, he was
evidently relying on a teleological account of human nature at this point.
He thought of human nature as being equipped with innate guides to what
is harmful or beneficial, and, as he had explained in the *Meditations*, he
thought of the senses as having a function that is accommodated to that
design.[59]

This natural teleology has to be exploited even in the youngest children,
at birth. Otherwise their survival would be at risk. Descartes thinks of
the newborn baby as having a set of innate dispositions that protect the
child and guide it naturally during its early years. Feelings of pain help
it avoid harmful things, and feelings of pleasure guide it to things which,
for the most part, are beneficial. This inbuilt guidance system would not
be enough for survival unless it were reinforced by some kind of internal
motivation toward the satisfaction of primitive needs. The emotions or
passions serve this function. Descartes thinks of love, for example, as
being one of the most basic emotions, which becomes operational as soon
as a child begins to be fed.

It seems to me that the first passions that our soul had, when it began to be joined to
our body, must have occurred when some blood, or some other juice which entered
the heart, was a more appropriate food than usual for maintaining the heat in the heart
which is the principle of life. This caused the soul to join itself willingly to this food,
that is, it loved it. At the same time, the spirits flowed from the brain to the muscles that
were able to press or agitate the parts of the body from which that food had come to

the heart, to cause them to send more of it there. . . . That is why this same movement of spirits has always accompanied the passion of love since then.   (xi. 407–8)

This describes an elementary feedback mechanism by which a young infant is motivated by a naturally endowed primitive feeling to seek things that support its survival. The same natural disposition works in the opposite direction for avoiding harms, and the relevant passion in that case is called hatred.

The final essential thread in this account of emotions is the Cartesian theory of conditioning. If someone's emotional life remained as undeveloped as it was at birth, with warm positive feelings toward mother's milk and an aversion to strong tastes, it would be impossible to develop the Cartesian 'physical' theory into a theory of human emotions. However, Descartes assumes that imagination and memory provide a link between innate responses, which are present from birth, and other emotional responses that are learned as one develops. Those that are innate are reinforced by practice, so that as a child grows into adulthood he or she continues to experience emotional responses that duplicate those of infancy.

Our soul and our body are so linked that, if we have once joined some bodily action with a certain thought, one of them does not occur subsequently without the other also occurring. We see this, for example, in those who have taken some medicine with great revulsion when they were ill, and cannot afterwards eat or drink anything that has a similar taste without immediately feeling the same revulsion. Likewise, they cannot think of their revulsion from medicines without the same taste returning in their thought.   (xi. 407)

This innate connection between specific thoughts or feelings and bodily states tends to continue indefinitely unless changed by new connections that displace them. However, the primitive connections can also be expanded to include novel relations between mental states and bodily states, even in the case of stimuli that have no natural connection with the feelings they trigger. Descartes had noticed that animals can be conditioned to respond to novel stimuli, long before Pavlov studied the same phenomenon in the twentieth century and gave his name to it. 'This is so certain that if you whipped a dog five or six times to the sound of a violin, I believe that it would begin to howl and run away when it hears that music again' (i. 134). Evidently, the same kind of conditioning works in the case of human beings. 'If people have at some time in the past enjoyed dancing while a certain tune was being played, then the desire to dance will return to them as soon as they hear a similar tune again. On the contrary, if others have never heard the music for a galliard without falling into some misfortune, they would infallibly become sad as soon as they heard it again' (i. 134).

There is one major assumption at the heart of this theory, something that Descartes cannot explain and that he has to accept as a natural fact: that there are relatively few, primitive, innate connections between certain mental states and certain bodily states, and that the reality of mind-body interaction depends essentially on that natural condition. Once that is accepted, Descartes' account of the emotions presupposes only that human beings are capable of acquiring new connections between specific thoughts and bodily states. This extra claim is supported by the experience of animal conditioning. Since each individual's emotional responses are determined by his or her own personal history, it is not surprising that different people react very differently to the same situation. Descartes gives examples of people who, as children, were frightened of cats or got a headache from the smell of roses, and for whom cats or roses remained forever after a trigger for aversion (xi. 429). Given the diversity of human experiences, the general principle that he presupposed had to acknowledge significant variations among individuals. 'I shall be content to repeat the principle on which everything that I have written about the causes of the passions rests: that our soul and body are so linked that, once we have joined some bodily action with a specific thought, neither of them occurs to us subsequently without the other also occurring, and that it is not always the same actions which are joined with the same thoughts' (xi. 428).

The *Passions of the Soul* was not exactly the completion of the *Principles* that Descartes had hoped to achieve. He was not in a position to realize that such a project would have required better optical instruments, such as a microscope, and significant advances in both chemistry and physiology, which were simply not available in 1649. Instead, the *Passions* brought his discussion of conditioning to the attention of the public, and it also provided his best attempt yet to construct a theory of how mind and body interact. The residual dualism of a mind and body remained unchallenged.[60] He had reached the limits of his theory of animal functioning. Any further progress would have required a reconsideration of the dualism of mind and body that he had defended in the *Meditations*. That this was the natural next step was more likely to have been noticed by his critics than by his supporters. For example, the Minim friar Father Maignan wrote from

Rome (in September 1649), asking how Descartes explained intellectual and voluntary actions. 'Knowing well that the actions of the senses, both internal and external, consist only in local motions, as Mr. Descartes and Mr. Hogelande explain, does the same explanation apply (to intellectual and voluntary actions), as some people believe here?'[61]

Descartes was not prepared to follow that line of inquiry, at least not publicly. Had he done so, he would also have provided support for the worst fears of his critics – that he was really an 'atheist' in disguise.

Death in Sweden

A man born in the gardens of Touraine ... cannot easily leave this country [the United Provinces] to go and live in a country of bears, among the rocks and the ice. (April 1649)[1]

I T is difficult to know why Descartes ever went to Sweden. One possible reason is that he could not resist the temptation of being honoured by Queen Christina, and that he was led to a premature death by vanity. Had he been asked directly, he would hardly have accepted that interpretation of events. He might have argued instead that he was predestined to die in Sweden and that it was impossible for him to avoid his fate. These twin themes, of destiny and the passions, were among the subjects of his philosophical reflections during the summer of 1649, when he was struggling with competing desires of unequal strength – a dominant desire to remain in Egmond, and a reluctant willingness to travel to Stockholm.

During those months, Descartes was editing the *Passions of the Soul* and was drafting the material that appeared in the final part of that book. One of the topics that arose naturally in that context was the influence of fortune in human lives. He had nothing but contempt for the suggestion that there is some kind of world power called 'fortune' that determines our fate and over which we have no influence. He wrote in the *Passions*: 'The common opinion that there is a fortune which is external to us, and which determines as it wishes what events happen or do not happen, should be rejected completely' (xi. 439). Such a 'power' was one of those mysterious scholastic entities against which he had argued for almost two decades. He suggested instead that a Christian philosopher should accept the universal influence of divine Providence. However, this Providence was also bound to appear, from the perspective of human beings, as an equally immutable fate. According to Descartes, we have no way of knowing what God has decided about future events, and we can do absolutely nothing to modify the effects of divine Providence. This amounted to substituting a kind of Christian fatalism for the mysterious determinism of fortune.

Descartes had endorsed this general principle in response to one of his correspondents who was a soldier and who had asked his opinion about the wisdom of remaining in the army. He had little respect for the life of a soldier, so that the merits of such a career could not decide the question. 'Idleness and licentiousness are the two primary motives which attract most men to that career now.'[2] He considered instead the relative danger associated with army life, and speculated that the life of a soldier was no more dangerous than that of a civilian because all human lives are equally exposed to unpredictable deaths.

We should be prepared to accept death without regret, whenever it comes, because it can come at any moment. . . . if we eat a morsel of bread, it may be poisoned; if we walk along the street, a tile may fall from some roof which would flatten us, and so on for other eventualities. That is why, since we live among so many inevitable dangers, it seems to me that wisdom does not prevent us from exposing ourselves also to the danger of war, when a good and just cause obliges us to take part in it.   (v. 557–8)

Given our inability to control natural events and the apparent predetermination of divine Providence, Descartes argued that the only thing within our control is what depends on our own will.[3] Our decisions, therefore, must be made within the limited space made available by our knowledge and our desires, and these are the only things for which we can be held morally responsible. That is the conclusion to which he was drawn in the *Passions*: 'we can be praised or blamed justifiably only for those actions that depend on free will' (xi. 445).

This Cartesian analysis locates each person within a divinely controlled, naturally determined, but unpredictable universe. The scope of our control is limited to estimating the relative probability of different events based on previous experience, and then adjusting our own desires to coincide as much as possible with what we believe will benefit us. To illustrate this point, Descartes uses the example that was uppermost in his mind at the time, that of taking a potentially hazardous journey.

For example, assume that we have some business to conduct in a place to which we could travel by two different routes, one of which is usually much safer than the other. Although the decree of Providence may be such that, if we take the safer route, we will certainly be robbed on the journey while, on the contrary, we could take the other route without any danger, we should still not be indifferent about the choice we make, nor should we fall back on the immutable fatality of this decree. Reason dictates that we choose the route that is usually safer, and our desire should be satisfied by doing so, no matter what evil may befall us.   (xi. 439–40)

Although Descartes does not mention, in this context, the fact that we have no way of knowing the decrees of divine Providence, his argument assumes such ignorance on our part. He concludes, therefore, that we should always follow what seems, on the evidence available, to be the most reasonable course of action. In doing so, we govern our own desires in accordance with our reason, even if the unpredictable outcome turns out to be worse than what would have resulted from a different choice.

This framework of divine Providence and natural determinism still left some room for the interplay of human emotions and desires, which was the primary topic of *The Passions of the Soul*. One desire that was readily recognized by anyone familiar with royal families and the trappings of court life was the desire to be esteemed by others. According to the *Passions*, self-esteem is based on goods such as 'intelligence, beauty, riches, honours, etc. which are usually valued more in proportion to their scarcity among people' (xi. 449). Descartes defined vanity or pride as unjustified self-esteem. He conceded that vain people might have some genuine basis for thinking highly of themselves. However, they would still fall into the vice of vanity if they thought more highly of themselves than their achievements deserved.[4]

Descartes' communications with other scholars during the previous two decades do not suggest that he suffered fools gladly. Quite the opposite. When engaged in controversy, he tended to present himself as merely defending his reputation, searching for the truth impartially, or being dutiful toward those whom God had established as lawful governors. There was no hint of recognition, on his part, that he was haughty, arrogant, or excessively sensitive to criticism. Thus if he had been pressed for an explanation of the manifestly unreasonable decision to spend the winter in Sweden, in relatively poor health, Descartes would almost certainly have offered a morally commendable motive for an adventure that bordered on recklessness. For example, he might have appealed to the concept of duty. Yet it is unclear how an ageing French philosopher could have had any genuine duty to provide philosophy lessons to a foreign queen who showed little understanding or appreciation of his work. He might have combined duty with friendship by referring to Chanut, who had asked him almost as a special favour to indulge the queen's whims and, perhaps, to help cement the cordial diplomatic relations that were developing between the two kingdoms of France and Sweden. Whatever reason he might have offered, he cannot have relied on the penchant for travel that he displayed in his youth; it had been clear for quite some time that he wished to avoid onerous journeys, especially by sea.

In these circumstances, it is difficult to avoid the conclusion that a strong desire to be honoured – almost anywhere, by any royal person – was part of his motivation. There were signs of this already in 1647, when he was so disappointed with the almost meaningless parchment he had received from Paris. His threat to leave Holland had similar connotations of regret that his philosophical genius was not adequately acknowledged by Dutch theologians. In fact, during much of his life he seemed to complain of a failure by others, in France and in the United Provinces, to appreciate his contributions to philosophy. Now perhaps, in the far North, the Queen of Sweden might eventually provide the public recognition that he thought he deserved. She might also provide the financial security that had eluded him for so long, and which he may have considered even more necessary with his advancing age.

The Reluctant Traveller

None of these considerations, however, was enough to persuade Descartes to make a firm decision. He was extremely reluctant to leave Egmond, even if the tentative plan was merely to visit Stockholm for a relatively short time and then return to his refuge in Holland. He gives the impression of having agreed to accept Queen Christina's invitation in April 1649, when he wrote to Brasset (in The Hague) and to Clerselier and Picot (who were both in Paris) that he had reached a decision. He pondered the various options available at the time. It was impossible to return to France in the short term, until the political disturbances associated with the Fronde were resolved, and Descartes had no way of knowing then that such a resolution was going to take another four years. His preferred option was to remain in Egmond – which, 'although it does not have as much honey as God promised the Israelites, it is plausible to think that it has more milk.'[5] When he wrote to Clerselier the same day, his provisional decision was qualified by continuing uncertainty and a distinct lack of enthusiasm for the projected journey. 'I will just tell you that . . . I have decided to embark on the journey to which I was invited by the recent letters, although initially I was more opposed to it than you could imagine.'[6] Even when the decision was made in principle, it still remained to agree on a suitable time to travel and, especially, to plan his return to the United Provinces within a relatively short time. Since Picot had provided a suitable valet on his last journey to Paris, he renewed that request, asking if he could borrow the services of Picot's current valet, whom he had spotted during the Paris visit. Henry Schluter was a German who (according to Baillet) knew some Latin, French, and Flemish in addition to his native language, and he had attended college for a period. Picot had no objection to lending him to Descartes for a period of six months to a year.[7]

Meantime, Chanut arrived in The Hague on the end of May 1649, on his way to Paris.[8] He planned to report to the regent on his diplomatic work in Sweden, to get new instructions for co-operation between Sweden and France, and he obviously envisaged returning to Stockholm sometime during the year, since his wife and family had remained there. Descartes had tipped off a number of people to watch out for Chanut's arrival and to alert him so that he would not miss the opportunity of discussing his own plans with someone who had extensive experience of living among 'the rocks and the ice'. It is not clear whether they met in The Hague or in Egmond, but, whatever the venue, the two exiled Frenchmen managed to discuss their apparently shared destiny. Descartes wrote to Elizabeth, a week later, to say that he was relieved by Chanut's account of life in Sweden. However, the reluctant traveller seems to have been still hoping to escape his fate if Queen Christina failed to confirm that she required his services. Despite the earlier decision, therefore, he decided not to leave immediately but to await confirmation of the original invitation from Stockholm.

I persist in the plan to go to Sweden, on condition that the queen continues to show that she wants me to go there. Mr. Chanut . . . when passing through here eight days ago on his way to France, spoke to me so positively about this marvellous queen that the journey there no longer seems as long or as troublesome as it did previously. However, I shall not depart until I receive once more some news from that country, and I shall try to wait for Mr. Chanut's return so that I can travel with him, for I hope that they will send him back to Sweden.[9]

This ambivalence continued for three months. Meantime, Descartes also thought of another excuse for not going to Sweden – it might reflect poorly on Queen Christina if she were to devote too much time to study and if she associated publicly with a Roman Catholic in an explicitly Lutheran kingdom. Having mentioned some of these difficulties to Chanut, Descartes decided to write to the queen's librarian, Freinsheim, and to ask him about his new scruples. As usual, he declared that he was ready to embark immediately, at the queen's command, but he needed to satisfy himself once more about some residual reservations.

Mr. Chanut will confirm that, before he arrived here, I had prepared my few travel accoutrements, and that I tried to overcome all the difficulties that a man like me faces, at my age, when he has to leave his usual residence to undertake such a long journey. However, despite the fact that he found me thus prepared to depart and that I also found that he was willing to use all kinds of reasons to persuade me to travel, in case I had not decided to do so, nevertheless, because he did not tell me that there was an order from her majesty to command me to make haste and that much of the summer has still to come, I mentioned a difficulty to him which he thought it best that I should ask you to clarify.[10]

Having explained this new 'difficulty' – about not compromising the good name of the queen by association with someone who had been involved in a number of public controversies with Protestant theologians – Descartes claimed, somewhat implausibly, that he was still ready to leave immediately, even without waiting for Chanut's return, if the queen wished him to do so. Once Freinsheim replied toward the end of July, confirming the queen's interest in having the French philosopher come to Stockholm, the unfortunate Descartes had exhausted all his remaining excuses. He now felt obliged to keep his indiscreet promise.

During this period of procrastinating, Descartes continued observing variations in barometric pressure, and he wrote to Carcavi, in Paris, asking if there was any news from the Auvergne about the experiment that had reportedly been done by Périer at Pascal's request. As already indicated, the famous experiment had been concluded on 22 September 1648, and it was published in Paris in November of the same year. Had Mersenne still been alive, he would surely have arranged to have a copy of the results sent to Descartes, even without waiting for him to request it. Carcavi provided the next best thing, a reasonably detailed and accurate description of the experiment and its results.[11]

In his attempt to fill Mersenne's role, Carcavi was bold enough to mention once again the strained relationship between Descartes and Roberval and, at the instigation of the Paris mathematician, to request a truce.

The same gentleman [i.e., Roberval] also told me, because you call him your enemy, that he never had any other intention except to honour you. He has also asked me to write to you, formally, as I do below ... in the hope of re-establishing peace between you, which may have been unwittingly damaged by the good Father Mersenne who sometimes understood things a bit crudely and often wrote about them in a way that reflected his own understanding rather than the way things were in fact. The same Mr. Roberval told me, therefore, that if you call him your enemy because he sought you out to tell you about something that seemed not quite right in your *Geometry* ... that this enmity was not reciprocal, because it survives only in your belief about him, since he is willing in all other ways to respect your achievements and status, as he has told you himself face to face.[12]

This apparently genuine attempt at a reconciliation was rebuffed by Descartes with the contemptuous comment that he never paid those who displeased him the honour of esteeming them worthy of his hatred! In the case of Roberval, and the suggestion that Mersenne might have been partly responsible for their quarrel, he was very explicit.

I can also assure you that the Reverend Father Mersenne did nothing to influence my judgment about the animosity of the said Mr. Roberval. Instead, he always hid it as much as the laws of friendship allowed. It was Roberval himself who declared his animosity so explicitly and in words that were so rash and so conceited that, if he now speaks in a different manner, I have reason to think that his only motivation is to be less suspected of calumny when he says something unfavourable about me. For the same reason, I want everyone to know how annoyed and angry he is with me. He may be someone whose profession requires him to appear learned. However, having attacked me five or six times to show how learned he is, he forced me on as many occasions to discover his mistakes, as he does once again with his three objections that you have taken the trouble to include in your letter.[13]

Although he could not respond positively to the peace overtures from Roberval, Descartes was able to inform Carcavi that the Latin version of his *Geometry*, which had been translated by Van Schooten, had finally appeared. Unfortunately, Van Schooten's Latin was not very stylish, and since Descartes was unable 'to see it before publication without being obliged to change everything in it' (v. 392), he excused himself completely from the work involved and tolerated its publication without any corrections.[14]

After what seemed like a relatively quiet summer in 1649, with little new work to report and most of his efforts devoted to revising the *Passions of the Soul* before releasing it for publication, Descartes eventually made final preparations for his departure to Stockholm.

Leaving Egmond

Descartes mentioned in passing, when writing to Chanut in March 1649, the danger of losing his life at sea in a shipwreck.[15] This was more than a casual reference to the dangers associated with sea travel in the seventeenth century, because he wrote about the same concern as he was about to embark for Sweden at the end of August. Before leaving, he took time to review his outstanding debts and arrange for their repayment if he were to die en route. As usual, he charged Picot with his financial affairs. 'Since I am about to depart for Stockholm, and since I may die on the journey, I am writing this letter to advise you that I borrowed money on many occasions from Mr. Anthony Studler van Zurck....' (v. 407)[16] These letters had the formal character and legal effect of a last will and testament. 'If God takes me from this world, he [Van Zurck] may contact my brothers and advise them' about his legal claim on Descartes' estate. He then bids what reads like a final adieu to Picot, very reminiscent of his final message to Beeckman before travelling to Denmark in 1619. 'I pray that God may keep you in good health for a long time, and I assure you that I have now and shall continue to have a very sincere and very perfect affection for you as long as my soul retains some memory of the things of this world.'[17]

Descartes also turned his attention to one of his other stalwart friends of many years, Cornelis van Hogelande, to whom he entrusted a trunk containing some of his personal papers. These were mostly letters written by Descartes' correspondents. Since the original authors might not agree to have them read by others, Descartes advised that, in the event of his death, Van Hogelande should burn all of them – with one exception. He should preserve the letters written by Voetius to Mersenne, when Voetius inquired secretly and mischievously about Descartes' alleged atheism, and he would find them 'inserted into the lid of the trunk'. Descartes instructed: 'I want them preserved for use as a protection against his calumnies' (v. 410). However, Descartes left the final decision about all the other material to his trusted Dutch friend. 'You may also read all the other letters or allow them to be read by some discreet friends before burning them, or you may even burn only those that you choose. For I leave the whole matter to your discretion' (v. 410).

Having made these detailed arrangements, Descartes travelled on 1 September 1649 to Amsterdam, where he met some local friends who gathered to wish him bon voyage. One of them, Bloemaert, arranged to have painted quickly a portrait of the departing philosopher.[18] Having made his farewells, he travelled by sea with Picot's valet and arrived in Stockholm in early October.[19] Although Chanut was still in Paris, he had left letters with his wife, Penelope, to welcome Descartes to Sweden and to offer him accommodation in his home.[20] Accordingly, Descartes lodged with Madame Chanut and her two children, and began almost immediately to instruct the queen in Cartesian philosophy.[21] His original reservations about the journey were unfortunately confirmed soon after his arrival. Christina had invited a number of scholars from different European centres to come to Sweden, where she had vague ambitions to found an academy that could exploit the library that had been looted by Swedish troops from Rudolph II's Prague. They included Isaac Vossius (1618–1689) – a prominent Dutch philologist – who accepted her invitation, and Claude Saumaise (1588–1653), who rejected it. There was a serious danger that the visiting scholars would be exhibited merely as ornaments to her majesty's ego, and that they would find little incentive or opportunity to engage in genuine scholarly work.

Christina arranged for Descartes to provide philosophy discussions in her library at five o'clock in the morning. After the first two sessions, he was already concerned about the wisdom of the whole enterprise, and he began to make plans to leave as soon as he could extricate himself diplomatically from a very disappointing situation. While he could hardly express these reservations to people he barely knew in Stockholm, he felt free to reveal his more personal concerns to his trusted correspondent in the German lands, Princess Elizabeth.

The queen is very much taken with the study of languages. However, since I do not know if she has ever learned anything about philosophy, I cannot judge how much she will acquire an interest in it nor whether she will be able to devote much time to it or, consequently, whether I will be able to satisfy her or be of any use to her. Her great enthusiasm for learning languages motivates her, at present, to study Greek especially, and to gather many ancient books.[22]

Descartes considered telling the queen more or less frankly about his reservations and, in that way, he thought he could at least satisfy the demands of duty. That might also have provided him, he thought, with an opportunity 'to return so much sooner to my solitude, without which it is difficult to make any progress in the search for truth' (v. 430). Whatever might happen, Descartes thought that nothing could persuade him to remain in Sweden beyond the following summer. Thus, within a week of his arrival, Descartes was already planning for his departure as soon as possible. Elizabeth reinforced his conviction by agreeing that even the queen could not keep him in Sweden, and by discussing the possibility of his departure 'this winter'.[23]

Queen Christina, however, had different plans. She thought up various inducements to change his mind, such as naturalizing him as a Swedish subject or inducting him into the Swedish nobility. This seems to have had the opposite effect to what was intended and to have made him even more anxious to depart, to France, to the Palatinate, or to the United Provinces, and to consider an earlier departure date, such as January 1650 – exploiting the excuse that this was a suitable time for sea voyages from Sweden.[24] Christina must have noticed the reluctance that even Descartes could no longer camouflage by his customary diplomatic language. She therefore excused him from all court duties, apart from giving her philosophy lessons, and she recommended that he take four to six weeks to become acquainted with his new country of residence. That meant that, beginning about the middle of October, Descartes was left to reside with Madame Chanut and her family, with no significant role at the royal court, and with little opportunity to pursue the incomplete projects that he had brought with him from Holland. The loneliness and bleakness of his situation must have been too much even for someone who notoriously relished the solitude of Egmond.

One slight source of relief was that, among the letters from Chanut that awaited his arrival in Stockholm, there was an indirect invitation from Pascal to continue the barometric observations that they had been making in parallel. If Chanut and Descartes were to co-operate, there would then be three complementary sets of observations, in Stockholm, Paris, and the Auvergne.[25] Since Chanut was still in Paris, Descartes had to assume responsibility for these observations until the end of 1649. He was also distracted temporarily from boredom when he heard about the publication of *The Passions of the Soul*, in late November, which Brasset and his daughter were happy to receive as a gift through the intervention of Van Zurck.[26] Descartes arranged with his friends in Leiden and Paris to distribute further copies of the new book on his behalf. The beneficiaries included the chancellor in Paris, the duke of Luynes, Abbé d'Estrées (who had arranged the reconciliation with Gassendi), Habert de Montmor, and others.

Descartes had occasion to meet the French ambassador to Poland, Viscount de Brégy, who had come to Stockholm on a diplomatic mission in September and was thus one of the more obvious members of the expatriot French community in that city. The exiled philosopher seems to have appreciated his company. However, he was cautious enough before accepting his friendship to inquire about him with Picot, to whom he explained that he could give his reply confidentially without mentioning the name of the person about whom they were corresponding.[27] When the time came for Brégy's return to Poland, he set sail for Danzig in particularly bad weather. Descartes told him about the local celebrations in honour of the queen's twenty-third birthday on 18 December. They sang a Te Deum, both in honour of her majesty's birthday and in thanksgiving for the restoration of peace throughout Europe. Descartes mentions, in a postscript, that he is enclosing a few verses for a ballet to be danced the next day, when the celebrations were expected to continue.[28]

One cannot avoid the impression that Descartes was completely out of his natural environment in this context. He was living as a guest of Madame Chanut, in the extremely cold and dark Swedish winter. He had little time or perhaps even motivation to do any serious intellectual work. His company was confined to a few French natives, about whom he felt so hesitant that he wrote to Picot in Paris to check their status. As an ultimate indignity, he was cajoled into participating in the frippery of the Swedish court despite his protests for many years that the avoidance of such social blandishments was his main reason for leaving Paris.

The situation improved significantly with the eventual return on 20 December of Chanut, who had meantime been promoted to the rank of ambassador. The royal court was riven with jealousy between Swedish nobles and foreign scholars, and despite attempts by various French nationals who tried to persuade Descartes to settle in Stockholm, their entreaties convinced him merely to defer his departure until early summer.[29] When asked about a new book by a Jesuit priest, Gregory of Saint Vincent – which discussed the impossible aim of squaring a circle – Descartes commented on Roberval's alleged refutation of the work.[30]

I am currently in a country that is so far away that I have no hope here even of seeing the writings that you ask me about. Apart from the fact that it would be difficult to do so here, I would not have much free time to study them. For that reason, if you write to Father Gregory of Saint Vincent, please assure him of my very humble service. Let him know on my behalf that, although I do not approve of his squaring the circle, nevertheless I do not believe that Mr. Roberval has enough intelligence to refute it. Thus, as long as he does not have a stronger adversary than Roberval, he will not find it difficult to defend his position.[31]

This is obviously one of those polite forms of refusal that cannot be taken literally. It was probably true that Descartes could not have located such an obscure work in Stockholm. However, the main reasons for not consulting it were that he had lost interest in mathematical work many years earlier and, even more importantly, that he knew that all attempts to square the circle were doomed to failure. When he said that he was too busy, he was simply exploiting the courtesies of politeness. He may also have been signalling a significant decline in his intellectual energies. One thing is obvious, however, about this reply; he grasped the opportunity presented, once again, to scorn the mathematical abilities of Roberval.

The fact that Descartes was not very busy during the winter of 1649–50 is clear from his letter to the French ambassador to Poland, in January 1650. He had given the queen her early morning instruction only four or five times during the previous month. In the two weeks prior to writing, the queen had been out of town. Even Chanut had seen little of her since his return just before Christmas. In fact, the whole atmosphere of the city seemed to resonate with the extreme cold of the winter, and the intellectual activity one might have expected of resident scholars was immobilized like the frozen waters.

Since I wrote to you on 18 December, I have seen the queen only four or five times, and it was always in the morning in her library, accompanied by Mr. Freinsheim, with no opportunity to discuss the matters that affect you. Two weeks ago she went to Uppsala, and I did not follow her there; nor have I seen her since her return (which was only on Thursday evening). I know that our ambassador has also seen her only once before this trip to Uppsala, apart from his first audience, when I was present. . . . it seems to me as if men's thoughts freeze here during the winter in addition to the water. . . . However, I assure you that my desire to return to my solitude increases more and more every day, and I do not even know if I can wait here until your return. . . . I am not in my element here, and I desire only the peace and rest which are goods that the most powerful kings on earth cannot give to those who, themselves, do not know how to find them.[32]

The murmurings against foreigners who were suspected of having a disproportionate influence on the young queen continued unabated. When Saumaise's son wrote to Brégy about the local rumours, he mentioned threats on the lives of foreign nationals, even if he qualified his stories as the babbling of the inebriated.[33] Descartes, meantime, made sure that

Picot looked after his friends in France who had not yet received a copy of the *Passions*.[34] His thoughts were focused resolutely on the future, on a possible relocation to France or, more likely, a return to the welcome solitude of Egmond.

Death in Stockholm

Heroic figures of the past were expected to die a heroic death, just as saints were supposed to expire in the odour of sanctity. Descartes invoked the first model in his efforts to comfort Princess Elizabeth about the execution of her uncle, Charles I, by commending the merits of a quick public death in contrast with an extended mortal illness. In doing so, he gave some hints about how he would have preferred to die himself had he pursued a military career.

Although there seems to be something more terrifying about this death [of Charles I], which is so violent, than the death one awaits in bed, it is nevertheless more glorious, happier, and sweeter when it is properly understood, so that those of its features which especially frighten ordinary people should provide a consolation for your highness. There is great glory in dying in circumstances such that one is universally regretted, praised, and pitied by all those who have any human emotion. It is certain that, without this ordeal, the clemency and other virtues of the late king would never have been so widely noticed and so much admired.[35]

There was no hope that Descartes could have emulated the glorious death of the king of England, as if he were still a soldier in the service of his prince and ready to lay down his life for a worthy cause. The sudden, public death of a warrior was impossible for a philosopher in the frozen but relatively peaceful wilderness of Sweden.

However, there was another model available of how to die well, which was exemplified in the terminal illness of the Calvinist theologian Jacques Rivet. Rivet's death at the age of seventy-eight, in January 1651, was preceded by a week of dying during which he prayed continuously with his family by his bedside. This was such an exemplary Christian death that his followers arranged to publish, almost immediately, a detailed account of his death for the edification of other Christians.[36] Rivet was suffering from a bowel obstruction, which provided an opportunity to his friends to reflect on the misery and insignificance of human life in comparison to the divine if one's life can be ended by a piece of human excrement. Rivet prayed, as he lay dying: 'O God, do not withdraw your protection from these

Provinces, nor remove from them your candlestick.'[37] He remembered his friends, such as Anna Maria van Schurman, 'to whom he had always given his sincere love and affection and who had honoured him with her saintly friendship', and to whom he bequeathed a copy of the Bible in unpointed Hebrew.[38] The Calvinist theologian was attended by a Roman Catholic doctor, Balthasar van der Cruyce (or de la Croix), despite the difference in religious allegiance between patient and physician, and he died in peace, prayerfully, on 7 January 1651.

Descartes' death one year earlier was reported by his friends and followers as if it conformed to the pattern of Rivet's Christian departure in the company of trusted friends. Chanut had contracted a flu-like infection about the middle of January, after taking a walk with Descartes.[39] Two weeks later, Descartes – who was still living in Chanut's house – fell victim to the same infection, just as his host was recovering.[40] The queen's primary physician, a Frenchman named M. du Ryer, was temporarily out of the city, and she sent her next in line, a Dutch Calvinist named Mr. Wuelles, to offer Descartes medical assistance. The unco-operative patient had never accepted blood-letting as an appropriate remedy for infections, as if a fever would depart by flowing out of the body as blood was released. In contrast with Chanut, who had accepted the physician's therapy and recovered (though hardly as a result of the physician's intervention), Descartes declined initially to allow his arm to be bled. He hoped to recover naturally. If not, he was resigned to face death.

Baillet presents Descartes' death as the characteristic passage to the other world of a fervent and pious Catholic. The Feast of the Purification occurs in the Roman Catholic liturgical calendar on 2 February. Baillet describes Descartes as having his confession heard and receiving communion on that day, almost in anticipation of his impending illness. Throughout the following days, the patient remained in bed with a high fever. Baillet reports implausibly that, during his final days, 'all his thoughts were directed only to piety, and they were concerned only with the greatness of God and the misery of mankind.'[41] By the eighth day of the fever, the dying philosopher acceded to the entreaties of his friends, and finally allowed the physician to bleed him twice. Those in attendance said the prayers for the dying, and Descartes dictated a letter for his brothers. Among other things, he asked them to provide financial support for his nurse, 'whom he had always cared for during his life' (v. 470). When asked for consent to be given the annointing of the dying, Descartes is reported to have opened his eyes and raised them to heaven in an expression of acceptance of God's will.[42] He passed his final hours reportedly 'in continuous acts of piety and religion', assisted by Chanut's chaplain, surrounded by his friends who recited appropriate prayers. According to Clerselier, Descartes accepted his imminent death in words such as the following: 'My soul, you have been held captive a long time. This is the time for you to leave prison and to relinquish the burden of this body. You must suffer this rupture with joy and courage.'[43] Descartes seems to have lapsed into unconsciousness during the final night, and he died in the early hours of 11 February 1650, just short of his fifty-fourth birthday.

The funeral was held on 13 February, according to the rite of the Catholic Church, during which the coffin was carried by Chanut's secretaries and by his son, Martial. There were only a few mourners at the funeral. They included Chanut, the chaplain who assisted at Descartes' death – an Augustinian priest named Father François Viogué – and his borrowed valet, Henry Schluter. The French philosopher was buried in the cemetery of the orphans' hospital. The son of Saumaise reported that this graveyard was reserved for children who had died without being baptized, and for those who had died of the plague – in other words, the two types of people with whom no one wished to be associated after death.[44] This decision by Chanut symbolized the ambiguity of Descartes' status within his church. If he was buried with children who had died before baptism, he was similar in death to those who were doomed to eternal exclusion from heaven (according to the theology accepted at that time by the church). If he was buried in consecrated ground reserved for children who had died after baptism, his posthumous association with them suggested that he was destined to spend eternity in heaven because of his innocence and uncontaminated holiness. Even in death, it seems, Descartes was ambiguously compared either with non-believers or with holy innocents.

Reburial in France

Within days of his death, Chanut got to work on Descartes' books and papers, and he wrote a number of letters to inform some of Descartes' closest friends of his premature death. In keeping with his long established practice of reading little, Descartes had few books in his personal library. Those he did have, and his personal papers, were set aside to be forwarded to his family in Brittany. With an eye to future possible use, Chanut wrote

to Princess Elizabeth on 19 February, asking permission to retain the
letters that she had sent to Descartes and that Descartes had evidently
brought with him to Sweden. Chanut couched his request in the diplomatic
language in which he had been professionally trained.

Among his papers were found a quantity of letters, which your royal highness paid him
the honour of writing to him and which he considered precious, since some of them
were carefully folded with other important papers. I put them all aside and I took them
from the trunk without including them in the inventory. I have no doubt, Madame, that
it would benefit your reputation if it became known that you had serious and learned
correspondence with the most gifted man who has lived for many centuries. I also
knew from Mr. Descartes himself that your letters were so full of light and intelligence
that it could only redound to your glory if they were published.[45]

Having explained that he had not compromised the privacy of the letters,
Chanut hoped for a favourable response. Elizabeth refused, however, and
Chanut had no option but to return to Princess Elizabeth in a bundle all
her letters to Descartes.[46] In doing so, the French ambassador added a
diplomatic protest and made sure to tell Elizabeth that, as he was dying,
Descartes had asked him to inform the princess that he died 'with the same
respect for her royal highness that he had had during his life'. However,
neither flattery nor entreaties worked. Elizabeth recovered the original
letters that she had sent Descartes and kept them.

Chanut also wrote to Huygens, although it took some weeks for news
of Descartes' death to reach him. Huygens replied in July to express his
inconsolable grief. 'Just as the profusion of tears which are only a useless
liquid console the afflicted, I thought that by speaking as best I could about
such a great friend – the loss of whom can never be adequately regretted in
public or in private – I might be able to mitigate the bitterness in my heart'
(v. 479). He found a way to alleviate his sorrow by writing several poems,
any of which could have served as Descartes' epitaph.[47] His famous son,
the physicist Christian Huygens, also composed a poem in French that
concludes with the lines: 'O Nature, mourn and be the first to grieve /
The great Descartes, and show your sorrow. / When he died, you lost
the light / It was only by means of his flame that we were able to see
you.'[48]

Descartes' discussions with Pascal, and their competing intuitions about
the factors that influence air pressure, had spurred both men to continue
making barometric observations even after Descartes' arrival in Stockholm. Now that Descartes had died, Chanut had to write to Pascal's

brother-in-law, Périer, to inform him too of the death of his collaborator. 'A few days after I wrote to you . . . we lost Mr. Descartes as a result
of a sickness similar to what I had some days previously. I still sigh when
writing about it.'[49] Chanut took advantage of the opportunity not only to
praise his departed friend, but also to emphasize their joint conclusion, in
opposition to Pascal, that barometric pressure is affected by variations in
temperature, humidity, and wind speed.

Meanwhile, Chanut retained possession of Descartes' papers or, at least,
of those that he had brought from Egmond to Stockholm, and he planned
to pass them on to his brother-in-law, Claude Clerselier.[50] He had no
opportunity to do this until he returned to Paris in 1653, when he travelled
by sea to Rouen and then by boat and barge to Paris. The boat sank
in the river Seine, near the Porte de l'Ecole, and its contents remained
at the bottom of the river for three days. When they managed to retrieve
the trunk containing Descartes' papers, they were sufficiently wet that it
required a team of assistants to spread them out to dry. In the course of
these primitive efforts at recovery, many of the pages were separated and
confused, which helps to explain the problems involved subsequently in
distinguishing one letter from another.

Within a year of Descartes' death, Queen Christina had both arranged
for her official coronation and begun to consider abdicating the throne
and joining the Catholic Church.[51] She had her cousin, Karl Gustav,
appointed heir to the crown, and, following a delay of three years, she
finally abdicated in June 1654. She left Sweden almost immediately and
was officially received into the Catholic Church in Brussels, on her journey
south to Rome. Meantime, Chanut also left Sweden and was appointed
French ambassador to the United Provinces in 1653. Many of the scholars
whom the queen had invited to Stockholm had either left or died. Chanut
remained in his new diplomatic post in The Hague for two years, and later
returned to Paris, where he died in 1662.

By this time, Descartes' reputation had sufficiently improved that the
idea of returning his remains to his native country was much less controversial than it might have been when he died. The French ambassador to
Sweden at that time, M. le Chevalier de Terlon, fully supported the idea,
and on 1 May 1666 Descartes' body was exhumed from the relatively
anonymous grave where it had lain for sixteen years. His remains were
placed in a new coffin, and the long return journey to Paris began in June
1666. Those who accompanied the coffin travelled by sea to Copenhagen,

and then overland to Paris. The travel plans were delayed in the Danish capital for three months, and there were further delays, caused by customs inspections, as the cortege moved from one country to another. The coffin arrived eventually in Paris in January 1667, and was lodged temporarily in Saint Paul's Church while a suitable, permanent resting place was sought. Following consultation with the religious community of Saint Geneviève, it was decided to rebury Descartes in the Church of Saint Geneviève de Mont. On Friday 24 June 1667, Descartes' remains were recovered from Saint Paul's Church and received into what was supposed to be his final resting place. The community of Saint Geneviève chanted the Vespers of the Dead, with lit candles and a solemn procession. The next morning, there was planned a funeral oration to celebrate the life and achievements of a great Catholic philosopher. However, the oration was cancelled at the last minute, for fear of censors who might have infiltrated the congregation, so that the final 'adieu' was limited to a pontifical High Mass and blessing. Those in attendance included some of the most prominent supporters of Cartesianism in France: Jacques Rohault, Claude Clerselier, and Habert de Montmor. Clerselier provided a suitable epitaph, which was inscribed on a marble stone to mark the place where Descartes was buried in the knave of the church.

Descartes' reburial in Paris was motivated partly by the wishes of his philosophical supporters that his status as a great philosopher be recognized in his native country. However, there was also an element of settling old scores about his religious orthodoxy and of acknowledging publicly that he had died as a Catholic philosopher, despite having spent twenty-two years abroad in either a Calvinist commonwealth or a Lutheran kingdom. Those who arranged the funeral requested testimonies from a number of people about how orthodox and faithful he had been in his religious practices. Among those who were asked to contribute was Queen Christina. She obliged promptly, from her temporary residence in Hamburg, although her testament did not arrive in Paris until three months after the funeral, in September 1667. Christina wrote:

We hereby make known that, having been invited to honour with a sign of our esteem the memory of Mr. Descartes – who justly acquired the title of 'the great philosopher of our century' – we did not wish to refuse to the memory of such a great man the honour of our approval. . . . We therefore admit that his reputation and writings formerly made us wish to know him. . . . When he agreed to spend some time at our court, we wished to receive from such a good teacher a smattering of philosophy and mathematics, and we used our leisure hours in this pleasant occupation, to the extent that our great and important affairs permitted. However, we were sad to find ourselves deprived by death of such a great and illustrious teacher ... and, moreover, we certify by these presents that he contributed greatly to our glorious conversion and that Providence used him ... to provide us with the first light of Catholicism. His grace and mercy later caused us to embrace the truths of the Catholic, Apostolic, and Roman religion which the said Mr. Descartes had always constantly professed and in which he died with all the signs of genuine piety ... 30 August 1667 at Hamburg.[52]

Unfortunately, the Church of Saint Geneviève was not to be the final resting place for Descartes' mortal remains. Even the integrity of his remains had been questioned since their removal to France in a casket designed for ease of transport rather than for the preservation of an integral corpse.[53] The tomb in the Church of Saint Geneviève survived until 1792, when the church fell into disuse following the French Revolution. The National Convention decided, 2 October 1793, to transfer his remains to the Pantheon. Before this plan was implemented, however, the remains were moved once again to a temporary tomb in the Jardin Elysée des Monuments Français, where they remained until 1816. The politicians of the day evidently lost enthusiasm for their original decree, that 'René Descartes merited the honours due to great men' and that 'the body of this philosopher shall be transferred to the French Pantheon.' Twenty-seven years later, it was suggested that he be reburied in the Père Lachaise cemetery. This plan was also abandoned in due course, and Descartes' remains were reburied for the last time in the nave of the former Benedictine monastery of Saint-Germain-des-Prés. On 26 February 1819, Descartes' remains were finally interred together with the remains of two famous Benedictines, Jean Mabillon (1632–1707) and Bernard de Montfaucon (1655–1741). Mabillon and Montfaucon had both been members of one of the most celebrated Benedictine communities in France, at St. Maur in Paris. It was suppressed during the Revolution, and its demise was officially acknowledged in 1818, when Pope Pius VII dissolved the community.

The fate of Descartes' remains reflects his life-long penchant for changing residence and his ambivalent relationship with both France and the Catholic Church. He failed to be honoured among the 'great men' who deserved burial in the Pantheon, and he found a final resting place, following five burials, beneath a bust of Mabillon in the church of a former Benedictine monastery in Paris.

Condemnation by Rome

In 1663, exactly thirty years after he had suppressed publication of *The World*, Descartes was accorded the dubious accolade that he had success-fully evaded during his lifetime. He thereby joined those whom he had ear-lier described as 'innovators', including Bruno, Campanella, Vanini, and Galileo. During his life, he had not only withheld *The World* from publi-cation but he had also officially denied the motion of the Earth. Given the theory of vortices defended in *The Principles of Philosophy*, Baillet thought that this denial of the Earth's motion might look like dissimulation to later generations, had Descartes not taken the trouble to anticipate sus-picions and to clarify his intentions.[54] However, Descartes had explained his apparently persuasive resolution of this dilemma in reasonably clear terms in a letter in 1644.

As regards Rome's censure concerning the Earth's movement, I see no likelihood of that because I very explicitly deny such a movement. I accept that, initially, I might seem to deny only the word 'movement' in order to avoid censure since I retain the Copernican system. But once my reasons are examined, I am confident that they will be found to be serious and solid, and that they will show clearly that it is more necessary to say that the Earth moves, if one adopts the system of Tycho, than if one accepts the Copernican system when it is explained as I explain it. If one cannot adopt either of those two systems, it would be necessary to go back to that of Ptolemy. I do not think that the Church ever requires us to do that, since that system is manifestly contrary to experience. All the scriptural passages that are contrary to the Earth's motion have nothing to do with astronomy; they concern only a manner of speaking. Thus, since I prove that, if one speaks accurately, one must say that the Earth does not move when one adopts the astronomical system that I explain, I comply fully with those scriptural passages.[55]

This had been Descartes' defence against incurring a censure from Rome since 1633. During the following seventeen years, he carefully avoided endorsing the Copernican system without the qualifications just men-tioned. Thus, if the Bible suggests that the Earth does not move, such texts should be understood as meaning that, when described from the perspective of people who live on the Earth, it does not move in relation to its immediate environment. However, the Bible was not intended to teach astronomy. If we have reason to believe that the Earth does move (in some technical sense of the term 'move' that is defined by natural philosophers), the traditional interpretation of the Bible (expressed in the language of the uneducated) is consistent with the technical claims of early modern astronomy.

Although Descartes escaped the official attention of the Roman censor until 1663, the Congregation of the Holy Office was prompted to open a case against him by reports from two theological examiners, Father Stefano Spinula and Father Agostino Tartaglia.[56] Spinula reported that he had read two of Descartes' books, *The Principles of Philosophy* and *The Passions of the Soul*, and that he had found five theses in each work from which conclusions that were inconsistent with the Catholic faith could easily be deduced. For his part, Tartaglia consulted the *Meditations* and the Latin edition of the *Discourse on Method, Dioptrics and Meteors* (which was published under the title *Specimens of Philosophy*), and he also found a number of theses that he described as 'insufficiently safe' and 'not sufficiently consistent with sacred doctrine'.

While Spinula mentioned the Earth's circular motion around the Sun among the questionable doctrines that he identified, the main focus of the two reports was not on Descartes' endorsement of the Copernican system. Instead, he attracted the attention of scholastic theologians by two other discussions that were primarily philosophical in the traditional sense. One was his venture into the theology of the Eucharist, and the other was his account of human nature. The official examiners were concerned about his general theory of the physical world (that he denied the 'prime matter' of Aristotle, that he denied that material things have substances that are distinct from their properties, and that he claimed that the material world extends indefinitely into space). They were particularly concerned about the possible implications of that natural philosophy for Trent's theology of the Eucharist. For example, Descartes seemed to claim that the properties of bread and wine were not 'real accidents' and, therefore, that they could not exist apart from the bread and wine of which they were properties. The examiners were equally worried about the Cartesian account of the mind (whether it was sufficiently independent of the human body), and about his account of free will and human knowledge.

Once these reports were submitted in September 1663, the Congregation of the Holy Office decided on 10 October that some of Descartes' works were dangerous to the Catholic faith, and the Congregation of the Index announced the decision. The long list of books proscribed by the Congregation of the Index, including Descartes', was introduced by the phrase: 'the following publications are banned.'

The following books of René Descartes, until they are corrected:

First Philosophy, in which God's existence and the distinction of the human soul from the body is demonstrated. To which are added various objections of learned men, together with the author's replies. Amsterdam, 1650.

Comments on a Certain Manifesto towards the end of 1654.

Letter to Father Dinet of the Society of Jesus, the Provincial Superior of the Province in France.

Letter to the very famous man, Gisbertus Voesius [sic].

The Passions of the Soul, a book written in French by the same author. Now made available in Latin to a wider world by H.D.M.I.V.L. Amsterdam, 1650.

Philosophical Works.

By decree of 20 November 1663.[57]

Decisions of the *Index of Forbidden Books* were understood strictly in the tradition of church law. That meant that only those editions of a book that were specifically mentioned in the *Index* were banned. Evidently, there were many editions available, in 1663, of Descartes' works. What initially looks like a list of different publications is in fact simply the two books that had been consulted by Tartaglia.

The 1650 Latin version of the *Meditations* was the third edition that was published in Amsterdam by Louis Elzevier.[58] Since Descartes had died earlier that year, the publisher decided to include a few supplementary texts that he had originally published independently. These included the *Comments on a Certain Manifesto*, which represented Descartes' attempt to defend the substance dualism of the *Meditations* against Regius' reduction of thought to some kind of activity in the brain. This should have seemed, even to Roman censors, to be a genuine effort by Descartes to defend the church's teaching about the immortality of the human soul rather than an insidious effort to compromise its spirituality. Likewise, the *Letter to Voetius* would hardly have attracted the attention of Roman censors as a separate text, unless the Vatican wished to defend in public a notorious Calvinist critic of 'papism'. The only rationale for including these specific items on the *Index* was that they were included in the 1650 edition of the *Meditations*. Apart from that, the only other book identified on the list was the Latin translation of the *Passions* (1650). That text is explicitly dualist in the opening sections of Part I, and, although Descartes presented the work as that of a natural philosopher, there are no explicit passages in which he rejects anything that was taught as a matter of faith by the various councils of the Catholic Church.

Why the condemnation of these two books? The most likely reason is that Descartes' metaphysics was open to the kind of interpretation that had been developed by Regius. In that sense, the Roman censors joined forces with Descartes' Calvinist critics and concluded that, despite his vociferous protests, he was potentially an atheist in disguise, that he weakened rather than strengthened the church's teaching about the immortality of the human soul, and that his discussion of matter cast doubt on the Eucharistic theology that was taught by the Council of Trent.

A Cartesian Sect

Within a short time of his death, those who supported Cartesian philosophy assumed a sufficiently distinct identity that they came to be described, especially by their critics, as a 'sect'. Claude Clerselier was a central figure in the normalization of Cartesian philosophy and its integration into the intellectual life of Parisian salons. One of his first tasks was to arrange for publication of material that had come to light in Stockholm and Leiden after Descartes' death. Clerselier collected as many letters as possible written to and by Descartes, and he published them in three large volumes in Paris in 1657, 1659, and 1667.[59] Since this edition was intended for French readers, one might have assumed that letters originally written in Latin would have been translated into French. This was done, somewhat freely, by the editor, although only in the second and third volumes. The other important new book to emerge, during these years, was part of the treatise on human nature, *l'Homme*, and the surviving sections of *The World*, both of which were published in Paris in 1664. A physician from Saumur in the Loire valley, Louis de la Forge, helped edit the material on the human body and provided some of the illustrations that have accompanied the text ever since.[60]

With the publication of new work and the frequent republication of earlier texts by Descartes, the scene was set for a burgeoning interest in Cartesian philosophy. Many of those who contributed to this development were sufficiently independent that they came to be recognized as distinct voices in the confluence of ideas that invigorated the second half of the seventeenth century. For example, Spinoza and Malebranche could hardly be described simply as Cartesians, as if they merely repeated or reworked ideas that had already been suggested by Descartes. Many others also contributed to the consolidation of a distinctively Cartesian approach to philosophy. These included Jacques Rohault, Pierre-Sylvain Régis, Claude Gadroys, Louis de la Forge, Antoine le Grand, and Nicholas-Joseph Poisson in France, and in the Netherlands, Arnold Geulincx, Adriaan Heereboord, Johannes de Raey, and Johannes Clauberg. Others again were sufficiently impressed by Cartesian ideas that they owe at least the inspiration for their success to Descartes, such as Antoine Arnauld and Christiaan Huygens.[61] Their combined work exceeded even the most extravagant expectations of an author who seemingly cherished his solitude, as a necessary condition for completing his life's work, more than the recognition of his contemporaries.

Descartes died as he had lived: alone, except for one or two close friends; geographically isolated; in exile from his native country, in a kingdom that was officially Lutheran; still reflecting the bitterness and stubbornness of a life filled with controversy; and still failing to be acknowledged for his mathematical and philosophical genius.

Appendix 1

Descartes' Principal Works

Title	Date of Composition/ Translation	Published
Compendium Musicae	1618 (November/ December)	1650
Regulae ad directionem ingenii	1619–28	1684 (Dutch) 1701 (Latin)
Le Monde, ou Traité de la Lumiere	1630–33	1664
L'Homme. Et un traitté de la formation du foetus.	1630–33, 1639?–48	1662 (Latin) 1664 (French)
Discours de la methode pour bien conduire sa raison, & chercher la verité dans les sciences. Plus la Dioptrique, les Meteores, et la Geometrie, qui sont des essaies de cete methode.	1633–37	1637
Traité de la Mechanique	1637	1665 (English) 1668 (French)
Meditationes de prima philosophia in qua Dei existentia et animae immortalitas demonstratur (first edition)	1640–41	1641
Meditationes de prima philosophia, in quibus Dei existentia et animae humanae a corpore distinctio, demonstrantur (second edition)	1641–42	1642
Epistola ad celeberrimum virum D. Gisbertum Voetium	1642–43	1643

(continued)

Title	Date of Composition/ Translation	Published
Specimina Philosophiae: seu Dissertatio de Methodo . . . Dioptrice et Meteora.	1640–44	1644
Principia Philosophiae	1640–43	1644
Les Principes de la Philosophie, escrits en Latin, et traduits en François par un de ses amis	1644–46	1647
Les Meditations Metaphysiques de René Des-Cartes touchant la premiere philosophie, Dans lesquelles l'existence de Dieu, & la Distinction réelle entre l'ame & le corps de L'homme, sont demonstrées	1644–46	1647
Querela Apologetica ad amplissimum Magistratum Ultrajectinum	1647 (French and Dutch)	1656 (Latin)
Notae in Programma quoddam, sub finem Anni 1647	1647	1648
Geometria, a Renato Des Cartes anno 1637 Gallice edita; nunc cum notis . . . in linguam Latinam versa . . . F. a Schooten	1639–47	1649
Les Passions de l'ame	1645–49	1649
La Recherche de la vérité	Date of composition unknown	1684 (Dutch) 1701 (Latin)

Appendix 2

Places Where Descartes Lived

Note: some of the places and dates are only approximate, especially for the years when Descartes was travelling in Europe. This list includes foreign travel, but not relatively brief local journeys, such as visits to The Hague or Amsterdam, during periods when he was renting accommodation elsewhere in the United Provinces.

Place	Date
La Haye (France)	1596–1609/10?
Châtellerault (France)	1609/10–1607
College of La Flèche (France)	Easter 1607–September 1615
Poitiers (France)	1615–December 1616
Breda (United Provinces)	1618 (early)–April 1619
Copenhagen (Denmark), Frankfurt (Germany)	April–July/September 1619
Neuburg (Germany)	10 November 1619
Germany	November 1619–November 1620?
United Provinces?	November 1620–Spring 1622?
Brittany and Poitou	Spring 1622–Spring 1623?
Paris	March–September 1623?
Travels to Italy	September 1623–May 1625
Paris	1625–1627
Brittany	Winter 1627–28?
Dordrecht (Holland)	October 1628
Paris	November 1628–March 1629
Franeker (United Provinces)	April–September 1629
Amsterdam	October 1629–May 1630
Leiden	May/June 1630
Amsterdam	Summer 1630?–Summer 1631
Denmark	Summer 1631

(*continued*)

Descartes in the United Provinces.

Place	Date
Amsterdam	Summer 1631–May 1632
Deventer	May 1632–February 1634
Amsterdam	March/April 1634–April 1635
Utrecht	April 1635–January 1636
Leiden	January–April 1636
Near Alkmaar (Egmond?)	April 1636–December 1638
Santpoort	January 1639–April 1640
Leiden	April 1640–April 1641
Endegeest	April 1641–May 1643
Egmond aan den Hoef	May 1643–June 1644
Paris and Brittany	July–October 1644
Egmond-Binnen	November 1644–June 1647
Paris and Brittany	June–September 1647
Egmond-Binnen	October 1647–May 1648
Paris	May–August 1648
Egmond-Binnen	September 1648–September 1649
Stockholm (Sweden)	September 1649–February 1650

Notes

Preface and Acknowledgments

1. Baillet (1691), i. pp. i, x, xii.
2. Adam (1910), p. i.

Introduction

1. Copernicus (1978), p. xx.
2. Copernicus (1978), 13, 14.
3. Kepler (1992), 48.
4. Kepler (1992), 60.
5. Galilei (1957), 203, 212.
6. Fourth session (8 April 1546). Tanner (1990), ii, 664; and Blackwell (1994), 15.
7. Foscarini's *Letter concerning the Opinion of the Pythagoreans and Copernicus about the mobility of the Sun and the new Pythagorean System of the World* is translated in Blackwell (1991), 217–51. Campanella's *Defence of Galileo the Mathematician from Florence* is translated in Campanella (1994).

Chapter 1

1. The term 'plague' was used for any contagious and mortal disease, including scarlet fever and typhus. There was a large outbreak of bubonic plague in Europe in 1625–6, which particularly affected Burgundy and the Loire valley. See Bercé (174), i. 20, and Collins (1995), 43–4.
2. See Chapter 4.
3. This was expressed by Montaigne (1993: 542): 'What good did their great erudition do for Varro and Aristotle? Did it free them from human ills? . . . Could logic console them for the gout – and did they feel it any the less because they knew how that humour lodged in their joints?'
4. For details, see Chapter 14.
5. Descartes, Cathérine (1745), 239.
6. Descartes to Van Schooten, 9 April 1649 (v. 338).

7. Joachim Descartes was appointed on 6 December 1585 and took up his post 14 February 1586. Ropartz (1877), 11.

8. Only three children survived, and thus René was the youngest (see family tree).

9. Descartes to Elizabeth, May 1646, and Descartes to Chanut, 1 Feb. 1647 (iv. 409, 605–6).

10. v. 470.

11. The parish church of his grandmother was Notre Dame de La Haye, which was marginally closer to her home, but Descartes was baptized in the somewhat larger church of St. George. The town of La Haye has since been renamed in honour of its most famous citizen as 'Descartes'.

12. Mousnier (1990).

13. Ariès (1986), iii. 76.

14. Mousnier (1974), 183.

15. Montaigne (1993), I. xxiii (p. 132).

16. Mousnier (1984), ii. 310.

17. On the widespread buying and selling of offices, see Mousnier (1971).

18. See especially Mousnier (1990) and Collins (1995).

19. Mousnier (1971), 110.

20. This is not the same person as Jeanne Sain, wife of René Brochard and grandmother to René Descartes. I am grateful to Theo Verbeek for drawing my attention to Thouverez (1899), and to the confusion of the two people with the same name that is repeated in Armogathe et al. (1988).

21. Session VII, 3 March 1547; Denzinger (1960), 843a–870.

22. 'Canon 2: If anyone says that true and natural water is not necessary for baptism . . . let him be anathema.' Denzinger (1960), 858.

23. 'Canon 8: If anyone claims that the baptized are free from all the precepts of the Church . . . so that they are not required to observe them, unless they choose by their own initiative to submit to them, let him be anathema.' Denzinger (1960), 864.

24. The *Chambre des comptes* audited accounts of the royal tax officials and had jurisdiction over applications for tax exemption in the province.

25. They also had two others, Claude (b. 1604) and François (b. 1609), about whom little is known.

26. Erasmus (1530), 50. 'A child sitting with those who are older than him should never speak unless forced by necessity or invited to do so. . . . Silence adorns women, but even more so children.'

27. Erasmus (1530), 8.

28. Descartes to Chanut, 6 June 1647 (v. 57).

29. The prominence of the Jesuits in education did not mean that they were the only providers of education in France in the early seventeenth century. There were other colleges that were established and operated by local authorities, and there were colleges, such as the famous college at Saumur, that were explicitly Huguenot. Even among Catholic educators, the Oratorians developed a network of colleges in France in the later seventeenth century. During the period when

Descartes attended, however, La Flèche was genuinely among the best schools in the country.

30. Louis XIII subsequently approved this in 1618, as a result of which the college was renamed Louis-le-Grand.

31. The title in Latin was *Ratio Studiorum*, which I translate here as *Syllabus of Studies*.

32. Pasquier (1602), 122.

33. Ariès (1973), 241.

34. 'Let the practice of speaking Latin be especially strictly guarded excepting in those classes in which the pupils do not know Latin: so that it never is allowed to use the vernacular language in any matter which pertains to class, . . . let the master always use Latin.' Fitzpatrick (1933), 198–9.

35. Louis de la Roche-Thévenin, who was a student from 1611 to 1616, wrote to his father complaining about his Greek studies and the verses he had to compose. See Gaston-Chérau (1949), 430–1.

36. Soarez (1577), 1, 8.

37. Fitzpatrick (1933), 211–12.

38. Quintilian talks about the 'lucidity and clarity' (*dilucida, aperta*) required by a lawyer in a statement of the facts of a case, and of the 'clear and distinct' (*distincta, perspicua*) arguments that should be constructed on that basis, in Quintilian (1921), IV, ii. 36, and V, xiv. 33.

39. Quintilian (1921), VI, ii. 26. Even the indirectness with which we stir up an emotional response in ourselves, an important feature of the Cartesian account of the passions, is found in the same discussion by Quintilian (1921), VI, ii. 29: 'But how are we to generate these emotions in ourselves, since emotion is not in our own power?'

40. Quintilian (1921), V, xii. 2.

41. Fitzpatrick (1933), 175.

42. Dainville (1978), 324–5.

43. Ibid., 328.

44. Fitzpatrick (1933), 149.

45. Ibid., 151.

46. Montaigne (1991: 606) comments sceptically: 'Aristotle is the god of scholastic science: it is heresy to discuss his commandments. . . . What Aristotle taught is professed as law – yet like any other doctrine it may be false'.

47. See Melanchthon (1999).

48. See, for example, Des Chene (1996).

49. Aquinas (1968) and Siger de Brabant (1911).

50. Copenhaver and Schmitt (1992), 103–112.

51. Denzinger (1960), no. 738 (p. 272).

52. Fitzpatrick (1933), 168.

53. Descartes wrote to Father Hayneuve, a Jesuit priest, in 1640 that he 'was educated in one of your colleges for almost nine years' (22 July 1640: iii. 100). Cf. Descartes to Father Grandamy [2 May 1644?]: 'I would be delighted to return to La Flèche where I spent eight or nine years in my youth' (iv. 122). Descartes to Bourdin

[9 February 1645], quoted in note 59, mentions only eight years. The arguments for
the chronology proposed by Rodis-Lewis (1995: 25–7) seem persuasive. Descartes'
older brother, Pierre, began to attend La Flèche only when he was twelve years old
(on the assumption that he began soon after the opening of the college in February
1604).

54. Rochemonteix (1889), i. 130.
55. Ibid., ii. 23; Gaston-Chérau (1949), 419–22.
56. Dainville (1978), 526–33.
57. Fitzpatrick (1933), 153, 173.
58. Descartes to Charlet, 9 February 1645 (iv. 156, 158).
59. See Descartes to Father Bourdin, 9 February 1645, where Descartes expressed
    the reflected honour of having Father Charlet as a relative: 'Besides, I am indebted
    to him for my education – which he directed for eight years – during my whole
    youth when I was at La Flèche and where he was rector' (iv. 160–1).
60. Scaglione (1986), 115, gives the following mix of pupils in a Bordeaux college in
    1644–48: 45 percent sons of bourgeois functionaries, 21 percent sons of merchants,
    8 percent sons of nobles, and 6 percent sons of peasants.
61. Rochemonteix (1889), i. 126.
62. Montaigne (1993), I, xxvi (p. 169).
63. On 15 June 1637, Descartes sent a copy of the *Discourse and Essays* to Father Noël,
    who by then had become rector of La Flèche College.
64. A book about the life and spiritual teaching of Father Lallemant was published
    in Paris in 1694 and reprinted in many subsequent editions. When *The Principles
    of Philosophy* was published in 1644, Descartes asked Father Bourdin to forward
    copies of the new book to Fathers François, Dinet, Charlet, and Vatier, among
    others. Descartes to Bourdin, October 1644 (iv. 143–4).
65. Baillet (1691), ii. 484.
66. Fitzpatrick (1933), 140.
67. Ariès (1973), 56–101.
68. Gaston-Chérau (1949) reports '*la paume, balles et battoirs*' among the games played
    by Louis de la Roche-Thévenin.
69. Fitzpatrick (1933), 241.
70. Fitzpatrick (1933), 142. Richeome (1604) provides an extremely detailed and
    extensive summary (almost one thousand pages) of this kind of mariology.
71. Ignatius (1963), 30.
72. Ibid., 36, 47.
73. Ibid., 15.
74. Ibid., 122.
75. Gaston-Chérau (1949), 418.
76. See, for example, Pasquier (1602), 11, where a Jesuit is credited with the following
    conversation: 'For three years we have failed to kill the Queen of England and
    Count Maurice of Nassau. Those were two strikes that unfortunately failed, and
    we are prepared to try again, in those cases or elsewhere whenever we think it best
    and wherever we have an opportunity.'
77. Rochemonteix (1899), I, 130.

78. *In anniversarium Henrici Magni obitus diem* (1611).
79. The languages in which the poems were written reflects the relative prominence of the three languages in the school curriculum. Approximately 83 percent were written in Latin, 11 percent in Greek, and only 5 percent in French.
80. 'Funeral oration for the anniversary of the late King, Henry the Great, given at the Church of St. Thomas at La Flèche, 4 June,' *In anniversarium* (1611), 305.
81. Ibid., 307.
82. 'La France avoit des-ia respandu tant de pleurs / Pour la mort de son Roy, que l'empire de l'onde / Gros de flots revageoit à la Terre ses fleurs, / D'un Deluge second menaçant tout le monde, / L'ors que l'Astre du iour, qui va faisant la ronde / Autour de l'univers, meu des proches malheurs. / Qui hastoient devers nous leur course vagabonde, / Luy parla de la sorte, au fort de les douleurs. / France, de qui les pleurs, pour la mort de ton Prince, / Nuisent par leur excez à toute autre Province, / Cesse de l'affliger sur son vuide tombeau, / Car Dieu l'ayant tire tout entier de la Terre, / Au Ciel de Iupeter maintenant il esclaire, / Pour servir aux mortels de coeleste flambeau.' *In anniversarium* (1611), 163. There have been suggestions that this sonnet may have been composed by Descartes, but there is no independent evidence to support the claim.
83. Descartes was asked, in 1638, to recommend a school where a young pupil could be well educated in philosophy. He wrote as follows. 'Although I do not think that everything they teach in philosophy is as true as the Gospel, nevertheless, because it is the key to the other sciences I think it is important to have studied the whole course in the way they teach it in Jesuit schools before lifting one's mind above the pedantry in order to become truly wise. I should give this honour to my teachers, that there is nowhere in the world where I think they teach better than at La Flèche' (11 October 1638: ii. 378). Descartes goes on to praise his former school because of the variety of students from different parts of the country and from various social ranks who study there, and for the spirit of equality that pervades the Jesuit schools.
84. A copy of the poster was recently discovered glued to the back of another notice, and it has been published with a translation and notes by Armogathe et al. (1988), 122–45.
85. Montaigne (1991), I. xxvi (p. 167).
86. Ibid., p. 190.
87. Ibid., p. 194.
88. Ibid., p. 172.
89. Ibid., I. xxv (p. 159).

Chapter 2

1. *On the Difficulty of Choosing One's Way of Life*, in Brosse (1611), ii. 658.
2. For the following, I rely on Israel (1982 and 1995).
3. Here and throughout the book, I reserve the name 'Holland' for the single province of that name rather than for the United Provinces as a whole.

4. Descartes advised Ferrier (18 June 1629) to travel overland from Paris to Calais, and to travel by sea 'for a day or two' until he reached Dordrecht or Rotterdam (i. 14).

5. Descartes to Beeckman, 26 March 1619 (x. 158).

6. The dispute between Catholic theologians began with the publication of *Concordia liberi arbitrii cum gratiae donis* (1588), by the Jesuit Luis Molina (1536–1600); the other side of the debate was defended by a Dominican friar, Domingo Bañez (1528–1604).

7. Baillet (1691), i. 40, says that Descartes went to Breda in May 1617, although he seems to have been in Brittany in October and December 1617. It is unclear when he arrived in the United Provinces, except that he was certainly there by October 1618.

8. Twenty-eight years later, Descartes refers to the time 'when I was once a soldier at Breda.' Descartes to Willem, 15 June 1646 (iv. 436).

9. Beeckman (1939–53), i. 237.

10. Beeckman raised the question as follows. If we know how far a body falls in two hours, calculate the distance the same body will fall in one hour. He comments on Descartes' reply: 'This was shown by M. Perron, when I gave him the opportunity by asking him if someone could know how much space is traversed by a falling body in an hour, if they know how much space is traversed in two hours, according to my principles, namely, that what is once set in motion continues in motion forever in a vacuum, assuming that there is a vacuum between the earth and the falling stone' (x. 60).

11. Stevin (1966) v. 413–64.

12. Beeckman to Mersenne, 7 October 1631 (CM, iii. 203).

13. For example, Descartes to G. Brandt, 18 July 1643. Descartes had sent his watch to have a chain fitted, and he wrote in Dutch: 'Excuse me if I write so poorly in Dutch' (iv. 18, 649)

14. Euclid (1574, 1603). John Pell wrote to Charles Cavendish in 1646, following a meeting with Descartes, that 'he says he had no other instructor for Algebra than the reading of Clavy Algebra above thirty yeares ago' (iv. 730–1).

15. Descartes acknowledged in June 1645 that 'Viète was undoubtedly a very good mathematician, although the writings we have from him are merely unconnected pieces which do not compose a perfect body and in which he did not try to make himself understood by everyone.' Descartes to [Haestrecht?] [June 1645?] (iv. 228). When an edition of Viète's work was published by Elsevier in Leiden, in 1646, Descartes had no interest in getting a copy from Mersenne, to whom he wrote (2 November 1646): 'I do not believe that there is anything in Viète that I should learn, and I am not interested in having books simply to decorate a library' (iv. 554).

16. Quoted in Bos (2001), 146, from François Viète, *The Analytic Art*, trans. T. Richard Witner (Kent, Ohio: Kent State University Press, 1983), 32.

17. Descartes to Beeckman, 26 March 1619 (x. 158).

18. The concluding phrase used in letters to Beeckman, 'love me,' was also used by Descartes when writing to other friends. He concluded a letter to Mersenne

(22 July 1633) with the words: 'Meantime, I ask you to love me and to believe that I am your very humble and affectionate servant' (i. 268). Likewise, he wrote to Plemp (3 October 1637): 'Goodbye, and continue to love me' (i. 412).

19. Fermat was born on 20 August 1601 and, once he purchased his office in the Toulouse parliament in 1631, was secure enough financially to marry the following year at the age of thirty-one.

20. Beeckman recorded in his *Journal*: 'Mr. René Descartes of Peron, who in 1618 had written a Treatise on Music for me, in which he shared his opinions about that subject with me and which has been inserted into this work; this same man, I say, came to Dordrecht to visit me on 8 October 1628, having first travelled from Holland to Middelburg to look for me there.' Beeckman (1939–53), iii. 94.

21. 'He (i.e., Descartes) is the same one to whom I communicated, ten years ago, what I had written about the causes of the sweetness of harmonies. . . .' Beeckman to Mersenne (March 1629), CM, ii. 218. See also editors' notes in Descartes (1964–74), i. 31.

22. Beeckman to Mersenne (1 October 1629), CM, ii. 283–4.

23. Descartes to Mersenne (18 December 1629): 'I have recovered one month ago the original text of the little treatise in which I explain it [namely, musical intervals], from which you have already seen an extract. It had rested for eleven years in the hand of Mr. Beeckman, and if that is enough time for prescription he has a right to claim it as his own' (i. 100). Descartes informed Mersenne (January 1630) that he no longer had anything further to do with Beeckman (i. 111), and in a letter of 18 March 1630 he quoted in Latin from the retrieved manuscript that he claimed to have in his hands (i. 133).

24. Cf. *Discourse on Method*: 'I may be mistaken, and what I think is gold and diamonds may be merely pieces of copper and glass' (vi. 3).

25. See Chapter 11 of this volume.

26. See Evans (1973).

27. Thoren (1990), 376–415.

28. Evans (1973), 188.

29. Yates (1979), 28.

30. Cf. Descartes to Mersenne, 25 December 1639: 'As regards the arguments of Raymond Lull, they are only sophisms and I do not think much of them' (ii. 629).

31. See Hilgarth (1971). The subtitle of Sanchez's book includes: 'in which the *Brief Art* of the illustrious and most pious doctor Raymond Lull is explained.'

32. Agrippa (1993), li.

33. Ibid., 3.

34. Ibid.

35. Ibid., 37.

36. Ibid., 441.

37. Ibid., 450.

38. Ibid., 443–4.

39. Ibid., 594.

40. Ibid., 597.

41. Ibid., 600.

42. The first edition appeared in 1558, and the second edition in 1589. Della Porta (1619), "Preface to the Reader," 3.
43. Della Porta (1658), 1–2.
44. Ibid., 4.
45. 'Every natural substance (I mean a compound body) is composed of matter and form, as of her principles.' Della Porta (1658), 6; Latin text, 9.
46. Della Porta (1658), 364–5, 376; Latin text, 547, 566–7.
47. The *Ars brevis*, in a French translation of 1632, defines the purpose of the art as follows: 'Le sujet de cet art, est de respondre de toutes sortes de questions, supposé que l'on sçache ce qui se dict par le terme ou le mot.'
48. I borrow from Jama (1998) for the following.
49. Baillet (1691), i. 85.
50. Baillet, ibid., quotes the phrase in quotation marks from his copy of Descartes' *Olympica* (since lost).
51. Pierre de la Brosse (1611), ii. 658.
52. This is discussed in detail in Flanagan (2000), 165–74.
53. Dee (1564), 3.
54. This is especially so in the *Propaedeumata Aphoristica* (1558). For an analysis of Dee's intellectual development, see Clulee (1988).
55. For the influence of Della Porta on the early notebooks of Descartes, see Shea (1988), 78.
56. He returns to a discussion of Charron's views about animal intelligence many years later. See Chapter 11, this volume.
57. Richeome (1604).
58. Ibid., 936.
59. Borell (1670: 8), places Descartes 'at the Battel of Prague', while Adam (1937: 19) claims that he could not have been present there since he went travelling in March 1620.
60. Baillet (1691), i. 103.

Chapter 3

1. Baillet (1691), I, 105–6. See also Bercé (1974), i. 20.
2. Descartes to his brother, Pierre, 3 April 1622 (i. 1–2), and Descartes to his father, 22 May 1622 (i. 2–3); Baillet (1691), ii. 460.
3. Westfall (1988), 47.
4. 11 October 1638 (ii. 388).
5. *Meteors*, vi. 316: 'In the same way I remember seeing one time in the Alps, around the month of May, that when the snow was heated and made heavy by the sun the least movement of the air was enough to make it fall in a great mass which was called, I think, an avalanche; when it resounded in the valleys, it was fairly similar to the sound of thunder.'
6. Council of Trent, session 4 (8 April 1546), Tanner (1990), ii. 665. This was expanded to require religious to have the approval of their superiors, and to prevent books being published without their authors' names by holding readers legally

responsible, as the putative authors, for any book in their possession that lacked the real author's name.

7. 'It is forbidden to everyone, on pain of their lives, to hold or to teach any maxims contrary to the ancient, approved authors, or to engage in any disputation apart from those that are approved by the doctors of the Faculty of theology. . . . 4 September 1624.' Quoted in Adam (1910), 87, note.

8. To avoid confusion, it should be noted that the Franciscans were founded by Saint Francis of Assisi in the thirteenth century, and there were numerous efforts subsequently to return to the simple lifestyle that he prescribed for his followers. One of these reforming attempts was made successfully by another Saint Francis, who was the founder of the Minims.

9. Vanini, about whom one author wrote that 'modesty was not his dominant quality' (Vaïse 1864: 12), took the name 'Julius Caesar' instead of Lucilio later in life. For his life and trial, see Lenoir (1939), Vaïse (1864), and Schramm (1709).

10. Heresy had been included on the original charge, but was subsequently deleted. See Lenoir (1939), 21–2.

11. Lenoir (1939), 83, and *Life of Vanini*, 102, 99.

12. *Life of Vanini*, 25.

13. While a number of authors refer to Mersenne's *Quaestiones celeberrimae in Genesim* (p. 671), the edition I consulted at the British Library made no reference to this unmentionable crime.

14. 'Perduto é tutto il tempo / Che in amar non si spende.' Quoted by Vanini in Dialogue LX, *Opere*, 523, from Tarquato Tasso's *L'Aminta*, in Tasso (1992), act I, scene I, lines 30–1. The Reynolds translation from 1628 gives the following version: 'Thou wouldst with sighes repent thy time misspent / and onely call a lovers life Content.' Donno (1993), 4.

15. This is quoted from the obliterated passage from Mersenne in the *Life of Vanini*, p. 25.

16. Vaïse (1864), 29.

17. This is examined in detail, with specific references to the Vanini's publications, in Raimondi (1998).

18. Raimondi (ibid.: 191) quotes the advice from R. Thuillier's history of the Minims in France, *Diarium Patrum, Fratrum, Sororum Ordinis Minorum Provinciae Franciae* (Paris: Giffart, 1709).

19. 'We reject as erroneous and contrary to the truth of the Catholic faith every doctrine or proposition rashly asserting that the substance of the rational or intellectual soul is not of itself and essentially the form of the human body, or casting doubt on this matter.' Council of Vienne, 1311–13 (Tanner, 1990: i. 362). The fifth Lateran Council, 1512–17, at session 8 (19 December 1513), rejected the 'extremely pernicious' doctrine that the rational soul is 'mortal, or only one among all human beings.' It decreed that 'the soul not only truly exists of itself and essentially as the form of the human body . . . but it is also immortal.' Tanner (1990), i. 605.

20. Silhon (1991), 28; and Silhon (1634), 103.

21. For details of publications, see Yates (1972), 235–8.

22. Ibid., 42.

23. Ibid., 45.
24. Ibid., Appendix, pp. 258, 257, 252.
25. Ibid., Appendix, p. 257.
26. *Nouvelle Caballe*, vol. 1, 123.
27. Ibid., 120.
28. *Effroyables pactions*, 303. The focus of Descartes' *Meditations* (1641) is the existence of God and the immortality of the soul.
29. Ibid., 277–8.
30. E. Fournier (vol. 1, 116, note) lists a number of them, including one written in Latin in 1622 and published the following year in a French translation as: *Advertissement pieux et très utile des frères de la Rosée-Croix, escrit et mis en lumière pour le bien public par Henry Neuhous de Dantzic* (Paris, 1623).
31. For a survey of Naudé's life and writings, see Rice (1939).
32. Naudé (1623), 1.
33. Ibid., 107–8.
34. Mersenne (1623), col. 716, where he refers to the 'errors and stupidity' of Fludd.
35. Garasse (1623), 83–92.
36. Rice (1939: 63) compares the rule proposed by Naudé in *Instruction to France* (p. 4) – that one should reject as false any opinion that fails to satisfy a criterion of being 'reasonable' following a 'diligent investigation' – with the first rule later proposed by Descartes in the *Discourse* (vi. 18).
37. Naudé (1625), and translated into English as Naudé (1657).
38. Naudé (1623), 26–36. He quotes Bacon (p. 43) to support the claim that the fourth kind of natural magic 'is nothing other than a practical physics'.
39. Baillet (1691), i. 108.
40. The ability of the Rose Cross members to move about invisibly provoked Henri Brasset, who worked in the French embassy in The Hague, to suggest their involvement in the escape of Charles I from imprisonment in Hampton Court on 21 November 1647, despite the extremely tight security in which he was held by the parliamentarians. Brasset to Descartes, 4 December 1647 (v. 93).
41. Schoock (1643), p. 15 of the unpaginated Preface; Verbeek (1988), 160–1.
42. On 21 May 1639.
43. In *De docta ignorantia* (1440). Descartes later comments on the reliance by scholastic philosophers on forms and qualities as explanations, possibly punning on the title of Cusa's work, that their 'ignorance is not at all learned, but ought to be described instead as vain and pedantic' (iii. 507).
44. He wrote to Constantijn Huygens, 9 March 1638, that he had read Campanella's *De sensu rerum* 'fifteen years ago' (i.e., in 1623) and that he had forgotten its contents completely (ii. 659).
45. Bernardino Telesio (1508–1588) was an Italian critic of Aristotle. Sebastianus Basson published a systematic critique of Aristotelian natural philosophy in 1621: *Twelve Books against the Natural Philosophy of Aristotle*. I discuss Vanini in Chapter 8. Some of the same names reappear in Martin Schoock's critique of Descartes at the height of the Utrecht crisis. Schoock wished to argue that the rejection of Aristotle and the cultivation of novel philosophies by Descartes was comparable

to the initiatives of other well-known dissenters, among whom he lists Ramus, Patrizzi, Telesio, Basso, Lull, and the Rose Cross fraternity. See Schoock (1643), Preface; Verbeek (1988), 183.

46. Campanella had reissued *De sensu rerum* (Paris, 1636) and dedicated it to Richelieu. However, the books sent by Huygens and offered by Mersenne could also have been copies of an earlier publication entitled *Real Philosophy* (Frankfurt, 1623).

47. Descartes to Mersenne, 15 November 1638 (1ii. 436).

48. Editors' note, *CM*, i. 145, and letter 32, pp. 248–9.

49. See Cornier to Mersenne, 16 March and 22 March 1626: *CM*, i. 418, 429–30.

50. See, for example, Guez de Balzac (1624).

51. See letters v and xxvi, in *Letres de Phyllarque a Ariste* (1628), part I, 27, 161–2.

52. Guez de Balzac (1638b), ii. 185, 186–7. I have modernized the spelling.

53. See iii. 360, 385–6.

54. Descartes to Villebressieu, [summer 1631] (i. 213).

55. I, 6; and Balzac to Descartes, 30 March 1626 (i. 569–71).

56. Descartes to [Pollot?], [1648?] (v. 558–9).

57. For the siege of La Rochelle, see Crété (1987) and Collins (1995), 29.

58. Recorded in his *Political Testament* and quoted in Crété (1987), 11.

59. Baillet (1691), i. 158.

60. For the history of the manuscript of the *Rules*, see Van Otegem (2002), ii. 659–61.

61. For a modern critical edition, see Giovanni Crapulli's edition, listed here as Descartes (1966). There is a French translation by Jean-Luc Marion, listed as Descartes (1977).

62. See especially Jean-Paul Weber (1964).

63. See Wallace (1992a, 1992b).

64. Alquié adds a note (1963: i. 63) to say that Descartes changed his mind about this later, in the metaphysics. However, I think his later writings are consistent with this insight about concept formation, including the concepts used in metaphysics.

65. De Caus (1615), "Letter of Dedication" (unpaginated).

66. Ibid., 3, 4.

67. Ibid., Book II, Problem I (unpaginated).

68. Ibid., Problem XXVII.

69. There is an extensive literature on this topic. See, for example, Levack (1987).

70. The account of diabolic possession at an Ursuline convent in Loudon, from 1632 to 1638, was more notorious than other cases but not atypical. See De Certeau (1970). Craig Stephenson drew my attention to this incident.

71. For example, Saint Francis de Sales encouraged those attending Mass to say the rosary in private when they could neither see nor hear the priest because there was a rood-screen between them and the altar, and they could not understand him either, since the services were celebrated in Latin. Ariès (1986), iii. 74.

Chapter 4

1. The exact date is not clear. Descartes refers, in the *Discourse*, to the decision 'three years' (vi. 60) previously not to publish *The World*. This dates the composition of

the *Discourse* at 1636, which coincides with the evidence available from correspondence at that time. He also says, in Part III of the *Discourse*, that 'it is exactly eight years since this desire made me resolve to move away from all the places where I had acquaintances and to retire here' (vi. 31). Thus, he probably moved to the United Provinces in 1628.

2. Descartes to Mersenne, 4 March 1630: 'I may leave this country completely within a month or two' (i. 125); Descartes to Mersenne, 18 March 1630: 'I am getting ready at the moment to travel to England in five or six weeks time' (i. 130). However, he also wrote to Balzac, 15 April 1631, that in the two years since he had left France he had never been tempted, even once, to return there (i. 197–8).

3. In a letter dated 2 December 1630, Descartes asked Mersenne not to tell anyone where he was staying and to suggest that he may already have left for England (i. 189). The original reasons for moving to the United Provinces are confirmed in a letter to Huygens, 12 June 1637. 'When I decided to leave my country and to distance myself from my acquaintances, in order to lead a more tranquil and peaceful life than I had led previously, I would never have decided to retire to these provinces and to prefer them to many other places (where there was no war in progress and where the purity and freshness of the air seemed more appropriate to intellectual work), had I not been persuaded by my great respect for his Highness [Prince Frederik Hendrik of Nassau] to entrust myself enormously to his protection and government. Since then I have enjoyed fully the leisure and peace that I hoped to find in the protection of his military power. . . .' (i. 638)

4. When Mersenne planned to take a trip to Italy in 1639, Descartes advised him that Italy was very unhealthy for French people, and he hinted that he himself might have gone to live there, rather than in the United Provinces, had he not been afraid of such illnesses. Descartes to Mersenne, 13 November 1639 (ii. 623).

5. Descartes to Mersenne, 18 March 1630 (i. 130).

6. Suggested by Theo Verbeek (private communication). Descartes later wrote, in the *Dioptrics*: 'About thirty years ago, a man named Metius, from the town of Alkmaar in Holland, a man who never studied but whose father and brother were professors of mathematics, and who particularly enjoyed making mirrors and burning glasses . . . happened by chance to look through two lenses. . . .' (vi. 82)

7. By 1638, Descartes had changed his mind about Ferrier's skills when he wrote to Mersenne (31 March): 'As regards Ferrier, let him be. It seems as if he will succeed at nothing, and I think that the most modest turner or blacksmith would be more capable than he is of demonstrating the effect of the lenses' (ii. 85).

8. Descartes to Mersenne, 25 November 1630 (i. 182). There are other references to this provisional metaphysics in Descartes to Mersenne, March 1637 (i. 350).

9. Descartes often mentioned his reluctance to become involved in theology, in which he claimed not to be competent. See, for example, Descartes to Mersenne, 15 April 1630 (i. 144), and Descartes to Mersenne, 27 May 1630: 'The question: *whether it is consistent with the goodness of God that men are damned for eternity* [in Latin], comes from theology. That is why you might allow me, please, to say absolutely nothing

about it' (i. 153). Descartes to Mersenne, 6 May 1630: 'I do not wish to become involved with theology' (i. 150).

10. Henri Regnier, or Henricus Reneri, was reared as a Catholic in the Spanish Netherlands, but later converted to Calvinism and went to live in the United Provinces. He studied at Leiden, where he registered as a student of theology (15 March 1616) and later as a medical student (13 October 1629). Cohen (1920), 448.

11. Although the letter is written in French, Descartes lapses into Latin in the final paragraph to state that 'if something is moved in a vacuum, it is moved perpetually and in exactly the same way' (i. 29).

12. Descartes to Mersenne, 4 March 1630 (i. 127). Kepler's work was *De nive sexangula & grandine acuminata* (1611).

13. vi. 115 ff.; and Descartes to Mersenne, 31 March 1638 (ii. 87).

14. Descartes to Mersenne, 4 March 1630 (i. 125).

15. Descartes to Mersenne, 18 March 1630 (i. 135).

16. Descartes to Mersenne, 15 April 1630 (i. 136).

17. Descartes (1936), i. 144; Theo Verbeek, private communication.

18. Baillet links this move with a vacancy caused by the death of François Burgersdijck. However, Burgersdijck died only five years later. Baillet (1691), i. 199–201.

19. He wrote to Mersenne (March 1638) in praise of Descartes: 'He is my light, my sun, and as Virgil says in the *Bucolics*, I can say of him too: He will always be a god to me, that is, by understanding the word "god" as the most eminent among all mortals in virtue and understanding' (ii. 102).

20. Descartes to Mersenne, 27 May 1630 (i. 154)

21. Descartes to Mersenne, 23 December 1630 (i. 194); Descartes to Mersenne, October 1631 (i. 219).

22. Descartes to Mersenne, 15 April 1630 (i. 139).

23. Descartes to Huygens, 1 November 1635 (i. 331). In a letter to Mersenne, 31 March 1638, he wrote: 'I admit that Kepler was my first teacher in optics and I believe that, up to now, he was the most knowledgeable of all about the subject' (ii. 86).

24. John Pell to William Cavendish, 12 March 1646 (iv. 731).

25. Baillet (1691), i. 260.

26. Descartes to Ville-Bressieux, summer 1631: 'I have returned to wait for you in Amsterdam, where I have arrived in good health' (i. 215). Beeckman mentions Descartes' indisposition in a letter to Mersenne, 7 October 1631: 'Mr Descartes, with whom I dined in Amsterdam a few days ago, is recovering from a rather serious illness' (CM, iii. 203).

27. The problem is a general version of the following question, in which only four lines are involved. Given four straight lines, find the locus of points from which a line can be drawn to each of the four lines so that the product of two of these new lines bears some constant proportion to the product of the other two lines. Pappus wished to generalize this problem to finding a locus for indefinitely *n* lines.

28. Descartes to Golius, January 1632 and 2 February 1632 (1. 232–6, 236–42). Descartes had evidently been working for some time on a number of problems

about light, including those that eventually appeared in the *Dioptrics* (1637). In a letter to Mersenne, June 1632 (i. 255), he decided to withhold publication of the sine law and effectively to separate *The World* from some of his work in dioptrics.

29. In July 1633, Descartes regrets that three of Mersenne's letters were lost in transit, and he wants to know the dates on which they were sent, so that he might identify the messenger responsible for losing them (i. 266–7).

30. Morin (1631), 1–2, 5.

31. Ibid., 11.

32. Ibid., 80–1: 'Quinta ratio valde notanda desumitur ab Astrologia, totius physicae capite ad quam prae caeteris scientiis spectat definire, quo in Mundi loco sit Terra omnium influentiarum coelestium receptaculum, sive passivum subjectum.'

33. Galileo's book was published in Florence in 1632. Gassendi wrote to him from Lyons, 1 November 1632, that his personal copy, which arrived in October, was still the only one available in France.

34. Descartes to Mersenne, November or December 1632 (i. 261).

35. Denzinger (1960), 786. This passage is also translated in Blackwell (1991), 183.

36. 'Joshua declaimed: Sun, stand still over Gibeon, and moon, you also, over the Vale of Aijalon. And the sun stood still, and the moon halted, till the people had vengeance on their enemies.' Joshua 10:12–13.

37. Blackwell (1991), 128.

38. Galileo was judged 'strongly suspected of heresy, namely of having believed and held the doctrine which is false and contrary to the Sacred and Divine Scriptures, that the sun is the centre of the world and does not move from east to west and that the earth moves and is not the centre of the world; and that any opinion may be held and defended as probable after it has been declared and defined as contrary to the Holy Scriptures.' Blackwell (1991), 132.

39. Descartes to Mersenne, February 1634 (i. 282). On this question, see Westfall (1988).

40. Descartes to Mersenne, April 1634 (i. 288). The 'churchman' in question was either Tommaso Campanella or Paolo Antonio Forcarini. See Blackwell (1994).

41. Galileo's position is best expressed in his *Letter to the Grand Duchess Christina*, in Galilei (1957), 175–216, and is analysed in McMullin (1967), 33–5, and Blackwell (1991), 53–85.

42. 'The loss of the letters I wrote you towards the end of November makes me think that they were intentionally withheld by some inquisitive person who found a way of taking them from the messenger and who, perhaps, knew that I had planned to send you my treatise about that time. Thus if I had sent it to you, it would very likely have been lost. I also remember that I had earlier failed to receive four or five of your letters, which should alert us not to write anything that we would not be willing to share with everyone' (i. 292).

43. Van Otegem (2002), ii. 540–1.

44. When writing about the publication of the *Principles* in 1644, Baillet claims that it was not 'son fameux traité *du Monde*, qui n'a jamais vû le jour, si ce n'est après avoir été réduit en fort petit abrégé, qui parût pour la première fois l'an 1664 d'une

manière très-imparfaite, sous le titre *du Monde ou Traité de la Lumière*.' Baillet (1691), ii. 222.

45. This was first published in a Latin translation prepared by F. Schuyl, as *De Homine* (Leiden, 1662). The French text was edited by Clerselier, with notes prepared by Louis de la Forge, and it was published together with *Un Traité de la Formation du Foetus* in 1664.

46. Galileo is usually credited for having been the first to raise this question, in *The Assayer* (1623). The possible disparity between appearance and reality in our sensations subsequently became a famous philosophical problem, under the title of primary and secondary qualities, for seventeenth-century authors such as Robert Boyle and John Locke. For Galileo's discussion, see Galilei (1957), 274–9.

47. Quintilian (1921), V, x. 12.

48. Molière (1971), ii. 1173.

49. The extent to which animal spirits in motion were expected to explain all animal motions is clear from the following: 'You will have no difficulty in concluding from the foregoing that the animal spirits are able to cause movements in all bodily parts in which the nerves terminate, even though anatomists have failed to find any that are visible in parts such as the eye, the heart, the liver, the gall bladder, the spleen, and so on' (xi. 138). The fact that these nerve connections were invisible to the naked eye and had not yet been observed by anatomists (because the microscope had not yet been invented) did not deflect Descartes from his claim. He was proposing a model or hypothesis about how such movements could occur, and the failure of anatomists to see the corresponding ducts did not count against the explanation.

50. For example, he writes about God uniting 'a rational soul to this machine' (xi. 143, 177, 183), and he concludes the *Treatise* with a sentence to introduce the second part, 'the description of the rational soul' (xi. 200). Evidently, this part was never written or, at least, has not survived. Descartes also leaves room for a 'soul' at critical points in his discussion of sensation (xi. 147, 159).

Chapter 5

1. Descartes encountered serious objections later to the metaphysical discussions that were outlined in Part IV of the *Discourse on Method*, and he may have been protecting himself from the ire of theological critics by publishing his book anonymously.

2. He had acknowledged this in a letter to Mersenne, April 1634: 'all the things that I explain in my treatise, among which was also the view about the earth's movement, are so interrelated that it is enough to know that one of them is false to conclude that all the reasons that I used are unconvincing; and although I thought that they were supported by very certain and very evident demonstrations . . . ' (i. 285).

3. Descartes to Mersenne, 15 May 1634 (i. 299).

4. Beeckman (1939–53), iii. 308, 356, 389.

5. Morin (1634).

6. Descartes to Huygens, 5 October 1646 (iv. 518).

7. Descartes to Mersenne, 5 October 1646 (iv. 511).

8. Descartes to Golius, 16 April 1636, refers to the 'extraordinary cold' of the previous winter (i. 316).

9. Huygens to Descartes, 14 August 1640 (iii. 153), and Descartes to Huygens, [August 1640?] (iii. 158). At this time they were discussing the book before its publication in 1641 as: *The Use and Nonuse of the Organ in the Churches of the United Netherlands [Gebruyck of ongebruyck van 't Orgel in de Kercken der Vereenighde Nederlanden]* (Leiden: Elzevier). Huygens endorsed the orthodox view that music is inappropriate in churches if it is offered merely as entertainment. However, if it is used to assist people to have the appropriate emotions when praying, then it should enjoy the same contingent justification as singing rather than merely reciting the psalms.

10. Descartes to De Wilhem, 23 May 1632 (i. 253). David le Leu de Wilhem was a councillor to the prince of Orange who married Constantia, Huygens' sister, in 1635.

11. Descartes to Golius, 16 April (i. 315). In his letter to Huygens, 1 November 1635, Descartes reminds his correspondent of 'three mornings' that they had spent together discussing optics (i. 591).

12. Baillet (1691), ii. 89–90; Cohen (1920), 485.

13. Saumaise to Rivet, [April 1640] (iii. 862).

14. Baillet (1691), ii. 89.

15. Ibid., ii. 91. Baillet reflected on this question in the Preface (vol. 1, p. ix), where he refers to Descartes' 'secret marriage as something doubtful and a genuine stain on his celibacy.' Toward the conclusion of the biography, Baillet (1691: ii. 502) comments again on the unique blemish on his celibacy as 'less a proof of his inclination towards sex than of his weakness.'

16. Baillet (1691), ii. 89. Italics added.

17. Schoock (1643), 265–6; Verbeek (1988), 317.

18. Baillet (1691), ii. 91.

19. Cohen (1920), 359.

20. See Tomalin (2002), 236–51, which mentions that one of Pepys' famous scientific contemporaries, Robert Hooke, also 'regarded the young female inmates of his house as his natural prey' (248–9). Saumaise commented, in 1640, that pregnancy among unmarried servants was not unusual, and that the French understood the misbehaviour of the men involved as 'gallantry' (Saumaise to Rivet, [April 1640], iii. 862).

21. See the information collected in Schama (1987), 455.

22. Adam (1937), 89.

23. Huygens wrote to Descartes on 18 September, when he was assisting Prince Frederik Hendrik at the siege of Breda: 'I am no further from you than the distance from here to Alkmaar' (i. 641). His anonymous correspondent may have been Cornelis van Hogelande (a Catholic medical doctor at Leiden), who may have sent him medical books by canal from Leiden to Amsterdam and onward to Alkmaar (see i. 581–2).

24. Much depends on which water had to be crossed. If the books travelled by canal, they may have come from Leiden. However, if Helena was still living in Deventer, they may just as easily have travelled by the Zuider Zee.

25. See Descartes to Mersenne, 15 September 1640: 'Fifteen days ago I decided to send you the letters included with this one, but I left this town suddenly before I had sealed them' (iii. 175).

26. Baillet (1691), ii. 90. Francine died either on September 7 or on September 17, depending on whether Baillet translated the old style dates that were used in Amersfoort into the new calendar used in France. If she died on September 7, 'on the third day of her illness', it is not clear why Descartes would have set off on his journey three days before Francine got sick. If she died on September 17, he would have returned to Leiden while the young child was dying. The three days quoted by Baillet correspond to the normal progression of scarlet fever. It may be that Descartes did travel from Leiden because of Francine's illness and death, and that Baillet was slightly confused about the precise date of her death.

27. Huygens to Descartes, 28 October 1635, refers to '*ce malheur publique*' (i. 325). Cf. Israel (1982), 329.

28. Baillet (1691), ii. 241.

29. Ibid., ii. 211–12.

30. Helena died in 1683 and was buried in Egmond aan den Hoef. I am indebited to Jeroen van de Ven for providing the detailed information about Helena Jans and her relationship with Descartes.

31. This correspondence first came to light when it was edited on behalf of the Buxton family by Leon Roth and published in 1926. Although I have consulted Roth (1926), all the letters have been reprinted in the revised edition of Descartes' works (edited by Adam and Tannery). For the sake of simplicity, I give references to that edition.

32. That he was in Utrecht in March 1635 is confirmed by a letter from Anna Maria van Schurman to Rivet, 18 March (OS?) 1635. See Bos (2002), liii.

33. 'Compose' here is intentionally ambiguous. Descartes had worked on many of the issues that are discussed in the published *Meteors* for some years before its publication, especially the application of the law of refraction to explaining the rainbow. The explanation of parhelias began in 1629.

34. Huygens to Descartes, 28 October 1635 (i. 589).

35. 'Since the condemnation of Galileo, I have revised and completely finished the treatise that I had begun earlier' (i. 322).

36. Roth (1926), 17, note; Descartes to Huygens, 28 March 1636 (i. 601–3); Descartes to Mersenne, March 1636 (i. 338–41).

37. Despite the fact the Elzevier was much more famous, Jan Maire had a significant number of international authors on his list, including John Selden, Francis Bacon, Francis Gomar, and Claude Saumaise. For the status of Jan Maire and the printing history of the 1637 book, see Brown (1990).

38. Descartes to Huygens, 31 March 1636 (i. 605); 11 June 1636 (i. 605); 13 July 1636 (i. 610).

39. Descartes to Huygens, 30 October 1636 (i. 613–14).

40. Descartes to Huygens, 1 January 1637 (1. 615), and Huygens to Descartes, 5 January 1637 (1. 345).

41. Beaugrand (1636), a short book of twenty-seven pages with his own signature on the accompanying privilege.

42. Mersenne to Descartes, 15 February 1637 (i. 659–62).

43. Descartes to Huygens, 27 February 1637, gave a similar justification for his choice of a title for the Preface. He wrote to Huygens, in a much more conciliatory tone than to Mersenne: 'Since I did not intend to explain my whole method but only to say something about it, and I do not like to promise more than I deliver, that is why I wrote "discourse on method". Whereas I wrote simply "the Dioptrics" and "the Meteors" because I tried to include in them everything that is relevant to my subject. . . . I also think that I should omit all the gloss that I had included at the end and leave simply these words: Discourse on the Method, etc. together with the Dioptrics, the Meteors and the Geometry, which are illustrations of this method' (i. 620–1). The same idea is shared with an anonymous friend in April (?) 1637: 'I propose . . . a general method, which I truly do not teach, but for which I try to provide some justification in the three treatises that follow and which I join to the discourse in which I speak about it. . . . ' (i. 370)

44. The text was found almost immediately after his death in 1650 and was subsequently published in various editions.

45. Descartes to Huygens, 29 March 1637 (i. 627–9).

46. Huygens to Descartes, 24 March 1637 (i. 626–7). See Descartes to Plemp (3 October 1637), in which he acknowledges: 'I am not unaware of the fact that my *Geometry* will have very few readers' (I, 411).

47. Writing to an anonymous correspondent (April 1637?), Descartes identifies some elements of the objectionable draft privilege: that he would seem to readers to be praising himself, that he would be described as the inventor of many fine things, and that he would promise to publish other treatises, although he wrote the opposite in the 'discourse which serves as a preface' (i. 369).

48. Descartes to Huygens, 27 February 1637 (i. 619–20).

49. His letter to Huygens on the death of his wife (20 May 1637) indicates that he has withdrawn 'rather a long distance from the world' (i. 371), and that he is living near Alkmaar (i. 634). Another letter to Colvius, 14 June 1637, shows that he had been travelling 'for more than six weeks' (i. 379). He probably departed from Leiden at the end of April 1637.

50. CM, vi. 138.

51. The original privilege was published in full in the Latin edition of the text (1644), and it explicitly names 'Des Cartes' as the author (vi. 518). Descartes used an abbreviated version in which his anonymity was protected in the 1637 edition, which referred simply to 'the author of the book entitled *Discourse on the Method, etc.*' (vi. 515).

52. In 1636, Louis XIII had approved 'his Highness' as the official French form of address for his ally against the Spanish, Prince Frederik Hendrik. The States General followed suit in 1637 by amending 'his Excellency' to 'his Highness'. See Israel (1995), 537.

53. The title of this edition was: *Specimina Philosophiae, seu Dissertatio de Methodo recte regendae rationis, & veritatis in scientia investigandae; Dioptrice, et Meteora*. A Latin version of the *Geometry* was prepared by Van Schooten and published by Jan Maire in 1649.

54. Those interested in the history of science or mathematics are an obvious exception. There is an English translation available in Descartes (2001). However, the translator has inexplicably changed the order in which the essays appeared in the first edition and in the standard editions of this book by putting the *Geometry* in second place.

55. The first edition of the book included two separately paginated parts. The essays were 413 pages long, while the *Discourse* was only 78 pages in length. Despite this, the essays are often described as appendices to the *Discourse on Method*. See, for example, Gleik (2003), 36, where Descartes' *Geometry* is characterized as 'a small and rambling text, the third and last appendix to his *Discours de la Méthode*'.

56. Plemp (1632). Plemp's reliance on traditional medicine is reflected in his very extensive library. See Tricot-Royer (1925). For his preference for Galen over Vitello or Kepler, see Book II, Chapter 7.

57. If the sticks are bent by an angle a and the distance between the two hands is d, then the distance between the blind man and the object is $d \sin (90 - a) / 2$.

58. Descartes to Ferrier, 8 October 1629 (i. 32) and 13 November 1629 (i. 53).

59. This sentiment is repeated in the final sentence of the *Meteors*: 'I hope that those who have understood everything in this treatise will see nothing in the clouds, in future, of which they will not be able easily to understand the cause nor anything that provides them with a subject for admiration' (vi. 366).

60. There is also a reference to 'another treatise' (the unpublished *World*) in which he has explained comets (vi. 323).

61. See p. 224, this volume.

62. He had also written his earlier unpublished *World* in French. Writing to Father Vatier, 22 February 1638, Descartes excused his failure to discuss God's existence adequately in the *Discourse* by claiming that 'it did not seem appropriate to include these thoughts in a book in which even women could understand something and, at the same time, the most subtle minds would also find things to occupy their minds' (i. 560).

63. Descartes to Deriennes, February 27, 1638 (i. 458).

64. I have borrowed from the invaluable work of Bos (2001), and have consulted Costabel (1990).

65. The title of the first chapter in Book I reads: 'Problems that can be constructed without using anything other than circles and straight lines' (vi. 369).

66. See p. 108, this volume.

67. See Balzac to Descartes, 30 March 1628 (i. 570); Descartes to Mersenne, 15 April 1630 (i. 144) and 25 November 1630 (i. 182).

Chapter 6

1. Compare James Joyce, *Finnegans Wake*: 'A hundred cares, a tithe of troubles and is there one who understands me?'

2. For example, he wrote to Balzac, one of his most loyal friends in France, on 14 June 1637 and gave as his address 'Holland'. Descartes wrote to Mersenne, 29 June 1638, that his letters had to pass through Haarlem to reach him, without telling his correspondent where exactly he was, and that he should address them to a priest, Mr. Bloemaert, who would ensure their safe delivery (ii. 191). The same concerns emerged in August 1638, when Descartes had reason to worry that some letters between Mersenne and himself had got lost or had been intercepted in transit. He advised him (23 August 1638) that letters sent through Haarlem would not be lost, although he should also ensure that they were properly sealed (ii. 338).

3. However, he had not yet moved when he wrote to Huygens, 5 July 1637 (i. 641).

4. Huygens to Descartes, 18 September 1637 (i. 641). The original phrase occurred in the *Discourse* when Descartes was describing the way in which God might have created matter 'in imaginary spaces' (vi. 42). Huygens reuses the same phrase, in a letter to Descartes on 23 November 1637, when informing him that a package had taken eighteen days to arrive at Breda from the 'imaginary spaces' where he lived (i. 461).

5. Descartes to Huygens, 29 January 1639 (ii. 676).

6. This is repeated in Descartes to Mersenne [October 1637]. 'Whatever the quality of the objections that may be made to my writings, please oblige me by sending them all to me, and I shall not fail to answer them – at least if they or their authors are worth the slightest bother, and if they agree to have me publish them when I have gathered enough to compose an appropriate volume' (i. 453–4).

7. He had sent a copy to the *Stadtholder* through Huygens, and had asked Huygens to give copies to the French ambassador for presentation to the king and to Richelieu (Descartes to Huygens, June 1637: i. 387). However, the ambassador's premature death at Breda probably frustrated that plan. Descartes also sent copies to Cardinals Baigné and Barberini, and he was happy that the papal nuncio in France might ensure their safe delivery in Rome (Descartes to Mersenne, December 1638: ii. 464–5).

8. Descartes to Father Noël [October 1637] includes the suggestion that Cartesian physics might be integrated into the Jesuit curriculum. 'It seems to me that no one has more interest in examining this book than the members of your society. For I see already that so many people are beginning to accept its contents that, especially in the case of the *Meteors*, I do not know how they will be able to teach this material in future, as they do every year in most of your colleges, unless they either refute what I wrote or else accept it' (i. 455). Descartes makes a general exception for 'the Jesuit Fathers and those of the Oratory' when he asks Mersenne (1 March 1638) not to forward any more unwelcome criticisms (ii. 25). One year after publication, he asked Mersenne (27 July 1638) whether the Jesuits at La Flèche were teaching his *Meteors* or refuting it, and he suggested that one could find out by consulting their 'public theses, which occur at about this time of year' (ii. 267–8).

9. For example, Alphonse Pollot (1602–1668), to whom Descartes sent a copy of the *Geometry*, with this comment: 'I think it is a great honour that you wish to take the trouble to examine my *Geometry*. I shall reserve for you one of the six copies that were destined for the first six people who would seem to me capable of understanding it'

(Descartes to Pollot, 12 February 1638: i. 518). Reneri provided copies on behalf of Descartes to Pieter Cornelisz Hooft and other prominent people in June 1637 (Hooft, *Briefwisseling*, ii. 934–5; quoted in Cohen 1920: 507).

10. The same general encouragement is repeated in Descartes to Mersenne, January 1638. 'I hope that you will continue always to tell me frankly what is said about me, either favourably or otherwise; you will have more opportunity in future to do so than ever before because my book has arrived in Paris' (i. 485).

11. Similar descriptions of himself as a reluctant protagonist are frequently repeated. For example: 'It is not my style to spend time refuting other people's views' (Descartes to Plemp, 23 March 1638: ii. 64); 'it is entirely against my character to reproach others and I think I have never done so as much as in this case' (Descartes to Mersenne, 3 May 1638: ii. 131).

12. Descartes to Mersenne, 5 October 1637 (i. 449).

13. Descartes to Van Beverwijck, 5 July 1643 (iv. 6). There was a sound basis for this complaint, because Plemp had published his own objections to Descartes and mere summaries of Descartes' replies in the first edition of his *De fundamentis medicinae, libri sex* (Leuven, 1638). The point here is simply that Descartes was so upset that he was still complaining about the injustice involved six years later. See Descartes to Colvius, 5 September 1643 (iv. 717–18).

14. He wrote to Plemp later about dissecting the heart of an eel 'before seven or eight o'clock this morning', on 23 March 1638 (ii. 66).

15. It was called the 'fallacy of affirming the consequent'.

16. The Aristotelian character of the *Meteorologicorum Libri Sex* is evident from his definition of meteors as 'imperfectly mixed bodies' (p. 1).

17. In *Anti-Aristarchus* (p. 2), Froidmont lists those who support the movement of the Earth, including Galileo, Foscarini, Gilbert, and 'many others throughout Europe today'. He repeats some of the standard arguments against the Earth's motion, including the objection that if the Earth revolved so quickly, buildings would collapse (p. 57). One of his basic arguments was that the Copernican theory was contrary to Scripture, and that for those who accepted the infallibility of the Pope, it was close to heresy to defend Galileo (pp. 26–9).

18. Plemp to Descartes, 15 September 1637 (i. 399).

19. In scholastic theories of perception, it was assumed that the form of what is perceived must travel from the object of perception to the observer's senses. That led them to postulate form-preserving images that travelled somehow from the objects of perception to the senses, and these were called intentional species.

20. Descartes to Plemp, for Fromondus, 3 October 1637 (i. 415–16).

21. The abuse of Scripture to support scientific or philosophical views continued to rankle with Descartes. He commented on work by Comenius [August 1638]; 'I think, however, that if one wishes to derive from Holy Scripture knowledge of truths that pertain only to the human sciences and which are not relevant to our salvation, that is equivalent to using it for an objective that was not intended by God and therefore abusing it' (ii. 348).

22. Morin to Descartes, 22 February 1638 (i. 537–57). This lengthy letter requires twenty pages in the standard edition.

23. Morin seems to have been genuinely open to the possibility of getting replies from Descartes, and he concludes his letter by saying that 'among all the men of letters that I know, you are the one that I admire the most' (i. 557).

24. Descartes wrote a twenty-four-page response, 13 July 1638 (ii. 221). He asked Mersenne (31 March 1638) to tell Morin that 'he had received his discourse very gladly, and that he would not fail to reply to it as carefully, as civilly, and as soon as possible' (ii. 85).

25. One might compare Descartes' efforts in this regard with those of Robert Boyle in 'On a Good Hypothesis and an Excellent Hypothesis' (Boyle 1979: 119), or with the much later and more famous defence of the same procedure by Christiaan Huygens in the Preface to his *Treatise on Light* (1690). See Boyle (1962), pp. vi, vii.

26. It is one of the ironies of this correspondence that Descartes addresses directly a challenge that was raised much later by Martin Schoock, in *Admiranda Methodus* (1643). Schoock criticized the alleged demand by followers of Descartes for a degree of certainty in natural philosophy that was impossible to realize. He contrasted the certainty of divine revelation with the relative uncertainty of medical science and then added: 'Just as it would be a mistake to demand of medicine a degree of certainty that is comparable to the dogmas of theology, so likewise one could not excuse those who would demand, for all the dogmas of physics, that their demonstrations would achieve the exactitude that is found only in mathematics.' Schoock (1643), 123; Verbeek (1988), 241–2.

27. Morin to Descartes, 12 August 1638 (ii. 292).

28. Descartes to Morin, 12 September 1638 (ii. 367). He had used the same expression, about an unknown 'philosophical entity', at ii. 364. Descartes often rejected suggestions that he should borrow scholastic terms to develop his explanations, because he objected not to the words used, but to the various entities that they denoted. Thus he wrote to the Jesuit, Father Ciermans (23 March 1638) that he did not wish to return to 'all the qualities and forms that I abhor' (ii. 74).

29. Descartes to Mersenne, 15 November 1638 (ii. 437).

30. Roberval arrived in Paris after assisting at the siege of La Rochelle in 1627, and there became acquainted with a number of mathematicians, including Hardy, Picot, Mydorge, and Étienne Pascal. He was among the first group of intellectuals appointed to the Académie royale des Sciences in 1666.

31. Fermat to Mersenne, April or May 1637 (i. 354–61).

32. Fermat to Mersenne, April or May 1637 (i. 355), where he refers to the 'brief time that Mr. Beaugrand gave me to glance over' the treatise on dioptrics.

33. Ibid. (i. 355). Descartes had contrasted, in Rule 4 of the *Rules*, the methodical search for the truth that he recommended with the hit-or-miss strategy followed by others who hoped to stumble by accident on the truth (x. 371).

34. Descartes wrote (December 1637) that Beaugrand's *Geostatics* was worthless, and that when he claims to 'provide (in a preface) the means of finding tangents to all

curves which will be better than mine, it is no less ridiculous than the captains of Italian comedies' (i. 479). He asked Mersenne to keep this letter 'between ourselves', but the letter found its way back to Beaugrand. By contrast, Descartes wrote two letters to Mersenne to be forwarded to Fermat, on 5 October 1637 and January 1638, but by 25 January he was complaining that he had received no reply and that he had no intention of reading any more material by Fermat until he received replies to earlier letters. It appears that Descartes' letter of January 1638, for Fermat, was forwarded to him only in May of that year.

35. This was the *Methodus ad disquirendum maximam et minimam et de tangentibus linearum curvarum* (*Oeuvres*, i. 133–6.).

36. By this stage Descartes knew the identity of the author, but thought it a sign of civility to pretend otherwise, 'so that he will realize that I respond only to his writing' (i. 503).

37. Descartes against Roberval and Pascal, 1 March 1638, in which he refers to the 'defenders' of Fermat (ii. 2), and to the fact that Fermat 'has friends who are taking great pains to defend him' (ii. 12). Descartes goes on to say that, since they have taken the side of Fermat, in support of a position 'as unsustainable from his side as could be imagined', he hopes they would not be his judges (ii. 13). The reference to 'friends' of Fermat is repeated in Descartes to Mydorge (1 March 1638: ii. 22) and in Descartes to Mersenne (1 March 1638: ii. 26). Descartes says that he knows only two people in Paris who would be competent in this context, Mr. Mydorge and Mr. Hardy. He follows through on this estimate by writing to Mydorge, the same day, listing all the correspondence between Fermat and himself, and asking that he and Hardy adjudicate the controversy (Descartes to Mydorge, 1 March 1638: ii. 15). Descartes later acknowledged to Mersenne that Roberval and Pascal did not have 'the special relation with Mr. Fermat that your letter made me imagine' (Descartes to Mersenne, 31 March 1638: ii. 90). This gave him reason to hope that they would quickly see the truth. Roberval also set the record straight, in a letter to Mersenne in April 1638, by explaining that he and Pascal 'know Mr. Fermat and Mr. Descartes only by reputation' (ii. 114).

38. 'Combat' is used in Descartes to Roberval and Pascal (1 March 1638: ii. 12), and the language of 'seconds' in a duel is used in Descartes to Huygens (March 1638: ii. 49).

39. Descartes to Mersenne, 1 March 1638 (ii. 26–7). See also Descartes to Mersenne, 11 October 1638: 'I beseech you to retain in your own hands all the papers that I sent you which contain geometrical solutions, without giving them anything other than copies if they request them. And if you have loaned them some which they refuse to return, I ask you to request them for me' (ii. 400–1).

40. This low opinion was repeated after his death. Descartes expressed regret when he heard that Beaugrand had died in December 1640 (iii. 277). However, when Mersenne forwarded one of Beaugrand's letters to Descartes the following year, he was scathing in his comments. 'I am surprised that you decided to send me one of Mr. N's letters after his death, since you did not think it was worth my while seeing them when he was still alive. Since this man was never capable of

writing anything except such impertinent paralogisms when he was searching for the truth, it would have been a miracle had he found it when his only intention was to slander someone whom he hated. I have nothing to reply to this letter, except that there is not a single word in it against me that is not false and without proof. I would be very sorry if you took the trouble to send me his other letters, because we have enough paper here for its most ignoble of uses and his letters are no good for anything else.' Descartes to Mersenne, September 1637 (iii. 437).

41. Descartes to Mersenne, 29 June 1638 (ii. 189); to Mersenne, 1 March 1638 (ii. 32); to Mersenne, 31 March 1638 (ii. 96). However, Descartes later requested that some of the offensive comments about Beaugrand be deleted or moderated (Descartes to Mersenne, 27 July 1638: ii. 271–2).

42. Descartes hoped that Mydorge would adjudicate the merits of both sides and would favour Descartes (ii. 15).

43. Descartes to Mersenne, 15 November 1638, where he is surprised that Fermat was still objecting to the *Dioptrics* although 'he does not understand at all what he thinks he has refuted' (ii. 445).

44. Descartes to Mersenne, 30 April 1639. He wrote to Debeaune the same day: 'I think it would be poor form if I stopped to chase a little dog who only barks at me and does not have enough strength to bite' (30 April 1639: ii. 542).

45. See Mahoney (1994), 393, and the text from Fermat's letter to Mersenne, September 1637, quoted on p. 370: 'I planned to let you know my thoughts on that subject later; but, apart from the fact that I cannot satisfy myself yet, I shall await all the experiments that you have done or that you will do, following my request, on the various proportions between angles of incidence and those of refraction.'

46. *Algebra ofte Nieuwe Stel-Regel* (1639).

47. There were detailed diplomatic messages sent in both directions, with Huygens helping to find a compromise and Van Zurck acting as an intermediary, before the precise conditions of the contest were agreed upon and the terms of reference and identity of the jury were decided. The compromise reached by the two parties accepted the professors of mathematics at Leiden, Andreas van Berlikom (secretary of the city of Rotterdam), and Bernard Schotanus (professor of law and mathematics at Utrecht); ii. 725.

48. Descartes to Regius, 24 May 1640 (iii. 69).

49. He was inaugurated on 16 September 1638.

50. 'Mr Reneri came here and brought me the exact height of the Utrecht tower. It is exactly 350 royal feet, including the weather-cock at the top' (Descartes to Mersenne, 23 August, 1638: ii. 330–1). Reneri's visit is also confirmed by Descartes to Huygens, 19 August 1638: 'I had written the first part of this letter when Mr Reneri arrived here and told me that Mr Pollot is among the prisoners taken at Callo [the Callo fort near Antwerp had been lost by the Dutch on 14 June]' (ii. 672–3).

51. Saumaise wrote (7 March 1638) that Descartes had 'a large number of followers in these quarters, so much so that his book is read publicly in the Utrecht Academy by a professor of philosophy called Reyneri'. Quoted in Cohen (1920), 509.

52. Regius to Descartes [early February 1639]: 'I hope to avail of your permission during this week, which concludes our vacation. . . . I will spend two or three days in your company, to consult you about various plans that I have' (ii. 527).

53. Regius and Aemilius to Descartes, 29 March 1639 (ii. 528–9). Aemilius published a book of orations in 1651, in which he dedicated a poem to Reneri as follows: 'To the shades of Henricus Reneri, Professor of Philosophy at Utrecht University, who lived intimately with the most noble man, René Descartes, the Atlas and unique Archimedes of our time, from whom he learned to penetrate the secrets of nature and the limits of the heavens.' Aemilius (1651), 412. The poem and oration had been printed together in 1639.

54. Letter to Descartes, reported by Baillet (1691), ii. 35. Erik-Jan Bos (Regius 2002: 26) suggests that this letter was probably written in the first half of September, since Regius' son was born 23 September and died three days later.

55. It was established as an 'Illustrious School' on 20 August 1634 and as a university on 16 March 1636.

56. In Regius (2002: xxxiii), Bos corrects Clerselier's mistake of identifying 'Mr. R.' as Regius rather than Reneri.

57. Descartes to Mersenne, 9 January 1639 (ii. 481). Descartes' estimate was accurate. There was a Latin edition of the book (apart from the *Geometry*), under the title *Specimina Philosophiae*, in 1644, and a French edition of the same selected texts appeared only in 1658. For a full history of its publication, see Van Otegem (2002), i. 29–78.

58. Descartes to Mersenne, 20 February 1639 (ii. 525).

59. Descartes to Huygens, December 1638 (ii. 456), where he explained that Thomas Harriot's book had fallen behind the few books he kept in his study and that it had lain there hidden from view for six months.

60. Mersenne sent a copy of the French edition of Edward Herbert's book *On Truth*, but Descartes could not find time to read it (Descartes to Mersenne, 27 August 1639). He describes himself, on that occasion, as studying 'without a book' (ii. 571). Three months later he says that he could not hope to read Bouillau's *Philolai sive dissertationis de vero systemate mundi, libri iv* (1639) for another six months (Descartes to Mersenne, 13 November 1639: ii. 622), although he had said the previous December that he wanted to read it 'as soon as it is published' (Descartes to Mersenne, December 1638: ii. 464). He declined to read Campanella (Descartes to Mersenne, 15 November 1638: ii. 436) and Fermat (Descartes to Mersenne, 9 February 1639: ii. 502).

61. Cf. Descartes to Mersenne, 27 May 1638: 'I no longer wish to study that science' (ii. 149); and Descartes to Mersenne, 12 September 1638: 'However, please do not expect anything else from me in geometry. For you know that for a long time I have protested that I do not wish to exercise it and I think I can honestly put an end to it' (ii. 360–1). Even as early as December (?) 1633, Descartes had written similar comments to Stampioen (i. 275).

62. Descartes to Huygens, 5 October 1637 (i. 434).

63. Letter published in Jurgens and Mesnard (1975).

64. Descartes to Mersenne, 30 April 1639 (ii. 530) and 19 June 1639 (ii. 563).

65. Descartes to Mersenne, 19 June 1639 (ii. 567).

66. Descartes to Mersenne, 15 November 1638 (ii. 443).

67. For example, he wrote about Galileo (11 October 1638) that he saw nothing in his books that would cause him envy, that his best work was in music (confusing Galileo with his father, who had written about musical theory), and that there was a much better chance that Galileo had borrowed from him than the reverse! (ii. 388–9)

68. Baillet (1691), ii. 446.

69. Quoted by Adam and Tannery, ii. 642.

70. Bannius wrote to William Boswell (an English diplomat living at The Hague), 15 January 1638, that Descartes had visited him at Haarlem on January 13 and that they had discussed musical theory together (ii. 153). Descartes writes about Bannius as 'not only a Catholic but also a priest, who I think has a benefice at Haarlem. He is very expert in the practice of music' (Descartes to Mersenne, 27 May 1638: ii. 150). The following year, on 15 October 1639, Descartes and Bannius met again 'at midday' to discuss music (CM viii. 536).

71. Descartes attended this service on 9 November 1639, as a public celebration of the victory of the Dutch over the Spanish fleet at Duins, 21 October 1639.

72. Descartes to Plemp, August 1638 (ii. 344).

73. Descartes to Mersenne, 27 July 1638 (ii. 267).

74. Descartes to Mersenne, 15 November 1639 (ii. 443) and 9 January 1639: 'Given the few copies that the publisher says he had sold, I do not see any real likelihood that he will have it reprinted' (ii. 481).

75. He did not observe this self-imposed interruption, for he wrote to Mersenne again one month later, on 9 February, although he repeated the request not to forward any writings and even to discourage potential correspondents from sending him anything (ii. 498–9).

76. Descartes to Huygens, 29 January 1639 (ii. 675–6).

77. Descartes to Mersenne, 27 February 1637 (i. 350).

78. Descartes to Wicquefort, 2 October 1640 (Bos and Vermeulen 2002: 102) and 5 October 1640 (iii. 735).

79. Descartes to Mersenne, 11 March 1640 (iii. 39).

80. Huygens gave as his address 'the fort of Nassau on the island of Voorn'. The De Voorn fortress was situated between the Maas and Waal Rivers, near Heerewaarden, and was also the return address for Huygens to Descartes, 6 June 1643. See Verbeek et al. (2003), 83.

81. Descartes to Mersenne, 20 February 1639 (ii. 525).

82. Apart from Huygens and Mersenne, who often asked Descartes to reconsider his decision not to publish *The World*, Pollot (I, 518), Saumaise (Cohen: 1920; 509), and Rivet (CM, vii. 185–6) all referred to the unpublished work. Mersenne even suggested that if the prince of Orange were to use his influence, Descartes might relent and agree to publish. He suggested this to Rivet, who at the time was governor to the prince's children (CM, viii. 182–3).

Chapter 7

1. Descartes to Mersenne, 16 October 1639 (ii. 596). He also wrote to Mersenne, 27 August 1639, that 'metaphysics is a science that almost no one understands' (ii. 570).

2. Descartes to Gibieuf, 18 July 1629. Although he did not specify that the treatise in question was on metaphysics, it seems clear from corroborating evidence that it was. He wrote: 'I am waiting to bother you when I have completed a little treatise that I am beginning. I would not have asked you anything about it until it was finished if I had not feared that the length of time involved would cause you to forget that you promised me to correct it and to add the final touches to it. I do not hope to finish it for two or three years and I may decide to burn it then or, at least, it will not escape from my hands and from those of my friends without being examined in detail. For, if I am not skilled enough to produce something worthwhile, I shall try at least to be wise enough not to publish my imperfections' (i. 17).

3. Descartes to Mersenne, 15 April 1630 (i. 144). In Part IV of the *Discourse on Method*, he wrote about his first months in the United Provinces: 'I do not know if I should tell you about the first meditations that I did there, because they are so metaphysical and unusual that they may not be to everyone's taste' (vi. 31).

4. It is clear why he refused to publish *The World*. He wrote to Mersenne, December 1640, that 'nothing has prevented me so far from publishing my Philosophy apart from the prohibition on the Earth's movement' (iii. 258). Descartes then explained that he accepted the infallibility of the church, that he did not doubt the reasons that supported his cosmology, and therefore that these two truths must be compatible. However, he did not wish to put himself at risk of censure from the church while the question of compatibility was being resolved. The question raised here is why he was so fearful of a censure.

5. Mersenne to Rivet, 15 September 1639 (CM viii. 511).

6. In a letter to Mersenne, 15 April 1630, Descartes mentions that he could not have found the foundations of his physics if he had not studied metaphysics (i. 144). There was an obvious sense in which the laws of nature and other basic assumptions about matter and explanation, which were included in *The World*, were foundations of his natural philosophy. Thus, Descartes seems to have been willing, in 1640–41, to reveal his metaphysical foundations while still reserving for later publication (in the *Principles of Philosophy*, 1644) the fundamental physical assumptions of his natural philosophy.

7. There were Latin editions published in 1624 and 1633, and Descartes acknowledges having read the Latin edition previously (Descartes to Mersenne, 19 June 1639: ii. 566). The French edition, *De la Verité, en tant qu'elle est distincte de la Revelation, du Vray-semblable, du Possible et du Faux*, was published in Paris in 1639.

8. Descartes to Mersenne, 27 August 1639 (ii. 570–1) and 16 October 1639 (ii. 596–8).

9. Descartes to Mersenne, 13 November 1639 (ii. 622).

10. Descartes uses the term 'essay' here in the sense of an attempt to write metaphysics or a sample of his efforts to do so. In the same paragraph, he assured Mersenne that he was not as deprived of books as might have been thought, since he had a copy of Aquinas' '*Summa* [presumably the *Summa of Theology*] and a Bible that I brought from France' (ii. 630).

11. Descartes to Mersenne (March 1637) (i. 349–50).

12. Descartes explicitly endorses this interpretation in his replies to Burman in April 1648. 'There is a summary of these *Meditations* in that section of the *Discourse on Method* which ought to be explained by the *Meditations* themselves' (v. 153).

13. For example, Descartes to Mersenne, 11 March 1640: 'I cannot say how much weight is required to equal the force of a hammer stroke because that is a factual question, in which reasoning is useless without the experience' (iii. 34–5); 'I cannot determine the speed with which every heavy body descends initially, because that is a completely factual question' (iii. 36). The same comment appears about the urine of a mad person (iii. 49), and about the declination of a magnetic needle (iii. 85).

14. Silhon (1634), 5.

15. Ibid., 178–9.

16. Sextus Empiricus (1562). That this is the principal source of sceptical objections is acknowledged in Schoock (1643), 96–7, 173–4; Verbeek (1988), 228, 268, which is discussed in Chapter 8.

17. De Gournay (2002). This interpretation of De Gournay has been developed by Eileen O'Neill.

18. 'Anybody can provide as many examples as he pleases of the ways our senses deceive or cheat us. . . .'; 'why should we therefore not doubt whether our thinking and acting are but another dream; our waking, some other species of sleep?' 'If this appearance has once deceived me, if my touchstone regularly proves unreliable and my scales wrong and out of true, why should I trust them this time, rather than all the others?' Montaigne (1991), 669, 674, 634–5.

19. Descartes to Mersenne, 30 July 1640 (iii. 121).

20. Richeome (1621).

21. Denzinger (1960), par. 738; Richeome (1621), 217.

22. Richeome (1621), 230–1.

23. Ibid., 24.

24. Ibid., 28.

25. Ibid., 44. I am using the word 'animal' here as an abbreviation for 'nonhuman animal' and as a translation of the French term '*bête*'.

26. La Mothe le Vayer (1647), 12.

27. Ibid., 252.

28. This interpretation is confirmed by Descartes to Mersenne, September 1641, in which he writes following the publication of the *Meditations*: 'In publishing it, I did what I thought I was obliged to do for the glory of God and the demands of my conscience' (iii. 436). The motto of the Jesuits was then, and still remains: 'For the greater glory of God.'

29. See Descartes to Mersenne, 19 January 1642, where he uses the 'war and peace' metaphor to comment that the Jesuits seem not to want 'peace' as long as they deal with him indirectly through Father Bourdin (iii. 481).

30. Descartes to Mersenne, 22 July 1640 (iii. 94–6). Descartes' frequent feigning not to know something that he obviously knows raises a general problem about how to read his letters. For example, he wrote to Mersenne, 22 December 1641, that he had pretended that he would not even dare ask that his letter be shown to the Jesuit provincial superior, while simultaneously suggesting that he would be disappointed if Mersenne were not able to arrange for that to happen (iii. 470).

31. The proverb quoted in Latin is from Plautus, *Amphitruo*, II, 2, 707. Clerselier may have modified the allusion, in the Latin text, to the Jesuits as hornets by translating this phrase into French as: 'although I have known for a long time that one should not draw one's adversaries on oneself' (iii. 103).

32. Descartes to Mersenne, 22 July 1640 (iii. 95). His later contrast with critics in Utrecht is discussed at length in Chapter 8.

33. Descartes to Mersenne for Bourdin, 29 July 1640 (iii. 105–18).

34. Descartes to Mersenne, 30 August 1640 (iii. 160, 168)

35. See a similar scheming letter to Mersenne, December 1640 (iii. 253–5). Descartes repeatedly alleged that objections voiced by one Jesuit were likely to represent the views of the whole Society, although he knew that this was not true. He was evidently using this ploy to provoke the Jesuits into writing some kind of official response to his *Meditations*. He repeated the same idea, and withdrew it in the face of the evidence, in replying to Father Bourdin's objections (vii. 452, 453), and in his letter to Father Dinet (vii. 544).

36. Descartes to Mersenne, 22 December 1641 (iii. 469).

37. In a letter to Mersenne, 30 September 1640 (iii. 185), Descartes mentioned this strategy. By December of that year, he was reconsidering the idea (iii. 251), and in Descartes to Mersenne, 22 December 1641, he admits to having given it up entirely (iii. 470). However, he asked Mersenne, 19 January 1642 (iii. 480–1), not to reveal his change of mind to the Jesuits and to encourage them to believe that he still planned to target their philosophy.

38. Descartes to Huygens, 22 January 1642 (iii. 775, 776). Descartes was living at Endegeest at that time, but it was close enough to Leiden that the latter could be used as a penultimate address.

39. He attributes to Descartes the unquestioned assumption that 'nothing belongs to the body apart from what I previously understood as belonging to it' (vii. 497), to which Descartes' reply is completely unsatisfactory.

40. He concluded his prolix replies to Bourdin with the comment: 'Since he says he is my friend and since I deal with him in as friendly a manner as possible ... I commend our bricklayer to his superior' (vii. 561).

41. The Sorbonne's monopoly in granting degrees was a source of bitter controversy with the Jesuits. See, for example, the collection of defensive tracts published on behalf of the Sorbonne under the title: *Traictez pour la Deffence de l'université de Paris, contre les Iesuites* (1643). The sharpness of the exchanges seems to have

increased with the passing of time. In 1663, a pamphlet was published in Paris that was subsequently translated into English as: *A Truth Known to very Few: viz. That the Jesuits are down-right compleat Atheists: Proved such, and condemned for it by Two Sentences of the Famous Faculty of Sorbonne* (1680).

42. Descartes to Mersenne, 11 March 1640 (iii. 36–7).

43. Descartes to Mersenne, 1 April 1640 (iii. 50). The following month he had moved to Leiden, but was still toying with the idea of visiting England. On this occasion he had been invited by Kenelm Digby, but Descartes thought it would be best, if he were to go there, to travel for personal reasons rather than simply because he was invited by someone else. Descartes to Mersenne, 11 June 1640 (iii. 87). I discuss Digby's relations with Descartes in Chapter 10.

44. Descartes to Pollot, 7 May 1640 (iii. 62). See also Descartes to Mersenne, 11 June 1640, in which he refers to his change of residence as the reason why he had not replied to letters since March (iii. 72).

45. Regius to Descartes, 5 May 1640 (iii. 61); Descartes to Regius, 24 May 1640 (iii. 63).

46. Descartes to Regius, 24 May 1640 (iii. 70). I discuss Descartes' relations with Van Schurman in Chapter 9.

47. Bos (2002), 49, speculates that Descartes may have been planning merely to visit his daughter Francine, who had died in Amersfoort on 7 September 1640, since there is no other indication of his having plans to live there.

48. Descartes to Mersenne, 30 July 1640 (iii. 126–7).

49. Descartes to Huygens, August 1640 (iii. 159), where he mentions a trip of four or five months; and Descartes to Mersenne, 15 September 1640 (iii. 178), where he mentions the proposed date of departure.

50. Descartes to Mersenne, 30 September 1640 (iii. 183–4).

51. Descartes to Mersenne, 30 September 1640 (iii. 185).

52. Descartes to Mersenne, 28 October 1640, in which he promised to send it 'in eight or nine days at the latest. . . . I wish to have a copy made first' (iii. 216). Descartes to Mersenne, 11 November 1640: 'I sent my *Metaphysics* yesterday to Mr. Huygens to forward to you' (iii. 235).

53. The proposed title was evidently in Latin: *Renati Descartes Meditationes de prima Philosophia* (iii. 235).

54. Descartes to Gibieuf, 11 November 1640 (iii. 237).

55. Decartes to Mersenne, 11 November 1640 (iii. 239–40).

56. Descartes to Mersenne, 24 December 1640 (iii. 265, 267).

57. Huygens to Descartes, 17 July 1641 (iii. 770), and Descartes to Huygens, 29 July 1641 (iii. 772). Descartes had a good excuse for not consulting Barlaeus. He had invited him to submit objections to the *Meteors* in 1639, but, despite having kept the manuscript for over a year, he had produced nothing. Besides, given his theological leanings, Barlaeus was most unlikely to react favourably to the *Meditations*.

58. Descartes to Mersenne, 24 December 1640 (iii. 265–6). This point is repeated in Descartes to Mersenne, 28 January 1641, when he suggests, as a title for the

Second Meditation: 'The Human Mind, that it is better known than the body', 'so that people will not think that I wished to prove its immortality' (iii. 297).

59. Descartes to Mersenne, 11 November 1640 (iii. 239).

60. See Descartes to Mersenne, 31 December 1640 (iii. 271–7).

61. Descartes to Mersenne, 21 January 1641 (iii. 282).

62. Hobbes to Mersenne for Descartes, 7 February 1641 (iii. 303).

63. Descartes to Mersenne for Hobbes, 21 January 1641 (iii. 287). The controversy continued in correspondence exchanged by Hobbes and Descartes through the intermediary of Mersenne: Hobbes to Mersenne for Descartes, 7 February 1641 (iii. 300); Descartes to Mersenne for Hobbes, 18 February 1641 (iii. 313); Descartes to Mersenne, 4 March 1641, in which only part of the letter was for Hobbes (iii. 321–6); Hobbes to Mersenne for Descartes, 30 March 1641 (iii. 341); Descartes to Mersenne for Hobbes (iii. 353).

64. Descartes to Mersenne, 28 January 1641 (iii. 293). Even on first reading, on 22 January 1641, Descartes was reluctant about this 'Englishman' and suspected that he was not worth replying to (iii. 283).

65. Descartes to Mersenne, 4 March 1641: 'I was the first to write it' (iii. 322); Hobbes to Mersenne for Descartes: 'when you say that I could have borrowed a hypothesis from him which he had published first, you will be my witness, I hope, that it is seven years since I discussed with you in your lodging the reflection of the rainbow' (iii. 342).

66. Descartes to Mersenne, 4 March, 18 March, and 31 March 1641 (iii. 330–1, 334, 349). Arnauld received his doctorate on 19 December 1641.

67. Descartes to Mersenne, 18 March 1641 (iii. 334–40).

68. Descartes to Huygens, 29 July 1641 (iii. 771) and 26 April 1642 (iii. 785); Descartes to Mersenne, 22 July 1641 (iii. 416).

69. See the letters from Gassendi quoted in iii. 363–5.

70. When Princess Elizabeth got a copy of the French translation of the *Meditations*, she commented that Gassendi, 'who has a great reputation for his knowledge, wrote objections that – apart from the Englishman – were less reasonable than all the others.' Elizabeth to Descartes, 5 December 1647 (v. 97).

71. Descartes to Mersenne, 23 June 1641 (iii. 384).

72. Descartes mentions the possibility of getting an official endorsement in many letters following the initial criticism by Bourdin, although the Sorbonne is not always explicitly mentioned. Descartes to Mersenne, 30 July 1640 (iii. 126–7); Descartes to Mersenne, 30 September 1640 (iii. 184); Descartes to Mersenne, 11 November 1640 (iii. 233); Descartes to Mersenne, 31 March 1641 (iii. 350); Descartes to Mersenne, 21 April 1641 (iii. 359); Descartes to Huygens, 29 July 1641 (iii. 771).

73. See Armogathe (1994).

74. 'As regards my *Metaphysics*, I have stopped thinking about it since the day I sent my reply to Hyperaspistes. . . . thus I cannot reply to any of the things you asked me about it, eight days ago, except to ask you not to think any more about it than I do.' Descartes to Mersenne, September 1641 (iii. 436).

75. Descartes to Mersenne, 23 June 1641 (iii. 388) and 22 July 1641 (iii. 415); Descartes to Hygens, 29 July 1641 (iii. 771).

76. Descartes to Mersenne, 17 November, 1641 (iii. 448) and 19 January 1642 (iii. 484); Descartes to Regius (November 1641): 'The printing of my *Meditations* was completed three months ago in Paris, but I have not received a copy yet. For that reason I have agreed to have a second edition done in this country' (iii. 445).

77. Descartes to Mersenne, 17 November 1641 (iii. 449).

78. Descartes to Huygens, 26 April 1642 (iii. 784). The first part is paginated 1–496; the second part, containing the Seventh Objections, Descartes' replies, and the Letter to Father Dinet, is paginated 1–212.

79. This is developed at great length in the Seventh Replies, vii. 536–61. The letter to Father Dinet also claimed that 'all the principles of the philosophy that I am preparing' are contained in the *Meditations* (vii. 602).

80. Descartes used this metaphor on two occasions, in his replies to Hobbes (vii. 172) and in his letter to Father Dinet (vii. 574).

81. Descartes to Mersenne, 16 October 1639 (ii. 599): 'I had much less difficulty reading it [Herbert's *On Truth*] in French than I had earlier in going through it in Latin.' See also Descartes to Pollot, 1 January 1644 (iv. 73). Among the 498 letters in the Adam and Tannery edition, only 63 are written in Latin.

82. Many texts clarify this position. For example: 'When we say that some idea is innate in us, we do not think that it is always present to us; in that sense no idea would be innate. We mean only that we have within us a power to produce the idea in question' (vii. 189); 'by "innate ideas" I have never understood anything else apart from what he himself [i.e., Regius] explicitly claims as true . . . namely: "that we have in us a natural power by which we are capable of knowing God." I have never either thought or written that the ideas in question are actual. . . . I cannot refrain from laughing when I see the large number of arguments which this gentleman . . . has laboriously put together to prove that infants in their mother's womb have no actual knowledge of God, as if he were thereby launching a magnificent attack on me' (viii-2. 366). See also Descartes to Hyperaspistes, August 1641: 'I do not think, as a result, that an infant's mind meditates about metaphysical questions in its mother's womb' (iii. 423).

83. Descartes spelled that out in reply to Hobbes: 'For who is there who does not perceive that there is something that they understand? Who therefore does not have the form or idea of understanding and, by extending this indefinitely, does not form the idea of God's understanding, and by a similar procedure an idea of the other attributes of God?' (vii. 188)

84. Oliver Ranner has reminded me that it is also found in Aristotle. See Aristotle (2000), 178 (1170a): 'if someone who sees perceives that he sees, and one who hears that he hears, and one who walks that he walks, and in the case of other activities there is similarly something that perceives that one is engaged in them, so that, if we perceive, we perceive that we perceive, and if we think, we perceive that we think; and if to perceive that we perceive or think is to perceive that we exist (since we saw that to exist is to perceive or think).'

85. The relevant text from Augustine reads: 'So far as these truths are concerned, I do not at all fear the arguments of the Academics when they say, What if you are mistaken? For if I am mistaken, I exist. He who does not exist clearly cannot be mistaken; and so, if I am mistaken, then, by the same token, I exist.' Augustine (1998), 484.

86. Descartes acknowledged to Mersenne, December 1640, that he had also asked him about this passage and had repeated the request later (iii. 261), to which Descartes replied with the reference to *The City of God*. See also Descartes to Mersenne, 21 January 1641 (iii. 283, 284), and Descartes to Mersenne, 21 April 1641 (iii. 358–9).

87. As Mersenne had noticed, there is not a word about the 'immortality' of the soul in the *Meditations*. Descartes replied that he had aimed merely to show that the soul is distinct from the body, and that philosophy could not support religious belief any more than that. Descartes to Mersenne, 24 December 1640 (iii. 265–6). Fowler (1999: 29) also points out that the word 'immortality' never occurs in any of the six meditations.

88. There is much less agreement about the general structure of Descartes' argument than this suggests. Here I draw on the analysis in Clarke (2003).

89. Descartes to Reneri for Pollot, April or May 1638 (ii. 38). See also Descartes' reply to Hobbes, where he argues: 'Since, however, we do not know a substance itself immediately through itself, but only by the fact that it is the subject of certain acts, it is very reasonable and in keeping with common usage that we apply different names to those substances that we recognize as the subjects of completely different acts or accidents, so as to examine later whether those different names signify different things or one and the same thing' (vii. 176).

90. The similarity with saint Anselm seems to have been pointed out by Mersenne, to whom Descartes replied (December 1640) that he would consult Anselm's text at the first opportunity (iii. 261).

91. Morin's book was published in Paris in 1635, with the title (in Latin): *That God Exists, and that the world was created by him in time, and is governed by his providence. Some selected theorems against Atheists.* In contrast with Descartes, Morin had received official church approval for his work. Descartes told Mersenne, 31 December 1640, that he would not object to seeing Morin's book (iii. 275). Mersenne obliged by sending a copy to Huygens, for forwarding to Descartes (Descartes to Mersenne, 21 January 1641: iii. 283).

92. Descartes to Mersenne, 28 January 1641 (iii. 293–4). Descartes also thought it was a mistake on Morin's part to make claims about infinity, something he carefully avoided doing himself, but that Mersenne should keep these criticisms confidential because he did not wish to offend the author.

93. The premise is that various ideas contain different degrees of intentional reality, and that the degree of intentional reality present in any idea must be explained in terms of its cause. Since the idea of God contains, intentionally, the reality of an infinite being, it must be the case that such an infinite being exists. Otherwise, we could offer no adequate explanation of how we came to have an idea of an infinite being.

94. He apologized for a delay in replying to a letter from Mersenne on March 25 because he was in the process of moving; Descartes to Mersenne, 11 June 1640 (iii. 72). On 31 March 1641, he told Mersenne that he had moved from Leiden, although it was not necessary to change the address on letters since the messenger knew where he lived (iii. 350–1). By April 1641, he was writing to Huygens from Endegeest (iii. 767–8).

95. Descartes to Mersenne, 11 March 1640 (iii. 35–6).

96. Huygens sent letters addressed to Descartes to Van Hogelande's house in Leiden, 24 July 1640; 27 April 1642 (iii. 750, 787). Descartes wrote to De Wilhem, 6 June 1640, that he and Van Hogelande would go to Gillot's house on 14 June, thereby suggesting that Descartes was not living with Gillot at that time.

97. Descartes to De Wilhem, 6 June 1640 (iii. 91). Johanna died in 1656.

98. Descartes to De Wilhem, 24 June 1640 (iii. 93).

99. He died on 18 October. Baillet reports that he was buried in the Church of the Franciscans at Nantes, 20 October 1640, and that Descartes had written to him on 28 October, ten days after he died. Baillet (1691), ii. 94.

100. Descartes appointed Jacques Bouexic de la Villeneuve as his legal representative in Rennes after his father's death. See Baillet (1691), ii. 95, and Descartes (2003), 45; Descartes to Pollot, 7 December 1648 (v. 235).

101. Descartes to Mersenne, 15 September 1640 (iii. 176) and 4 March 1641, (iii. 332).

102. Descartes to Mersenne, 4 March 1641, where he refers to a 'counsellor and the others who wish to come to visit' (iii. 332). The 'counsellor' may have been Jacques Vallée des Barreaux (1599–1673). On 23 June 1641, Descartes wrote to Mersenne: 'Mr. Picot is here at Leiden and seems to want to remain there. We often meet together. His two companions come and go and I think they will return to France soon' (iii. 388).

103. For Picot and his friends Jacques Vallée des Barreaux (1599–1673), Damien Milton (1618–90), and Jacques Bordier († 1660), see Descartes (2003), 284–7.

104. Descartes to Huygens, 8 December 1647 (v. 653).

105. Descartes to Mersenne, 21 January 1641 (iii. 282) and 4 March 1641 (iii. 319).

106. The castle had been occupied by Nicolas van Schouwen until his death in 1638. It was inherited by his nephew, Pieter van Foreest van Schouwen, in March 1639. Since he was living in Rome and still a minor, he could not officially assume ownership until he reached the age of twenty-five. However, he died on 11 January 1644, before reaching his legal maturity. Descartes evidently rented the castle during this period when there was only a provisional owner. For information on the Schouwen family, see v. 579–80.

107. Baillet (1691), ii. 167.

108. Descartes to Mersenne, 29 January 1640 (iii. 9–10); 11 June 1640 (iii. 78); 6 August 1640 (iii. 146); 30 August 1640 (iii. 163–4); 15 September 1640 (iii. 180).

109. Descartes to Mersenne, 29 January 1640 (iii. 15).

110. Descartes to Mersenne, 11 March 1640 (iii. 42), and Descartes to Huygens, 12 March 1640 (iii. 746).

111. Descartes to Meyssonnier, 29 January 1640 (iii. 18), and Descartes to Mersenne, 1 April 1640 (iii. 49).

112. Eustace of St. Paul died in Paris the same month, on 26 December 1640.
113. Villiers to Mersenne, 9/10 December 1640: CM, x. 319.
114. Descartes to (Father Charlet?), (December 1640?), (iii. 270).
115. Descartes to Mersenne, 22 December 1641 (iii. 470).

Chapter 8

1. Schook (1643), 262; Verbeek (1988), 316.
2. Schoock (1643), p. 17 of unpaginated Preface; Verbeek (1988), 16.
3. Descartes to Huygens, 26 April 1642 (iii. 784).
4. Descartes referred to the anonymous university as the 'most recently founded' in the United Provinces. That was enough to provide a unique identification. Utrecht had become a university in 1636. All the others were founded much earlier – Groningen in 1614, Franeker in 1586, and Leiden in 1575.
5. 'In all the meetings that took place, he sat as judge and at the same time as the most bitter accuser, while the physician was not heard and was not even present. Who would doubt, then, that he had any difficulty in leading his colleagues to the conclusion he wanted and that he was able to overcome resistance by the sheer number of his followers?' (vii. 589)
6. Verbeek (1988), 86.
7. Regius (2002), 24.
8. Verbeek (1988), 87–8.
9. Descartes to Regius, 24 May 1640 (iii. 66–70), and Regius to Descartes, 30 May 1640 (iii. 71).
10. Descartes to Regius (June 1640) (iii. 63–5). Here I follow the revised date suggested in Regius (2002), 51.
11. Regius (1640).
12. Descartes to Regius [April 1641] (iv. 239–40), redated by Verbeek (1988: 451–2).
13. Descartes to Regius [May 1641] (iii. 369, 371, 375)
14. Regius (1641), 3, 9–10.
15. Voetius' views were drafted as corollaries to Regius and were scheduled to be presented on 28 December 1641. They included his critiques of (a) the suggestion that the unity of human nature is accidental, (b) the Copernican system, and (c) the denial of substantial forms (iii. 487–8). Voetius was persuaded not to present these publicly, but in early January 1642 he returned to the same themes under the title: *Appendix ad Corollaria theologico-philosophica nuperae disputationi de Jubileo Romano, De rerum naturis et formis substantialibus* (excerpts quoted in iii. 511–20). See also Verbeek (1988), 98–9, 100–2, 103–15.
16. Regius to Descartes, 24 January 1642 (iii. 490).
17. Regius to Descartes, 5 March 1642 (iii. 534).
18. Letter to Father Dinet: 'he convened his academic senate and complained about a pamphlet published by one of his colleagues against him, and said that it should be proscribed and that all the philosophy that disturbed the peace of the university should be eliminated' (vii. 589).

19. The committee also included Meinardus Schotanus (theology), Guilielmus Stratenus (medicine), and Arnold Senguerd (philosophy). See Verbeek (1988), 74.

20. Descartes to Pollot, March 1642 (iii. 550).

21. Descartes to Regius, April 1642 (iii. 558).

22. Quoted in Descartes, *Correspondance*, v. 209–10.

23. Descartes to Mersenne, 7 December 1642 (iii. 598).

24. Descartes repeats this altruistic justification for replying to Voetius in a letter to Mersenne, 23 March 1643 (iii. 642–3).

25. These letters are now lost. Descartes quotes from them in his letter to the French ambassador, La Thuillerie, 22 January 1644 (iv. 88), and in his *Apologetic Letter* (viii-2. 205–6). He told Van Hogelande where to find these letters among the papers that he entrusted to him, in a suitcase that was to be opened after his death. Descartes to Van Hogelande, 30 August 1649 (v. 410).

26. Mersenne to Voetius, 13 December 1642 (iii. 602–4).

27. Huygens to Descartes, 7 January 1643 (iii. 802).

28. Descartes to Samuel Maresius [late January or early February 1643] (iii. 605–7). The book in question was *De Confraternitate Mariana* (On the Marian Confraternity).

29. The toleration of Catholicism in districts recovered from the Spanish continued to be a contentious issue in subsequent alliances between France and the United Provinces, and it was one of the reasons why the *Stadholder* often found himself at odds with a changing majority, of Counter-Remonstrants or Arminians, in the largest province (Holland). In the 1635–36 campaign, Richelieu insisted on toleration of the Catholic religion in captured territories.

30. One cannot assume that he wrote the book in the order in which it was published. However, the sections on magnetism eventually appeared in the final part, Part IV, sections 139 ff.

31. Descartes to Colvius, 5 September 1643, repeats this assessment. Descartes found 'nothing solid' in Kircher (iv. 718).

32. Descartes to Mersenne, 23 June 1641. He qualified his lack of interest in Jansen with the phrase: 'I would be happy to know where it was published so that I can get a copy if I need one' (iii. 387).

33. Gassendi's book was *De motu impresso a motore translato, epistolae duae* (Paris, 1642).

34. Descartes to Mersenne, 2 February 1643 (iii. 615). Gassendi had accepted the decision by the committee of cardinals to punish Galileo for his disobedience, without conceding that their decision was an article of faith (pp. 155–7); hence Descartes' lack of sympathy for his new book on motion, including the Earth's motion.

35. Descartes to Huygens, 18/19 February 1643: 'I have little trust in experiments that I have not done myself. . . . artisans implement so poorly what they are told to do' (iii. 617).

36. Descartes to Colvius, 20 April 1643 (iii. 646–7).

37. Descartes to Colvius, 20 April 1643 (iii. 647).

38. Schoock (1643). Rivet refers to its appearance in a letter to Sarrau, 30 March 1643, in Bots and Leroy (1978–82), i. 434.

39. Schoock was appointed to Deventer in 1638, and at Groningen in 1640. See Verbeek (1998), 49–50.

40. Schoock (1643), pp. 33, 46, 49 of unpaginated Preface, 43, 124; Verbeek (1988), 165, 168, 200, 208, 242.

41. Schoock (1643), 262; Verbeek (1988), 316.

42. The query about practising religion is in Schoock (1643), 265–6; Verbeek (1988), 317, while the comparison to Vanini is found in Schoock (1643), 262; Verbeeck (1988), 316.

43. Schoock (1643), pp. 61–2 of unpaginated Preface; Verbeek (1988), 171.

44. Schoock (1643), 211; Verbeek (1988), 287.

45. Schoock (1643), p. 13 of unpaginated Preface; Verbeek (1988), 160. Descartes replies to this comparison to Vanini in the *Letter to Voetius* (viii-2. 142).

46. Schoock (1643), 142; Verbeek (1988), 251.

47. Schoock (1643), 123; Verbeek (1988), 241–2. See also pp. 74–5, 218. Descartes' similar reply to Mersenne is quoted earlier on p. 167.

48. Schoock (1643), 96–7, 173–4, 177–89; Verbeek (1988), 228, 268, 270–6.

49. Descartes to Mersenne, 23 March 1643 (iii. 642–3); to Colvius, 23 April 1643 (iii. 646–7); to Huygens, 22 May 1643 (iii. 814–15).

50. Descartes to (Samuel Maresius) (late January or early February 1643): 'What I am most pleased about is that what I shall write will be published in Latin and in Dutch, because I think it is important that people are disabused of the excessively high opinion they have of this man [Voetius]' (iii. 607).

51. Mill wrote in Chapter 2 of *On Liberty* (Mill, 1989: 20): 'But the peculiar evil of silencing the expression of an opinion is, that it is robbing the human race; posterity as well as the existing generation; those who dissent from the opinion, still more than those who hold it. If the opinion is right, they are deprived of the opportunity of exchanging error for truth; if wrong, they lose, what is almost as great a benefit, the clearer perception and livelier impression of truth, produced by its collision with error.'

52. *Letter to Voetius* (viii-2. 20).

53. Ibid., viii-2. 20; 'I have not yet published a philosophy that could have followers' (viii-2. 24); 'since you have never seen it [my philosophy], because I have not published it, you obviously cannot know it' (viii-2. 38).

54. Ibid., viii-2, 20.

55. This partisan portrait of a dispute-prone Voetius is confirmed by a relatively independent witness, Samuel Sorbière: 'He was always at odds with one of his colleagues or with some other learned man. I saw him implacably opposed sometimes to Vedelius and Maresius, sometimes to Regius and Descartes, at other times again to Borel, Courçelles and an infinity of others with whom he delighted in having rows.' Sorbière (1660a), 182.

56. Descartes repeats this charge of interfering in the affairs of another republic toward the conclusion of his *Letter*. 'Were you not too inquisitive into the affairs of another republic when, in these same theses, you accused of idolatry the leading citizens of 's-Hertogenbosch' (viii-2. 192).

57. Israel (1995), 542. Given the delicate balance that was under negotiation at the time between provincial autonomy and national unity, Descartes was able to claim

five years later, in his *Apologetic Letter to the Magistrates of Utrecht*, that Voetius had evidently slandered these worthy citizens in his ill-tempered public criticism of their conduct (viii-2. 239).

58. Huygens had been attacked by Voetius earlier, because of his support for the use of the organ in Reformed churches.

59. Huygens to Descartes, 6 June 1643 (iii. 678).

60. Colvius to Descartes, 9 June 1643 (iii. 680–2).

61. Mersenne to Rivet, 29 May 1643: 'It is most unfortunate in this world to be classified as an atheist who should be burned after having done everything in one's power to prove the existence of God' (CM, xii. 194).

62. See Raimondi (1998) and the discussion in Chapter 3, this volume.

63. Descartes to M. de la Thuillerie, 22 January 1644 (iv. 86). He repeated this complaint later in the same letter: 'he clearly claimed that I teach atheism here surreptitiously and in a completely occult style, just like Vanini who was burned at Toulouse' (iv. 89).

64. Descartes to Mersenne, 30 May 1643 (iii. 674), where Descartes explains that he has travelled from his new residence in Egmond to Amsterdam to finalize publication of the letter with Louis Elzevier in Amsterdam.

65. The *Historical Narrative* was dated 28 September/8 October 1643, but was probably made public only in October of the same year. See Descartes to De Wilhem, 7 November 1643 (iv. 34).

66. The immediate reason for moving may have been the expiration of his lease at Endegeest. That leaves open the question why he moved so far north to the relative isolation of Egmond.

67. Descartes to Mersenne, 30 May 1643: 'It is four or five weeks since I wrote to you, because I have changed my residence and I am now in a district a bit further away, where I receive letters that you have sent to Leiden only about eight days after they arrive there' (iii. 672).

68. Descartes to the *Vroedschap* of Utrecht, 6 July 1643 (iv. 9–12), which was written in Dutch.

69. Descartes to Graswinckel, 17 October 1643, in which Descartes describes him as a 'good angel whom God has sent from heaven to assist me' (iv. 19).

70. Descartes to Pollot, 17 October 1643 (iv. 24); Descartes later wrote to Huygens that 'Pollot is working on my behalf, I would not say like a brother, for I do not receive such support from mine, but like a friend who is more solicitous for my interests than I could ever be myself.' Descartes to Huygens, 15 November 1643 (iv. 764).

71. Brasset to Descartes, 10 November 1643 (iv. 653).

72. Descartes to De Willem, 26 February 1644 (iv. 98–9). The text of the ambassador's letter is reproduced in iv. 96.

73. Descartes to Pollot, 15 January 1644 (iv. 81).

74. Descartes to Pollot, 22 January 1644 (iv. 82).

75. This is a summary rather than an exact translation of the text, which is reproduced in iv. 198–9.

76. Descartes to Tobias Andreae, 26 May 1645 (iv. 215).
77. Descartes to Huygens, 4 August 1645 (iv. 261).
78. I rely on the revised dating and analysis of Bos (1996). The *Letter* was probably written in French, although Descartes arranged for a Dutch translation to be submitted as well. However, he accepted responsibility only for the original French version. See viii-2. 275.
79. The Preface to the first volume of Voetius' disputations was dated 1 October 1647.
80. Descartes to Bourdin, 7 September 1642 (iii. 575–7).
81. Descartes to Dinet, October 1644 (iv. 142–3).

Chapter 9

1. Descartes, writing from Paris to Princess Elizabeth in The Hague (July 1644), (v. 64–5). On the redating of this letter, from July 1647 to July 1644, see v. 553.
2. Catherine Descartes (1637–1706) recorded this version of events in a poem. See Catherine Descartes (1745), 248.
3. Since there are no independent indications of financial support for his former nurse throughout her life, the death-bed wish may have been a result of the dying philosopher's feverish imagination.
4. Charles Adam (1937b) makes a valiant effort to situate Descartes in a context of feminine friendships that include his grandmothers, his sister, his niece Catherine, Picot's sister, Clerselier's sister (Marguerite, who married Pierre Chanut), Huygens' sister (Constantia, who married de Wilhem), Van Schurman, and Princess Elizabeth.
5. It is difficult to gauge the depth or extent of Descartes' emotional attachment to Helena. The most obvious interpretation of the available evidence is that he observed the social proprieties by helping to provide financially for her to have a respectable marriage with someone else.
6. Baillet (1691), i. 258.
7. Cohen (1920), 475, quotes J. de Bois as describing the friendship in these terms.
8. Huygens to Descartes, 15 February 1644 (iv. 769).
9. This included the period when Descartes knew her. Van Schurman later moved to Friesland with Labadie. For Van Schurman's biography, I have borrowed from her autobiography, *Eukleria* (1673), and from Birch (1909), Irwin (1977), Brink (1980), and de Baar (1996).
10. Voetius (1648–67), iii. 29.
11. Beardslee (1965), 328. The excesses of the age are listed in detail in Voetius (1648–67), iv. 325–492.
12. Van Schurman (1641). This was translated into French as *Question celebre* (1646), and into English as *The Learned Maid* (1659). There is a modern English translation in Van Schurman (1998).
13. Van Schurman (1641), 9.
14. Ibid., 12–13.
15. Ibid., 16–18, 30.

16. Descartes to Regius, 24 May 1640: 'When these theses are being disputed [those of 10/20 June 1640], I can visit Utrecht if you wish, but only on condition that no one knows about it and that I can remain hidden behind the curtain where Miss Schurman usually hears the lectures' (iii. 70).

17. The journal of François Ogier (quoted in iv. 660) recalls a visit with Descartes in The Hague, during which Descartes told his guests that he 'did not have much respect for Miss Schurman, and that she was also a great friend of this minister [i.e., Voetius]'.

18. Descartes to Mersenne, 11 November 1640 (iii. 231).

19. Quoted from Foucher de Careil, *Descartes et la Princess Elizabeth* (Paris: Germer-Baillière, 1879), 150–2, in iv. 700–1.

20. Van Schurman (1650), 319.

21. Maurits Huygens (1595–1642) had died on 24 September, and Descartes wrote to Huygens on 10 October 1642 (iii. 798–9).

22. Descartes to Pollot, 6 October 1642 (iii. 577).

23. I follow the revised dating in Descartes (2003), 65.

24. Descartes to Elizabeth, 28 June 1643 (iii. 692).

25. In more technical language, they have no properties in common that are relevant to explaining how they interact. According to Descartes, mind and body have in common the property of being substances, of existing, etc., but none of these common features could explain how they interact.

26. Cf. Descartes to Reneri for Pollot [April/May 1638]: 'Of course one may wonder whether the nature that thinks may perhaps be the same as the nature that occupies space, so that there is one nature that is both intellectual and corporeal' (ii. 38).

27. Descartes to Elizabeth [November 1643] (iv. 38–42), and Elizabeth to Descartes, 21 November 1643 (iv. 44–5).

28. The printing of the *Principles* was completed on 10 July 1644, by Elzevier in Amsterdam. It is discussed in more detail in Chapter 10.

29. For example, in Elizabeth to Descartes, 16 May 1643 (iii. 662); 20 June 1643 (iii. 685); 5 July 1643 (iv. 3); 1 August 1644 (iv. 133).

30. Descartes later provided a theory of why people in radically different social positions cannot love each other, in a letter to Chanut, 1 February 1647. 'It is also true that ordinary language usage and the demands of civility do not allow us to tell someone that we love them if they are very much superior to us socially. We are allowed to say only that we respect, honour, and esteem them and that we are zealous and devoted to serving them. The reason for this, it seems to me, is that friendship between people makes those in whom it is reciprocated in some way equal to each other. Thus, if one tries to be loved by some great person, if one says that one loves them, they could think that one treats them as an equal and that one harms them' (iv. 610).

31. Elizabeth to Descartes 16 May 1643 (iii. 660); 20 June 1643 (iii. 684); 28 October 1645 (iv. 322). On 30 September 1645, and on 15 April 1646, she again refers to her 'stupidity' (iv. 302, 404).

32. Elizabeth wrote to Descartes, 1 August 1644, asking for 'rules for the preservation of my health' (iv. 133). Descartes is now writing, on 18 May 1645, to explain that Pollot had promised to keep him informed about her health and, since he had heard nothing further from him, he had assumed that all was well. Descartes to Elizabeth, 18 May 1645 (iv. 200).

33. Descartes to Elizabeth, May or June 1645 (iv. 219).

34. Descartes to Elizabeth, May or June 1645 (iv. 221).

35. Henricus Bornius to Gassendi, 16 June 1645 (quoted in iv. 238, note).

36. Elizabeth to Descartes, 22 June 1645 (iv. 234). Descartes refers to his garden studies in reply, June 1645 (iv. 238).

37. Descartes to Elizabeth, 21 July 1645 (iv. 251–3).

38. Part III of the *Discourse* (vi. 24–8) includes four maxims as a provisional personal code, the last three of which are: once decided on a certain course of action, not to change direction in midcourse; to accept that there is nothing that is completely in his control except himself, and to change himself and adjust his desires rather than attempt to change the world; and finally, to pursue the search for truth as much as possible as his primary vocation in life.

39. Descartes to Elizabeth, 1 September 1645 (iv. 282).

40. Descartes to Elizabeth, 1 September 1645 (iv. 286).

41. This is repeated in his next letter of 15 September: 'All our passions represent the goods that they incite us to pursue as much greater than they really are' (iv. 294–5).

42. Descartes to Elizabeth, 1 September 1645: 'I was uncertain whether Your Highness was at The Hague or at Rhenen' (iv. 281).

43. Elizabeth to Descartes, 15 September 1645 (iv. 290).

44. Elizabeth to Descartes, 30 September 1645: 'How can one measure the evils that one causes to the public, in comparison with the good that one would derive from it, without the latter appearing greater since one has a much more distinct idea of it? And what measure shall we use to compare things that are not equally well known to us, such as what we deserve and what those with whom we live deserve?' (iv. 303)

45. Descartes to Elizabeth, 6 October 1645 (iv. 314).

46. Descartes to Elizabeth, 3 November 1645 and January 1646 (iv. 330, 351). Elizabeth's letter of 30 November 1645 (iv. 335) continues the discussion.

47. Descartes to Elizabeth, 6 October 1645 (iv. 308).

48. Descartes to Elizabeth, 3 November 1645 (iv. 333).

49. Elizabeth to Descartes, 30 November 1645 (iv. 336).

50. Descartes to Elizabeth, January 1646 (iv. 351).

51. These suggestions are found in Descartes' letters of June 1645 (iv. 237); 15 September 1645 (iv. 296); 3 November 1645 (iv. 334); May 1646 (iv. 415).

52. Descartes to Elizabeth, 6 October 1645 (iv. 310).

53. Ibid., (iv. 312).

54. Descartes to Chanut, 15 June 1646, mentions that while he was growing plants to assist research in natural philosophy, he took time to ponder some questions

about morality. 'Thus I drafted this past winter a little treatise on the nature of the passions of the soul, without however having any plan to publish it . . .' (iv. 442)

55. Elisabeth to Descartes, 25 April 1646 (iv. 404), and Descartes to Elizabeth [May 1646] (iv. 407).

56. The text quoted from Elizabeth's letters implies that Descartes listed five primitive passions in his draft. These were increased to six in the final version of the theory, *The Passions of the Soul* (xi. 380, 443).

57. Descartes to Elizabeth, July 1647 (v. 65). He adds that he thought this type of control of the body by the mind was much more plausible and reasonable than the opposite experience, when those who are persuaded by an astrologer or a physician that they are going to die at a certain time fall ill and die as a result of the prediction. Descartes had referred to this earlier (iii. 15).

Chapter 10

1. Kenyon (1986), 18–20, 222–6.

2. Baillet (1691), ii. 191; Descartes to Mersenne, 30 May 1643 (iii. 674), when he visited Amsterdam for a day to consult with Louis Elzevier about printing his response to Voetius. He suggested that letters be sent to Elzevier, in Amsterdam, for forwarding to his address.

3. Descartes to Mersenne, 30 May 1643: 'It is four or five weeks since I wrote to you, the reason being that I have changed residence and I am now in a district that is a bit isolated, where I do not receive the letters that you have sent to Leiden until eight days after they have arrived there' (iii. 672). He gave the same indications of delays in receiving letters to Huygens, 24 May 1643 (iii. 816).

4. Gassendi (1644), 4.

5. Rivet to Sarrau, 24 August 1643: Bots and Leroy (1978–82), ii. 81.

6. Huygens to Descartes, 23 November 1643 (iv. 768).

7. *Disquisitio Metaphysica. Seu Dubitationes et Instantiae, Adversus Renati Cartesii Metaphysicam, & Responsa* (Amsterdam: Johannes Blaeu, 1644). Heereboord had a copy on 25 February 1644 (iv. 62). Rivet informed Sarrau, 16 March 1644, that the printing had been completed. Bots and Leroy (1978–82), ii. 227.

8. Descartes to Huygens, 26 February 1644 (iv. 770).

9. Digby to Hobbes, 14 October 1637: Hobbes, *Correspondence*, i. 51.

10. This whole episode is recounted in Des Maizeau's 'Life of St. Evremond', which is published in the first volume of St. Evremond's *Oeuvres*. See St. Evremond (1709), I, xxv–xxvi.

11. Ibid., xxv.

12. Ibid., xxvi.

13. Descartes to Mersenne, 13 October 1642 (iii. 582) and 20 October 1642 (iii. 590). These were delayed responses to reports of Digby's week in jail.

14. The book was published in Paris by Gilles Blaizot.

15. Descartes wrote to Newcastle, 23 November 1646: 'I very much regret that I cannot read Mr. Digby's book, because I do not understand English' (iv. 572).

For Elizabeth's offer to have part of it translated into Latin, see her letter to Descartes, 24 May 1645 (iv. 210).

16. *De Mundo Dialogi Tres* (Paris: Denis Moreau, 1642). He was also known in Latin as Thomas Anglus and in English as Thomas Blacklow. On p. 58, he acknowledged Digby as his patron.

17. Huygens to Descartes, 7 October 1642 (iii. 795). Huygens informed Descartes in the same letter of the death of his only brother, Maurits, who had died 24 September.

18. Descartes to Huygens, 10 October 1642 (iv. 796).

19. White (1642), 394, and the *Principles*, Part I, chapter 41 (viii-1. 20).

20. White (1642), 256–9.

21. Descartes to Mersenne, 20 October 1642 (iii. 590).

22. Descartes to Huygens, 24 May 1643 (iii. 816). Huygens acknowledged this, and expressed his anticipation of the imminent publication of 'your Physics', on 6 June 1643 (iii. 820).

23. Huygens to Descartes, 7 January 1643, and Descartes to Huygens, 14 January 1643 (iii. 802, 803); and Descartes to Colvius, 5 September 1643 (iv. 718). Kircher's book, entitled *Magnes sive de Arte Magnetica*, was published in Rome, 2 May 1641. See also Descartes (2003), 16, note *a*.

24. Descartes to Huygens, 20 September 1643 (iv. 753). He also wrote to an unnamed priest that he could explain the tides more satisfactorily once his 'Principles' were published, which he expected would be 'within a short time' (iv. 67).

25. Huygens to Descartes, 5 October 1643 (iv. 756).

26. Huygens to Descartes, 23 November 1643 (iv. 767).

27. The French version of this text, published three years later, adds another reason for this decision. The inadequacy of Descartes' knowledge was due to a 'lack of experiences' (ix-2. 310).

28. The discussion of magnetism appears in the *Principles* in Part III, paragraphs 87–93, and Part IV, paragraphs 133–83.

29. Huygens to Descartes, 15 February 1644 (iv. 769). He eventually undertook this travel in October 1644, after Descartes' visit to France. The book by Mersenne was *Universae Geometriae mixtaeque Mathematicae Synopsis* (Paris: Anthony Berthier, 1644).

30. Mersenne to Descartes [early 1644] (iv. 69).

31. *Momenta Desultoria* was edited by Caspar Barlaeus and published in Leiden by the Elzevier brothers in 1644. It was an extensive collection (322 pages); the poem in praise of Descartes appears on pp. 202–3.

32. Later editions of his book included an extra foreword explaining that it was written in reply to an earlier book by a Jesuit, entitled *Question: S'il est meilleur de communier souvent, que rarement*. Arnauld (1703), 167.

33. Descartes to Picot, 1 April 1644 (iv. 103).

34. *De libero arbitrio libri tres* (Paris: Sebastian Cramboisy, 1643).

35. Descartes to Grandamy, 2 May 1644: 'I am currently in a place where I have many distractions and little leisure, for I recently left my usual residence to find a way to travel to France, where I plan go go within a short time' (iv. 122).

36. *Epistolicae Quaestiones, cum doctorum responsis* was published in 1644, and included contributions from Van Schurman, Vossius, Hensius, Colvius, and Salmasius.

37. Descartes to Van Beverwijck, 5 July 1643 (iv. 5).

38. Descartes to Tobias Andreae, 27 May 1644 (iv. 123).

39. Descartes to De Willem, 9 July 1644, in which he confirms having the same devotion to others that he had 'in Holland', and that he is concerned that he might be suspected of forgetting his friends 'in travelling by sea' (iv. 126).

40. Descartes to Willem, 9 July 1644 (iv. 126).

41. Descartes to Father Dinet, 9 February 1645: 'I went to France last summer because of my personal affairs, but having concluded them quickly, I returned to this land of Holland, where nonetheless I am detained by no reason except that I can be more easily free to dedicate myself to my studies, because the customs of this country do not encourage mutual visiting as freely as in France' (iv. 159–60).

42. Baillet (1691), ii. 219.

43. Descartes to Dinet, October 1644 (iv. 142), and Descartes to Bourdin, October 1644 (iv. 143).

44. 'Now that I have eventually published the principles of this philosophy . . . you are one of those to whom I wish most of all to present a copy, both because I owe you all the fruits that I can derive from my studies, given the care you took of my instruction when I was young . . . ' (Descartes to Charlet, October 1644: iv. 140).

45. Digby (1644), p. 3 of unpaginated Preface.

46. Ibid., 352.

47. Ibid., 415.

48. Ibid., 415–16.

49. Ibid., 416.

50. Descartes uses the same argument in a subsequent letter to Father Mesland, (9 February 1645), when he explains how we have the same body over time, even if all its parts are gradually replaced, because it is joined with the same soul (iv. 166–7).

51. The official certification that a book contains nothing objectionable to the Catholic Church was called a '*nihil obstat*' (literally: 'nothing prevents' the publication). The *nihil obstat* signed by H. Holden certified that 'nothing contained in either of those two treatises . . . doth any way tende to the disadvantage of the faith or pietie of our Catholike Roman church, whereof this author professeth him selfe a dutiful & obedient child' (Paris, 10 November 1644).

52. Digby (1658). This was republished in twenty-nine editions.

53. Ibid., 75.

54. Baillet (1691), ii. 246.

55. Descartes to Picot, 8 November 1644 (iv. 147).

56. Baillet (1691), ii. 246.

57. Ibid., ii. 286.

58. Descartes to Chanut, 26 February 1649 (v. 291), when he was explaining to Chanut how unnecessary it was for Queen Christina to read the *Meditations* if she was reading the French edition of the *Principles*. 'Although the first part [of the *Principles*] is merely a summary of what I wrote in my *Meditations*, it is still not necessary,

in order to understand it, to read these *Meditations* because many people find that they are much more difficult and I would be worried that her Majesty might get tired of them.'

59. In the following pages, I refer in parentheses to the *Principles* by part and paragraph number, to facilitate identification of references in the Latin and French texts and in contemporary translations.

60. The second and third laws of *The World* are reversed, and the original formulation of each law is amended as follows. 'The first law is that every thing, insofar as it is simple and undivided, remains always in the same state insofar as it can, and it is never changed except by external causes' (II, 37). 'Another law of nature is: no part of matter, when considered separately, ever tends to continue moving in an oblique path but only in a straight line' (II, 39). 'The third law of nature is: whenever a body that is moved meets another body, if it has less force to continue in a straight line than the other body has to resist it, then it is deflected elsewhere and, while it retains its motion, it loses only the determination of its motion. If however it has a greater force, then it moves the other body with itself and it loses as much of its own motion as it contributes to the other body' (II, 40).

61. 'If we consider what should be understood by motion, not as it is commonly used but according to the truth of the reality . . . we can say that it is the translation of one part of matter or of one body from the vicinity of those bodies which are immediately close to it and which are considered to be at rest to the vicinity of others' (II, 25).

62. Thus, 'the location [of a body] in the philosophical sense should be determined, not by bodies that are very far away, such as the fixed stars, but by those that are contiguous to what is said to move. Moreover, if one understands location in a non-technical sense, there is no reason to think of the fixed stars rather than the Earth as immobile; that would make sense only if one thinks that there are no other bodies beyond the stars from which they recede and in relation to which they can be said to move and the Earth can be said to be at rest, in the same sense in which the Earth is said to move in relation to the fixed stars. However, it is unreasonable to believe that.' (III, 29). Descartes later added, in the French edition, that one could think of the Earth as being in motion if one used the term 'motion' loosely, 'in the same way that one can sometimes say, about those who are asleep and are lying in a boat, that they move from Calais to Dover because they are in a boat which transports them there' (ix-2. 115).

63. He refers to these letters, which are now lost, in Descartes to Charlet [9 February 1645] (iv. 156); Descartes to Dinet [9 February 1645] (iv. 159); and Descartes to Bourdin [9 February 1645] (iv. 160).

64. Descartes to Charlet [9 February 1645] (iv. 157–8).

65. Descartes to Dinet [9 February 1645] (iv. 159).

66. This is reflected, for example, in the contrasting accounts by two contemporaries. François Poulain de la Barre was a Catholic priest who became a Calvinist and then offered a detailed critique of the Catholic position. According to Poulain de la Barre, Christ is present spiritually or symbolically in the Eucharist. Samuel Sorbière, in his discourse concerning his conversion to Catholicism, argued that

the words of Christ, 'This is my body,' must be understood in their 'proper sig-nification' (i.e., literally). See Poulain de la Barre (1720) and Sorbière (1654), 137.

67. Council of Trent, session XIII (11 October 1551): Decree on the Most Holy Eucharist, Chapter 1: 'There is no inconsistency between these two things: that our Saviour always sits at the right hand of the Father in Heaven in his natural mode of existence and, at the same time, that he is present to us sacramentally by his substance in many different places by a mode of existence which, although we can hardly express it in words, is still possible for God. . . .' Denziger (1960), 874.

68. The Council of Trent used the term 'transubstantiation' to refer to what it called 'the conversion of the whole substance of the bread into the substance of the body of Christ Our Lord, and of the whole substance of the wine into the substance of his blood.' Denziger (1960), 877.

69. Descartes to Mesland, 9 February 1645 (iv. 165–70).

70. Descartes to Mesland [1645/1646] (iv. 346).

71. Descartes to Clerselier, 2 March 1646 (iv. 372–3).

72. Descartes assumes in the *Meditations* that a stone is a substance (vii. 44). Accord-ingly, he wrote to Father Gibieuf [19 January 1642]: 'From the mere fact that I conceive of two halves of the same part of matter, in spite of how small they may be, as two complete substances, . . . I conclude with certainty that they are really divisible' (iii. 477). For a detailed discussion of the use of the term 'substance', see Clarke (2003b), 207–34.

73. Descartes to *** [1646?] (iv. 375).

74. Baillet (1691), ii. 205.

75. Mersenne (1624), Part II, 451: 'this truth could not be as we believe it to be if we accepted that the substance of bread is the same as the substance of Our Lord's body, because that undermines transubstantiation and every form of substantial change.'

76. Gassendi to Rivet, 5 February 1645: Gassendi (1658), vi. 217.

77. Charles Cavendish to John Pell, 26 August 1644: 'if we should remove into Hollande I should be in hope to see you, and intended to see De Cartes, but you write he is gone to Paris. I desire your judgment of De Cartes his new booke. Doutelesse he is an excellent man.' Halliwell (1841), 83. Pell had informed him a few days previously that 'Des Cartes himself is gone into France'. Pell to Charles Cavendish, 17 August 1644: Halliwell (1841), 80.

78. He asked twice, with a repeat letter in case the first one was lost by messengers. 'I desire you will doe me the favoure to send me one of De Cartes his new bookes, *De Principiis Philosophiae*, without anie addition of his olde worckes, except he hath either added or altered something in the matter.' Charles Cavendish to John Pell, 5 August 1644 (Halliwell 1841: 78). He made the same request on 18 August 1644 (Halliwell 1841: 79).

79. Charles Cavendish to John Pell, 17 September 1644: Halliwell (1841), 84.

80. Charles Cavendish to John Pell, 20 October 1644: Halliwell (1841), 85.

81. Descartes to Mesland, May 1645 (iv. 216–17).

82. Descartes to *** [June 1645] (iv. 223).
83. The use of '*ermitage*' is found in Descartes to Chanut, 6 March 1646 (iv. 378).
84. For his work on plants, see Regius to Descartes, 18 November 1644 (iv. 148), and Baillet (1691), ii. 248–9.
85. Descartes to Tobias Andreae, 16 July 1645 (iv. 247).
86. *La methode et invention nouvelle de dresser les chevaux* (Antwerp, 1657).
87. Descartes to Newcastle [April 1645]. (iv. 188–92). This first letter to Newcastle seems to have resulted from a conversation they had at Egmond, and included discussion of a range of physiological questions about heat in animals, fevers, animal spirits, and the cause of sleep.
88. Descartes to Newcastle, October 1645 (iv. 326).
89. Descartes to Newcastle, October 1645: 'The treatise on animals . . . presupposes many experiences without which it is impossible for me to complete it and which I have not yet had the opportunity to perform – nor do I know when I shall have such an opportunity. I cannot promise to publish it for quite some time. . . . However, the treatise on animals that I am thinking about, and which I have not been able to complete yet . . .' (iv. 326, 329).
90. Sorbière to Petit, 20 February 1657, in Sorbière (1660), 689.
91. Borel (1670), 8.
92. One was a Dutchman called Bils, who worked in Rouen and Rotterdam, and another was Swedish, Peter Ossemius in Upsalla. See Sorbière (1660a), 123, 140.
93. Sorbière (1660a), 124.
94. Borel (1670), 8.
95. Baillet (1691), ii. 467. Baillet links this disregard for other authors with the line in the *Discourse on Method* where Descartes says: 'If one spends too much time travelling, one eventually becomes a stranger in one's own country' (vi. 6).
96. Descartes to Picot, 2 November 1646 (iv. 563).
97. Descartes to Pollot, 18 May 1645 (iv. 204–5).
98. Descartes to Pollot, 24 May 1645 (iv. 206–7).

Chapter 11

1. Descartes to ***, 5 October 1646 (iv. 517).
2. Baillet (1691), ii. 248.
3. Descartes to Clerselier, June/July 1646 (iv. 443): 'My hope of being in Paris soon is the reason why I am less anxious to write to those whom I hope to have the honour of seeing there.' In fact, Descartes deferred this visit until the following year.
4. Sorbière to Patin, in Sorbière (1660a): 'When I lived in Leiden, he operated a charitable medical practice and all he asked of the poor people whom he treated was that they would give him a faithful report of the success of his remedies. . . . he was often in his laboratory and I saw him many times in the vestibule of his house . . . distributing drugs from his well supplied cabinet, from eight to nine o'clock in the morning and from one to two o'clock in the afternoon' (pp. 444, 445; see also p. 138).

5. Sir William Petty to John Pell, 24 August 1644, in Halliwell (1841), 82, referred to Van Hogelande as 'a chymist and physician, Des Cartes his most intimate freind [sic] and correspondent, who hath promised at his next writing to send one [a copy of Pell's refutation of Longomontanus] to Des Cartes.'

6. Descartes to Clerselier, 2 March 1646 (iv. 372), where he thanks Clerselier for forwarding letters from his half-sister, Anne, and for agreeing to provide the same service for Descartes in return. These letters had previously been channeled through Mersenne, who was about to leave Paris on his travels. Since Descartes wrote to Anne only 'two or three times a year', he expressed the hope that this new arrangement would not bother his friend too much. See also Descartes to Mersenne, 14 December 1646 (iv. 748), where Descartes worries that letters to and from relatives in Brittany have been misdirected because of Clerselier's illness.

7. Descartes to De Willem, 15 September 1645 (iv. 300); Baillet (1691), ii. 279; Descartes to ***, 15 October 1645 (iv. 318).

8. Descartes to Chanut, 6 March 1646 (iv. 376–7).

9. Descartes to Chanut, 15 June 1646 (iv. 441).

10. Descartes to Chanut, 1 November 1646 (iv. 535).

11. Descartes to Mersenne, 7 September 1646 (iv. 497), in which Descartes tells the Minim friar that he is delighted to hear that he has returned to Paris. He acknowledges having received a letter from Mersenne while he was travelling, although he did not have any address to which he could reply.

12. Elizabeth to Descartes [July 1646] (iv. 448–9), and Descartes to Elizabeth [September 1646] (iv. 486–93).

13. Descartes to Princess Sophie [September 1646] (iv. 495–6).

14. Clerselier may have translated the whole text, and Descartes may have accepted the duke of Luynes' version of the six meditations, in deference to his social status. The six meditations conclude at page 90 of the standard Latin edition, while the whole book numbers 603 pages. Descartes to Clerselier, 10 April 1645 (iv. 193–4).

15. 'They [the two translators] had reserved for the author, as is appropriate, the right to review and correct the text. He used this opportunity to correct himself rather then their translation, and merely to clarify his own thoughts' (ix-1. 2).

16. Descartes to Huygens, 15 February 1644 (iv. 770).

17. Descartes to Clerselier, 20 December 1645 (iv. 338–9), and ix–1. 198–217.

18. Descartes to Clerselier, 12 January 1646 (iv. 357–8). This was further clarified in another letter of 23 February 1646, in which Descartes thanked his translator for reducing the sharpness of some of the terms he had used in his original replies, in 1641, to Gassendi's objections, and thus performing the roles of 'translator, apologist and mediator' (iv. 362).

19. Descartes to Clerselier, 9 November 1646 (iv. 563–4). The three unidentified religious sisters may have included any three of the following: the daughters of his brother, Pierre – Anne (who became a Carmelite) and Françoise (who became an Ursuline) – and the daughters of his older sister, Jeanne, both of whom, Henriette and Hélène, became Ursulines.

20. Descartes to Chanut, 1 November 1646 (iv. 535), and Chanut to Descartes, 1 December 1646 (iv. 583)

21. Descartes to Mersenne, 23 November 1646 (iv. 565–6), where he discusses Clerselier's illness in some detail and makes suggestions about how he should be treated, and again to Mersenne, 14 December 1646 (iv. 748): 'Please tell me how Mr. Clerselier is coping with the sickness, which I am very sorry to hear about.'
22. For a detailed account of its printing history, see Van Otegem (2002), i. 220–2.
23. Descartes to Picot, 17 February 1645 (iv. 180–1).
24. Descartes to Mersenne, 20 April 1646 (iv. 396).
25. Descartes to Clerselier, 2 March 1646 (iv. 373).
26. Baillet (1691), ii. 272. Baillet extends the religious analogy by referring to Regius first as a 'martyr' and later as a 'schismatic' (ii. 271).
27. Regius to Descartes, 6 July 1645 (iv. 241–2). I follow the redating of the correspondence proposed by Regius (2002), 57–9 and 185–6.
28. Regius to Descartes, 23 July 1645 (iv. 254).
29. Descartes to Regius, [July or early August] 1645 (iv. 256).
30. Regius (1646), p. 2 of unpaginated dedication: 'If I walk in the footsteps of the most noble and incomparable philosopher, René Descartes, or if I follow my own path or proceed by a route that differs from the common views of those who acknowledge that they are occult and not understood . . . I do so in the interests of philosophical freedom. . . .' This was not the explicit acknowledgement that he had promised Descartes, but rather an ambivalent indication that he may or may not differ from Cartesian philosophy.
31. Regius (1646), Chapter 12, 'De Homine', extends from p. 245 to p. 306.
32. Ibid., 245: 'Frustra itaque quaeritur, quomodo mens cogitet; cum illa hoc per suam essentiam jam explicatam faciat, ut corpus per extensionem, seu essentiam extensam, se extendit.'
33. Ibid., 249.
34. Ibid., 248–9.
35. Ibid., 246.
36. Ibid., 284, 290.
37. For this reading of how the human will moves the body, see Clarke (2003), 135–57.
38. Regius (1646), 254.
39. Ibid., 298.
40. Ibid., 251.
41. Descartes to Huygens, 17 February 1645 (iv. 776–7).
42. Descartes to Chanut, 6 March 1646 (iv. 376–7), and Descartes to Huygens, 11 March 1646 (iv. 786–7), when he wrote: 'I have been planning to travel to The Hague for a long time, but the bad weather has kept me here. I hope it will not last forever and that I shall see you soon.'
43. 'Illi mors gravis incubat / Qui, notus nimis omnibus, / Ignotus moritur sibi.' Descartes to Chanut, 1 November 1646 (iv. 537), quoted from Seneca, Thyestes.
44. Baillet (1691), ii. 449, 450.
45. 'His habit of meditating made him very reserved and a little taciturn.' Ibid., ii. 466.
46. Ibid., ii. 466–7.
47. Ibid., ii. 428.

48. Ibid., ii. 460.
49. Descartes to Mersenne, 20 April 1646 (iv. 403). He later told him that he had read only 'the first five or six pages' (to Mersenne, 7 September 1646: iv. 499) and 'the first four or five pages' (to Mersenne, 5 October 1646: iv. 509).
50. Chanut to Descartes, 25 August 1646 (iv. 474). Descartes had written, 15 June 1646, that he would be willing to publish something else 'if the aversion I have to seeing how few people bother to read my writings did not make me negligent' (iv. 442).
51. Descartes to Mersenne, 12 October 1646 (iv. 527).
52. Descartes to De Willem, 15 June 1646 (iv. 436).
53. See Descartes to [Newcastle] [October 1645]: 'The preservation of health has always been the principal objective of my studies, and I have no doubt that there is a way of acquiring much knowledge of medicine which has been lacking up to now. However, since the treatise on animals that I am thinking about, and which I have not yet found a way of completing, is only a prelude to achieving this knowledge, I refrain from boasting that I already possess it' (iv. 329).
54. Descartes to Huygens [January 1646] (v. 262–5). Erik-Jan Bos provided information on the redating of these letters and on the details of the incident.
55. Descartes was writing in January 1646, and the *Stadtholder* died on 14 March 1647.
56. Descartes to Huygens, 11 March 1646 (iv. 786).
57. Descartes to Chanut, 6 March 1646 (iv. 377–8).
58. Descartes to Mersenne, 2 March 1646 (iv. 364), and Descartes to Cavendish, 30 March 1646 (iv. 380–8). He refers to the nine-year lapse of time in his letter to Mersenne, 20 April 1646 (iv. 398).
59. Descartes to Cavendish, 30 March 1646 (iv. 380).
60. Descartes to Mersenne, 2 March 1646 (iv. 363).
61. Descartes to Mersenne, 20 April 1646 (iv. 391–2).
62. Descartes to Mersenne, 2 November 1646 (iv. 547).
63. Descartes to [Cavendish], 2 November 1646 (iv. 559). Later in the same letter, he makes explicit that the impedence of the air 'cannot be determined by reasoning but only by experience' (iv. 560). The emphasis on experience was not confined to the oscillation of pendulums. Descartes advised Princess Elizabeth that, in political questions, it was 'better to be guided by experience than by reason, because one rarely interacts with people who are perfectly reasonable'. Descartes to Elizabeth [May 1646] (iv. 412).
64. Descartes to Mersenne, 20 April 1646 (iv. 392). Descartes repeated this charge to Mersenne, 2 November 1646 (iv. 550–1), that there was no merit in reading Roberval at all and that the only reason he bothered to do so was because of Mersenne's requests.
65. Roberval against Descartes [September 1646] (iv. 507).
66. Descartes to Cavendish, 15 May 1646 (iv. 418).
67. Descartes to Mersenne, 5 October 1646 (iv. 513).
68. Elizabeth to Descartes, 25 April 1646 (iv. 404). When Elizabeth was about to return the manuscript to Descartes in April, she had mislaid the name of the

contact person in Alkmaar (Mr. Adam Spijcker) through whom her letters could reach their destination, and she decided to hold onto the manuscript lest it be lost. See Descartes to a lawyer, 17 April 1646 (iv. 390). Descartes also refers to the draft manuscript in a letter to Chanut, 15 June 1646: 'I outlined this winter [1645–46] a little treatise on the passions of the soul, without having any intention however of publishing it' (iv. 440).

69. Descartes to Elizabeth [May 1646] (iv. 407).

70. See Van Otegem (2002), ii. 488.

71. Descartes to Elizabeth, 6 October 1645 (iv. 310): 'Since your highness took the trouble to read the treatise that I had drafted previously, concerning the nature of animals, you already know how I think that different impressions are formed in their brain.'

72. Descartes to Elizabeth [May 1646] (iv. 408, 409–10).

73. Descartes to Mersenne, 7 September 1646 (iv. 497).

74. Descartes to Mersenne, 5 October 1646 (iv. 510–11).

75. The breach of their friendship is made explicit in his letter to Mersenne, 2 November 1646: 'I think it is best if everyone knew that we are no longer friends' (iv. 552).

76. Descartes to Father Charlet, [14 December 1646] (iv. 588): 'I can tell you, in truth, that if I had followed only my own inclination, I would never have published anything.'

77. Descartes to Elizabeth [December 1646] (iv. 590).

78. Descartes to Mersenne, 7 September 1646 (iv. 498).

79. Descartes to [Noël], 14 December 1646 (iv. 584), where he regrets the delay in receiving the letter that arrived only on 6 December. The two books were: *Aphorismi physici seu physicae peripateticae principia breviter ac dilucide proposita* (La Flèche, 1646) and *Sol Flamma, sive Tractatus de Sole, ut flamma est, ejusque pabulo* (Paris, 1647).

80. Descartes to Mersenne, 23 November 1646 (iv. 567).

81. Descartes to Noël, 14 December 1646 (iv. 586).

82. Descartes to Elizabeth [December 1646] (iv. 591).

83. This had originally appeared in the *Letter to G. Voetius* in 1643 (viii-2. 163), and is repeated in the Preface to the French edition of the *Principles of Philosophy* (ix-2. 19).

84. Baillet (1691), ii. 323–4. The illustrations had been printed to accompany the text in the Latin edition, but it was felt that this was likely to be too expensive and to cause further delays in the French edition. The printer therefore collected all the illustrations at the back of the book. For the history of its printing, see van Otegem (2002), i. 301–3.

85. Elizabeth to Descartes [May 1647] (v. 48).

86. For these details, see Verbeek (1992), 54.

87. Voetius (1648–69), volume I, appeared on 1 October 1647. See Verbeek (1992), 54–7, for a summary of relevant theses about Descartes.

88. The text was written in Latin and published by Louis Elzevier, in Amsterdam, as *Notae in Programma quoddam, sub finem Anni 1647, in Belgio editum, cum hoc Titulo'*,

after which he reproduces the title of Regius' pamphlet. Before publication, he sent a draft copy with a request for advice to Van Hogelande or some other Dutch correspondent, without identifying the original author who was the target of his comments. Descartes told his correspondent that the author of the manifesto wished to remain anonymous but that he would be recognized readily from his style. Descartes to [Van Hogelande?] [December 1647] (v. 109–10). However, when Descartes sent a copy of the *Comments* to Princess Elizabeth, 31 January 1648, he had no difficulty in identifying the object of his criticisms. 'I am sending with this letter a booklet of little significance. . . . The insults of Mr. Regius forced me to write it and it was published sooner than I expected. They have even added some verses and a preface of which I disapprove (although the verses are by Mr. Heydanus, who did not dare to put his name to them – as he ought not to have done)' (v. 114).

89. Regius (1648), 7.
90. Ibid., 8.
91. Ibid., 9.
92. Ibid., 12, 13.
93. Descartes to Mersenne, 2 November 1646 (iv. 555).
94. Descartes to Newcastle, 23 November 1646 (iv. 569), where he acknowledges that the letter received was dated 5 January 1646.
95. Subtitle of the *Meditations* (second edition).
96. Montaigne (1991), 524.
97. Charron (1654), 56.
98. Descartes to Newcastle, 23 November 1646 (iv. 573). Later in the same letter he identifies one of the 'others' when he links 'Montaigne and Charron' together as common opponents (p. 575).

Chapter 12

1. Descartes to Elizabeth, 10 May 1647 (v. 19).
2. Descartes to Mersenne, 23 November 1646 (iv. 567); Descartes to Huygens, February 1647 (iv. 790); and Descartes to Elizabeth [March 1647] (iv. 624).
3. Descartes to Huygens, 4 February 1647 (iv. 791).
4. Reported by Baillet (1691), ii. 449, from a lost letter of 1 March 1647.
5. Baillet (1691), ii. 450, based in part on a lost letter to Picot, 26 April 1647 (iv. 640).
6. Descartes to Elizabeth [March 1647] (iv. 624). He told Mersenne, 26 April 1647, that he hoped to be in Paris within six or seven weeks (iv. 639).
7. Chanut to Descartes, 1 December 1646 (iv. 581–3).
8. Descartes to Chanut, 1 February 1647 (iv. 601).
9. This theory was also outlined in the *Principles*, Part IV, paragraphs 189 and 190. Since Descartes had the incomplete French translation at hand, he referred Chanut to 'my French *Principles*' for further assistance (iv. 602)
10. When he heard about Clerselier's illness in November 1646, Descartes expressed a general scepticism about physicians and specific concerns about blood-letting.

'I fear only that the doctors' ignorance will cause them to make mistakes that will injure him. They were right to bleed him at the beginning . . . but because they are great supporters of blood-letting at Paris, I am afraid that when they notice that the blood-letting helped him they may continue with the same therapy and that will greatly weaken the brain without improving his bodily health.' Descartes to Mersenne, 23 November 1646 (iv. 565).

11. Descartes to Elizabeth [March 1647] (iv. 625).
12. Chanut to Descartes, 11 May 1647 (x. 617).
13. Descartes to Chanut, 6 June 1647 (v. 50–1).
14. I am grateful to Theo Verbeek for information about this appointment. The title of 'Professor Extraordinary' implied that the holder was less than a full or 'ordinary' professor and that he was paid correspondingly less. Heereboord's appointment as assistant regent or assistant dean of the *Statencollege* provided a supplementary salary.
15. Descartes to Pollot, 8 January 1644: 'I have just read the theses of a professor of philosophy at Leiden, in which he declares his support for me and cites me with much more praise that Mr. Regius ever did. He did this without having consulted me, when I knew nothing about it, because the theses were printed three weeks ago and I received them only yesterday. However, they will greatly anger my enemies. . . . I am told that there is also someone at Groningen who wishes to support me. These events do not affect me very much. For my adversary [i.e., Voetius], however, who I think does not sleep as well as I do, they are revolutionary' (iv. 78).
16. Descartes to Pollot, 8 January 1644: 'some time ago this professor arranged other disputations, concerning substantial forms, in which he seems to support Aristotle. . . . ' (iv. 78)
17. Amyraut (1641).
18. This disputation was held on 22 March 1644. See Heereboord (1664), 341, and Verbeek (1992), 37–8.
19. Quoted by Verbeek (1992), 117.
20. Ibid.
21. Quoted by Verbeek (1992), 43–4, and by Descartes in his letter to the Leiden University curators, 4 May 1647 (v. 5).
22. Descartes to Heereboord, 19 April 1647 (iv. 632). Descartes mentions a previous letter (now lost) that he had sent to Heereboord, in which he inquired about theological disputes at Leiden. On this occasion, he concentrates on a disputation that had been scheduled for 27 March and had, unknown to him, been deferred until 16 April, in which Descartes was mentioned as the source of the exaggerated idea of the human will. He asked Heereboord to inquire of others who may have attended the disputation to find out what was said, if he had not been present himself.
23. Descartes had contrasted the apparently unlimited scope of the will with that of the understanding in the context of explaining, in the Fourth Meditation, how human beings fall into error. Even when we lack clear and distinct ideas, we may still exercise our will by making a judgment. 'I experience the will alone, or freedom

of choice, as being so extensive in my own case that I conceive the idea of nothing greater, so that it is principally because of this faculty that I understand myself as being in some sense the image and likeness of God. For although the will is incomparably greater in God than in me ... when it is considered formally and in a strict sense, however, it does not seem to be greater' (vii. 57).

24. Descartes wrote in similar terms to Huygens, 12 May 1647 (v. 648–50). He had no objection to Calvinist theologians reading his books or publishing alternative views themselves. What he objected to were the 'outrageous calumnies' involved in accusing him publicly of blasphemy and other crimes, and threatening to examine him in a Calvinist synod.

25. Descartes to the Leiden University curators, 27 May 1647 (v. 35–9).

26. Descartes to De Willem, 24 May 1647 (v. 33).

27. Wevelichoven had acknowledged politely Descartes' original letter of complaint, on 20 May 1647 (v. 31 2), and this prompted the further request from Descartes, 27 May 1647 (v. 40).

28. Voetius (1647–67). The Preface to the first volume was dated 1 October 1647.

29. Quoted by Verbeek (1992), 58.

30. Heereboord (1659), 18.

31. Revius (1648).

32. Ibid., 27.

33. Brasset to Descartes, 27 July 1648 (v. 216). Brasset passed on the information he had received from Pollot, while Descartes was in Paris. See Verbeek (1992), 129, note 119.

34. Descartes to Elizabeth, 10 May 1647 (v. 15), and Elizabeth to Descartes [May 1647] (v. 46).

35. Elizabeth to Descartes [May 1647] (v. 47).

36. Descartes to Picot, 8 June 1647 (v. 63), and Baillet (1691), ii. 323.

37. Baillet (1691), ii. 324.

38. Ibid., ii. 325 .

39. Le Tenneur, a mathematician from the Auvergne, wrote to Mersenne on 13 September, with the prayer that 'God would not deprive the public of a hand which is as useful as yours, and which serves the public every day with such great service in the excellent books that you produce constantly.' He was able to write, on 21 October, to express his great happiness that the threat of gangrene had passed. Both letters are quoted in v. 77–8. See also Descartes to Mersenne, 13 December 1647, at the beginning of which Descartes wrote: 'I was very glad to see some of your writing because I learned that your inexpert bleeding had not deprived you of the use of your hand.' E.-J. Bos and M. van Otegem (2002), 5.

40. Baillet (1691), ii. 325.

41. Jacqueline Pascal to her sister Gilberte, Pascal (1998), i. 14–15.

42. Magno's work was entitled *Demonstratio ocularis*; it was published in Warsaw in 1647, and a copy was sent to Roberval almost immediately. See Desnoyers to Mersenne, CM, xv. 311–14.

43. There is a fuller account of this controversy, with the focus on Pascal, in Clarke (2003a).

44. Pascal (1998–2000), i. 433.
45. Ibid., i. 426–37.
46. These doubts began to emerge in the seventeenth century, and they were raised even by well-known experimental scientists such as Robert Boyle, who supported Pascal's general theory but was worried that some of his experiments were only thought experiments. For example, in *Hydrostatical Paradoxes* (1666), Boyle questioned whether Pascal had done the experiment that required someone to sit fifteen or twenty feet under water with a tube in contact with his thigh. Alexandre Koyré raised similar doubts whether glass makers in the 1640s could have constructed a glass tube thirty or forty feet long, with sufficiently strong sides to support a column of water of the same length. See Boyle (1999–2000), v. 206, and Koyré (1956), 270–1.
47. Pascal (1998–2000), i. 373.
48. Ibid., 394–5, 387.
49. Ibid., i. 396.
50. Huygens to Descartes, 14 November 1647 (v. 651–2).
51. Descartes to Huygens, 8 December 1647 (v. 653).
52. Descartes to Mersenne, 13 December 1647 (v. 98).
53. Descartes to Mersenne, 13 December 1647: 'I advised Mr. Pascal to experiment if the mercury rises as much when one is high up on a mountain as when one is at the bottom, and I do not know if he has done the experiment yet' (v. 99). Since Mersenne had died in 1648, Descartes wrote to Carcavi in Paris, 11 June 1649, still asking whether the experiment had been done or not. 'I hope you will not find it unacceptable if I ask you to tell me about the results of an experiment which, I am told, Mr. Pascal performed or had arranged to be performed on the Auvergne mountains, to find out if mercury rises higher in a tube at the bottom of a mountain and to what extent it rises more than when it is higher up the mountain. I should be entitled to get the information from him rather than from you, because I was the one who suggested, two years ago, that he do this experiment and that I had no doubt about its success, although I had not done the experiment myself' (v. 366).
54. Descartes to Carcavi, 17 August 1649 (v. 391).
55. Carcavi to Descartes, 24 September 1649 (v. 412). Pascal remained in Clermont from May 1649 to November 1650, whereas Descartes died 11 February 1650.
56. This debate is discussed in detail in Shapin and Schaffer (1985).
57. Brasset wrote to Brisacier, 14 October 1647, that Descartes had passed through The Hague on his return journey to Egmond, where he would 'practise his philosophy during the winter' (v. 80).
58. Baillet (1691), ii. 331.
59. Huygens to Descartes, 8 December 1647 (v. 653).
60. This was sparked by a lecture she heard at Uppsala on 17 September 1647 by Johann Freinsheim (1608–1660), who had been professor of politics and rhetoric at the university and, in 1647, became court librarian and historiographer to the queen. He remained in Sweden until after Descartes' death, and took up a post as counsellor to Princess Elizabeth's brother, the elector of Palatine, in 1651. Chanut's letter was delayed in transit, and he wrote a second time, on 9 November, to remind

Descartes of the royal request, although the reclusive and dutiful Frenchman had not yet received the first letter.

61. Descartes to Chanut, 20 November 1647 (v. 87), and Descartes to Elizabeth [20 November 1647] (v. 89–92), in which he alerts Elizabeth to sharing his letters with a second royal correspondent.

62. This must have been his dominant impression of Descartes, since he wrote to Rivet, 15 December, wondering how Descartes would cope 'in his solitude' with the attacks from Revius (v. 95).

63. Brasset to Rivet, 15 January 1648 (v. 111).

64. Descartes to Elizabeth [31 January 1648] (v. 114).

65. Elizabeth to Descartes, 5 December 1647 (v. 97).

66. Descartes to Elizabeth, 25 January 1648 (v. 111–12). The first reason offered was that it would have been impossible to include all the truths that were required in such a treatise without provoking a hostile reaction from the schoolmen (especially those in Leiden and Utrecht). The other equally unconvincing reason was that much of what he planned for this treatise had been dealt with adequately in the *Principles*, which was now available in a French edition for all to read.

67. Descartes to Mersenne, 23 November 1646: 'It is twelve or thirteen years since I described all the functions of the human body, but the paper on which I wrote is so confused that I would have great difficulty myself in reading it' (iv. 566–7).

68. Descartes to an unknown correspondent [March 1648] (v. 261).

69. Descartes also refers to this in reply to a query from Burman, in Descartes (1976): 'Indeed, in the *Treatise on Animals*, on which he worked this winter, he [the author] noticed the following: when he wished merely to explain animal functions, he realized that that could hardly be done without having to explain how an animal is formed from an egg' (v. 170–1).

Chapter 13

1. Descartes to Chanut, written from Egmond (v. 293).

2. Descartes to Mersenne, 31 January 1648: 'this year the winter has been the mildest that I have ever seen in this country' (v. 115). Brasset, in his letter to Descartes of 4 December 1647, advised that if Chanut mentioned the cold weather they experience in Sweden, Descartes could counter with the cold temperatures they experience 'in Holland' (v. 92). This must have been a general comment about their usual winter weather conditions, rather than a specific comment about conditions in December 1647.

3. He reported to Mersenne the following month that, despite the fact that 'it has not been very cold this winter', the mercury had risen 'more than fifteen lines'. Descartes to Mersenne, 7 February 1648 (v. 119).

4. Father Noël published three books in 1648, the first of which was written in Latin under the title: *Gravitas comparata, seu Comparatio Gravitatis Aëris cum Hydargyri gravitate* (Paris, 1648). Mersenne sent a copy to Huygens, 2 May 1648, requesting that he read the book himself and then forward it to Descartes.

5. Descartes to Pollot, 7 February 1648 (v. 123).

6. He refers to his summary statement of events in Utrecht in the letter to Pollot just cited (v. 123). Brasset wrote to Chanut in Stockholm, 28 February 1648, that Descartes was very strongly inclined to leave the United Provinces, and added: 'I have just read the taunt directed to his minister [Voetius] at Utrecht. It is a rather churlish *remember me*' (v. 132).

7. See Verbeek (1992), 75. For the context in which this book was written, see also John Cottingham's introduction to Descartes (1976).

8. Descartes to Elizabeth, 28 June 1643 (iii. 695).

9. This reflection on the relative value of different parts of his oeuvre was offered in the context of explaining his research on animals during the winter of 1647–48 (v. 171).

10. Compare the *Discourse*, Part I, from eleven years earlier: 'But once I learned, as something that is very certain, that the path to heaven is just as open to the most ignorant as to the most learned, and that the revealed truths which lead there are beyond our understanding, I did not dare subject them to the feebleness of my reasoning, and I thought that one needed to have some extraordinary assistance from heaven and to be more than human in order to study them successfully' (vi. 8).

11. Baillet (1691), ii. 339–40.

12. Descartes to Chanut, 31 March 1649 (v. 328–9).

13. See Bercé (1974), Foisil (1970), and Parchnev (1963).

14. Brasset to Descartes, 7 February 1648 (v. 121) and 30 April 1648 (v. 179).

15. Descartes to Picot, 4 April 1648 (v. 140).

16. Baillet (1691), ii. 339.

17. Chanut had written to Descartes on 4 April, and when the letter arrived at The Hague, Brasset asked M. van Zurck to deliver it by hand when Descartes was passing through the city on 8 May. Since Descartes was leaving that morning for Rotterdam, he took Chanut's letter with him to Paris, from which he replied about the middle of May. See v. 180 note, 183 note.

18. Descartes to Chanut, May 1648 (v. 183).

19. Arnauld to Descartes, 3 June 1648 (v. 184), and Descartes to Arnauld, 4 June 1648 (v. 194).

20. In a letter to an unknown correspondent, March/April 1648, he had written: 'You see the power you have over me, when you make me transgress the boundaries of philosophizing which I have set for myself' (v. 139).

21. Descartes to Arnauld, 4 June 1648 (v. 194). Descartes quoted the decision of the Council of Trent, session XIII (11 October 1551), Chapter 1, in which the Council decreed: 'Nor is there any inconsistency in the fact that Our Saviour always sits at the right hand of the Father in heaven in his natural mode of existence, and that, nevertheless, he is sacramentally present to us in many places, in his substance, in a mode of existence that we can hardly express even in words....' Denziger (1960), par. 874 (p. 304).

22. Arnauld to Descartes, July 1648 (v. 215).

23. Cf. the clarification offered in the *Conversation with Burman*. When Burman asked Descartes to explain how body and mind could interact if their natures were as different as he claimed, he replied: 'This is very difficult to explain. However, experience suffices in this context, because it is so clear in this case that it cannot possibly be denied, as is apparent in the case of the passions, etc.' (v. 163).

24. Arnauld (1990), 153.

25. A similar conclusion appears in the final sentence (numbered 7) of Wittgenstein's *Tractatus*: 'What we cannot speak about we must pass over in silence.' Wittgenstein (1963), 151.

26. Descartes to Mersenne, June/July 1648 (v. 202–8).

27. Descartes to Picot, 6 September 1648 (v. 229–30).

28. Descartes to Carcavi, 11 June 1649 (v. 365).

29. Carcavi to Descartes, 9 July 1649: 'There is a Minim friar in Rome, called Father Maignan, who is more intelligent that Father Mersenne. . . .' (v. 371) Carcavi later offered a gloss on this evaluation of Mersenne. In reply to Descartes' defence, he argued that Mersenne was well intentioned but did not always distinguish clearly between personal and scientific disagreements. 'As regards Father Mersenne, I accused him only of what everyone who knew him noticed, namely, that he was always absolutely blameless in his intentions, which were directed exclusively towards a search for the truth. . . . however, he seemed to me not always to distinguish adequately between those who dispute about some scientific questions and others who fight with each other about their honour.' Carcavi to Descartes, 24 September 1649 (v. 414)

30. Baillet (1691), ii. 342. The meeting is confirmed by Sorbière's Preface to the complete works of Gassendi, published three years after his death. See Gassendi (1658), I, p. 19 (unpaginated).

31. Elizabeth to Descartes, 30 June 1648 (v. 195).

32. Descartes to Elizabeth, June/July 1648 (v. 198). Elizabeth's reply to this letter refers to the 'unexpected disturbances in France which . . . force you to return to Holland' (v. 209).

33. Elizabeth to Descartes, 23 August 1648 (v. 226).

34. Descartes to Elizabeth, October 1648 (v. 232).

35. Descartes to Picot, 6 September 1648 (v. 227–8).

36. Descartes to Picot, 7 December 1648 (v. 235).

37. Editors' note, v. 229.

38. Descartes to Picot, 6 September 1648 (v. 220).

39. These letters to Picot are reported in Baillet (1691), ii. 368, and date from December 1648 and 21 February 1649 (v. 280).

40. Descartes to Chanut, 26 February 1649 (v. 292–3).

41. Descartes to Chanut, 26 February 1649 (v. 293).

42. Chanut to Descartes, 27 February 1649 (v. 295).

43. Descartes to Chanut [23 April 1649] (v. 351–2), in which he explains how Fleming arrived unannounced in Egmond and why Descartes assumed that his invitation to accompany him to Stockholm was merely an expression of extreme courtesy.

44. Descartes to Chanut, 31 March 1649 (v. 324), which replies to Chanut's letter of 27 February.

45. Brasset to Descartes, 2 March 1649 (v. 296–7); More to Descartes, 11 December 1648 (v. 235) and 5 March 1649 (v. 298). More wrote two other letters later, 23 July (v. 376–90) and 21 October 1649 (v. 434–43). Descartes drafted a reply to the first in August 1649 (v. 401), at the beginning of which he explained that he was preparing for his journey to Sweden. However, he did not send any further replies to More; the draft response was found in his papers after his death. See Alan Gabbey's notes on this correspondence in v. 628–47.

46. Descartes to Arnauld, 29 July 1648 (v. 224).

47. Descartes' conversation with Burman, 16 April 1648 (v. 152): 'The same thing can be said about body and its extension, and about all things. For the author does not claim to have an adequate knowledge of anything.'

48. Descartes to More, 15 April 1649 (v. 347).

49. See van Otegem (2002), i. 338–9. The printing was most like done initially by Elzevier in Amsterdam, and then published with a new title page by H. le Gras in Paris.

50. Van Otegem (2002: I, 340–1) speculates that this correspondent may have been Henri Maresius (1629–1725), who was interested in arranging for publication of the Latin edition of the *Passions* (which appeared in 1650 from L. Elzevier at Amsterdam).

51. Baillet (1691), ii. 394.

52. Descartes to Clerselier, 23 April 1649 (v. 353–4).

53. It is also possible that this 'correspondence' was invented by Descartes as an appropriate Preface to his book. Without independent evidence concerning the alleged correspondent, it is impossible to trust it.

54. *** to Descartes, 23 July 1649 (v. 325); Descartes to Clerserlier, 23 April 1649 (v. 353–4).

55. Descartes to Freinsheim, June 1649 (v. 363–4). Freinsheim's reply reached The Hague toward the end of July and was forwarded by Brasset to Egmond. See Brasset to Madame Chanut, 30 July 1649 (v. 364, note). Once that was received, Descartes felt free to release the text to his editor.

56. This is confirmed by Descartes to Carcavi, 17 August 1649 (v. 391): 'As regards my treatise on the passions, it is true that I promised a long time ago to send it to a friend who planned to arrange for its publication. However, I have not sent it to him yet.' This is inconsistent with Descartes' letter of 14 August 1649 (xi. 326), in which he apparently agrees to send the manuscript to his correspondent. He may have given the manuscript directly to Elzevier in Amsterdam before his departure for Sweden on 1 September 1649.

57. The definition provided in *The Passions of the Soul* (Part I, par. 27) is: 'Perceptions or feelings or emotions of the soul which are referred specifically to the soul and which are caused, maintained, and strengthened by some movement of the spirits' (xi. 349). The term 'spirits' refers, as usual, to a very fine fluid that travels throughout the tubes that serve as nerves in Cartesian physiology.

58. This is repeated, slightly more clearly, in Part II, par. 137: 'As regards the function of the emotions, it is noticeable that, in accordance with nature's institution, they are all related to the body and are provided to the soul only insofar as it is united with the body. Hence their natural function is to stimulate the soul to assent and contribute to actions which can be used to preserve the body or to make it in some sense more perfect' (xi. 430).

59. In the *Meditations*, Descartes argued that mistaken perceptions – such as feeling pain in an amputated limb – occur because nature has designed our system of perceptions so that the information it provides is more likely to be beneficial to each organism, in most circumstances, than any alternative system. See the Sixth Meditation (vii. 83–5).

60. The dualism of mind and body was accepted as an underlying assumption at the beginning of the *Passions*, in Part I, paragraphs 2 and 3. 'There is no better way to acquire knowledge of our passions than by examining the difference between the soul and the body. . . . Everything in us, which is such that we cannot in any way conceive of it as capable of belonging to the body, should be attributed to our soul' (xi. 328, 329).

61. Carcavi to Descartes, 24 September 1649 (v. 413).

Chapter 14

1. Descartes to Brasset, 23 April 1649 (v. 349).

2. Descartes to [Pollot?], possibly 1648 (v. 557).

3. Descartes endorses, in the *Discourse*, the Stoic philosophers who believed that 'there was nothing completely in their power apart from their own thoughts' (vi. 26).

4. *Passions of the Soul*, Part III, par. 157 (xi. 448–9).

5. Descartes to Brasset, 23 April 1649 (v. 349).

6. Descartes to Clerselier, 23 April 1649 (v. 353).

7. Descartes to Picot, 23 April 1649 (v. 358), and Baillet (1691), ii. 457.

8. Descartes to Picot, 7 and 14 May 1649 (v. 358–9). Chanut had left Stockholm on 1 May, and he spent two days in The Hague (28 and 29 May 1649) before continuing his journey to Paris.

9. Descartes to Elizabeth, 6 June 1649 (v. 359–60).

10. Descartes to Freinsheim, June 1649 (v. 362).

11. Carcavi to Descartes, 9 July 1649 (v. 370). Carcavi added that he was awaiting publication of the *Passions*, and of the Latin translation of the *Geometry* that had been prepared by Van Schooten.

12. Carcavi to Descartes, 9 July 1649 (v. 373).

13. Descartes to Carcavi, 17 August 1649 (v. 394).

14. Descartes had written to Mersenne the previous year with concerns about Van Schooten's ability to translate the *Geometry* accurately. However, on that occasion he conceded that Van Schooten's incompetence would coincide with his own desire not to make the book clear enough to provide ammunition to critics. 'That is why

I did not want to see the translation by Van Schooten, although he wanted me to do so. For, if I began to correct it, I could not have prevented myself from making it clearer than it is at present, which is something that I do not wish to do. Since Van Schooten is not skilled in Latin, I am certain that his translation will be rather obscure and that it will possibly include equivocations which will provide a pretext for quibbling to those who look for it. However, I cannot be held responsible, since his Latin is not at all similar to mine' (v. 143). In the course of writing about this stategy to Mersenne, Descartes had referred to his critics, including Roberval, as 'monsters'.

15. Descartes to Chanut, 31 March 1649 (v. 329).

16. Descartes wrote two interdependent letters to Picot on 30 August 1649. In one of them, he advised Picot of the complex arrangements he had made about repaying his debts to Anthony Studler van Zurck (1608?–1666), who had acted as an informal banker for Descartes. Picot was asked to realize the money from Descartes' properties in France and to pay Van Zurck directly. However, if that failed and if the property was about to be inherited by Descartes' family, he provided Van Zurck with another letter that could then be used to make a claim against his estate.

17. Descartes to Picot, 30 August 1649 (v. 408). Cf. his final adieu to Beeckman, 29 April 1619: 'I do not want to lose any opportunity of writing to you, to show my affection for you and to show that my memory of you cannot be erased by any of the distractions that occur during my travels' (x. 164).

18. Baillet (1691), ii. 387.

19. Descartes to Elizabeth, 9 October 1649 (v. 429), where he tells her that he had arrived four or five days before. During this interval, Carcavi wrote again, mentioning that people in Paris did not know whether he was in Egmond or in Sweden. Carcavi to Descartes, 24 September 1649 (v. 412).

20. Descartes to Clerselier, 6 November 1649 (v. 447).

21. When Baillet was writing his life of Descartes, which he claimed to have completed in one year, one of Chanut's sons, Martial, was Visitor General of the Carmelites and was based at Issoire, while the second son, Hector, had died as counsellor in the Grand Conseil. Baillet (1691), ii. 387.

22. Descartes to Elizabeth, 9 October 1649 (v. 430).

23. Elizabeth to Descartes, 4 December 1649 (v. 452).

24. Descartes to Picot, 9 October 1649 (v. 432–3).

25. Pascal wrote in the Appendix to the 1663 edition of the *Traitez de l'Equilibre des liqueurs et de la pesanteur de la masse de l'air* about his request to Chanut in 1649: 'I also was honoured to write to Mr. Chanut . . . who was then Ambassador to Sweden, who favoured me by agreeing to my request to send me in parallel the observations made by himself and Mr. Descartes at Stockholm, from 21 October 1649 to 24 September 1650, as I also sent him mine' (quoted in v. 448).

26. Brasset to Descartes, 27 November 1649 (v. 450). See also Descartes to Picot, 4 December 1649 (v. 452).

27. Descartes to Picot, 4 December 1649 (v. 455). 'To enable you to write to me more freely, there will be no need to name him in your letter, because I shall understand

well enough who you are writing about. I expect that you will see him in Paris soon, because of his father's death.'

28. Descartes to Brégy, 18 December 1649 (v. 455–7). It remains unclear whether these verses were composed by Descartes or by someone else.

29. Descartes to Picot, 25 December 1649 (v. 461–2).

30. His work was examined subsequently in a book written by Father Francis Xavier Aynscom, *Francisci Xaverii Aynscom, e Societate Jesu, Expositio et Deductio geometria quadraturarum circuli R. P. Gregorii a Sancto Vincentio ejusdem Societatis, cui praemittitur liber de Natura et affectionibus rationum ac proportionum geometricarum* (Antwerp, 1656).

31. Descartes to an unidentified correspondent, possibly Van Schooten, 1649/50 (v. 465).

32. Descartes to Brégy, 15 January 1659 (v. 466). Chanut returned to Stockholm on 20 December and had an audience with the queen on 23 December. Descartes mentions that he has had only one audience with the queen since then.

33. Saumaise to Brégy, 29 January 1650 (quoted in v. 468). His father had been attempting for some time to join his son in Stockholm, and he arrived there eventually in August 1650 (v. 469).

34. Descartes to Picot, 15 January 1650 (v. 469).

35. Descartes to Elizabeth, 22 February 1649 (v. 282).

36. *Les dernieres heures de Monsieur Rivet* (1651).

37. Ibid., 16.

38. Ibid., 54.

39. Baillet (1691), ii. 410. According to Baillet, Chanut fell ill on 18 January and had recovered by 24 January.

40. Chanut to M. de Brienne, 12 February 1650, and Chanut to Elizabeth, 19 February 1650 (v. 470–71).

41. Baillet (1691), ii. 419,

42. Descartes (1657), vol. 1 (Preface), and Baillet (1691), ii. 423.

43. Descartes (1657), Preface to vol. 1, quoted in v. 482.

44. Saumaise to Brégy, 19 February 1650 (v. 476).

45. Chanut to Elizabeth, 19 February 1650 (v. 471).

46. Chanut to Elizabeth, 16 April 1650 (v. 472–4).

47. The poems were composed on 15, 17, 21, 25, and 31 March 1650. I am indebted to Erik-Jan Bos for this information.

48. Epitaph for Descartes by Christian Huygens, written to his brother Constantijn, 29 March 1659 (v. 480).

49. Chanut to Périer, 28 March 1650 (v. 475).

50. For the history of these papers, see the Introduction to Descartes (2003), pp. xvi–xxi.

51. The coronation was on October 20/30, 1650.

52. Arckenholtz (1751), vol. 4, 19–20 (note).

53. Baillet (1691: ii, 436) reports that the French ambassador to Sweden kept a bone from his finger as a souvenir, and Arckenholtz (1751: iv. 232) reports that Isaac

Planstrom, an officer in the Stockholm guards, stole the philosopher's cranium from his coffin and substituted another in its place. Adam (1910), 629, discusses the probability that the cranium returned from Sweden and stored in the Museum of Natural History, Paris, is that of Descartes.

54. Baillet (1691), i. 251.
55. Descartes to an unknown correspondent [1644?] (v. 55).
56. Armogathe and Carraud (2001).
57. *Index* (1664), 393–4.
58. The 1650 edition includes the dedication to the Sorbonne, the Preface to the Reader, and the Synopsis, together with: (1) six meditations; (2) the first four sets of objections and replies; (3) Descartes' note, translated from French, which explains why he omitted the Fifth Objections and his letter in reply to Gassendi's *Instances*; (4) the Sixth Objections and Replies; (5) *Comments on a Certain Manifesto*; and (6) an Appendix containing (a) the Fifth and Seventh Objections and Replies, (b) the letter to Father Dinet, and (c) the letter to Voetius.
59. Descartes (1657, 1659, 1667).
60. La Forge published his own summary of Descartes' theory of mind two years later. See La Forge (1666, 1997).
61. Some of these authors are discussed in Clarke (1989).

Bibliography

Primary Sources

Aemilius, Antonius (1651). *Orationes*. Utrecht: Gisbertus à Zyll et Theodorus ab Ackersdyck.

Agrippa, Henry Cornelius (1993). *Three Books of Occult Philosophy*. Trans. James Freake, ed. Donald Tyson. St. Paul, MN: Llewellyn Publications. (First ed. in Latin 1531, in English 1651).

Anonymous (1611). *In anniversarium Henrici Magni obitus diem. Lacrymae collegii Flexiensis regii Societatis Jesu*. La Flèche: Jacob Reze.

Anonymous (1623). *Effroyables pactions faites entre le Diable et les prétendus invisibles avec leurs damnables instructions, perte deplorable de leurs escoliers, et leur miserable fin*. Reprinted in Édouard Fournier, ed., *Variétés historiques et littéraires*, vol. 9 (Paris: Pagnerre, 1859), 275–307.

Anonymous (1624). *Examen sur l'inconnue et nouvelle caballe des frères de la Rozée-Croix, habituez depuis peu de temps en la ville de Paris. Ensemble l'histoire des moeurs, coustumes, prodiges et particularitez d'icieux*. Paris. Reprinted in Édouard Fournier, ed., *Variétés historiques et littéraires*, vol. 1 (Paris: Jannet, 1855), 115–26.

Anonymous (1643). *Traictez pour la Deffence de l'université de Paris, contra les Iesuites*. Paris.

Anonymous (1680). *A Truth Known to very Few: viz. That the Jesuits are down-right compleat Atheists: Proved such, and condemned for it by Two Sentences of the Famous Faculty of Sorbonne*. London: T. Dawks.

Aquinas, Thomas (1968). *On the Unity of the Intellect against the Averroists*. Trans. Beatrice H. Zedler. Milwaukee, WI: Marquette University Press.

Arckenholtz, Johann Wilhelm (1751). *Memoires concernant Christine Reine de Suede pour servir d'Eclaircissement a l'histoire de son regne et principalement de sa vie privée, et aux evenemens de l'histoire de son temps civile et littéraire*. 4 vols. Amsterdam and Leipzig: Pierre Mortier.

Aristotle (2000). *Nichomachean Ethics*. Trans. Roger Crisp. Cambridge: Cambridge University Press.

Arnauld, Antoine (1703). *De la frequente Communion, ou les sentimens des Peres, des papes, et des Conciles, touchant l'usage des Sacrements de Penitence & d'Eucharistie sont fidellement exposez*. Lyon: Leonard Plaignard. (First ed. 1644).

Arnauld, Antoine (1990). *On True and False Ideas*. Trans. S. Gaukroger. Manchester: Manchester University Press. (First ed. 1683).

Arnauld, Antoine, and Pierre Nicole (1996). *Logic or the Art of Thinking*. Trans. Jill Vance Buroker. Cambridge: Cambridge University Press. (First ed. 1662).

Augustine, Saint (1998). *The City of God against the Pagans*. Trans. R. W. Dyson. Cambridge: Cambridge University Press.

Ausonius (1991). *The Works of Ausonius*. Edited with an introduction and commentary by R. P. H. Green. Oxford: Clarendon Press.

Baillet, Adrien (1691). *La Vie de Monsieur Des-Cartes*. 2 vols. Paris: Daniel Horthemels.

Basso, Sebastianus (1621). *Philosophiae naturalis adversus Aristotelem libri xii*. Geneva: Peter de la Roviere.

Beardslee, John, ed. (1965). *Reformed Dogmatics*. New York: Oxford University Press.

Beaugrand, Jean de (1636). *Geostatice, seu de vario pondere gravium secundum varia a terrae [centro] intervalla*. Tussamus du Bray.

Beeckman, Isaac (1939–53). *Journal tenu par Isaac Beeckman de 1604 à 1634*. Ed. Cornelis de Waard. 4 vols. The Hague: Martinus Nijhoff.

Beverwijck, Johannes van (1644). *Epistolicae Quaestiones, cum doctorum responsis*. Rotterdam: Arnold Leers.

Borel, Pierre (1670a). *Historiarum, & Observationum Medicophysicarum, Centuria iv; Renati Cartesii vita*. Frankfurt: L. S. Cornerum.

Borel, Pierre (1670b). *A Summary or Compendium of the Life of the most Famous Philosopher Renatus Descartes*. London: George Palmer.

Botois (Bootius), Gerard and Arnold (1641). *Philosophia Naturalis Reformata. Id est, Philosophiae Aristotelicae accurate examinatio. Et novae verior introductio*. Dublin: Societas Bibliopolarum.

Bots, Hans, and Pierre Leroy, eds. (1978–82). *Correspondance intégrale d'André Rivet et de Claude Sarrau, 1641–1550*. 3 vols. Amsterdam: APA–Holland University Press.

Boyle, Robert (1979). *Selected Philosophical Papers of Robert Boyle*. Ed. M. A. Stewart. Manchester: Manchester University Press.

Boyle, Robert (1999–2000). *The Works of Robert Boyle*. Ed. M. Hunter and E. B. Davis. 14 vols. London: Pickering and Chatto.

Brosse, Pierre de la [Petrus Brossaeus] (1611). *Corpus omnium veterum poetarum Latinorum secundum seriem temporum, et quinque libris distinctum, in quo continentur omnia ipsorum opera, seu fragmenta quae reperiuntur, cui praefixa uniuscuiusque poetae vita*, 2nd ed. Geneva: Samuel Crispin.

Campanella, Thomas (1993). *La Città del Sole*. Ed. Davide Sala. Sommacampagna: Demetra. (First ed. 1602).

Campanella, Thomas (1994). *Apologia pro Galileo: A Defence of Galileo the Mathematician from Florence*. Trans. Richard J. Blackwell. Notre Dame and London: University of Notre Dame Press. (First ed. 1616).

Caus, Salomon de (1624). *Les raisons des forces mouvantes, avec diverses machines tant utiles que plaisantes: ausquelles sont adjoints plusieurs desseins de Grotes & Fontaines*. Paris: Charles Sevestre.

Caussin, Nicolas (1624). *La Cour Sainte.* Paris: Sebastien Chappelet.

Caussin, Nicolas (1634). *The Holy Court.* Trans. Thomas Hawkins. London: John Cousturier.

Caussin, Nicolas (1649). *The Christian Diary.* London: John Williams.

Caussin, Nicolas (1714). *The Penitent: or, Entertainments for Lent.* Translated by B. B. [Basil Brook]. London: Gosling.

Chanet, Pierre (1646). *De l'Instinct et de la connoisssance des animaux.* La Rochelle: Toussaincts de Govy.

Charron, Pierre (1654). *De la Sagesse. Trois Livres.* Leiden: Jean Elzevier.

Charron, Pierre (1729). *Of Wisdom Three Books.* Trans. George Stanhope. London: n.p.

Copernicus, Nicholas (1978). *On the Revolutions.* Translation and commentary by Edward Rosen. Baltimore and London: Johns Hopkins University Press. (First ed. 1543).

Dee, John (1564). *Monas Hieroglyphica.* Antwerp: G. Silvius.

Descartes, Cathérine (1745). 'Relation de la mort de M. Descartes.' In *Bibliothèque Poétique*, vol. 3. Paris: Briasson, 238–50.

Descartes, René (1641). *Meditationes de prima philosophia, in qua Dei existentia, & animae immortalitas demonstratur.* Paris: Michael Soly.

Descartes, René (1642). *Meditationes de prima philosophia, in quibus Dei existentia, & animae humanae à corpore distinctio, demonstrantur.* Amsterdam: L. Elzevier.

Descartes, René (1644). *Principia Philosophiae.* Amsterdam: Louis Elzevier.

Descartes, René (1650). *Meditationes De Prima Philosophia, in quibus Dei existentia, & animae humanae à corpore distinctio, demonstrantur.* 3rd ed. Amsterdam: Louis Elzevier.

Descartes, René (1657–67). *Lettres de Mr Descartes.* Ed. Claude Clerselier. 3 vols. Paris: Angot.

Descartes, René (1665). *Discourses of the Mechanicks: A manuscript of Monsieur Des-Cartes.* In *Mathematical Collections and Translations,* by Thomas Salusbury, vol. 2. London: William Laybourn, 311–18.

Descartes, René (1859–60). *Oeuvres inédits de Descartes.* Ed. Foucher de Careil. Paris: Auguste Durand.

Descartes, René (1936). *Descartes: Correspondance.* Ed. Charles Adam and G. Milhaud. 8 vols. Paris: Félix Alcan.

Descartes, René (1961). *Compendium of Music.* Trans. Walter Robert. Rome: American Institute of Musicology.

Descartes, René (1963). *Oeuvres philosophiques de Descartes.* Edited and annotated by F. Alquié. 3 vols. Paris: Éditions Garnier Frères.

Descartes, René (1966). *Regulae ad directionem ingenii.* Ed. Giovanni Crapulli. The Hague: Martinus Nijhoff.

Descartes, René (1976). *Descartes' Conversation with Burman.* Translated with an Introduction by John Cottingham. Oxford: Clarendon Press.

Descartes, René (1977). *Règles utiles et claires pour la direction de l'esprit en la recherche de la verité.* Translated by Jean-Luc Marion, with mathematical notes by Pierre Costabel. The Hague: Martinus Nijhoff.

Descartes, René (1990). *Abrégé de Musique, suivi des Éclaircissements physiques sur la Musique de Descartes du R. P. Nicolas Poisson.* Translation and notes by Pascal Dumont. Paris: Méridiens Klincksieck.

Descartes, René (2001). *Discourse on Method, Optics, Geometry, and Meteorology,* rev. ed. Trans. Paul J. Olscamp. Indianapolis: Hackett.

Descartes, René (2003). *The Correspondence of René Descartes 1643.* Ed. T. Verbeek, E.-J. Bos, and J. van de Ven. Utrecht: Zeno Institute for Philosophy.

Digby, Kenelm (1644). *Two Treatises in the one of which, The Nature of Bodies; in the other, the Nature of Mans Soule: is looked into in way of discovery, of the Immortality of Reasonable Soules.* Paris: Gilles Blaizot.

Digby, Kenelm (1658). *A Late Discourse Made in a Solemne Assembly of Nobles and Learned Men at Montpellier in France, Touching the Cure of Wounds by the Powder of Sympathy; with Instructions how to make the said powder, whereby many other secrets of Nature are unfolded.* Trans. R. White. London: R. Lowndes and T. Davis.

Donno, Elizabeth Story, ed. (1993). *Three Renaissance Pastorals: Tasso, Guarini, Daniel.* Binghamton, New York: Medieval and Renaissance Texts and Studies, vol. 102.

Erasmus, Desiderius (1530). *De civilitate morum puerilium.* Cologne: Joannes Gymnicus.

Erasmus, Desiderius (1532). *A Lytell booke of Good Manners for Children.* Trans. Robert Whytyngton. London.

Erasmus, Desiderius (1967). *Erasmus on His Times: A Shortened Version of the 'Adages' of Erasmus.* Cambridge: Cambridge University Press. (First ed. 1500).

Euclid (1574). *Euclidis Elementorum libri XV. Accessit XVI de solidorum regularium comparatione.* Ed. Christopher Clavius. Rome: Vincent Accoltus.

Fermat, Pierre (1891–1912). *Oeuvres de Fermat.* Ed. Paul Tannery and Charles Henry. Paris: Gauthier-Villars.

Fitzpatrick, Edward A. (1933). *St. Ignatius and the Ratio Studiorum.* New York and London: McGraw-Hill.

Fromondus, Libertus (1627). *Meteorologicorum Libri Sex.* Antwerp: Plantiniana.

Fromondus, Libertus (1631). *Anti-Aristarchus sive Orbis-Terrae immobilis.* Antwerp: Plantiniana.

Galilei, Galileo (1957). *Discoveries and Opinions of Galileo.* Edited and translated by Stillman Drake. New York: Doubleday.

Garassus, François (1623). *La doctrine curieuse des beaux esprits de ce temps, ou pretendus tels.* Paris: Sebastien Chappelet.

Gassendi, Pierre (1641). *Viri Illustris Nicolai Claudii Fabricii de Peiresc. Senatoris Aquisextiensis.* Paris: Sebastian Cramoisy.

Gassendi, Pierre (1642). *De motu impresso a motore translato. Epistolae duae.* Paris: Louis de Heuqueville.

Gassendi, Pierre (1644). *Disquisitio Metaphysica. Seu Dubitationes, et Instantiae: Adversus Renati Cartesii Metaphysicam, & Responsa.* Amsterdam: Johannes Blaeu.

Gassendi, Pierre (1657). *The Mirrour of True Nobility & Gentility. Being the Life of the Renowned Nicolaus Clausius Fabricius Lord of Peiresk, Senator of the Parliament of Aix.* Trans. W. Rand. London: Humphrey Moseley.

Gassendi, Pierre (1658). *Opera Omnia*. 6 vols. Lyon: Laurentius Anisson.

Gassendi, Pierre (1962). *Disquisitio Metaphysica*. Latin text, French translation by Bernard Rochot. Paris: Vrin.

[Goulu, Dominique] (1628). *Letres de Phyllarque a Ariste*. Paris: George Verd.

Gournay, Marie le Jars de (2002). *Apology for the Woman Writing and Other Works*. Edited and translated by Richard Hillman and Colette Quesnel. Chicago and London: University of Chicago Press.

Guez de Balzac, Jean Louis (1624). *Lettres de Sieur de Balzac*. Paris: Toussaint du Bray.

Guez de Balzac, Jean Louis (1638a). *The Letters of Mounsieur de Balzac*. Trans. 'W.T.' London: W. Edmonds.

Guez de Balzac, Jean Louis (1638b). *New Epistles by Mounsieur D'Balzac*. Trans. Richard Baker Knight. London: Eglesfield, Crooke and Serger.

Halliwell, James Orchard, ed. (1841). *A Collection of Letters Illustrative of the Progress of Science in England from the Reign of Queen Elizabeth to That of Charles the Second*. London: Historical Society of Science.

Heereboord, Adrianus (1665). *Meletemata Philosophica*. Leiden: Francis Moyard.

Hobbes, Thomas (1994). *The Correspondence*. Ed. Noel Malcolm. 2 vols. Oxford: Clarendon Press.

Huygens, Constantijn (1644). *Momenta Desultoria: Poematum Libri XI*. Ed. Caspar Barlaeus. Leiden: Bonaventure and Abraham Elzevier.

Huygens, Constantijn (1911). *De Briefwisseling van Constantijn Huygens (1608–1687)*. Ed. J. A. Worp. 's-Gravenhague: M. Nijhoff.

Huygens, Christiaan (1962). *Treatise on Light*. Trans. S. P. Thompson. New York: Dover. (First ed. 1690).

Huygens, Constantijn (1964). *The Use and Nonuse of the Organ in the Churches of the United Netherlands*. Trans. Ericka E. Smit-Vanrotte. New York: Institute of Medieval Music.

Ignatius of Loyola (1963). *The Spiritual Exercises*. Trans. Thomas Corbishley. London: Burns and Oates. (First ed. 1548).

Kepler, Joannes (1992). *New Astronomy*. Trans. William H. Donahue. Cambridge: Cambridge University Press. (First ed. 1609).

Kepler, Joannes (1997). *The Harmony of the World*. Trans. E. J. Aiton, A. M. Duncan, and J. V. Field. Philadelphia: American Philosophical Society. (First ed. 1619).

La Forge, Louis de (1666). *Traitté de l'esprit de l'homme et de ses facultez et fonctions, et de son union avec le corps. Suivant les principes de René Descartes*. Paris: T. Girard.

La Forge, Louis de (1997). *Treatise on the Human Mind (1666)*. Trans. D. M. Clarke. Dordrecht/Boston/London: Kluwer.

La Mothe le Vayer, François de (1647). *Petit Discours Chrestien de l'Immortalité de l'Ame, avec Corollaire, & un Discours Sceptique sur la Musique*. 3rd ed. Paris: Antoine de Sommaville. (First ed. 1637).

Lipstorp, Daniel (1653). *Specimina Philosophiae Cartesianae. Quibus accedit euisdem authoris Copernicus redivivus*. Leiden: Joannes et Daniel Elsevier.

Louis de Grenade [Luis Sarria] (1583). *La Guide des pecheurs, composée en espagnol par R. P. F. Louis de Geenade, traduite en français par N. Colin.* Paris: Le Fizelier.

Lull, Ramon (1578). *Ars brevis illuminati doctoris magistri Raymundi Lull.* Paris: Aegidius Gorbinus.

Lull, Ramon (1632). *Le fondement de l'artifice universel, de l'illuminé docteur Raymond Lulle.* Trans. R. L. sieur de Vassi. Paris: Champenois.

Lull, Ramon (1985). *Selected Works of Ramon Llull.* Edited and translated by Anthony Bonner. 2 vols. Princeton, NJ: Princeton University Press.

Melanchthon, Philip (1999). *Orations on Philosophy and Education.* Ed. S. Kusukawa, trans. S. F. Salazar. Cambridge: Cambridge University Press.

Mersenne, Marin (1623). *Quaestiones celeberrimae in genesim, cum accurata textus explicatione.* Paris: Sebastian Cramoisy.

Mersenne, Marin (1624). *L'Impiété des Deistes, et les plus subtils Libertins découverte, & refutee par raisons de Théologie & de Philosophie.* 2 vols. Paris: Pierre Billaine.

Mersenne, Marin (1625). *La vérité des Sciences. Contre les Septiques ou Pyrrhoniens.* Paris: Toussainct du Bray.

Mersenne, Marin (1932–91). *Correspondance du P. Marin Mersenne, religieux minime.* Ed. C. de Waard, R. Pintard, R. Rochot, and A. Beaulieu. Paris: Presses Universitaires de France and Editions du CNRS.

Mill, J. S. (1989). *On Liberty and Other Writings.* Ed. Stefan Collini. Cambridge: Cambridge University Press.

Montaigne, Michel de (1991). *The Complete Essays.* Trans. M. A. Screech. London: Penguin. (First ed. 1580).

Morin, Jean-Baptiste (1631). *Famosi et antiqui problematis de telluris motu, vel qiete; hactenus optata solutio.* Paris: Published by the author.

Naudé, Gabriel (1623). *Instruction à la France sur la vérité de l'histoire des Frères de la Roze-Croix.* Paris: François Iulliot.

Naudé, Gabriel (1625). *Apologie pour tous les grands personages qui ont esté faussement soupçonnez de Magie.* Paris: François Targa.

Naudé, Gabriel (1657). *The History of Magick by way of Apology for all the Wise Men who have unjustly been reputed Magicians, from the Creation, to the present Age.* Trans. J. Davis. London: John Streater.

Pascal, Blaise (1998–2000). *Oeuvres complètes.* Ed. Michel Le Guern. 2 vols. Paris: Gallimard.

Pasquier, Étienne (1602). *Le Catechisme des jesuites; un examen de leur doctrine.* Villefranche: Guillaume Grenier.

Pasquier, Etienne (1975). *The Jesuites Catechisme 1602.* Ilkey (Yorkshire) and London: Scolar Press.

Plemp, Vopiscus Fortunatus (1648). *Ophthalmographia sive Tractatio de Oculo.* 2nd ed. Louvain: Jerome Nemparaeus.

Porta, John Baptista della (1619). *Magiae naturalis libri viginti, in quibus scientiarum naturalium divitiae, & deliciae demonstrantur.* Hanover: Daniel and David Aubriorum and Clement Schleichius.

Porta, John Baptista della (1658). *Natural Magick by John Baptista Porta, a Neapolitane: in twenty Books . . . wherein are set forth All the Riches and Delights of the Natural Sciences.* London: Thomas Young and Samuel Speed.

Poulain de la Barre, François (1720). *La Doctrine des protestans sur la liberté de lire l'Ecriture Sainte, le service divin en langue entendue, l'invocation des saints, le sacrement de l'eucharistie.* Geneva: Fabri & Barrilot.

Prévot, Jacques, ed. (1998). *Libertins du XVIIe siècle*, vol. 1. Paris: Gallimard.

Quintilian, M. Fabius (1921). *Institutio Oratoria.* Trans. H. E. Butler. 4 vols. London and Cambridge, MA: Heinemann and Harvard University Press.

Regius, Henricus (1640). *Spongia qua eluuntur sordes Animadversionum quas Jacobus Primirosius Doctor Medicus adversus Theses pro Circulatione sanguinis in Academia Ultrajectina disputatas nuper edidit.* Leiden: W. Christiaens for J. Maire.

Regius, Henricus (1641). *Physiologia, sive Cognitio sanitatis. Tribus disputionibus in Academia Ultrajectina publice proposita.* Utrecht: Aeg. Roman.

Regius, Henricus (1646). *Fundamenta Physices.* Amsterdam: Louis Elzevier.

Regius, Henricus (1648). *Brevis Explicatio Mentis Humanae, sive animae rationalis: Ubi explicatur, quid sit, & quid esse possit.* Utrecht: Theodore Ackersdicius.

Regius, Henricus (2002). *The Correspondence between Descartes and Henricus Regius.* Ed. Erik-Jan Bos. Utrecht: Zeno.

Revius, Jacobus (1648). *Methodi Cartesianae Consideratio Theologica.* Leiden: Jerome de Vogel.

Richeome, Louis (1604). *Le Pelerin de Lorete.* Bordeaux: S. Millanges.

Richeome, Louis (1621). *L'Immortalitaté de l'ame, declaree avec raisons naturelles tesmoignages humains et divins pour la Foy Catholique contre les Athees et Libertins.* Paris: Nicolas Buon.

(Rivet, Andrew) (1651). *Les dernieres heures de Monsieur Rivet vivant, Ministere de la Parole de Dieu.* Delf: Arthur Woodward. Translated into English by 'G.L.' as: *The Last Houers of the Right Reverrent Father in God, Andrew Rivet, in his life time Dr. and Professour Honorable of Divinity, in the University of Leyden.* The Hague: Samuel Broun, 1652.

Roman Catholic Church (1664). *Index librorum prohibitorum.* Edition authorized by Pope Alexander VII. Rome: Holy Office.

Roth, L. (1926). *Correspondence of Descartes and Constantijn Huygens 1635–1647.* Oxford: Clarendon Press.

Saint-Evremond, Monsieur de (1709). *Oeuvres meslées de Mr. de Saint-Evremond.* 2nd ed., revised and corrected. 3 vols. London: Jacob Tonson. (Author also known as Charles de Saint Denis).

Saint-Evremond, Monsieur de (1726). *Oeuvres de Monsieur de Saint-Evremond, avec la vie de l'auteur par Mr. Des Maizeaux.* 3 vols. Amsterdam: Covens & Mortier.

Saint-Evremond, Monsieur de (1728). *The Works of Monsieur de St. Evremond. With the Life of the author by Mr. Des Maizeaux F.R.S..* 2nd ed. 3 vols. London: J. and J. Knapton.

Sanchez, Jerome (1613). *Generalis et admirabilis methodus, ad omnes scientias facilius, et citius addiscendas.* Tyrasona: Carolus a Lauayen.

Schoock[ius], Martinus (1643). *Admiranda Methodus Novae Philosophiae Renati Des Cartes*. Utrecht: J. van Waesberge.

Schurman, Anna Maria van (1641). *Dissertatio de ingenii mulieribus ad Doctrinam, & meliores litteras aptitudine*. Leiden: Elzevier.

Schurman, Anna Maria van (1646). *Question celebre. S'il est necessaire, ou non, que les Filles soient sçavantes*. Paris: Rolet le Duc.

Schurman, Anna Maria van (1650). *Opuscula Hebraea, Graeca, Latina, Gallica, Prosaica & Metrica*. 2nd ed. Leiden: Elzevier.

Schurman, Anna Maria van (1659). *The Learned Maid; or, Whether a Maid may be a Scholar? A Logick Exercise Written in Latine by that Incomparable Virgin Anna Maria à Schurman of Utrecht*. London: John Redmayne.

Schurman, Anna Maria van (1673). *Eukleria, seu Melioris Partis Electio*. Altona: Cornelius van der Meulen.

Schurman, Anna Maria van (1998). *Whether a Christian Woman Should Be Educated and Other Writings from Her Intellectual Circle*. Trans. Joyce L. Irwin. Chicago and London: University of Chicago Press.

Seneca, Lucius Annaeus (1969). *De vita beata*. Ed. Pierre Grimal. Paris: Presses Universitaires de France.

Sextus Empiricus (2000). *Outlines of Scepticism*. Edited and translated by Julia Annas and Jonathan Barnes. Cambridge: Cambridge University Press.

Siger de Brabant (1911). *Quaestiones de anima intellectiva*. In P. Mandonnet, ed., *Siger de Brabant et l'Averrroisme Latin au XIIIème Siècle*, vol. 2. Louvain: Institut Supérieur de Philosophie.

Silhon, Jean de (1991). *Les Deux Vérités*. Paris: Fayard. (First ed. 1626).

Silhon, Jean de (1634). *De l'immortalité de l'ame*. Paris: Pierre Billaine.

Soarez, Cyprian (1577). *De arte Rhetorica Tres, ex Aristotele, Cicerone, & Quintiliano praecipue deprompti*. Salamanaca: M. Gastius.

Sommervogel, Carlos, ed. (1892–1932). *Bibliothèque de la Compagnie de Jésus*, new ed. 11 vols. Brussels and Paris: Schepens and Picard.

Sorbière, Samuel (1654). *Discours sur sa conversion à l'Eglise Catholique*. Lyon: Guillaume Barbier.

Sorbière, Samuel (1660a). *Relations, Lettres, et Discours de Mr. de Sorbiere*. Paris: Robert de Ninville.

Sorbière, Samuel (1660b). *Lettres et Discours, sur diverses matieres curieuses*. Paris: François Clousier.

Stevin, Simon (1966). *The Principal Works of Simon Stevin*, vol. 5. Ed. E. Crone et al. Amsterdam: C. V. Swets and Zeitlinger.

Tanner, Norman P., ed. (1990). *Decrees of the Ecumenical Councils*. 2 vols. London and Washington, DC: Sheed and Ward and Georgetown University Press.

Tasso, Torquato (1957). *L'Aminta*. Ed. Angelo Solerti, Introduction by A. Gareffi. Manziana, Italy: Vecchiarelli Editore.

Théophile de Viau (1660). *Le Parnasse des Poetes Satyriques*. Paris. (First ed. 1622).

Vanini, Giulio Cesare (1990). *Opere*. Ed. G. Papuli and F. P. Raimondi. Galatina: Congedo Editore.

Vieta, Francis (1591). *In artem analyticem Isagoge.* Turonis: Mettayer.

Voetius, Gisbertus (1648–69). *Selectarum Disputationum Theologicarum.* 5 vols. Utrecht and Amsterdam: J. van Waesberge.

White, Thomas (1642). *De Mundo Dialogi Tres.* Paris: Dionysius Moreau.

Wittgenstein, Ludwig (1963). *Tractatus Logico-Philosophicus*, 2nd impression. Trans. D. F. Pears and B. F. McGuinness. London: Routledge and Kegan Paul.

Secondary Works

Adam, Charles (1910). *Vie & Oeuvres de Descartes: étude historique.* Paris: Léopold Cerf.

Adam, Charles (1937a). *Descartes: sa vie et son oeuvre.* Paris: Boivin.

Adam, Charles (1937b). *Descartes: ses amitiés féminines.* Paris: Boivin.

Åkerman, Susanna (1991). *Queen Christina of Sweden and Her Circle.* Leiden and New York: E. J. Brill.

Anonymous (1730). *The Life of Lucilio (alias Julius Caesar) Vanini, Burnt for Atheism at Thoulouse. With an Abstract of his Writings.* Trans. from French. London: W. Meadows.

Ariès, Philippe (1973). *L'Enfant et la vie familiale sous l'ancien régime.* Paris: Editions du Seuil.

Ariès, Philippe, et al. (1986). *Histoire de la vie privée: Vol. III: De la renaissance aux Lumières.* Paris: Éditions du Seuil.

Ariew, Roger, John Cottingham, and Tom Sorell, eds. (1998). *Descartes' Meditations: Background Source Materials.* Cambridge: Cambridge University Press.

Armogathe, Jean-Robert (1977). *Theologia cartesiana: L'explication physique de L'Eucharistie chez Descartes et Dom Desgabets.* The Hague: Nijhoff.

Armogathe, Jean-Robert (1994). 'L'approbation des Meditationes par la faculté de théologie de Paris (1641).' *Bulletin cartésien, 21*, 1–3.

Armogathe, J.-R., Vincent Carraud, and Robert Feenstra (1988). 'La Licence de droit de Descartes: un placard inédit de 1616.' *Nouvelles de la République des Lettres, 1*, 122–45.

Armogathe, J.-R., Giulia Belgioioso, and Carlo Vinti (1999). *La biografia intelletuale di Réne Descartes attraverso la correspondance.* Naples: Vivarium.

Armogathe, J.-R., and Vincent Carraud (2001). 'La première condamnation des Oeuvres des Descartes, d'après des documents inédits aux Archives du Saint-Office.' *Nouvelles de la république des lettres, 2*, 103–37.

Augur, Léon (1962). *Un savant méconnu: Gilles Personne de Roberval (1602–1675).* Paris: Blanchard.

Baar, Morgan de, et al., eds. (1996). *Choosing the Better Part: Anna Maria van Schurman (1607–1678).* Dordrecht: Kluwer.

Barbour, James Murray (1951). *Tuning and Temperament.* East Lansing: Michigan State University Press.

Belgioioso, Giulia, ed. (1990). *Descartes: il metodo e i saggi: atti del convegno per il 350° anniversario della pubblicazione del* Discours de la Méthode *et degli* Essais. 2 vols. Rome: Istituto della Encyclopedia Italiana.

Bercé, Y.-M. (1974). *Histoire des croquants: Étude des soulèvements populaires aux xviie siècle dans le sud-ouest de la France*. Paris and Geneva: Librairie Droz.

Birch, Una Constance (1909). *Anna van Schurman: Artist, Scholar, Saint*. London: Longmans, Green and Co.

Blackwell, Richard J. (1991). *Galileo, Bellarmine, and the Bible*. Notre Dame, IN, and London: University of Notre Dame Press.

Bonansea, Bernardino M. (1969). *Tommaso Campanella: Renaissance Pioneer of Modern Thought*. Washington, DC: Catholic University of America Press.

Bordo, Susan, ed. (1999). *Feminist Interpretations of René Descartes*. University Park: Pennsylvania State University Press.

Bos, Erik-Jan (1999). 'Descartes's *Lettre Apologétique aux Magistrats d'Utrecht*: New Facts and Materials.' *Journal of the History of Philosophy*, *37*, 415–33.

Bos, Erik-Jan, and Corinna Vermeulen (2002). 'An Unknown Autograph Letter of Descartes to Joachim de Wicquefort.' *Studia Leibnitiana*, *34*, 100 9.

Bos, E.-J., M. van Otegem, and T. Verbeek (2002). 'Notes sur la correspondance de Descartes.' *Archives de Philosophie*, *65*, 5–14.

Bos, Henk J. M. (1990). 'The Structure of Descartes' *Géométrie*.' In Belgioioso (1990), vol. 2, 349–69.

Bos, Henk J. M. (2001). *Redefining Geometrical Exactness: Descartes' Transformation of the Early Modern Concept of Construction*. New York: Springer-Verlag.

Brink, J. R., ed. (1980). *Female Scholars: A Tradition of Learned Women before 1800*. Montreal: Eden Press.

Brown, Barbara Traxler (1990). '*Discours* and *Essäis de la Méthode*: An Evaluation within Jan Maire's Publishing Activities, 1636–1639.' In Belgioioso (1990), vol. 2, 119–35.

Certeau, Michel de (1970). *La Possession de Loudun*. Paris: Julliard.

Christensen, Thomas, ed. (2002). *The Cambridge History of Western Music Theory*. Cambridge: Cambridge University Press.

Clarke, Desmond M. (1989). *Occult Powers and Hypotheses: Cartesian Natural Philosophy under Louis XIV*. Oxford: Clarendon Press.

Clarke, Desmond M. (2003a). 'Pascal's Philosophy of Science.' In N. Hammond, ed., *The Cambridge Companion to Pascal*. Cambridge: Cambridge University Press, 102–21.

Clarke, Desmond M. (2003b). *Descartes's Theory of Mind*. Oxford: Clarendon Press.

Clulee, Nicholas H. (1988). *John Dee's Natural Philosophy: Between Science and Religion*. London: Routledge.

Cohen, Gustave (1920). *Écrivains Français en Hollande dans la première moitié du xviie siècle*. Paris: Édouard Champion.

Collins, James B. (1995). *The State in Early Modern France*. Cambridge: Cambridge University Press.

Copenhaver, Brian P., and Charles B. Schmitt (1992). *Renaissance Philosophy*. (A History of Western Philosophy, vol. 3). Oxford: Oxford University Press.

Costabel, Pierre (1990). 'La *Géométrie* que Descartes n'a pas publiée.' In Belgioioso (1990), vol. 2, 371–85.

Crété, Liliane (1987). *La vie quotidienne à La Rochelle au temps du grand siège 1627–1628.* Paris: Hachette.

Dainville, François de (1978). *L'Education des jésuites (xvie–xviiie siècles).* Ed. M.-M. Compère. Paris: Éditions de Minuit.

Denzinger, Henry (1960). *Enchiridion Symbolorum definitionum et declarationum de rebus fidei et morum,* 31st ed. Ed. Karl Rahner. Fribourg: Herder.

Des Chene, Dennis (1996). *Physiologia: Natural Philosophy in Late Aristotelian and Cartesian Thought.* Ithaca and London: Cornell University Press.

Evans, R. J. W. (1973). *Rudolph II and His World: A Study in Intellectual History 1576–1612.* Oxford: Clarendon Press.

Feingold, Mordechai (1999). 'Descartes and the English: The Cavendish Brothers.' In Armogathe et al., eds. (1999), 697–711.

Ferrier, Francis (1979). *Un Oratorien ami de Descartes. Guillaume Gibieuf et sa philosophie de la liberté.* Paris: Vrin.

Flanagan, Owen (2000). *Dreaming Souls: Sleep, Dreams, and the Evolution of the Conscious Mind.* New York and Oxford: Oxford University Press.

Foisil, Madeleine (1970). *Le révolte des Nu-Pieds et les révoltes normandes de 1639.* Paris: Presses Universitaires de France.

Fowler, C. F. (1999). *Descartes on the Human Soul.* Dordrecht/Boston/London: Kluwer.

Fumaroli, Marc (1980). *L'Âge de l'éloquence: Rhétorique et 'res literaria' de la Renaissance au seuil de l'époque classique.* Geneva: Droz.

Gaston-Chérau, Françoise (1949). 'Pages de la vie de collège.' In *Mélanges dédiés à la mémoire de Félix Grat,* vol. 2. Paris: Mme Pecqueur-Grat, 413–43.

Gaukroger, Stephen (1995). *Descartes; An Intellectual Biography.* Oxford: Clarendon Press.

Gleick, James (2003). *Isaac Newton.* London and New York: Fourth Estate.

Grimaldi, N., and Marion, J.-L. (1987). *Le Discours et sa méthode.* Paris: Presses Universitaires de France.

Harth, Erica (1992). *Cartesian Women: Versions and Subversions of Rational Discourse in the Old Regime.* Ithaca and London: Cornell University Press.

Hilgarth, J. N. (1971). *Ramon Lull and Lullism in Fourteenth-Century France.* Oxford: Clarendon Press.

Irwin, Joyce (1977). 'Anna Maria van Schurman: From Feminism to Pietism.' *Church History, 46,* 48–62.

Irwin, Joyce (1980). 'Anna Maria van Schurman: The Star of Utrecht (Dutch, 1606–1678).' In Brink (1980), 68–85.

Israel, Jonathan I. (1982). *The Dutch Republic and the Hispanic World 1606–1661.* Oxford: Clarendon Press.

Israel, Jonathan I. (1995). *The Dutch Republic: Its Rise, Greatness, and Fall 1477–1806.* Oxford: Clarendon Press.

Jardine, N. (1984). *The Birth of History and Philosophy of Science.* Cambridge: Cambridge University Press.

Java, Sophie (1998). *La Nuit des Songes de René Descartes.* Paris: Aubier.

Jurgens, Maleleine, and Jean Mesnard (1975). 'Quelques pièces exceptionelles découvertes au minutier central des notaries de Paris (1600–1650).' *Revue d'histoire littéraire de la France*, *79*, 739–54.

King, Peter, and Michael Winter (1998). *The Netherlands: World Bibliographcial Series*, vol. 88. Oxford: Clio Press.

Lenoir, Ernest (1939). *Trois Novateurs, Trois Martyrs. Vanini, Campanella, Giordano Bruno*. Paris: Rieder.

Levack, Brian P. (1987). *The Witch-hunt in Early Modern Europe*. London and New York: Longman.

McMullin, Ernan, ed. (1967). *Galileo: Man of Science*. New York and London: Basic Books.

Mahoney, Michael Sean (1994). *The Mathematical Career of Pierre de Fermat 1601–1665*, 2nd ed. Princeton, NJ: Princeton University Press.

Mehl, Édouard (2001). *Descartes en Allemagne 1619–1620*. Strasbourg: Presses Universitaires de Strasbourg.

Moore, James (1996). 'Metabiographical Reflections on Charles Darwin,' in Shortland and Yeo (1996), 267–81.

Mousnier, Roland (1964). *L'Assassinat d'Henri iv 14 Mai 1610*. Paris: Gallimard.

Mousnier, Roland (1971). *La vénalité des offices sous Henri iv et Louis xiii*. Paris: Presses Universitaires de France.

Mousnier, Roland (1979/84). *The Institutions of France under the Absolute Monarchy 1598–1785*. Vol. 1: *Society and the State*, trans. Brian Pearce; vol. 2, *The Organs of State and Society*, trans. Arthur Goldhammer. Chicago and London: University of Chicago Press.

Mousnier, Roland (1980/90). *Les institutions de la France sous la monarchie absolue 1598–1789*, 2 vols. 2nd ed. Paris: Presses Universitaires de France.

Ong, Walter Jackson, S.J. (1958). *Ramus, Method, and the Decay of Dialogue*. Cambridge, MA: Harvard University Press.

Osler, Margaret, J., ed. (2000). *Rethinking the Scientific Revolution*. Cambridge: Cambridge University Press.

Otegem, Matthijs van (2002). *A Bibliography of the Works of Descartes (1637–1704)*. 2 vols. Utrecht: Leiden-Utrecht Research Institute of Philosophy.

Parchnev, Boris (1963). *Les soulèvements populaires en France de 1623 à 1648*. Paris: S.E.V.P.E.N.

Petersson, Robert Torsten (1956). *Sir Kenelm Digby: The Ornament of England 1603–1665*. London: Jonathan Cape.

Raimondi, Fancesco Paolo (1998). 'Vanini et Mersenne.' In *Vanini*, ed. Jean-Pierre Cavaillé and Didier Foucault: a special edition of *Kairos*, no. 12, pp. 181–253.

Rice, James V. (1939). *Gabriel Naudé 1600-1653*. Baltimore and London: Johns Hopkins University Press and Oxford University Press.

Rochemonteix, Camille de (1889). *Un collège des jésuites au xviième et au xviiième siècles*. 4 vols. Le Mans.

Rodis-Lewis, Geneviève (1995). *Descartes: Biographie*. Paris: Calmann-Lévy.

Sambuc, Félix (1869). *Jean de Labadie; sa vie et ses écrits*. Strasbourg: Heitz.

Saxby, T. J. (1987). *The Quest for the New Jerusalem: Jean de Labadie and the Labadists, 1610–1744*. Dordrecht: Nijhoff.

Scaglione, Aldo (1986). *The Liberal Arts and the Jesuit College System*. Amsterdam: John Benjamins Publishing Company.

Schama, Simon (1987). *The Embarrassment of Riches: An Interpretation of Dutch Culture in the Golden Age*. London: Collins.

Schramm, Johannes Mauritius (1709). *De vita et scriptis famosi athei Juliii Caesaris Vanini*. Custrini: Godfrey Heinichius.

Sebba, Gregor (1987). *The Dream of Descartes*. Ed. Richard A. Watson. Carbondale and Edwardsville: Southern Illinois University Press.

Shapin, S., and S. Schaffer (1985). *Leviathan and the Air-Pump: Hobbes, Boyle, and the Experimental Life*. Princeton, NJ: Princeton University Press.

Shea, William R. (1988). 'Descartes and the Rosicrucian Enlightenment.' In R. S. Woolhouse, ed., *Metaphysics and Philosophy of Science in the Seventeenth and Eighteenth Centuries*. Dordrecht: Kluwer, 73–99.

Shea, William R. (1991). *The Magic of Numbers and Motion*. Canton, MA: Science History Publications.

Shortland, Michael, and Richard Yeo, eds. (1996). *Telling Lives in Science: Essays on Scientific Biography*. Cambridge: Cambridge University Press.

Stewart, William McC. (1938). *Descartes and Poetry*. Reprinted from *The Romantic Review* (October 1838), 212–42.

Thomas, Roy Digby (2001). *Digby: The Gunpowder Plotter's Legacy*. London: Janus.

Thoren, Victor E. (1990). *The Lord of Uraniborg: A Biography of Tycho Brahe*. Cambridge: Cambridge University Press.

Thouverez, E. (1899). 'La famille Descartes.' *Archiv für Geschichte der Philosophie, 12*, 505–28.

Tomalin, Claire (2002). *Samuel Pepys: The Unequalled Self*. London: Penguin.

Tricot-Royer, L. (1925). *La Bibliothèque de Vopiscus Fortunatus Plempius*. Brussels: Goemaere.

Vaïse, Emile (1864). *Lucilio Vanini, sa vie, sa doctrine, sa mort, 1586–1619*. Toulouse: Charles Douladoure.

Verbeek, Theo (1988). *René Descartes et Martin Schoock: La Querelle d'Utrecht*. Paris: Les Impressions Nouvelles.

Verbeek, Theo (1992a). *Descartes and the Dutch: Early Reactions to Cartesian Philosophy, 1637–1650*. Carbondale and Edwardsville: Southern Illinois University Press.

Wallace, William A. (1992a). *Galileo's Logical Treatises*. Dordrecht and London: Kluwer.

Wallace, William A. (1992b). *Galileo's Logic of Discovery and Proof*. Dordrecht and London: Kluwer.

Weber, Jean-Paul (1964). *La constitution du texte des Regulae*. Paris: Société d'Éditions d'Enseignement Supérieur.

Westfall, Richard S. (1988). 'Galileo and the Jesuits.' In R. S. Woolhouse, ed., *Metaphysics and Philosophy of Science in the Seventeenth and Eighteenth Centuries*. Dordrecht: Kluwer, 45–72.

Wymeersch, Brigitte van (1996). *Descartes et l'évolution de l'esthétique musicale.* Liège, Belgium: Mardaga.

Yates, Frances A. (1979). *The Occult Philosophy in the Elizabethan Age.* London: Routledge and Kegan Paul. Reprinted in Routledge Classics, 2002.

Yates, Frances A. (1986). *The Rosicrucian Enlightenment.* London: Routledge and Kegan Paul. (First ed. 1972).

Index